Tenth Edition

Psychology and Work Today

An Introduction to Industrial and
Organizational Psychology

Tenth Edition

Psychology and Work Today

An Introduction to Industrial and
Organizational Psychology

Duane P. Schultz
University of South Florida

Sydney Ellen Schultz

Prentice Hall
Boston   Columbus   Indianapolis   New York   San Francisco   Upper Saddle River
Amsterdam   Cape Town   Dubai   London   Madrid   Milan   Munich   Paris
Montreal   Toronto   Delhi   Mexico City   Sao Paulo   Sydney
Hong Kong   Seoul   Singapore   Taipei   Tokyo

Editorial Director: Leah Jewell
Executive Editor: Jeff Marshall
Project Manager, Editorial:
  LeeAnn Doherty
Editorial Assistant: Amy Trudell
Director of Marketing: Brandy Dawson
Marketing Manager: Nicole Kunzmann
Marketing Assistant: Jen Lang
Senior Managing Editor:
  Maureen Richardson
Project Manager, Production:
  Annemarie Franklin
Senior Operations Supervisor:
  Sherry Lewis
Operations Specialist: Amanda Smith
Art Director, Cover: Jayne Conte

Cover Design: Axell Designs
Manager, Visual Research:
  Beth Brenzel
Manager, Rights and Permissions:
  Zina Arabia
Image Permission Coordinator:
  Debbie Hewitson
Manager, Cover Visual Research &
  Permissions: Karen Sanatar
Cover Art: Bigstockphoto.com
Full-Service Project Management:
  Shelley Creager/Aptara®, Inc.
Composition: Aptara®, Inc.
Printer/Binder: Edwards Brothers
Cover Printer: Coral Graphics

This book was set in 10/12 Latin by Aptara®, Inc.

Credits and acknowledgments borrowed from other sources and reproduced, with permission, in this textbook appear on appropriate page within text or on page 411.

Library of Congress Cataloging-in-Publication Data

Schultz, Duane P.
  Psychology and work today : an introduction to industrial and organizational psychology /
Duane P. Schultz, Sydney Ellen Schultz. -- 10th ed.
    p. cm.
  Includes bibliographical references and index.
  ISBN-13: 978-0-205-68358-1
  ISBN-10: 0-205-68358-4
  1. Psychology, Industrial. I. Schultz, Sydney Ellen, II. Title.

HF5548.8.s356 2010
158.7--dc22   2008055733

Prentice Hall
is an imprint of

To David B. Quinty in appreciation for his sound judgment, management skills, and unflagging good will.

Brief Contents

Contents

Preface

Most of the students taking this introductory course in industrial-organizational (I-O) psychology will work for some kind of organization. Many are already employed while attending college. Our goal in this book is to show them how I-O psychology directly influences their lives as job applicants, trainees, employees, managers, and consumers. In brief, we are teaching students about the nature of work in modern society.

Our focus is on the practical and the applied rather than the scientific ideal. We believe that students must be introduced to topics such as training needs analysis, for example, but they also should know that in the reality of the workplace, training needs analyses are rarely conducted because companies are reluctant to spend money on them.

Students should learn about the major theories, models, research techniques, and findings of the science of I-O psychology so that they can develop an understanding of the aims and goals of the field. They must also be aware, however, that I-O psychology in practice is tempered by the conditions and demands of organizational life. Therefore, we have chosen to discuss theories, methods, and research results within the framework of actual work situations and job-related problems.

Virtually all of the research we cite deals with employees on the job, not college students performing simulated work tasks in the psychology department laboratory. We describe I-O psychology programs in action, showing how they are developed and implemented in a variety of organizational settings, using workers who differ by gender, age, culture, ethnicity, and socioeconomic status.

To reflect the globalization of the workplace and the interrelationships among today's economies, we have included research conducted on employees in nearly 50 countries in North and South America, Europe, Asia, Africa, and Australia. A list of these countries is included at the end of this preface.

Thus, the tenth edition of *Psychology and Work Today* continues to recognize not only the diversity of the workforce, but also the impact of changing economic conditions and the effects of state-of-the-art technology. We have written this text primarily for students who are not psychology majors but who make up the majority of the enrollment in courses in I-O psychology, business psychology, personnel psychology, and applied psychology in psychology departments and business schools at the community college, college, and university levels.

The changes in this edition mirror the dynamic nature of the field. Chapters have been rewritten and reorganized to incorporate the results of more than 400 new studies reflecting findings and trends within twenty-first-century I-O psychology. Some of the highlights of this edition include

- job preferences and attitudes of today's college students and the challenges for I-O psychologists
- advantages and disadvantages of Web-based research, recruiting, job training, and socialization
- puzzle interviews
- diversity training
- the growing "digital divide" between employees with computer skills and those without such skills
- work teams
- advertising targeted to ethnic groups
- personality factors and job performance
- gender and racial bias in performance evaluation
- impression management
- transformational leadership
- organizational justice
- organizational citizenship behavior
- bullying, incivility, and harassment in the workplace
- work–family balance
- human factors in health care
- neuromarketing

The chapters include outlines, summaries, annotated reading lists, and key terms. Definitions for the key terms are presented in the top margins and are cumulated in a glossary at the back of the book. Review questions challenge students to analyze material from the chapter; these questions are also suitable for class discussion and written assignments. The popular *Newsbreak* feature has been expanded. These brief sections offer informal discussions of real-world job issues, such as how *not* to interview, work–family balance, the effectiveness of vacations, the applications of virtual reality, and the impact of social networking sites such as MySpace.

An instructor's manual and test bank accompany the text and are available through the Instructor's Resource Center and www.pearsonhighered.com

We would like to thank the many students and colleagues who wrote to us about the book and who offered valuable suggestions for the new edition. In addition, several reviewers provided perceptive feedback on the manuscript, and we are appreciative of their efforts. They include

Shawn R. Charlton, *University of Central Arkansas;*
Kim Cummings, *University of Tampa;*
George Diekhoff, *Midwestern State University;*
Donald A. Hantula, *Temple University;*
Brian Johnson, *University of Tennessee-Martin;*
Bryan Kennedy, *Athens State University;*
Hollie G. Smith, *Stephen F. Austin State University.*

Duane P. Schultz
Sydney Ellen Schultz

The tenth edition of *Psychology and Work Today* includes research from the following countries:

Argentina	France	Nepal	South Korea
Australia	Germany	Netherlands	Spain
Austria	Greece	New Zealand	Sweden
Belgium	Hong Kong	Norway	Switzerland
Brazil	India	Pakistan	Taiwan
Canada	Iraq	Peru	Thailand
China	Ireland	Portugal	Turkey
Colombia	Israel	Russia	United States
Ecuador	Italy	Scotland	Uruguay
Egypt	Japan	Singapore	Vietnam
England	Malaysia	South Africa	Wales
Finland	Mexico		

Tenth Edition

Psychology and Work Today

An Introduction to Industrial and
Organizational Psychology

PART ONE

The Practice of Industrial-Organizational Psychology

The work of industrial-organizational (I-O) psychologists will affect your behavior and your physical and emotional well-being, both on and off the job, whether you are applying for your first job, advancing in your career, or planning for your retirement. In chapter 1 we describe the scope of I-O psychology. In chapter 2 we review the research methods I-O psychologists use to collect data, draw conclusions, and make recommendations to management, thus applying their findings to all facets of organizational life.

Principles, Practices, and Problems

CHAPTER OUTLINE

WOULD YOU WORK IF YOU DIDN'T HAVE TO?

Suppose you won $10 million in a lottery. Would you still keep your job? It may surprise you to know that many people do keep working, even when they don't need the money. We're not talking about movie stars or athletes or superstar musicians. No, we're talking about people in traditional jobs who continue to work hard even though they have more than enough money to live comfortably for the rest of their days. Why do they keep working? Because they love what they do.

Think about the CEOs of large corporations, many of whom receive multimillion dollar salaries. Yet they keep working. Or consider wealthy Wall Street traders who rarely take vacations and who regularly put in long hours, driven by the same intensity they had before they became so successful. Many surveys have been taken of the rest of us, the people working at less glamorous jobs such as teacher, computer programmer, lab technician, or auto mechanic. Results consistently show that approximately three fourths of the people questioned would continue to work even if they suddenly became financially secure and no longer needed the salary from their job.

Some people get so much more from their jobs than just a paycheck. Those who are fortunate enough to have found the type of work that suits their abilities experience a high degree of personal satisfaction, fulfillment, and the pride of accomplishment. These feelings provide their own reward, distinct from income. Thus, work is related not only to economic well-being but also to emotional security, self-esteem, and contentment. Your job can give you a sense of identity and status, defining for you and for others who and what you are. Your work can give you the chance to learn new skills and master new challenges. It can bring positive social experiences, satisfying your need to belong to a group and providing the security that comes from being an accepted and valued member of a team. A job can furnish the opportunity to form friendships and to meet people of diverse backgrounds.

On the other hand, if you are not one of the lucky ones who love what they do, your job can be tedious, monotonous, and even hazardous to your health. Some work environments pose physical dangers; others produce stress, anxiety, and dissatisfaction. If you are bored with your job, thwarted in your plans for advancement, or angry with your boss, you may bring your discontent home at the end of the workday and take out these negative feelings on your family and friends.

Long-term research has linked work-related stressors with physical and emotional health. Studies conducted in workplaces show that positive social interactions at work are associated with improved cardiovascular functioning and strengthened immune systems (Heaphy & Dutton, 2008). Other research indicates that work is central to psychological health, feelings of satisfaction and accomplishment, and emotional well-being (Brustein, 2008). The single most reliable predictor of a long life is satisfaction with one's job. People who are satisfied with their work tend to live longer than people who are dissatisfied with their work.

Finding the kind of work that is compatible with your interests, skills, and temperament is among the most significant endeavors you will ever undertake. For that reason, this course in industrial-organizational (I-O) psychology may be the most personally relevant course of your college career. You will find that I-O psychology will have an impact on your future from the day you apply for your first job until the day you announce your retirement. The findings and practices of I-O psychologists, in conjunction with your own skills and motivation, will determine the positions for which you are hired, the way you are expected to perform your job duties, your rank and compensation, your ultimate level of responsibility, and the personal happiness you derive from your work.

I-O PSYCHOLOGY ON THE JOB

I-O psychologists working in the area of human resources, or employee selection, help initially with the difficult task of choosing a job. Your first formal contacts with I-O psychology outside the classroom are likely to be with recruitment Web sites, application forms, interviews, psychological tests, and other employee selection measures. I-O psychologists have devised these selection measures to help employers determine whether you are the right person for their job and whether that job is the most suitable one for you.

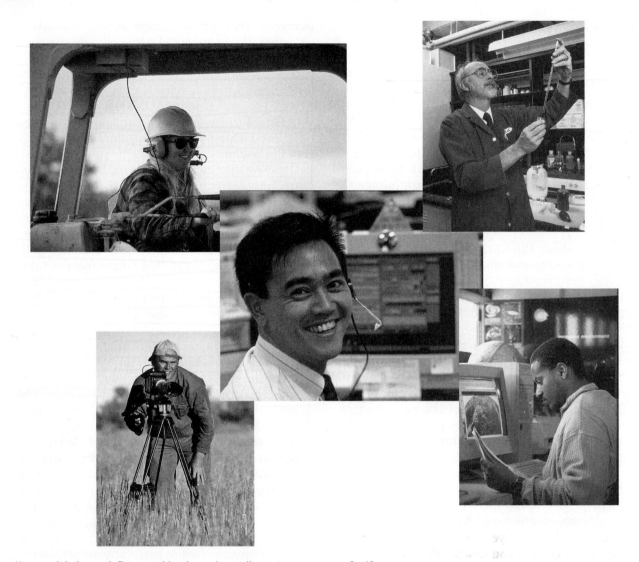

Your work helps to define your identity and contributes to your sense of self-esteem.

After you have satisfied yourself and the organization that the position is appropriate, your advancement will depend on your performance in training programs and on the job. Your employer will use assessment criteria developed by I-O psychologists.

Because of your college training, you will likely qualify for management positions within the corporate hierarchy. These jobs require you to be aware of and sensitive to the diverse motivational factors and personal concerns that affect the people who work for you. To learn how to lead and to motivate your subordinates to put forth their best efforts, you will need to understand the findings of I-O psychologists on these factors.

Even if you have no direct subordinates—if, for example, you are an engineer, information technology specialist, or accountant or if you are self-employed—you will benefit from a knowledge of human relations skills. Knowing how to get along with others can mean the difference between failure and success.

Ideally, you will feel some commitment to your employer and will want to see the organization prosper so that it continues to provide opportunities for your own advancement. The company's output must be produced efficiently and at a high level of quality. The physical plant, equipment, and working conditions should foster a productive working climate. I-O psychologists help design manufacturing

You've Got to Find What You Love

That's what Steve Jobs told the graduating class at Stanford University a few years ago, and he was talking from his own experience. "I was lucky," he said. "I found what I loved to do early in life." When he was 20 years old, Steve Jobs, along with Steve Wozniak, founded Apple Computers in his parents' garage. Ten years later the company had more than 4,000 employees and Steve Jobs was a billionaire. Then he was fired by the new president and board of directors he helped put in place. He was 30 years old and worth more money than he ever dreamed of earning in his life. And he was absolutely miserable.

"What had been the focus of my entire adult life was gone, and it was devastating." Jobs could have done anything he desired—gone anywhere, bought anything—and never work again. Instead, he started a new software company and then developed Pixar, which quickly became the most successful film animation studio in the world.

"Sometimes life hits you with a brick," he said, describing being fired from Apple. "I'm convinced that the only thing that kept me going was that I loved what I did. You've got to find what you love. And that is as true for your work as it is for your lovers. Your work is going to fill a large part of your life, and the only way to be truly satisfied is to do what you believe is great work. And the only way to do great work is to love what you do. If you haven't found it yet, keep looking. Don't settle. As with all matters of the heart, you'll know when you find it. And like all great relationships, it just gets better and better as the years roll on. So keep looking until you find it."

Source: Steve Jobs, commencement address, Stanford University, June 14, 2005.

and office environments to maximize productivity. In addition, a company's output must be effectively packaged, advertised, and marketed. Psychologists play a role in all these activities.

Thus, at all levels of modern organizational life, psychologists provide essential services to both employees and employers. I-O psychology serves these two masters—you and your company. As it benefits one, it automatically benefits the other.

We offer a note of caution, however. As vital as I-O psychology is, as influential as it will be throughout your working career, it is primarily a tool. And any tool is only as valuable as the skill of the person using it. If the methods and findings of I-O psychology are used improperly by management or are misunderstood by employees, they can do more harm than good. Therefore, it is important for you to know something about I-O psychology, if only for self-defense.

I-O PSYCHOLOGY IN EVERYDAY LIFE

There is more to I-O psychology than its application to the workday world. It also affects attitudes and behavior in other areas of life. Consider how you started your day. What governed your choice of toothpaste or bath soap? Why did you choose a particular brand of breakfast cereal this morning? Most likely your decisions were influenced by the psychological image created for the product, by the perceived attractiveness of the package, or by the emotional need a particular brand was intended to satisfy. Did an ad or a slogan tell you that you would be more popular or successful if you wore these jeans or drove that car? I-O psychologists have helped develop advertising and marketing techniques to create, identify, and influence these needs.

Similar psychological techniques are used to promote and sell political candidates. Opinion polls and focus groups inform political leaders about how voters feel about a candidate's stands on various issues. Polling techniques are also used to determine ratings for television programs.

I-O psychologists assist engineers in the design and layout of displays and controls, such as those on the instrument panel of your car or in various consumer appliances. Psychologists ensure that the controls are comfortable to operate and that the visual displays are easy to interpret. The shape and color of familiar highway signs resulted from I-O

How Not to Get Hired, Part 1: What Not to Say in Your Interview

The following activities were reported by managers and executives dealing with job applicants.

- "One candidate sang all of her responses to the interview questions."
- "One individual said we had nice benefits, which was good because he was going to need to take a lot of leave in the next year."
- "One person brought his mother to the job interview and let her do all the talking."

- "A person said he had no relevant experience for the position he was interviewing for, but his friend did."
- "One job-seeker said he should get the job because he had already applied three times and felt that it was now his turn."

Would you hire any of these people?

Source: Biz Tidbits, September 2, 2007.

psychology research. Psychologists have been involved in the design of aircraft cockpits, cell phones, microwave ovens, and computer monitors and keyboards to make them more user-friendly and efficient.

WHAT I-O PSYCHOLOGY MEANS TO EMPLOYERS

Why are the services of I-O psychologists used by so many different types of organizations? Because they work. They promote efficiency, improve morale, and increase corporate profits. Consider the problem of employee absenteeism. Workers who fail to show up cost the company a great deal of money. Techniques devised and applied by I-O psychologists to reduce absenteeism can result in substantial savings. A bank in Canada with 30,000 employees estimated that it saved $7 million in one year by heeding a consulting psychologist's advice to install a computerized absentee-reporting system. The psychologist's fee and the cost of the system were considerably less than the amount saved.

Another costly problem in organizations is turnover. When employees quit, the company loses the investment made in recruiting, selecting, and training them. Then it must hire and train replacements. An I-O psychologist studied the situation in a company and suggested ways to deal with the high incidence of quitting. Implementing these rec-

ommendations led to a 10% reduction in turnover and a cost saving of $100,000 within the first year. Other research found that regularly scheduled surveys of employee attitudes, formal communication programs between management and workers, and employment tests resulted in more than a 20% increase in company profits (Rynes, Brown, & Colbert, 2002).

Enhancing job satisfaction is a major concern in business today. Corporate leaders call on I-O psychologists to improve the attitudes of workers toward their jobs and their organizations. Enhanced satisfaction with work can reduce grievances and other labor disputes and decrease absenteeism, turnover, work slowdowns, faulty products, and accidents.

Appropriate employee selection methods, such as psychological tests, designed and monitored by I-O psychologists help ensure that the most qualified applicants are hired. For example, researchers compared federal government employees who were hired on the basis of their cognitive ability (intelligence) test scores with employees hired on the basis of level of education and work experience. The tests were found to be far superior for selecting better and more productive workers, and the cost savings were substantial.

These examples indicate the importance of the work of I-O psychologists to all types of employing organizations. I-O psychology contributes

I-O psychology The application of the methods, facts, and principles of the science of psychology to people at work.

to organizational efficiency and improves the bottom line on the company's financial report.

AN OVERVIEW OF THE DEVELOPMENT OF I-O PSYCHOLOGY

Psychology is the science of behavior and mental processes. **Industrial-organizational (I-O) psychology** involves the application of the methods, facts, and principles of psychology to people at work. That fact that psychology is a science tells us how it operates. A science deals with facts that can be seen, heard, touched, measured, and recorded. Hence, a science is empirical, which means that it relies on verifiable observation, experimentation, and experience, not on opinions, hunches, pet notions, or private prejudices. A science is objective in its approaches and results.

It is important to remember that science is defined by its methods, not by its subject matter. In methods and procedures, I-O psychology attempts to be just as scientific as physics or chemistry. When psychologists observe the behavior of people at work, they do so in the best traditions of science: objectively, dispassionately, and systematically.

The subject matter of I-O psychology is also objective. Psychologists observe and analyze overt human behavior, such as movements, speech, writings, and other creative works, to analyze and understand the people who are the focus of these observations. These overt behaviors are the only aspects of human existence that can be objectively seen, heard, measured, and recorded. Something more must be involved, however, because psychology is also the science of cognitive processes. Psychologists must study intangible qualities such as motives, emotions, needs, perceptions, thoughts, and feelings. These facets of our inner life cannot be observed directly.

Motivation, for example, cannot be seen. It is an internal driving force inaccessible to observation. Its effects, however, can be seen. An angry person may display that emotion in such behaviors as a flushed face, rapid breathing, and clenched fists. A person driven by a high need to achieve suc-

cess exhibits that motivation in behaviors that differ from those of a person content merely to get along, whether on the job, at a party, or under observation in a psychology experiment.

Psychologists cannot see intelligence directly, but they can observe the overt behavioral manifestations of different levels of intelligence. Psychologists can objectively record that one person performs at a higher level than another person on a test of cognitive abilities and can then infer that the first person is more intelligent. Inference based on the objective observation of behavior enables us to draw conclusions regarding personal factors or conditions, even when we cannot see them directly.

This is how I-O psychologists conduct their work. They observe the behavior of employees on the job under well-controlled and systematic conditions. They record behavioral responses such as the number of parts produced each hour on an assembly line, the number of keystrokes per minute made by a computer clerk, or the quality of telephone service provided to customers by airline reservations agents. They vary the conditions under which a job is performed and measure any resulting differences in performance. Using these and other techniques, I-O psychologists observe, to achieve a better understanding of human behavior. They look, listen, measure, and record objectively and precisely, adhering to the principles of the scientific method.

How did I-O psychology become so necessary to modern organizational life and to daily life in general? The field was formed and fashioned of necessity. An urgent, practical problem needing a novel solution gave the initial impetus to the field, and the demands of crisis and need have continued to stimulate its growth and influence.

Pioneers in Personnel Selection

Industrial psychology had its formal beginning in the early years of the twentieth century. The honor for sparking the development of the field is usually given to Walter Dill Scott (1869–1955). A college football player at Northwestern University, Scott

Hawthorne studies A long-term research program at the Hawthorne, Illinois, plant of the Western Electric Company. It documented the influence of a variety of managerial and organizational factors on employee behavior.

graduated from a theological seminary and intended to be a missionary in China. By the time he was prepared to undertake this calling, however, he learned that there were no vacancies for missionaries in China. And so he became a psychologist instead.

Scott was the first to apply psychology to advertising, employee selection, and management issues. At the turn of the twentieth century, he spoke out on the potential uses of psychology in advertising. Encouraged by the response of business leaders, Scott wrote several articles and published a book titled *The Theory and Practice of Advertising* (Scott, 1903), which is generally considered to be the first book about using psychology to help solve problems in the business world. In 1919 Scott formed the first consulting company in industrial psychology, which provided services to more than 40 major American corporations, primarily in the area of personnel selection.

In 1913 Hugo Münsterberg (1863–1916), a German psychologist teaching at Harvard University, wrote *The Psychology of Industrial Efficiency*. Münsterberg was an early advocate of the use of psychological tests to measure a prospective employee's skills and to match that person with the requirements of a particular job. He conducted considerable research in real-world work situations and workplaces, with the goal of improving on-the-job efficiency. His writing, research, and consulting activities helped spread the influence of industrial psychology, and he became a celebrity—America's most famous psychologist. Münsterberg befriended kings, presidents, and movie stars, and he was one of only two psychologists ever accused of being a spy (the accusation was untrue).

World War I and the Testing Movement

The work of Scott and Münsterberg provided a beginning for the field, but it was an urgent request by the U.S. Army during World War I (1917–1918) that marked the emergence of industrial psychology as an important and useful discipline. Faced with the task of screening and classifying millions of men recruited for military service, the army commissioned psychologists to devise a test for identifying people of low intelligence so that they could be eliminated from consideration for training programs. Two tests resulted from their efforts: the Army Alpha, designed for recruits who could read and write, and the Army Beta, which used mazes, pictures, and symbols for recruits who could not read. The Army Beta was also suitable for immigrants who were not fluent in the English language.

Additional tests were prepared for selecting candidates for officer and pilot training and for other military classifications that required special abilities. A personality test, the Personal Data Sheet, which could be administered to large groups of people at one time, was developed to detect neurotic tendencies among army recruits.

After the war, businesses, manufacturing concerns, school systems, and other organizations that needed to screen and classify large numbers of people demanded more and better testing techniques. The tests devised for the army were adapted for civilian use, and new ones were designed for a variety of situations. Enthusiasm for psychological testing spread throughout the United States. Soon millions of schoolchildren and job applicants routinely faced batteries of psychological tests. Thus, the initial contributions of industrial psychologists focused on issues of personnel selection—evaluating individuals and placing them in the appropriate grades, jobs, or training programs.

The Hawthorne Studies and Motivational Issues

The scope of the field broadened considerably with one of the most significant examples of psychological research ever undertaken on the job. The investigation lasted from 1929 to 1932 and was conducted by psychologist Elton Mayo, head of Harvard University's Department of Industrial Research. Called the **Hawthorne studies** because they were conducted at the Hawthorne, Illinois,

Newsbreak

First Jobs: We All Have to Start Somewhere

Brad Pitt dressed up in a chicken suit and stood outside a fast-food fried chicken restaurant to attract customers before he made it big as an actor. Michael Dell washed dishes at a Chinese restaurant before he became a billionaire in the computer industry. Filmmaker Quentin Tarantino was an usher in a theater showing X-rated movies and a clerk in a video store before he became a movie and TV producer. Comedian Chris Rock started out as a busboy at Red Lobster restaurant before he rose to fame on a Jay Leno show, telling jokes about his job there.

You've probably never heard of Jim Skinner, but he earned more than $15 million a year as president of McDonald's. He served in the U.S. Navy for 10 years, then started up the corporate ladder as a management trainee sweeping floors, cleaning bathrooms, and making fries and hamburgers at McDonald's.

Terry Lundgren shucked oysters and waited tables as his first job while working his way through college. Tired of the food service business by the time he graduated, he worked at several companies and eventually became president of Macy's department store. In 2006, his take-home pay was $9 million. "I always loved what I did from the very beginning," Lundgren said. "I always worked hard. I feel very fortunate. I never take any of this for granted, especially from where I started."

Where are you starting from? Where do you want to go from there? Whatever your goal, chances are the work of I-O psychologists can help you reach it.

Sources: Celebrity first jobs (2007). Retrieved from www.forbes.com; MSNBC.com, May 11, 2007; Kirdahy, M. (2007, October 26). CEO's first jobs. Retrieved from www.forbes.com

plant of the Western Electric Company, this long-term research program took industrial psychology beyond employee selection and placement to the more complex problems of motivation, interpersonal relations, and organizational dynamics (Roethlisberger & Dickson, 1939; see also Hsueh, 2002).

The research began as a straightforward investigation of the effects of the physical work environment on employee efficiency. The researchers asked questions such as these: What is the effect on productivity if we increase the lighting in the workroom? Do temperature and humidity levels affect production? What will happen if management provides rest periods for the workers?

The results of the Hawthorne studies surprised both the investigators and the plant managers. The researchers found that social and psychological factors in the work environment were of potentially greater importance than physical factors. For example, changing the level of illumination in a workroom from very bright to dim did not diminish worker efficiency. More subtle factors were operating to induce these workers to maintain their original production level, even under nearly dark conditions.

With another group of workers, lighting was increased and production levels rose. The researchers made other changes—rest periods, free lunches, a shorter workday—and with the introduction of each change, production increased. However, when all the benefits were suddenly eliminated, production continued to increase. The researchers concluded that physical aspects of the work environment were not as important to employees as management had assumed and that social and psychological factors were more important.

For example, researchers conducted "20,000 interviews of workers and found that it was not the substance of the interviews but the very fact of being interviewed (i.e., being given attention, scrutinized, surveyed, watched, listened to) that defused their griping and made them more docile and 'better adjusted'" (Lemov, 2005, p. 65). In other words, just the fact of being questioned or observed on the job as part of a research program persuaded many workers that management cared about them, that their boss was truly interested in them as individuals and not merely as interchangeable cogs in the great industrial machine.

The Hawthorne studies opened up new areas for I-O psychologists to explore, such as the nature of leadership, the formation of informal groups among workers, employee attitudes, communication patterns, and other managerial and organizational variables now recognized as influences on efficiency, motivation, and job satisfaction. Although the Hawthorne studies have been criticized for a lack of scientific rigor, there is no denying their impact on the way psychologists view the nature of work and on the scope and direction of I-O psychology. For more information on the Hawthorne studies and their impact on management issues today, log on to www.library.hbs.edu/hc/hawthorne/

World War II and Engineering Psychology

World War II (1941–1945) brought more than 2,000 psychologists directly into the war effort. Their major contribution was the testing, classifying, and training of millions of recruits in various branches of military service. New skills were required to operate sophisticated aircraft, tanks, and ships, and the military needed to identify persons capable of learning to perform these tasks.

The increasingly complex weapons of war sparked the development of a new field: engineering psychology. Working closely with engineers, psychologists supplied information about human abilities and limitations for operating high-speed aircraft, submarines, and other equipment and thus influenced their design.

I-O psychology achieved greater stature as a result of these contributions to the war effort. Government and industry leaders recognized that psychologists were equipped to solve many practical business problems. The wartime experience also demonstrated to many psychologists, who before the war had worked in the relative isolation of their university laboratories, that there were vital and challenging problems in the real world that they could help solve.

Later Developments in I-O Psychology

The explosive growth of I-O psychology since the end of World War II in 1945 paralleled the growth of U.S. business and technical enterprise. The size and complexity of modern organizations placed additional demands on the skills of I-O psychologists and provided phenomenal opportunities for the development of the field. New technologies meant that employees needed enhanced and redesigned training programs. The advent of computers, for example, generated the need for programmers and technical support personnel and changed the way many jobs were performed. Psychologists had to determine the abilities required for these jobs, the kinds of people most likely to have these abilities, and the best ways to train the new employees.

The demands on engineering psychologists also increased. Innovations such as supersonic aircraft, missiles, advanced weapons systems, and information technology required additional training to achieve maximally effective operation. Engineering psychologists became involved in the design of industrial robots and high-tech office equipment and in the redesign of workspaces for automated operations.

Organizational issues have also assumed greater importance (the *O* side of I-O psychology). Human relations skills are recognized by managers and executives as vital to maintaining high job performance of their employees. The nature of leadership, the role of motivation and job satisfaction, the impact of the organizational structure and climate, and the processes of decision making are continuously being analyzed. In recognition of the significance of organizational variables, the Division of Industrial Psychology of the American Psychological Association (APA) became the Society for Industrial and Organizational Psychology (SIOP).

CHALLENGES FOR I-O PSYCHOLOGY

Factors such as the rapidly changing nature of work, technological advances, and a more diverse population mean new demands and responsibilities for I-O psychologists. One challenge relates to the kinds of jobs available, the ways in which they will be performed, and the type of employee who will perform them.

The Virtual Workplace

It has become commonplace for organizations to have large numbers of employees who work off-site.

Employees telecommute from a home office, e-mail or text-message from a car, phone from an airplane while traveling on business, or teleconference from a hotel room or vacation spot. This dramatic shift in where and how people work is an effect of the information age. Many jobs can be performed anywhere within electronic reach of the home office or the actual workplace thanks to e-mail, voicemail, pagers, cell phones, laptop computers, and personal data systems.

To function efficiently and productively, these virtual workplaces require at least three types of information access: (1) online material that can be downloaded and printed; (2) databases on customers and products, and automated central files, that can be accessed from remote locations; and (3) a means of tracking employees and their work assignments at any time of day.

The downside of electronically connected virtual workplaces is that employees are often expected to work, or to be available, beyond the normal working hours of the organization. Some companies require their employees to carry phones or beepers at all times, keeping them effectively tethered to the office with no way to escape the demands of their jobs. As a writer for the *New York Times* noted, "The 24/7 culture of nearly round-the-clock work is endemic to the wired economy." When 985 I-O psychologists were asked to name the trends most likely to affect the future of the field, 37% chose the impact of technology and Internet-related developments as most important (Waclawski, Church, & Berr, 2002).

Virtual Employees

Not only are more people performing their work at locations away from the office, but they are less likely to be full-time employees who can expect to remain with the same employer for the duration of their career. Whereas previous generations of workers presumed a kind of unwritten psychological contract with their employer—"If I do my job well, my company will keep me on until I'm ready to retire"—today's workers have no such certainty of lifelong job security. The notion of long-term loyalty and commitment to one organization faded in the closing decades of the twentieth century during a frenzied period of corporate mergers and acquisitions, downsizing, and plant closures in which millions of workers and managers lost their jobs.

More of today's employees are likely to be contingent workers, freelancers, independent contractors, or part-time seasonal labor. The largest single private employer in the United States is Manpower, Inc., a temporary staffing agency. Millions of Americans work on a freelance basis. At the professional level, the U.S. Department of Labor estimates that more than 8 million people can be classified as independent contractors.

Many workers, especially younger ones, report that they prefer contingent work because it provides flexibility, independence, challenges, and the opportunity to continually upgrade their work experience and job skills. Many corporations also prefer this arrangement because they save on administrative expenses and taxes and do not have to provide benefits such as insurance or pension plans.

Research has shown, however, that the use of temporary workers can have negative effects on an organization's full-time employees. In a survey of 415 full-time workers employed by several organizations, investigators found that the use of contract workers resulted in a decrease in the full-time workers' loyalty to the organization. The full-time workers also reported that their relations with management had deteriorated (Davis-Blake, Broschak, & George, 2003).

In addition, many organizations expect their full-time employees to train and supervise temporary workers. They also hold their full-time employees accountable for tasks assigned to temporary workers. Thus, organizations increase both the workload and the responsibility of full-time employees; rarely are these employees compensated for the extra demands placed on them. In a study of 568 employees in eight companies in Belgium, investigators confirmed that full-time employees believed they had a more demanding workload than part-time employees (DeCuyper & DeWitte, 2006). Surveys have also shown that many full-time employees think their jobs are higher in prestige than those of temporary workers. Such attitudes are hardly a basis for viewing temporary workers as equals and can lead to unpleasant relationships in the workplace.

Newsbreak

Temporarily Yours

"Ten years ago, I took a job stuffing envelopes. It was a necessity: I had just graduated from college and had no idea what I wanted to do with my life, but the lenders who had financed my college education weren't sympathetic to my existential crisis. The job came through a temporary-employment agency, which paid me $7.25 an hour to cram manila envelopes with a company's pap. I lasted one day. Since then, the temp world has changed dramatically. . . ."

Temporary employment has grown in part because employers are more cautious about committing themselves. "They want to try people out before hiring them," said James Essey, president of the Tempositions Group of Companies in Manhattan [New York]. Many companies also prefer temps because they may not have to give them full benefits, or any benefits at all.

But it is not only employers who are fickle. Many young people engage in serial workplace monogamy, refusing to enter into serious relationships until they have sowed their corporate oats. "You test each other out, like a trial marriage," said Georgia Ellis, a vice president at Fifth Avenue Temporary Services in Manhattan. "And it doesn't look bad on your résumé, because it doesn't look like you've jumped from place to place. You have an excuse. You're a temp."

Kristin Robinson, 29, has morphed into what is known as a "permanent temp"—one with a long-term assignment. For the last two years, Ms. Robinson, who is also an actress, has had a continuing temporary position as a graphic artist, three days a week, at Andersen Consulting in Manhattan. She freelances the other two days from connections made at other temp jobs. The freedom, she said, is invaluable: "I try to be respectful and give notice, but if I need to leave I leave. And I don't take work home."

Most young corporate nomads, some of whom are actors, musicians, and writers, want to focus on their "real" careers without having to ask, "Do you want fries with that?" They thrive on the flexibility and often use their day jobs as floating office spaces for managing the rest of their lives.

And if they're unhappy in a job, they can simply walk away. Suzanne Lynn, 27, said she left a Greenville, South Carolina, law firm for lunch and, angry about being yelled at, didn't come back. Her agency understood and handed her another assignment. With that kind of freedom and unconditional love, temporary work might be the wave of the future.

Source: Ellin, A. (1999, April 18). *New York Times.*

Worker Involvement

The ways in which organizations today conduct business are changing drastically, both in existing jobs and in new jobs that are being created. As a result, employees at blue-collar, supervisory, and upper-management levels are facing revolutionary challenges.

The days when a worker could be taught how to perform a simple task and then be told to keep doing it that way without question are disappearing. Today's workers want quality management. Their key words are "empowerment," "involve-

ment," and "participation." Not only are workers expected to master the tasks of a single job, but they are also expected to assemble a cluster of personal skills, or skill sets, that they can transfer from one job to another. They must continually upgrade these skills and learn to participate in decision-making teams to determine how the work is best carried out. Today's workers are also assuming increased responsibility in the production or service process, even in selecting and hiring new workers.

This involvement of workers affects the ways managers perform their jobs. No longer can managers rule by command, telling their employees what to do and when and how to do it. Now they function more as guides and mentors than as traditional leaders. These changes require substantial adjustments for workers and managers and are, in part, a response to technological change in the workplace.

New Technology Requires New Skills

A radical change in the workplace stems from advances in microelectronics: word processors, computers, and industrial robots. Work environments large and small have become automated; sophisticated equipment has taken over functions once performed by humans. Most office workers today use word-processing or data-processing equipment that has eliminated clerical jobs requiring lower-level skills. Workers must be technically proficient in systems and procedures unknown to previous generations of employees. Computers, faxes, modems, cell phones, electronic notebooks, e-mail, and the Internet have changed the functions of many jobs and created others that never existed before. Some companies use electronic equipment as job perks. For example, both Ford and Delta Air Lines provide their employees—whether they work in offices, on the factory floor, or in the maintenance hangar—with computers and printers for home use, plus free access to the Internet.

As a result of the reduction in the number of manufacturing jobs and the demands of modern technology, there are fewer job opportunities for computer-illiterate or poorly educated men and women. Consider the job of longshoreman, or stevedore, whose tasks were once described as requiring considerably more brawn than brain. Forty years ago, it took 500 men 3 months to unload a 900-foot cargo ship. Today, using automated equipment, 10 workers can unload a container ship in 24 hours. Their work requires skills not needed 40 years ago, such as the ability to run computerized inventory checks on a ship's cargo.

As many as 25 million Americans over the age of 17 are functionally illiterate, which means they do not have sufficient writing and reading comprehension skills to fill out an application for a job. Basic math skills are also lacking. Studies have shown that when people in their twenties are asked to make change from a two-item restaurant bill, only some 20% can so correctly.

From an employer's standpoint, it is increasingly difficult to recruit entry-level workers who possess the basic skills needed to learn to perform many jobs. A telecommunications company in the northeastern United States had to interview and test 90,000 job applicants to find 2,000 who could be trained for a job that did not even require a high school diploma. General Motors found that workers who lacked appropriate reading, writing, and math skills had difficulty completing the training programs provided every few years to update skills and become familiar with new manufacturing processes. By 2012, the United States will face a shortage of 10 million workers able to perform high-tech jobs (Salzberg, 2007).

The Global Workplace

Your job may be going overseas, but you'll still be here—and unemployed. A large number of U.S. companies are outsourcing or offshoring jobs such as customer relations, tech support, and call centers by having them performed by workers in other countries. IBM, for example, has sent thousands of high-paying information technology jobs to China, where the tasks can be done for a fraction of the pay required by U.S. workers. Microsoft has exported jobs to India where the annual salary for a computer programmer is $40,000, compared with $80,000 for a programmer in the United States. Globalization means shifting jobs to places with lower labor costs and less competition. This phenomenon leaves thousands of highly skilled workers in need of retraining to develop job skills compatible with the current needs, and pay scales, of business and industry today

Ethnic Diversity in the Workplace

Another change in the workplace is demographic. A significant shift has occurred in the ethnic composition of the workforce. Persons of African, Asian, and Hispanic heritage now constitute at least 35% of all new workers. Furthermore, half of all new employees are women. White male workers

Will There Be Jobs for You? The Hottest Careers for College Graduates

As some U.S. jobs are being outsourced, others are being eliminated altogether. Still others are being changed so completely by new technology that old skills no longer apply. How can you predict what jobs will be ready for you when you graduate, prepared to begin your working career? Research conducted at Harvard University and at the Massachusetts Institute of Technology about the kinds of jobs likely to be exported found that the most important factor was whether a job could be "routinized," that is, "broken down into repeatable steps that vary little from day to day. Such a job is easier to replace with a clever piece of software or to hand over to a lower-paid worker outside the U.S." (Coy, 2004).

OK, so where does that leave you? According to College Board, the company that gives the test of the same name, the fastest growing jobs for college graduates between now and 2014 are the following:

- Network systems and data communications analysts
- Computer software engineers
- Network computer systems administrators
- Database administrators

This does not mean that there will not be many jobs in other areas, such as general managers, teachers, and social workers, but the fastest growing occupations are in information technology and related fields.

Source: College Board, Ten Hottest Careers for College Graduates, 2007.

---

are becoming a minority. Organizations large and small are becoming increasingly sensitive to the needs and concerns of a workforce that consists of many cultures and backgrounds.

Up to 800,000 immigrants enter the United States every year. Most of them are eager to work, but many lack English-language training and other literacy skills. They may also be unfamiliar with corporate work habits. This situation presents an additional challenge to business and industry.

All these changes in the workplace and in the composition of the workforce pose opportunities for I-O psychologists in selecting and training workers, redesigning jobs and equipment, refining management practices, raising morale, and dealing with health and safety issues. These challenges suggest that the twenty-first century is an exciting time to consider a career as an I-O psychologist.

Different Generations—Different Values

For the first time in history, people belonging to distinct cultural groups—different generations with diverse backgrounds, expectations, and needs—

are occupying the same workplaces. Of course, there have always been older, middle age, and younger employees working for the same organization, but never have the differences among the age groups been so divisive and potentially distracting as they are today. The four generations identified in today's workforce are the Silent Generation, Baby Boomers, Generation X, and Generation Y. Keep in mind that these generalizations describe many, but certainly not all, members of a generation. There are exceptions in each category, and you may be among them.

The so-called Silent Generation was born between 1922 and 1945. Most are at the end of their working careers or have already retired, but some retain positions of power and leadership. They tend to be hardworking, respectful of authority, and loyal to their employer, and they believe that their employer will be loyal in return and take care of them to and through retirement. Typically, they have worked for only one or two employers in their career.

The Baby Boomers were born between 1946 and 1964. As the largest generation, they had to

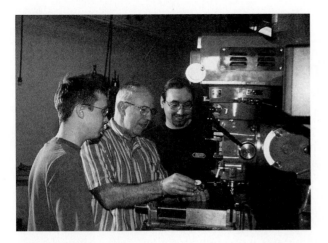

Older workers can serve as mentors or trainers for younger workers.

become extremely competitive to find jobs and promotions. Many became workaholics, spending up to 60 hours a week in the office. They sacrificed time with their families to keep their jobs or to obtain greater pay and promotions.

Generation X, born between 1965 and 1979 (the product of Boomer parents), deliberately chose not to follow their parents' lives of total commitment to work. They tend to be more open to nontraditional work, are sophisticated users of computer technology, and are likely to question authority and to value autonomy and independence in their work and in their private lives.

Members of Generation Y, born after 1980, are entering the workforce in increasing numbers. By 2012 they will constitute more than half of the U.S. workforce. They have been called the most praised generation: They are more self-centered and require more constant adulation, feedback, and recognition from their bosses (Zaslow, 2007). "Boomer parents have taught their kids that they're wonderful, so they enter the workforce thinking they should be showered with things that they want" (McCormack, 2007, p. 1). "They've got high self-esteem," a journalist wrote, "having grown up singing songs with lyrics like 'I am special.' They're entrepreneurial and want meaningful work right away; they're enthusiastic about work, but not willing to pay dues performing menial jobs. They want feedback from and interaction with managers. They'd rather have free time than money, so they're not willing to work 60-hour weeks. They saw parents get laid off by companies

that were supposed to take care of them, so they feel little loyalty to employers and switch jobs or career paths every few years" (Rexrode, 2007). Log on to www.employeeevolution.com to learn what Generation Y thinks and says about their place in the world of work.

Surveys of members of Generation Y show that more than 90% of them say they are looking for the kind of job that offers a flexible schedule, requires creativity, and allows them to have an impact on the world. They also want co-workers who make work fun (Belkin, 2007). As they enter the workforce in ever-increasing numbers, organizations must adapt to their special needs, which means ever more challenges and job opportunities for I-O psychologists. So if you want to consider a career in I-O psychology, we offer some information to get you started.

CAREERS IN I-O PSYCHOLOGY

The minimum requirement for working as an I-O psychologist is a master's degree. Most master's degree students work full time or part time while in school. Of all the graduate degrees granted in I-O psychology each year, two-thirds are at the master's level. The majority of I-O master's degree graduates find professional jobs in their specialty areas at competitive salaries in industry, government, consulting firms, and research organizations. Their most marketable skills that can be applied to the job are in the areas of psychological test and survey construction and validation, human resources selection and placement, performance appraisal, fair employment practices, and employee training. College course work in motivation, job satisfaction, and organizational development are also useful on the job. Thus, a master's degree program in I-O psychology provides valuable preparation for a productive and rewarding career. However, the higher positions in businesses and universities typically require a doctoral degree, which requires from three to five years of graduate study.

The number of graduate students in I-O psychology continues to grow, with the bulk of the increase being among students at the master's level. These students have a sound practical reason for their choice. The U.S. Bureau of Labor Statistics expects an increase in job opportunities for psychologists in business and research, in nonprofit organizations, and in computer firms.

Newsbreak

But What Can I Do with a BA in Psychology?

Fewer than half of all psychology graduates with bachelor's degrees go on to attend graduate school. What happens to them? Where do they find work? What sort of career opportunities can they expect? Relax. If this is your situation, the future looks promising, even if you're not planning on studying for a master's or doctoral degree.

Psychology majors with 4-year degrees find employment in all sectors of the economy. Approximately 50% work for private corporations, 15% are employed by government agencies, 14% find jobs in education, 12% run their own businesses, and 9% work for charitable organizations. Of those in the corporate sector, most are in managerial positions; the rest work in sales, human resources, training, and other staff functions.

Nearly half of all BA graduates in psychology report that their job duties are closely related to their course work. They also say that their jobs have high career potential. When employers were asked what skills and abilities they were looking for in job applicants with bachelor's degrees in psychology, they answered that they wanted people with high interpersonal skills and a strong work ethic. Specifically, they sought new college graduates who could get along with others, be a team player, and had the desire to learn new skills. So, yes, even if you do not plan on graduate school, good jobs are out there for you, but work on your "people skills" and be willing to keep learning.

Sources: Landrum, R. & Harrold, R. (2003). What employees want from psychology graduates. *Teaching of Psychology, 30,* 131–133; Van Wagner, K. (2007). Career options with a bachelor's degree in psychology. Retrieved from, www.about.com/psychology

The training requirements for a career in I-O psychology are difficult, but the rewards can be great. I-O psychologists have higher salaries than those of any other group of psychologists. In 2006 the median annual income for I-O psychologists with doctoral degrees in the United States was $98,500; at the master's level the median annual income was $79,000. In contrast, in 2007 the average reported starting salary was $74,000 for all psychologists with PhDs and more than $55,000 for those with MAs (APA Research Office, 2007; Khanna & Medsker, 2007). Other rewards for I-O psychologists are notable: stimulating work, challenging responsibilities, and intellectual growth. As Ann Howard, a past president of the Society for Industrial and Organizational Psychology, commented, it is a field in which "you can make things happen. You put in a program, and you see some results. You might see better people selected, or job satisfaction go up, or turnover go down. But you've made something happen, and that's a very exciting kind of reward."

I-O psychologists work in business, industry, government agencies, service organizations, con-sulting firms, and universities. Many of the psychologists who teach courses in I-O psychology also undertake research and consulting activities. Employment opportunities, as reflected in examples of job titles, responsibilities, and types of organizations, are shown in Table 1-1.

Women play an increasingly important role in psychology today. In 1970, only 20% of the doctoral candidates who received PhDs in psychology were women. By 2005, that number had increased to 72%, and more than half expressed an intention to work in I-O psychology (Cynkar, 2007). Partly as a result of an intensive recruiting effort for minority graduate students, 22% of all graduate students in I-O doctoral programs represent ethnic minorities (Avery & Hysong, 2007).

I-O psychologists are affiliated primarily with four divisions of the APA: SIOP, Division of Military Psychology, Division of Applied Experimental and Engineering Psychologists, and the Society for Consumer Psychology. Many academic and research-oriented I-O psychologists are also affiliated with the American Psychological Society.

TABLE 1-1
Places of Employment and Job Responsibilities of Selected I-O Psychologists

Human Resources Consulting Firm
Conduct test development and validation, interview training, assessment center design, performance appraisal system design, career development programs, and attitude surveys

Market Research, Consulting, and Promotional Services Firm; Marketing Research Project Director
Apply social science research skills to proposal development, analysis, writing, and presentations

International Airline, Assessment Center Specialist for Overseas Development
Coordinate and supervise assessment center for evaluation of employees being considered for promotion: develop assessment materials, make recommendations to improve effectiveness, select and train staff to become qualified assessors

Management Consulting Firm, Senior-Level Manager
Oversee projects involving the systems approach to training, training technologies, and management and career development training

Human Resource Research and Consulting Associates, I-O Project Manager
Work with interdisciplinary staff (psychologists, sociologists, computer science specialists, and educators) on information systems, test development, survey design, and equal employment issues, including providing expert witness testimony in selected court cases

Employee Decisions Consulting Firm, Director of Human Resources
Provide services in counseling, coaching executive candidates for job interviews, assessment and test interpretation, and career development

Pharmaceutical Firm, Manager of Psychological Services
Design psychological strategies for employee testing and job analysis, assess legal considerations in hiring, research and recommend changes in corporate compensation procedures, develop and monitor performance appraisal practices

Public Utility (Gas and Electric Company), Executive Consultant in Organization Planning and Development
Work with unions, line operations, human resource departments, and senior management groups to redesign human resource systems and implement major organizational changes

Electronics Corporation, Team Leadership and Communication Trainer
Implement self-directed production work teams: train workers in manufacturing team concepts, problem-solving techniques, leadership development, communications, and cooperative decision making; monitor and evaluate programs and document results

Telecommunications Company, Human Resource Research Intern
Serve as a predoctoral intern (for person admitted to doctoral candidacy at an accredited university) to conduct research on human resource programs while working with licensed I-O psychologists and human resource professionals

State College, Assistant Professor of Psychology
Teach courses in organizational behavior, group processes, and tests and measurements; direct undergraduate research projects

Question 2

PRACTICAL PROBLEMS FOR I-O PSYCHOLOGISTS

No field of study is free of internal and external problems. I-O psychologists face several difficulties, all aggravated by the very factor that has made the field so successful, namely, the demand for its services.

Fraudulent Practitioners

More than any other science, psychology has been victimized by quackery, that is, by the illicit and fraudulent practice of psychology by people who have little or no professional training. This problem is particularly apparent in clinical psychology,

Newsbreak

What I Did Last Summer

Andrew Braaksma, a junior at the University of Michigan, worked long hours in the summer at a hot, dirty, and demanding job on an automobile plant assembly line. "For a student like me," he said, "who considers any class before noon to be uncivilized, getting to a factory by 6 o'clock each morning, where rows of hulking, spark-throwing machines have replaced the lush campus and cavernous lecture halls of college life, is torture. There my time is spent stamping, cutting, welding, moving or assembling parts, the rigid work schedules and quotas of the plant making days spent studying and watching 'SportsCycle' seem like a million years ago."

It's the kind of work Andrew does every summer to make enough money for another year of college tuition, and it has taught him some valuable lessons. "Factory life has shown me what my future might have been like had I never gone to college in the first place. After a particularly exhausting string of 12-hour days at a plastics factory, I remember being shocked at how small my check seemed. I couldn't believe how little I was taking home, after all the hours I spent on the sweltering production floor."

Andrew also learned about another kind of stress that affects blue-collar workers, knowing that the plant could close down next week or next month and the whole factory moved to Mexico or some other country. And that means your job is gone forever and even if you are lucky enough to find another one, the odds are good that it's not going to pay nearly as much as the job you lost.

"Many people pass their lives in the places I briefly worked, spending 30 years where I spent only 2 months at a time. My lessons about [the benefits of an] education were learned at the expense of those who weren't fortunate enough to receive one."

One of his coworkers told him, "This job pays well, but it's hell on the body. Study hard and keep reading."

Andrew hasn't yet found the kind of work he wants to commit to, but he has certainly found what he would not want to do.

Source: Braaksma, 2005, p. 17.

---

where untrained people set themselves up as "counselors" and "therapists" and often do great harm to emotionally disturbed persons who are seeking help.

Quackery also affects I-O psychology. Mary Tenopyr, a past president of SIOP, wrote:

> A major complication in the lives of psychologists in business is the ill-trained or unscrupulous person who offers psychological-type services to companies. . . . Some of the most difficult situations I have had to cope with in my career have resulted from the actions of pseudopsychologists who have captured the ears of high-level managers. (Tenopyr, 1992, p. 175)

An uninformed business organization can be just as gullible as an individual. Unethical testing or consulting firms have sold their so-called services to industry and made quick money—and a quicker getaway—before the company realized it had been duped. Not only is such unethical behavior dangerous and unfair to business (consider, for example, all the competent people who were not hired because they performed poorly on the quack's phony test), but it is also harmful to psychology as a science and profession. If a company is damaged by the charlatan's actions, the field as a whole receives the blame. Executives of an organization defrauded in the past will be reluctant to consider legitimate psychological services in the future.

Credentials and Certification

The problem of the phony practitioner has been reduced in clinical psychology because many states license or certify psychologists in the same way they license physicians. It is illegal for people to represent themselves to the public as psychologists or to use any of the tools of psychology unless they have met the licensing or certification requirements, which usually are a graduate degree and satisfactory performance on an exam covering knowledge of all areas of psychology.

Such procedures were established specifically to protect the public from charlatans in the areas of clinical and counseling psychology. The question of licensing I-O psychologists is controversial within the profession. Many I-O psychologists who practice in states that offer licensing have chosen to apply for it. Although many SIOP members are licensed, SIOP takes the position that they need not be.

A business must exercise care when seeking the services of a psychologist. It is not enough to flip through the pages of the telephone directory or enter the words *I-O psychology* on a search engine. The educational and professional qualifications of anyone called a psychologist must be examined carefully.

Question 2

Communicating with Management

All sciences develop a specialized technical jargon that its members use to communicate with one another. Sometimes this vocabulary is not understood by those outside the discipline. Because I-O psychologists must work closely with people who are not psychologists, that is, with managers and employees, they must make the effort to communicate clearly their ideas, activities, and research results. Recommendations of I-O psychologists will be of no value to an organization if they cannot be comprehended; their reports will be filed in the nearest wastebasket. I-O psychologists must be able to present their contributions in a way that can be understood by those who are using their services.

Question 2

Worker Resistance to New Ideas

This problem might be called, "I've always done it this way, and I'm not going to change now!" Psychologists who work in business and industry often meet this attitude—a resistance to change, an unwillingness to try something new or consider novel ideas. When an I-O psychologist recommends altering the usual way of performing a job, workers sometimes view the suggestion as a threat. Employees who are told to modify their work habits to conform to the potentially more efficient system proposed by the psychologist may actively resist because they believe that the company is try-

ing to get them to work harder for the same pay. Insecure workers may also feel that management is criticizing their past job performance. Resistance to change is a serious problem at all levels, from the worker on the assembly line or the phone bank to the CEO at corporate headquarters.

If the findings of I-O psychologists are to have any impact, they must have the support of the managers and employees who will be affected by them. Psychologists need the cooperation of those employees whose jobs will be changed. They must show considerable human relations skills, patience, and persuasiveness in addition to their technical expertise.

Research or Application?

The question of research versus application continues to concern I-O psychologists in their relations with management. Some managers complain that too little of the research published in I-O psychology journals is oriented toward the practical, real-world problems with which they deal every day (Lawler, 2007; Madigan & Dickson, 2007). This may explain why most human resources managers do not read the published literature in I-O psychology; they find it too technical, difficult to understand, and impractical or irrelevant to their needs (Rynes, Giluk, & Brown, 2007; Shapiro, Kirkman, & Courtney, 2007). Psychologists who work for organizations can help alleviate this problem. Through clear and direct writing, they can interpret research findings in a way that human resources managers find useful and applicable to their everyday problems on the job.

In addition, there are serious differences between academic I-O psychologists and psychologists who work in applied settings. Although they may receive the same training, once they leave graduate school, their employment experiences and values diverge. Researchers are popularly seen as interested only in theories and methods, not in anything relevant. In contrast, practitioners are viewed as problem-solvers who ignore research findings. Although much academic research may appear to have no immediate application, psychologists who work directly for organizations know that the two functions, research and application, are interdependent. Without research, there would be no reliable information to apply to critical problems on the job. This point is often overlooked by managers who demand immediate solutions to specific problems and who cannot understand the hesitation of the psychologist who tells them that the answer can come only from research.

The conflict between research and application arises because organizations often need prompt answers. Production schedules and contract deadlines do not always wait for the design and execution of a research study. Managers facing time constraints may have unrealistic expectations and become impatient when the company psychologist—their so-called expert on human behavior—cannot provide a quick fix.

We are not suggesting that whenever I-O psychologists are asked a question, they run to the laboratory to begin a month-long experiment. The history of psychology already provides a wealth of empirical data about human behavior in a variety of situations, and well-trained psychologists know how to apply these findings to specific problems in the workplace. The value of such data, however, depends on the similarity between the situations in which they were obtained and the present situation. For example, studies about how college sophomores learn complex material are not as relevant to the learning abilities of employees in a chemical company as is research conducted on the learning abilities of employees in a steel company. The steel company research, performed in an actual work setting, will probably provide more useful results. But a learning study conducted in another chemical company will be even more applicable. And a study conducted on the very workers whose learning habits are in question will be the most useful of all.

Properly devised research can be of immense value to an organization's productive efficiency. Sometimes, however, circumstances do not allow sufficient time or resources for research to be undertaken. The needs of the workplace often call for compromise, patience, and understanding by both managers and psychologists. The fundamental issue is not research *versus* application but research *plus* application. The two functions are compatible and complementary.

AREAS OF I-O PSYCHOLOGY

In this chapter we noted in general how I-O psychology affects many aspects of the relationship between you and your work. In the following chapters we describe the specific interests of I-O psychologists.

Techniques, Tools, and Tactics of Science (Chapter 2). Psychologists study human behavior through the tools and techniques of science. To understand their work, we must become acquainted with the ways in which they perform research, analyze data, and draw conclusions.

Recruiting and Selecting Employees (Chapters 3 and 4). Some executives and personnel managers say they can judge job applicants by a handshake, eye contact, or style of dress. However, selecting and evaluating employees are complex processes that continue long after initial recruitment and hiring. Throughout your career, questions of promotion and salary increases will arise. Many of the selection devices such as interviews and psychological tests that were used when you were first hired are relevant to subsequent career decisions. Thus, it is important to understand the selection process. It is to your advantage that your potential employers choose the most valid techniques available. Improper matching of the person and the job can lead to inefficiency and dissatisfaction for you and your employer.

Appraising Employee Performance (Chapter 5). Periodic evaluation of the quality of your job performance will continue throughout your working career. Promotions, pay increases, transfers, and dismissals will be based on these appraisals. These decisions should be made as fairly and objectively as possible and not be subject to the personal likes and dislikes of your supervisor. I-O psychologists have devised appraisal methods for many types of jobs. Your future satisfaction and security depend on these appraisals, so it is important that your company have a fair and appropriate system for evaluating job performance and that you understand how that system works.

Employee Training and Development (Chapter 6). Virtually every new employee receives some sort of job training. Inexperienced workers must be taught the specific operations they are expected to perform, and they may also need training in good work habits. Experienced workers who change jobs must be taught the policies and procedures of their new employer. Workers whose jobs are altered by changing technology require retraining. As the machinery of production and the dynamics of organizational life become more complex, the demands made on employees to learn and on employers to teach increase in scope and significance.

Organizational Leadership (Chapter 7). One of industry's greatest challenges is selecting, training, and developing effective leaders. The problem is of concern to you for two reasons. First, as an employee you will work under a supervisor or manager, and your efficiency and satisfaction will be affected by his or her leadership style. Second, because most business leaders come from the ranks of college-educated persons, you will most likely serve at some level of management in the course of your career. Psychologists are concerned with the abilities of leaders in various situations and the effects of different leadership styles on subordinates. To continue growing, an organization must place its most competent people in positions of leadership, and they must exercise their skills in the most effective manner.

Motivation, Job Satisfaction, and Job Involvement (Chapter 8). Vital to the efficiency of any organization are the motivations of its employees, the satisfaction employees receive from their work, and the extent of employee commitment to the company. Many aspects of the work environment affect motivation, satisfaction, and involvement: the quality of leadership, advancement opportunities, job security, and characteristics of the physical and psychological work climate. Negative aspects of a job can produce undesirable effects, such as absenteeism, turnover, low productivity, frequent accidents, and labor grievances. I-O psychologists work to identify and modify conditions that can impair the quality of working life before they have serious psychological and economic consequences for employees and employers.

Organizational Psychology (Chapter 9). Few people work in isolation. Whether work is in a classroom, a department store, or a software company, it takes place within a particular organizational climate or culture. This culture includes the formal structure and policies of the organization, the nature of its leadership, and the informal groups that arise among workers. Informal groups may dictate norms and behaviors that are at variance with company policy.

Working Conditions (Chapter 10). The physical aspects of the work environment were the first factors to be studied by I-O psychologists. Much research was conducted on lighting, temperature, noise, workspace design, and working hours. Later, attention shifted to more complex social and psychological conditions of work. A job's psychological climate, including factors such as fatigue and boredom, may be more important than the physical climate, because psychological effects are subject to greater individual variation.

Employee Safety and Health Issues (Chapter 11). In addition to the tragic physical and personal consequences of industrial accidents, economic losses cost organizations billions of dollars in lost work hours, employee compensation, and the expense of hiring and training new workers. Because most accidents are caused by human error, the work of I-O psychologists is crucial in reducing the accident toll. Psychologists are also involved in efforts to deal with alcohol and drug use on the job and with violence in the workplace.

Stress in the Workplace (Chapter 12). Job-induced stress has widespread effects on physical and mental health. Stress can interfere with job performance and lead to serious illness. Many organizations attempt to deal with the effects of stress through counseling programs and by redesigning jobs to be less stressful.

Engineering Psychology (Chapter 13). The design of the tools and equipment needed to perform a job is directly related to the physical work environment, to employee motivation and morale, and to job safety. As the machinery of the manufacturing, transportation, and service industries becomes more complex, so do the demands placed on the human operators of the equipment. The job of the engineering psychologist is to ensure the best working relationship between person and machine by taking account of the strengths and weaknesses of both.

Consumer Psychology (Chapter 14). The work of consumer psychologists is important to you if you are employed by a company that manufactures and sells consumer products and services, and if you want to be a smart and informed buyer. Psychologists are involved in defining the markets for consumer goods, determining the effectiveness of advertising campaigns, and analyzing the motivations and needs of the buying public.

Summary

Work provides a sense of personal identity, defines social status, contributes to self-esteem, and satisfies the need for belonging to a group. **Industrial-organizational (I-O) psychology** is defined as the application of the methods, facts, and principles of the science of behavior and mental processes to people at work. As a science, psychology relies on observation and experimentation and deals with overt human behavior—behavior that can be observed objectively.

Industrial psychology began in the early twentieth century and grew under the impetus of the two world wars. A major change in industrial psychology came with the recognition of the influence of social and psychological factors on worker behavior, as demonstrated by the **Hawthorne studies** of the 1920s and 1930s. Engineering psychology emerged out of the development of the sophisticated weaponry of World War II. Organizational psychology developed in the 1960s in response to concern about the organizational climate in which work takes place.

Continuing challenges for I-O psychologists relate to virtual workplaces and virtual employees, the demands of new skills, the ethnic and generational diversity of the workforce, the changing nature of work itself, and the globalization of work.

To work professionally as an I-O psychologist, you need a master's degree, but you will find a position of greater responsibility with a doctoral degree. I-O psychologists in organizations face several problems brought about, in part, by the demand for their services. These practical problems include fraudulent practice of I-O psychology by persons who are not professionally trained, the difficulty of translating technical jargon so that ideas can be communicated to management, the unwillingness of managers and workers to try new ways of doing things, and the necessity of balancing research and timely solutions to problems.

Areas of I-O psychology discussed in the following chapters are employee selection, psychological testing, performance appraisal, training and development, leadership, motivation and job satisfaction, organizational psychology, working conditions, safety and health, stress, engineering psychology, and consumer psychology.

Key Terms[1]

Hawthorne studies
Industrial-organizational (I-O) psychology

Review Questions

1. Describe some ways in which the kind of work you do affects your life off the job.
2. How will the findings of I-O psychologists influence the way in which you perform your job?
3. How does I-O psychology influence everyday life, even away from work?
4. Give examples of ways in which I-O psychology can save money for your employer.
5. Explain how psychology as a science deals with aspects of behavior such as motivation, emotion, and intelligence, which cannot be objectively observed.
6. How did World War I influence the development of I-O psychology?
7. In what ways did the following individuals contribute to the development of I-O psychology: (a) Walter Dill Scott, (b) Hugo Münsterberg, (c) Elton Mayo?
8. Explain how the results of the Hawthorne studies opened new areas for I-O psychologists to explore.

---

[1]Key terms are defined at the top of the page on which they are first mentioned. These definitions are cumulated in alphabetical order in the Glossary section at the back of the book.

9. Describe the impact of World War II on the development of I-O psychology.

10. What are some advantages and disadvantages of electronically connected virtual workplaces?

11. In what ways can the hiring of temporary workers affect a company's full-time employees?

12. How have the trends toward virtual employees, virtual workplaces, and globalization changed the ways in which jobs are performed?

13. What challenges does the changing ethnic composition of the U.S. workforce offer for I-O psychologists?

14. Distinguish between the four generations in today's workforce.

15. Describe some of the characteristics of your generation. Do you think this is a fair description of yourself?

16. What kinds of jobs could you obtain with a bachelor's degree in psychology? Suppose you earned a PhD in I-O psychology; for what kinds of jobs would you be qualified?

17. What unique problems do I-O psychologists face in today's workplace? Which of these problems do you think is the most serious?

18. Describe the controversy between research and application.

Additional Reading

Benko, C., & Weisberg, A. (2007). *Mass career customization: Aligning the workplace with today's nontraditional workforce.* Cambridge, MA: Harvard Business School Press. Offers a program for dealing with the needs of a diverse, multigenerational workforce as well as changes in attitudes and family structures.

Bowe, J., Bowe, M., & Streeter, S. (Eds.). (2000). *Gig: Americans talk about their jobs at the turn of the millennium.* New York: Crown. Contains 126 oral history interviews from a wide cross section of the U.S. workforce ranging from an air force general to a movie director, a lawn maintenance worker, and a waitress. Interesting themes include job satisfaction or dissatisfaction, personal identification with one's work, negative features of glamorous jobs, and appealing features of repetitive jobs.

Fraser, J. A. (2001). *White-collar sweatshop; The deterioration of work and its rewards in corporate America.* New York: Norton. A grim portrait of the American workforce as full of stressed-out people caught up in a race they cannot win. Blames the situation of lengthening workdays, fears of layoffs and replacement by temporary workers, dilution of employee benefits, and the pervasive technology that allows the job to follow employees home.

Hedge, J. W., Borman, W. C., & Lammlein, S. E. (2005). *The aging workforce: Realities, myths, and implications for organizations.* Washington, DC: American Psychological Association. Examines the changing nature of the workforce including age stereotyping and employment discrimination, the effect of aging on job performance and motivation, and the resulting challenges for management.

Koppes, L. L. (Ed.). (2007). *Historical perspectives in industrial and organizational psychology.* Mahwah, NJ: Erlbaum. Reviews the history of selected topics in I-O psychology including personnel selection, job analysis, motivation, and leadership; a valuable resource for understanding the growth of the field.

Rogelberg, S. G. (Ed.). (2007). *Encyclopedia of industrial and organizational psychology.* Thousand Oaks, CA: Sage Publications. A comprehensive, well-organized overview of the variety of topics of interest to I-O researchers and practitioners.

CHAPTER 2

Techniques, Tools, and Tactics

CHAPTER OUTLINE

Scientific method   A controlled, objective, and systematic approach to research.

WHY STUDY RESEARCH METHODS?

Why study research methods? To put the question more bluntly, what's in it for you? Why do you need to know about how psychologists collect and analyze research data? Although you may not be interested in becoming an I-O psychologist, most likely you will have to deal with the findings of I-O psychologists. As a manager, you may interact with psychologists to find solutions to management problems, and you will be responsible for making decisions based on the recommendations of the company psychologist or of the consulting psychologist your organization has hired.

Suppose, for example, that you are put in charge of implementing a new manufacturing process to produce color monitors for computers. A modern production facility must be designed and built, and part of your job will be to facilitate the changeover from the old process to the new. You will have to consider several issues. How will workers react to an abrupt change in the way they do their jobs? Will they be sufficiently motivated to operate the new equipment and maintain a high standard of production? Will they need retraining? If so, how and where should the training be undertaken? How will the new process affect the company's safety record? These are just a few of the questions you will be expected to answer. If you make a bad decision or a misjudgment, the cost to you and your company will be high.

Using information based on psychological research, I-O psychologists may be able to help you. But if you are to evaluate their advice and recommendations, you must understand how they studied the problems and arrived at their conclusions. At some time you may be asked to decide whether a research program is worth the time and money. Knowledge of research methods will help you make this decision more wisely.

Our goal in this chapter is not to train you to conduct research but to acquaint you with the requirements, limitations, and methods of the scientific approach. By applying the **scientific method** to problems that are too often dealt with by intuition or guesswork, I-O psychologists make a distinctive contribution to improved management and work practices. If you understand their research tools, you will be able to ensure that they are used properly on the job.

Requirements of Psychological Research

Three requirements of scientific research are objective observation, control, and duplication and verification.

Objective Observation.   A basic requirement and defining characteristic of scientific research in any discipline is objective observation. Ideally, researchers base their conclusions on objective evidence, which they view without preconceived ideas or biases. For example, when a psychologist chooses a particular test, training method, or workspace design, that choice cannot be determined by private hunches, by the recommendation of some prestigious authority, or even by past research. The decision should be based on an objective evaluation of the facts of the present situation.

Control.   A second requirement of psychological research is that observations must be well controlled and systematic. The conditions under which objective observations are made should be predetermined so that every factor that could possibly influence the outcome is known to the researcher. For example, if psychologists are studying the effects of background music on the efficiency of employees in data-entry jobs, they must control the experimental situation so that no factors other than the music can affect worker productivity.

Duplication and Verification.   The systematic control of objective observation allows for the fulfillment of a third research requirement, that of duplication and verification. By carefully controlling conditions, a scientist working at another time and place can duplicate the conditions under which the earlier experiment was conducted. We can have more confidence in research findings if they have been verified by other investigators. Verification is possible only under carefully controlled conditions. Thus, psychological research in any setting requires systematic planning, control of the experimental situation so that the findings can be duplicated and verified, and objective observation.

Limitations of Psychological Research

Psychologists face many challenges in designing and executing a psychological research program within the confines of a university laboratory. But when they undertake a study in the real-life setting of a factory or office, the problems are magnified.

Not All Behavior Can Be Studied. One obvious limitation is that research methods cannot be applied to every problem. For example, social psychologists cannot conduct controlled observations of how people behave in riots. The situation is too complex and dangerous to arrange in advance. Similarly, in industry it is not feasible to conduct systematic research on some mechanical safety devices that might expose workers to possible injury. There is a limit to what people should be asked to risk in the interest of scientific research.

Observing Behavior Can Change It. The act of observing people in an experiment can interfere with or change the behavior that is being studied. For example, if employees are asked to take a personality test as part of research on job satisfaction, they may deliberately distort their test responses because they do not want to answer personal questions or because they don't like their boss or the company psychologist. For another example, consider research to investigate the effects of jet engine noise on the efficiency of airline mechanics. If the mechanics are aware that they are part of a psychological research study, they may deliberately work faster or slower than they would on a normal workday when they were not being observed.

The Hawthorne Effect. Sometimes employee behavior changes just because something new has been introduced into the workplace. This phenomenon was first observed during the Hawthorne experiments and has come to be called the Hawthorne effect. Recall from chapter 1 that one of the Hawthorne studies involved increasing the level of lighting in a work area. Production rose with each increase in illumination and then remained high even when the lighting level was reduced. It didn't seem to matter whether the light was brighter or dimmer. It was the change— something new happening in the workplace—that affected worker productivity. The psychologist conducting research must determine whether the differences observed in the behavior of the subjects result from the actual working conditions under study or if they arise from the novelty of the change itself, independent of working conditions.

Artificial Settings. Some studies must be conducted in artificial settings. Management may not allow psychologists to disrupt production by experimenting with various work procedures on the assembly line or in the office. As a result, research may have to be conducted in a simulated job environment. In such cases, research results will be based on performance in a situation that is not identical to the job environment in which the findings are to be applied. This artificiality may reduce the usefulness of the research findings. A comparison of several hundred studies of the performance of work teams in organizations found that research carried out in laboratory settings yielded results that differed from research conducted in field or on-the-job settings, even though all the research programs were studying the same variables. Thus, *where* the research was done affected the outcomes (Bell, 2007).

College Students as Subjects. The problem of artificiality is complicated by the fact that much research in I-O psychology is conducted in universities and relies on college students as subjects. A review of five leading journals showed that in 87% of the studies, students were used as subjects. Most studies comparing the characteristics and behaviors of student and nonstudent samples reveal important differences between the two groups. For example, in one study experienced business managers and college students performed the same task: evaluating applicants for a management position. Students rated the applicants much higher and deserving of higher starting salaries than did the business managers.

Thus, college students may behave differently from employees and managers on the job, and these differences limit the generalizability of the research findings. Although some I-O psychologists argue that

Experimental method   The scientific way to determine the effect or influence of a variable on the subjects' performance or behavior.

Independent variable   In an experiment, this is the stimulus variable that is manipulated to determine its effect on the subjects' behavior.

Dependent variable   In an experiment, this is the resulting behavior of the subjects, which depends on the manipulation of the independent variable.

research conducted in university laboratories can be generalized to human resources and organizational issues, other psychologists maintain that the differences are so great that only the most cautious generalization is acceptable. To maximize the usefulness of the findings we discuss in this book, we rely primarily on research that studies employees and managers in actual work situations.

THE EXPERIMENTAL METHOD

Several research methods are available to psychologists who conduct studies in the workplace. Selecting the most effective technique is one of the first issues to be resolved in any research program. In most cases, the technique will be determined by the nature of the problem to be investigated. We discuss the following techniques: experiments, naturalistic observations, surveys, and Web-based research.

The **experimental method** is simple in its basic concept but can be difficult to implement. The

purpose of an experiment is to determine the effect or influence of a variable on the performance or behavior of the people being studied (the subjects).

Psychologists distinguish two variables in an experiment. One is the stimulus, or **independent variable**, the effects of which psychologists are interested in determining. The other is the participants' resulting behavior, called the **dependent variable** because it depends on the independent variable. Both variables can be objectively observed, measured, and recorded.

Designing an Experiment

Consider the following experiment. Management is concerned about the poor productivity of a group of workers who assemble television sets. Company psychologists are asked to study how output could be increased. At first they suggest a number of factors that could be responsible for the low level of production, such as low pay, inadequate training,

Newsbreak

How Not to Get Hired, Part 2: It's Your E-mail Address, Dude!

Are you proud of your e-mail address? Do you think it's clever, funny, or offbeat? That it reflects who you are and what you're about? Well, potential employers might not agree. They are likely to turn down your application, not on the basis of your qualifications but because they were turned off by the way you chose to represent yourself to the big wired world.

Steve Watkins reviewed 300 e-mailed résumés in his search for a network administrator. He was appalled by some of the addressees and compiled examples for his Web site. He changed the domain names to "@domain.com," to protect the innocent.

If you recognize your e-mail address in this list, Watkins said, "we have already filled our position—and it wasn't with you, Dude."

IBFreakin@domain.com
2hot4u@domain.com
SleazyLiza@domain.com
Hottie@domain.com
DrinkMoreBeer@domain.com
Joe6Pack@domain.com
Dude@domain.com
SleepyHead@domain.com

Source: Watkins, S. (2002, November 5). Top 10 ways *not* to get hired. Retrieved from lowendmac.com/practical/02/1105.html an unpopular supervisor, and obsolete equipment. After they inspect the workplace, however, the psychologists suspect that the problem is insufficient lighting. They design an experiment to test this hypothesis.

The two variables in the experiment are easy to identify and measure. The independent variable is the level of lighting. This is the stimulus variable, which the psychologists will increase during the experiment to determine the effects. The dependent variable is the workers' response rate—in this case, their measured rate of production with the changed lighting.

The psychologists arrange for the lighting level in the workroom to be increased, and they measure production before the experiment and after 2 weeks of the brighter lighting. Prior to the change in lighting, each worker assembled an average of three television sets an hour. Two weeks later, individual production averaged eight units an hour, a considerable increase.

Why Did Production Increase?   Can we conclude that the change in the independent variable (the brighter lighting) brought about the change in the dependent variable (the greater productivity)? No. We cannot draw this conclusion on the basis of the experiment as described.

How do we know that some factor other than lighting was not responsible for the higher production? Perhaps the boss was nicer to the workers during the 2-week experiment because he knew the company psychologists were hanging around. Maybe the workers purposely produced more because they thought their jobs were being threatened. Maybe sunny weather made the workers happier, or perhaps production increased because of the Hawthorne effect, the fact that some change had been introduced to break the usual monotony of the workday. Many other factors could account for the increase in production. The psychologists must be certain that nothing operated to influence the subjects' behavior except the stimulus being manipulated.

The Element of Control.   An essential feature of the scientific method was omitted from the experi-

ment: the element of control. Controlling the experimental conditions ensures that any change in the behavior or performance of the research participants is solely attributable to the independent variable.

To produce this necessary control, psychologists use two groups of subjects in an experiment: the **experimental group**, which consists of the subjects exposed to the independent variable, and the **control group**. The experimental and control groups should be as similar as possible in every respect except that the control group is not exposed to the independent variable. To conduct the experiment properly, then, the psychologists must separate the workers into these two groups. Worker productivity is measured before and after the experimental period. The production level of the control group serves as a standard against which to compare the resulting performance of the experimental group.

If the groups of workers are similar and if the performance of the experimental group at the end of the experiment is significantly higher than that of the control group, then we can conclude that the improved lighting was responsible for the increased production. Extraneous factors, such as the weather, the supervisor's behavior, or the Hawthorne effect, could not have influenced the subjects' behavior. If any of these factors had been influential, then the performance of both groups would have changed similarly.

Selecting the Subjects

The people in the control group and the experimental group must be as similar as possible. There are two methods experimenters can use to ensure this: the random group design and the matched group design.

The **random group design** involves assigning subjects at random to the experimental and control groups. In our experiment, if the company employed 100 assemblers of television sets, the psychologists would arbitrarily assign 50 to the experimental condition and 50 to the control condition. Because the basis

Matched group design   A method for ensuring similarity between experimental and control groups that matches subjects in both groups on characteristics, such as age, job experience, and intelligence, that could affect the dependent variable.

for dividing the workers into experimental and control conditions is random, we may assume that the groups are essentially similar. Any possible influencing variables, such as age or length of job experience, should be evenly distributed over the two groups because these factors were not allowed to influence the assignment of the subjects.

In the **matched group design**, to ensure similarity between experimental and control groups, subjects in one group are matched with subjects in the other group on the basis of characteristics that could affect their performance (the dependent variable). For our experiment, the psychologists could find pairs of subjects who are matched on age, job experience, intelligence, and supervisor ratings; then they could assign one member of each pair to each group. In this way, the experimental and control groups would be as alike as possible.

Although desirable, the matched group technique is costly and difficult to carry out. To find enough pairs of subjects, the researchers would need an even larger pool of potential participants from whom to choose. Also, it becomes extremely complicated to equate pairs of subjects on more than one factor. Matching people on length of job experience alone presents few problems, but matching them on several factors at the same time is cumbersome.

A Sample Experiment: The Effects of Training Conditions on Turnover and Productivity

As a classic example of a typical experiment,[1] let us consider the research conducted in a factory in which sewing machine operators produced women's lingerie. Management had asked a consulting psychologist to find out why 68% of the sewing machine operators quit within a year. After taking a survey of employee attitudes and interviewing the supervisors, the psychologist hypothesized that the reason for the high turnover was insufficient job training.

---

[1]From "Effect of Training on the Productivity and Tenure of Sewing Machine Operators," by J. Lefkowitz, 1970, *Journal of Applied Psychology, 54*, pp. 81–86.

The psychologist devised a study to investigate the effects of several training conditions on the rate of turnover as well as on the rate of productivity. Note that the initial problem leading to the research was the high number of people quitting. In the process of designing an experiment to focus on this problem, the psychologist realized that with little extra effort, data could also be secured on a second dependent variable: the level of production.

Subjects and Experimental Design.   The subjects were 208 female employees hired in 1 year as trainees. The dependent variables were (1) job turnover, defined as the percentage of workers who quit in their first 40 days on the job, and (2) productivity, defined in terms of daily output figures in the first 40 days on the job. The psychologist chose the 40-day period because company records showed that most terminations occurred during that time. The dependent variables were easy to observe, measure, and record with precision.

The independent variable was the level of training. The psychologist specified four training periods. The company's standard practice was to provide 1 day of training for new employees, conducted in a special training facility. This 1-day training was designated as the control condition against which other training periods would be compared.

Trainees assigned to Group I took the standard 1-day training course. Group II received 2 days of training in the training facility, and Group III received 3 days of training in the training facility. Group IV had 3 days of training, but part of it was conducted in the training facility and part of it took place in the workroom.

Workers were assigned to each of the four conditions on the basis of the date of their initial employment with the company. Those hired during the first month of the study were placed in Group I, those hired during the second month in Group II, and so on; the cycle was repeated throughout the year the study was in progress. Statistical comparisons of each group's initial performance demonstrated the similarity.

Naturalistic observation   The scientific observation of behavior in its natural setting, without any experimental manipulation of the independent variable.

FIGURE 2–1   Turnover rates of four training conditions.

Results.   The results of the turnover study revealed that the longer the training received in the training facility (Groups I, II, and III), the lower the rate of turnover (see Figure 2–1). The 3-day training period combining on-the-job experience with the training facility (Group IV) did not reduce the turnover rate when it was compared to the 3-day training period conducted wholly in the training facility (Group III). As you can see, however, comparing Groups I and III shows that the additional days of training reduced turnover from 53% to 33%.

The second part of the study (the effect of training on productivity) produced unexpected complications. The data showed that the longer the time spent in the training facility, the lower the average daily rate of production (see Figure 2–2). The 3 days of training in the facility and on the job (Group IV)

led to greater productivity than did the 3 days of training in the facility alone (Group III).

Thus, the independent variable (the different training levels) produced conflicting results on the dependent variables. Greater time in the training room resulted in lower turnover, but it also yielded lower productivity. It is at this point—interpreting the research results—that the training and experience of the I-O psychologist are put to their most severe test. Experiments do not always turn out the way the researcher hopes. Hypotheses are not always confirmed. Results are not always clear and consistent, and considerable interpretive skill is necessary to relate the data to the job or the problem being studied and to explain the options to management.

The psychologist conducting this experiment evaluated the productivity and turnover data and concluded that the 3-day integrated training condition (Group IV) would be the most profitable for the company. It yielded a close second-highest level of production and a close second-lowest rate of turnover.

Keep in mind that research proceeds on two levels: first, designing the experiment and second, interpreting and implementing the results. At both levels, psychologists depend on the cooperation of managers and workers who understand the requirements of psychological research.

THE NATURALISTIC OBSERVATION METHOD

In the study of human behavior at work, it is not always possible to bring the relevant variables under the precise control required by the experimental method. Also, it may be more useful to study behavior as it occurs in real life. One of the limitations of the experimental method is artificiality. To avoid this, psychologists sometimes prefer to observe behavior in its natural setting without introducing any manipulation of the independent variable. This is the essence of the method of **naturalistic observation**. Although this method does not involve manipulation of the

FIGURE 2–2   Production levels of four training conditions.

independent variable, the psychologist is still able to maintain some control over the situation.

One advantage of naturalistic observation is that the behaviors being observed and the situations in which they are observed are typical of what occurs in everyday life. The findings of naturalistic observation can be more readily generalized and applied to real life because that is where they were obtained. After all, ordinary daily activities occur in situations that are not under the stringent control necessary in the experimental method.

This advantage is also a major weakness. Because researchers do not manipulate the independent variable, it is sometimes difficult to conclude with assurance what brought about any resulting change in the subjects' behavior or performance. Another limitation is that the observation cannot be repeated. It is impossible to duplicate the exact conditions that prevailed during the initial observation.

The experimental method also has problems, as we noted. Nevertheless, when the experimental method can be used, it is a better choice than naturalistic observation, because the experimenter can control and systematically manipulate the independent variable. However, both methods, when applied with precision and interpreted with care, are valuable in the study of human behavior in the workplace.

A Sample Controlled Observation: The Friendly Behaviors of Convenience Store Clerks

A nationwide chain of convenience stores instituted a training program to teach its clerks to be friendly toward customers.[2] The company wanted to determine whether the friendly behaviors would lead to an increase in sales and thus justify the expense of the training. Arranging an experiment would have been difficult and might not have been informative. The company could have compared sales at two stores, one that had clerks trained to be friendly and one that did not, but that might have meant a loss in sales at the control group store and the possible alienation of customers.

---

[2]From "Untangling the Relationship Between Displayed Emotions and Organizational Sales: The Case of Convenience Stores," by R. I. Sulton and A. Rafaeli, 1988, *Academy of Management Journal, 31,* pp. 461–487.

The company could have designed a laboratory experiment in which people would pose as courteous clerks and rude clerks. Persons playing the role of customer would be asked if they thought they would buy more from the courteous clerks than from the rude clerks, but that would have been too artificial a situation. Also, the results would not tell the company anything about the impact of friendly behavior on actual sales.

Research Design. The psychologists decided to conduct a naturalistic observation in which the behavior of 1,319 clerks in 576 convenience stores was secretly watched by trained observers during 11,805 transactions with customers. The clerks had been informed that their level of courtesy would be monitored at some time, but they were not told when and how the observations would take place.

The observers, chosen to fit the profile of a typical customer, pretended to be making purchases. They spent from 4 to 12 minutes in each store, depending on how many real customers were present. The more crowded the store, the longer the observers could linger without causing the clerks to be suspicious. Observers reported that they thought clerks were suspicious of them in fewer than 3% of the observations; these data were excluded from consideration. The clerks' friendly behaviors, as recorded by the observers, included smiling at customers, greeting customers, thanking customers, and maintaining eye contact with customers. These behaviors, along with the sales figures for each store, were the dependent variables.

Although no independent variables were manipulated, factors that might have influenced behavior and sales were controlled. For example, the proportion of female clerks to male clerks was considered to control for variation in courteous behavior by gender; past research had suggested that women tend to be more courteous than men in any setting. The proportion of female to male customers was recorded to control for gender differences in purchasing behavior. Why? Because if some stores were patronized primarily by women, for example, and if women typically made more purchases than men did, then the sales figures for those stores would be higher, independent of the clerks' behavior.

The stores for the observations were selected at random, but all were in heavily populated urban districts. None was in a suburban or rural area

> **Survey research method**   Interviews, behavioral observations, and questionnaires designed to sample what people say about their feelings or opinions, or how they say they will behave in a given situation.

where the sales pattern might differ from that of an urban area. Researchers recognized that people in various regions of the United States have different buying habits, independent of the company's training program; therefore, the data from four sectors—Northeast, South, Midwest, and West—were analyzed separately. Taking the research out of the laboratory and conducting it in the real world still permitted the psychologists to control relevant variables and make objective observations.

Results.   To the researchers' surprise, the findings showed that the higher the incidence of courteous behaviors, the lower the sales. Analysis of the data revealed that a store's level of sales influenced the clerks' behaviors, and the courteous behaviors taught in the training program did not lead to increases in sales. The busier the store (the higher the sales), the less time the clerks had to be courteous. In stores with lower sales, clerks had time to be friendlier. The results also confirmed that female clerks were more courteous than male clerks and that clerks in the West were more courteous than those in the Northeast.

The behavior being observed in this example was not as well controlled as it could have been under laboratory conditions, but the greater realism afforded by the real-life situation offset this disadvantage. In many cases, the nature and complexity of the phenomena under investigation determine the most appropriate method of study. In other instances, the psychologist must decide whether to sacrifice some measure of control for greater applicability.

SURVEYS AND OPINION POLLS

Surveys and opinion polls rely on the observation of behavior as it is revealed in the subjects' responses to personal interviews and questionnaires. The focus in the **survey research method** is not on what people do (as in experiments or naturalistic observations) but on what they say they will do.

Survey questionnaires and interviews have many applications in I-O psychology. Psychologists

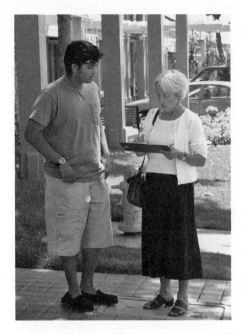

The focus of the survey method is on what people tell interviewers they will do rather than on what they actually do.

use surveys to ascertain factors that contribute to job satisfaction and morale. Some large organizations maintain a staff of poll-takers to conduct periodic employee surveys on a variety of work-related issues. This polling gives employees the chance to air gripes and complaints (a form of upward communication). It also assesses reactions to changes in work procedures and policies and provides the opportunity for employee participation in policymaking. As a result, surveys have the potential for raising employee morale, reducing turnover, and avoiding costly union grievance procedures. In some plants, maintaining an open channel of communication between employees and employers has prevented unionization. Workers who believe their opinions are heard and valued by management are less likely to feel the need for union representation.

Advertising and motivation research firms use survey techniques to uncover consumer preferences. For example, Campbell Soup questioned more than 100,000 consumers to determine their food likes and dislikes. On the basis of the survey results, the company changed the seasonings in its frozen dinners and introduced a line of low-salt soups.

In addition, public opinion polls are routinely used in political campaigns to assess voter reaction to candidates and to the issues in their platforms.

Problems with Surveys. Even the best polling organizations have difficulty, however, with the precise measurement of personal opinions and attitudes. In some cases, people deliberately lie when they are asked questions in a survey; or they may say they will do one thing and then do something else. People change their minds; for example, they tell an interviewer in October that they will vote Republican, then they vote Democratic in the November elections.

People may say they prefer a particular brand of clothing or automobile because they believe this choice will make them appear sophisticated. They may claim to drink an expensive imported beer, for example, but if interviewers could look in the refrigerator, they might find cans of an inexpensive local brew instead.

Sometimes people express an opinion in response to a survey question even when they do not have one, because they do not want the interviewer to think they are uninformed. An analysis of 37 surveys showed that 64% of the respondents claimed to have read the magazine article the poll-takers were questioning them about. In reality, no such article had ever been published. The results also showed that people were more likely to be honest in their responses when they completed a questionnaire in private than when they were asked the same questions in a face-to-face interview.

These difficulties with the survey method can explain some lost elections, failed businesses, and bad management decisions. The fault lies not with the method itself but with the complex, subjective, and sometimes perverse nature of our attitudes, preferences, and behaviors. Keep in mind, however, that properly designed surveys can be highly accurate, and they succeed more often than they fail.

Interviews

Four basic ways to collect survey data are personal interviews, paper-and-pencil questionnaires, Web-based surveys, and telephone surveys. The personal

Telephone surveys offer a low cost per interview and the likelihood that an interviewer can contact hundreds of people in the course of a workday.

interview, the most expensive and time-consuming technique, requires a face-to-face meeting with respondents.

Finding and training capable interviewers is vital because their appearance, manner, and behavior can influence the way people cooperate with them and answer their questions. Research has shown that people respond differently to interview questions, depending on the interviewer's age, race, and gender. More subtle interviewer variables can also affect survey results. For example, say an interviewer asking questions about drug use shows by smiling or frowning apparent agreement or disagreement with what the respondent is saying. That respondent may change subsequent answers because of his or her perception of the interviewer's opinion about drug use.

Personal, or face-to-face, interviews offer several advantages over other ways of collecting survey data. In general, personal interviews have higher response rates (some as high as 90%) than telephone questionnaires or mailed questionnaires. Personal interviews can reach persons who are unable to read. In addition, interviewers are available to clarify questions the respondents may have about the process.

A disadvantage of these interviews is that some people are uncomfortable disclosing personal information in a face-to-face situation. Also, many people now choose to live in gated or enclosed housing communities or in secure apartment or condominium complexes. Interviewers may find it difficult to reach people at these economic levels.

Newsbreak

The Guy Who Knew He Was Right

The year was 1936 and everyone agreed that President Franklin D. Roosevelt was going to lose his bid for reelection. The largest, most prestigious public opinion polling organization, The Literary Digest, had never been wrong. The company had correctly predicted the five previous elections, down to precise percentage points, and the company's polls showed that Roosevelt was going to lose. It was a done deal.

But from a tiny office above a store in Princeton, New Jersey, the brash 35-year-old head of an upstart polling company in business only a year, announced that his poll results showed that Roosevelt would win. The establishment laughed at him. What could he know? Come election day, Roosevelt won in the biggest landslide of any presidential election in history, and so George Gallup, and his Gallup Poll, were launched, on their way to becoming a major force in public opinion polling.

How did Gallup do it? By taking an objective, scientific approach to the measurement of public opinion. As a former editor of the University of Iowa's student newspaper, Gallup had written an editorial urging students to "Doubt everything. Question everything. Be a radical!" He received his PhD in applied psychology in 1928 with a dissertation titled, "An Objective Method for Determining Reader Interest in the Content of a Newspaper." For Gallup, the only way to measure public opinion accurately was through what he called a "laboratory attitude of mind," using researchers trained in the scientific method.

Which was how he called the 1936 election correctly when others got it wrong. The Literary Digest had mailed survey questionnaires to millions of homes throughout the country to people selected from telephone directories and lists of automobile registrations. The problem with this approach was that the nation was in the midst of the Great Depression, and many voters could not afford cars or phones.

Gallup, in contrast, sampled only 2,000 people, but these were carefully chosen to be a representative sample of the entire U.S. voting population, and they were interviewed individually by his pollsters. The majority of them said they planned to vote for Roosevelt. And so George Gallup won the polling election over The Literary Digest and changed the way public opinion was sampled for the next 70 years.

Sources: Blackwell, J. (2007). 1935: The Poll That Took America's Pulse. Retrieved from www.capitalcentury.com/1935.html; Igo, S. (2006). A gold mine and a tool for democracy: George Gallup, Elmo Roper, and the business of scientific polling, 1935–1955. *Journal of the History of the Behavioral Sciences, 42,* 109–145.

Paper-and-Pencil Questionnaires

Questionnaires offer a cheaper and more convenient way to obtain information from large numbers of people over a wide geographical area. I-O psychologists today frequently use questionnaires to collect information from employees. Because employees can remain anonymous, they are more likely to respond freely and openly. Also, because employees can take their time, they can formulate their answers more carefully. Thus, the views reported in questionnaires are often more reliable than those expressed in a personal interview.

The major disadvantage of questionnaire surveys is that the response rate is typically only 40% to 45%. Follow-up procedures are sometimes used to try to secure additional returns. A reminder letter or postcard can be mailed to all questionnaire recipients explaining the importance of the survey and requesting cooperation. Letters sent by registered mail and follow-up telephone calls can also be used to encourage compliance. Some companies offer incentives for responding to a survey. A few hold contests with valuable prizes as inducements for returning the questionnaires. Most companies offer only a token payment, such as a dollar bill, which is often sufficient to make respondents feel guilty if they take the money and do not answer the questions.

Web-Based Surveys

Most organizations today use electronic methods to conduct polls of their employees. Questions are posted through e-mail, intranet, or Internet services, and employees respond by using their keyboards to enter their answers. Electronic polls can be completed more quickly than face-to-face polls. Companies such as Allstate, Duke Power, IBM, and Xerox routinely conduct electronic surveys and post the results online, accessible to all their employees.

I-O psychologists have conducted research to compare responses to paper questionnaires with responses to computer-administered questionnaires. Several studies have reported no significant differences. Other studies comparing paper-and-pencil questionnaires with Web-based questionnaires showed that employees in the United States, Japan, and France preferred online survey approaches to the paper-and-pencil format. A significant age difference

was found; employees younger than 50 preferred the online approach, whereas employees older than 50 preferred the paper-and-pencil technique (Church, 2001). Later research supported the finding that the majority of employees preferred the online survey approach. No significant differences in that preference were found by gender, race, or military versus nonmilitary status (Thompson, Surface, Martin, & Sanders, 2003).

Research comparing Web-based and telephone surveys found that Web-based surveys produced more reliable data and were less expensive and less time-consuming to conduct than telephone surveys (Braunsberger, Wybenga, & Gates, 2007).

Despite the popularity of Web-based surveys, there are several disadvantages to this approach. Since these surveys are faster and less expensive to conduct than other types of surveys, management has tended to solicit employee opinions just because it can be done so easily. Sometimes management does not have a clear objective in mind about how it intends to use the survey results. Employees complain about being questioned too

Newsbreak

Push Polls: Truth, or Out-of-Context?

In addition to collecting information from voters, public opinion polls can provide information. And some of it may be false or distorted information about a political candidate that can ruin his or her chances of winning. These polls are called push polls, because they are designed to see if certain negative information can push voters away from one candidate in favor of the candidate who is paying for the poll.

Here's how they work. A polling firm hired by Congressman Green, let us say, calls several thousand registered voters in the congressional district. The callers are asked if they intend to vote for Green or for the opponent, Candidate Brown. Voters who say they plan to vote for Brown or who have not yet made up their minds are asked a question of this type: "If I told you that Brown was once arrested for fraud—for cheating senior citizens out of their life savings—would that make a difference in your vote?"

Note how the question is phrased. The pollster is not saying that Brown had actually been arrested on such charges—which, in truth, he had not. But merely by raising the issue, the pollster implies clearly that Brown had been arrested. In this way, thousands of people in the voting district can be fed false information about an opposition candidate in the otherwise innocent guise of taking a poll.

Push polls have been used by candidates of major political parties at all levels of government. And, as you might expect, their use has raised ethical questions. One poll-taker criticized this questionable practice in the trade journal *Campaign Elections*: "The truth is that polls are being used in today's campaigns as much to shape public opinion as to simply report it. Some polling may be used to mislead the public by skewing questions or reporting results out of proper context."

frequently and seeing no action taken in response to their opinions and suggestions. When they believe that their input is not being considered or appreciated, they are likely to disregard future surveys. A study of 661 civilian and military employees of a large military organization showed that people were far more likely to respond to a survey if they knew that the organization had acted on their responses to previous surveys (Kroustalis, Behrend, Meade, & Surface, 2007).

There are also concerns about what has been called ballot stuffing; that is, employees making repeated responses to the same survey. This, of course, can bias the results. Employees are also concerned about privacy. Even if they do not provide their names when responding to a company survey,

Newsbreak

Call Me "Unresponsive"

"Blame me, if you wish, for the poor showing of conservatives in opinion polls. I refuse to respond to telephone polls. It's not that I'm unpatriotic, or that I don't want my opinion to count. I vote in every election, and it's partly because my name appears on voter lists that I get so many calls—about one or two a week. I used to respond to pollsters. Why did I swear off them?

- Polls take up my time. The calls interrupt me, whatever I'm doing. What right does Gallup or whoever have to something of mine that he intends to turn around and sell to political parties and publications?

- How do I know it's Gallup or Harris or Fox News or Time/CNN or whoever at the other end of the line? Back when I did answer polls, one pollster asked me what bank I went to and how often I visited it. Thus began my refusals.

- Some questions are too personal, or even dangerous, to answer—like the bank questions. I've also been asked the number of people in my household, whether I have a dog and a gun, and my total household income. These touchy questions get asked late in a poll, since it's harder to stop answering midway than never to begin answering at all.

- Many pollsters are nice, but some are rude. One waited until 10 minutes into our conversation before hitting me with the family income stuff. When I declined to answer, she blew up. She said I had to answer or the entire in-depth survey and her time would be wasted. So both of us had wasted our time.

- Some pollsters are salespeople. Under the pretense of polling, a caller might ask, for instance, if you belong to a church, then if you believe in God, and then if you would like to visit his group's new chapel or buy its religion book.

- Many pollsters try to influence opinion. They may ask if you are aware of the horrible things their political opponents have done lately. They don't really want a yes or no; they want to open a discussion in which they mold your views and maybe get a contribution from you for their cause.

- Poll responses often aren't private. They can be recorded and circulated, with respondents' names attached. One evening at a Republican Party caucus, I was treated to a computer printout of a poll taken in my neighborhood. Whom did we intend to vote for, Candidate A, Candidate B, No Opinion, or Refused to Answer? There it was—my entire block, house by house, with my address listed as Refused to Answer. But wasn't it fun gawking at the political leanings of all those people I knew? . . . I do my part by taking opinion poll results with a grain of salt. Others might do likewise."

Source: Dickerson, G. (1999, July 13). *New York Times*.

> **Open-end questions** Survey questions to which respondents state their views in their own words. They are similar to essay questions on college exams.
>
> **Fixed-alternative questions** Survey questions to which respondents limit their answers to the choices or alternatives presented. They are similar to multiple-choice questions on college exams.

can they be certain that their anonymity is protected? Such fears prevent some employees from expressing an opinion that they believe may be contrary to company policy. Despite these disadvantages, Web-based surveys have quickly become the most frequently used approach to employee polling.

Telephone Surveys

Telephone surveys offer the advantage of a low cost per interview and the possibility that a single interviewer can contact several hundred people a day. Telephone surveys have been aided by computerized phone systems that speed up the contact process. Telephone surveys cost approximately half as much as personal interviews and they obtain comparable data. As you probably know from your own experience, however, it is difficult to reach some people by telephone because modern technology makes it easy for them to avoid unwanted callers. One survey researcher described it as follows: "The majority of American households now have answering machines, caller ID, or both, and substantial numbers of households use them to screen out unwanted calls. Many survey professionals report anecdotally that telephone response rates have plummeted over the last decade" (Tourangeau, 2004, p. 782).

The widespread use of cell phones has created problems for this type of survey. Survey and polling organizations are not allowed to use computer dialing (so-called robo-dialing) to call cellular telephone numbers. Many people have given up their traditional landline phones and use only cell phones; thus, these people are not likely to be included in a telephone survey sample. In one government study, researchers found that nearly one third of respondents between the ages of 18 and 29 use cell phones exclusively (Graff, 2007; Thee, 2007).

Survey Questions

With any survey, regardless of the method used to collect the data, two basic problems must be resolved: (1) what questions will be asked and (2) who will be questioned. In general, surveys use either open-end questions or fixed-alternative questions.

With **open-end questions**, which are similar to the essay questions on college exams, respondents present their views in their own words without any restrictions. They are encouraged to answer as fully as they desire and to take as much time as they need. If the questionnaire contains many open-end questions, the process will be time-consuming. The usefulness of the replies depends on how skillfully the subjects verbalize their thoughts and feelings. Open-end questions place considerable pressure on interviewers to be complete and accurate in recording the answers.

Fixed-alternative questions, like multiple-choice exam questions, limit a person's answer to specific alternatives. A typical open-end question might be: How do you feel about raising taxes to provide money for schools? A fixed-alternative question on the same topic might be this: With regard to raising taxes to provide more money for schools, are you in favor _____, opposed _____, or undecided _____? Thus, the respondent is faced with a finite number of choices and a restricted way in which to answer.

Fixed-alternative questions simplify the survey and allow more questions to be asked in a given period of time. Also, answers to fixed-alternative questions can be recorded more easily and accurately than can answers to open-end questions. A disadvantage is that the limited number of alternatives may not accurately reflect the respondent's opinion. A person could be in favor of higher school taxes under some circumstances and opposed to them under others. When answers are restricted to yes, no, or undecided, people cannot make these feelings known to the interviewer. If enough people in the sample have such unexpressed reservations, the results will be misleading.

Usually it is a good idea to pretest survey questions on a small sample of respondents to make sure that the questions are worded clearly. If subjects misinterpret a question or detect unintended meanings, the results may be biased. For example, a survey by the National Center for Health Statistics

Probability sampling   A method for constructing a representative sample of a population for surveys or polls. Each person in the population has a known probability or chance of being included in the sample.

Quota sampling   A method for constructing a representative sample of a population for surveys or polls. Because the sample must reflect the proportions of the larger population, quotas are established for various categories such as age, gender, and ethnic origin.

questioned Americans about "abdominal pain" until poll-takers discovered that a number of people—enough to skew the survey results—did not understand the phrase: They did not know where the abdomen was located or even what it was. When respondents were shown a diagram of the body and the abdominal region was pointed out, their answers turned out to be quite different.

The wording of survey questions presents a challenge for I-O psychologists because approximately 25% of the U.S. workforce is functionally illiterate. People who cannot read and comprehend questionnaire items and instructions will not be motivated to complete the survey and may not have the ability to do so properly even if they wanted to.

Sampling Methods

Suppose a consulting psychologist is asked by the Texas state legislature to determine the opinions of automobile owners about a proposed increase in the fee for a driver's license. To question every car owner in the state would be tedious and difficult, even with sufficient time and money, and it would not be possible to locate and interview everyone. Nor is it necessary. With careful planning, surveying a representative sample of car owners will provide the desired information and predict the responses of the total population.

To select a sample of car owners in Texas, the psychologist could stop people at shopping centers, gas stations, or busy intersections. However, this would not guarantee that the people would be typical, or representative, of all car owners in the state. The people encountered at a high-end shopping mall in the suburbs of Dallas or Houston, for example, would be more likely to represent a higher income bracket than the state's large and diverse population. Is there a better way to identify a representative sample of the population for the survey?

Two ways to construct a representative sample of a population are probability sampling and quota sampling. In **probability sampling**, each person in the population has a known probability or chance of being included in the sample. By securing from the state department of motor vehicles a list of all automobile owners, the researcher can select, say, every 10th or 25th name, depending on how large a sample is needed. In this way, every person in the population of registered car owners has the same chance (1 in 10 or 1 in 25) of being included in the sample. This method is satisfactory as long as there is a list of everyone in the population. If we wanted to study all eligible voters in the United States, this method would not be useful because only registered voters are listed.

In **quota sampling**, the researcher attempts to construct a duplicate in miniature of the larger population. If it is known from census data that in Texas 20% of all car owners are college graduates, 50% are men, 40% are of Hispanic origin, and so on, then the sample must reflect these proportions. Interviewers are given quotas for people to interview in the various categories and must find appropriate respondents. Because the persons questioned are chosen by the interviewers, however, their personal feelings and prejudices can affect the selection of the sample. One interviewer may prefer to talk only to people who appear well dressed; another might select only women.

Employee Attitudes Toward Surveys

Some employees decline to respond to surveys; this refusal can bias the results. In some instances, employees may not have received a questionnaire, or they may have misplaced it and forgotten about it. But others adamantly refuse to participate in any survey by their employer about their attitudes, opinions, interests, and feelings. The number of noncompliant employees has been rising, often because managers survey their employees too frequently, asking for information so often that employees become annoyed. When the response rate to an organization's questionnaires is thus reduced, the resulting data can provide managers with misleading information.

In a study of 194 employees, investigators found that people who said they would not fill out a company survey differed in important ways from people who agreed to answer the company's questions (Rogelberg, Luong, Sederburg, & Cristol, 2000). The noncompliant employees were found to have a greater stated intention of quitting their jobs. Compared with the employees who did complete the survey, the noncompliant employees were less committed to the company and less satisfied with their work. Furthermore, these employees placed a low value on the responses the company had made to previous surveys. In this instance, then, the replies that management received to its survey came primarily from employees who were highly satisfied with their jobs and supportive of the organization. Therefore, the company did not obtain a representative selection of their employees' views.

Similar results were obtained in a study of 96 health care workers in the Netherlands. Those who said they were more likely to respond to employee surveys held far more positive attitudes toward their work and their organization than did those who said they were less likely to participate (Taris & Schreurs, 2007). In a study of more than 11,000 employees of a large U.S. company, researchers found that by adding a modest financial incentive for participation (up to $1 in this instance), the survey response rate increased significantly (Rose, Sidle, & Griffith, 2007).

For current survey results on a variety of issues, and to participate in surveys, log on to one of these Web sites: www.ropercenter.uconn.edu, www.gallup.com, or www.pollingreport.com

VIRTUAL LABORATORIES: WEB-BASED RESEARCH

I-O psychologists use the Web to conduct research 24/7. In a virtual laboratory, they can run faster and less costly studies, and draw upon a larger and more diverse pool of subjects, than in a university laboratory or an organizational setting. Web-based research has included questionnaires for job applicants, surveys of employee attitudes, and psychological tests, as well as interactive experiments in which employees respond to stimuli presented on their computer screens. A review of the articles published in APA journals over a 2-year period showed that the majority of the studies were "straightforward translations of the traditional psychological measures and methods for use on the Web. These studies were designed to ask the same kinds of questions and to employ methods that one

typically uses in the psychological laboratory" (Skitka & Sargis, 2006, p. 535).

The linking, or networking, of individual laboratories into a so-called NetLab makes it possible to conduct large-scale studies that collect data from thousands of research participants from different companies and different countries. NetLabs can operate virtual reality group experiments in which subjects respond to simulations of situations in their actual work environment.

Virtual research offers additional advantages over traditional hands-on research conducted in a workplace or a college laboratory. As one researcher noted, "Surveys and experiments can be delivered quickly to anyone connected to the Web and data can be saved automatically in electronic form, reducing costs in lab space, dedicated equipment, paper, mailing costs, and labor" (Birnbaum, 2004, p. 804). Recruiting subjects with a diverse range of personal characteristics—age, gender, level of education, type of work, income, social class, and nationality—can be done far more easily on the Web. Much psychological research has been performed with college students because they are so readily available on college campuses, where most studies are undertaken. In contrast, "Internet chat rooms and bulletin boards provide a rich sample of human behavior that can be mined for studies of communication, prejudice, and organizational behavior, among other topics" (Kraut, et al., 2004, p. 105).

Consider the example of the graduate student who wanted to study older people who had expressed an interest in genealogy. Instead of placing notices or advertisements in publications dealing with genealogy and asking people to respond—a process that could have taken several months—the researcher made inquiries to online genealogy groups and enrolled more than 4,000 people for the study in less than a week (Birnbaum, 2004).

Critics of Web-based research note that it is impossible to assess the honesty and accuracy of responses on criteria such as age, gender, and ethnic origin, or to know whether subjects are cheating by being coached or are giving obviously incorrect or frivolous responses just to be contrary. Also, people who are computer literate and comfortable interacting with Internet sources are likely to differ in their educational and socioeconomic characteristics from people who are not so familiar with computers. Thus, the respondents are, in a sense, self-selected and not representative of the population as a whole. However, proponents of Web-based research point out that college students—the typical subjects for psychological research studies—are also not representative of the general population.

Critics also note that the rate of response to online surveys is lower than the rate for surveys conducted in person or by telephone. The dropout rate is higher for Web-based research than for laboratory studies. It is far easier for an anonymous participant to log off than for a college student to walk out of an experiment being conducted by his or her professor. Nevertheless, a growing number of studies comparing online research with laboratory research and with job-site research show that the results from all types are similar and consistent (see, for example, Birnbaum, 2004; Gosling, Vazire, Srivastava, & John, 2004; Kraut, et al., 2004).

To learn more about Web-based research, including information on how to do it, as well as results from studies in a variety of areas of psychology, go to www.psych.hanover.edu/research/exponnet.html

ANALYZING RESEARCH DATA

In psychological research, as in research in any science, collecting the data is only the first step in the scientific approach to solving problems. Assume that we have conducted an experiment to measure the productivity of 200 assembly-line workers or have administered an aptitude test to 200 applicants for sales jobs. What have we learned? So far, we have simply amassed numbers—the raw scores. Now we need to analyze and interpret these data so that we may draw conclusions about their meaning and apply the results to current situations. To do so, we apply statistical methods to summarize and describe the data.

Descriptive Statistics

You are already familiar with the word *descriptive*. When you describe a person or an event in words, you try to convey a mental picture or image. Similarly, when psychologists use **descriptive statistics**, they are trying to describe or represent their data in a meaningful fashion. Let us examine some research data and see how statistics can describe them.

To evaluate a new test for job applicants that was designed to predict their success in selling satellite TV systems, a psychologist administered the test to 99 applicants. The test scores are shown in Table 2–1. Looking at this swarm of numbers you can see why it is important to have a way to summarize and describe them. It is not possible to make sense of the data as they are. You cannot formulate a useful prediction or make a meaningful evaluation of the potential job performance of these applicants as a whole by looking at a table of individual numbers.

One way to describe the data is to construct a **frequency distribution**, or bar graph, by plotting the number of times each score occurs (see Figure 2–3). For convenience in dealing with so many scores, we can group them in equal intervals. Grouping the scores is not required, but it does make the data easier to work with. The graph offers a clearer idea of the test performance of the job applicants than does the table of raw scores. Also, the graph provides useful information about group performance by showing that most of the subjects who took the test scored in the middle range.

Mean, Median, and Mode.   Scientific analysis of data requires that the raw scores also be summarized and described quantitatively. We must be able to represent the data with a single number, a measure of the central tendency of the distribution. To find the typical score in a distribution, we can calculate the mean, median, or mode.

The most common and useful measure of central tendency is the arithmetic average, or **mean**, which is calculated by adding the scores and dividing the resulting sum by the total number of scores. The mean for the group of 99 job applicants is 11,251 divided by 99, yielding 113.6 as the average score. Thus, averaging reduces raw data to a single number. The mean provides the basis for many higher level statistical analyses.

The **median** is the score at the midpoint of the distribution. If we arrange the 99 scores in order

Median   The score at the midpoint of a statistical distribution; half the scores fall below the median and half above.

TABLE 2–1

Raw Scores of 99 Job Applicants on Satellite TV Sales Test

141	91	92	88	95	113
124	119	108	146	120	123
122	118	98	97	94	89
144	84	110	127	81	120
151	76	89	125	108	90
102	120	112	89	101	118
129	125	142	87	103	147
128	94	94	114	134	114
102	143	134	138	110	128
117	121	141	99	104	127
107	114	67	110	124	122
112	117	144	102	126	121
127	79	105	133	128	118
87	114	110	107	119	133
156	79	112	117	83	114
99	98	156	108	143	99
96		145		120	

FIGURE 2–3   Distribution of scores on satellite TV sales test (grouped data).

Mode   The most frequently obtained score in a distribution of data.

Normal distribution   A bell-shaped distribution of data in which most scores fall near the center and few fall at the extreme low and high ends.

Skewed distribution   An asymmetrical distribution of data with most scores at either the high or the low end.

from lowest to highest, the median is the score obtained by the 50th person. Half the job applicants scored higher than the median and half scored lower. In this sample, the median is 114, which is close to the mean. The median is a useful measure when dealing with skewed distributions.

The **mode** is the most frequently obtained score in the distribution; a distribution may have more than one mode. For the job applicant scores, the mode is 114. The mode is seldom applied to describe data, but it is useful in certain work situations. For example, a store manager who wants to stock an adequate inventory of computer games would want to know which games were being purchased more frequently than others.

Normal Distributions and Skewed Distributions.   In Figure 2–3 you can see that most of the job applicants achieved test scores in the middle of the distribution and that only a few scored very high or very low. Many measurements approximate this bell-shaped distribution. In general, this normal curve of distribution occurs when a large number of measurements are taken of a physical or psychological characteristic. Whether we measure height, weight, or intelligence, for example, a

sample of sufficient size will yield a distribution in which most scores fall near the middle and few fall at the extreme low and high ends.

The **normal distribution** is predicated on the random nature and size of the sample tested. If the sample is not representative of the population but is biased in one direction or another, the distribution will not approximate a normal curve.

Suppose we administered an IQ test to a group of high school dropouts, persons with little formal schooling and little experience in taking standardized tests. Such a group is not typical or representative of the general population, so the distribution of their test scores will not look like the normal curve. When measurements are taken from specially selected groups, the distribution will most likely be an asymmetrical or **skewed distribution** (see Figure 2–4). In dealing with skewed distributions, the median is the most useful measure of central tendency. The mean is affected by a few extreme scores in either direction and thus may provide a misleading description of the data. The median is less affected by extreme scores.

No doubt you have heard people say that statistics lie. Although statistics can be used to mislead people, the fault is usually in applying them inappropriately, and not with the statistical techniques

FIGURE 2–4   A skewed distribution

Standard deviation   A measure of the variability of a distribution; the standard deviation is a precise distance along the distribution's baseline.

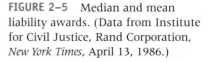

FIGURE 2–5   Median and mean liability awards. (Data from Institute for Civil Justice, Rand Corporation, *New York Times*, April 13, 1986.)

themselves. Consider the data in Figure 2–5, for example, which represent median and mean monetary awards in corporate liability cases over a period of 24 years. The mean, or average, awards increased from about $60,000 to $250,000, whereas the median awards decreased slightly during that time period. Interpretation of these data sparked a controversy. Lawyers, who benefit from larger liability awards to their clients, argued that the liability judgments did not increase over the 24-year period. Insurance companies, who have to pay these liability awards, argued that there had been a fivefold increase. The lawyers were using *median* liability awards; the insurance companies were citing *mean* liability awards. Both sides were technically correct, although the median is the better measure with a skewed distribution. As an employee, manager, voter, and consumer, you will find that it pays to be skeptical when you hear about "average" figures. Ask which average is being used. Is it the median or the mean?

Variability and the Standard Deviation.   Calculating and diagramming the central tendency of a distribution is not enough. More analysis is needed to provide a comprehensive description of a distribution of scores. We must also have a numerical indication

of the spread of the scores around the center if we are to make good use of the data.

Consider the normal distributions in Figure 2–6. If we took the mean or median as the measure of central tendency of these distributions, we would conclude that the distributions are identical. The means and medians are the same for both curves. You can see, however, that the distributions are not identical. They differ in their spread, or variability. The basic measure of variability is the **standard deviation** (SD), a precise distance along

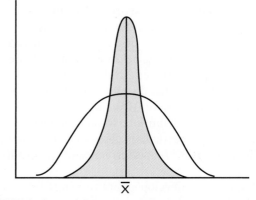

FIGURE 2–6   Normal curves with the same central tendency but different variability.

Correlation   The relationship between two variables. The strength and direction of the relationship is expressed by the correlation coefficient.

Statistical significance   The level of confidence in the results of an experiment. Significance is based on the calculation of probability values.

FIGURE 2–7   Normal distribution of IQ scores showing standard deviation units.

the distribution's baseline. Once we determine this distance, we can learn a great deal about the data and describe them more meaningfully.

Let us examine the distribution of IQ scores presented in Figure 2–7. The data form a normal curve with a mean of 100 and a standard deviation of 15. Knowing that the SD is 15 tells us that an IQ score of 115 is +1 SD unit, or distance, above the mean of 100. An IQ score of 130 is +2 SD units above the mean, and so on. Similarly, an IQ score of 85 is 1 SD distance below the mean (–1 SD).

With the standard deviation, we can determine the percentage of scores in the distribution that fall above or below any particular raw score. Tables based on the mathematical formula for the normal distribution give us the percentage of cases, or frequency of scores, that fall between standard deviation units. For example, as you can see in Figure 2–7, 99% of the population has IQ scores below 145, 97.5% below 130, and 84% below 115. These percentages hold for any measured variable as long as the distribution of the data follows the normal curve. If we know the standard deviation of a distribution, we can determine the meaning of any particular score. We can tell where it falls in terms of the performance of the group as a whole.

Suppose we develop an aptitude test for dental school students that we will use to measure the motor skills needed to manipulate the implements

used in dental surgery. Your roommate takes the test and obtains a score of 60. This number by itself tells us nothing about your roommate's aptitude relative to that of all the other students. However, if we know that the distribution of test scores follows the normal curve, that the mean is 50, and that the standard deviation is 10, then a score of 60 (+1 SD from the mean) indicates that only 16% of the students scored higher and 84% scored lower. Your roommate might make a pretty good dentist after all.

There is a method by which raw scores can be converted to standard deviation scores; this allows us to interpret each raw score in the distribution. The standard deviation also permits us to compare the performance of individuals on two or more measures that use different scoring systems. By converting the distributions on all tests to standard deviation units, we can compare performance on one test with performance on another test because the scores will be expressed in the same terms.

Correlation.   We have been discussing the statistical treatment of one variable at a time, such as a set of test scores from a group of job applicants. I-O psychologists more often are concerned with the relationships between two or more variables. Any situation in which a prediction must be made about whether a person is likely to succeed on the job involves matching two or more variables. For example, an employee's performance on a selection test must be compared with a later measure of actual job performance. That is the only way the psychologist can determine whether that selection technique is a valid means of choosing the best people for the job. (We discuss the concept of validity in more detail in chapter 4.) Psychologists use the correlational method to investigate relationships among variables.

A **correlation** tells the researcher two things: (1) the direction of the relationship between the variables and (2) the strength of that relationship. The direction of the relationship may be positive or negative, depending on whether high scores on one

Inferential statistics   Methods for analyzing research data that express relationships in terms of probabilities.

Probability   The idea that the differences between the means of experimental and control groups could have occurred by chance.

Meta-analysis   The large-scale reanalysis of the results of previous research studies.

variable are accompanied by high scores or low scores on the other variable. In a positive relationship, increasing scores on one variable are accompanied by increasing scores on the other variable. For example, a positive correlation between employees' test scores and supervisors' ratings of the employees' job performance tells us that the higher the test score, the higher the supervisory rating. As one variable increases, so does the other. We can predict that job applicants who do well on the aptitude test will likely perform well on the job. In other words, applicants who earn a high test score are apt to get a high rating from their supervisor. In a negative correlation, increasing scores on one variable are accompanied by decreasing scores on the other variable. Applicants who got high scores on the selection test would be likely to receive low ratings from their supervisors. In other words, those who do well on the test tend to do poorly on the job.

Through the application of the statistical formula for the correlation coefficient, we can calculate the direction and strength of the relationship between the variables. Positive correlations range from zero to +1.00. Negative correlations range from zero to −1.00. A correlation coefficient of 1.00 indicates just as strong a relationship or correspondence as a coefficient of +1.00. Only the direction is different. In both cases, performance on one variable, such as job ratings, can be predicted from performance on the other variable, such as test scores. The closer the correlation coefficient is to +1.00 or −1.00, the more accurately we can predict performance on one variable from performance on the other. Correlation is a valuable and widely used tool in I-O psychology, and we shall see its use in many examples throughout this book.

Inferential Statistics

In the typical psychology experiment, researchers are interested in comparing the performance levels of two groups—the experimental group and the control group. In an experiment to test the value of a new training method, for example, the job performance of the experimental group, which has had the training, is compared with the control group, which has not been exposed to the new training. An important decision rests on this comparison. Should the new training method be implemented throughout the organization? The decision hinges on the size of the difference between the two groups on their job performance.

Levels of Significance.   How do I-O psychologists know when the difference between the two groups is large enough to justify the cost of establishing the training program throughout the company? They must determine the level of **statistical significance** of the difference between the means of the two groups. Their answer will be expressed in terms of probabilities rather than certainties. The problem is this: Is the difference between the means of the groups large enough so that it is unlikely it could have occurred by chance?

Probability.   Psychologists apply techniques of **inferential statistics** to the data from the experimental and control groups, to calculate a **probability** value for the difference between the means. This number represents the probability that the difference could have occurred by chance. Psychologists recognize two levels of statistical significance: a probability (p) of .05 and a p of .01. A probability value of .01 means that a difference as large as that obtained in the experiment would occur by chance only 1 time of every 100. Thus, a difference at this level of significance could be attributed to the new training method used with the experimental group and not merely to chance. If the probability value was .05, we would have a little less confidence in the results, because this would tell us that there was a probability of 5 in 100 that the difference could have occurred by chance.

Meta-Analysis.   In I-O psychology, **meta-analysis** is a level of analysis higher than significance testing. Meta-analysis involves the large-scale reanalysis of previous studies to determine overall trends. This technique has been adopted by many psychologists as a way of reaching more objective conclusions about issues on which a considerable body of research data exists. Meta-analysis has been used in fields as diverse as I-O psychology, economics, and medical research.

Meta-analysis has been used successfully in a wide range of research including employee selection techniques, leadership traits, and the relationships among job satisfaction, job performance, turnover, and absenteeism. The method allows researchers to "understand, analyze, and interpret their research findings [and] translate conflicting results from single studies into conclusive and credible answers to their research questions, thereby making their research more relevant to practitioners" (Le, Oh, Shaffer, & Schmidt, 2007, pp. 9, 14).

Regardless of the specific techniques used to analyze research data, statistical tools help the I-O psychologist reach informed decisions and recommendations about crucial problems in business and industry. The use of statistics does not eliminate the need for human decision making, but it does help guide the researcher, manager, or executive in that task. Statistical tools are means to an end, not an end in themselves.

Summary

In psychological research, observations must be objective, well controlled and systematic, and capable of being duplicated and verified. Research has several limitations. For example, some problems are too complex to investigate by psychological research methods. The act of observing some behaviors may interfere with them. The novelty of change may alter behavior more than the actual change itself (the Hawthorne effect). Also, some research must be conducted in artificial settings, which limits the generalizability of the findings.

In the **experimental method**, psychologists investigate one influencing variable while holding all others constant. The variable being investigated is the **independent variable**; the behavior that results is the **dependent variable**. Two groups of subjects are used: the **experimental group** and the **control group**. The groups must be as similar as possible—a condition brought about by **random group design** (assigning subjects at random to the two groups) or by **matched group design** (matching the subjects in the groups on a number of personal characteristics).

Naturalistic observation involves observing behavior in its everyday setting. The experimenter can control the independent variables but cannot manipulate them with the precision permitted by the experimental method.

Survey research methods focus on attitudes and opinions. Survey techniques include personal interviews conducted face-to-face, paper-and-pencil questionnaires, Web-based questionnaires, and telephone surveys. Research conducted in the United States, Japan, and France has shown that employees prefer online surveys to paper-and-pencil surveys. Employees younger than the age of 50 are more likely to prefer online surveys. Survey questions can be **open-end**, allowing respondents to answer in their own words, or **fixed-alternative**, restricting respondents to a few choices. Representative samples of the people to be questioned in a survey can be selected through **probability sampling** in which each person in the population has a known chance of being included in the sample, or through **quota sampling** in which a replica in miniature of the larger population is constructed. George Gallup applied an objective, scientific approach to public opinion polling by using representative samples of the population.

Employees who refuse to answer survey questions may be more dissatisfied with their jobs than are employees who are willing to answer questions. Psychologists also conduct Web-based research in virtual laboratories, where large and diverse subject populations can be studied. Comparisons of Web-based research with laboratory research show that more subjects can be studied in less time in Web-based research, which also produces data that are more reliable.

The raw data obtained in a research project can be summarized, described, and analyzed by **descriptive statistics**. Data can be presented in graphs or reduced to a few meaningful numbers.

Three ways to measure the central tendency of a distribution of data are the **mean**, **median**, and **mode**. When sufficient data are collected from a representative sample of the population, they form a bell-shaped or **normal distribution**, in which most of the scores fall in the center or average range. To measure a distribution's variability, psychologists use the **standard deviation**, which is a distance along the distribution's baseline. The standard deviation provides information on the percentage of scores that fall above or below any particular raw score. The **correlation coefficient** denotes the direction and strength of the relationship between two variables and enables psychologists to predict performance on one variable from performance on another variable.

Inferential statistics are used to determine the level of **statistical significance** of the difference between the means of two groups by indicating whether the difference is so large that it is unlikely to have occurred by chance. **Meta-analysis** is a technique for averaging the results of a large number of studies, thereby making the research findings more relevant to practitioners.

Key Terms

control group	inferential statistics	probability
correlation coefficient	matched group design	probability sampling
dependent variable	mean	quota sampling
descriptive statistics	median	random group design
experimental group	meta-analysis	scientific method
experimental method	mode	skewed distribution
fixed-alternative questions	naturalistic observation	standard deviation
frequency distribution	normal distribution	statistical significance
independent variable	open-end questions	survey research method

Review Questions

1. Of what value to you is a knowledge of psychological research methods as you begin your working career?
2. Describe three basic requirements of psychological research.
3. What is the Hawthorne effect and how can it limit the results of psychological research?
4. Distinguish between dependent and independent variables and between random group design and matched group design.
5. In what ways do experimental groups differ from control groups? What is the purpose of having a control group in an experiment?
6. How would you design an experiment to determine why a group of experienced computer operators who had worked for a company for 5 years suddenly began making data-entry mistakes when their department was moved to a new workplace?
7. Describe advantages and limitations of the naturalistic observation method.
8. What are some of the uses of surveys and public opinion polls? Discuss some of the problems that can limit their usefulness.
9. Describe four methods used to collect survey data. Note the advantages of each.
10. If your job was to conduct a market survey of BMW car owners to find out what changes they wanted to see in new models, what survey research method would you use? Why?
11. How did Gallup change the way in which public opinion polls were conducted?
12. What are push polls? How can they influence the outcome of elections?
13. Differentiate between open-end and fixed-alternative survey questions.
14. Discuss the differences between probability sampling and quota sampling.

15. Why has it become difficult to conduct polls and surveys by telephone?

16. Describe advantages and limitations of conducting psychological research in virtual laboratories.

17. What is the difference between descriptive statistics and inferential statistics?

18. In your opinion, would the world be a better place without statistics? Defend your answer, showing appropriate data.

19. What can the standard deviation reveal about your performance on an IQ test?

20. What does a correlation of +.85 indicate about the relationship between your IQ score and your boss's rating of your job performance?

Additional Reading

Birnbaum, M. H. (Ed.). (2000). *Psychological experiments on the Internet*. Orlando, FL: Academic Press. Discusses advantages and disadvantages of Web-based research and offers examples from cross-cultural studies.

Cohen, B. H. (2007). *Explaining psychological statistics*. New York: Wiley. A comprehensive statistics textbook for students who have a minimal background in the field.

Evans, A. N., & Rooney, B. J. (2007). *Methods in psychological research*. Thousand Oaks, CA: Sage Publications. Guides the student through the research process from reading the literature to writing a report.

Gavin, H. (2008). *Understanding research methods and statistics in psychology*. Thousand Okas, CA: Sage Publications. A guide to qualitative and quantitative research methods; includes access to an interactive student Web site.

Igo, S. E. (2006). "A gold mine and a tool for democracy": George Gallup, Elmo Roper, and the business of scientific polling, 1935–1955. *Journal of the History of the Behavioral Sciences, 42*, 109–134. Describes early polling techniques and sampling methods and the underlying assumptions about human behavior.

PART TWO

The Development of Human Resources

The area of I-O psycholeferred to as human resources includes selecting, training, and evaluating new and current employees. When you apply for a job, you become part of an extensive selection process. An organization that is hiring new employees may use techniques ranging from application blanks to sophisticated psychological tests.

Once hired, you must be trained to perform the job efficiently. The company wants to match your skills with the job's requirements. Selection and training techniques are also used when you are being considered for promotion. And when you do advance to a more responsible job, you must be trained for this new role. Periodically, your supervisor will evaluate your performance. You will want this appraisal to be as fair and objective as possible and to provide you with feedback about your progress on the job. Employee selection, training, and appraisal methods determine the kind of job for which you will be hired and the way in which you will perform your duties.

Chapters 3 and 4 deal with problems of selection. Chapter 3 discusses application blanks, interviews, letters of recommendation, and assessment centers. Chapter 4 describes cognitive ability (intelligence), interest, aptitude, personality, and honesty tests used for selection purposes. Performance appraisal methods are covered in chapter 5, and training techniques in chapter 6.

Employee Selection Principles and Techniques

CHAPTER OUTLINE

WHAT'S YOUR IDEAL JOB?

What are you looking for in a job? High salary? Stock options? A comprehensive health insurance plan? A reserved parking space? Although it may be easy to identify the single most important factor for you as an individual, there is no single answer for all employees. I-O psychologists have identified a number of job characteristics likely to be important to employees; some of these are listed here. How would you rank them for yourself?

_____ Challenging, interesting, and meaningful work.

_____ High salary

_____ Opportunities for advancement

_____ Job security (no danger of being laid off or fired)

_____ Company stock options

_____ Satisfactory working hours

_____ Pleasant working conditions

_____ Compatible co-workers

_____ Signs of respect and appreciation from one's boss

_____ Opportunity to learn new skills

_____ Fair and loyal supervisor

_____ Being asked one's opinion on work issues

_____ Assistance with personal problems

When more than 3,000 job-seekers were asked what they were looking for in their work, they reported that the following factors were personally important (Howard, Erker, & Bruce, 2007).

Opportunities to learn and grow	78%
Interesting work	77%
Good manager/boss	75%
Organization you can be proud to work for	74%
Opportunity to advance	73%
Promise of stability/job security	70%
Creative or fun workplace culture	67%
Compatible work group/team	67%
Balance between work and personal life	65%
Opportunity for accomplishment	64%

How did your rankings of what you want in your job compare with the factors identified by the psychologists and by the job-seekers? In part, the degree of similarity in job preferences depends on your age and your generation. As noted in chapter 1, people included in Generation Y (born after 1980), for example, are likely to want a flexible work schedule that allows them to express their creativity and co-workers who will make work fun.

Surveys have identified other work characteristics prized by members of Generation Y, who will constitute more than half the workforce by the year 2012. They have a need to stay connected through instant messaging, instant games, and instant media. They are multitaskers who seem to work best, and to find the greatest fulfillment, as part of a team, and they expect instant recognition and reward for their efforts. Other surveys report that Generation Y members expect the latest in company-provided technology for communication, as well as higher pay. They believe their jobs should provide them with meaningful and challenging work, and they want to be given responsible assignments as soon as possible. They do not think they should have to work at low-level routine tasks initially to prove themselves (Balderrama, 2007; Barreto, 2007; Erickson, 2006).

Employee preferences can be influenced by factors such as level of education. College graduates have different expectations from those of high school graduates, who in turn have different preferences from those who did not complete high school. Not all college graduates have the same preferences. Engineering and computer science majors differ from liberal arts majors, and A students differ from C students. Preferences of white-collar workers differ from those of blue-collar workers, and technical personnel's differ from managerial personnel's.

Employee preferences change as a function of economic conditions. In an economic downturn when jobs are scarce, new employees may be more interested in pay and job security and be more willing to remain with an organization even if it does not allow fulfillment of their goals and preferences. In a robust economic climate when jobs are plentiful, issues such as challenging work or the opportunity to develop new skills rank higher in preference than security or salary.

Many people enter an organization with unrealistic or inflated expectations about the nature of the job and the company, which may explain why so many people leave their first job: The discrepancy between expectations and reality is too great. In one meta-analysis of 111 studies, investigators showed that unrealistic job expectations led to lower job satisfaction and lower commitment to the goals of the organization and to higher expressed intention to quit (Zhao, Wayne, Glibkowski, & Bravo, 2007).

Expectations begin to clash with reality from the outset, when you have your first contact with a potential employer—typically at your initial meeting with the company recruiter. This marks the first opportunity for each to size up the other, and it is an important step in the preselection process.

THE RECRUITMENT PROCESS

I-O psychologists are concerned with several issues in the recruitment process: sources employees use to find out about jobs, characteristics of recruiters, recruiting on college campuses, and the kinds of information provided to job applicants.

Sources for Recruiting

The traditional recruiting sources available to organizations include online search services, help-wanted advertisements in newspapers, referrals from current employees, employment agencies and search services, placement services of professional associations, job fairs, and outplacement agencies. Another popular source for recruiting is the college campus. Almost half of all large corporations actively recruit managerial and professional employees through on-campus interviews.

Referrals from current employees have long been used by organizations, which often award cash bonuses to their employees for successful referrals. This is an easy, low-cost approach that generally yields reliable results. In a study of 9,008 applicants for jobs at a call center, researchers found that those who had been referred to the company by high-performing existing employees were significantly more likely to be accepted than those referred by low-performing employees (Yakubovich & Lup, 2006).

Organizations are increasingly using Web-based recruitment methods to provide information to prospective employees about available jobs, as well as information about the organization itself. Such recruiting Web sites offer several advantages over more traditional approaches. First, they can transmit a great deal of information in a cost-effective way. Second, they can give the impression that

Using technology to recruit

the organization is sophisticated and up-to-date technologically, which is especially important to younger workers.

Recruiting Web sites also offer advantages to job-seekers. Applicants can quickly and readily use these online resources to learn about a prospective employer. By submitting application blanks and other materials online, and by responding to questions online, application costs can be reduced and companies can make job offers more rapidly.

Results from a study of 48 college students indicated that students were able to learn quickly and easily about an organization's culture and values from its Web site in matters such as emphasis on teamwork, growth, expansion, decisiveness, creativity, and innovation on the job (Braddy, Meade, & Kroustalis, 2006). In a study 814 college students, researchers found that student intention to pursue employment with a particular organization was significantly influenced by the information and image the organization presented on its recruitment site. Students who had a more positive attitude toward the site were more likely to apply for a job with that organization (Allen, Mahto, & Otondo, 2007).

Some companies, including Hewlett-Packard, Microsoft, and Verizon, have conducted virtual job fairs in which they present material about their organization and the specific jobs they want to fill. Prospective employees who "attend" these online job fairs can communicate with the company's executives in real time, similar to instant messaging. Organizations have also established recruiting Web pages on such popular social networking sites as MySpace, Facebook, and YouTube (Athavaley, 2007).

Recruiter Characteristics

The behavior and personal characteristics of company recruiters can have a significant impact on how college seniors choose their first job. Psychologists have found that characteristics likely to induce graduating seniors to accept a job offer include behaviors such as smiling, nodding, maintaining eye contact, demonstrating empathy and warmth, and showing thoughtfulness.

Researchers conducted a meta-analysis of 71 studies and found that applicants were influenced more by the recruiter's behavior than by the characteristics of the job for which they were applying. The most successful recruiters, in terms

Realistic job previews   A recruitment technique that acquaints prospective employees with positive and negative aspects of a job.

of the number of new employees they brought to the organization, were judged by the applicants to be the most personable, friendly, and helpful. The quality of personableness was seen as more important than the recruiters' status in the organization or their race or gender (Chapman, Uggerslev, Carroll, Piasentin, & Jones, 2005).

Other research on job applicants at on-campus placement centers showed that college seniors preferred recruiters to spend the interview period providing information about the company, soliciting information about the applicant, and answering the applicant's questions. When the college seniors thought that corporate recruiters were spending too much time talking about irrelevant topics, they were significantly less likely to accept a job offer.

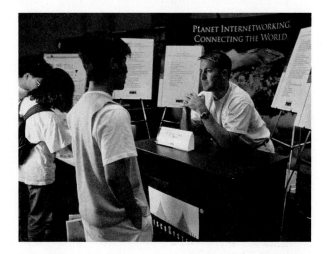

On-campus job fairs give college students the opportunity to obtain information on a variety of careers.

On-Campus Recruiting

College recruiting may not be living up to its potential, and companies may not be realizing full value from their recruitment programs. Fewer than half of corporate recruiters receive training in the proper techniques for interviewing job applicants. Recruiters tend to form a positive or negative impression about an applicant's qualifications in the first few minutes of an interview, hardly sufficient time to collect information on which to base a recruiting decision.

Recruiters also tend to spend more time talking with applicants they consider to be qualified and less time with applicants they dismiss on the basis of a superficial judgment. Often, recruiters do not follow the corporate script about the topics to be covered in an interview, and sometimes they fail to discuss important issues with applicants. All these points reflect a lack of interviewing skills.

A major difficulty faced by corporate recruiters on campus is finding job candidates who have a realistic view of the business world. This is another reason why college recruiting often produces less than satisfactory results. During the campus recruitment interview, many students obtain a false picture of the job and the organization, sometimes because they have had no experience in corporate

life and, therefore, do not know what questions to ask the recruiter. Students want to make a good impression and may try to hide attitudes and characteristics they think the recruiter might not like. Another reason for a misleading image of an organization or a job is the fault of the recruiters. Their goal is to find people with promise for their company; to accomplish this, they may paint an idealized picture of their organization and of the new graduate's first job in it.

Thus, each side may be guilty of misleading the other. The result, when the match turns out to be less than perfect, is likely to be dissatisfaction. The obvious way to avoid misleading situations is greater honesty, with each party being open about good and bad points. Some corporations present a realistic preview of the job as part of their organizational entry procedures.

Realistic Job Previews

Realistic job previews provide information that is as accurate as possible about all aspects of a job. Such information can be supplied through a brochure or other written description of the job, through a film or video, or through an on-the-job sample of the work

Newsbreak

If It Sounds Too Good to Be True . . .

"Here's what Marc Russell was promised for his first job out of college: a position in a fast-growing consulting company helping Fortune 500 companies solve complex business problems and technological needs, with amply opportunity for rapid career advancement, international travel and stock options. This fairy tale gave way to a scary truth: He spent three months in an empty room in the Seattle suburbs waiting his turn to play Battle Zone on the company's fast computer. That was the good part.

"His longest trip was from Seattle to Portland. He got all of 10 stock options, which he has since lost. His biggest project was working for the King County Jail, where his keenest insight was that the corndogs don't have sticks. He wrote software tracking inmate movement. (How far could they go?) And there was this spooky perk no one warned him about: 'the client threatened to keep us there [in the jail] if he didn't get what he wanted,' Russell says of the prison administrator. 'He was only half joking.'"

And so it often goes: The dream job the recruiter promises turns out to be a nightmare. It happens more often than you might think. One executive recruiter advises that you should do everything you can to find out, before you accept the job, whether the promises exceed the realities.

Source: When employers promise the moon (2003, November 2). *St. Petersburg (FL) Times*; adapted from the *Wall Street Journal*.

to see if the applicant can perform the required tasks. The purpose of a realistic job preview is to acquaint prospective employees with both positive and negative aspects of the job. The hope is that this practice will reduce overly optimistic or unrealistic expectations about what the job involves.

Consider the example of Lindblad Expeditions, a cruise ship company that takes people to offbeat travel destinations such as Antarctica or the Galapagos Islands. Everyone who applies for a job with Lindblad receives a DVD that shows what the work actually involves. There is a scene of crew members cleaning toilets and an interview with a crew member who washes 5,000 dishes every day. "Be prepared to work your butt off," one employee tells the prospects. The DVD is "meant to scare you off," says the company CEO. And it works. Most applicants drop out after viewing this dose of reality. How much better for you and the company to find out the job is not appropriate before you sign up, fly off to Alaska, and board ship, only then to realize that it's not at all what you expected (Simon, 2007).

Research has shown that the use of realistic job previews correlates positively with job satisfaction, job performance, organizational commitment, and reduced turnover (Ganzach, Pazy, Ohayun, & Brainin, 2002; Kammeyer-Mueller & Wanberg,

2003). Realistic job previews have also been found to reduce the number of applicants initially accepting jobs, because potential employees learn, even before starting a job, whether certain aspects of the work situation are unappealing or otherwise not appropriate for them.

AN OVERVIEW OF THE SELECTION PROCESS

Proper selection methodology involves more than placing an ad in a newspaper or with an online search service, having people come to the office to fill out an application blank, and conducting a brief interview. A successful selection program includes several additional procedures. Suppose that the head of the human resources department is told that 200 new employees must be hired to operate the complex machinery that is being installed to produce digital cameras. How will these workers be found?

Job and Worker Analyses

Ideally, the first step is for I-O psychologists to investigate the nature of the job. The organization will not know what abilities potential employees

Job analysis   The study of a job to describe in specific terms the nature of the component tasks performed by the workers.

Selection ratio   The relationship between the number of people to be hired (the number of jobs) and the number available to be hired (the potential labor supply).

should have unless it can describe in detail what they are expected to do to perform the job effectively. I-O psychologists undertake a process called **job analysis** to determine the specific skills necessary to the job. From the job analysis, a profile of worker qualifications can be developed.

Once these abilities have been specified, the human resources manager must determine the most effective means of identifying these characteristics in potential employees. Does the job require the ability to read complex diagrams? To manipulate small parts? To demonstrate knowledge of electronics? And how will the company find out whether an applicant has these skills? In a survey of more than 3,000 employees, investigators found (perhaps to no one's surprise) that the more complex the skill requirements for a job are, and the more demanding the job is, the greater will be the number, variety, and complexity of the selection methods used for that job (Wilk & Cappelli, 2003).

The necessary background characteristics and aptitudes, as revealed by the job and worker analyses, must be assessed or evaluated in each applicant. For example, specific questions may be asked in an interview or appropriate psychological tests may be administered. Cutoff test scores or levels for the various abilities will be established. A minimum score on a test or a fixed number of years of education or experience will be proposed, and no one who falls below that level will be hired. I-O psychologists may have to evaluate present workers in the same or similar jobs to determine where the cutoff scores should be set.

Recruitment Decisions

Recruitment decisions are next. Should the company recruit new employees through print or online ads? Through an employment agency? Through referrals from current employees? The number of potential employees attracted by these efforts affects the caliber of those ultimately offered jobs. If ads and referrals bring in

only 250 applicants for the 200 jobs, the company must be less selective in hiring than if there were 400 applicants to choose from. I-O psychologists call this the **selection ratio**, the relationship between the number of people to be hired and the number who are available to be hired. Thus, the potential labor supply directly affects the strictness of the requirements established for the job. If there is a shortage of applicants and the jobs must be filled within a few weeks, some requirements (perhaps the cutoff score on a test of cognitive abilities) may be lowered.

A shortage of job applicants may also force the company to expand its recruiting campaign and to offer higher wages, enhanced benefits, or improved working conditions to attract and retain new employees. Thus, the size of the labor supply can greatly influence not only recruitment and selection procedures but also features of the job itself.

Selection Techniques

Selecting the new employees and classifying them as suitable or unsuitable for the job are accomplished by a variety of techniques, including application blanks, interviews, letters of recommendation, assessment centers, and psychological tests. Hiring decisions typically are based not on a single technique but on a combination of methods. In addition, testing for drug use is now widespread for many types of jobs (see chapter 12). Some jobs also have physical requirements and may require tests of strength and endurance.

The next step in the selection process is to test the selection procedures to determine if they succeeded in identifying the best workers for the jobs. In our example, after the initial 200 workers have been hired, the human resources department must track their progress to see how they perform on the job. This is the major test of the worth of a selection program.

Every new selection program must be investigated to determine its predictive accuracy or validity. This is done by evaluating the performance of

Adverse impact   When a minority group of
job applicants or employees is treated
markedly worse than the majority group in
staffing decisions.

the employees selected by the new procedures. For
example, after the new workers are on the job for 6
months, their supervisors can be asked to rate their
job performance. By comparing these ratings with
performance on the selection techniques, we can
determine how the two measures correlate. We
want to know whether the selection techniques
were able to predict which of the applicants turned
out to be the better workers.

Suppose we learn that the employees who
received high ratings from their supervisors had
performed an average of 10 points above the cutoff
score on a test of manual dexterity and had earned a
high school diploma. Employees who received low
ratings from their supervisors performed within 1 or
2 points of the cutoff score on the manual dexterity
test and had not completed high school. These findings tell us that the two factors (manual dexterity
and a high school diploma) were able to distinguish
between potentially good and potentially poor
workers. In the future, then, the human resources
department can use these criteria with confidence
to select the best people for these jobs.

Keep in mind that to evaluate employee selection procedures we must have some measure of job
performance with which to compare performance
on the selection techniques. Some ways to appraise
and measure work performance are discussed in
chapter 5.

FAIR EMPLOYMENT PRACTICES

Successful employee selection programs must conform to the regulations of the Equal Employment
Opportunity Commission (EEOC), established in
1972, and the provisions of the 1964 and 1991 Civil
Rights Acts. All job applicants, regardless of race,
religion, gender, or national origin, are guaranteed
equal opportunities in seeking and maintaining
employment. Discrimination in hiring is unethical,
immoral, and illegal. Such discrimination has been
greatly reduced over the past few decades as a
result of this legislation. However, examples of
prejudice and discrimination can still be found in
the workplace.

One investigator found that employers were
50% more likely to call job applicants for interviews if they had "White-sounding" names such
as Brad or Kristen, than if they had "Black-sound-
ing" names such as Tyrone or Tamika (Ferdman,
2003). This finding held true even when the background information on the application form was
the same for all applicants, regardless of name.

Researchers studied 114 Hispanic employees
who spoke with a pronounced Spanish accent.
Even in an area where more than half the population was Hispanic (in this case, Miami, Florida),
the employees reported experiencing discrimination on the job. Not surprisingly, this led to feelings
of stress and decreased reported job satisfaction
(Wated & Sanchez, 2006).

In an analysis of the hiring decisions made
for 357 applicants for high-level management
positions in the U.S. government civil service,
investigators reported these results: Selection
panels composed of people of different races and
genders reacted more favorably to female job
applicants but more negatively to Black and
Hispanic applicants. In addition, African-American
men on the selection panels were significantly
less likely to hire African-American male job
applicants than were female or White members of
the selection panels (Powell & Butterfield, 2002).

Adverse Impact on Minority Groups

When any minority group of job candidates is
treated markedly worse than the majority group,
that minority group is said to be the target of
adverse impact in the selection process. Any
selection rate for a minority group that is less than
80% of the selection rate for the majority group is
evidence of adverse impact. Let us say that a
company had 200 job applicants (100 Blacks and
100 Whites) and hired 100 of them (20 Blacks and
80 Whites). In this instance, 80% of the White
applicants were hired but only 20% of the Black
applicants. The selection rate for Blacks was only
one fourth, or 25%, of that for Whites, much less
than the 80% rule for showing adverse impact. This

Reverse discrimination The phenomenon that may occur when recruiting, hiring, promoting, and other human resources decisions in favor of members of a minority group result in discrimination against members of the majority group.

company could be challenged in court for maintaining vastly different rejection rates for minority and majority applicants.

Reverse Discrimination

The impetus to recruit, hire, and promote members of minority groups and to implement EEOC rulings has sometimes resulted in discrimination against members of the majority group. An organization may be so intent, for example, on increasing the number of women in its ranks to meet federal guidelines that it denies equal opportunities to men. This phenomenon, called **reverse discrimination**, has also occurred in graduate and professional schools, where some White applicants have been denied admission in favor of minority applicants whose grades and test scores were not as high as those of the White applicants. Reverse discrimination may also operate in promotion decisions on the job when women and ethnic minorities are offered greater opportunities for advancement than are similarly qualified White men.

Equal opportunity programs can stigmatize persons hired or promoted on an affirmative action basis. Employees who are members of the majority group may come to believe that preferential hiring practices for women and minorities led to the hiring of unqualified people. As a result, some White men feel resentful. A backlash against affirmative action programs has been expressed by dissatisfied employees, employers, and political leaders.

Increasing Diversity at Work

Most organizations today target women as well as ethnic and racial minorities in their employee selection campaigns by using appropriate photographs in recruitment ads and by employing female, Black, and Hispanic recruiters. The majority (78%) of the Fortune 100 companies show women and minorities in their recruitment materials based on the premise that the only way to attract a diverse workforce is to show examples of the company's commitment to diversity (Avery & McKay, 2006).

Are these efforts effective?

Despite the proliferation of diversity research and diversity training programs in the past 20 years and four decades of anti-discrimination legislation and affirmative action programs, women, minorities, and other non-dominant group members remain woefully underrepresented in key organizational positions, confined by glass ceilings and walls; held to higher performance stands; and [still] sometimes subjected to virulent harassment, discrimination, and exclusion (Bell & Berry, 2007, p. 21).

Yes, diversity in the composition of the workforce can be readily seen, but full acceptance of women and minority employees in many workplaces has yet to be achieved.

Other Targets of Discrimination

Discrimination Against Older Workers The workforce in the United States is aging. Most employers, however, still prefer to hire younger workers, despite consistent evidence from I-O psychology research that older workers are often more productive than younger workers and have lower absenteeism and turnover rates. In general, older employees do not suffer from poorer health, diminished vigor, or declining mental abilities when compared with younger employees.

A meta-analysis of 380 studies showed that older workers are good organizational citizens. They show far less drug use, tardiness, and absenteeism than younger workers. They also exhibit less aggression and are better able to control their emotions on the job (Ng & Feldman, 2008).

Nevertheless, stereotypes about older workers persist. Older workers tend to receive more negative performance evaluations than younger workers, appraisals that are likely based more on age than on actual work performance. Older workers are protected by law against age discrimination in hiring and promotion. The Age Discrimination in Employment Act of 1967 legislated against using

Newsbreak

Are We Still at the Back of the Bus?

We are unable to get taxis to pick us up in front of office buildings. We are frisked and detained on suburban commuter trains. We are watched in department stores and mistaken for coat-check clerks and restroom attendants while lunching in the best restaurants. We are directed to freight elevators and delivery windows by receptionists who fail to recognize us in our own company offices. We are black professionals in corporate America.

Although I am at my desk each morning facing the same corporate challenges as my white co-workers, a great deal of my job-related stress comes from sources totally unrelated to my job. My father dreamed of the day when his son would work in a towering office with a city view. What he didn't know was that arriving there would not be the end of the struggle for black Americans.

Even though I have been the beneficiary of affirmative action, I can acknowledge some of its flaws—its tendency to create resentment among white men and its potential for generating a sense of "group entitlement" among minorities and women. But my experiences as a corporate lawyer, professor, and black professional in a mostly white environment have shown me that workplace bias in America, even today, is so intractable that it justifies establishing affirmative action as a permanent policy.

For those who believe I am overzealous in suggesting the permanent enforcement of affirmative action, I offer an incident that took place soon after I started a new job as a corporate lawyer in Manhattan.

A receptionist with a security guard in tow came running past my secretary's desk just as I was joining a conference call with a client in my office.

"Excuse me, Larry, but I've got security here," the receptionist said breathlessly, interrupting our call. "Did you see a delivery boy get past reception and come through here with a purple bag?"

I looked to the corner where a Bergdorf Goodman [an upscale department store] bag sat with a hat that I had bought for my wife.

"That's the boy!" shouted the security guard, pointing to me.

When the receptionist saw the shopping bag, recognition and relief washed over her face. "That's so funny," she laughed while closing the door. "We thought you were a delivery boy. Sorry to bother you."

The client looked at me with the slightest hint of skepticism.

Source: Graham, L. O. (1995, May 21). The case for affirmative action. *New York Times*.

---

age to deny employment opportunities to people in the 40- to 65-year-old age bracket. The act was amended in 1978 to increase the age at which employees could be forced to retire from 65 to 70.

Discrimination Against Workers with Disabilities. Approximately one fifth of the U.S. population has some form of disability, and disabled persons have the highest unemployment rate of any group of working age. Only about one third of all disabled persons who want to work have found full-time jobs, despite legislation designed to foster employment opportunities (Fassinger, 2008).

Employees with physical and mental disabilities are protected by federal laws against job discrimination. The Vocational Rehabilitation Act of 1973 made it mandatory for organizations to recruit, hire, and promote qualified disabled persons. The 1990 Americans with Disabilities Act (ADA) prohibits employers, state and local governments, employment agencies, and labor unions from discriminating against qualified individuals with disabilities in job application procedures, hiring, firing, advancement, compensation, job training, and other conditions of employment. The act requires employers to make reasonable accommodations to the physical or mental impairments of a qualified applicant or employee with a disability, if the accommodations would not impose an undue hardship on normal business operations.

In one case of reasonable accommodation, a supermarket employee who experienced fatigue due to lupus (a tubercular disease) was provided with a stool so that she could perform her cashier's job without having to stand throughout her shift. Accommodations for other persons with disabilities include providing oral or Braille instructions to visually impaired job applicants or employees, and constructing ramps and other structural modifications for people who use wheelchairs.

An unintended consequence of making accommodations for disabled workers may be resentment among workers who do not have such disabilities (see, for example, Colella, Paetzold, and Belliveau, 2004). Another issue is that the disabled employee's co-workers may believe that they have to work harder because the disabled employee is working fewer hours.

Prejudice against hiring disabled workers still occurs, even though it is at variance with their actual job performance. Research by I-O psychologists shows that disabled employees perform as well as or better than nondisabled employees. Many large U.S. corporations, such as DuPont, 3M, and McDonnell Douglas, routinely hire disabled workers because they have found that disabled persons make good employees. Companies such as McDonald's and Marriott routinely hire people with mild to moderate cognitive impairments and find them to be as productive as their other employees. Nevertheless, fewer than 20% of the people of working age who can be classified as mentally disabled have found jobs, and half of these jobs are in federally subsidized programs. Such jobs include janitor, gardener, grocery store clerk, office receptionist, toll collector, and fast-food restaurant cook.

Passage of the 1990 ADA has led to the filing of thousands of formal job discrimination complaints and lawsuits against employers. Unfortunately, the prospect of legal challenges has made many organizations even more wary of hiring disabled persons. This fear of litigation may explain why the number of disabled persons in the workforce has not increased over the past decade. Russell Redenbaugh, a member of the U.S. Civil Rights Commission who himself is disabled, has concluded that the effect of the ADA has been a complete disappointment.

Discrimination Against Female Workers. Women continue to confront discrimination in the workplace, particularly when they apply for what are still considered to be traditionally male jobs. However, the amount of discrimination is declining, albeit slowly. Nevertheless, the gender pay gap remains a problem. Women continue to earn less than men, on average, for the same or similar kinds of work (Blau & Kahn, 2007).

Pregnant women face additional discrimination. In one study investigators found that pregnant job-seekers experienced significantly greater overt hostility and discrimination than women who were not pregnant. The hostility was higher when the pregnant women applied for so-called masculine jobs and lower for traditionally feminine jobs such as maid or kindergarten teacher (Hebl, King, Glick, Singletary, & Kazama, 2007). Research with male and female college students, and with full-time employees, found bias in job selection against women who were mothers; they were perceived to be less competent and less committed to their work than female applicants who had no children (Heilman & Okimoto, 2008).

Discrimination Based on Sexual Orientation. Gay men and lesbian women face discrimination in hiring in public agencies and private companies; to date, no federal civil rights legislation protects them from workplace discrimination. However, several states now include sexual orientation among the protected categories in their civil rights laws, and a growing number of cities have passed ordinances forbidding job discrimination against gay people.

Many U.S. corporations have implemented antidiscrimination policies with regard to gay persons. Some companies, such as AT&T, Xerox, Lockheed, and Levi Strauss, sponsor support groups and networks for their gay employees. The major American automakers (Ford, General Motors, and Chrysler), as well as IBM, Citigroup, and some local governments, offer standard fringe benefits to partners of employees in same-sex relationships.

Research with 379 gay and lesbian employees showed that those who believed their work environment was sufficiently supportive to allow them to publicly acknowledge their sexual identity were high in measured job satisfaction and low in anxiety. They also experienced more favorable reactions from co-workers, less job discrimination, and fairer

Job analysis The study of a job to describe in specific terms the nature of the component tasks performed by the workers.	**Work analysis** The study of certain tasks and skills that workers can transfer from one job to another.

treatment from supervisors than did gay employees who worked in less supportive environments (Griffith & Hebl, 2002).

Other research, involving 534 gay, lesbian, and bisexual employees, found that those who were most fearful of "coming out" on the job had lower levels of job satisfaction and higher levels of stress-related physical complaints. In addition, those who believed that their co-workers and supervisors were supportive reported less fear and stress on the job, and a greater willingness to disclose their orientation, than those who did not receive such support (Ragins, Singh, & Cornwell, 2007).

To learn about a potential employer's diversity policies with regard to gender orientation, log on to www.gaybusinessworld.com or www.hrc.org; the latter is the Web site of the Human Rights Campaign.

Discrimination Based on Physical Attractiveness. Some job applicants have a more pleasing appearance than others in terms of currently accepted cultural standards. This type of judgment, called "beautyism" by some, affects hiring and promotion decisions in the business world. Many people believe that physically attractive persons also possess more desirable personal and social traits, an attitude summed up by some I-O psychologists as "what is beautiful is good." Physically attractive persons are perceived as more sociable, dominant, and mentally healthy than less physically attractive persons.

In a meta-analysis of studies dealing with the biasing effects of physical attractiveness in the workplace, researchers found that company recruiters and human resources mangers were just as susceptible as were college students to being influenced in hiring decisions by the physical attractiveness of the job applicants. This research also showed that the biasing effects were strong for both male and female applicants. However, the results also demonstrated that the biasing effects of attractiveness have decreased over the past few decades (Hosodo, Stone-Romero, & Coats, 2003).

An applicant's height may serve as an advantage in selecting, hiring, and promoting decisions. A meta-analysis of studies involving 8,590 research participants indicated that height was significantly related to ratings of job performance, leader emergence, and income. Taller people ranked higher on all three measures than did less tall people (Judge & Cable, 2004).

Research has also shown that retail sales personnel discriminate against obese shoppers in subtle ways. For example, when dealing with obese persons sales personnel smile less, make eye contact less frequently, act less overtly friendly, spend less time interacting, and act less polite than when dealing with people of more average weight (King, Shapiro, Hebl, Singletary, & Turner, 2006).

JOB AND WORK ANALYSIS

The purpose of **job analysis** is to describe in specific terms the nature of the component tasks performed by workers on a particular job. A job analysis includes information about the tools or equipment used, the operations performed, the education and training required, the wages paid, and any unique aspects of the job such as safety hazards.

Many I-O psychology practitioners prefer to use the term **work analysis** instead of job analysis. Work analysis focuses on certain tasks and skills that can be transferred from one job to another. In today's job market, employees must develop and continue to refine a diverse package of skills that they can apply to different jobs. Unlike some workers in previous generations, employees in the twenty-first century cannot expect to spend their working lives performing routine and repetitive tasks.

We mentioned earlier the value of job and work analyses in employee selection. Unless a company knows precisely what a job entails and what is required for successful performance of the tasks, it has no way of knowing what qualities to look for in applicants for that job.

Job and work analyses have other important uses in organizational life. To establish a training program for a particular job, for example, the

The Americans with Disabilities Act of 1990 prohibits employers from discriminating against qualified persons who have disabilities.

nature of the job and the skills it requires must be known. A company cannot expect to train a person to perform a job unless the tasks and operations required for job success can be described. Job analysis can also aid in efforts to design a job or a workspace for more efficient performance. For example, say a job analysis reveals that a lathe operator has to walk 50 yards from the machine to the storage shelves every time it is necessary to replenish the supply of raw materials. Redesigning the work area can eliminate this wasted time and effort. Job analysis can also uncover safety hazards or dangerous operating procedures.

I-O psychologists have devised a number of techniques for conducting job and work analyses. One approach is to refer to previously compiled analyses. The U.S. Department of Labor has developed the Occupational Information Network (O*NET), a database that summarizes such information. It defines, classifies, and describes a variety of occupations. This online database is updated frequently to provide employers with examples and analyses of the knowledge, skills, and abilities employees need to perform these jobs. It is an inexpensive, user-friendly tool for analyzing thousands of jobs and has had a strong impact on both research and application. It has also been shown to be useful in other cultures. Research comparing O*NET descriptions for the same jobs in the United States, New Zealand, China, and Hong Kong found

no significant differences in the knowledge, skills, and abilities needed for successful job performance (Taylor, Kan Shi, & Borman, 2008). In general, the O*NET provides the following information for each job.

- **Personal requirements:** the skills and knowledge required to perform the work
- **Personal characteristics:** the abilities, interests, and values needed to perform the work
- **Experience requirements:** the training and level of licensing and experience needed for the work
- **Job requirements:** the work activities and context, including the physical, social, and organizational factors involved in the work
- **Labor market:** the occupational outlook and pay scales for the work

Table 3–1 shows examples from the O*NET of the knowledge required to perform different types of tasks. Table 3–2 presents descriptions of verbal, quantitative, and cognitive abilities needed for various tasks. To learn more about O*NET and the jobs it describes in such detail, go to www.online. onetcenter.org/

Other techniques for conducting job and work analyses for specific jobs include interviews, questionnaires, observation, activity logs, and critical incidents.

Interviews. The use of interviews for job and work analyses involves extensive meetings with the persons directly connected with the job (the so-called subject matter experts). These include the workers performing the job, their supervisors, and the instructors who trained the workers for the job. Job analysts may supplement interviews with questionnaires. The persons being interviewed should be told the purpose of the interview and why it is important to answer the questions fully and honestly. The questions should be carefully planned and clearly worded to elicit as much information as possible.

Questionnaires. Two types of questionnaires are used in job analysis: the unstructured questionnaire and the structured questionnaire. In the unstructured, (or open-end) approach, the subject matter experts (workers, supervisors, and trainers) describe in their own words the components of the job and the tasks performed.

TABLE 3–1	
O*NET Job Descriptions and Levels of Knowledge	
Category and Operational Definition	**Level of Knowledge**
Administration/Management—Knowledge of principles and processes involved in business and organizational planning, coordination, and execution. Includes strategic planning, resource allocation, manpower modeling, leadership techniques, and production methods.	*High*—Managing a $10 million company. *Low*—Signing a pay voucher.
Clerical—Knowledge of administrative and clerical procedures and systems such as word processing, filing and records management, forms design, and other office procedures and terminology.	*High*—Organizing a storage system for company forms. *Low*—Filing letters alphabetically.
Sales/Marketing—Knowledge of principles and methods involved in showing, promoting, and selling products or services. Includes marketing strategies, product demonstration and sales techniques, and sales control systems.	*High*—Developing a marketing plan for a nationwide phone system. *Low*—Selling cakes at a bake sale.
Computers/Electronics—Knowledge of circuit boards, processors, chips, and computer hardware and software including applications and programming.	*High*—Creating a program to scan for computer viruses. *Low*—Operating a VCR to watch a prerecorded tape.
Engineering/Technology—Knowledge of equipment, tools, and mechanical devices and their applications.	*High*—Designing a clean, efficient power plant. *Low*—Installing a door lock.

When the structured questionnaire approach is used, the people being interviewed are provided with descriptions of tasks, operations, and working conditions and are asked to rate the items or to select those items that characterize the job. Research has shown, however, that people can be careless in providing ratings, which can lead to less-than-accurate job and work analyses.

A widely used questionnaire is the Position Analysis Questionnaire (PAQ), which consists of 194 job elements related to specific behaviors and activities. The job elements are organized into six categories of job behavior: information input, mental processes, work output, relationships with other persons, job context, and other job activities and conditions. Employees and supervisors rate each element for its importance to the job in question. Such quantifiable ratings have an obvious advantage over the kind of information yielded by the unstructured questionnaire. As with other types of surveys conducted today, job analysis questionnaires can be administered online as well as in printed versions.

Direct Observation. A third approach to job and work analyses is direct observation of workers as they perform their jobs. Because people may behave differently when they know they are being watched, the job analysts must remain as unobtrusive as possible. Also, they should observe a representative sample of workers and make observations at various times throughout the workday to take account of changes caused by factors such as fatigue.

Direct observation is typically conducted through electronic performance monitoring. (We discuss in chapter 5 the use of this technique for employee performance evaluation.) For example, trucking companies use onboard computers to monitor running time, downtime, and speed. Cable television companies monitor maintenance workers electronically to record the time spent per service call.

Systematic Activity Logs. With systematic activity logs, workers and supervisors maintain detailed written records of their activities during a given time period. If prepared with care, these logs can

Critical-incidents technique   A means of identifying specific activities or behaviors that lead to desirable or undesirable consequences on the job.

TABLE 3–2

O*NET Examples of Specific Work Abilities

Abilities	Level
VERBAL	
Oral comprehension—The ability to listen to and understand information and ideas presented through spoken words and sentences.	*High*—Understanding a lecture on advanced physics. *Low*—Understanding a television commercial.
Written comprehension—The ability to read and understand information and ideas presented in writing.	*High*—Understanding a book on repairing a missile guidance system. *Low*—Understanding signs on the highway.
Oral expression—The ability to communicate information and ideas in speaking so that other people will understand.	*High*—Explaining advanced principles of genetics to 1st-year college students. *Low*—Cancelling newspaper delivery by phone.
Written expression—The ability to communicate information and ideas in writing so that other people will understand.	*High*—Writing an advanced economics textbook. *Low*—Writing a note to remind your spouse to take something out of the freezer to thaw.
QUANTITATIVE	
Mathematical reasoning—The ability to understand and organize a problem and to select a mathematical method or formula to solve the problem.	*High*—Determining the math required to simulate a spacecraft moon landing. *Low*—Determining the cost of 10 oranges when priced at 2 for 29 cents.
Number facility—The ability to add, subtract, multiply, and divide quickly and correctly.	*High*—Manually calculating the flight path of an aircraft, considering speed, fuel, wind, and altitude. *Low*—Adding 2 and 7.

---

reveal details about a job that are not otherwise obtainable.

Critical Incidents.   The **critical-incidents technique** is based on the identification of those incidents or behaviors that are necessary to successful job performance. The goal is to have subject matter experts indicate the behaviors that distinguish good workers from poor workers. The critical-incidents technique focuses on specific actions that lead to desirable or undesirable consequences on the job. A single critical incident is of little value, but hundreds of them can effectively describe the unique behaviors required to perform the job well. (We note in chapter 6 that critical

incidents can also be used to identify areas where employee retraining might be needed.)

Job analysis continues to be an important part of the employee selection process. Every employing organization must be able to justify each of its job requirements to show that whatever it asks of a job applicant is related directly to the abilities required to perform the job. The company must not set arbitrary qualifications that can be used to discriminate against groups of workers and to deny them equal opportunity for employment. Detailed job and work analyses provide justification for determining specific job requirements. For example, if a company is charged with sex discrimination because female employees are paid less than male employees for what appears to be the same job, the company has to show that the men are performing different tasks that justify the greater pay. A job analysis can provide that information. Therefore, organizations take seriously the task of job analysis. Equal employment opportunity and successful selection programs are not possible without it.

Let us consider some specific employee selection techniques currently in use: biographical information, interviews, references, and assessment centers. Psychological tests for employee selection are discussed in chapter 4.

BIOGRAPHICAL INFORMATION

The collection of biographical information, or biodata, on the backgrounds of job applicants is a common method of employee selection. The rationale for this technique is the belief that past experiences or personal traits can be used to predict work behavior and potential for success. Because many behaviors, values, and attitudes remain consistent throughout life, it is not unreasonable to assume that behavior in the future will be based on behavior in the past.

Application Blanks

The initial determination about your suitability for employment is likely to be based on the information you supply on a company's application blank. Today, fewer organizations use the standard paper forms, instead, they rely on applications completed online.

Home Depot, among other companies, uses in-store kiosks at which prospective employees complete an application online. Most of the 40,000 people Home Depot hires every year are processed electronically. Other companies, including Blockbuster and Target, use in-store kiosks to process 80% of the hourly employees they hire. Some firms even provide a realistic job preview, using short videos to show what life on the job is really like and to highlight what workers are expected to do. Home Depot shows that their jobs include heavy lifting and working some weekends, conditions a person would surely like to know about before filing an application.

Applicants may also answer a series of true-false and multiple-choice questions, devised by I/O psychologists, dealing with personality and ethics issues. Some questions are asked several times, with different wording. In only a few minutes after an application is completed online, the store manager receives a color-coded score for the applicant. A green score is considered so good that the manager will often try to interview the applicant before he or she leaves the store. Yellow scores are considered borderline. Persons who receive red scores, typically 30% of all Home Depot applicants, will not be working for the company.

One problem with application blanks, whether completed online or on paper, is the honesty of the applicant's responses. Is the information the applicant supplies complete and correct? Did the person actually graduate from the college indicated on the form? Did he or she really supervise 50 workers in the previous job? Is the reported annual salary correct or exaggerated? A sizable number of job applicants provide misleading or fraudulent information, especially about their previous job title, pay, and degree of responsibility. A few years ago, the newly hired football coach at a major university was fired after only 5 days on the job. It turned out that he had not won three football letters as an undergraduate, as he had claimed. In fact, he had never even played football. In addition, he had not received a master's degree, although he had so stated on his application form. Yet, he had been a successful football coach for more than 20 years! Until he went to his new job, however, no one had bothered to check the information he had been providing on applications and résumés.

Similar situations occur in the corporate world. The CEO of Bausch & Lomb was found to have lied about receiving an MBA degree. Although he was not fired, he did lose a $1.1 million bonus for the year. The chief financial officer of Veritas Software resigned when it was learned that he had also lied about earning an MBA.

Many organizations attempt to confirm the accuracy of biographical information by contacting former employers and the persons named as references. However, many companies are reluctant to release personal information for fear of lawsuits. A former employee may sue a company for providing unfavorable information, claiming libel or slander. Therefore, many employing organizations hesitate to supply more than limited factual data, such as job title and dates of employment. Few give evaluative information, such as performance ratings, or answer questions about why the employee left or whether the company

Biodata inventory An employee selection technique covering an applicant's past behavior, attitudes, preferences, and values.

Newsbreak

How Not to Get Hired, Part 3: Prooofread Your Résumé

It pays to proofread your résumé and review your answers on an application blank to correct typographical errors, misspellings, and awkward phrasing. Consider carefully the image your résumé or application presents to a prospective employer. The following items are taken from actual résumés, application forms, and cover letters to employers. Do you think any of these people were hired?

"I received a *plague* for Salesperson of the Year."

"I'm a *rabid* typist."

"I have the ability to meet deadlines while maintaining my *composer*."

"I have an excellent eye for *derail*."

"Please excuse any spelling errors on this résumé since spelling is not my strong *suite*."

"Objective: To obtain a position that allows me to make use of my *commuter* skills."

"I have formed a partnership with three business *collies*."

And to close a cover letter, one job-seeker wrote: "Thank you for your consideration. I hope to hear from you *shorty*."

To make the best impression, consider a professional résumé writing service such as Pathfinder Writing and Career Services at www.pathfindercareers.com

---

would rehire the employee. Thus, it is difficult for an organization to verify certain kinds of information provided on an application blank.

Biodata Inventories

The **biodata inventory** is a more systematized form of application blank. Typically, biodata questionnaires are longer than application blanks and seek greater detail about a person's background and experiences. The rationale for this extensive probing is that on-the-job behavior is related to attitudes, preferences, and values, as well as to past behavior in a variety of situations.

The FBI uses a 47-item biodata inventory to select special agents. A sample question is similar to the following, in which applicants are asked to choose the alternative that best describes what gives them the most pride in their work. Applicants are cautioned to answer honestly; "doing otherwise will negatively affect your score."

- Having been able to avoid any major controversies
- Having gotten where I am on my own
- Having been able to work smoothly with people
- Having provided a lot of new ideas, good and bad
- Having been able to do well whatever management has requested

Considerable research is required to determine the background experiences and preferences that correlate with job success. The process of validating items on a biodata inventory is similar to that for any selection technique. Each item must be correlated with a measure of job performance.

Research on biodata inventories confirms their high predictive value. Nevertheless, as with standard application blanks, faking can be a problem. Some applicants deliberately distort their answers to put a more positive spin on their work and life

Impression management Acting deliberately to make a good impression, to present oneself in the most favorable way.

experiences. Advising applicants that their answers will be checked sometimes reduces this problem. Also, written notice that a scale to detect faking is built into the questionnaire, or that the scoring system will deduct points for dishonest answers (such as in the FBI questionnaire), can be effective.

Although biodata have been found to be valid predictors of job success, the biodata inventory technique is not used extensively. Some managers claim that they do not have the time, money, or expertise to develop inventories. Others are skeptical of the research showing the utility of biodata inventories. It seems that the I-O psychologists working for these companies or conducting research on biodata have not been effective in communicating the value of biodata inventories to the persons who are in a position to apply them. This situation illustrates the gap that sometimes arises between research and application in I-O psychology, which we discussed in chapter 1. Researchers have developed a highly successful employee selection tool—the biodata inventory—but it is seldom used in the workplace. Psychologists need to provide data that persuade human resources managers that this technique for selecting the best employees will save more money in the long run than the initial costs of developing and implementing the inventory.

INTERVIEWS

The personal interview is a widely used employee selection technique. Regardless of any other techniques that are part of an organization's selection program, almost every prospective employer wants the chance to meet an applicant in person before offering a job. The employment interview, like the college recruiting interview, is a two-way process. Its purpose is to allow a company to evaluate a candidate's suitability for employment. But it also offers the opportunity for candidates, if they ask the right questions, to determine whether the company and the job are right for them. Research has shown that job applicants have more favorable attitudes toward interviews than toward any other

selection technique, including biodata inventories and psychological tests (Posthuma, Morgeson, & Campion, 2002).

Interviews, if conducted properly, can supply a great deal of information to employers, including feedback on social skills, the ability to work with others, team focus, job knowledge, and specific job skills.

Making a Good Impression

The impression you make during an interview will be a decisive factor in whether the organization offers you a job. I-O psychology research has shown that interviewers' assessments of job applicants are often influenced more by their subjective impressions of the applicants than by such specifics as work history, academic qualifications, or extracurricular activities. Personal qualities, such as perceived attractiveness, sociability, and skill at self-promotion, are often key factors in an interviewer's hiring recommendations.

Of course, as you probably know from your own experience, it is possible to act deliberately so as to make the right impression, that is, to present yourself in the most favorable light. I-O psychologists call this skill **impression management** and have noted two approaches job applicants can take: ingratiation and self-promotion. Ingratiation refers to ways of behaving that attempt to persuade the interviewer to like you. For example, you may compliment the interviewer's style of dress or appear to agree with his or her opinions and attitudes. Self-promotion tactics include praising your accomplishments, character traits, and goals. Self-promotion tactics are used more frequently than ingratiation behaviors and result in higher ratings from interviewers (Ellis, West, Ryan, & DeShon, 2002; Posthuma, Morgeson, & Campion, 2002).

Psychologists have identified another construct, called self-monitoring, that influences the image people present to others. Self-monitoring refers to the extent to which people observe, regulate, and control the image of themselves they choose to display in a public setting such as a job

Unstructured interviews   Interviews in which the format and questions asked are left to the discretion of the interviewer.

Newsbreak

How Not to Get Hired, Part 4: Are You Having Fun Yet?

Would you show up for a job interview wearing a bathing suit? Would you tilt way back in your chair and prop your feet on the interviewer's desk? Yes, people have actually done those things. Here are descriptions of other not-too-bright interview behaviors taken from the files of corporate interviewers.

- The reason the applicant took so long to answer my question became apparent when he began to snore.
- When I gave the applicant my business card at the beginning of the interview, she immediately crumpled it and tossed it in the wastebasket.
- The interview was going well until the applicant told me that he and his friends always

wore the clothing my company manufactured. At that point I told him that we made office products, not clothing.
- She had arranged for a pizza to be delivered to my office during the interview.
- Without asking if I objected, he casually lit a cigar and tossed the match onto the carpet. He did not seem to understand why his behavior annoyed me.
- The applicant was asked to bring a résumé and two references to the interview. She arrived with résumé in hand—and two friends.
- The applicant answered my first few questions then picked up his cell phone and called his parents to tell them the interview was going well.

---

interview. Those who are high self-monitors present themselves in whatever way best fits the social climate around them. Low self-monitors remain more true to themselves and behave much the same way in all situations. They do not try to present a different self according to the situation.

As you could guess, high self-monitors have a competitive edge in the workplace. In a meta-analysis of 136 samples of more than 3,000 people, researchers found that high self-monitors tended to receive more promotions and higher performance ratings than did low self-monitors (Day, Schleicher, Unckless, & Hiller, 2002). Similarly, we could suggest that high self-monitors would tend to receive higher ratings and hiring recommendations in job interviews.

There is also the matter of deliberately distorting or faking answers during an interview—what we might otherwise call *lying*. In a study of 1,346 college seniors interviewing for jobs, investigators

found that more than 90% of the seniors admitted they had faked or embellished their answers to the interviewers' questions (Levashina & Campion, 2007). Are you surprised that the figure is that high? Or are you surprised that it's not higher?

Unstructured Interviews

Four types of interviews common in the business world are the standard, or unstructured, interview; the patterned, or structured, interview; the situational interview; and the puzzle interview.

The **unstructured interview** can be little more than a general conversation. There is little advance planning or formal structure. The format and questions are left to the discretion of the interviewer. Therefore, it is possible that interviewers conducting separate unstructured sessions with the same applicant will receive completely different impressions. Thus, a basic weakness of the

The standard application blank may include questions about one's life history, work experience, specific skills, interests, community activities, and career goals.

unstructured interview is its lack of consistency in assessing candidates. Interviewers may be interested in different aspects of an applicant's background, experience, or attitudes. Recommendations of the interviewers may then reflect more of the biases and prejudices of the interviewers than the objective qualifications of the applicants.

A classic study on this topic, published in 1929, asked 12 interviewers to independently rate 57 applicants on their suitability for a sales job (Hollingworth, 1929). Although the interviewers were experienced sales managers who had conducted many interviews with job applicants, there was a significant lack of agreement among them. Some applicants who were ranked first by one interviewer were ranked last by another. The results of the judgments made about a single applicant are shown in Figure 3–1. You can see that the ratings for this person range from a low of less than 5 to a high of 55. This information would be of no help to a manager trying to decide whether to hire this applicant because it offers no firm basis on which

to judge the person's suitability. In addition to a lack of consistency, or reliability, the predictive validity of the unstructured interview is low.

Training interviewers in the kinds of questions to ask and how to ask them can improve the usefulness of the unstructured interview. Trained interviewers are far less likely to digress into conversation about non-job-related issues than are untrained interviewers. In addition, trained interviewers are able to elicit more pertinent information from the job applicants, information that can be used as the basis for deciding whether to offer an applicant a job.

Despite the recognized limitations of low reliability and validity, unstructured interviews are used far too often by employing organizations.

Structured Interviews

The **structured interview** uses a predetermined list of questions that are asked of every applicant. Thus, the interview procedure is standardized so that the resulting assessment of job candidates is less open to interviewer bias. In conducting a structured interview, the interviewer follows a printed form that contains the questions to be asked. The applicant's responses are recorded on the same form. The interview session has been described as being like an elaborate application blank that the interviewer completes on the basis of what the applicant says.

The following structured interview questions are typical of those used by organizations selecting college graduates for management positions. Because the items deal with work experience, they are intended for graduates who have held at least one job since graduation.

1. What was your first job after completing college?
2. What were your major accomplishments on that job?
3. What were some of the things you did less well, things that point to the need for further training and development?
4. What did you learn about yourself on that job?

Situational interviews Interviews that focus not on personal characteristics or work experience but on the behaviors needed for successful job performance.

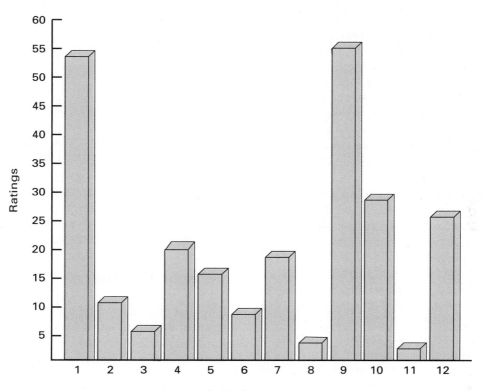

FIGURE 3–1   Data from a classic study showing ratings of one applicant by 12 interviewers.

5. What aspects of the job did you find most challenging?
6. What sort of work would you like to be doing 5 years from now?

Because all applicants are asked the questions in the same sequence, there is a more reliable basis for comparison of the candidates than with the random questioning procedures of the unstructured interview.

Structured interviews are a considerable improvement over unstructured interviews and have the potential for higher predictive validity. Research has shown that structured interviews can be as valid predictors of job success as cognitive ability tests. Structured interviews are high in reliability as well. If used properly, structured interviews have the potential for making hiring decisions much easier.

Despite the proven success of structured interviews, however, they are seldom used in the workplace. They are viewed as too expensive and time-consuming to develop and as impinging too much on the autonomy and independence of the interviewers, who resent having to stick to a prepared script. This is another example of a well-proven technique that is not widely applied, another instance of the difficulty I/O psychologists have in communicating research results to managers and of the problems managers have in accepting what psychological research has confirmed.

Situational Interviews

A **situational interview** is developed specifically to meet the requirements of a particular job. Interview questions are not designed to inquire about general work experience or personal characteristics and abilities but, rather, about the specific behaviors needed for successful performance of the job in question. These behaviors are determined by a job analysis conducted by the critical-incidents technique.

The first step in developing the situational interview is to prepare a list of critical incidents that differentiate between successful and unsuccessful employees currently on the job. These incidents are typically identified by supervisors who have a comprehensive knowledge of the job. The supervisors determine benchmarks for scoring the incidents, assigning a score of 5 to those behaviors displayed by successful employees, 3 to behaviors displayed by average employees, and 1 to behaviors displayed by poor employees. The incidents are rephrased as questions to be asked in the situational interview; therefore, they represent issues directly related to how an applicant would behave on the job. The numerical benchmarks make it possible to score the interview objectively.

Once constructed, situational interviews are easy to administer and interpret. Because the interview questions are clearly and directly related to job behaviors, they can increase the motivation of job applicants to answer accurately and completely.

Situational interviews are used most often to select workers for skilled and semiskilled factory jobs, for sales jobs, and for first-line supervisory positions. Situational interview results correlate positively with measures of later job performance and, in some instances, are more valid than structured interviews. For higher level leadership positions, behavior-description interviews have proved more useful than situational interviews. In this approach, applicants are asked to relate actual events from their past work experience that might be relevant to the job for which they are applying.

Puzzle Interviews

Puzzle interviews, as you probably guessed from the name, involve asking job applicants to solve puzzles such as these: Why are manhole covers round? How do you weigh an airplane without a scale? This type of interview question, popularized by Microsoft in the 1990s, is assumed to be a way of determining an applicant's ability in such areas as critical thinking, creativity, flexibility of thought, and ability to reason under pressure. The technique

has become popular in many companies, including law firms, banks, insurance companies, airlines, advertising agencies, and the military. Despite widespread use of the puzzle interview, there has been little research to validate the approach.

Researchers asked 76 college students puzzle questions such as the following. Be warned, however, that the researchers did not provide the answers (Honor, Wright, & Sablynski, 2007).

1. You have a 3-quart bucket, a 5-quart bucket, and an infinite supply of water. How can you measure out precisely 4 quarts?

2. How many gas stations are there in the United States? Please give an estimate and describe how you arrived at your estimate.

3. You have a bucket of jellybeans in three colors: red, green, and blue. With your eyes closed, you must reach in the bucket and extract some jellybeans. What is the minimum number of jellybeans you can take out to be certain of getting two of the same color?

The results showed that a subject's performance in solving the puzzles was related to cognitive ability. Potential employees who performed well on these types of questions considered the questions to be fair. This, in turn, increased the perceived attractiveness of the organization using the technique.

Online Interviews

In online interviewing, computer software is used to conduct the initial interview. Applicants answer a fixed sequence of multiple-choice questions. All applicants for a specific position are asked the same

The personal interview is part of virtually every employee selection program.

questions in the same order. Questions on sensitive issues, if appropriate, can be included in an online interview; in contrast, many interviewers are hesitant to ask about personal matters in the traditional face-to-face interview situation. Corporate users of online interviews report that most applicants are comfortable with this type of screening and are willing to respond with honesty and candor.

Online screening is now conducted routinely by Target, Macy's, Home Depot, and other large retail chains. Home Depot's in-store computer kiosks allow selected applicants to complete an interview in less than an hour. The company reported that turnover dropped by more than 11% during the first year of the online interview program. Also, managers saved time because they no longer had to interview applicants and score tests. Personal interviews are conducted only with applicants who complete and pass the online screening.

The Interviewer's Judgments

Several factors can bias an interviewer's judgment about a job applicant. We discuss here the influence of prior information, the so-called contrast effect, and interviewers' personal prejudices. These factors can be reduced or minimized by training interviewers to recognize them.

Prior Information. Interviewers generally have some prior information about job candidates, such as recruiter evaluations, application blanks, online screening results, or the results of psychological tests. The nature of that prior information can predispose an interviewer to have a favorable or unfavorable attitude toward an applicant before he or she even arrives for the interview. For example, applicants who performed well in preliminary recruitment screening are generally rated higher by interviewers than are those who did less well in preliminary screening.

The Contrast Effect. Interviewers see many job applicants, often one after another. How they evaluate a particular applicant may depend on their standards of comparison, that is, the characteristics of the applicants they interviewed previously. For example, after having interviewed three undesirable candidates, an interviewer may rate the next candidate in line as more favorable than the candidate's qualifications merit. That same average candidate might have been rated less

favorably if the previous candidates had all been highly qualified.

This contrast tendency highlights the importance of a person's place in an interviewer's schedule. It also means, as we noted earlier, that interviewers do not always have objective standards for the type of person considered to be a suitable employee. Applicants are not evaluated on an absolute basis, or on their merits alone; rather, they are judged relative to the other applicants interviewed during the same time period. Thus, the standard for the acceptable employee may change frequently.

Interviewers' Prejudices. Another factor that affects interviewers' judgment is their personal likes and dislikes. For example, men sometimes think that women are incapable of performing certain jobs. Interviewers of both genders are more likely to hire women for so-called traditional female jobs, such as schoolteacher or nurse, than for traditional male jobs, such as those in management or engineering. Conversely, some female interviewers are reluctant to consider men for teaching or counseling jobs.

Racial and ethnic prejudice can skew interviewers' evaluations of job candidates, although this bias may not be quite as strong today as it was toward previous generations of employees. In a large-scale study in which 708 recruiters interviewed 12,203 applicants, there was no evidence that either difference or similarity in race or gender between interviewers and applicants had any effect on the ratings given (Sacco, Scheu, Ryan, & Schmitt, 2003). However, a more recent study in which experienced police officers assessed videotaped responses of other police personnel being interviewed for promotion indicated that racial bias did have a significant effect. White assessors rated White candidates for promotion more highly than Black candidates; Black assessors rated Black candidates higher (Buckley, Jackson, Bolino, Veres, & Field, 2007).

Interviewers can also prejudge applicants who display certain qualities or traits and refuse to consider their other abilities or characteristics. They may also recommend hiring some applicants merely because they display some quality the interviewers like, such as a shared interest in baseball, even though it may bear no relation to job performance. The phenomenon of generalizing from one trait or characteristic to the entire person in a positive or a negative direction is called

| **Halo effect**   The tendency to judge all aspects of a person's behavior or character on the basis of a single attribute. | **Assessment center**   A method of selection and training that involves a simulated job situation in which candidates deal with actual job problems. | **Situational testing**   An early term for the assessment-center technique; employees are placed in a simulated job setting so their behavior under stress can be observed and evaluated. |

the **halo effect**. It influences the decision-making process whenever people have to make personal judgments about others.

As difficult and error-prone as the interview can be, it remains part of virtually every selection program in business, industry, education, and government. The danger lies in placing too much emphasis on its results. If used wisely, however, and in conjunction with other valid selection measures, the interview can be of help to both organization and applicant. Its predictive accuracy can be greatly improved by the use of structured and situational techniques and by appropriate training of interviewers.

REFERENCES AND LETTERS OF RECOMMENDATION

At one time, employee selection programs routinely involved obtaining information about job applicants from persons who knew something about the applicants' background, skills, and work history, such as former teachers, employers, co-workers, and friends. The purpose was to examine other people's impressions of the applicants and to verify the information the applicants reported. Often, though, such references presented a false picture of the applicant. The person providing the reference sometimes deliberately responded in a misleading manner. Past employers wanted to be kind and to say only favorable things about former employees. Current employers who hoped undesirable employees would leave wrote glowing letters of recommendation. Professors wrote positive letters because they knew students would be able to read their files in the university placement center.

The usefulness of references is also limited now because many organizations are no longer willing to supply evaluative information of any kind about former employees for fear of lawsuits. If a company makes a false statement about why a former employee was fired, for example, the employee can sue the company for defamation of character. Thousands of such lawsuits have been filed against U.S. corporations. The mere threat of legal action has prevented many companies from cooperating in even the most basic reference-checking effort (Korkki, 2007).

Companies are advised to refuse to reveal any information about former employees beyond dates of employment, job title, and final salary. If a company chooses to discuss the job performance of a fired employee, it should have for its own protection written evidence from objective performance appraisals. Specific instances regarding performance should be documented by date, time, and place. In addition, managers and supervisors should assume that anything they include in a letter of recommendation may one day be scrutinized by a judge and jury.

Even though the amount and kind of information obtained from references is minimal, many employers still make at least a cursory attempt to check references. Because of the legal complications, however, references are used less frequently today as a selection technique than they were in the past.

ASSESSMENT CENTERS

The **assessment center** is a widely used method of selection that places candidates who are being considered for hiring or for promotion in a simulated job situation so that their behavior under stress can be observed and evaluated. This approach, initially called **situational testing**, was developed by the German army in the 1920s to select officer candidates of high quality. It was first used extensively in the United States by psychologists during World War II when it was adopted as a selection technique by the Office of Strategic Services (OSS), the forerunner of today's Central Intelligence Agency (CIA).

Assessment centers usually involve 6 to 12 candidates at a time who are evaluated as they work through a series of exercises over a period of several days. Candidates are interviewed extensively and may be given intelligence and personality tests, but most of their time is devoted to exercises designed to simulate the actual problems of high-level jobs. The major techniques for eliciting these work

In-basket technique An assessment center exercise that requires job applicants to process memos, letters, and directives found in a typical manager's in-basket.

Newsbreak

Recommendation Letters: What If the Employee Is Dangerous?

Around the Allstate Insurance Company office in Tampa, Florida, where he worked, Paul Calder had frequently seemed to be acting weird. He told people he was an alien. He wrote strange words on his computer screen and refused to let the boss see them. He threatened to kill a masseuse who refused to give him a refund. And then he brought a gun to work.

"I was reasonably sure I had a total lunatic on my hands," his boss said. "A nut case."

The boss was afraid to fire Calder because he believed the employee was capable of killing him and others in the office, but he knew somehow he had to get rid of Calder. So he made up a story about a corporate restructuring that would eliminate Calder's job and offered him severance pay if he would resign. When Calder chose to resign, the boss wrote him a letter of recommendation that was bland and innocuous, as most such letters are nowadays. It did not indicate that there was anything at all wrong with Paul Calder. The letter said Calder resigned because of organizational restructuring and that his resignation "is in no way a reflection upon Paul's job performance."

To do otherwise—to put an employee's faults and failings on paper—is to open yourself and your organization to a lawsuit for libel or slander.

It has become prudent in corporate life today to say nothing about an ex-employee but the bare facts: job title and dates of employment.

Paul Calder found a job with another Tampa insurance company, but his bizarre behavior continued and he was fired. Several months later, he returned to that office to see the people who had fired him. He carried a 9-mm handgun. He killed three men and wounded two women, then he drove to nearby Clearwater and killed himself.

Charles Cullen, a 44-year-old male nurse, may have murdered as many as 40 people over 11 years while he held nine different hospital jobs. No hospital would have hired him had they known that he had attempted suicide three times, been committed to mental institutions on four occasions, and was suspected of killing four elderly patients in intensive care units. And he had also been seen running around his neighborhood at night, chasing cats.

Yet no hospital at which he had worked, including those that had fired him, reported to prospective employers anything negative about Cullen's record for fear of being sued for slander. The only information hospitals were willing to provide was job title and dates of employment. As a result, Cullen "got away with murder" for a long time.

Sources: Dougherty, L. (1995, August 8). Shooting victims' families can sue Allstate. *St. Petersburg (FL) Times*.

samples are the in-basket exercise and the leaderless group discussion.

The In-Basket Technique

When the **in-basket technique** in used, each applicant is presented with the sort of in-basket that is found on virtually every managerial desk, whether in the form of a work tray or in the files on a computer. In the assessment center exercise, the in-basket contains the typical problems, questions, and directives that managers would expect to find when they returned to the office from vacation. The applicants must process this material in a fixed period of time, demonstrating precisely how they would handle the questions and problems on the job. After the

Leaderless group discussion   An assessment center exercise in which job applicants meet to discuss an actual business problem under the pressure of time. Usually, a leader emerges from the group to guide the discussion.

exercise, applicants may be required to justify their decisions during interviews with assessors.

The employee selection program at AT&T relies heavily on the in-basket exercise. Each candidate, playing the role of a manager, must process 25 items (e-mail messages, executive orders, and correspondence) in 3 hours. Trained assessors observe the candidates to see if they are systematic, establish priorities, delegate authority to subordinates, or become enmeshed in trivialities.

Leaderless Group Discussions

In the **leaderless group discussion**, applicants meet as a group to discuss an actual business problem. For example, they may be given information about a group of subordinates from among whom they must select one for promotion. As the meeting proceeds, the candidates are observed to see how they interact and what leadership and communications skills each person displays.

In the leaderless group discussion exercise at AT&T, a group of six candidates is told that they are managers of a corporation and that they must develop a plan to increase profits, and they must complete the plan within a specific amount of time. They are given information about the company and the market, but no person is appointed leader and no rules are established about how to accomplish their goal. Usually, one candidate assumes the leader's role, and that person's capabilities can be evaluated. The other group members are assessed on their cooperation in performing the tasks assigned to them by the leader.

To induce additional pressure, participants are notified frequently of changes in costs or market conditions, sometimes immediately after the total problem has been solved. The new information must be processed and incorporated into the planning. All the while, the clock ticks, the assessors watch, and the stress increases. Some participants become angry and disrupt the group's ability to function cohesively. The contrast between those who can operate well under stress and those who cannot becomes obvious.

Assessment centers also obtain work samples through oral presentations and role playing. In the oral presentation exercise, job applicants are given a packet of information about some aspect of corporate operations, such as the development of a new product or a new sales campaign. They must organize this material and present it to the group, a task typical of executive responsibilities. In role playing, the candidate acts out the role of manager in a simulated job situation, showing, for example, how he or she would conduct a job interview, fire an incompetent worker, or deal with an irate boss.

Computers and video cameras may be used in assessment centers as a way of reducing costs. Information is provided to applicants on computer terminals. Assessors videotape the candidates' behavior for later and more extensive evaluation.

Predictive Validity of Assessment Centers

Although researchers are not certain which attributes or dimensions of behavior are being evaluated by assessment center techniques, they have found the techniques to be useful in predicting subsequent job success, not only for managers and executives but also for entry-level positions. For example, 585 applicants for the police force in Israel participated in a 2-day assessment center exercise. On-the-job evaluations made 2 to 4 years later revealed that assessment center results correlated highly with training and job performance. The level of the applicants' performance in the assessment center exercise was a valid predictor of their later success on the job (Dayan, Kasten, & Fox, 2002).

Similar results have been obtained in studies of managers in the United States and the Netherlands: Investigators found significant positive correlations between assessment center performance and later job performance, job satisfaction, promotions, and salary increases (Jansen & Stoop, 2001; Waldman & Korbar, 2004). A study of 137 employees in Ireland showed that assessment center performance predicted the degree to which employees' personal characteristics meshed with the organization's culture. This relationship was maintained throughout a 6-year period of employment (Garavan, 2007). In a meta-analysis of 26 studies, researchers found a significant positive correlation between assessment center performance and supervisor ratings of on-the-job performance (Hermelin, Lievens, & Robertson, 2007). Another meta-analysis of assessment centers identified four dimensions that accounted for most of the predictive validity of the assessment center technique: the candidate's ability to solve problems, influence others, organize and plan, and communicate effectively (Arthur, Day, McNelly, & Edens (2003).

Some research has indicated that performance on assessment center tasks tends to demonstrate fewer differences in leadership behaviors and skills between Black applicants and White applicants than is shown on tests of cognitive ability (Goldstein, Yusko, & Nicolopoulos, 2001). Other research, however, has found a higher level of adverse impact in assessment center evaluations of Black job applicants than of Hispanic or female applicants (Dean, Roth, & Bobko, 2008). The evidence is not clear, and some I-O psychologists have concluded that assessment center exercises are an equitable way to evaluate the management skills of candidates of different racial and ethnic backgrounds because the exercises focus directly on the ability to perform job-related tasks.

Gender and age differences also influence performance in assessment center exercises. In a study of 1,857 officer candidates for the army in Britain, assessment center ratings for women were higher than for men on such factors as drive, determination, and oral and social interaction skills. As leaders, the women were rated higher in being helpful, sensitive, and kind (Anderson, Lievens, van Dam, & Born, 2006).

In a study of 371 managers in Canada, aged 21 to 57 years, older managers who scored high in dominance and exhibition (the tendency to be demonstrative and noticeable and to engage in social activities) were rated much higher in assessment center performance than younger managers

who scored high on the same factors. Apparently, older managers expressed those traits in a more mature and effective manner in the assessment center tasks than younger managers did (Krajewski, Goffin, Rothstein, & Johnston, 2007).

Employee Attitudes Toward Assessment Centers

Some job candidates, particularly those who perform poorly, resent assessment center exercises. Many people believe that a poor evaluation in an assessment center marks the end of their career, no matter how excellent a record they have compiled in their years with the company. Some candidates believe that success in the assessment center depends more on being articulate and personable than on actual competence at managerial tasks. There may be some truth to these charges. Interpersonal skills do count strongly in these assessments, and active and forceful participation is rewarded. However, assessment center ratings are also based on organizational and decision-making skills, as well as on motivation.

Participation in assessment centers can lead to changes in candidates' perceptions of their interpersonal and administrative skills. Those who perform well tend to believe they have the ability to develop and refine their skills. Those who do poorly tend to have lowered expectations for promotion.

In a study of 189 newly hired supervisors, investigators found that those who performed poorly in an assessment center program designed for training were far less likely to initiate a scheduled feedback call with a mentor to help them improve than did those who performed well. This finding suggests that the supervisors who could benefit most from help on the job were the least likely to take advantage of it, due to their reaction to their poor performance in the assessment center exercises (Abraham, Morrison, & Burnett, 2006).

Summary

Employee preferences for work may vary by age. Sources for recruiting employees for jobs include Web-based recruitment sites, referrals from current employees, job fairs, and help-wanted ads.

Realistic job previews provide accurate information about positive and negative aspects of a job.

An organization's employee selection program requires several steps: conducting job and work analyses, establishing requirements and cutoff levels, recruiting, administering selection devices, and validating the selection devices by determining how they correlate with measures of subsequent job performance.

Equal employment opportunity legislation mandates fair employment practices in hiring. Selection techniques should be job related and should minimize **adverse impact** on minority groups. Companies must also try to prevent **reverse discrimination** against qualified members of the majority group. Fair employment practices appear to have had a minimal impact on organizational effectiveness. Targets of discrimination may include minorities, older workers, women, disabled persons, gay persons, and unattractive people.

Job analysis involves a detailed description of the component tasks performed on a job. Job analysts can use already published work analyses available on O*NET, interview the people directly concerned with the job, observe workers performing the job, have workers keep a systematic activity log, or record critical incidents related to successful job performance. On the basis of the information collected, a job specification can be written that defines the characteristics to be sought in job applicants.

Application blanks on paper or online provide information about job candidates that can be directly related to their probability of success on the job. **Biodata inventories** are useful in predicting job success and are similar to psychological tests in objectivity and types of questions. Because many companies are reluctant to release information on former employees for fear of lawsuits, it can be difficult to confirm the accuracy of information provided on applications.

Although the face-to-face or online interview consistently receives unfavorable evaluations in research on employee selection, most companies continue to use it. The weakest type of interview is the **unstructured interview**; the **structured interview** is a more valid predictive device but it is seldom used because it seems too expensive and time-consuming. All interviews exhibit weaknesses: failure of interviewers to agree on the merits of a job candidate, failure of interviews to predict job success, subjectivity of interviewers' standards of comparison, and interviewers' personal prejudices. In the **situational interview**, questions related to actual job behaviors are developed from a critical-incidents job analysis; this may be the most valid type of interview for predicting an applicant's potential for job success. In puzzle interviews, applicants are asked to solve puzzles as a way of determining their critical thinking skills and their ability to reason under pressure. Interviewers' judgments can be biased by prior information, the contrast effect, the **halo effect**, and personal prejudices.

Letters of recommendation are part of most employee selection programs. They are limited, however, because of the recognized tendency of writers to be overly kind and the reluctance of employers to reveal more than basic, factual information so as to avoid lawsuits.

In **assessment centers**, job candidates perform exercises that realistically simulate problems found on the job. Through the use of the **in-basket technique**, the **leaderless group discussion**, oral presentations, and role playing, applicants are assessed by trained managers on their interpersonal skills and their leadership and decision-making abilities. Assessment centers are valid predictors of success in training programs and job performance.

Key Terms

adverse impact	in-basket technique	situational interviews
assessment center	job analysis	situational testing
biodata inventory	leaderless group discussion	structured interviews
critical-incidents technique	realistic job previews	unstructured interviews
halo effect	reverse discrimination	work analysis
impression management	selection ratio	

Review Questions

1. Discuss the factors that can influence employee preferences, that is, what applicants are looking for in a job.

2. What are some of the advantages of recruitment Web sites over other sources for recruiting job applicants?

3. How might a company's recruiter be responsible for creating job dissatisfaction among new employees?

4. Do you prefer online job applications and interviews or the more traditional person-to-person approach? Why?

5. What are realistic job previews? How do they help both applicants and companies?

6. How does the selection ratio affect recruitment and hiring decisions?

7. How is the validity, or predictive accuracy, of a new selection program determined?

8. Describe how the concept of adverse impact can influence the hiring of minority-group job applicants.

9. How might reverse discrimination influence the hiring of majority-group applicants?

10. What is the effect of ethnic diversity in the workplace on the recruiting of minority applicants?

11. What forms of discrimination, other than racial prejudice, are still found in the workplace? How might these be reduced?

12. Describe the basic techniques of job analysis.

13. Distinguish between job analysis and work analysis. Describe the role of O*NET in conducting such analyses.

14. What are the advantages and disadvantages of biodata inventories? Why are they rarely used?

15. Distinguish between unstructured, structured, and situational interviews. Which approach is the least valid for predicting job success? Which is the most frequently used?

16. Describe the nature and purpose of puzzle interviews. Do you believe they are a fair way to assess a job applicant's suitability for a position? Why?

17. Why are manhole covers round? What might your answer to this question tell a prospective employer about you?

18. What are two types of impression management? How do they differ from self-monitoring?

19. How are the questions used in situational interviews developed? How do situational interviews differ from behavior-description interviews?

20. What factors can influence an interviewer's judgment about a job applicant? Define the contrast effect. Define the halo effect.

21. What is the major problem with obtaining references and letters of recommendation for job applicants? If you were an employer, how would you deal with this issue?

22. When were assessment centers first used in the United States? For what purpose were they devised?

23. Describe two major techniques used in assessment centers.

24. Are assessment centers useful predictors of job performance at all levels?

25. Why do some candidates resent assessment center evaluations? How do you feel about assessment center evaluations? Do you think they provide a fair appraisal of a job candidate's abilities?

Additional Reading

Karsh, B. (2006). *Confessions of recruiting director: The insider's guide to landing your first job*. Upper Saddle River, NJ: Prentice Hall. Explains the basic steps to getting the job you want: writing a good résumé and cover letter, networking, interviewing, and more.

Kravitz, D. A., & Klineberg, S. L. (2000). Reactions to two versions of affirmative action among Whites, Blacks, and Hispanics. *Journal of Applied Psychology, 85,* 597–611. Reviews responses of American-born White, Black, and Hispanic job applicants in the Houston, Texas, area to different types of affirmative-action recruitment plans.

Peterson, N. G., Mumford, M. D., Borman, W. C., Jeanneret, P. R., & Fleishman, E. A. (Eds). (1999). *An occupational information system for the 21st century: The development of O*NET.* Washington, DC: American Psychological Association. Describes the development and validation of this global database of job descriptions; the successor to the Dictionary of Occupational Titles (DOT).

Sacektt, P. R., & Lievens, F. (2008). Personnel selection. *Annual Review of Psychology, 59,* 419–450.

Reviews recent developments in personnel selection including improvements in measurement and validity of specific techniques, predictors of job success, and bias and adverse impact.

Thornton, G. C., & Rupp, D. E. (2006). *Assessment centers in human resource management.* Mahwah, NJ: Erlbaum. A review of the literature on the practice and evaluation of the assessment center method of employee selection; describes validation issues, innovative applications, and feedback, and provides sample cases.

C H A P T E R   4

Psychological Testing

CHAPTER OUTLINE

Standardization   The consistency or uniformity of the conditions and procedures for administering a psychological test.

Objective tests   Tests for which the scoring process is free of personal judgment or bias.

Subjective tests   Tests that contain items such as essay questions. The scoring process can be influenced by the personal characteristics and attitudes of the scorer.

Test norms   The distribution of test scores of a large group of people similar in nature to the job applicants being tested.

Standardization sample   The group of subjects used to establish test norms. The

If you think you'll be finished taking tests when you graduate, think again. You will be taking tests for many more years. How well you perform on them can determine the path of your career, and even your life. Do you plan to continue your education in graduate school to get a master's degree in psychology? Perhaps a law degree or an MBA? Graduate and professional schools all have admissions and certification tests.

Do you expect to find a full-time job right after graduation? Not many organizations will hire you until they see how you score on their tests for job applicants. Once you're hired, you'll be required to take tests for training programs and possible promotions. Even NFL football teams administer psychological tests to prospective players. One team uses personality tests to detect whether a player might tend to be overly aggressive and likely to cause trouble on or off the field.

Psychological testing is big business in today's workplaces. I-O psychologists are responsible for designing, standardizing, and scoring the tests that will play an important part in your future. There is no escaping psychological tests, so you should want to learn something about them.

CHARACTERISTICS OF PSYCHOLOGICAL TESTS

Carefully developed and researched psychological tests have several characteristics that set them apart from the tests published in the Sunday newspaper or on a self-help Web site, the ones that ask, "Are you a good spouse?" or "What is your sex quotient?" A good test involves more than a list of questions that appear to be relevant to the variable being measured. A proper psychological test is standardized, objective, based on sound norms, reliable, and valid.

Standardization

Standardization refers to the consistency or uniformity of the conditions and procedures for administering a psychological test. If an employer or human resources department expects to compare the performance of several job applicants on the same test, all applicants must take that test under identical circumstances. This means that every student or job applicant taking the test reads or listens to the same set of instructions, is allowed the same amount of time in which to respond, and is situated in a similar physical environment.

Any change in testing procedure may produce a change in individual test performance. For example, if the air conditioning system in the testing room breaks down during a summer day, the people taking the test may not perform as well as people who took the test under more comfortable conditions. If an inexperienced or careless tester fails to read the complete instructions to a group of job applicants, then those applicants are not taking the test under the same conditions as other applicants.

Appropriate testing procedures are designed into a test by its developers, but maintaining standardized conditions is the responsibility of the persons administering the test. Therefore, the training of test administrators in proper procedures is vital. An excellent test can be rendered useless by an untrained or inattentive tester. Computer technology is helping to maintain standardized conditions of test administration. Computer-assisted testing ensures that everyone taking the test receives the same instructions in the same format.

Objectivity

Objectivity refers primarily to the scoring of the test results. For a test to be scored objectively, the scoring process must be free of subjective judgments or biases on the part of scorers; anyone scoring the test will obtain the same result.

In your college career you have taken both objective and subjective examinations. With **objective tests** (such as those containing multiple-choice and true-false items) scoring is a mechanical process that requires no special training or knowledge. A clerk in a company's human resources department, an undergraduate grader in the psychology department, or a computer program can score an objective test accurately as long as a scoring key with the correct answers has been provided.

Scoring **subjective tests** (such as those containing essay questions) is more difficult, and the results can be influenced by the scorer's personal characteristics, including a like or dislike for the person who took the test. For a fair and equitable assessment of a job applicant, then, an objective test is more desirable.

Test Norms

To interpret the results of a psychological test, a frame of reference or point of comparison must be established so that the performance of one person can be compared with the performance of others. This is accomplished by means of the **test norms**, the distribution of scores of a large group of people similar in nature to the job applicants being tested. The scores of this group, called the **standardization sample**, serve as the point of comparison in determining the relative standing of the applicants on the ability being tested.

Suppose a high school graduate applies for a job that requires mechanical skills and achieves a score of 82 on a test of mechanical ability. This score, alone, tells us nothing about the level of the applicant's skill, but if we compare that score of 82 with the test norms—the distribution of scores on the test from a large group of high school graduates—then we can ascribe some meaning to the individual score. If the mean of the test norms is 80 and the standard deviation is 10, we know immediately that an applicant who scores 82 has only an average or moderate amount of mechanical ability. With this comparative information, we are in a better position to evaluate objectively the applicant's chances of succeeding on the job relative to the other applicants tested.

The most widely used psychological tests have sets of norms for men and women, for different age groups, for various racial and ethnic groups, and for levels of education. The adequacy of a test's norms can determine its usefulness in any employee selection program.

Reliability

Reliability refers to the consistency or stability of response on a test. If a group of applicants takes a cognitive ability test one week and achieves a mean score of 100, and repeats the test a week later and earns a mean score of 72, something is amiss. The test is unreliable because it yields inconsistent measurements. It is common to find a slight variation in test scores when a test is retaken at a later date, but if the fluctuation is great, something is wrong with the test or the scoring method.

Three ways to determine reliability are the test-retest method, the equivalent-forms method, and the split-halves method. The **test-retest method** involves administering a test twice to the same group of people and correlating the two sets of scores. The closer the correlation coefficient (called, in this case, the reliability coefficient) approaches a perfect, positive correlation of +1.00, the more reliable the test is considered to be. In choosing a test for employee selection, the reliability coefficient ideally should exceed +.80, although in practice a value of approximately +.70 is considered acceptable. This method has several limitations, however. It is uneconomical to ask employees to take time from their jobs to take the test twice. Also, the effects of learning (remembering the test questions) and the influence of other experiences between the two testing sessions may cause the group to score higher the second time.

The **equivalent-forms method** for determining reliability also uses a test-retest approach, but instead of using the same test a second time, a similar form of the test is administered. The disadvantage of the equivalent-forms method is that it is

Split-halves method   A way to determine test reliability that involves administering a new test to a group of subjects, dividing in half the total number of items, and correlating the two sets of scores.

Validity   The determination of whether a psychological test or other selection device measures what it is intended to measure.

Criterion-related validity   A type of validity concerned with the relationship between

test scores and subsequent job performance.

Predictive validity   An approach to establishing criterion-related validity in which a new test is administered to all job applicants,

Newsbreak

Too Smart for The Job?

Bob Jordan wanted to be a police officer in New London, Connecticut, the town where he lived. He applied for the job, took the Wonderlic Personnel Test, and waited to be called for an interview. No call came. He was sure he had passed the test—the questions seemed so easy— and when he heard that other people who had applied at the same time had been hired, he went to the police station to find out what had happened to his application. He was advised that he did not "fit the profile" of a successful police officer. Had he performed poorly on the test? Had he scored so low that he was considered unfit for training or too dumb to ever learn how to do the job? No. Bob's problem was that he scored too high.

Too high? He was too smart? Yes. The test norms for the Wonderlic provide an optimum range of scores for a variety of jobs. If your score is too low, the norms suggest that you lack the ability to succeed on the job. And if you score too high, the test makers say that you are too intelli-

gent, that you will be bored by the job and will probably quit before long. According to the test manual, "Simply hiring the highest scoring employee can be self-defeating." Bob Jordan scored six points too high to be considered a good candidate for the job.

An interview with the deputy police chief revealed more information. "Bob Jordan is exactly the type of guy we would want to screen out. Police work is kind of mundane. We don't deal in gunfights every night."

Jordan was so angry that he did what any good American does when he feels he is being treated unfairly. That's right. He sued, claiming he was discriminated against because of his level of intelligence. But a judge ruled that since the police department treated all highly intelligent job applicants the same, it had not discriminated against him. The judge noted that the decision to disqualify Jordan might have been unwise, but Jordan had not been denied equal protection. He now works as a prison guard.

Source: Allen, M. (1999, September 9). Help wanted: The not-too-high-Q standard. *New York Times*.

difficult and costly to develop two separate and equivalent tests. In the **split-halves method**, the test is taken once, the items are divided in half, and the two sets of scores are correlated. This method is less time-consuming than the other methods because only one administration of the test is required. There is no opportunity for learning or recall to influence the second score.

Validity

Validity is the most important requirement for a psychological test or any other selection device;

that is, the test or selection device must be shown to measure what it is intended to measure. I-O psychologists consider several different kinds of validity.

Criterion-Related Validity.   Suppose that an I-O psychologist working for the U.S. Air Force develops a test to measure the proficiency of radar operators. The test will be considered valid if it measures those skills needed for competent performance on the job. One way to determine this is to correlate test scores with some measure, or criterion, of subsequent job performance. If persons

and all applicants are hired, regardless of test scores. Later, when a measure of job performance can be obtained, test scores are correlated with job performance to see how well the test predicted job success.

Concurrent validity A way to establish criterion-related validity that involves administering a test to employees on the job and correlating their scores with job performance data.

Rational validity The type of validity that relates to the nature, properties, and content of a test, independent of its relationship to job performance measures.

who score high on the radar operator proficiency test also perform well on the job, and if those who score low on the test perform poorly on the job, then the validity coefficient between test scores and job performance will be high. We will know that the test truly measures the skills needed to be a good radar operator and is a valid predictor of job success. Validity coefficients of +.30 to +.40 are considered acceptable for employee selection tests. This approach to defining and establishing validity is called **criterion-related validity**. It is not concerned with the nature or properties of the test itself but rather with the relationship between test scores and later measures of job performance.

Two approaches to establishing criterion-related validity are predictive validity and concurrent validity. **Predictive validity** involves administering the new test to all job applicants for a specified period and hiring them all, regardless of their test scores. At a later date, when some measure of job performance such as production figures or supervisor ratings can be obtained on each worker, the test scores and the job performance criteria are correlated to determine how well the test predicted job success. In most organizations, top management is unwilling to use this approach because obviously some of the people hired will turn out to be poor workers.

Concurrent validity is more popular with management than is predictive validity. It involves giving the test to employees already on the job and correlating the scores with job performance data. The disadvantage of this method is that by testing only current workers, the validation sample contains mostly the better employees. Poorer workers will probably already have quit or been fired, demoted, or transferred. Therefore, it is difficult to establish by the concurrent validity method whether the test is truly distinguishing between good and poor workers.

Another problem with concurrent validity is that applicants for a job and employees already on the job have different motivations and are likely to perform differently on psychological tests. Applicants may be more highly motivated

to perform well on employment tests than current workers, who may feel more secure in their work situation.

The job performance criterion most often used in the establishment of criterion-related validity is ratings assigned by a supervisor to an employee's present level of job performance. Such ratings are made routinely as part of the employee performance appraisal process for all types of jobs. (We discuss performance appraisal in chapter 5.)

Rational Validity. I-O psychologists are also interested in **rational validity**, the kind of validity that relates to the nature, properties, and content of a test, independent of its relationship to measures of job performance. In some employment situations it is not feasible to establish criterion-related validity, perhaps because the company is too small to support the expensive and time-consuming validation process or because the job has no precedent. In the initial selection of the original U.S. astronauts, for example, before any spaceflights had taken place, there were no measures of job performance that could be correlated with test scores.

Two approaches to establishing the rational validity of a test are content validity and construct validity. In **content validity**, the test items are assessed to ensure that they adequately sample the knowledge or skills the test is designed to measure. This assessment can be accomplished by conducting a job analysis and determining if the test items are related to all those abilities needed to perform the job. With a word-processing job, for example, test questions about word-processing computer software are job-related, whereas questions about musical abilities may not be. In the classroom, if your professor announces that you will be tested on the first three chapters of this book, then questions about information from other chapters would not be considered content valid.

Construct validity is an attempt to determine the psychological characteristics measured by a test. How do we know that a new test developed to measure intelligence or motivation or emotional stability really does so? One way to measure construct validity statistically is to correlate scores on the new test with scores on established tests that are known to measure these variables. If the correlation is high, then we can have some confidence that the new test is measuring the trait it claims to measure.

Face Validity.   **Face validity** is not a statistical measure but a subjective impression of how well the test items seem to be related to the job in question. Airline pilots would not think it unusual to take tests about mechanics or navigation because these topics are directly related to the job they expect to perform, but they might balk at being asked if they loved their parents or slept with a light on in their room. Such questions might be related to emotional stability, but they do not appear to be related to flying an airplane. If a test lacks face validity, applicants may not take it seriously, and this may lower their test performance.

The best psychological tests include in their manuals the results of validation studies. Without this information, the human resources or personnel manager can have little confidence that the tests in the company's employee selection program are actually measuring the qualities and abilities being sought in new employees. Test validation is expensive, but proper validation procedures will more than pay for themselves.

Validity Generalization.   I-O psychologists used to follow a doctrine of situational specificity, which recommended validating a test in every situation— that is, in every job and every organization—for which it was chosen as a selection device. Tests were assumed to be differentially valid, which meant that a test appropriate for selecting laboratory technicians in one company was not automatically considered valid for selecting technicians in another company. Therefore, no test could be used with confidence for employee selection without first determining its validity in the given instance, no matter how valid the test had proven for other, similar jobs.

The idea of situational specificity or differential validity has been replaced by **validity generalization**. On the basis of meta-analyses of previous validation studies, I-O psychologists have concluded that tests valid in one situation may also be valid in another situation. In other words, once established, the validity of a test can be generalized.

The Society for Industrial and Organizational Psychology (SIOP) supports validity generalization. It has also been endorsed by the National Academy of Sciences and is included in the Standards for Educational and Psychological Testing of the APA. Validity generalization is widely accepted not only for tests but also for biodata, assessment centers, interviews, integrity tests, and other selection devices. Many large corporations and government agencies apply the concept of validity generalization in their selection programs.

Validity generalization has important practical implications for psychological testing as an employee selection technique. Organizations have realized that if tests no longer require expensive validation procedures for every job at every level, then they can improve their selection programs by including tests, while saving time and money.

FAIR EMPLOYMENT PRACTICES

One result of fair employment legislation has been an increase in validity research to document whether a test is discriminatory. If studies show that applicants of all races who score below a certain level on a test perform poorly on the job, then the test is not discriminatory by race. I-O psychology research confirms that tests with high validity coefficients have relatively low levels of adverse impact. Criterion-related validation procedures (correlating test scores with job performance measures) are required, when feasible, by the guidelines of the Equal Employment Opportunity Commission (EEOC). Rational validation procedures may also be used to meet EEOC requirements.

A test that is found to be valid for one group is expected to be valid for another. Research has

Validity generalization The idea that tests valid in one situation may also be valid in another situation.

Newsbreak

How to Lose Your Job: What Your MySpace Profile Tells the World

Stacy Snyder was a 25-year-old senior at Pennsylvania's Millersville University and a student teacher at a local high school. She was doing well and enjoying her work until the day she was abruptly fired from her job. She was warned not to try to enter the school building ever again and was denied her teaching credentials, which meant she would never get another teaching job.

What had she done? Robbed a bank, seduced a student, gotten caught using illegal drugs? No. She had posted a picture of herself on her MySpace profile. Taken at a recent costume party, it showed Stacy wearing a pirate's hat and drinking something that could have been a soft drink from a plastic cup. Why should anyone lose a job, and a career, because of a fairly innocent picture? Unfortunately, she had captioned it "drunken pirate," although there was nothing in the photo that made her appear to be drunk. No matter.

When high school officials saw that picture, they pronounced it "unprofessional," and declared that it could promote underage drinking. The university agreed.

There are no secrets when you leave a digital footprint online. Employers, and prospective employers, routinely check the entries on your blogs and social networking sites. Any type of post that someone might consider unsavory, obscene, inappropriate, suggestive, or otherwise inappropriate can follow you for years and get you fired or affect your future employment opportunities. "Putting something on the Internet is no different than leaving it on a table at a coffee shop at the mall," said the director of the APA's Ethics Office. "Anybody can stop by and take a look." So remember, once those pictures of you or comments about you are out there, they can be viewed by anybody at any time.

Sources: Chamberlin, J. (2007). Too much information. *APA Grad Psych, 5(2)*, 14–16; Stross, R. (2007, December 30). How to lose your job on your own time. *New York Times*.

demonstrated that racial differences among average test scores are not the result of test bias but arise from educational, social, and cultural differences. A group of internationally known scientists issued the following statement, published in 1994 in the *Wall Street Journal*:

> Intelligence tests are not culturally biased against American blacks or other native-born, English-speaking peoples in the U.S. Rather, IQ scores predict equally accurately for all such Americans, regardless of race and social class.

A report prepared by the APA's Board of Scientific Affairs in 1996 concluded that cognitive ability tests are not biased against African Americans. In other words, the tests do not discriminate against minority groups. Rather, they reflect in quantitative terms the discrimination that has been created by society over time. Therefore, the consistent finding that Blacks score, on the average, some 15 IQ points, or one standard deviation, below Whites on tests of cognitive ability, is a reflection of societal discrimination and not bias or discrimination on the part of the tests themselves (Roth, Bevier, Bobko, Switzer, & Tyler, 2001; Sackett, Borneman, & Connelly, 2008).

However, the empirical demonstration of validity does not guarantee that a test will not be

Race norming   A controversial practice, now outlawed, of boosting test scores for minority job applicants to equalize hiring rates.

Banding   A controversial practice of grouping test scores for minority job applicants to equalize hiring rates.

declared discriminatory and barred from further use. This occurred with the General Aptitude Test Battery (GATB) used by the U.S. Employment Service. The GATB is a test of cognitive functioning; it also assesses manual and finger dexterity. More than 750 validity studies have confirmed the high validity of the test as a screening instrument for employment. Test validities for Whites and minorities were comparable, although minority job applicants showed lower average scores and hence were less likely to be hired.

To avoid the adverse impact that would result from continued use of the GATB, the U.S. Employment Service adopted the controversial practice of **race norming**. Scores for minority applicants were adjusted upward to equalize hiring rates. Thus, political, social, and legal imperatives were given precedence over scientific ones. The Civil Rights Act of 1991 prohibits the practice of race norming, specifically banning any form of score adjustment based on race, color, religion, gender, or national origin.

With race norming outlawed, the technique of **banding** was suggested. This was another attempt to equalize hiring rates by race by compensating for the consistently lower scores obtained by minorities on cognitive ability tests. Let us consider a simplified example. A company's human resources director could examine the test scores of job applicants and decide to band, or group together, all applicant scores between, say, 91 and 100, calling this range of scores Band 1. Band 2 would encompass all scores between 81 and 90, Band 3 the scores between 71 and 80, and so on. Of course, any bandwidth could be selected; that is, Band 1 might just as easily include all scores between 81 and 100.

To equalize hiring rates by race, then, all applicants included in Band 1 would be considered equal in terms of the ability being tested. No distinction would be drawn between the applicant with a score of 100 and the applicant with a score of 91 if both were in the same band. Furthermore, the order of selection within a band would not necessarily be by test score, but, rather, could be by

race. Thus, the person who scored 100 would not always be selected over the person who scored 91; within that band, hiring decisions could be made by racial or ethnic background.

Probably to no one's surprise, studies showed that job applicants who stood to benefit from banding were more likely to believe it was an equitable technique. Many organizations today continue to use banding, but it remains a widely debated and highly emotional issue among the people who develop and use psychological tests for selection purposes (Aguinis, 2004; Campion, et al., 2001).

Discrimination against disabled job applicants and employees has been substantially reduced in recent years as a result of EEOC regulations and the Americans with Disabilities Act of 1990. Many psychological tests were modified for disabled persons and have been supported by empirical validation studies.

For visually handicapped persons, test questions can be presented orally, in large print, or in Braille, and people can be allowed more time in which to complete the test. Test questions relating to color, shape, and texture cannot be used with persons who were born without sight and have never seen colors and objects. Applicants with hearing disabilities can be given written instead of oral test instructions.

OVERVIEW OF A TESTING PROGRAM

The basic steps in establishing a testing program are essentially those necessary for any kind of employee selection program. The first requirement is to investigate the nature of the job for which testing will be used. Once job and worker analyses have been conducted, the appropriate tests to measure the behaviors and abilities related to job success must be chosen or developed.

Where do I-O psychologists find appropriate tests? They can use tests already available or develop new tests specifically for the job and company in question. The best tests include information on reliability, validity, and test norms. Additional evaluative information is provided by the periodically revised *Mental Measurements Yearbook*, which can be accessed at www.unl.edu/buros. This invaluable resource, begun in 1938, offers current reviews of nearly 4,000 commercially available tests.

There are several issues to consider in deciding whether to use a published test or develop a new one. Cost is always important. It is less expensive to purchase a test than to construct one, especially if only a small number of employees are to be selected. Time is also important. If the organization needs qualified workers as soon as possible, management may be unwilling to wait for a test to be developed. This situation is an example of the frequent conflict between research and application in I/O psychology, which we discussed in chapter 1. As one I/O psychologist (who is both a researcher and a practitioner) noted, "Time and money are usually far more salient organizational criteria in decision making than reliability and validity. Practitioners seemingly are engaged in the continuous art of compromise, navigating what they should be doing through the organizational seas of what they are allowed to do" (Muchinsky, 2004, p. 176).

If an organization decides to develop its own test for a particular job, the I-O psychologist overseeing the project will prepare a list of suitable test items. Then the test must be validated to determine whether it measures what it is supposed to measure. An item analysis will show how effectively each test item discriminates between those who score high on the total test and those who score low. This evaluation involves correlating a person's response on each item with the response on the test as a whole. A perfectly valid test question is one that was answered correctly by everyone who scored high on the complete test and was answered incorrectly by everyone who scored low. Only items with a high correlation coefficient will be retained for the final version of the test.

The level of difficulty of each item must be determined. If the majority of the test questions are too easy, then most people will obtain high scores. The resulting range of scores will be too narrow to distinguish those who are high on the trait or skill being measured from those who are only moderately high. A test in which most items are too difficult presents the opposite problem. It will be difficult to distinguish between those who possess extremely low ability and those who possess moderately low ability.

Much of this validity research requires the determination of some measure of job performance, a criterion with which the test scores can be correlated. Ideally, the test will be administered to a large group of applicants and all will be hired regardless of the test scores. At this point, the value of the test is unknown, so it makes little sense to base hiring decisions on its results. Later, after workers have been on the job long enough to develop some competence, their job performance will be assessed, and these ratings will be compared with the test scores. Economic and time constraints usually preclude this approach to establishing predictive validity. The more common method is to test workers already on the job.

Once the validity and reliability of a new test have been found to be satisfactory, a cutoff score must be set. No one scoring below this level will be hired. The cutoff score depends partly on the available labor supply. The greater the number of applicants, the more selective a company can be. The higher the cutoff score, the higher the quality of the applicants hired. However, by being increasingly selective, the organization must spend more money to recruit and evaluate more applicants to find sufficient numbers who meet or exceed the

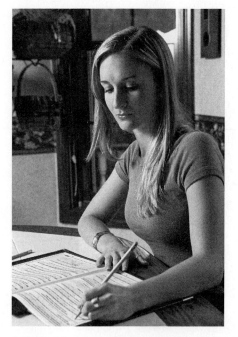

Because individual tests are costly and time-consuming to administer, they are used mostly for vocational counseling and for selecting management personnel.

cutoff score. There is a point of diminishing returns at which the increase in the quality of new hires is less than the cost of recruitment and selection.

Most of the procedures for establishing cutoff scores involve job analyses and criterion-related validity studies to determine the minimum acceptable level of job performance. One frequently used technique asks employees and supervisors to assess the probability that a minimally competent person would answer each test item correctly.

TYPES OF PSYCHOLOGICAL TESTS

Psychological tests can be categorized in two ways: (1) how they are constructed and administered and (2) the skills and abilities they are designed to measure.

Individual and Group Tests

Some tests are designed so that they can be administered to a large number of people at the same

Newsbreak

How Common is Common Sense?

If you are planning to go to graduate school to earn an MBA, you will probably be required to take the Graduate Management Admission Test (GMAT), the standard test used by business school admissions departments since 1954. This 4-hour test assesses verbal, math, and analytical writing skills. It includes 41 verbal questions, 2 essays, and 37 quantitative questions.

The test is reliable and valid; it is known to predict success in MBA programs. But it is less successful in indicating which of those thousands of MBA students will go on to pursue successful business careers. The test cannot identify the seemingly lazy student who will become, at age 27, CEO of a start-up company worth millions. Nor does the test distinguish the all-*A* student who will never rise above a paper-pushing job in middle management.

The business school at the University of Michigan is trying to change that situation by adopting a new kind of selection test, one that focuses on "practical intelligence," otherwise known as common sense. The test was developed by Robert Sternberg, a Yale psychologist, who argues that traditional admissions tests do not pinpoint the ability to advance practical ideas and develop the analytical and creative skills that lead to success in the corporate world.

The practical intelligence test for business school admissions presents applicants with a set of realistic business scenarios, including financial statements, press releases, news articles, and other market information. The applicants are then given a problem to solve by answering a series of questions. The goal of the test is to evaluate an applicant's ability to handle changing situations, learn from misjudgments, and cope with less-than-adequate information—the same everyday challenges that managers confront on the job.

So far, the test has proven to be highly successful as a supplement to the GMAT in predicting grades in business school; the higher the test scores, the higher the grade-point averages. The test has also shown to have less gender and racial disparity than the GMAT. Women scored significantly higher than men on the test of practical intelligence, and Blacks scored only slightly lower than Whites. On the standard admissions test, Black students scored substantially lower than White students.

The research will follow several successive classes of MBA students as they enter the workplace so that their on-the-job performance can be correlated with test scores to determine the test's validity.

Sources: Hedlund, J., Wilt, J., Nebel, K., Ashford, S., & Sternberg, R. (2006). Assessing practical intelligence in business school admissions: A supplement to the Graduate Management Admissions Test. *Learning and Individual Differences, 16*, 101–127. Kuncel, N., Crede, M., & Thomas, L. (2007). A meta-analysis of the predictive validity of the Graduate Management Admissions Test (GMAT) and undergraduate grade point average (UGPA) for graduate student academic performance. *Academy of Management Learning and Education, 6*, 51–68.

Group tests Psychological tests designed to be administered to a large number of people at the same time.

Individual tests Psychological tests designed to be administered to one person at a time.

Computerized adaptive tests A means of administering psychological tests in which an applicant's response to an item determines the level of difficulty of succeeding items.

time. These **group tests** can be given to 20, 200, or 2,000 applicants simultaneously. The only limitation is the size of the testing room or the number of computerized testing stations available.

Individual tests are administered to one person at a time. Because this makes them more costly than group tests, they are used less frequently by employing organizations. Usually they are reserved for selecting senior management personnel. Individual tests are more popular for vocational guidance and counseling and for diagnostic work with patients.

Computerized Adaptive Tests

Designed for large-scale group testing, **computerized adaptive tests** provide an individual testing situation in which the applicant takes the test at a computer terminal. This approach is sometimes referred to as tailored testing because the test is tailored, or adapted, to the person taking it.

If you were given a standard cognitive ability test in paper-and-pencil format, you would have to answer questions designed to sample the full range of your intelligence. Some questions would be easy because your level of intelligence is higher than the level at which the questions are targeted, whereas other questions would be more difficult because they are at or above your level of intelligence. To complete the test, you must spend time answering all the questions, even the simple ones.

In computerized adaptive testing, you do not have to waste time answering questions below your level of ability. The computer program begins with a question of average difficulty. If you answer correctly, the program proceeds to questions of greater difficulty. Had you answered incorrectly, the program would have given you a less difficult question.

Computerized adaptive testing has other advantages. Testing can be done at any time during the selection process; it is not dependent on finding a qualified test administrator and scheduling a testing session. Because a range of abilities can be measured in a relatively short time, there is less

opportunity for the applicant's interest and motivation to diminish. Immediate results are available to the human resources department.

Computers also allow for the use of different types of test items. For example, computerized adaptive tests of spatial ability allow the use of three-dimensional objects moving in space instead of two-dimensional stationary images. Questions can be presented with full-motion video and stereo sound. Test-takers can use a standard keyboard response or a joystick, mouse, or trackball to respond to test questions. Other advantages include worldwide use of a test, instant updating of items without having to reprint paper copies, and instant scoring so that decisions about an applicant's suitability can be made more rapidly (Kersting, 2004a; Naglieri et al., 2004).

Computerized adaptive testing requires a larger initial investment than does a paper-and-pencil test, but it is more economical in the long run. Consultants estimate that the U.S. Department of Defense could save $5 million annually by computerizing the basic enlistment test given to military recruits.

Comparisons of the same tests given in paper-and-pencil format and computerized adaptive versions show little difference in the resulting scores. In one large-scale comparison, 425 employees of a call center took a paper-and-pencil version of a test measuring aspects of personality and judgment. A group of 2,544 job applicants also took the test. A separate group of 2,356 applicants took a Web-based version of the same test that included the same items. The results showed no significant differences in mean scores between the paper-and-pencil and computer versions of the test (Ployhart, Weekley, Holtz, & Kemp, 2003).

One growing problem with computerized tests is that many tests are available on Internet sites and can be accessed from any computer terminal. As they are not administered in a controlled environment, such as a company's human resources office or testing room, ample opportunity exists for cheating. For example, for an intelligence test, an applicant could

Speed tests   Tests that have a fixed time limit, at which point everyone taking the test must stop.

Power tests   Tests that have no time limit. Applicants are allowed as much time as they need to complete the test.

consult source books or have someone else present to help with the answers (Tippins, et al., 2006).

A growing number of retail stores provide on-site stations or kiosks at which job applicants can take brief psychological tests. A comparison of applicants taking such employment tests with applicants taking tests on Internet sites showed no significant differences in test performance. When given the choice between the two modes, the majority of White, Asian, and male applicants preferred the Internet testing option (Robie & Brown, 2007).

Another source of concern is whether Web-based testing might result in adverse impact because of age and race differences in computer access and computer literacy. This could result in what some researchers have called a "digital divide," in which people who own and can use computers have an advantage over those who do not. A large-scale U.S. public opinion poll on the use of, and the attitudes toward, information and communications technology (including, for example, computers, cell phones, and text messaging) found that 49% of Americans used such technology only occasionally. Some 15% reported that they had never used such technology or had no interest in doing so. People in the latter category tended to be female, in their mid-60s or older, and showing lower levels of income and formal education (Horrigan, 2007).

Speed and Power Tests

The difference between speed tests and power tests is the time allotted for completion of the tests. A **speed test** has a fixed time limit, at which point everyone taking the test must stop. A **power test** has no time limit. Applicants are allowed as much time as they need to complete the test. A power test often contains more difficult items than does a speed test. Large-scale testing programs often include speed tests because all test forms can be collected at the same time.

For some tasks, working speed is an important component of successful job performance. A test for a computer keyboarding job would contain relatively easy questions. Given enough time, most

people would be able to respond correctly. The important predictive factor for keyboarding or word processing is the quality of the work that can be performed in a given period: in this case, data-entry accuracy and speed. A power test would not be able to evaluate this skill properly.

WHAT DO TESTS MEASURE?

A more familiar distinction among psychological tests for employee selection is in terms of the characteristics or behaviors they are designed to measure. The basic categories are tests of cognitive abilities, interests, aptitudes, motor skills, personality, honesty, and situational judgment.

Cognitive Abilities

Cognitive ability tests (intelligence tests) are widely used for employee selection because they are highly effective in predicting success in the workplace. Research studies involving thousands of people in the military services and in a variety of civilian jobs have shown consistently that cognitive ability tests are highly valid for predicting success in job training programs and in actual job performance (Hough & Oswald, 2000; Schmidt & Hunter, 2004).

In a meta-analysis of thousands of studies conducted over a period of 85 years, researchers compared the predictive validities of 19 selection techniques. They found that cognitive ability tests had the highest validity for predicting success in job training and performance (Schmidt & Hunter, 1998). An additional meta-analysis of studies of more than 75,000 people in a variety of jobs in Britain lends further support to the predictive value of cognitive ability tests for success both on the job and in training programs (Bertoa, Anderson, & Salgado, 2005).

In other meta-analyses, researchers reviewed studies of 12 occupational groups in Belgium, France, Germany, Ireland, the Netherlands, Portugal, Spain, Britain, and the Scandinavian countries. The researchers concluded that tests of cognitive ability were highly valid predictors of suc-

Interest tests Psychological tests to assess a person's interests and preferences. These tests are used primarily for career counseling.

cess in training programs and job performance for all the countries and occupations included in the studies (Salgado, Anderson, Moscoso, Bertua, & Fruyt, 2003; Salgado, et al., 2003).

And if you've been wondering whether it takes a different kind of intelligence, or cognitive ability, to succeed in the workplace than the type needed to succeed in college, I/O psychologists have the answer. A meta-analysis of 163 samples involved 20,352 research participants who took the Miller Analogies cognitive ability test; the test is used for the selection of graduate students and for employees for jobs of moderate to high levels of complexity in business and industry. Investigators found no significant differences between the abilities needed to succeed in academia and to succeed in the world outside the classroom (Kuncel, Hezlett, & Ones, 2004).

It may not surprise you to learn that there is a high positive correlation between performance on cognitive ability tests and level of education. People who score higher on such tests are more likely, given the opportunity, to graduate from high school and complete at least some years of college. This helps explain why employers often set educational requirements for certain jobs. The completion of more years of formal schooling can provide critical information about a job applicant's level of cognitive ability (Berry, Gruys, & Sackett, 2006).

Let us now consider some of the major tests used in the workplace today. The Otis Self-Administering Tests of Mental Ability is useful for screening applicants for jobs such as office clerk, assembly-line worker, and first-line supervisor. This group-administered test takes little time to complete. It is less useful for professional or high-level managerial positions because it does not discriminate well at the upper range of intelligence.

The Wonderlic Personnel Test, a reliable 50-item measure of general mental ability, is the most popular test for selection, placement, promotion, and reassignment. It is applicable to more than 140 jobs in business and industry, such as flight attendant, bank teller, store manager, and industrial engineer. Because the test has a 12-minute time limit, it is an economical screening device. Test items measure the ability to understand instructions, to solve job-related problems, and to propose ideas that can be applied to new work situations. Test norms are based on more than 450,000 working adults. Computer- and hand-scoring versions are available.

Wonderlic scores show a high positive correlation with scores on the Wechsler Adult Intelligence Scale, a longer and more complex, individually administered test. A hiring kit to facilitate employer compliance with the Americans with Disabilities Act of 1990 offers large-print, Braille, and audiotape versions of the test. Since its introduction in 1937, the Wonderlic has been administered to more than 130 million job applicants throughout the world. In a study of college-age applicants to a computer applications training center, investigators found no significant differences between mean scores of persons who took the computerized version and scores of those who took the print version (Dembowski & Callans, 2000). A study of 1,277 job applicants reported no significant gender or race differences in test performance (Buttigieg, 2006).

The Wechsler Adult Intelligence Scale-Revised (WAIS-R) is a lengthy (approximately 75 minutes), individually administered test used primarily for jobs that require a comprehensive psychological assessment, such as senior management personnel. Its administration, scoring, and interpretation require a well-trained and experienced clinical examiner. The WAIS-R includes 11 subtests, as follows: the verbal subtests are information, digit span, vocabulary, arithmetic, comprehension, and similarities; the performance subtests are picture completion, picture arrangement, block design, object assembly, and digit symbol. Separate verbal and performance measures of cognitive ability can be obtained as well as an overall IQ score. Computer scoring and interpretation are available.

Interests

Interest tests, which tend to be used more for career counseling than for employee selection, include items about daily activities from among

Can You Pass This Test? "If a Train Travels 20 Feet in One Fifth of a Second . . ."

The Wonderlic Personnel Test has been used to evaluate more then 130 million job applicants throughout the world. Chances are good that you may have taken it. There are 50 questions (a perfect score is 50), but not many people answer all of them correctly. The average score in the United States is 21.6. Minimum scores have been established for many occupations. For example, the minimum score considered appropriate for corporate executive or sales manager is 28; for nursing jobs it is 26; bank teller, 23; cashier, 20; and factory worker, 17. The only way to review the actual questions is to take the test, but here are some examples of the types of questions used. The answers are provided so you can check your score.

1. Assume the first two statements are true. Is the final one true, false or not certain?

   The boy plays baseball.
   All baseball players wear hats.
   The boy wears a hat.

2. Paper sells for 21 cents a pad. What will four pads cost?

3. How many of the five pairs of names listed below are exact duplicates?
   a. *Nieman, K M.*
      Neiman, K. M.
   b. *Thomas, G K.*
      Thomas, C. K.
   c. *Hoff, J. P.*
      Hoff, J. P.
   d. *Pino, L. R.*
      Pina, L. R.
   e. *Warner, T. S.*
      Wanner, T S.

4. "Resent" and "reserve." Do these words:
   a. *Have similar meanings*
   b. *Have contradictory meanings*
   c. *Mean neither the same nor opposite*

5. A tram travels 20 feet in one fifth of a second. At this same speed, how many feet will it travel in three seconds?

6. When rope is selling at $.10 a foot, how many feet can you buy for 60 cents?

7. The ninth month of the year is:
   a. *October*
   b. *January*
   c. *June*
   d. *September*
   e. *May*

8. Which number in the following group represents the smallest amount?
   a. *7*
   b. *8*
   c. *31*
   d. *33*
   e. *2*

9. In printing an article of 48,000 words, a printer decides to use two sizes of type. Using the larger type a printed page contains 1,800 words. Using smaller type, a page contains 2,400 words. The article is allotted 21 full pages in a magazine. How many pages must be in smaller type?

10. Three individuals form a partnership and agree to divide the profits equally. X invests $9,000, Y invests $7,000, Z invests $4,000. If the profits are $4,800, how much less does X receive than if the profits were divided in proportion to the amount invested?

11. Assume the first two statements are true. Is the final one true, false, or not certain?
    Tom greeted Beth.
    Beth greeted Dawn.
    Tom did not greet Dawn.

12. A boy is 17 years old and his sister is twice as old. When the boy is 23 years old, what will be the age of his sister?

Answers

1. True	7. d
2. 84 cents	8. e
3. One	9. 17
4. c	10. $560
5. 300 feet	11. Not certain
6. 6 feet	12. 40 years old

Source: Sample questions from *New York Times*, November 30, 2003.

Aptitude tests Psychological tests to measure specific abilities, such as mechanical or clerical skills.

Personality tests Psychological tests that assess personal traits and feelings.

Self-report personality inventories Personality assessment tests that include questions dealing with situations, symptoms, and feelings. Test-takers are asked to indicate how well each item describes themselves or how much they agree with each item.

which applicants select their preferences. The rationale is that if a person exhibits the same pattern of interests and preferences as people who are successful in a given occupation, then the chances are high that the person taking the test will find satisfaction in that occupation. Remember, however, that just because a person shows a high degree of interest in a particular job, it is no guarantee that he or she has the ability to be successful in that job. What interest test scores show is that the person's interests are compatible with the interests of successful people in that career. If a test shows that a person has no interest in a field, then the chances of succeeding in it are limited.

Two frequently used interest tests are the Strong Interest Inventory and the Kuder Occupational Interest Survey. The Strong is a 291-item, computer-scored group test that covers occupations, school subjects, leisure activities, types of people, and work preferences. Items are rated as "like," "dislike," or "indifferent." Scales for more than 200 vocational, technical, and professional occupations are grouped around six themes on which test-takers are ranked from low interest to high interest: artistic, conventional, social, realistic, investigative, and enterprising. In addition, many of the test's occupational scales are gender-differentiated; that is, they have separate norms for males and females. Research on the Strong has shown that people's interests tend to remain stable over time.

The Kuder items are arranged in 100 groups of three alternative activities. Within each forced-choice trio, applicants select the most preferred and least preferred activities. The test can be scored for more than 100 occupations. Typical groups of items are as follows:

Group 1	Group 2
Visit an art gallery.	Collect autographs.
Browse in a library.	Collect coins.
Visit a museum.	Collect butterflies.

Both of these interest inventories are used primarily for career counseling, where the focus is on trying to select the right kind of occupation for an individual. One problem with using interest tests for personnel selection is the possibility that applicants will fake their responses to make themselves appear more suitable for a particular job. Presumably, when a person is taking an interest test for the purpose of career counseling, he or she will answer more honestly because the results will be used to select a broad area of training and employment rather than a particular job.

Aptitudes

For many jobs, **aptitude tests** are administered to applicants to measure specific skills. Sometimes such tests must be specially designed for a particular job, but there are tests available that measure general clerical and mechanical aptitudes.

The Bennett Mechanical Comprehension Test consists of 68 pictures with questions about the application of physical laws or principles of mechanical operation (see Figure 4–1). Tape-recorded instructions are provided for applicants who have limited reading skills. The Bennett is designed for individual or group administration; it takes 30 minutes to complete. The test is used for jobs in aviation; construction; chemical plants; oil refineries; utilities; glass manufacturing; steel, paper, and plywood manufacturing; and mining.

Personality

Certain personality characteristics can contribute to job satisfaction and job performance. For example, empathy and nurturance are important traits for counselors to have; autonomy and persistence are vital to investigative reporters; and orderliness and precision are needed by accountants. **Personality test** scores have been found to correlate with job success in virtually all occupations. The predictive validities of personality test scores can be as high as those for assessment centers and biodata questionnaires (Tett & Christiansen, 2007).

Two approaches to personality assessment are self-report inventories and projective techniques. **Self-report personality inventories** include

Projective techniques   A personality assessment technique in which test-takers project their feelings onto an ambiguous stimulus such as an inkblot.

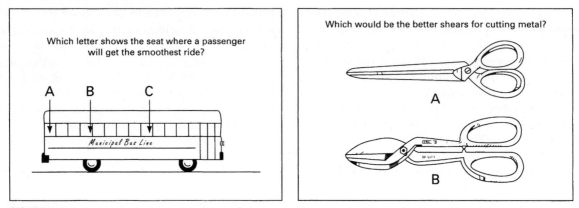

FIGURE 4–1   Sample items from Bennett Mechanical Comprehension Test. (Reproduced by permission. Copyright 1950, renewed 1967; 1941, renewed 1969; 1942, renewed 1969; 1967, 1968, 1980 by The Psychological Corporation, San Antonio, Texas. All rights reserved.)

items dealing with specific situations, symptoms, or feelings. Applicants are asked to indicate how well each item describes them or how much they agree with each item. Honesty of responses may be the major problem with self-report personality tests. Test questions are often transparent, so people can usually figure out how to respond to make themselves appear to possess whatever qualities they think the organization wants.

Projective techniques for personality testing present applicants with an ambiguous stimulus such as an inkblot. The task is to tell what is seen in the figure or picture. The rationale is that people will project their thoughts, wishes, and feelings onto the stimulus in an effort to give it meaning. These tests cannot be faked because there are no right and wrong answers.

The best known projective technique is the Rorschach Inkblot Test in which subjects are shown 10 standardized inkblots and asked to describe what they see in each. In the Thematic Apperception Test (TAT), subjects are asked to respond to 30 ambiguous pictures of people and situations.

Projective tests are time-consuming and must be administered individually. Examiners must be thoroughly trained and experienced. Because few of the tests have objective scoring keys, there is ample opportunity for subjective bias to affect the scoring and interpretation of the results. Although projective techniques are sometimes used for employee selection at the executive level, research shows that they have low validity.

Self-Report Inventories.   The Guilford-Zimmerman Temperament Survey is a widely used paper-and-pencil personality test. The 300 items are statements rather than questions, and the applicant responds by checking "yes," "?," or "no." Here are three sample items:

> You start work on a new project with a great deal of enthusiasm.
>
> You are often in low spirits.
>
> Most people use politeness to cover up what is really cutthroat competition.

The test yields separate scores for 10 independent personality traits. As a check against faking or carelessness in responding, there are three falsification scales based on answers to selected items.

The Minnesota Multiphasic Personality Inventory (MMPI-2) is a frequently used personality test for employee selection and for clinical diagnostic work. The test is widely used in screening for jobs that require a high level of psychological adjustment, such as police officer, firefighter, air traffic controller, and airline flight crew member. The test consists of 567 statements answered by "true," "false," or "cannot say." The items cover

TABLE 4–1

Simulated Items from the Minnesota Multiphasic Personality Inventory (MMPI)

Answer "true" or "false."

At times I get strong cramps in my intestines.
I am often very tense on the job.
Sometimes there is a feeling like something is pressing in on my head.
I wish I could do over some of the things I have done.
I used to like to do the dances in gym class.
It distresses me that people have the wrong ideas about me.
The things that run through my head sometimes are horrible.
There are those out there who want to get me.
Sometimes I think so fast I can't keep up.
I give up too easily when discussing things with others.

physical and psychological health; political and social attitudes; educational, occupational, family, and marital factors; and neurotic and psychotic behavioral tendencies. A number of items can be scored to determine whether the person taking the test was faking, careless, or misunderstood the instructions. Sample items from the test are shown in Table 4–1.

A shorter version of the MMPI was published in 2008. It contains 338 items and can be completed in 35 to 40 minutes instead of the 60 to 90 minutes required for the longer version. A Spanish-language edition of the MMPI uses item scenarios common to Hispanic cultures and has become the most widely used personality test for Spanish-speaking clients (Butcher, Cabiya, Lucio, & Garrido, 2007).

One problem with any test as popular as the MMPI-2 is that some people will take it more than once if they apply to different organizations that use

it. Among a sample of nearly 2,000 workers in the nuclear power industry, more than 200 persons were found to have taken the MMPI four times, 102 had taken it five times, 26 had taken it six times, and 3 had responded to all 567 items seven times. The scores of these examinees showed that repeated administrations of the test resulted in less extreme scores. One reason for this finding is that the job applicants became more test-wise with each additional exposure to the test. This problem is not unique to the MMPI; it applies to any psychological test used by a large number of employers.

The Big Five Personality Factors. Predictive validities for self-report personality tests are generally in the low to moderate range. However, research using self-report inventories to assess the so-called Big Five personality factors has shown higher validities. These basic personality factors are listed and described in Table 4–2.

TABLE 4–2

The Big Five Personality Factors

Factor	Description
Neuroticism	Worried, insecure, nervous, highly strung
Extraversion	Sociable, talkative, fun-loving, affectionate
Openness	Original, independent, creative, daring
Agreeableness	Good-natured, softhearted, trusting, courteous
Conscientiousness	Careful, reliable, hardworking, organized

The original test for the Big Five factors was the NEO Personality Inventory; NEO is an acronym derived from the initial letters of the first three factors: neuroticism, extraversion, and openness. The test consists of 240 items and takes 40 minutes to complete. A more recent version, the Five-Factor Model Questionnaire (FFMQ), was developed specifically to assess personality in the workplace (Gill & Hodgkinson, 2007).

Two of the Big Five factors, conscientiousness and extraversion, have been found to be particularly effective in predicting job performance. Conscientiousness includes such characteristics as being responsible and dependable, able to plan, organized, and achievement-oriented. Conscientiousness has been found to be a valid predictor for many occupations, including managerial, sales, professional, law enforcement, and skilled and semiskilled jobs.

Extraversion, which includes the characteristics of sociability, talkativeness, ambition, assertiveness, and high activity level, correlates highly with success for salespersons and managers. In a study of nearly 4,000 managers in the United States and Japan researchers found that extraversion was highly predictive of successful job performance in both cultures (Robie, Brown, & Bly, 2005). Extraversion also shows a high positive correlation with success in obtaining a job. College seniors who score high in extraversion and conscientiousness are far more likely to find jobs after graduation than those who score low on these factors. In a survey of 1,886 high-level managers, investigators found that those who scored high in agreeableness, openness to experience, and neuroticism were more likely to be seeking to change jobs than were those who scored low on those factors (Boudreau, Boswell, Judge, & Bretz, 2001).

Extraverts do very well in sales jobs. A study of 164 telemarketing sales representatives showed that those who scored high in extraversion had better sales records than those who scored low. Extraverts also scored higher in striving for status, that is, in working to perform at a higher level than their peers (Barrick, Stewart, & Piotrowski, 2002).

In a meta-analysis of 222 correlations from leadership studies, researchers found that extraversion was the most consistent correlate with leadership skill, followed by conscientiousness and openness to experience. The factor of agreeableness was the least relevant of the Big Five factors in predicting leadership success (Judge, Bono, Ilies, & Gerhardt, 2002). Research involving 131 employees and 167 supervisors in a health and fitness center showed that extraversion and emotional stability were highly predictive of successful job performance (Judge & Erez, 2007).

The traits of agreeableness and conscientiousness were found to be highly valid predictors of successful performance when a job involved participation as a member of a work team. For example, a study was conducted of 79 four-person human resources work teams. High scores on agreeableness and conscientiousness were closely related to task achievement, getting along well with other group members, and dealing effectively with conflicts (Neuman & Wright, 1999).

Much additional research has been done on the role of conscientiousness as it relates to work behavior. For example, research has demonstrated that conscientiousness is a consistent predictor of job performance. Employees who score high in conscientiousness are "predisposed to be organized, exacting, disciplined, diligent, dependable, methodical, and purposeful. Thus, they are more likely than low conscientiousness workers to thoroughly and correctly perform work tasks, to take initiative in solving problems, to remain committed to work performance, to comply with policies, and to stay focused on work tasks" (Witt, Burke, Barrick, & Mount, 2002, p. 164). Research on 2,518 employees in a variety of occupations also found that those high in conscientiousness scored high on measures of job success (Smithikrai, 2007).

In a study of 1,673 clerical, sales, and production workers, and truck drivers, investigators found that those who scored high in conscientiousness and in agreeableness received higher ratings of job performance from supervisors than workers who scored high in conscientiousness but low in agreeableness (Witt, Burke, Barrick, & Mount, 2002). A related study of 491 workers in a variety of jobs—including sales, technical support, and software engineering—found that conscientiousness was highly and positively related to high job performance, but only among employees who also scored high in social skills. Those who scored high in conscientiousness but low in social skills received lower ratings from supervisors (Witt & Ferris, 2003). Again, conscientiousness is the key factor;

Proactivity A tendency to take action to try to influence or change one's environment.

social skills help, but they are not sufficient to compensate for a lack of diligence.

In a study of 900 managers in Britain, both conscientiousness and extraversion correlated positively with managerial level. Those who scored highest on those two factors advanced to higher managerial positions than did those who scored lower (Moutafi, Furnham, & Crump, 2007). Other research showed that entrepreneurs (people who start and manage their own businesses) scored significantly higher on conscientiousness and openness to experience than did managers who worked for an organization (Zhao & Seibert, 2006).

It has also been found that extraversion and emotional stability correlate positively with a person's level of job satisfaction and degree of commitment to the organization, and negatively with burnout and a desire to change jobs. Conscientiousness "may best predict how well one does at work, but extraversion and emotional stability are more important for understanding how one feels about work" (Ozer & Benet-Martinez, 2006, p. 412).

Other studies have found that conscientiousness is a highly valid predictor of successful performance for U.S. employees working for multinational corporations in other countries, whether they are newly hired or long-term employees (Caligiuri, 2000). In research showing a negative correlation, low scores on conscientiousness were found to be a valid predictor of dysfunctional behaviors such as alcoholism, substance abuse, and reckless driving. People scoring high in conscientiousness were much less likely to exhibit these behaviors than were people scoring low (Sarchione, Cuttler, Muchinsky, & Nelson-Gray, 1998). In view of these and many other similar studies, it is reasonable to conclude that conscientiousness is a desirable characteristic for employees to show and for employers to seek in job applicants.

The factor of openness to experience may also have predictive utility in the workplace, at least for some types of jobs. In a study of 166 managers for firms in Europe, who were participating in a cross-cultural training program in Japan, researchers found that those who scored higher in openness to experience received significantly higher ratings from the instructors in the training program than did those who scored lower in openness (Lievens, Harris, Van Keer, & Bisqueret, 2003). Openness was also related to on-the-job creativity. When the supervisors of 149 office workers were asked to rate their employees on creativity—described as suggesting new ideas to improve performance, for example—the employees judged most creative had scored significantly higher on openness to experience than those rated less creative (George & Zhou, 2001).

Openness to experience, and emotional stability, were found to be vital factors in learning how to fly airplanes. A study of 91 civilian student pilots showed that students with higher levels of openness to experience and emotional stability required significantly less time to learn the necessary skills than did those who scored lower on these factors (Herold, Davis, Fedor, & Parsons, 2002).

Inventories have been developed to measure other specific personality characteristics, such as introversion, self-esteem, sociability, emotional maturity, and proactivity. **Proactivity** refers to a tendency to take action to try to influence or change one's environment. The Proactive Personality Scale consists of 17 items to which respondents indicate the extent of their agreement or disagreement. Sample items include the following (Seibert, Kraimer, & Crant, 2001, p. 874):

- No matter what the odds, if I believe in something I will make it happen.
- Nothing is more exciting than seeing my dreams turn into reality.
- I am always looking for better ways of doing things.

Being proactive can determine how successful you will be in searching for a job. A study of 180 graduating college seniors showed that those who scored high on the Proactive Personality Scale were significantly more successful in finding satisfying employment than did those who scored low

Integrity tests   Paper-and pencil tests designed to detect employee theft, assess attitudes toward dishonesty, and measure relevant personality variables such as a tendency toward delinquency.

Situational judgment tests   A means of assessing behavior and performance in job-related situations.

(Brown, Cober, Kane, Levy, & Shalhoop, 2006). A 2-year investigation of 180 full-time employees found that those who scored high on the Proactive Personality Scale at the beginning of the study were rated higher by supervisors 2 years later on factors such as innovation, career initiative, and learning the political landscape of the workplace. These characteristics were associated with greater career progress and career satisfaction over the course of the study (Seibert, Kraimer, & Crant, 2001).

Other research supports the relationship between being proactive at work and receiving high ratings from supervisors on job performance. Employees who scored high in proactivity also tended to establish stronger social support networks on the job, which allowed them to pursue initiatives beyond their immediate tasks. This led to positive changes in job satisfaction which, in turn, improved performance ratings (Thompson, 2005). In a study of 282 wire-makers in Britain, researchers found that proactive behavior on the job could be enhanced or increased by job autonomy and trust in one's co-workers. The higher the job autonomy and the greater trust in co-workers, the higher the proactive behavior (Parker, Williams, & Turner, 2006).

A final observation on the role of personality in the workplace concerns the predictive value of personality over time. For example, do you think your personality at age 18 will influence the situations you find yourself in when you are older? Researchers in New Zealand measured the traits of positive and negative emotionality in 910 18-year-olds; negative emotionality was described in terms of aggression, alienation, and high stress reactions. The same research participants were surveyed 8 years later on the job. Those who scored high on negative emotionality at the age of 18 were generally unsuccessful in their careers. They held low-prestige jobs, were dissatisfied with those jobs, and had difficulty paying bills and getting ahead financially. The researchers noted that "alienated and hostile adolescents appear trapped in a self-fulfilling and vicious cycle. Their personality dispositions lead them to work experiences that undermine their ability to make a suc-

cessful and rewarding transition into the adult world (Roberts, Caspi, & Moffitt, 2003, p. 593). Those who scored high on positive emotionality at age 18 reported success, happiness, and financial rewards on the job by age 26. They were also engaged in more stimulating work, which at least partially explains their job satisfaction.

Honesty

U.S. companies lose billions of dollars every year to theft, embezzlement, and other forms of employee dishonesty. The polygraph (the so-called lie detector) has been discredited as an effective means of detecting employee theft. A more valid way to predict and detect employee dishonesty is with **integrity tests**, a paper-and-pencil approach developed as an alternative to the polygraph. I-O psychologists estimate that every year more than 15 million employees and job applicants take integrity tests. Currently, some four dozen such tests are in use.

There are two types of integrity tests: (1) overt integrity tests, which directly assess attitudes toward theft and other dishonest behaviors and (2) personality-oriented integrity tests, which measure general delinquency, impulse control, and conscientiousness. Both types of test appear to be valid predictors of theft and of such counterproductive behaviors as absenteeism, drug abuse, malingering, and violent behaviors (Ones & Viswesvaran, 2007). These tests have also been found predictive of general job performance as assessed by supervisor ratings (Berry, Sackett, & Wieman, 2007; Rynes, Brown, & Colbert, 2002).

Research evidence suggests that most integrity tests are probably measuring the Big Five factor of conscientiousness, which would explain why the tests are such valid predictors of job performance (Marcus, Lee, & Ashton, 2007).

Situational Judgment

Situational judgment tests have become increasingly popular. These consist of a series of job-related situations designed to test judgment in the workplace. Applicants choose from among several alternatives to decide which would be the best way and which would be the worst way to respond to the problem. Another approach asks applicants to rate the effectiveness of each of a number of options offered as potential responses to the situation described.

One of the situational judgment tests in current use is the Supervisory Practices Tests, which assesses how well a candidate for a supervisory position responds to situations that involve making decisions about other people. Test 905 is a situational judgment test used by the U.S. Office of Personnel Management to assess the human relations skills and promotion potential for first-line supervisory jobs in the federal civil service.

A meta-analysis of studies involving more than 10,000 people found that the situational judgment test has high predictive validity for a wide range of jobs. Validity levels are comparable to those for assessment centers, structured interviews, and biographical inventories. Situational judgment tests also correlate highly with cognitive ability tests (McDaniel, Morgeson, Finnegan, Campion, & Braverman, 2001) and with the Big Five personality factors (McDaniel, Hartman, Whetzel, & Grubb, 2007). In a study of 823 employees in a government agency, a transportation company, and a manufacturing concern, researchers found that a situational judgment test was a valid predictor of job performance in all three kinds of organization (Clevenger, Pereira, Wiechmann, Schmitt, & Harvey, 2001).

PROBLEMS WITH USING PSYCHOLOGICAL TESTS

Use of psychological tests poses two categories of problems: recurring limitations and ethical and privacy issues.

Recurring Limitations

Uncritical Use.   A common danger with psychological tests is uncritical or inappropriate use by trusting human resources managers who may be taken in by slick brochures and promises of instant success in solving problems of employee selection and equal employment opportunity. A manager may choose a test because it is new, without investigating the test's norms, reliability, or validity. A

test may continue to be used despite negative information about its dependability because the employment office is unaware of the research. Often, there are no data to support a test because no research has ever been conducted on it. The harm generated by an improper testing program affects not only the organization but also applicants, who may be unfairly disqualified from a job by an ineffective test.

Rejection of Qualified Applicants.   Even the best psychological tests are not perfectly valid. No validity coefficients for tests reach a perfect positive correlation of +1.00. There is always some margin for error in the prediction of job success. Sometimes unqualified persons will be hired, and sometimes otherwise qualified applicants will be incorrectly identified as unqualified or ineligible on the basis of their test performance. (This type of error also applies to other selection techniques.) In a study of 754 applicants for jobs at a U.S. government agency, investigators found that those who had failed the selection tests believed that the tests were less fair than did those who had passed the tets (Schleicher, Venkataramani, Morgeson, & Campion, 2006).

False-positive and similar errors can be reduced when tests with the highest predictive validities are chosen for the selection program. To minimize such errors, an employee selection program should not be based on a single technique. The use of several techniques allows for the compilation and evaluation of much more information about an applicant.

Faking.   Organizations using tests for employee selection must be sensitive to the possibility of faking. In one study, the responses of 1,023 people who took a personality test for the purpose of contributing to research on counseling, where there was no incentive for giving a false personal impression, were compared with the responses of 1,135 job applicants, some of whom may well have had a reason for faking. The test responses of the two groups were found to differ significantly, which the investigators said indicated the existence of faking (Stark, Chernyshenko, Chan, Lee, & Drasgow, 2001). In more recent research, when applicants' and nonapplicants' personality test scores were compared, applicants were found to score significantly higher than nonapplicants on extraversion, emotional stability, conscientiousness, and openness. These are traits applicants would expect an employer to be looking for in its employees (Birkeland, Manson, Kisamore, Brannick, & Smith, 2006).

Current thinking among researchers and practitioners is that faking can be expected on personality tests used for job selection but that overall, faking may not represent a major problem. Some I-O psychologists suggest that the ability to distort and dissemble can be a socially useful skill in the workplace as a means of adapting to challenging and stressful demands, and as a way of promoting oneself and advancing in one's career (Hogan, Barrett, & Hogan, 2007; Morgeson, et al. 2007).

Whatever the ultimate truth about faking on personality tests, it seems impossible to eliminate it. Put yourself in this situation: Imagine that you desperately need a job and apply for a sales position. You are given a test that includes the following questions:

I enjoy meeting new people.	Yes_____	No_____
I get along well with most people.	Yes_____	No_____
I find it easy to talk to people.	Yes_____	No_____

You can easily anticipate the way the company expects salespersons to answer. Unless these characteristics apply to you, however, your answers will provide the company with a false impression. You may be hired, but you probably will not be successful or satisfied with the job because it requires abilities that you do not possess. In the long run, then, faking test responses works to your disadvantage, but it is hard to convince some avid job-seekers of this in advance.

Retaking Selection Tests.   Some job applicants, particularly those applying for government jobs (from the local to the federal level) take selection tests repeatedly in the hope that their scores will improve sufficiently to receive a job offer. As you might expect, with continued practice on selection devices such as cognitive ability tests, scores do improve. It's not that the applicants get smarter but that they become more familiar with the kinds of questions being asked. Also, with repeated exposure to the test items, applicants may become less anxious about the testing experience.

To investigate the effects of retaking such tests, the scores of 1,515 applicants to a law enforcement agency were examined. The tests in questions were for cognitive ability and oral communication skills. More than 40% of those who were hired had taken the tests more than once. The scores on both tests increased significantly between the first and second testing experiences, and between the second and third testing experiences. Also, those who took the tests more than once performed better in the training program and were less likely to quit than were those who took the tests only once. The researchers describe these findings as the "persistence" effect, suggesting that applicants who "had to persevere to gain entry into training (repeat testers) were, on average, more motivated to perform than were those who gained entry after a single test" (Hausknecht, Trevor, & Farr, 2002), p. 251).

A meta-analysis of 50 studies involving more than 134,000 job applicants confirmed the value of retaking cognitive ability tests. Test scores increased approximately one fourth of a standard deviation on the second taking and up to one fifth of a standard deviation by the third attempt (Hausknecht, Halpert, DiPaolo, & Gerrard, 2007).

Ethical and Privacy Issues

Ethical Issues.   The APA is concerned about the ethical practices of all psychologists, whether engaged in clinical practice, in academic laboratory research and teaching, or in employee selection. Principles for proper conduct state that psychologists must protect the dignity, worth, and welfare of the persons with whom they deal. Unfortunately, this ideal is sometimes violated in applying psychological tests to employee selection. The APA ethics code describes safeguards for the distribution and use of psychological tests.

1. *Test users.* Persons who administer and interpret psychological tests should be aware of the principles of psychological measurement and validation and the limitations of test interpretation. They must avoid bias and should consider more than one means of assessment. They must adhere to standardized test administration procedures and make every effort to achieve accuracy in recording and scoring test results.

2. *Test security.* Actual test questions should never be reprinted in a public medium such as a newspaper or magazine. It is permissible to publish sample questions (similar to real questions) but not items used in the actual scoring of a test. [The examples in this chapter are sample questions.] Tests should be sold only to professionals who will safeguard their use.

3. *Test interpretation.* Test scores should be given only to those qualified to interpret them. They should not be given to anyone outside the human resources department, such as the applicant's potential supervisor, unless the supervisor has been trained to interpret the scores. The person being tested has the right to know the test score and what it means.

4. *Test publication.* Tests should not be released for use without adequate background research to support the test developers' claims. Informative and current test manuals containing reliability, validity, and normative data should be made available. Advertisements should describe tests accurately, without emotional or persuasive appeals.

Newsbreak

Who Says the Question Is Relevant?

When Sibi Soroka applied for a job as a security guard at Target Stores in California, he didn't know he would be asked about his religious beliefs or his sexual orientation. And he didn't like it when he was. As part of the employment screening process, Soroka had to take Psychscreen, a personality test used by Target, which contains items from two well-known psychological tests, the Minnesota Multiphasic Personality Inventory and the California Psychological Inventory.

Soroka felt that his privacy had been invaded when he was asked if he believed there was a devil and a hell in an afterlife. He was also asked whether he was strongly attracted to members of his own sex or if he dreamed a lot about sex. Questions like these were entirely too personal, he said, and besides, what did his religious beliefs or sexual behavior have to do with being a security guard? Soroka sued Target for violating his right to privacy.

The trial judge denied Soroka's motion for an injunction to prohibit further use of the personality test by Target and ruled that Psychscreen was not an unreasonable device for screening job applicants. Soroka appealed his case to the California Court of Appeals, which ruled in his favor. Psychscreen's questions about religion and sexual orientation, wrote the judges in a 39-page decision, violated a job applicant's right to privacy, unless the company could prove that such information was directly related to job performance.

The appeals court ruling did not object to psychological screening of the store's security guards; it acknowledged that Target had a legitimate and justifiable interest in hiring emotionally stable applicants. Nor did the court find fault with the idea of using personality tests to select guards. What it did criticize was asking questions about sexual orientation and religion when the company could not provide any empirical demonstration of a compelling interest in that kind of personal information about an applicant.

Although Target appealed to the California Supreme Court, it made an out-of-court settlement with Soroka before a decision could be rendered. Between the legal fees and the undisclosed amount of the settlement, plus the public notoriety, the use of Psychscreen turned out to be an expensive selection technique for this company.

Source: Brown, D. C. (1993). Target Stores settle out of court in Soroka v. Dayton Hudson. *The Industrial-Organizational Psychologist, 31*(2), 88–89; Jackson D. N., & Kovacheff J. D. (1993). Personality questionnaires in selection: Privacy issues in the Soroka case. *The Industrial-Organizational Psychologist, 30*(4), 45–50.

Privacy Issues. One aspect of psychological testing that has come under attack is the use of questions about personal or intimate issues. Critics charge that such personal probing is an unnecessary invasion of privacy. Individual freedom is violated when organizations request or require information that cannot be shown to be related to performance of the job for which the person is applying. Few people question the right of an organization to investigate the background, training, abilities, and personality of job applicants. But personal questions about sexual orientation, religion, political beliefs, and health have been successfully challenged in court as unwarranted invasions of privacy. Even if such questions were related to job performance, there remains the issue of how much of ourselves we should be required to reveal to a potential employer.

Summary

Psychological tests must meet criteria regarding: standardization, objectivity, norms, reliability, and validity. **Standardization** refers to the consistency of procedures and conditions under which people take tests. **Objectivity** involves accurate and consistent test scoring that is unbiased by the scorer's personal characteristics and beliefs. **Test norms** are the scores of a group of people who are similar to persons taking the test; norms serve as a point of comparison for individual test scores. **Reliability** refers to the consistency of responses; it can be determined by the test-retest, equivalent-forms, or split-halves methods. **Validity** is concerned with how well a test measures what it is intended to measure. **Criterion-related validity** is determined by the methods of predictive or concurrent validity. **Rational validity** is established by **content** or **construct validity**. The concept of **face validity** refers to how relevant the test appears to the person taking it. **Validity generalization** indicates that a test valid for one job may be valid for other jobs, and a test valid for one ethnic group may be valid for others.

Fair employment legislation prohibits the use of tests to discriminate against job applicants because of race, color, religion, gender, or national origin. A valid test may be declared discriminatory if adverse impact on minority groups can be demonstrated. **Banding** involves grouping test scores to equalize hiring rates for minorities; banding compensates for lower scores obtained by minority applicants on cognitive ability tests.

To establish a testing program, I-O psychologists conduct job and worker analyses, develop suitable tests, conduct an item analysis of each test question, determine the level of difficulty of each question, establish the test's reliability and validity, and set cutoff scores.

Psychological tests differ in terms of how they are constructed and administered and in terms of the type of behavior they measure. Categories include **individual** and **group tests, computerized adaptive tests,** and **speed** and **power tests.** Psychological tests can measure cognitive ability, interests, aptitudes, personality, honesty, and situational judgment. Cognitive ability tests show high correlations with performance in job training programs as well as in actual job performance. Personality characteristics are assessed by **self-report inventories** or **projective techniques**. The Big Five personality factors—especially extraversion, conscientiousness, agreeableness, and openness to experience—are valid predictors of job success. **Proactivity** is related to finding satisfying jobs and performing well in them. **Integrity tests** are designed to predict and detect employee dishonesty. Two types of integrity tests are overt integrity tests and personality-oriented integrity tests. **Situational judgment tests** have high predictive validities for a wide range of jobs.

Psychological tests can be of great value in employee selection because of their objectivity and validity. Limitations of tests include uncritical use, unfair rejection of applicants, and faking of responses. Ethical issues include invasion of privacy and confidentiality of test questions and answers.

Key Terms

aptitude tests
banding
computerized adaptive tests
concurrent validity
construct validity
content validity
criterion-related validity
equivalant-forms method
face validity
group tests
individual tests
integrity tests

interest tests
objective tests
personality tests
power tests
predictive validity
proactivity
projective techniques
race norming
rational validity
reliability
self-report personality
   inventories

situational judgment tests
speed tests
split-halves method
standardization
standardization sample
subjective tests
test norms
test-retest method
validity
validity generalization

Review Questions

1. Why are standardization and objectivity important in psychological testing?

2. Distinguish three ways of establishing the reliability of a psychological test.

3. Define criterion-related validity, rational validity, and face validity.

4. How would you establish the criterion-related validity of a new psychological test being developed to assess applicants for sales jobs?

5. What is validity generalization and what practical implications does it have for psychological testing as a selection technique?

6. Is the practice of race norming still in use? Why or why not?

7. Describe the technique and purpose of banding.

8. Discuss the steps involved in establishing a testing program.

9. In what ways are computerized adaptive testing programs superior to paper-and-pencil testing programs?

10. Discuss the problems and limitations of computerized testing.

11. How do speed tests differ from power tests? Which approach is used most frequently in large-scale testing programs?

12. How do interest tests differ from aptitude tests? Give an example of each type.

13. How good are tests of cognitive ability in predicting success in training programs and in subsequent job performance? Suggest a type of job for which these tests would be inappropriate or of no value.

14. Give an example of a projective technique. Give an example of a self-report personality inventory. Which is more useful for personnel selection? Why?

15. What are the so-called Big Five personality factors? Which ones do you think are the most useful for predicting job performance?

16. For what type of job would you hire someone with a high score in extraversion? With a high score in conscientiousness?

17. What is proactivity? How does it relate to job performance?

18. What kinds of on-the-job behaviors are integrity tests designed to predict?

19. How do overt integrity tests differ from personality-oriented integrity tests?

20. What aspects of job performance are involved in situational judgment testing? Do the results of such tests correlate positively with cognitive ability test scores or with the Big Five factors?

21. Discuss the problems and limitations in using psychological tests for selection purposes.

22. What can happen when a job applicant takes the same selection tests several times? In general, how do people who are hired after retaking these tests perform in training programs?

Additional Reading

Hogan, R. (2007). *Personality and the fate of organizations*. Mahwah, NJ: Erlbaum. Links personality measurement to issues such as leadership, team performance, organizational processes, and managerial competence.

Hornaday, J. A., & Gibson, L. A. (1998). *The Kuder book of people who like their work*. Atlanta: Motivation Research Corp. A collection of nearly 1,500 job descriptions provided by people who are satisfied with their work. Employees describe their job duties, a typical day, and the abilities and personality characteristics required for job success.

Kaplan, R. M., & Saccuzzo, D. P. (2005). *Psychological testing: Principles, applications, and issues* (6th ed.). Belmont, CA: Wadsworth. A popular textbook reviewing all types of psychological tests.

Morgeson, F., Campion, M., Dipboye, R., Hollenbeck, J., Murphy, K., & Schmitt, N. (2007). Reconsidering the use of personality tests in personnel selection contexts. *Personnel Psychology, 60,* 683–729. Examines the use of personality measures for hiring and promotion decisions; focuses on issues such as validity, faking of responses, and ensuring that test questions are job-related.

Wainer, H. (2000). *Computerized adaptive testing: A primer* (2nd ed.). Hillsdale, NJ: Erlbaum. An accessible state-of-the-art guide to the elements of computerized adaptive testing including computer technology, test development, statistics, and test theory.

CHAPTER 5

Performance Appraisal

CHAPTER OUTLINE

Performance appraisal The periodic, formal evaluation of employee performance for the purpose of making career decisions.

There's no getting away from it. Someone somewhere will always be monitoring or evaluating your performance at something. Maybe it's your roommate, a classmate or team member, a friend, lover, spouse, or boss. Someone is assessing your behavior and appraising your abilities, whether informally or formally.

Throughout your career, your performance will be monitored and appraised, and your level of salary, rank, and responsibility will depend on how well you satisfy the established criteria for job performance. Of course, the **performance appraisal** of your work is nothing new to you. It has been going on since you started school. Your performance has been appraised through classroom examinations, term papers, standardized tests, and oral presentations—all techniques designed to gauge or assess the quality of your work. In principle, they are similar to the techniques used on the job, and the results of these evaluations obviously have an important bearing on your future.

Although you may not take formal examinations during your years with an organization, performance appraisals at work are just as important as those in college. Your pay raises, promotions, and job duties affect not only your income and standard of living but also your self-esteem, emotional security, and general satisfaction with life. Performance appraisals can also determine whether you keep your job. In a sense, then, you are never finished passing tests; once you have been evaluated and hired by a company, your performance will continue to be assessed.

Keep in mind that performance appraisal can be as beneficial to you as to your company. Just as classroom tests show where you stand and where you need improvement, so the effective performance appraisal program can help you assess your competence and personal development on the job. Performance appraisal will reveal your strengths and weaknesses, thereby enhancing your self-confidence in some areas and motivating you to improve your performance in others.

FAIR EMPLOYMENT PRACTICES

The Equal Employment Opportunity Commission (EEOC) guidelines apply to any selection procedure that is used for making employment decisions, not only for hiring but also for promotion, demotion, transfer, layoff, discharge, or early retirement. Therefore, performance appraisal procedures must be validated like tests or any other selection device. Employers who base their personnel decisions on the results of a well-designed performance review program that includes formal appraisal interviews are much more likely to be successful in defending themselves against claims of discrimination.

Racial and Gender Bias. Most performance evaluation programs are based on supervisor ratings, which are subjective human judgments that can be influenced by personal factors and prejudices. Race and gender discrimination persist in job assignment, pay, promotion, and other personnel decisions. In a meta-analysis of 92 studies, researchers found that White employees were generally judged to be performing at higher levels on the job than were Black employees (McKay & McDaniel, 2006). A study of 448 upper-level managers reported that women were held to higher standards than men for promotion. Women who had received promotions needed to show higher performance evaluations than men did for promotion to the same level. In other words, women had to work harder and perform better than men to earn a promotion (Lyness & Heilman, 2006).

Age Bias. Evidence with regard to age bias shows that older workers tend to receive significantly lower ratings than do younger workers on measures of self-development, interpersonal skills, and overall job performance. In a survey of 185 mangers and 290 employees of a large multinational corporation, investigators found that older employees who had younger managers received the lowest performance evaluation ratings (Shore, Cleveland, & Goldberg, 2003). Recall from chapter 3 that job proficiency does not necessarily decline with age. In some cases, then, raters may be basing their assessments on their expectations of an older worker's skills rather than on the worker's actual job performance.

Criteria for Compliance. Performance appraisal systems, which depend on having one person evaluate another, provide opportunities for unfair treatment in terms of pay, promotion, and other job outcomes. For organizations to ensure compliance with fair employment practices, performance appraisals should be based on job analyses to document specific critical incidents and behaviors that are related to successful job performance. Appraisers should focus on these actual job behaviors rather than on personality characteristics. They should review the ratings with the employees who are being evaluated and offer training and counseling to employees who are not performing well.

In addition, appraisers should be trained in their duties, have detailed written instructions about how to conduct the evaluation, and observe the workers on the job. It is vital that all relevant notes, records, and supporting documentation be well organized and maintained to ensure the accuracy and objectivity of the appraisals and to support the company's position in any future legal challenges from workers who claim they were treated unfairly.

WHY DO PERFORMANCE APPRAISALS?

The overall purpose of performance appraisal is to provide an accurate and objective measure of how well a person is performing the job. On the basis of this information, decisions will be made about the employee's future with the organization. In addition, performance evaluations are often used to validate specific selection techniques. Thus, there are two broad purposes for conducting performance appraisals: (1) administrative, for use with personnel decisions such as pay increases and promotions, and (2) research, usually for validating selection instruments. Let us consider the purposes of performance appraisal in more detail.

Purposes of Performance Appraisal

Validation of Selection Criteria. Chapters 3 and 4, showed that in order to establish the validity of employee selection devices, the devices must be correlated with some measure of job performance. Whether I-O psychologists are concerned with

psychological tests, interviews, application blanks, or some other technique, they cannot determine the usefulness of these measures until they examine the subsequent performance of the workers who were selected and hired on the basis of those techniques. Therefore, a major purpose of performance appraisal is to provide information for validating employee selection techniques.

Training Requirements. A careful evaluation of employee performance can uncover weaknesses or deficiencies in knowledge, skills, and abilities. Once these are identified, they can be corrected through additional training. Occasionally, an entire work crew or section is found to be deficient on some aspect of the work routine. Information of this sort can lead to the redesign of the training program for new workers and the retraining of current workers to correct the shortcomings. Performance appraisal can also be used to assess the worth of a training program by determining whether job performance improved after the training period.

Employee Improvement. Performance appraisal programs should provide feedback to employees about their job competence and their progress within the organization. I-O psychologists have found that this kind of information is crucial to maintaining employee morale. Appraisals can also suggest how employees might change certain behaviors or attitudes to improve their work efficiency. This purpose of performance appraisal is similar to that of improving training. In this instance, however, a worker's shortcomings can be altered through self-improvement rather than through formal retraining. Workers have a right to know what is expected of them—what they are doing well and how they might improve.

Pay, Promotion, and Other Personnel Decisions. Most people believe they should be rewarded for above average or excellent performance. For example, in your college work, fairness dictates that if your performance on an exam or term paper is superior to that of others taking the course, you should receive a higher grade. If everyone received the same grade regardless of academic performance, there would be little incentive for continued hard work.

In employing organizations, rewards are in the form of salary increases, bonuses, promotions, and transfers to positions providing greater opportunity for advancement. To maintain employee initiative and morale, these changes in status cannot depend on a supervisor's whim or personal bias; rather, such changes must be based on a systematic evaluation of employee worth. Performance appraisals provide the foundation for these career decisions and help to identify employees with the potential and talent for contributing to the company's growth.

Opposition to Performance Appraisal

Not everyone is in favor of formal performance appraisal systems. Many employees—especially those affected most directly by such ratings—are less than enthusiastic about them. The list of critics also includes labor unions and managers.

Labor Unions.   Labor unions, which represent approximately 11% of the U.S. workforce, require that seniority (length of service) rather than assessment of employee merit be taken as the basis for promotion. However, length of job experience alone is no indication of the ability to perform a higher-level job. For example, a worker with 10 years of experience in an auto body plant may know everything about the assembly line. But unless the company has a formal, objective evaluation of that worker's competence in other areas—such as the ability to get along with people or the verbal skills to write reports for management—there is no basis for concluding that the worker will make a good supervisor.

Senior people should be given the first opportunity for promotion, but they must qualify for that promotion because of their abilities, not solely because of length of service. Performance evaluations can provide a reliable basis for decisions.

Employees.   Few people like being tested or evaluated, particularly if they anticipate an unfavorable

Newsbreak

Rating Your Professors: Tough or Cool?

Paul Trout is unhappy about his performance appraisals. Not the ones he gives to his students as a professor at Montana State University, but the ones they give him. At the end of every semester, at colleges throughout the United States, students have the opportunity to evaluate how well their teachers are doing their job.

Do the instructors show concern for the students? How thoroughly do they know the subject matter? Can they communicate the material clearly and with enthusiasm? Do they grade assignments and tests promptly and fairly? Are they available to discuss students' problems? These are just some of the questions students use to rate their professors. The evaluations are factored into the college's decisions about contract renewals, promotions, salary increases, and tenure.

At Montana State, faculty members need to maintain an average score of 3.6, on a 4-point scale, to qualify for a pay raise. "To get scores this high," Professor Trout said, "I have to make a lot of students happy." And to make them happy, he cannot be too demanding. He has to be careful about the amount of work he requires, about his expectations for student performance, and about the standards he sets for grading. A reputation as a tough grader can be costly.

Research on student evaluations shows that students consistently assign low ratings to teachers who set high standards and strict course requirements. Teachers known to offer easy courses receive higher ratings. Have performance appraisals become nothing more than popularity contests?

According to Trout, "To get high scores, most instructors have to please [their students] or at least not upset them. Even a few students, angry about a demanding workload or a *C* grade, can have a devastating effect on evaluation scores simply by giving an instructor a zero on every item, as some disgruntled students do."

Is this how you would like your work performance to be evaluated? And what kind of ratings will you give your professor when this semester ends?

Source: Trout, P. (2000, March 24). Students give top teachers low marks. *St. Petersburg (FL) Times*; Munsey, C. (2007). Why your evaluation counts, *GradPsych, 5(2)*, 21.

rating. Not many people are so confident of their skills that they expect consistently to receive praise from their superiors. And few of us welcome criticism, no matter how objective it is or how tactfully it is offered. Because many of us would rather not be assessed and be told of our weaknesses or deficiencies, we may react with suspicion or hostility to the idea of performance appraisals.

Managers. Managers who have had unsatisfactory experiences with inadequate or poorly designed appraisal programs may be skeptical about their usefulness. Some managers dislike playing the role of judge and are unwilling to accept responsibility for making decisions that affect the future of their subordinates. This tendency can lead managers to inflate their assessments of the workers' job performance, giving higher ratings than deserved. Also, managers may be uncomfortable providing negative feedback to employees and may lack the skills to conduct the postappraisal interview properly.

Despite these sources of opposition to performance appraisal, it remains a necessary activity in organizational life. Its critics overlook the point that some form of appraisal is inevitable. Some basis must be established for employee selection and training and other personnel decisions. These determinations should not be based on personal likes and dislikes. Job competence must be measured in a way that reflects, as objectively as possible, the qualities and abilities required to do the job.

OBJECTIVE PERFORMANCE APPRAISAL TECHNIQUES

Industrial-organizational psychologists have developed a number of techniques to measure job performance. The specific technique used depends on the type of work being evaluated. The abilities needed to work satisfactorily on an assembly line differ from those required on a sales job or a high-level administrative position. The performance measures chosen must reflect the nature and complexity of the job duties. For example, repetitive assembly-line work can be assessed more objectively than the daily activities of a bank executive.

Performance measures may be described as either objective or judgmental. Proficiency on production jobs is more readily appraised by objective performance and output measures. Assessing competence on nonproduction, professional, and managerial jobs, however, requires more judgmental and qualitative measures.

The measurement of performance on production jobs is relatively easy in principle. It typically involves recording the number of units produced in a given time period. Such measures of quantity are widely used in industry in part because production records are readily available. In practice, performance appraisal of production jobs is not so simple, particularly for nonrepetitive jobs. Quality of output must also be assessed.

Output Measures

Consider the productivity of two employees doing word processing. One enters 70 words a minute and the other enters 55 words a minute. If we use quantity as the sole measure of job performance, we must give the first worker the higher rating. However, when we examine the quality of their work, we find that the first worker averages 20 errors a minute and the second makes none. We must now adjust the performance evaluations to reflect the quality of output, and the second worker should receive the higher rating.

Even though we have corrected the output data to compensate for the different quality of performance, we must also consider the possibility that other factors can influence or distort the performance measure. Perhaps the employee who made so many keyboard errors works in a vast, open room surrounded by many other employees and a lot of noisy office equipment. The other employee being evaluated may have a private office and few distractions. Or perhaps one is responsible only for short, routine business letters and the other transcribes technical reports from the engineering department. It would be unfair to assign performance ratings without correcting for differences in office environment and level of difficulty of the job tasks.

Another possible contaminating factor is length of job experience. In general, the longer employees are on a job, the greater is their productivity. The performance appraisals of two otherwise identical workers doing the same job may be expected to differ if one has 2 years of experience and the other 20 years.

Therefore, many factors have to be recognized in evaluating performance on production jobs. The

Some routine production jobs can be evaluated in terms of the number of units produced in a given period.

more of these influences that must be taken into account, the less objective is the final appraisal. The impact of these extraneous factors requires raters to make personal judgments. Thus, even with production jobs in which a tangible product can be counted, performance appraisal may not always be completely objective. In repetitive jobs, such as assembly-line work, subjective judgments may have less impact on the final appraisal. In these instances, a straightforward record of quantity and quality of output may suffice as a measure of job performance.

Computerized Performance Monitoring

Computers are a normal part of the work environment for millions of people the world over, largely in word-processing, data-entry, insurance, and customer-service jobs. Many organizations have programmed their computers to monitor employees' on-the-job activities. Every time a worker produces a unit of work, such as a keystroke, it is automatically counted and stored, providing an objective measure of job performance. Computers can record the number of keystrokes per unit of time, the incidence of errors, the pace of work over the course of a shift, and the number and length of work breaks or rest pauses. Many workers who use computer terminals are subject to this continuous monitoring and evaluating of their job performance by the so-called electronic supervisor, the machine that is always watching. It detects and remembers everything.

Computers are also being used to assess workers in telecommunications jobs, such as airline and hotel reservations agents. An airline based in San Diego, California, monitors its reservations agents throughout the work period, timing their calls and comparing their performance with company standards for the number of seconds spent on each inquiry and the number of minutes allotted for rest breaks. Employees who exceed the standards receive demerits and unfavorable ratings.

Attitudes Toward Computerized Monitoring. How would you like to have every moment of your behavior throughout the workday monitored and recorded? Would it bother you? It may surprise you to learn that a lot of employees, perhaps the majority, are not bothered by electronic performance monitoring. Some of them like it and prefer it to other forms of performance appraisal. Psychologists have found that a person's reaction to electronic monitoring depends on how the data compiled on their job performance are ultimately applied. When the information is used to help employees develop and refine job skills (instead of reprimanding them for taking long rest breaks, for example), most workers report a favorable attitude toward computerized monitoring.

Many employees like this high-tech performance appraisal technique because it ensures that their work will be evaluated objectively, not on the basis of how much their supervisor may like or dislike them. Also, employees believe that such objective measures can provide support for their requests for pay raises or promotions.

Stress and Computerized Monitoring. Having noted that many employees like computerized performance monitoring, it may seem contradictory to report that they also find it stressful, or so they claim in surveys asking whether the technique causes stress. Keep in mind, in trying to reconcile these disparate findings, that the research results may not be contradictory after all. It is quite conceivable that many employees prefer computerized monitoring over other, more subjective, forms of appraisal, yet still find it stressful. Indeed, it would be surprising if some workers did not claim that all forms of appraisal are stressful to some degree. (If you were asked on a questionnaire whether you find college exams to be stressful, you would probably answer yes.)

The monitoring of an individual's job performance is far more stressful for that employee than is monitoring the performance of the work group as a whole. In the latter case, each worker's performance is combined with that of other group members. Also, both field studies and laboratory studies show that people who work alone experience greater stress from computerized monitoring than people who work as part of a cohesive group, even when the group members are monitored individually. The social support provided by the other members of a close-knit work group helps to reduce the stress.

The knowledge of continuous monitoring, of knowing that every action one takes or fails to take is being recorded, can lead workers to focus more on the quantity of their output than the quality. Thus, the stress of computerized monitoring may result in a reduction of work quality, which has a negative effect on overall job performance and satisfaction.

As with many innovations in the workplace, computerized performance monitoring has both advantages and disadvantages. As advantages, the technique provides immediate and objective feedback, reduces rater bias in performance evaluations, helps identify training needs, facilitates goal setting, and may contribute to increases in productivity. However, computerized performance monitoring also invades workers' privacy, may increase stress and reduce job satisfaction, and may lead workers to focus on quantity of output at the expense of quality.

Job-Related Personal Data

Another objective approach to performance appraisal involves the use of personal data, such as

Newsbreak

The Electronic Black Box: Is Your Employer Watching You?

The reach of computerized performance monitoring is being widened as more and more jobs come online. The see-all, know-all electronic supervisor is now watching assembly-line workers, fast-food workers, machine operators, retail clerks, salespeople, accountants, personnel managers, and health care professionals.

Consider how the typical United Parcel Service (UPS) delivery person performs his or her job. Not so long ago, a driver picked up the packages for his or her route from the dispatcher in the morning and then worked alone, unobserved and unreachable, until returning at the end of the shift. Not anymore. Now the UPS driver carries a personal computer in a box, all day long. The screen shows tasks, each one timed to the minute. When the driver completes a delivery, he or she enters the details into the computer and the information is instantly transmitted to the supervisor. Thus, the supervisor knows at any time where each delivery person is and whether that person is on schedule.

There is no hiding. UPS drivers and millions of other workers are being watched over by what one writer called "the boss that never blinks," the boss that is always observing, recording, and measuring.

Long-distance truckers are another group being monitored electronically. They used to enjoy considerable freedom. You know the image—alone in their 18-wheel rigs, barreling down the highway, exchanging greetings in their own language on their CB radios, with no one to tell them what to do. Those days are gone. Those trucks now carry computers that are on all the time. Using satellite links and onboard recorders, employers can monitor a driver's speed, rate of braking, and time spent off the road at a stop. Some systems beep when a driver exceeds the prescribed speed or shifts improperly.

A trucker who hauls mattresses from Indiana to Florida told a reporter that the onboard computer saves time by keeping his daily logbook up-to-date and making it easier for him to get help when his truck has a breakdown, since the company is always aware of his location. Still, there is a downside. "You know they are always watching."

Source: In a nonstop economy, truckers keep rolling (1999, November 24). *New York Times*; Truckers face monitoring to make sure they rest (2000, February 26). *St. Petersburg (FL) Times*; Big brother in a black box (1999, August/September). *Civilization*, pp. 53–55.

How would you evaluate the job performance of a documentary filmmaker?

operate on each week? For business executives, tally the number of decisions they make each month?

And what about football players? Their jobs also differ in complexity from ordinary jobs as psychologists demonstrated in a study of 106 NFL players. Quarterbacks, for example, must quickly process information and make decisions for themselves and their teammates on every play. Wide receivers on the team have a less complex job. They engage in very little information processing as they carry out the specific assignments given to them for each play. The study showed that worker performance in complex jobs is much more strongly influenced by environmental factors, including the actions of other people, over which they have little control. This means that it is much more difficult to evaluate their performance as objectively as performance in less complex jobs (Stewart & Nandkeolyar, 2007).

In such situations, I-O psychologists must find some way to assess the merit of the person's work, not by counting or keeping a precise record of output but by observing work behavior over a period of time and rendering a judgment about its quality. To determine how effective or ineffective an employee is, the assessors must ask people who are familiar with the person and the work, usually a supervisor; but sometimes they must also ask colleagues, subordinates, and even the employee being evaluated.

absenteeism, earnings history, accidents, and advancement rate. It is usually easier to compile job-related personal information from the files in the human resources office than it is to measure and assess production on the job. I-O psychologists have found that personal data may provide little information about an individual worker's ability on the job, but these data can be used to distinguish good from poor employees. The emphasis here is on the distinction between *workers* and *employees*.

Highly skilled and experienced machine operators who are prone to excessive absenteeism and tardiness may be outstanding workers when they are actually on the job. They may be considered poor employees, however, because the company cannot rely on them to show up regularly and contribute to the efficiency of the organization. Job-related personal data are useful in assessing the relative worth of employees to an organization, but they are not a substitute for measures of job performance.

SUBJECTIVE (JUDGMENTAL) PERFORMANCE APPRAISAL TECHNIQUES

Jobs on which employees do not produce a countable product—or one that makes sense to count—are more difficult to assess. How would you evaluate the performance of firefighters? Count the number of fires they put out in a day? How would you appraise brain surgeons? By the number of brains they

Written Narratives

Although some organizations use written narratives, which are brief essays describing employee performance, to appraise performance, most apply numerical rating procedures. Although both narrative and rating approaches are subjective, the narrative technique is more prone to personal bias. An essay written by a supervisor can be ambiguous or misleading when describing an employee's job performance. Sometimes misstatements are inadvertent, but sometimes they are deliberate to avoid giving a negative appraisal. An article published in the *Harvard Business Review* listed some common expressions used in written performance appraisals—and suggested what the rater might have meant.

- "exceptionally well qualified" (has committed no major blunders to date)
- "tactful in dealing with superiors" (knows when to keep quiet)

- "quick thinking" (instantly offers plausible-sounding excuses for errors)
- "meticulous attention to detail" (a fussy nitpicker)
- "slightly below average" (stupid)
- "unusually loyal to the company" (no one else wants them)

In an attempt to reduce ambiguity and personal bias, various merit rating techniques have been developed to provide greater objectivity for judgmental performance appraisals.

Merit Rating Techniques

In many everyday situations we make judgments about the people with whom we come in contact. We assess them in terms of their appearance, intelligence, personality, sense of humor, or athletic skills. On the basis of these informal judgments, we may decide whether to like or dislike them, hire them, become friends with them, or marry them. Our judgments are sometimes faulty; a friend can become an enemy or a spouse an adversary in divorce court. Errors in judgment occur because the process is subjective and unstandardized. We do not always judge people on the basis of meaningful or relevant criteria.

The process of judgment in **merit rating** is considerably more formalized and specific because job-related criteria are established to serve as standards for comparison. Opportunity still exists for raters to impose personal prejudices on the process, but that is not the fault of the method. Merit rating is designed to yield an objective evaluation of work performance compared with established standards.

Rating Technique.   Performance **rating scales** are the most frequently used merit rating technique. The supervisor's task is to specify how or to what

degree the worker possesses each of the relevant job characteristics. To rate work quality based on observations of the worker's performance, the supervisor expresses a judgment on a rating scale such as shown in Figure 5–1. The worker in this example has been judged to exhibit a slightly above average level of task proficiency.

Some companies rate employees on specific job duties and on broader factors such as cooperation, supervisory skills, time management, communications skills, judgment and initiative, and attendance. In addition, many organizations compare current employee performance with their past evaluations, asking supervisors to indicate whether employees have improved, worsened, or shown no change since the last appraisal.

Supervisors may also be asked to note any particular strengths and to explain extenuating circumstances that might have affected a worker's performance. Some companies allow employees to add their own written comments to the evaluation form. A portion of a typical performance rating form is shown in Figure 5–2. Ratings are a popular way of evaluating performance for two reasons: (1) they are relatively easy to construct and (2) they attempt to reduce personal bias.

However, it is difficult to eliminate totally the influence of personal bias against the person being rated; it is still possible for a rater to make an unduly harsh evaluation or an undeserved positive one. A study of 104 officers in the U.S. Air Force showed that their ratings of the people assigned to give them briefings were influenced by whether they knew the persons in question. The factor of prior acquaintance resulted in more positive ratings of their competence (Scotter, Moustafa, Burnett, & Michael, 2007).

Ranking Technique.   In the **ranking technique**, supervisors list their workers in order from highest

1	2	3	4	5
Poor		Average		Excellent

FIGURE 5–1   Rating scale.

Name _____ Position _____ Time in Position _____ Date _____

Department _____ Location _____ Evaluator (Name/Title) _____

Type of Evaluation: Initial 6 Months ☐ Annual ☐ Other _____ Evaluation Period Dates _____

INSTRUCTIONS: Place a check mark (✓) in the box corresponding to the appropriate performance level. Possible elements to consider in evaluation are suggested.

PERFORMANCE RATING LEVELS ──

Commendable (C) Performance exceeded expectations for the position in most areas and results were fully accomplished in all other areas. Assignments always produce results above "good" performance standards established for this position.

Good (G) Performance met most of the expectations for the position. Overall performance was satisfactory. Assignments and major job duties are accomplished with minimal supervision and direction.

Needs Improvement (NI) Performance is below expectations. Work may lack consistency or require more frequent and closer supervision than normally expected. Attitude or attendance may affect performance.

Unsatisfactory (U) Performance does not meet minimum expectations. This may include below standard performance, lack of ability, lack of application, or disruptions in the workplace. After a final warning and if performance does not improve, the employee will be terminated.

PERFORMANCE RATING FACTORS (Use additional paper if necessary) ──────────────────────────

Specific Responsibilities and Duties _____	(C)	(G)	(NI)	(U)
1.				
2.				
3.				

PERFORMANCE RATING FACTORS (Continued) — (NA) Does Not Apply (S) Satisfactory (NI) Needs Improvement (U) Unsatisfactory

General Responsibilities and Requirements _____	(NA)	(S)	(NI)	(U)
1. Cooperation. Ability to demonstrate a spirit of willingness and interest when working with superior(s) and co-workers.				
2. Supervision. Ability to direct, control and train subordinates. Also consider degree to which assistants are helped to establish work objectives.				
3. Time Management. Ability to organize time effectively. Also consider ability to set priorities, anticipate problems, estimate time requirements, and meet deadlines.				
4. Communication. Ability to explain, convince and be understood in oral and written communications with employees at all levels. Also consider evidence of an understanding of people's views and of the effect of own actions on others.				
5. Judgment and Initiative. Ability to identify and appropriately solve or refer problems. Willingness to expand responsibilities.				
6. Attendance. Attendance and timeliness meet acceptable standards.				
Days Absent _____ Days Late _____				

FIGURE 5–2   Portion of a performance appraisal form.

to lowest or best to worst on specific characteristics and abilities and on overall job proficiency. You can see that there is a major conceptual difference between rating and ranking. In ranking, each employee is compared with all others in the work group or department. In rating, each employee is compared with his or her past performance or with a company standard. Thus, ranking is not as direct a measure of job performance as is rating.

An advantage of the ranking technique is its simplicity. No elaborate forms or complicated instructions are required. Ranking can be accomplished quickly and the technique is usually accepted by supervisors as a routine task. Supervisors are not

Paired-comparison technique A performance appraisal technique that compares the performance of each worker with that of every other worker in the group.

COMPLETE THIS SECTION

Principal Strengths _____

Areas for Development _____

Comments: _____

_____

Overall Performance Rating: ☐ Commendable ☐ Good ☐ Needs Improvement ☐ Unsatisfactory

Last Performance Review: ☐ Exceptional ☐ Commendable ☐ Good ☐ Needs Improvement ☐ Unsatisfactory

Date _____

Evaluated by (Name/Title): _____ _____ _____
                      Please print   Signature   Date

Signature of Reviewer: _____ _____
                                  Date

Signature of Employee: _____ _____
                                  Date

Note: Employee's comments, if any, should be attached to this form.

FIGURE 5–2 *Continued*

being asked to judge workers on factors such as initiative or cooperation, qualities they may not be competent to assess. Ranking has its limitations, however, when there are a large number of employees to appraise. Supervisors would have to know all the workers on their shifts quite well to make comparative judgments of their efficiency. With a work group of 50 or 100 subordinates, it becomes difficult and tedious to rank them in order of ability or merit. Another limitation is that because of its simplicity, ranking supplies less evaluative data than does rating. Worker strengths and weaknesses cannot be readily determined by ranking, and there is little feedback or information to provide to workers about how well they are doing or how they might improve their task performance.

The ranking technique for performance appraisal also makes it difficult for supervisors to indicate similarities among workers. For example, in ranking ten workers, a supervisor may believe that three are equally outstanding and two are equally poor, but there is no way to indicate this. The supervisor is forced to rank the workers from highest to lowest. Thus, only one of the three outstanding workers can be at the top of the list even though all three deserve it. These limitations make the ranking technique a crude measure of performance appraisal. It is usually applied only when a small number of workers are involved and when little information is desired beyond an indication of their relative standing.

Paired-Comparison Technique. The **paired-comparison technique** requires that each worker be compared with every other worker in the work team. It is similar to ranking, and the result is a rank ordering of workers, but the comparative judgments

Forced-distribution technique A performance appraisal technique in which supervisors rate employees according to a prescribed distribution of ratings, similar to grading on a curve.

Forced-choice technique A performance appraisal technique in which raters are presented with groups of descriptive statements and are asked to select the phrase in each group that is most descriptive or least descriptive of the worker being evaluated.

are more systematic and controlled. Comparisons are made between two people at a time, and a judgment is made about which of the pair is superior.

If specific characteristics are to be rated, the comparisons are repeated for each item. When all possible comparisons have been made, an objective ranked list is obtained that is based on the worker's score in each comparison. If a supervisor evaluates six workers by this technique, comparing each worker with every other worker, 15 paired comparisons must be made because there are 15 possible pairs. The following formula is used (N represents the number of persons to be evaluated):

$$\frac{N(N-1)}{2}$$

An advantage of the paired-comparison approach over the ranking technique is that the judgmental process is simpler. The supervisor has to consider only one pair of workers at a time. Another advantage is that it is possible to give the same rank to those of equal ability. A disadvantage lies in the large number of comparisons that are required when dealing with many employees. A supervisor with 60 employees would be required to make 1,770 comparisons. If the performance evaluation calls for the appraisal of, say, five separate traits or factors, each of the 1,770 comparisons would have to be made five times. The use of the technique is necessarily restricted to small groups or to a single ranking of overall job effectiveness.

Forced-Distribution Technique. The **forced-distribution technique** is useful with somewhat larger groups. Supervisors rate their employees in fixed proportions, according to a predetermined distribution of ratings. The standard distribution is as follows:

Superior	10%
Better than average	20%
Average	40%
Below average	20%
Poor	10%

If your college instructors grade on a curve, then you are already familiar with forced distribution. The top 10% of the class receive a grade of *A*, regardless of specific test scores. The next 20% receive *B*s, and so on, until all grades are forced into the categories of the distribution resembling the normal curve.

A disadvantage of the forced-distribution technique is that it compels a supervisor to use predetermined rating categories that might not fairly represent that particular group of workers. All workers in a group may be better than average or superior in job performance, and all deserve good ratings. However, the forced distribution technique dictates that only 30% can be rated as above average.

Forced-Choice Technique. One difficulty with the merit rating techniques we have discussed is that raters are aware of whether they are assigning good or poor ratings to employees. This knowledge may permit their personal biases, animosities, or favoritism to affect the ratings. The **forced-choice technique** prevents raters from knowing how favorable or unfavorable the ratings they are giving their employees are.

In the forced-choice technique, raters are presented with groups of descriptive statements and are asked to select the phrase in each group that best describes an employee or is least applicable to that employee. The phrases within each group are designed to appear equally positive or equally negative. For example, raters may be asked to choose one statement in each of the following pairs that best describes a subordinate.

Is reliable
Is agreeable

Is careful
Is diligent

Next, raters may be asked to select one statement in each of these pairs that least describes the subordinate.

Is arrogant
Is not interested in working well

Behaviorally anchored rating scale (BARS) A performance appraisal technique in which appraisers rate critical employee behaviors.

Is uncooperative

Is sloppy in his/her work habits

When given a number of sets of statements, it is difficult for supervisors to distinguish the items that represent desirable or undesirable characteristics. Therefore, they are less likely to deliberately assign favorable or unfavorable ratings.

When I-O psychologists develop statements for forced-choice rating scales, they correlate each item with a measure of job success. Although the statements in each pair may appear to be equally favorable or unfavorable, they have been found to discriminate between more efficient and less efficient workers.

Although the forced-choice technique limits the effect of personal bias and controls for deliberate distortion, it has several disadvantages and is unpopular with raters. Considerable research is necessary to determine the predictive validity for each item. Thus, the technique is more costly to develop than other methods of merit rating. The instructions can be difficult to understand, and the task of choosing between similar alternatives in a large number of pairs is tedious.

Behaviorally Anchored Rating Scale (BARS). A **behaviorally anchored rating scale (BARS)** attempts to evaluate job performance in terms of specific behaviors that are important to success or failure on the job rather than in terms of general attitudes or factors such as communications skills, cooperation, or common sense. The usual way to develop behavioral criteria is through the critical-incidents technique described in chapter 3 as a method of job analysis.

Supervisors familiar with the job observe the performance of their workers and note those behaviors necessary for effective job performance. A series of critical-incident behaviors are established; some of these are associated with superior performance and others with unsatisfactory performance. These behaviors, based on actual job behaviors, are used as standards for appraising worker effectiveness.

BARS items can be scored objectively by indicating whether the employee displays that behavior or by selecting on a scale the degree to which the employee displays that behavior. Figure 5–3 shows a fictitious BARS for the position of Superman or Wonder Woman, though there are not many applicants for those jobs.

Much of the success of the BARS approach depends on the observational skill of the supervisors in identifying behaviors that are truly critical to successful or unsuccessful performance on the job. If the list of critical incidents is inadequate, any performance appraisal based on these behaviors may be misleading. In some applications of the

Area of Performance	Degree of Performance				
	Far Excels Job Requirements	Exceeds Job Requirements	Meets Job Requirements	Needs Improvement	Does Not Meet Minimum Requirements
Quality of work	Leaps tall buildings in a single bound	Leaps tall buildings with running start	Can leap over houses, if prodded	Often stumbles into buildings	Is often knocked down by buildings
Promptness	Is faster than a speeding bullet	Is as fast as a speeding bullet	Would you believe a slow bullet?	Misfires frequently	Wounds self when handling a gun
Initiative	Is stronger than a locomotive	Is as strong as a bull elephant	Almost as strong as a bull	Shoots the bull	Smells like a bull
Adaptability	Walks on water	Strong swimmer	A good water treader	Favorite haunt is the water cooler	Passes water in emergencies
Communication	Talks with God	Talks with the angels	Talks to self	Argues with self	Loses most of these arguments

FIGURE 5–3 A satirical example of a behaviorally anchored rating scale (BARS).

Behavioral observation scale (BOS)   A performance appraisal technique in which appraisers rate the frequency of critical employee behaviors.

Management by objectives (MBO)   A performance appraisal technique that involves a mutual agreement between employee and manager on goals to be achieved in a given period.

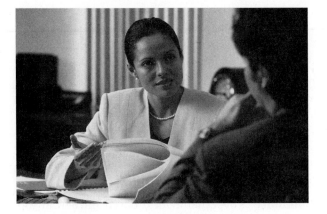

In a management by objectives (MBO) program, managers and employees meet to set goals and, later, to review the extent to which those goals were met.

BARS technique, behaviors are listed in terms of expectations; in this instance, the instrument is called a behavioral expectation scale (BES). One advantage of BARS and BES approaches to performance appraisal is that they meet federal fair employment guidelines. The criteria on which workers are assessed are job related because they derive from actual job behaviors.

The Royal Canadian Mounted Police developed a BARS approach to evaluating the job performance of candidates for promotion. In a study involving 6,571 police personnel, the BARS evaluations differentiated between successful and unsuccessful candidates and was not influenced by nonperformance factors such as gender (Catano, Darr, & Campbell, 2007).

Behavioral Observation Scale (BOS). In the **behavioral observation scale (BOS)** approach to performance appraisal, employees are also evaluated in terms of critical incidents. In that respect, the BOS is similar to the BARS. However, BOS appraisers rate subordinates on the *frequency* of the critical incidents as they are observed to occur over a given period. Ratings are assigned on a 5-point scale, and the evaluation yields a total score for each employee, obtained by adding the ratings for each critical incident. The behavioral incidents

for the rating scale are developed in the same way as those for the BARS, through identification by supervisors or other subject matter experts. Similarly, the BOS meets equal employment opportunity guidelines because it is related to actual behaviors required for successful job performance.

I-O psychology research comparing BARS and BOS techniques has been inconclusive. Some studies demonstrate the superiority of one technique over the other; other studies fail to confirm these findings.

Management by Objectives (MBO)

Management by objectives (MBO) involves a mutual agreement between employees and managers on goals to be achieved in a given time period. Instead of focusing on abilities or traits as in merit rating, or on job behaviors as in BARS and BOS, management by objectives focuses on results—on how well employees accomplish specified goals. The emphasis is on what employees do rather than on what their supervisors think of them or perceive their behaviors to be. Furthermore, MBO actively involves employees in their own evaluations; they are not simply graded or rated by others.

MBO consists of two phases: goal setting and performance review. In goal setting, employees meet individually with supervisors to determine the goals for which they will strive in the time before the next appraisal, usually 1 year, and to discuss ways of reaching those goals. The goals must be realistic, specific, and as objective as possible. For example, it is not enough for salespersons to say that they will try to sell more products. A fixed number of items or a dollar volume must be established as the goal.

In performance review, employees and supervisors discuss the extent to which the goals were met. Again, this is a mutual process involving both parties. The performance appraisal is based on job results, not on characteristics such as initiative or general skills.

Employees in MBO programs may feel pressured to set higher goals with each appraisal to

Peer rating   A performance appraisal technique in which managers or executives at the same level assess one another's abilities and job behaviors.

Self-ratings   A performance appraisal technique in which managers assess their own abilities and job performance.

show evidence of improvement. A supervisor may not accept last year's quota as a sufficient goal for this year's job performance. Thus, the goals may become increasingly unrealistic. Also, MBO is not useful for jobs that cannot be quantified. It would be silly to expect research chemists to agree to make five more scientific breakthroughs this year than last. The MBO technique satisfies fair employment guidelines and has been found to be effective in increasing employee motivation and productivity.

PERFORMANCE APPRAISAL METHODS FOR MANAGERS

The performance appraisal of managerial personnel presents problems not faced in the assessment of other employees. Merit rating techniques are often used to evaluate low- and middle-level managerial personnel, but additional appraisal methods are required. Paradoxically, senior executives are rarely evaluated. They seldom receive feedback or judgments about the quality of their job performance unless the company faces a crisis. Indeed, high-level management failure is sometimes rewarded with generous severance packages. Interviews with top executives have shown that at higher levels of management, performance reviews are less systematic and informative.

Evaluation Techniques

Assessment Centers.   Assessment centers (discussed in chapter 3 as an employee selection technique) are a popular method of managerial performance appraisal. Managers participate in simulated job tasks such as management games, group problem solving, leaderless group discussions, in-basket tests, and interviews. Recall that assessment centers do not assess actual job behavior but, rather, a variety of activities that are like those encountered on the job. Assessment-center evaluations appear to have high validity when used for performance appraisal purposes.

Evaluation by Superiors.   The most frequently used technique for the performance appraisal of managers is assessment by their superiors in the organization. Standard rating sheets are rarely used. Typically, the rater writes a brief descriptive essay about the person's job performance. An evaluation by an immediate superior is often supplemented by the judgments of executives at higher levels.

Evaluation by Colleagues: Peer Rating.   **Peer rating** was developed in the 1940s. It is a technique for having managers or executives at the same level assess one another in terms of their general ability to perform the job and their specific traits and behaviors. Although ratings given by peers and colleagues tend to be higher than ratings assigned by superiors, research shows a positive correlation between high peer ratings and subsequent promotion. However, peer ratings show a lower inter-rater reliability than do ratings by supervisors (Viswesvaran, Schmidt, & Ones, 2003).

Attitudes toward peer rating among managers are generally positive. Managers are far more favorable toward peer rating, however, when the evaluations are used for career development or improving job skills than when they are used for promotion or other career decisions.

Self-Evaluation.   Another approach to managerial performance appraisal is to ask people to assess their own abilities and job performance. One technique is similar to management by objectives (MBO), discussed earlier in this chapter. Managers and their superiors meet to establish goals for managerial performance—not specific production targets but personal skills to be developed or deficiencies to be corrected. After a time, the managers meet again with their superiors to discuss their progress.

Self-ratings tend to be higher than evaluations by superiors and to show greater leniency. Self-ratings also focus more on interpersonal skills, whereas ratings by superiors emphasize initiative and specific job skills. Leniency can be reduced if raters are told that their self-evaluations will be validated against more objective criteria.

In a study of 1,888 managers at a large accounting firm, researchers compared self-ratings and subordinate ratings collected twice during a 1-year period. Managers who rated themselves much higher than their subordinates did tended to show improvement in their own job performance over time. Those managers who rated themselves lower than their subordinates did tended to show a decline in job performance. These results suggested to the researchers that self-ratings can have a motivating effect for people who tend to overestimate their job performance (Johnson & Ferstl, 1999).

In another study, each of 110 supervisors in a state law-enforcement agency was rated on leadership ability by at least two subordinates. The supervisors who received feedback on these ratings later lowered their self-ratings. Supervisors who received no feedback did not change their self-ratings. The researchers concluded that the feedback from subordinates influenced the supervisors' view of their leadership ability (Atwater, Waldman, Atwater, & Cartier, 2000).

Evaluation by Subordinates.   Another approach to the performance appraisal of managers involves evaluation by subordinates, as used in the studies just described. The technique, sometimes described as upward feedback, is similar to having students evaluate their classroom instructors.

A study showing that subordinates' ratings lead to improved job performance involved 252 bank managers. In research conducted over a 5-year

---

Newsbreak

Rating Your Boss: Do You Really Want to Sign Your Name?

You know the drill. About every 6 months, your boss calls you in for a chat about how you're doing at your job. It's called a performance appraisal. You sit there, perhaps seething inside, while the boss tells you what you're doing wrong and how you could improve. And you're thinking how you'd like to tell the boss a thing or two about how he or she is doing.

Nowadays, some employees can talk back. Growing numbers of companies are asking workers to participate in an upward feedback appraisal process—that is, to appraise the performance of their supervisors and managers. These appraisals, or ratings, are then used to help determine promotions and pay raises for bosses. Does this sound great? A chance to get back at the supervisor? Maybe get that obnoxious guy fired? But suppose you had to sign your name to the appraisal? Would that affect your comments? Most likely it would, unless, of course, you had already lined up another job.

To test this hypothesis, a management professor at the University of Wisconsin asked 183 employees at an insurance company to rate 38 managers. The employees were all volunteers for the task and were told that the managers would take no reprisals, regardless of what the employees reported. To further reassure the employees, they were given the phone number of a contact in the human resources department whom they could call in the event of any backlash.

Half the employees in the study appraised their bosses anonymously. The other half signed their names to the evaluation form. Did the act of identifying themselves make a difference in the ratings? You bet it did! Employees who signed their names to the appraisal forms gave higher ratings to their managers than did the employees who were doing the ratings anonymously. All employees reported that they would feel much more comfortable rating their bosses if they could remain anonymous.

Upward feedback can be an effective tool for improving manager effectiveness. Just don't sign your name to the form.

Source: Antonioni, D. (1994). The effects of feedback accountability on upward appraisal ratings. *Personnel Psychology, 47,* 349–356.

360-degree feedback A multisource approach to performance appraisal that combines ratings from several sources such as superiors, subordinates, peers, and self.

period, psychologists found that managers who received poor to moderate ratings from subordinates at the beginning of the period showed far more improvement in subsequent ratings than managers who received higher initial ratings. Managers who met with subordinates to discuss their ratings improved more than managers who did not meet with subordinates (Walker & Smither, 1999).

In a study of 454 managers at a telecommunications firm, researchers found that ratings by subordinates were significantly more reliable when the results were used for developmental purposes than when they were used for administrative purposes (Greguras, Robie, Schleicher, & Goff, 2003).

360-Degree Feedback

Another approach to managerial performance appraisal involves combining evaluations from several sources into an overall appraisal. Any number of individual ratings sources can be so combined, but the ultimate multisource approach is called **360-degree feedback**. It combines the full circle of ratings from all sources—superiors, subordinates, peers, self, and even evaluations by the organization's customers or clients who have dealings with the person being rated.

Multisource feedback can provide information that would not otherwise be available about the people being rated, because it provides data from unique perspectives. For example, subordinates and peers have different experiences and relationships with their managers than do the managers' bosses. Multisource feedback may also reduce many forms of bias. If all parties are told that their ratings will be compared with ratings assigned by others, they are likely to be more objective in their assessments. When combined ratings are consistent, decisions about a manager's future with the organization can be made with greater confidence. Also, if ratings show a high level of agreement, a manager may be more willing to accept criticism because it comes from sources other than the immediate supervisor.

When ratings disagree, however, the manager may be reluctant to accept and act on criticism.

In a study of 1,883 managers working for a large U.S. utility company, the managers submitted self-ratings and were also rated by 2,773 subordinates, 12,779 peers, and 3,049 supervisors. The results showed that multisource ratings were not in agreement. Self-ratings were the least discriminating and correlated poorly with the other rating sources (Facteau & Craig, 2001).

Other researchers found that managers who rated themselves higher than other managers did were less satisfied with the 360-degree feedback approach than were managers who did not rate themselves higher than others (Craig & Hannum, 2006). Also, studies have shown that the 360-degree feedback approach to performance appraisal is more effective in individualistic cultures where there is less formal social stratification than in collectivist cultures that have a rigid social hierarchy (Shipper, Hoffman, & Rotondo, 2007).

In a 3-year study of two organizations—a large retail chain and a public school district—investigators found that leaders who improved their job performance over the period as a result of the feedback they had received in their appraisals behaved in ways that led to favorable changes in job satisfaction and in engagement among their subordinates. No such changes were reported among the subordinates of leaders who did not improve as a result of performance appraisal feedback (Atwater & Brett, 2006; Atwater, Brett, & Charles, 2007).

The use of 360-degree feedback is more costly than using appraisals from a single source, but the approach is growing in popularity. Surveys show that 360-degree feedback is already in use in nearly all of the Fortune 500 companies.

SOURCES OF BIAS IN PERFORMANCE APPRAISAL

Regardless of the sophistication of the techniques used, performance appraisal still involves one person judging, assessing, or estimating the characteristics

Halo effect   The tendency to judge all aspects of a person's behavior or character on the basis of a single attribute.

Constant bias   A source of error in performance appraisal based on the different standards used by raters.

Most-recent-performance error   A source of error in performance appraisal in which a rater tends to evaluate a worker's most recent job behavior rather than behavior throughout the period since the last appraisal.

and performance of another. Inevitably, human biases and prejudices affect the judgments. Some common sources of error that can distort performance appraisals include the halo effect, constant or systematic bias, most-recent-performance error, inadequate information error, average rating or leniency error, the rater's cognitive processes, the rater's personality, role conflict, and impression management.

The Halo Effect

The **halo effect** involves the familiar tendency to judge all aspects of a person's behavior or character on the basis of a single attribute. For example, if you find a person to be physically attractive, you may tend to think of that person also as friendly, likeable, and easy to get along with— generalizing from one attribute to personality characteristics and other abilities. A supervisor who scores an employee high on one factor of a merit rating scale may tend to grade that person high on all other factors. This distortion is particularly likely to occur when a high rating is given on one or two traits and the other traits to be rated are difficult to observe, unfamiliar, or not clearly defined.

One way to control for the halo effect is to have more than one person rate a worker, on the assumption that any personal biases will tend to cancel each other out. Another way is to have supervisors rate all subordinates on one trait or characteristic at a time instead of rating each person on all items at once. When workers are judged on a single characteristic, there is a smaller chance for one rating to carry over to other traits.

I-O psychology research suggests that the halo error may be less a problem than previously thought. The halo effect does not appear to diminish the overall quality of ratings, often cannot be detected, and may, in many cases, be illusory. Of course there are some people who truly are outstanding in all their attributes. In these cases, generalizing from one quality to others is not an error but a simple observation of fact.

Other Sources of Error

Constant or Systematic Bias.   **Constant bias** as a source of performance appraisal error has its basis in the standards or criteria used by raters. Some raters or supervisors expect more than others from their employees. Similarly, some college professors are known as easy graders and expect less from their students than those known as hard graders. The constant biasing error means that a top rating given by one supervisor may not be equivalent to a top rating given by another supervisor, just as an *A* from one professor may not mean the same as an *A* from another professor as an evaluation of merit or ability.

Constant bias can be corrected by requiring supervisors to distribute ratings in accordance with the normal curve. However, as noted with the forced distribution technique, this means that some workers will receive ratings that are undeserved.

Most-Recent-Performance Error.   Performance appraisals are usually made every 6 or 12 months. There is an understandable tendency to base ratings on workers' most recent behavior, without considering their performance throughout the entire rating period since the last appraisal. Naturally memory is clearer about events that have occurred more recently, but recent behavior may be atypical or distorted by extraneous factors. For example, if a worker performs poorly in the weeks just before an evaluation because of illness or marital problems, the results may overshadow a previous record of exemplary job performance. If a worker is aware that a performance evaluation is due, he or she may strive to work more efficiently just before the rating. In both cases, performance is not typical of the workers' overall job behavior, and a falsely low or high rating will result.

One way to reduce this **most-recent-performance error** is to require more frequent appraisals. By shortening the time between performance reviews, there is less of a tendency for supervisors to forget a worker's usual behavior. Making supervisors aware of the possibility that this type of error can occur can also be effective in reducing it.

Inadequate Information Error. Supervisors are required to rate employees at specified intervals whether or not they know enough about the employees to do so fairly and accurately. To admit to superiors that they lack adequate knowledge of their subordinates can be construed as a personal failing. The resulting appraisals, however, will be worth little to the organization or to the employees because they will not be based on a comprehensive knowledge of worker behavior.

A way to deal with this **inadequate information error** is to educate raters about the value of performance appraisals and the harm done by ratings based on incomplete information. Supervisors should be given the opportunity to decline to rate employees about whom they have little knowledge and the assurance that they will not be penalized for such refusal.

Average Rating or Leniency Error. Some raters are reluctant to assign extreme scores in either direction. The tendency is to be lenient and to assign average ratings to all workers. Particularly when dealing with a small number of employees, it is not unusual to find their ratings clustered around the middle of the scale, separated by no more than one or two points. Thus, the range of abilities indicated is restricted, and the ratings are so close that it is difficult to distinguish between good and poor workers. This **average rating error** does not reflect the range of differences that exist among workers, and the ratings provide no useful information to the company or to employees. The challenge for employers is to identify the raters who show this tendency and to take it into consideration when making personnel decisions based on their appraisals of subordinates.

Cognitive Processes of Raters. The cognitive or thought processes of raters underlie their judgments of worker effectiveness. Four cognitive variables that can influence evaluations of employee performance are category structures, beliefs, interpersonal affect, and attribution.

1. *Category structures.* The category structures that managers use in evaluating their employees can affect their assessments. When an appraiser thinks about a worker as belonging to a particular category, the information he or she recalls about that worker will be biased toward that category. For example, if an employee is perceived to be a team player, then this becomes a category in the rater's mental picture. The employee's job performance will likely be observed, interpreted, and remembered in terms of how a typical team player is expected to behave rather than in terms of how that employee actually behaves.

2. *Beliefs.* A related cognitive variable that can influence performance appraisals involves raters' beliefs about human nature. These ideas can lead raters to make evaluations in terms of how they view people in general rather than in terms of a specific worker's characteristics and behaviors. For example, supervisors who believe that people are basically good and trustworthy give more generous ratings than those who think that people are spiteful and narrow-minded. Managers who accept the idea of individual differences among people and who are tolerant of those differences may give different ratings from managers who believe most people are alike.

3. *Interpersonal affect.* The cognitive variable of **interpersonal affect** refers to one person's feelings or emotions toward another person. Common sense suggests that, except for those raters who can maintain impartiality and objectivity toward their subordinates, ratings will be influenced by the personal relationship between rater and ratee. In general, raters who have positive emotions or affect toward the persons they are rating give higher marks than do raters who have negative affect. Simply stated, we tend to be more lenient, forgiving, and generous toward people we like.

Attribution A source of error in performance appraisal in which raters attribute or assign positive or negative explanations to an employee's behavior.

Role conflict A situation that arises when there is a disparity between job demands and the employee's personal standards.

4. *Attribution.* The concept of **attribution** derives from social psychology research on the way people form impressions of other people. In performance appraisal, one person forms an impression of the abilities and characteristics of another. The rater mentally attributes or assigns reasons to the worker's behavior. These beliefs about why an employee behaves in a particular way can affect the rater's evaluation. For example, a supervisor may observe that two employees frequently seem tired. That supervisor may be lenient and understanding toward the tired employee who has young children but less forgiving of the tired employee who is known to enjoy late-night partying.

Attribution can also be influenced by interpersonal affect. Managers may attribute poor job performance to internal factors, such as lack of motivation or inadequate skills, when they dislike (have negative affect toward) the person being rated. In other words, the managers appear to believe that the poor performance of the workers they do not like is the fault of the workers themselves. On the other hand, the poor performance of workers they do like may be attributed to external factors such as bad luck, a heavy workload, or equipment failure.

The attribution error can be reduced by having supervisors spend time performing the job they are evaluating. This experience exposes them to the kinds of external factors that can influence job performance. Raters should also be made aware of how their perceptions of a worker's behavior on the job can differ from the worker's own point of view.

Personality of Raters. It seems obvious that our personality can influence the way we judge or evaluate other people, not only in the workplace but in all areas of life. For example, a person who is vindictive or hostile toward others will view a person differently from someone who is caring and compassionate. Consider the characteristic

of self-monitoring. Recall from chapter 3 that self-monitoring refers to the way people act to control the image of themselves that they choose to display in public. High self-monitors present themselves in whatever ways they believe best fits the social situation around them. Low self-monitors stay more true to their own nature and behave generally the same way in all situations.

In a study of 210 people employed in government, manufacturing, or service jobs, all of whom had experience in giving performance evaluations, the researcher found that high self-monitors gave significantly more lenient and less accurate ratings than did low self-monitors. The researcher suggested that high self-monitors may be trying to avoid the disapproval of others. Nevertheless, this finding provides an example of how one facet of personality can influence the performance evaluation process (Jawahar, 2001).

Other research involved more than 500 rater-ratee pairs employed by an insurance company who were asked to assign peer ratings to one another. The results showed that when both members of the pair had scored high on the personality dimension of conscientiousness, the ratings they gave each other were significantly higher than those of pairs who had scored low on conscientiousness. In this case, the degree of personality similarity between rater and rater influenced subsequent evaluations (Antonioni & Park, 2001).

Role Conflict. **Role conflict** refers to the disparity or contradiction between the job's demands and the supervisors' standards of right and wrong. Sometimes the nature of a job requires supervisors to compromise those standards (chapter 12 shows how role conflict is a source of job stress). Supervisors who score high in role conflict tend to give performance evaluations that are higher than justified for several reasons: as a way of establishing control over the work situation, as a way of avoiding confrontation with subordinates that might result from giving them lower ratings, or as a way of obtaining subordinates' gratitude and goodwill.

For whatever reasons, role conflict, and the stress associated with it, may lead supervisors to give performance ratings that are higher than justified. Managers may inflate performance appraisals as a way of satisfying personal needs and dealing with organizational pressures.

Impression Management. Impression management involves behaving in ways designed to present ourselves to others in a favorable, positive way. We manage the impressions we make on others to get them to like us, to hire us, or to give us a good performance evaluation. Ingratiation and self-promotion are two approaches to making a good impression (see chapter 3). Another impression management technique that can influence performance appraisals is political skill: the ability to understand others and to use that understanding to influence them in ways designed to support the attainment of our goals.

In a study involving more than 350 employees in a state agency and in two retail organizations, researchers found that people high in political skill were much more likely to be perceived by their supervisors as not using ingratiation behaviors to curry favor for personal gain. Those low in political skill were seen as using ingratiation for their own advantage (Harris, Kacmar, Zivnuska, & Shaw, 2007; Treadway, Ferris, Duke, Adams, & Thatcher, 2007). Research conducted in Israel on 231 employees and supervisors showed that those who worked in highly formal, centralized, hierarchical organizations, such as the army, used impression management techniques significantly more often than did employees in less rigid, less formal, less bureaucratic organizations (Drory & Zaidman, 2007).

Newsbreak

How Not to Get Hired, Part 5: Leave That Bottle of Gin at Home

Here are more amazing things people actually said and did while interviewing for jobs, as told by the interviewers.

- A young woman came to the interview wearing headphones. She sat down and took out only the left earbud. When the manager asked if she wanted to take the entire headset off, she said, "Nah, it's cool. I can listen to you and my music at the same time."

- An applicant answered her cell phone during the interview and then asked the manager, "How much longer will we be? I have another interview to go to."

- An interviewee was asked if she was thirsty. She said yes and reached for the glass on the interviewer's desk. "No need to get me a glass," she said. "This will do."

- One person asked if it would be permissible to work from home so she could take an afternoon nap every day.

- An applicant who failed a typing test for a word-processing job asked if she could retake the test. When told that she could, she asked for a moment to settle her nerves. She reached into her purse, pulled out a bottle of gin, took a drink, and announced that she was ready.

- And perhaps we shouldn't mention the applicants who brought their dogs to the interview or the man who wore a woman's bright red shoes.

Source: Those cute red shoes? They're my wife's (2007, November). *Washingtonian*, pp. 106–107.

WAYS TO IMPROVE PERFORMANCE APPRAISALS

The fact that performance appraisals can be so easily biased is no reason to abandon hope of achieving more objective evaluations. We have noted steps that can be taken to reduce some sources of error. Providing training and feedback to raters, and allowing subordinates to participate, can also decrease errors, increase accuracy, and promote satisfaction with the evaluation process.

Training.   Training the persons who conduct performance appraisals involves two elements: (1) creating an awareness that abilities and skills are usually distributed in accordance with the normal curve, so that it is acceptable to find broad differences within a group of workers; and (2) developing the ability to define objective criteria for worker behaviors—the standards or average performance levels against which workers can be compared. I-O psychology research supports the idea that rater training can reduce errors in performance appraisal, particularly the leniency and halo errors. The more actively raters are involved in the training process, the greater the positive effects. Having raters participate in group discussions and in practice sessions about providing feedback to subordinates generally produces better results than having raters attend lectures about the rating process.

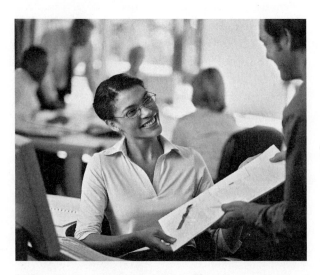

Positive feedback during postappraisal interview can lead to improvements in job performance.

Providing Feedback to Raters   Providing feedback to raters can also improve performance appraisal. In a classic study, marketing managers in a large high-tech company received feedback from trained raters about the evaluations those managers had given their subordinates. The feedback included information about how each manager's ratings differed from the ratings given by other managers. When these marketing managers evaluated their subordinates a year later, they assigned lower ratings than did a control group of marketing managers who had received no feedback about their earlier ratings. More than 90% of the managers in the experimental group said that the feedback had influenced their second set of ratings. The researchers concluded that the feedback had reduced the leniency error (Davis & Mount, 1984).

Subordinate Participation.   Allowing employees to participate in the evaluation of their own job performance has been shown to lead to improvements in the appraisal process. Allowing employees to have a say in how their job performance is assessed significantly increases satisfaction with and acceptance of the organization's performance appraisal system. Employee participation also leads to a heightened belief in the fairness and usefulness of the appraisal process and to an increase in motivation to improve job performance.

THE POSTAPPRAISAL INTERVIEW

The two goals of performance appraisal programs are to supply information to management for personnel decisions and to diagnose strengths and weaknesses of employees and provide them with the means for self-improvement. To fulfill the second goal, the job performance ratings and the recommendations of the appraisers must be communicated to the employees.

Offering Feedback.   Offering feedback to employees is usually accomplished during a postappraisal interview between worker and supervisor, a situation that can easily become antagonistic, even hostile, especially when a performance evaluation contains criticism. Negative feedback during a postappraisal interview can make employees angry and lead them to reject any criticism or suggestions. Employees may attempt to shift the blame for alleged deficiencies in job performance by dismissing the usefulness of the appraisal, downgrading the importance of the job, or criticizing the supervisor.

A meta-analysis of 131 studies showed that postappraisal information provided by computer instead of in a personal interview with a supervisor was considered more desirable by the employee and was more effective in improving job performance. Apparently, eliminating the face-to-face interview situation reduced any personal antagonism between worker and supervisor that might otherwise have interfered with the employee's acceptance of criticism (DeNisi & Kluger, 2000).

Not all workers will benefit from feedback, no matter how it is presented. This was demonstrated in a study of 329 tellers in a large international bank in Hong Kong. Researchers found that how bank tellers responded to feedback from their performance evaluations depended on their level of negative affectivity. Employees high in negative affectivity tended to be cynical and distrustful and to dwell on negative rather than positive work experiences. In addition, among the bank tellers who received high ratings, job satisfaction and organizational commitment increased for those who had scored low in negative affectivity. Similar increases did not occur in tellers who received high ratings and who had scored high in negative affectivity (Lam, Yik, & Schaubroeck, 2002).

A 1-year study of 176 managers showed that those who received favorable upward feedback from their subordinates tended to improve their job performance more than did those who received unfavorable upward feedback. Managers who received negative evaluations from subordinates tended to show a decline in their job performance (Smither & Walker, 2004).

Reacting to Criticism. The primary purpose of the postappraisal interview is to stimulate employees to improve their job performance. This expectation may be wishful thinking. Some workers, when criticized, will exaggerate their faults—coming to work late or showing sloppy work habits—as an imagined means of revenge. If workers are told that they request assistance too frequently, they may stop doing so and, as a result, make more mistakes. In such cases, criticism can lead to reduced motivation and job performance.

Perhaps it is unrealistic to expect that a brief meeting every 6 or 12 months will provide suffi-

cient impetus for employees to change. In addition, maybe it is not wise to believe that supervisors, unless they are specially trained, possess the insight and skill to diagnose the reasons for a worker's unsatisfactory job performance and to prescribe a program for improvement. If feedback on employee performance were provided more frequently than the formal postappraisal interview—and in a more competent manner—then employee motivation to change job behavior and to persist in that behavior could be enhanced.

Improving Postappraisal Interviews. Despite the limitations and problems of postappraisal interviews, they can be structured to fulfill the purposes for which they are intended. I-O psychologists have identified several factors related to successful postappraisal interviews. Employees are more likely to be satisfied with postappraisal interviews and to follow their supervisors' suggestions about improving job performance under the following conditions:

1. Employees should be allowed to participate actively in the appraisal process.
2. The postappraisal interviewer should adopt a positive, constructive, and supportive attitude.
3. The interviewer should focus on specific job problems rather than on the employee's personal characteristics.
4. The employee and the supervisor should establish jointly specific goals to be achieved in the period before the next appraisal.
5. The employee should be given the opportunity to question, challenge, and rebut the evaluation without fear of retribution.
6. Discussions of changes in salary and rank should be linked directly to the performance appraisal criteria.

PERFORMANCE APPRAISAL: A POOR RATING?

Performance appraisal may be one of the least popular features of modern organizational life. Here is the general attitude toward performance appraisal: "Oh, well, it's appraisal time again. I suppose we had better do it. But what the hell are we doing it for?" A survey of human resources managers found that 90% of them were dissatisfied with the performance appraisal system in their organizations. When asked what they would like to change, many said they would eliminate the programs entirely. Some executives express such a high level of dissatisfaction with performance appraisal that they no longer use the term; they call the process "performance management" instead (Toegel & Conger, 2003).

Why do performance appraisal programs get such a poor rating? We have already discussed the opportunities for personal bias and other errors to enter into the evaluations. Here are some additional reasons.

A Poor Rating From Managers. Consider the person who must make the ratings or conduct the observations and appraisals. Despite a great deal of impressive research supporting the benefits of performance appraisals made by subordinates or peers, the fact remains that on the job, most performance ratings are made by managers or supervisors. Performance appraisal requires their considerable time and effort—in addition to their other job duties. They must spend many hours observing subordinates to develop sufficient knowledge on which to base their assessments. They spend additional hours on paperwork, completing the appraisal forms, and yet more time in rater training programs.

In practice, some managers and supervisors resist appraisal programs and fill out the forms only when pressured by their superiors. Thus, the evaluations are often not thorough and systematic but are compiled in haste. Many supervisors loathe the idea of judging employees and taking responsibility for their progress in the organization; therefore, they are reluctant to give low ratings, even for poor performance.

Supervisors may deliberately delay providing feedback, particularly when the evaluation is negative. Or they may inflate the ratings or suppress unfavorable information. By pretending that the employee is performing at a higher level than actual job performance justifies, the supervisor eliminates the potential for confrontation and reduces the negative impact of an unfavorable appraisal.

A Poor Rating From Employees. Employees do not like performance appraisals, although most recognize that some means of evaluating job performance is necessary. They express concern about the effect of performance assessments on their career; they are apprehensive that a supervisor will use the appraisal to exaggerate misunderstandings or highlight personality clashes that have nothing to do with job competence. Employees are often not sufficiently informed about the criteria by which they are being judged or even precisely what is expected of them on the job. In addition, employees may be given low ratings for faults that lie within the organization or in the way jobs are structured. These are matters over which employees have no control but for which they may be blamed. In many organizations, the results of performance appraisal programs are never used to help make decisions about promotions or to help employees improve their skills, the major purposes for which such programs were developed.

Performance appraisal as conducted in organizations today is largely unsatisfactory, which may help explain why correlations between ratings and results-oriented job performance criteria (such as sales and output data) are relatively low. Nevertheless, assessments of employee ability at all levels of employment are necessary. The question is not whether to use an employee appraisal system but, rather, which is the most effective approach to use—and that question has yet to be answered.

Summary

Performance appraisal programs are used to validate employee selection criteria, determine the need for and success of employee training programs, improve employee behavior, determine promotions and pay raises, and identify employees with promotion potential. To ensure compliance with EEOC guidelines, performance appraisals must be based on job analyses, must focus on job behaviors rather than personal traits, and must be reviewed with the person being evaluated. Labor unions oppose performance appraisal because of their commitment to seniority as the basis for personnel decisions. Employees dislike performance appraisal because few people like to be judged or criticized. Managers dislike making appraisals that will affect their subordinates' careers.

Performance appraisals may be objective or judgmental. Objective appraisals include measurement of quantity and quality of output, computerized performance monitoring, use of data on accidents, salary, advancement, and absenteeism. Judgmental appraisal methods involve having supervisors assess their workers' ability to perform the job. These assessments are made by **merit rating techniques**, including **rating, scales, ranking, paired-comparison, forced-distribution**, and **forced-choice**, in which one person judges the abilities or characteristics of another. The **behaviorally anchored rating scale (BARS)** and the **behavioral observation scale (BOS)** approaches to merit rating attempt to evaluate performance in terms of specific behaviors critical to success or failure on the job. The BARS and BOS meet EEOC guidelines and can reduce rating errors. **Management by objectives (MBO)** involves mutual agreement between managers and employees about setting and achieving specific goals.

Evaluation of managerial performance can be accomplished through assessment centers or other evaluation techniques: assessment by supervisors, **peer rating**, rating by subordinates, or **self-ratings**. Combining ratings into an overall appraisal—**360-degree feedback**—is especially popular.

Sources of rater error in appraisals include the **halo effect, most-recent-performance error, inadequate information error, average rating error**, the rater's cognitive processes, the rater's personality, **role conflict**, and impression management. Three ways to improve performance appraisals are better training for raters, providing feedback to raters, and allowing employees to participate in their own ratings.

Results of performance appraisal must be communicated to employees to provide them with information about their strengths and weaknesses. Feedback should be given with tact and sensitivity, particularly when criticism is involved, because it can lead to defensiveness and a decline in job performance. Feedback sessions should be informal and frequent and focus on specific goals. Workers should be allowed to participate freely in the discussions.

Key Terms

attribution
average rating (leniency) error
behavioral observation scale (BOS)
behaviorally anchored rating scale (BARS)
constant (systematic) bias
forced-choice technique

forced-distribution technique
halo effect
inadequate information error
interpersonal affect
management by objectives (MBO)
merit rating
most-recent-performance error

paired-comparison technique
peer rating
performance appraisal
ranking technique
rating scales
role conflict
self-ratings
360-degree feedback

Review Questions

1. Why do Equal Employment Opportunity Commission guidelines apply to performance appraisal programs?

2. What has I-O research learned about race, gender, and age bias in performance appraisal?

3. What are the purposes of performance appraisal?

4. Why do employees and managers both object to performance appraisal programs?

5. In evaluating performance on production jobs, what factors other than worker output should be considered? Why?

6. What are the advantages and disadvantages of computerized performance monitoring? How

would you feel about having your work appraised in this way?

7. If you were a manager responsible for periodically evaluating the performance of your 23 employees, which merit rating technique would you most like to use? Which would you least like to use? Why?

8. Describe advantages and disadvantages of the ranking technique, the paired-comparison technique, and the forced-choice technique.

9. How would you construct a behaviorally anchored rating scale for evaluating your employees?

10. How do behaviorally anchored rating scales and behavioral observation scales differ? Which provides more accurate information?

11. How does the management by objectives approach to performance appraisal work? Is it likely to increase or decrease employee motivation and job performance?

12. If you were a manager, would you want your job performance to be evaluated by your superior, your peers, your subordinates, yourself, or all of the above? Explain the reasons for your choice.

13. What are the advantages and disadvantages of performance appraisals conducted by subordinates?

14. Discuss the results of research conducted on 360-degree feedback.

15. What is the halo effect? How might it influence the results of performance appraisals?

16. Distinguish between the following sources of error in performance evaluation: constant bias, most-recent-performance error, leniency error, and role conflict.

17. How can a rater's cognitive processes and personality influence the evaluations he or she makes?

18. Describe the techniques of impression management that can influence performance evaluation.

19. In what ways can performance appraisals and the postappraisal interview be improved?

20. In your opinion, what changes to the performance appraisal process might make employees and managers more receptive to the idea of performance evaluation?

Additional Reading

Atwater, L., Brett, J., & Atira, C. (2007). Multisource feedback. *Human Resource Management, 46,* 285–307. Discusses research findings and issues for organizations to consider in order to maximize the usefulness of a multisource feedback evaluation program.

Drory, A., & Zaidman, N. (2007). Impression management behavior. *Journal of Managerial Psychology, 22,* 290–307. Compares employees' impression management behavior in different organizations and offers a checklist of sample behaviors.

Ghorpade, J. (2000). Managing five paradoxes of 360-degree feedback. *Academy of Management Executive, 14(1),* 140–150. Notes the popularity of the 360-degree performance appraisal method in the Fortune 500 companies and discusses several problems relating to privacy, validity, and effectiveness.

Guerra-Lopez, I. (2008). *Performance evaluation: Proven approaches for improving program and orga-nizational performance.* San Francisco: Jossey-Bass. A handbook for students, teachers, researchers, and human resources personnel on using and improving performance appraisals.

Kessler, R. (2008). *Competency-based performance reviews: How to perform employee evaluations the Fortune 500 way.* Franklin Lakes, NJ: Career Press. Focuses on defining the specific competencies that help people become successful and then emphasizing these skills and abilities during the postappraisal interview to evaluate and motivate employees.

Shipper, F., Hoffman, R., & Rotondo, D. (2007). Does the 360 feedback process create actionable knowledge equally across cultures? *Academy of Management Learning & Education, 6,* 33–50. Acknowledges the problems of globalization and cultural differences and compares the 360-feedback process for employees in the United States, Ireland, Israel, Malaysia, and the Philippines.

C H A P T E R 6

Training and Development

THE SCOPE OF ORGANIZATIONAL TRAINING

Hamburger University does not have a football team. What it does have is a 130,000-square foot, state-of-the-art training facility with a faculty of 30 professors. Located in Oak Brook, Illinois, a suburb of Chicago, Hamburger U. was started more than 40 years ago by (who else?) McDonald's. Since then, more than 65,000 managers of the company's restaurants have graduated. In addition, Hamburger U. offers training for employees and franchise holders, who come from all over the world to attend courses. Classes are also given online in more than 25 languages. McDonald's has 10 other training centers in countries such as England, Japan, Germany, and Australia. It's expensive, but management believes that the training it offers is one of the main reasons for the organization's success. In the United States, the McDonald's curriculum is eligible for 46 credits at most colleges. In England, McDonald's trainees can earn credits toward a high school diploma (Hamburger University, 2008; Margulies, 2004; Wardell, 2008).

Training is big business. "When I look at the money we spend on education and training," said a chemical company executive, "I wonder whether we're running a chemical business or a college." From the high school dropout to the college graduate, from the long-time unemployed to the high-level executive, millions of people today are participating in some form of organizational training in their workplace. Employers spend some $55 billion annually on formal training programs and another $180 billion on informal on-the-job instruction.

Training often begins at an elementary level, teaching basic literacy and mathematics skills before offering instruction in specific job skills. When Motorola geared up to meet global competition by converting a plant to cellular technology, the company found that 60% of its workforce had difficulty doing simple arithmetic and reading and understanding English. Without remedial training in these skills, the employees could not be taught to perform their new jobs. Polaroid spent $700,000 to offer basic language and math instruction to 1,000 employees. Domino's Pizza teaches reading and math so that employees can follow instructions for making pizza dough.

Training for skilled, high-tech jobs is a priority in industry, government, and the military. Aerospace, telecommunications, and Web-based industries rely heavily on reprogrammable robots, multifunctional machinery, and computer-assisted design and manufacturing equipment. The companies need a highly trained workforce to design, operate, and maintain this sophisticated equipment.

As we described in chapter 1, the nature of work today has changed. People can no longer count on learning one job and keeping it until retirement. Workers must learn to think not of choosing a single career for a lifetime, but of having several careers during which they will master a cluster of skills that must be continually upgraded. Careers now require lifelong learning, which means that training has become even more vital today than it was for previous generations.

A Sample Training Program. A classic example of a high-level organizational training program involved the Western Electric Company, which established a company college, the Corporate Education Center, to provide instruction in engineering and management. The facility contained state-of-the-art equipment and offered more than 300 courses on a 190-acre campus, complete with dormitories.

Newly hired engineers participated in 6-week orientation programs, one during the first 6 months of employment and a second during the next 6 months. Engineers were able to choose among various courses in their specialty areas, classes designed to keep them up-to-date. Supervisors could select courses to upgrade their technical knowledge and managerial skills. The center provided management training at several levels to persons with promotion potential; courses ranged from planning and interdepartmental relations to urban affairs and I-O psychology.

This ambitious venture is not unusual in American business. Training centers have been established by organizations such as IBM, Xerox, General Electric, and Avis Rent A Car. So, do not be surprised if, during your first month on the job and periodically throughout your career, you find yourself back in the classroom.

Training for Disabled Employees. Many organizations provide specialized training for disabled employees. At McDonald's, more than 9,000 workers

Needs assessment   An analysis of corporate and individual goals undertaken before designing a training program.

New employees find themselves back in the classroom to learn about company policies and objectives.

with visual, hearing, orthopedic, or learning disabilities, or mental retardation, have been trained for various jobs at the company's fast-food restaurants. In an attempt to dispel stereotypes and to make all employees sensitive to the problems of being disabled, training is provided not only for the disabled employees but also for the employees who will be working with them. Over a 10-year period, more than 90% of the disabled persons who began training in a McJobs program completed it and became productive employees. The company believes that people with disabilities constitute a large pool of underused labor and is determined to train them to do whatever they are capable of doing.

Training and Fair Employment Practices.   Organizational training programs may have an adverse impact on minority employees. Performance in a training program is often used as a basis for career decisions about promotion, transfer, or dismissal—any technique that results in personnel decisions has the potential for discriminating against ethnic minority, female, older, or disabled employees. Therefore, training programs must meet equal employment opportunity guidelines and must be clearly related to job performance before their results can be applied to career decisions.

GOALS OF ORGANIZATIONAL TRAINING PROGRAMS

The first step in establishing a formal training program is the precise formulation of objectives. These objectives must be stated in terms of specific behavioral criteria, the acts or operations employees must perform on the job and the way they should perform them to maximize job efficiency. It is impossible to determine what the training program should include unless the organization knows what the program is supposed to accomplish. In other words, what knowledge, skills, and abilities are critical to learning how to perform the job successfully?

Needs Assessment.   The goals of the training program should be derived from the needs of the organization and the employees. A **needs assessment** should be conducted to determine corporate and individual goals and how a training program would help to achieve them. Such assessments are used to determine specific job components and the skills required to perform them.

Despite the recognized importance of conducting needs assessments, most companies do not do so, probably because the process is so time-consuming and expensive. In a meta-analysis of 397 studies of training programs, investigators found that only 6% of the programs reported conducting needs assessments prior to establishing the training program (Arthur, Bennett, Edens, & Bell, 2003).

Of course there are situations in which the need for a training program is obvious. For example, a company that automates a manufacturing process, eliminating a number of jobs, may choose to retrain its employees for other work. Rapid expansion that creates new jobs requires a program to train workers to fill the positions. A high accident rate may call for additional safety training. Frequent complaints from dissatisfied customers may lead to employee training in human relations skills. In the absence of a clear indication that training is needed, however, it is management's responsibility to analyze its operations periodically

Can Your Employees Read? Are You Sure?

Cindy Marano forgot her glasses when she left her office to go to lunch, otherwise she would never have noticed it. Marano, who directs a job training program in Washington, DC, could not read the menu posted on the wall of her local sandwich shop without her glasses. She asked the middle-age woman behind the counter to read it to her. At first, the woman pretended not to hear; then she became flustered and rude before finally asking another waitress to read the menu aloud. "Suddenly, the light went on for me," Marano said. The woman was unable to read. And Marano knew, from her work with the job training program, that many of the 40 million Americans who have trouble reading and writing are able to fake it on the job and conceal their handicap, as the waitress had done.

Marano also knew how expensive employee illiteracy is, costing the American economy $225 billion a year in lost productivity. Someone else very much aware of that cost is Peter Coors, CEO of Colorado's Coors Brewing Company. He calls employee illiteracy a crisis for American industry, and he has taken the lead in promoting corporate awareness and creating industry-based training programs to teach employees how to read.

With today's increasingly high-tech jobs, it is becoming harder to pretend you can read when you can't. Coors found that out when the company instituted a computerized inventory control system. The new system required forklift operators to punch information into a computer, and it soon became obvious that many of them could not do the job. Why? Because they could not recognize the letters on the computer keyboard or read the product codes on the items to be inventoried.

Even low-tech companies lose money to illiteracy. The Outback Steakhouse chain found that some of its cooks were mistakenly preparing more expensive instead of less expensive steaks because they could not read the waiters' orders. Outback started a training program to teach all employees a list of abbreviations, so that even workers for whom English was a new language could do their jobs without making costly mistakes. Other restaurant and fast-food chains use symbols instead of words on their computer screens.

Every company would operate more efficiently if all employees could read. It would be better for the employees, too. Sharon Thomas, a 34-year-old high school dropout living in Washington was on welfare for 15 years, until she learned to read and was hired for a well-paid job in construction. "I had a lot of hurdles to get over," she said, "but once I was in the workforce, I was so happy. I feel good about myself."

to determine if any aspect could benefit from additional training.

Organizational Analysis. A general organizational analysis can suggest broad training needs that can then be translated into specific needs of employees or work groups. The next step is a task analysis to identify the specific tasks performed on a job and the knowledge, skills, and abilities needed for those tasks. A person analysis is undertaken to determine which workers need retraining and what kind of training is necessary. These evaluations can be accomplished by job analysis methods, the critical-incidents technique, performance appraisal techniques, and self-assessments.

Job analysis is the most frequently used technique for determining training needs and objectives. It yields a detailed list of the characteristics needed to perform a job successfully and the sequence of operations required. From a job analysis, the company can determine how new training procedures can improve job performance.

The critical-incidents technique, which focuses on specific desirable or undesirable job behaviors, provides information on how employees are equipped to cope with significant workday events.

For example, how do assembly-line workers deal with jammed machinery? How do supervisors handle disputes among subordinates? How do managers deal with charges of sexual harassment? An analysis of critical incidents can alert the training director to areas in which additional training or instruction is needed.

Performance appraisals are an obvious source of information on training needs. They can document employee weaknesses and lead to recommendations for retraining to correct specific deficiencies. Self-assessment is based on the assumption that the person who is performing a job well is a good source of information about the skills needed to do that job and the areas in which training may be desirable.

STAFFING FOR ORGANIZATIONAL TRAINING

The quality of an instructor can have a tremendous impact on your performance as a student. Some teachers are able to bring the subject matter to life, to organize and present the material with enthusiasm, and to inspire interest among the class members. Other instructors teaching the same material can make the classroom experience frustrating, tiring, and boring. The most important factor in teaching anything at any level seems not to be competence or expertise in the subject matter. Although competence is necessary, the instructor must have the ability to teach—to impart information in a clear and compelling manner.

The same principle holds for organizational training. Too often, corporate training is conducted by people who have vast experience on the job but no ability to communicate their skills effectively to others. The solution is to use professional instructors, persons trained in teaching methods and in job skills. Larger organizations maintain full-time training staffs equipped to teach a number of subjects and job skills.

A meta-analysis of 136 studies involving more than 27,000 trainees demonstrated the importance of the teaching style and manner of the trainers. Those who were more relaxed and open, and who interacted more with the trainees, were found to be more effective as trainers (Sitzmann, Brown, Casper, Ely, & Zimmerman, 2008).

THE PRETRAINING ENVIRONMENT

The pretraining environment established by an organization includes those decisions and cues, communicated directly or indirectly to employees by supervisors and peers, which indicate the value management places on training programs. These factors may include organizational policies, supervisor attitudes toward training, resources available for training, and employee participation in needs assessments. Such cues influence the effectiveness of training programs because they tell employees how supportive the company is of training efforts.

The more training opportunities a company offers, the more likely its employees are to believe that training is an important and relevant activity for their careers. Trainees are also more likely to regard training as worthwhile and to be more motivated to achieve in training programs when they know their supervisors support training, know their posttraining skills will be assessed, and are given a realistic picture of what the training involves. When these conditions are not met—when the organization's pretraining attitude or climate is perceived as unsupportive—a training program is likely to be rendered ineffective before it even begins.

A number of psychological characteristics can influence employees' desire to learn from a training program as well as the amount and kind of material they are capable of learning. These attributes include individual differences in ability, pretraining expectations, motivation, job involvement, locus of control, and self-efficacy.

Individual Differences in Ability. Individual differences in training ability can be predicted through cognitive ability tests, biographical data, and performance in an initial training experience, such as a work sample. Trainability tests, such as work samples or minicourses, are also valid predictors of performance in a full course of training. Work samples, when used as measures of trainability, offer a short period of formal job skill instruction followed by a test of job performance in a training facility.

Pretraining Expectations. Employees' expectations about the outcome of training can influence a program's effectiveness. A study of 84 employees in a call center in Germany found that those employees whose expectations were being fulfilled by their training program learned significantly more than did those whose expectations were not being met (Rowold, 2007).

When a training program fails to live up to the trainees' expectations, the trainees are less likely to complete the program. Trainees whose expectations are not met but who do complete the program are likely to be dissatisfied on the job, to have a low sense of commitment to the organization, and to have a high rate of job turnover. In contrast, trainees whose pretraining expectations are met by the training program develop strong organizational commitment, a high sense of self-efficacy, and enhanced motivation to succeed.

Motivation. The motivation or desire to learn is vital to employees' success in a training program. Regardless of their ability, trainees will not learn unless they truly want to learn. Every occupation has people who have achieved success with less than an optimal level of ability but with a great drive or motivation to succeed.

Research has shown that trainees with higher motivation learn more in training programs than do trainees with lower motivation. Trainees who are highly motivated are more likely to complete the program and to apply their training on the job (Salas & Cannon-Bowers, 2001). Management can increase trainees' motivation by involving them in decisions about the training program, allowing them to participate in the needs-assessment process, and giving them a choice of training courses.

Job Involvement. Trainees who show greater job involvement—whose sense of self-identity is closely linked with their work—show higher motivation to learn than do trainees who are less involved. Long-term career plans are also a factor. Training opportunities may be wasted on employees who display low job involvement and a lack of career interest because their motivation to learn is likely to be low. Furthermore, employees with low job involvement have low potential for showing improvement in their job performance as a result of their training. Thus, pretraining programs to increase job and career involvement may be desirable for some employees.

Locus of Control. Another variable that affects trainee motivation is locus of control. People identi-

fied as having an internal locus of control believe that job performance and such work-related rewards as pay and promotion are under their personal control, dependent on their own behaviors, abilities, and efforts. People with an external locus of control believe that life events in and out of the workplace are beyond their control. They are dependent on such outside forces as luck, chance, or whether their boss likes them.

In a meta-analysis of studies on locus of control, researchers found that people who scored high in internal locus of control also scored higher on measures of job performance, job satisfaction, job commitment, and motivation than did those who scored low in internal locus of control (Ng, Sorensen, & Eby, 2006).

Employees who have an internal locus of control are likely to be highly motivated to succeed in a training program because they believe that mastering the job skills is under their control and within their capabilities. They are more likely to accept feedback during training and to take action to correct deficiencies. They also show higher levels of job and career involvement than do employees with an external locus of control.

Self-Efficacy. Another factor that influences employee motivation to succeed in training programs is self-efficacy, the belief in one's capacity to perform a task. It may be described as our sense of adequacy, efficiency, and competence in coping with life's demands. A study of 19,120 people in 25 countries demonstrated that self-efficacy existed in similar ways across these cultures (Scholz, Dona, Sud, & Schwarzer, 2002).

The relationship between self-efficacy and motivation to learn, and between self-efficacy and actual success in training programs, has been amply demonstrated. Several meta-analyses of studies dealing with self-efficacy beliefs concluded that efficacy beliefs contribute significantly to a person's level of motivation and performance in the workplace and in the classroom (Bandura & Locke, 2003). In turn, self-efficacy can be influenced by training. Certain types of training, such as behavior modeling, can be used to increase self-efficacy. Even simply telling trainees that the skill they are trying to learn can be mastered through practice can increase self-efficacy.

HOW PEOPLE LEARN: PSYCHOLOGICAL ISSUES

Psychologists have devoted considerable effort to the study of learning. The published literature in the field contains thousands of research reports on human and animal learning under various conditions. In this section we deal with several factors that relate to teaching methods and to the nature of the material to be learned.

Active Practice.   Practice may not always make perfect, as the saying goes, but it does help. For learning to be most effective, trainees must be actively involved in the learning process, not merely passive recipients of information. For example, it is not sufficient to read about the operation of a construction crane or to watch a video of someone operating it. The training program should provide the opportunity for the trainee to sit in the operator's cab and have hands-on practice of the skills required to perform the job.

Imagine learning to drive a car only by listening to a lecture and memorizing traffic regulations. This can make you a better driver, but you will not actually learn how to drive until you sit in the driver's seat and start practicing. The same principle holds for academic material. Actively taking notes during lectures, highlighting and outlining the textbook, and discussing questions with classmates facilitate learning much more than sitting passively in the lecture hall.

Massed and Distributed (Spaced) Practice.   Some tasks are learned more readily when the training program schedules one or a few relatively long practice sessions (massed practice). Other tasks require a large number of relatively short practice sessions (distributed, or spaced, practice). In general, spaced practice results in better learning, particularly for motor skills.

For jobs requiring relatively simple tasks, spaced practice interspersed with short rest periods is more effective. For more complex tasks, longer rest periods between the spaced practice sessions results in more effective learning.

The research evidence is less clear for the learning of verbal skills. Massed practice may be more useful, but much depends on the complexity of the task to be mastered and the type of material to be learned. Short, simple material can be learned well by massed practice because the sessions do not have to be too long for trainees to absorb the content. More difficult material must be divided into shorter units and learned by distributed practice.

Whole and Part Learning.   The concept of whole or part learning refers to the relative size of the unit of material to be learned. The training course content can be divided into small parts, each of which is studied individually, or the material can be learned as a whole. The decision depends on the nature and complexity of the material and the ability of the trainees. More intelligent trainees are capable of rapidly learning larger units of material than are less intelligent trainees. However, when slower learners are offered the chance to learn the same material in smaller units, they may be able to master it better than when forced to apprehend it as a whole.

Some skills are obviously better suited to the whole learning method. For example, when learning to drive a car, it serves no useful purpose to divide driving behavior into component skills. You do not practice separately and repeatedly movements such as fastening the seat belt, turning on the ignition, releasing the emergency brake, adjusting the rearview mirror, and moving the gearshift lever from park to drive. Driving is an interdependent flow of movements and actions that can be learned more effectively as a whole.

When a task requires the initial learning of several subskills, the part method is more efficient. For example, piano students confronting a new piece of music may choose at first to practice the right-hand and the left-hand parts separately. Trainees can practice these various subskills until a particular level of efficiency has been achieved before integrating them into the total behavior or operation.

Transfer of Training.   Organizational training often takes place in an artificial setting, a training facility that may differ in several ways from the actual job environment. This discrepancy between training and job situations must be bridged. The training program must ensure that there will be a transfer of training—a carryover of the skills mastered during the training program—to the job itself.

The issue is one of relevance: Is the information provided during the training program relevant and meaningful to actual job performance? Is there a correspondence between the behaviors and attitudes taught in the training sessions and the behaviors and attitudes needed to perform the job successfully? Can all the information mastered in the training facility be applied in the production facility or the office? In many instances, the answer to these questions is no.

If there is close correspondence between training requirements and job requirements, positive transfer will develop. The material learned during training will aid or improve job performance. The greater the similarity between the training and work situations, the greater will be the transfer. This question of similarity is important because of the growing use of virtual work environments for training purposes.

If there is little similarity between training situations and work situations, negative transfer will result. In that case, the skills learned in the training program will hamper or interfere with job performance, and these skills or behaviors must be unlearned or modified before employees can perform the job. A survey of 299 managers, supervisors, and employees in Nepal found that more than 70% of them rated positive transfer of training to actual job tasks as the most important criterion for evaluat-

ing the worth of a training program (Subedi, 2006).

Several conditions in the posttraining environment can facilitate positive transfer. The most important is supervisor support for and reinforcement of the behaviors and skills taught in the training program (Smith-Jentsch, Salas, & Brannick, 2001). Research on 182 employees of a food marketing company in Portugal confirmed the importance of supervisor support in facilitating transfer of training. In addition, investigators found that support from the organization and from co-workers aided in positive transfer, as did high self-efficacy among the trainees (Velada, Caetano, Michek, Lyons, & Kavanagh, 2007).

Also influential are the opportunity to apply on the job the skills learned in the training program and a follow-up discussion or assessment shortly after completing the training program. Another important factor is the overall organizational climate. The more supportive it is of training, the greater the opportunities for transfer of the training experience to the actual work situation.

A survey of 150 members of a training and development organization dealt with the judgments of training professionals about the effectiveness of on-the-job training programs. The trainers expected

Newsbreak

It's OK to Bring Your iPod to Work

People used to hide their iPods from their boss at work, and many still do, but a growing number of employees are being given iPods by their companies and told that it's OK to listen to them on the job. In fact, some employees are told they have to listen to them in order to download files of company training courses.

A semiconductor manufacturer in California spent $2.5 million to buy video iPods for its 8,500 employees, including those who work overseas, so they can view the training sessions. A fast-food restaurant in Tennessee distributes iPods to new employees with instructions on food preparation, so they can listen while they are actually in the kitchen and follow the procedures step by step.

Some employees report that they use their iPods to listen to training material off the job, during their commute to and from work, or even while working out at the gym. It's almost as though they don't want their bosses to see them using them at work for fear they will look like slackers.

Younger employees said they were happy with their new training tools, but not so for those over age 50, many of whom had no idea what the gadgets were or what they could be used for. They learned quickly, however. The only reported disappointment came when an employee was laid off or quit and had to return the iPod!

Source: Athavaley, A. (2006, October 25). The Boss Puts the iPod to Work. *Wall Street Journal.*

On-the-job training Training that takes place directly on the job for which the person has been hired.

that two thirds of the employees would apply what they learn in training programs directly to their jobs. However, a year after training only one third of the employees applied what they had learned in the training programs directly to their jobs. Thus, the effectiveness of transfer appears to decline over time (Saks & Belcourt, 2006).

Feedback. People learn more readily when they are given a clear idea of how well they are doing. Feedback (sometimes called "knowledge of results") indicates to the trainees their level of progress. Feedback is also important in maintaining motivation. If trainees are not provided with feedback during a training program, they might persist in learning and practicing inappropriate behaviors and incorrect techniques of job performance.

To be maximally effective, feedback must be offered as soon as possible after the inappropriate behavior occurs. If a sequence of operations is being practiced incorrectly, the desired change is more likely to be brought about if the trainees are told immediately. Overall training progress is greater when a program allows for frequent feedback. The more specific and detailed the correction, the more useful it will be.

Reinforcement. The greater the reward that follows a behavior, the more easily and rapidly that behavior will be learned. The reward, or reinforcement, can take many forms—a good test grade, a gold star on a chart, a pat on the back from a supervisor, or a promotion for successful completion of a training program. By establishing a program of reinforcement, management can maintain employee motivation and effectively shape behavior by rewarding only those actions that the trainees are supposed to learn and display.

The most frequently used reinforcers in business and industry are money (such as pay raises or bonuses), social recognition (compliments or expressions of approval), and positive feedback about job performance. In a meta-analysis of 72 studies conducted on the job, researchers found that money improved performance by 23%, social

recognition improved performance by 17%, and feedback improved performance by 10% (Stajkovic & Luthans, 2003). Together, the three types of reinforcers are powerful tools for changing on-the-job behavior so that employees may become more productive.

Reinforcement should be provided immediately after the desired behavior has occurred. The longer the delay between behavior and reinforcement, the less effective the reinforcement will be, because the trainee may fail to perceive the connection between the correct behavior and the reward for having behaved in that way.

In the early stages of training, reinforcement should be given every time the desired behavior is displayed. Once some learning has taken place, continuous reinforcement is no longer necessary. Then, partial reinforcement will be sufficient, for example, rewarding trainees every third or every tenth time they perform the appropriate behavior.

TYPES OF TRAINING PROGRAMS

Now that we have described the pretraining attributes of trainees and the psychological factors that affect learning, let us consider specific organizational training techniques. Each technique offers advantages and disadvantages, depending on the goals of the training program, the abilities of the employees, and the nature of the information to be learned.

On-the-Job Training

One of the oldest and most widely used training methods takes place directly on the job for which the worker is being trained. Under the guidance of an experienced operator, supervisor, or trained instructor, or following instructions on an iPod or similar device, trainees learn while working. They operate the equipment in the production facility or assist customers out on the sales floor and have the opportunity to develop proficiency while they work.

The major advantage of **on-the-job training** is economy; the organization does not have to establish, equip, and maintain a separate training facility.

Vestibule training   Training that takes place in a simulated workspace.

If current workers and supervisors serve as trainers, even the cost of a professional instructor is saved. A more obvious advantage is positive transfer of training. There is no concern about whether job performance in a training situation will carry over to the actual work situation because the training and job situations are the same. In terms of other psychological factors, active practice is provided from the outset. Motivation to learn should be high because the training situation is clearly relevant to the job situation. Feedback is immediate and visible. Good performance will elicit praise, and poor performance will show in a faulty product or dissatisfied customer.

On-the-job training can be expensive in the long run, however. Workers and supervisors must take time from their regular jobs to train new employees. This can lead to an overall reduction in productivity. Additional costs come with the slower work pace of the trainees and any damage they cause to equipment or product because of their inexperience. On certain jobs, permitting untrained workers to operate machinery may be hazardous not only to the trainees but also to other employees. Accident rates for trainees on the job are typically higher than accident rates for experienced workers.

In an on-the-job training program, new employees practice job skills under the supervision of an experienced worker.

Use of current workers or supervisors as trainers does not ensure adequate training for new employees. Because a person performs a job competently or has been on the job for a considerable time does not mean that person has the ability to teach the job to someone else. On-the-job training is often haphazard and inadequate, amounting to no more than the supervisor's saying to the trainees, "Go ahead and start. If you have any questions, come see me."

On-the-job training is also used at the management level. Much managerial and executive training and development occurs through informal and unstructured on-the-job experiences. Indeed, on-the-job experiences can contribute more significantly to the development of managerial ability than any formal classroom instruction.

Vestibule Training

Because on-the-job training has the potential for disrupting the production process, many companies prefer **vestibule training**. They establish a simulated workspace in a separate training facility. (A vestibule is a hallway or entrance foyer between the outer door of a building and its main rooms. In the early days of American industry, vestibule schools were organized just inside the doors of industrial plants to introduce new workers to their jobs with a few weeks of specialized training. The word *vestibule* is used in this context to denote that the training program is like an entryway or passageway the employee must cross before getting to the job itself.) Using the same kind of equipment and operating procedures as the actual work situation, a vestibule training program relies on skilled instructors, rather than experienced workers and supervisors, to teach new workers how to perform their jobs.

Because the sole purpose of vestibule training is training, there is no pressure to maintain a given level of productivity. Trainees do not have to be concerned about making costly or embarrassing errors or about damaging actual production equipment.

Apprenticeship　A training method for skilled crafts and trades involving classroom instruction and on-the-job experience.

Computer-assisted instruction (CAI)　A computer-based training method in which trainees learn material at their own pace and receive immediate feedback on their progress.

They can concentrate on learning the skills necessary to be successful on the job.

The greatest disadvantage of vestibule training is the cost. The organization must equip the facility and maintain a teaching staff. This expense is particularly burdensome when there are not enough new workers to make full-time use of the training facility. Furthermore, if the training situation does not correspond closely to the work situation, negative transfer of training will occur, and the trainees may need informal, on-the-job instruction once they start to work. This problem can be aggravated by the common business practice of using obsolete equipment, retired from the production floor, in the training facility. However, if a vestibule training program is properly designed, staffed, and equipped, it can be an effective training technique.

Apprenticeship

Perhaps the earliest recorded training method still in use today is the **apprenticeship** program for skilled crafts and trades in private-sector industries such as construction and manufacturing. Programs are available for plumbers, carpenters, electronics technicians, painters, and auto mechanics, among others. Conducted in the classroom and on the job, apprenticeship involves extensive background preparation in the craft as well as actual work experience under the guidance of experts.

Apprenticeships average 4 to 6 years. The standard procedure is for the trainees to agree to work for a company for a fixed period in return for a specified program of training and a salary, usually half that earned by skilled and licensed craftspersons. Trainees must complete their apprenticeship before they are allowed to join a union. Membership in a labor union is necessary to securing employment. Thus, apprentice programs constitute a joint effort by industry and organized labor to maintain an adequate supply of skilled workers.

In recent years, apprenticeships in the public sector have grown in popularity. A number of federal, state, and local government agencies have adopted them for skilled blue-collar jobs in civilian and military programs, such as building maintenance worker, highway maintenance worker, prison correctional officer, and firefighter. The Smithsonian Institution in Washington, DC, operates an apprenticeship program for carpenters, electricians, and plaster masons to build displays for its museums.

Computer-Assisted Instruction

Computer-assisted instruction (CAI), sometimes called computer-based training (CBT), is widely used by private- and public-sector organizations. In CAI, the program of instruction, usually on CD-ROM, serves as the teacher. Trainees interact with the material on computer terminals. Their responses are recorded and analyzed automatically, and the difficulty of each item presented is based on the correctness of the response to the previous item.

One of the most widespread uses of computer-based training is to teach computer literacy skills. With millions of workers now using computers daily on the job, the development of computer operating skills is critical. Another popular use of CAI is in training airline flight crews. The software used by airlines presents displays and touch-panel graphics to simulate the buttons, switches, dials, and signal lights in the cockpit. This type of instruction reduces the number of hours that pilots and copilots would otherwise have to spend in a more expensive flight simulator.

With CAI, trainees are actively involved in the learning process and work through material at their own pace. This means that the trainees, rather than the trainer, decide how long and how often to practice. Freedom to choose can have a downside, however, particularly for trainees who are not sufficiently motivated to work properly so as to learn the material. Research on 78 technical employees who volunteered for an online course on problem solving showed that some of them skipped practice sessions or moved too quickly through the course work to adequately understand the material. After the course, the trainees who obtained the lowest test scores were found to have completed less than 70% of the practice sessions and to have spent fewer than 6 hours working at what was scheduled as a 14-hour course. Those who spent the least time on the training also had low learning self-efficacy levels; that is, they were not sufficiently confident about their ability to learn the material (Brown, 2001).

Nevertheless, for people with the ability and motivation to succeed, computer-assisted instruction offers many advantages. Trainees receive immediate feedback on their progress and reinforcement for displaying mastery of a skill. The CAI technique offers more individualized instruction than does a traditional lecture-based training course. It is not unlike private tutoring by an excellent teacher who has a comprehensive knowledge of the subject, never becomes impatient or annoyed, and displays no prejudice or error. Because CAI keeps accurate records and maintains a current performance analysis on each trainee, the training staff is free to devote time to any unusual learning problems that arise.

In a meta-analysis of 96 studies involving more than 19,000 participants, researchers found that Web-based instruction was 19% more effective than classroom instruction in teaching declarative knowledge, that is, descriptions of facts, methods, and procedures. There were no significant differences between the two methods for teaching procedural knowledge: learning about how to actually perform those methods and procedures on the job. Also, no differences were found between Web-based instruction and classroom instruction on measures of employee satisfaction with the training program (Sitzmann, Kraiger, Stewart, & Wisher, 2006). In another study on CAI, investigators found that field workers from Hispanic ethnic groups who had little formal education or experience with computers were successful in learning safety procedures from Web-based instruction and in transferring this knowledge to on-the-job behaviors (Anger, et al., 2006).

Computer-assisted instruction can be used with even a small number of trainees, so a company does not have to make trainees wait until there are enough to fill a classroom and schedule a course. CAI can also be provided to a large number of trainees simultaneously in different locations. Studies have shown that the technique significantly decreases training time and provides positive transfer of training.

Net-Based Training

Net-based training involves the Internet and the intranet (the within-company site). The technique is a type of distance learning, and it is transforming traditional training programs by delivering up-to-the-minute programs on demand. Through net-based training, a company can provide training courses for any number of workers to access from their desks at work or at home, or from laptops and handheld computer devices while traveling. Instruction is being prepared for nearly every type of training, from certification in information technology to advanced accounting practices and course work for an MBA degree.

Net-based training offers the same advantages as computer-assisted instruction: active involvement of the trainees, the opportunity to proceed at their own pace, immediate feedback and reinforcement, and flexibility as to the time and place of training.

The cost of net-based training has been estimated to be 20% to 35% lower than the cost of traditional classroom instruction, where trainers and trainees must assemble on a prescribed schedule. The technique has become a cheaper, better, and faster way of reaching a wider range of employees.

Behavior Modification

The use of positive reinforcement to change behavior has many applications to organizational training. An assessment called a performance audit is conducted first to determine the problems or behaviors that can be modified to achieve more efficient job performance. A program of positive reinforcement is then introduced to reward employees for displaying the desired behaviors, such as reducing errors or decreasing production time per unit. Punishment or reprimands are not used because although they may temporarily eliminate an undesirable behavior, they may leave in its place anxiety, hostility, and anger. Providing positive reinforcement is much more effective in improving employee productivity and behavior.

Behavior modification A training program of positive reinforcement to reward employees for displaying desirable job behaviors.

A classic program of **behavior modification** was developed at Emery Air Freight, where the behavioral changes induced were directly connected to job performance. A performance audit revealed two problem areas: (1) despite the employees' belief that they were responding within 90 minutes to 90% of customer telephone inquiries, they were actually responding to only 30% of the inquiries within that time; and (2) employees were combining packages into containers for shipment only 45% of the time, whereas management expected containers to be used 90% of the time. The goals of the behavior modification training program were to have employees respond faster to customer inquiries and to use containers for shipment whenever possible.

Newsbreak

Coast-to-Coast Commuting: San Diego to Tampa?

Morgan Hezlep, 29 years old, was working for a San Diego company that designed health care software programs when she decided that she wanted to go back to college to finish her bachelor's degree. She couldn't quit her job to return to school full time because she needed the salary. And besides, she liked her work. Unfortunately, her company wanted to send her to Boston on a long-term assignment to work with a client establishing a new program.

Then it got more complicated. Morgan didn't want to move to Boston so her company agreed to fly her back and forth every week. That settled the job problem, but where could she take the classes to finish her degree? In Boston she would be working all the time, and in San Diego there were no colleges where she could attend weekends only.

Then she learned about an online degree program in computer science offered by Saint Leo University, located near Tampa, Florida. Morgan could do her course work online during the hours she spent in airports and commuting cross-country by plane. That system gave her about 16 hours a week to study the lectures provided on CD-ROMs and to write the required papers. "I left San Diego every Sunday," she said, "worked Monday through Thursday and flew back home to San Diego on Friday morning. I would get settled in [at the airport], put on my headphones, pop in a CD and begin class."

It took 2 years to complete the program. In addition to the CD-ROMs, there were weekly online seminars and discussions with professors and other students in a virtual classroom setting. Advisers were always available through a toll-free phone number, fax, or e-mail. Textbooks arrived by mail at the beginning of every course.

Along with her degree, Morgan accumulated more than 300,000 frequent-flyer miles, some of which she applied to the airfare to Tampa for her graduation—the only time she ever saw the campus.

Her new credentials helped her decide to enter a new field. She enrolled in law school and attended actual classes in real buildings every day. Morgan says that her study habits were greatly improved by her online learning experience. "With the online classes," she said, "I was forced to develop good study habits and time management skills. I think the experience made me a more disciplined student."

Source: Commuter school (2003, July 20). *St. Petersburg (FL) Times.*

Job rotation A management training technique that assigns trainees to various jobs and departments over a period of a few years.

Case studies A method of executive training in which trainees analyze a business problem and offer solutions.

Managers were taught a number of recognitions and rewards to bestow on employees as reinforcers, ranging from a smile and a nod to specific praise for a job well done. Financial incentives to improve performance were not used. Praise and recognition were found to be sufficient reinforcers for improving job performance and for bringing about positive changes in behavior. Managers were told to reinforce desirable behaviors as soon as they occurred and gradually to shift from constant reinforcement to occasional, or intermittent, reinforcement.

Employees were required to keep a detailed record of their accomplishments so that they could compare their performance with the company standards. This record keeping provided them daily feedback on their progress.

The company estimated that the improved productivity and response time saved $3 million in 3 years, considerably more than the cost of instituting the behavior modification program initially.

Job Rotation

Job rotation is a popular management training technique. It exposes trainees to different jobs and departments to acquaint them with all facets of the organization. The technique is frequently used with new college graduates who are just beginning their working careers. Through job rotation, trainees gain perspective on various aspects of organizational life. They have the opportunity to see and be seen by higher management in different departments and to learn through direct experience where they might best apply their knowledge, abilities, and interests.

The rotation phase of a management career may last several years, taking employees from one department to another or from one plant or office in the United States to others throughout the world. Such changes can promote the development of the management trainees' flexibility, adaptability, and self-efficacy as employees learn to deal successfully with new challenges. Job rotation programs are also used for skilled and semiskilled jobs. The programs allow workers to increase their skill levels in diverse occupations, and they serve to alleviate the boredom that can result from years of performing the same tasks.

Disadvantages of the job rotation technique include frequent moves, which can disrupt family life and interrupt a spouse's career. If the rotation period is too brief, there may not be sufficient time to become fully acquainted with a particular job. If top management is more interested in using management trainees as temporary office help, instead of considering them a rising group of managers in

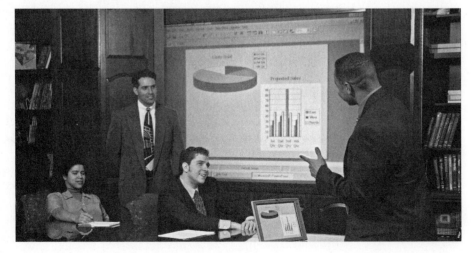

Role playing gives management trainees the chance to try out various supervisory behaviors and to receive feedback from other trainees and instructors.

Business games A training method that simulates a complex organizational situation to encourage the development of problem-solving and decision-making skills.

In-basket technique An assessment-center exercise that requires job applicants to process memos, letters, and directives found in a typical manager's in-basket.

Role playing A management training technique in which trainees play the role of a supervisor, acting out various behaviors in situations with subordinates.

need of mentors, the trainees will not have the opportunity to acquire the necessary skills to transfer to upper-management positions. This can defeat the purpose of the program.

Case Studies

The use of **case studies**, a method developed by the Harvard University School of Business, is popular in executive training programs. A complex problem, or case, of the kind faced daily by managers and executives, is presented to the trainees prior to a general meeting. The trainees are expected to familiarize themselves with the information and to find additional relevant material. When they meet as a group, each member must be prepared to interpret the problem and offer a solution. Through the presentation of diverse viewpoints, the trainees come to appreciate different perspectives on a problem and, consequently, different approaches to solving it. Usually the cases have no one correct solution. The group leader does not suggest an answer. The group as a whole must reach consensus and resolve the problem.

A limitation of the case study method is that the solution may not be relevant to the requirements of the job. There may be a discrepancy between the theoretical solution to the case problem and the solution that is practical for the organization. Therefore, actions taken on the basis of the case study solution proposed in the training program may not transfer positively to actions that are appropriate on the job.

Business Games

Business games attempt to simulate a complex organizational situation. They are intended to develop problem-solving and decision-making skills and to provide practice in using those skills in a situation in which a management trainee's mistake will not prove costly or embarrassing to the organization.

Trainees compete in teams, each team representing a separate, hypothetical business organization. The team companies are given detailed information about the operation of their organization, including data on finances, sales, advertising, production, personnel, and inventories. Each group must organize itself and assign various tasks and responsibilities to each member. As the teams deal with corporate problems, an instructor evaluates their reasoning processes and decisions. Teams may be required to consider additional problems based on the outcomes of their initial decisions.

Because the business problems presented to the trainees are so realistic, many trainees form an emotional commitment to their virtual company. They gain experience in making decisions on real-life problems under the pressures of time and the actions taken by rival organizations. For new employees, business games may provide their first exposure to actual job tasks and stresses managers face. This type of realistic job preview persuades some trainees that they would be happier in another line of work.

In-Basket Training

The **in-basket technique** was discussed in chapter 3 as a method of employee selection. The same technique is used to train prospective managers. Each trainee is given a stack of letters, memos, customer complaints, employee requests, and other items that present various problems typical of those dealt with by managers on the job. The trainees must take action on each item within a specified period. After completing the tasks, the trainees meet with a trainer to discuss their decisions and receive feedback on the outcomes.

Role Playing

In **role playing**, management trainees pretend to act out a particular role by displaying whatever behaviors they believe are appropriate in a given situation. For example, they may be asked to imagine themselves to be a supervisor discussing a poor performance appraisal with a subordinate. They act out these situations in front of a group of trainees and

Behavior modeling A management training technique in which trainees attempt to imitate the job behaviors of successful supervisors.

Executive coaching A management training technique involving personal sessions with a coach to improve a particular aspect of job performance.

instructors who offer comments on their performance. A trainee may play the role of supervisor at first, then the situation will be reversed and the same trainee will play the employee. Sessions can be videotaped for later analysis. Many people feel foolish or awkward acting out in front of a group, but once they begin, most people develop a sensitivity for the part and project their feelings onto it.

Role playing can be a valuable learning device. It enables trainees to understand the views of subordinates and acquaints them with the roles they will be expected to play as managers. It provides practical experience as well as feedback from other trainees and instructors. Trainees have the opportunity to practice job-related behaviors in a situation in which mistakes or inappropriate behaviors will not jeopardize interpersonal relations on the job.

Behavior Modeling

The **behavior modeling** approach to management training involves having trainees attempt to imitate or model their behavior on examples of exceptional job performance. It is a popular technique for teaching interpersonal and leadership skills. Behavior modeling is usually conducted with groups of 6 to 12 supervisors or managers. Sessions may last 2 to 4 hours a week for up to 4 weeks. In the intervals between training sessions, the trainees are on the job, applying what they have learned, which provides them with feedback from their subordinates.

The usual procedure is for a trainer, using a prepared script, to provide a general introduction. Then the trainees watch a video of a manager who is acting out appropriate procedures and behaviors for handling a job situation with a subordinate—for example, discussing poor job performance, excessive absenteeism, or low morale.

Next, the trainees engage in behavior rehearsal; they practice the behaviors they saw the model perform. Trainees are not being asked to play a role; instead, they are imitating the actual behaviors they will use on the job, the behaviors the

model has displayed. The trainer and the other trainees provide feedback by telling each trainee how closely he or she imitated the model's behavior and where the behavior diverged. This social reinforcement helps trainees gain confidence in their ability to display appropriate behavior.

The interpersonal and leadership behaviors learned by behavior modeling will transfer directly to the job because the modeled situations between manager and subordinate are actual job situations. Thus, there is a high degree of relevance between behavior modeling as a training technique and the job requirements, a condition that increases trainees' motivation to accept and apply the training.

Reports from organizations using behavior modeling show that the technique is effective in raising employee morale, improving communication with customers, increasing sales, decreasing absenteeism, enhancing supervisory skills, improving production quantity and quality, and reducing employee resistance to change.

Executive Coaching

Another approach to management training involves one-to-one training sessions in which a coach works with a manager to improve a particular aspect of the manager's job performance. Can the manager give a good speech? Can the executive use the Internet? Do performance appraisals show that colleagues and subordinates think the boss has lousy human relations skills? Get a coach!

Executive coaching is designed to solve individual problems as they arise. The most frequent use of executive coaching has been as a follow-up to poor ratings on 360-degree feedback appraisals. Because feedback alone is often not sufficient motivation for a manager to alter his or her behavior, a coach will be brought in to help interpret the feedback and work with the manager to devise strategies for eliciting the desired changes in behavior. Several sessions of coaching may be required to deal with perceived deficiencies.

One year after receiving executive coaching, 1,202 senior managers underwent a 360-degree performance evaluation. Those who had received the coaching were judged to be far more likely to set specific rather than general goals for their subordinates and to solicit ideas for improvement than were those who had received no coaching. The overall performance ratings of those who had received the coaching were also higher than those of the no-coaching control group (Smither, London, Flautt, Vargas, & Kucine, 2003). Most executives who have received coaching tend to agree with their coaches' recommendations and to rate the process as valuable to their career development.

Diversity Training

We described in chapter 1 how the nature of the workforce is changing to include more women and more ethnic minorities. To aid their employees in coping with an increasingly diverse workforce,

Newsbreak

Virtual Training: How Not to Crash a Multimillion Dollar Airplane

You've seen it in the movies. A jet fighter eases its way upward, below and behind a mammoth flying tanker loaded with aviation fuel. A long, thin tube with a funnel extends from the rear of the tanker aircraft. The fighter pilot maneuvers the jet so that its fuel tank port connects with the tiny funnel, while traveling at more than 500 miles an hour. It's called in-flight refueling, a tricky, delicate, and dangerous operation every fighter pilot has to learn.

Lt. Charlie Howard, a newly graduated 26-year-old pilot, is trying to perform the maneuver for the first time. He has listened to the lectures, read the operating manual, and paid close attention to the video showing a pilot's-eye view of the connection, but now he feels his fear mount as he closes in on the monster plane overhead. He never takes his eyes off the funnel. It's only 20 feet away. He draws closer. Suddenly, his plane is buffeted by high wind gusts and his body is slammed into the seat as the fighter bounces on an updraft. Frantically, Charlie forces the control stick forward, but it is too late. The wind whips faster than he can react, and his tiny plane smashes into the side of the tanker.

"Boom," rings a voice in his ear. "You're dead, Charlie. And so is everybody in the tanker. OK, let's try it again."

Charlie Howard is flying in a virtual aircraft, a flight simulator, wearing a head-mounted virtual reality apparatus that provides lifelike computer-generated images. The only damage he suffered from the "crash" was to his ego, and now he can try the maneuver again and again until he perfects it. Only then will he be permitted to try it in a real airplane.

The U.S. military has invested millions of dollars in virtual training for pilots, air-traffic controllers, and tank commanders, so they can learn their jobs without inflicting harm on themselves and others or damaging expensive equipment. Virtual reality allows researchers to shape the training to the specific needs of the various branches of the armed forces. U.S. Air Force psychologist Wesley Regian said, "People can practice one part of a more complicated task. Or simulations can start out easy—as with removing the wind in the refueling simulation—and increase in difficulty as a student grasps the basics."

One day Lt. Howard will practice refueling in a real plane under genuine wind conditions, but thanks to the I-O psychology research on virtual reality simulation devices, he will be well trained by then. He will have performed the required maneuvers many times already, and survived.

Diversity training   Training programs to make employees aware of their personal prejudices and to teach them to be more sensitive to the concerns and views of others.

many organizations have instituted **diversity training** programs to teach people to confront personal prejudices that could lead to discriminatory behaviors. Through lectures, videos, role-playing, and confrontational exercises, employees are learning, in a way, how it might feel to be a female worker being sexually harassed by a male boss, or a Hispanic worker receiving an unsatisfactory performance appraisal from a Black supervisor. Trainees are forced to deal with their own sexist and racist attitudes and to learn to be more sensitive to the concerns and viewpoints of others.

U.S. companies are spending up to $10 billion annually for diversity training. The success of diversity training depends on several factors: support from management, mandatory attendance, and the size of the organization. Large organizations with strong support from top executives, a staff of diversity specialists, and required attendance for all employees are the most likely to have successful diversity training programs. However, posttraining interviews with participants suggest that for some people these programs foster negative reactions as well as charges that the programs are offered only because it appears to be the politically correct thing to do.

An analysis of diversity training programs conducted by 830 U.S. companies over a period of 31 years found that mandatory attendance at such programs often resulted in less diversity in the workplace. Forced attendance at diversity training exercises led to a decrease of up to 7.5% in the number of women in management positions, a 10% drop in jobs for African-American women, and a 12% drop for African-American men. Similar declines were recorded for Asian and Hispanic managers; also reported was an overall backlash against the idea of artificially increasing diversity. Such training programs yielded more positive results when attendance was voluntary (Kalev, Dobbin, & Kelly, 2006; Vedantam, 2008).

In a study of 6,130 salespersons in 743 stores of a national retail chain, researchers found that differences in the number of sales per hour between

Black and White employees were highest in stores that did not have a favorable climate for a diverse workforce. The differences were significantly lower in stores with a pro-diversity climate (McKay, Avery, & Morris, 2008).

CAREER DEVELOPMENT AND PLANNING

Training methods are designed to improve employees' knowledge, job skills, and interpersonal relations. Most training programs are mandatory and are oriented toward a specific job or specific career stage, such as the entry-level worker, the employee who needs retraining, or the midcareer manager. Some organizations also offer personal development opportunities throughout an employee's career. These career development and planning efforts, which are strictly voluntary, involve a lifelong learning approach.

Organizations as diverse as General Electric, AT&T, Merrill Lynch, TRW, and Xerox operate career development centers. These centers provide information on company career paths and opportunities and offer counseling and self-analysis programs so that employees can determine how their personal goals coincide with organizational goals. Many companies sponsor workshops to assist employees in career planning and in the development of human relations skills. Employees are encouraged to set career objectives—for example, specifying where they hope to be within the corporate hierarchy in 5 years' time—and to review these goals periodically. Some companies offer tuition refund plans that enable employees to return to college or graduate school to upgrade job skills or to learn new skills. Employees are also encouraged to participate in in-house training courses.

One of the forces of change in the workplace today is the decline of the idea of a lifetime career with a single employer. Increasingly, employees may choose to or be forced to change careers several

Career self-management A lifelong approach to learning and skill enhancement initiated by the employee rather than by the organization.

times during the course of their working lives and to continually enhance and upgrade their personal package of skills. This necessity for lifelong learning increases the importance of career development and planning efforts.

A 13-month study followed 800 workers in several different organizations who were involved in career development and learning activities. The researchers reached the following conclusions (Maurer, Weiss, & Barbeite, 2003).

- Prior participation in career development activities was a good predictor of present and future intentions to undertake more such learning activities.
- High self-efficacy led to more favorable attitudes toward career development opportunities, which led, in turn, to higher levels of participation.
- The more supportive organizations are of career development activities, the greater are employee beliefs that their participation will lead to positive personal benefits.
- Older workers receive less organizational support and encouragement for career development activities and feel less capable of undertaking such activities.

In addition, the researchers reported that the major reason for intending to stay with a company, instead of looking for a job with another organization, was the opportunity for career growth, development, and learning provided by the present employer.

Career Self-Management

As a result of years of corporate mergers, restructuring, downsizing, and outsourcing, many companies today are less able or less willing to provide opportunities for the career development and growth of their employees. They are urging employees to take more responsibility on their own for actively planning and managing their careers. The term **career self-management** refers to the degree to which a person regularly and routinely

gathers information and formulates or revises plans for his or her own career through solving problems and making decisions. There has been little research, however, on the effectiveness of career self-management training.

Some organizations offer training to help employees assume this responsibility to upgrade their skills and learn new ones. One estimate is that approximately half of all U.S. corporations with a workforce exceeding 100 employees offers career self-management training. A typical program consists of three stages or programs presented on successive days:

1. Assessing career attitudes, values, plans, and goals
2. Analyzing how these goals have or have not been met by the current job
3. Discussing career strategies to create opportunities to meet one's plans and goals, whether on or off the job (This stage includes upgrading skills, soliciting feedback from colleagues and supervisors, networking, and being mobile in seeking new job opportunities.)

EVALUATING ORGANIZATIONAL TRAINING PROGRAMS

Many training programs and facilities appear impressive and sophisticated, and employees like many of them. Nevertheless, the outcomes or results of training programs should be evaluated in systematic and quantitative terms. One way to measure the worth of a program is to assess the following results: (1) changes in cognitive outcomes, such as the amount of information learned, (2) changes in skill-based outcomes, such as improvements in quantity and quality of production, and (3) changes in affective outcomes, such as positive attitudes and higher motivation. Unless such evaluative research is conducted, an organization will not know if its investment of time and money is effective.

Are employees learning the skills they need for their jobs? Are productivity, safety, and efficiency rising? Have communications and leadership skills improved? Have the attitudes of majority-group employees toward minority-group employees changed? To answer these questions, comparisons must be made of trained and untrained workers performing the same jobs. Or the same workers before and after training can be compared with a control group of workers who were not exposed to the training. Only through such research can an organization determine whether its training program should be modified, extended, or eliminated.

In a meta-analysis of 397 studies on training, investigators found what the researchers described as a medium to large positive effect of organizational training (Arthur, Bennett, Edens, & Bell, 2003). A survey of 150 members of a training and development organization showed that these training professionals believed that approximately half of all training efforts resulted in an improvement in employee and organizational performance (Katz, 2002).

Even with such a substantial investment at stake, most organizations do not make a systematic effort to evaluate their training programs. Or, they may accept subjective or intuitive evidence that the trainees are actually learning something. As a result, many organizations do not have a clear idea whether the millions of dollars they spend on training is worthwhile. This failure to examine the effectiveness of training programs is increasingly expensive as more and more training is dependent on computer technology.

In addition to cost, other factors help explain the lack of assessment of the effectiveness of training programs. Many training directors do not have the skills to conduct such research. Also, they may overestimate the usefulness of programs they have initiated and designed. Some companies offer

Newsbreak

Obsolete at Midlife? Retrain, Retrain, Retrain

Gary Herman is a 55-year-old systems analyst with the data services division of GTE in Tampa, Florida. He's concerned about his future because he's working in a field where the technology changes so fast and so radically that a person's skills can become obsolete in the space of only a year or two. He spends considerable time reeducating himself to stay marketable.

"People need to be retooled," said James Harris, Herman's boss. "If they don't choose to do that, they could lose their jobs. Either you retrain or you don't move along in your career. It's that simple."

Internet-based technological advancements pose continual challenges for people like Gary Herman. When his employer offered a 2-month course on state-of-the-art developments, he added those 8 hours per day of study time to his full-time work schedule. His boss had not told him to take the course. Herman knew it was up to him to take advantage of the opportunity to improve his skills. But he also knew that if his next performance appraisal, which included a critical skill reevaluation, did not show that he was making an effort to manage the direction of his career, he would not remain on his chosen career path with GTE and would no longer be marketable elsewhere.

"You have to adopt a pattern of lifelong learning in this field," said John Bonanno, executive director of Boston University's corporate education center. "A lot of what you learn today will, in two or three years, be obsolete."

But not everyone is capable of being retrained. GTE's training director, Rene Lutthans, found that 25% of the employees who participate in such training are unable to master the new skills. "The company tries to find a place for such people, but as projects are phased out, there are no guarantees of employment."

If you can't keep up, you're out. If you don't manage your own career, no one else will.

training not because management believes in it or expects it to meet specific corporate goals but merely because their competitors do it.

Some training programs are established because some new technique or management style has produced a flood of anecdotal reports in the popular media attesting to its value. One example was "time management," supposedly a method for learning to use one's time in the most efficient manner. Supporters claimed time management increased employee productivity and satisfaction and reduced stress. As the number of magazine articles and television reports about the success of time management grew, companies hired time-management consultants to train employees in this latest miracle cure for the ills of the workplace. The only problem was, time management did not work. No one knows how many companies initiated expensive time-management training programs and maintained them in the absence of data to support their effectiveness.

Assessing the behavioral changes that may occur after training can be difficult. If a worker operates a simple machine or assembles a part, the goal of the training program and the measurement of the outcome are relatively straightforward. The number of items produced per unit time by trained and untrained workers, or by workers trained by different techniques, can be determined objectively and compared. At this work level, training programs have been shown to be effective. When dealing with human relations, problem solving, or other management behaviors, it is far more difficult to assess the usefulness of the training.

Yet the face validity of management training remains high, despite the lack of supporting data. The programs are popular, everyone says they are necessary, and management looks good for providing them. However, the question remains: Are they truly worthwhile?

Training directors defend their programs by pointing out that management trainees are subsequently promoted to higher levels of responsibility. This is not a valid or sufficient measure of a training program's success, because usually only the most capable and promising candidates are chosen to participate in management training initially. These trainees are the ones most likely to be promoted anyway, even without the training programs. Training directors also like to boast that employees like the programs. That's nice, but feelings and other subjective reactions are no substitute for research to investigate whether training results in better job performance. Organizations must be willing to expend the resources necessary to evaluate their elaborate training and development programs. It makes little sense to continue to support such activities without empirical evidence of their worth.

Problems with organizational training provide many challenges for I-O psychologists:

- To identify the abilities required to perform increasingly complex jobs
- To provide job opportunities for unskilled workers
- To assist supervisors in the management of an ethnically diverse workforce
- To retrain workers displaced by changing economic, technological, and political forces
- To help organizations remain competitive in the international marketplace
- To conduct the necessary research to determine the effectiveness of training programs

Summary

Training and development take place from the first day on a job throughout a person's career at all levels of employment: from unskilled teenagers who need remedial work in basic math and language skills to seasoned corporate vice presidents. Fair employment legislation affects training programs because decisions on placement, promotion, retention, and transfer are often based on performance during training. Therefore, training has the potential to be discriminatory.

The first step in establishing a training program is to specify the training objectives. A **needs assessment** based on organizational, task, and worker analyses is conducted using the techniques of job analysis, critical incidents, performance appraisal, and self-assessment. The training staff should be knowledgeable about the subject matter, be able to communicate effectively, and have the requisite interpersonal skills.

Pretraining characteristics of trainees can influence how much they will benefit from a training program. Relevant attributes include individual differences in ability, pretraining expectations, motivation, job involvement, locus of control, and self-efficacy. Psychological factors involved in learning include active practice of the material, massed or spaced practice, whole or part learning, transfer of training, feedback, and reinforcement.

In **on-the-job training**, trainees learn while actually working at the job. **Vestibule training** takes place in a simulated work area. In **apprenticeship**, trainees undergo classroom instruction and work experience under the guidance of skilled craftspersons. In **computer-assisted instruction**, trainees interact with computer software that presents the material to be learned. **Net-based training** offers instruction over the Internet or the company's in-house intranet network. This makes training available both on and off the job, whenever and wherever the employees choose to log on. In **behavior modification**, trainees are reinforced, or rewarded, for displaying the desired behaviors.

Job rotation exposes trainees to various jobs at their level of employment. In **case studies**, man-agement trainees analyze, interpret, and discuss a complex business problem. **Business games** require groups of trainees to interact in a simulated business situation. The **in-basket technique**, also a simulation, asks trainees to respond individually to letters, memos, and other office tasks. In **role playing**, trainees act out the problems of workers and managers. **Behavior modeling** has trainees pattern their behavior on that of successful managers. **Executive coaching** offers one-to-one training to improve a particular aspect of a manager's job performance. It is frequently a follow-up to poor ratings on a 360-degree performance appraisal. In **diversity training**, employees learn to confront and deal with racist and sexist attitudes.

Career development and planning is a lifelong learning approach to enhancing job skills and abilities and fostering personal development. Through self-analysis and company counseling and training programs, employees are assisted through various career stages. **Career self-management** refers to lifelong learning and skill enhancement initiated by the employee rather than by the company.

Organizations rarely undertake systematic or quantitative evaluation of their training programs. Many training programs are continued because of subjective beliefs about their effectiveness rather than because of empirical evidence of actual behavior changes that result from training.

Key Terms

apprenticeship	computer-assisted instruction	needs assessment
behavior modeling	(CAI)	on-the-job training
behavior modification	diversity training	role playing
business games	executive coaching	vestibule training
career self-management	in-basket technique	
case studies	job rotation	

Review Questions

1. What is Hamburger U.? What does it say about the nature and extent of training in the workplace?

2. What are the purposes of a needs assessment, and how is it conducted?

3. What is the most frequently used technique for determining training needs and objectives?

4. Describe how performance appraisals and job analyses can be used to provide information about a company's training needs.

5. What factors in the pretraining environment influence employee beliefs about the value of the training program?

6. Discuss the influence on training of employees' pretraining expectations and motivation. In what ways can a company increase trainee motivation?

7. How is trainee motivation to perform well in a training program influenced by the factors of locus of control and self-efficacy?

8. Describe the effect on learning of active practice, massed versus distributed practice, and whole versus part learning.

9. How would you establish a training program to teach people to use bulldozers? To use computers?

10. What factors can hinder positive transfer from a training program to on-the-job performance?

11. What reinforcers are used in the workplace? What is their relative importance in improving job performance?

12. Describe the relative merits of vestibule training and on-the-job training.

13. What are the advantages and disadvantages of computer-assisted instruction as compared to more traditional instructor-led training?

14. Distinguish between behavior modification and behavior modeling.

15. How are case studies, business games, and role playing used in management training?

16. How does executive coaching differ from other management training techniques? In the study of senior managers who received executive coaching, how did their behavior change a year after the coaching?

17. Under what conditions does diversity training appear to lead to a decline in the number of minority employees in management positions? How do you explain these findings?

18. What factors can influence employee attitudes toward and participation in career development and planning activities?

19. What are the reasons for pursuing career self-management activities.

20. What conclusions can you draw about the necessity, value, extent, and worth of employee training programs?

Additional Reading

Fouad, N. A. (2007). Work and vocational psychology: Theory, research, and application. *Annual Review of Psychology, 58,* 543–564. Reviews the factors that affect career choice, including social and economic influences as well as gender, ethnicity, sexual orientation, and social class.

Killburg, R. R. (2000). *Executive coaching: Developing managerial wisdom in a world of chaos.* Washington, DC: American Psychological Association. A guide to the psychodymanics of executive behavior and job performance designed to help managers learn from mistakes and gain mastery over their organizationl roles.

Robinson, P., & Schiff, N. (2001). *If I don't do it now: Career makeovers for the working woman.* New York: Pocket Books. Practical advice for retraining women who want a new career.

Rothwell, W., & Kazanas, H. (2004). *Improving on-the-job training,* (2nd ed.). San Francisco: Jossey-Bass. Describes job training programs, key issues for managers, identifying work needs, training the trainers as well as the trainees, and evaluating results.

Salas, E., & Cannon-Bowers, J. A. (2001). The science of training. *Annual Review of Psychology, 52,* 471–499. Reviews training theory, need analysis, training and post-training conditions, and strategies for motivating trainees. Methods and instructional strategies discussed include distance learning, simulations, games, and team training.

PART THREE

Organizational Psychology

Organizational psychology focuses on the social and psychological climate at work. Few people work alone. Most of us work in groups, such as a crew on an assembly line or the staff of a department in a corporate office. We develop informal cliques that generate and reinforce standards, values, and attitudes that may differ from those of the organization. We are also influenced by the formal structure of the company that employs us. Like informal groups, these formal groups generate a psychological climate or culture of ideals and ideas that affect our feelings about our job. Thus, our attitudes and behaviors in the workplace are influenced by the social climate of the organization and the psychological characteristics of its members. Organizational psychologists study the relationships between these two sets of factors.

Leadership (chapter 7) is a major influence on work attitudes and behaviors. Organizational psychologists study the impact of various leadership styles and the characteristics and responsibilities of leaders.

Motivation, job satisfaction, and job involvement (chapter 8) relate to employee needs and the ways organizations can satisfy them. Employees identify with a job and with organizational goals, and the nature of this identification affects job performance and satisfaction.

Formal and informal groups and their psychological climate define the organization of an organization (chapter 9). Organizational style involves factors such as participatory democracy, adaptation to social and technological change, socialization of new employees, and efforts to improve the quality of working life.

Organizational psychology affects your working career directly. It influences your motivations, the style of leadership under which you function best, the leadership qualities you may display, and the structure of the organization for which you work. These factors determine the quality of your work experience, which, in turn, influences your general satisfaction with life.

CHAPTER 7

Leadership

THE QUALITY OF MODERN LEADERSHIP

Did you know that half of all new business ventures and start-up companies fail within their first 2 years? Did you know that only one third survive as long as 5 years? In most cases, these costly business failures can be traced to one source: poor leadership. And did you know that worker confidence in senior managers has declined to the point where only about one third of all employees trust the judgment of their company's executives?

Overall, survey and research results do not present a positive or favorable impression of leadership in the workplace today. More than half of all managers and executives may display, at times, some degree of incompetence. Thus, many employees—perhaps including you—probably work for someone who is an inept leader. Working for such a person can have a negative effect on how you perform your job and how you relate to the people and situations in your life off the job. Poor leadership hurts the company, too, by contributing to work slowdowns, poor customer service, sloppy work habits, and high absenteeism and turnover. The subordinates of a bad boss feel no commitment to their organization, report reduced job and life satisfaction, and experience high levels of stress.

In a poll of more than 700 people working at a variety of jobs, 31% said that their supervisor had sometimes given them the silent treatment, refusing to talk to them. In addition, 27% reported that their supervisor had made negative comments about them to co-workers or other managers, and 23% said they knew that their supervisors had blamed other people to cover up their own mistakes (Ray, 2006). These results and those of similar polls suggest that there are a lot of bad bosses in today's workplaces. But what do you think happens when bosses are surveyed about their own job performance? You guessed it. They think they're doing great. A 2007 poll of 2,000 managers conducted by *Business Week* reported that 90% believed they were in the top 10% of leaders in their organizations.

Although some leaders may be incompetent, others are clearly abusive. They may ridicule or berate subordinates in front of their co-workers or blame them for something they did not do. They may threaten to fire or demote them. Studies of abusive leaders in civilian and in military organizations, in the United States and in China, revealed that employees who face verbal abuse on the job develop anger and hatred toward their supervisors. They also resist their supervisors' requests and demands, express low levels of job and life satisfaction and high levels of stress, behave in counterproductive ways within the organization, and even become abusive in turn to their co-workers and family members (Aryee, Chen, Sun, & Debrah, 2007; Detert, Trevino, Burris, & Andiappan, 2007; Hoobler & Brass, 2006; Mitchell & Ambrose, 2007; Tepper, Moss, Lockhart, & Carr, 2007).

Abused workers are unhappy workers, and their organization is not functioning at its most productive or effective levels. On the other hand, consider the results of a meta-analysis of 106 studies involving more than 27,000 employees dealing with their level of trust in the organization's leadership. Employees who reported high levels of trust rated higher in job satisfaction, job performance, and organizational commitment (Dirks & Ferrin, 2002).

The quality of leadership is a critical factor in the workplace, in every worker's career, and in an organization's success or failure (Kaiser, Hogan, & Craig, 2008). It is not surprising, then, that organizations are greatly concerned with selecting, developing, and supporting their managers and executives and in making the best use of their leadership abilities on the job.

In addition to their research on selection and training, I-O psychologists have conducted considerable research on leadership techniques. They have explored the qualities and behaviors of successful and unsuccessful leaders, the effects of different leadership styles on subordinates, and the ways of maximizing leadership abilities.

Scientific Management

The ways in which leaders behave—the specific actions by which they play out their leadership roles—are based on certain assumptions about human nature. Consciously or unconsciously, leaders operate on the basis of some personal theory of human behavior, a view of what their subordinates are like as people. For example, managers who exercise close supervision on the job, who watch to make sure their employees are doing the work exactly as they have been instructed, hold a different

Newsbreak

When a Bad Boss Ruins Your Day

You've probably worked for someone like Ellen Brower at some time, or you've known someone who did. She is arrogant, abrasive, and abusive. She gets angry at the slightest provocation and chews out her employees in front of their colleagues, berating them as incompetent and stupid—and a lot worse. No matter how hard you work, no matter how good a job you do, it's never good enough. She's never satisfied.

You dread going to work, and maybe you have a headache or an upset stomach by the time you reach the office. You have trouble sleeping because of the stress at work, thanks to her. You plan to quit as soon as you can, but until then, you're likely to remain an unhappy employee who gets little from the job but a paycheck. And no amount of money, you tell yourself every day, is worth having to put up with a boss like her.

If you do work for someone like Ellen Brower, you're not alone. Psychologist Robert Hogan of the University of Tulsa says that as many as 7 of every 10 managers may be incompetent, exploiting, domineering, irritable, and untrustworthy. They refuse to delegate authority and have poor decision-making skills. In short, they are lousy bosses.

There are thousands of "bad boss" stories, like the one about the manager who would not let his employees phone for an ambulance when a co-worker collapsed at his desk with a heart attack. The boss insisted that they wait until quitting time so that they didn't disrupt the work routine! Besides, the boss said, "the guy was dead anyway." Or the insensitive department head who refused to believe a female employee who said she had missed work because she had suffered a miscarriage. He insisted that she obtain a written explanation from her physician. When she later requested bereavement leave to deal with her loss, he demanded to see the death certificate.

Approximately 75% of U.S. workers believe that the worst thing about their jobs, and the greatest single cause of stress, is their boss. The most common complaints from workers are that supervisors are unwilling to exercise authority, tyrannize subordinates, and treat employees as if they were stupid.

How did such incompetent people get to be in charge? Hogan says it's because many companies select their best workers and promote them to supervisory positions. The catch is that being the best worker may have nothing to do with having the skills and abilities needed for good leadership. "What these bad guys are good at," Hogan claims, "is sucking up to *their* boss. These people have good social skills. That's how they got their job." Clearly, it takes a lot more than social skills to make a good boss.

Source: A real piece of work: "Worst boss" contest lets employees vent (1997, October 16). *Washington Post*; Fishman, S. (2007, April 1). Boss science: The psychopathology of the modern American corporate leader, *New York Times Magazine*. Retrieved from nymag.com/guides/2007/officelife/30010/

view of human nature from that of managers who give their subordinates the freedom to work independently in whatever way they think best.

In the early years of the twentieth century, foremen (the first supervisory level over production workers) were promoted from the ranks of the workers and received little formal training for their leadership role. They had complete control over their subordinates' working lives. Foremen hired and fired, determined production levels, and set pay rates. There were few reins on their authority—no labor union, no industrial relations department, no human resources or personnel manager, no one to whom a worker could complain. Foremen usually gave hiring preference to their relatives and friends, and they applied a combination of autocratic behavior, aggression, and physical intimidation to force workers to meet production goals.

The management philosophy during that period was called **scientific management**, an approach promoted by Frederick W. Taylor, an engineer. Taylor's concern was finding ways to increase productivity by getting the workers and the machines they operated to run faster and more efficiently.

Scientific management regarded workers simply as extensions of the machinery they operated. No consideration was given to the employees as human beings, as people with different needs, abilities, and interests. Workers were considered to be lazy and dishonest and likely to have a low level of intelligence. This view was reinforced by research that psychologists were then conducting on the general level of intelligence in the U.S. population. The psychologist H. H. Goddard argued that people with low intelligence required supervision by people with greater intelligence. "Laborers," Goddard said, "are but little above the child [and] must be told what to do and shown how to do it" (Goddard quoted in Broad & Wade, 1982, p. 198). Therefore, the only way for an organization to increase productivity and efficiency was to compel workers to submit to the dictates of their supervisors and the requirements of the manufacturing process.

The Human Relations Approach to Leadership

It is difficult to imagine people working under the scientific management approach today. Most modern organizations regard the satisfaction of employee needs as a legitimate corporate responsibility. This changed view, called the human relations approach, arose in the 1920s and 1930s under the impact of the Hawthorne studies (discussed in chapter 1), which focused attention on workers instead of on the needs of the production equipment.

One change introduced into the work situation in the Hawthorne studies was the style of leadership. At the Hawthorne plant, workers had been dealt with harshly by supervisors who berated

them for dropping parts, talking on the job, and taking breaks. Workers had been treated like children who needed to be watched, shouted at, and punished. In the Hawthorne experiments, supervisors were trained to act differently—to allow workers to set their own production pace and to form social groups. Workers were permitted to talk to one another on the job, and their views about the work were solicited. The new supervisors treated them like human beings, not interchangeable cogs in some giant production machine.

Theory X and Theory Y

The scientific management and human relations approaches to leadership behavior were given formal expression by Douglas McGregor as Theory X and Theory Y (McGregor, 1960; see also Heil, Bennis, & Stephens, 2000). The **Theory X** approach to management assumes that most people are innately lazy and dislike work, avoiding it whenever they can. They must be coerced, watched, and scolded on the job to make them work hard enough to meet the organization's goals. Theory X assumes that most people have no ambition, avoid responsibility, and prefer to be led and directed. Indeed, they would not work at all without a dictatorial leader. Theory X is compatible with scientific management and with the classic organizational style known as **bureaucracy**.

Theory Y proposes that most people seek inner satisfaction and fulfillment from their work. Control and punishment are not necessary to bring about good job performance. According to Theory Y, then, people are industrious and creative and seek challenge and responsibility on the job. They function best under a leader who allows them to participate in setting and working toward personal and organizational goals. The Theory Y viewpoint is compatible with the human relations movement in management and with the participative, democratic style of organization. An example of the application of Theory Y is the management by

Early yrs of 20th century

Contingency theory A leadership theory in which a leader's effectiveness is determined by the interaction between the leader's personal characteristics and the characteristics of the leadership situation.

Path–goal theory A leadership theory that focuses on the kinds of behaviors leaders should exercise to allow their subordinates to achieve personal and organizational goals.

objectives (MBO) approach to performance appraisal (see chapter 5). MBO involves a high degree of employee participation in setting goals for job performance and personal growth.

The theoretical distinctions McGregor proposed have long been recognized as useful. How well have they been applied in the workplace? A contemporary scholar wrote that the Theory X view still persists, that is, the "view that workers are ordinarily passive and resistant to the legitimate expectations of management." But, he added, "McGregor's humanistic vision of organizations [his Theory Y concept] is closer to realization today than ever before" (Jacobs, 2004, pp. 293, 295).

LEADERSHIP THEORIES

I-O psychologists recognize that effective leadership depends on the interaction of three factors: the traits and behaviors of the leaders, the characteristics of the followers, and the nature of the situation in which leadership occurs. We describe several theoretical explanations of leadership: contingency theory, path–goal theory, leader–member exchange, and implicit leadership theory.

Contingency Theory

In **contingency theory**, developed by Fred Fiedler (Fiedler, 1978), leadership effectiveness is determined by the interaction between the leader's personal characteristics and aspects of the situation. Leaders are classified as primarily person-oriented or task-oriented. The type of leader who will be the more effective depends on the leader's degree of control over the situation.

Control is contingent on three factors: the relationship between the leader and followers, the degree of task structure, and the leader's authority or position power. If leaders are popular with their followers, are directing a highly structured or routine task, and have the authority or power to enforce discipline, then they have a high degree of control over the situation. This condition may be

described as favorable. For example, army sergeants who get along well with the soldiers in their squad are high-control and effective leaders.

On the other hand, if an unpopular president of a social club that has no formal goals has no authority to require attendance or collect dues, that president is a low-control leader in an unfavorable situation. According to contingency theory, the task-oriented leader will be more effective in extremely favorable or extremely unfavorable situations. When the situation is moderately favorable, the person-oriented leader will be more effective.

Contingency theory has stimulated a great deal of research, some of which is supportive and encouraging. However, most of that research was conducted in laboratory settings, not on the job. The validity of contingency theory remains in question, but over the years it has generated a great deal of theoretical and methodological inquiry (see, for example, Vroom & Jago, 2007).

Path–Goal Theory

The **path–goal theory** of leadership focuses on the kinds of behaviors a leader exercises to allow subordinates to achieve their goals. The theory states that leaders can increase their subordinates' motivation, satisfaction, and job performance by administering rewards that depend on the achievement of particular goals. In other words, effective leaders help employees reach personal and organizational goals by pointing out the paths they should follow and by providing them with the means to do so.

Four styles that leaders can adopt to facilitate employee attainment of goals are as follows (House, 1971; House & Mitchell, 1974):

- *Directive leadership.* The leader tells subordinates what they should do and how they should do it.

- *Supportive leadership.* The leader shows concern and support for subordinates.

Leader–member exchange A leadership theory that focuses on how the leader–follower relationship affects the leadership process.

- *Participative leadership.* The leader allows subordinates to participate in decisions that affect their work.
- *Achievement-oriented leadership.* The leader sets challenging goals for subordinates and emphasizes high levels of job performance.

The leadership style that will be most effective depends on characteristics of the situation and the attributes of the subordinates. Leaders must be flexible and should choose whichever style is called for. For example, employees who have a low level of the skills required to perform a task will function better under directive leadership. Employees who have high skills need less direction and function better under supportive leadership. Leaders must be able to perceive accurately the nature of the situation and the abilities of their subordinates and respond with the most appropriate approach.

Research findings on the path–goal theory are contradictory to date, but I-O psychologists are continuing to test and refine the theory.

Leader–Member Exchange

The **leader–member exchange** model deals with the ways in which the leader–follower relationship (the leader–member exchange, or LMX) affects the leadership process (Graen & Schliemann, 1978). The proponents of this model have criticized other leadership theories for focusing on average leadership styles or behaviors and for ignoring individual differences among subordinates. The relationship between each leader–subordinate pair (or dyad) must be considered separately because leaders behave differently with each subordinate.

Subordinates are of two types: the in-group employees, whom the supervisor views as competent, trustworthy, and highly motivated, and the out-group employees, whom the supervisor views as incompetent, untrustworthy, and poorly motivated. The LMX model also distinguishes two leadership styles: supervision, in which leadership is based on formal authority, and leadership, in which

influence is exerted through persuasion. With out-group subordinates, leaders use supervision and assign tasks requiring low levels of ability and responsibility. There is little personal relationship between leaders and out-group members.

With in-group subordinates, leaders practice leadership rather than supervision and assign members important and responsible tasks that require high levels of ability. Leaders and in-group members establish personal relationships in which in-group subordinates provide support and understanding.

On-the-job research has generally supported the leader–member exchange model for various levels of management. Research has shown that the quality of the leader–subordinate relationship can be improved through training, resulting in the display of more leadership than supervision. Significant improvements in job satisfaction and productivity and decreases in errors have been found among subordinates as a result of training to improve the quality of the LMX.

Studies of worker–supervisor dyads in a medical center and in a distribution company found that employees who believed they had a high LMX with their supervisors also believed they communicated with them more frequently than did those who believed they had a low LMX. In addition, employees in high LMX relationships who communicated frequently with their managers received higher performance ratings than did those in low LMX relationships who communicated frequently with their managers (Kacmar, Witt, Ziunuska, & Gully, 2003; Yrle, Hartman, & Galle, 2002).

Research conducted in China found that high LMX encouraged subordinates to seek out negative feedback from their supervisors about how they were performing their jobs. Because of the high LMX, the employees felt secure enough in their relationship with their boss to not only accept criticism but to actively ask for it (Chen, Lam, & Zhong, 2007).

Studies in companies in the United States showed that high LMX led to employees' high feelings of empowerment, both at individual and team levels. That appeared to lead, in turn, to greater job satisfaction and improved performance (Chen, Kirkman, Kanfer, Allen, & Rosen, 2007). Other research demonstrated that the higher the LMX, the more employees exhibited "organizational citizenship behavior," which refers to activities that go beyond the scope of the job and which are designed to enhance organizational performance as a whole (Ilies, Nahrgang, & Morgeson, 2007).

High LMX has also been shown to enhance employee attitudes toward both the organization and its customers and clients (Tangirala, Green, & Ramanujam, 2007). Additional research related high LMX to increased job satisfaction and performance among virtual employees who spent at least one fourth of their time telecommuting; thus they spent considerable time out of the office and away from direct contact with their leaders (Golden & Veiga, 2008).

Several factors have been found to influence the level of leader–member exchange. LMX is higher when a group's workers and leaders are of the same gender and when they share the same growth-need strength, that is, the need for achievement and accomplishment (Huang & Iun, 2006; Vecchio & Brazil, 2007). Personality also affects leader–member exchange. In one study LMX showed no relation to job performance for employees who

---

Newsbreak

Please Hold for the Deputy Assistant to the Assistant Deputy . . .

Suppose you were offered the following choice. Either a $2,000 pay raise or a new job title with the word *manager* in it—not a new job, just a new title. Which would you choose? When the president of On-Line Systems offered his sales force that choice, the $2,000 or the title "sales manager" instead of "salesman," almost everyone opted for the new label.

"The thing that makes people stay," he said, "is not necessarily money. Why do they stay, day after day, coming back to you? It's because they're happy. A showy title makes them feel appreciated."

Employees especially like ego-boosting titles that include the words *manager* or *director*. Managers get their phone calls returned. Clients respond faster to their e-mails and faxes than they do to those from someone with a lower level title. Being a manager means never being put on hold. All those advantages will make them more productive.

Companies that recruit on college campuses are aware of this phenomenon and have been upgrading the job titles for their starting positions. Instead of seeking a "sales representative," they want a candidate for their "management leadership development program." Same job, but different label. The result? Many more job applicants.

A sampling of ego-inflating job titles in major U.S. corporations include the following:

- Chief responsibility officer
- Chief vision officer
- Chief learning officer in charge of training
- Chief beer officer (for a major hotel chain) [Note: Some 5,500 people applied for this job!]

Nowhere is title inflation more blatant than in government bureaucracy. Consider these numbers at the federal level in Washington, DC:

484 deputy assistant secretaries

148 associate assistant secretaries

220 assistant assistant secretaries

82 deputy assistant assistant secretaries

Paul Light, a senior fellow at the Brookings Institution, who studies what he calls "job title creep," joked about his own job. He said that he needs to have a chief of staff, "but I won't really be somebody until I have a *deputy* chief of staff."

Source: Please hold for the Deputy Deputy (1999, March 14). *New York Times;* Needleman, S. (2007, December 26). What's in a title? Ego stroking, chiefly, *Wall Street Journal.*

Implicit leadership theory   A leadership theory that describes a good leader in terms of one's past experiences with different types of leaders.

scored high in extraversion; in contrast, employees who scored low in extraversion were influenced negatively by lower LMX levels. The researchers concluded that introverts have a greater need than do extraverts for leader support in order to perform well on the job (Bauer, Erdogan, Liden, & Wayne, 2006).

Other research has shown that when supervisors believed they were supported by their organization, a concept described in the study as perceived organizational support (POS), they were more supportive of their subordinates. This, in turn, enhanced LMX as well as subordinates' job satisfaction and performance. In other words, supervisors who felt supported by their superiors behaved in ways to support their subordinates, which improved the leader–member exchange (Erdogan & Enders, 2007; Shanock & Eisenberger, 2006). These on-the-job research findings have given the leader–member exchange model a practical advantage over most other leadership theories.

Implicit Leadership Theory

Implicit leadership theory defines leadership from the standpoint of the persons who are being led. According to this view, each of us develops, through our past experiences with different types of leaders, our own implicit theory or image of the ideal leader. If our new manager or boss fits that ideal view or perception, then we will consider him or her to be a good leader. If not, we will consider the new boss to be a poor leader (Lord, Brown, & Freiburg, 1999; Lord & Maher, 1993).

This theory suggests that anyone can be classified as a good leader if that person is perceived by subordinates as fitting their mental image of a good leader's personality. Thus, leadership would be highly subjective. There would be no objective criteria or characteristics that define a person as a good or bad leader. Instead, a person is only a good leader if his or her behavior matches our expectations.

Suppose, for example, that your experiences in the workplace have led you to believe that the ideal manager is kind and considerate and asks for your opinion before making decisions that affect your work environment. This type of leader may make you feel more like a partner than a subordinate. When your new boss turns out to be an authoritarian bureaucrat, you are likely to decide that he or she is not a good leader. A co-worker, however, may have thrived under a different kind of leader; perhaps this employee likes to be told what to do and does not want to participate in decision making. This co-worker may view the new boss as a good leader. According to the implicit leadership theory, then, it appears that great leaders exist only in the eyes of the beholder, that is, in the perceptions of their followers.

It does not follow, however, that a manager could display almost any type of behavior and still be perceived by someone among the subordinates as a good leader. In practical terms, legitimate leadership behavior is limited to attributes that are considered acceptable in the workplace. In a study of 939 workers in a variety of industries in England, a paper-and-pencil test was developed to measure implicit theories of leadership. The results identified four traits associated with good leadership and two traits associated with bad leadership. The positive characteristics were sensitivity, intelligence, dedication, and dynamism. The negative characteristics were tyranny and masculinity. These positive and negative attributes were consistent with employees at all working ages, career stages, and levels of employment (Epitropaki & Martin, 2004). Implicit personality theory is an unusual approach to leadership. Its usefulness in the workplace has yet to be determined.

LEADERSHIP STYLES

Much I-O psychology research focuses on leadership styles and the behaviors by which they are manifested on the job. Organizations are led by several types of leaders: authoritarian and democratic, transactional and transformational, and charismatic.

Authoritarian leadership   A leadership style in which a leader makes all decisions and tells followers what to do.

Democratic leadership   A leadership style in which a leader and followers discuss problems and make decisions jointly.

Transactional leadership   A leadership style that focuses on the social interactions between leaders and followers, based on followers' perceptions of and expectations about the leader's abilities.

Authoritarian and Democratic Leaders

Leadership in the workplace involves various styles along a continuum. The continuum ranges from a highly **authoritarian leadership** style, in which the leader makes all decisions and tells followers what to do, to a highly **democratic leadership** style, in which leader and followers discuss problems and jointly make all decisions that affect their work. The style that is most effective depends on the nature of the situation and the needs and characteristics of the followers.

In stressful work situations that require unusually rapid and highly efficient job performance, productivity and satisfaction are more likely to be maintained under authoritarian leadership. I-O psychologists suggest that employees who work under such conditions recognize that the nature of their work does not allow time for a participative approach. For example, firefighters must respond to a fire alarm immediately and follow the directions of their chief. They do not have time to hold a committee meeting to determine the best way to deal with the fire.

For police officers, who hold stressful jobs that require rapid decision-making skills and efficient job performance, authoritarian leadership is desirable. Often, law enforcement situations do not allow time for a more democratic approach.

Transactional and Transformational Leaders

Transactional leaders conduct their business by identifying the needs of their followers and bestowing rewards to satisfy those needs in exchange for a certain level of performance. Adhering to the path–goal theory, transactional leaders are expected to do the following: "set goals, articulate explicit agreements regarding what the leader expects from organizational members and how they will be rewarded for their efforts and commitment, and provide constructive feedback to keep everybody on task" (Vera & Crossan, 2004, p. 224).

Transactional leaders focus on increasing the efficiency of established routines and procedures and are more concerned with following existing rules than with making changes to the structure of the organization. Thus, they operate most effectively in organizations that have evolved beyond the chaotic, no-rules stage of entrepreneurial development that characterizes so many new companies. Transactional leadership establishes and standardizes practices that will help the organization reach maturity, emphasizing setting of goals, efficiency of operation, and increase of productivity.

Transformational leaders have more latitude in their behavior. They are not limited by their followers' perceptions. Rather than believing that they must act in accordance with what their followers expect of them, transformational leaders work to change or transform their followers' needs and redirect their thinking.

Transformational leaders challenge and inspire subordinates with a sense of purpose and excitement about what can be accomplished. These leaders create a vision of what the corporate culture can be and communicate it to their employees, stimulating them to develop their abilities while accepting feedback and suggestions. In a study of nearly 200 managers (from supervisors to CEOs) in a wide variety of industries, researchers found that transformational leaders scored higher on the personality factors of extraversion and agreeableness than did non-transformational leaders (Judge & Bono, 2000). A meta-analysis of 45 leadership studies showed that women are far more likely than men to be transformational leaders (Eagly, Johannesen-Schmidt, & Van Engen, 2003).

Studies of business executives, high-ranking military officers, and high-level administrators in government and universities have found that those described by their subordinates as transformational leaders were more effective on the job. They also had better relations with superiors and made greater contributions to organizational goals than did those described as transactional leaders. Employees reported that they worked harder for transformational leaders than for transactional leaders, were rated higher in job performance, and enjoyed greater job satisfaction (Bono & Anderson, 2005; Keller, 2006; Nemanich & Keller, 2007; Schaubroeck, Lam, & Cha, 2007).

Employees who worked for transformational leaders reported feeling more optimistic and enthusiastic on the job and rated their work more challenging and important. They also scored higher in psychological well-being than did employees working for transactional leaders (Arnold, Turner, Barling, Kelloway, & McKee, 2007; Bono, Foldes, Vinson, & Muros, 2007; Piccolo & Colquitt, 2006).

Research studies support the idea that transformational leaders are more effective in securing their subordinates' commitment to organizational changes and to achieving organizational goals (Colbert, Kristof-Brown, Bradley, & Barrick, 2008; Herold, Fedor, Caldwell, & Liu, 2008). Other research has demonstrated that transformational leaders inspire feelings of worker empowerment and identification with the leader and the work unit. They also motivate subordinates to think and act in ways beyond what they considered possible, thus bringing out the subordinates' best qualities. Transformational leadership is capable of producing greater creativity among subordinates as well as a belief in the importance of

their tasks (Bass, Avolio, Jung, & Berson, 2003; Bono & Judge, 2003; Kark, Shamir, & Chen, 2003; Shin & Zhou, 2003). The greater effectiveness of transformational leaders has been demonstrated in a wide range of employing organizations and in several countries including the United States, India, Spain, Japan, China, and Austria.

Charismatic Leaders

Often, transformational leaders display **charismatic leadership**. Charismatic leaders have a broad knowledge of their field, a self-promoting personality, a high energy level, and a willingness to take risks and use unconventional strategies. They use their power effectively to serve others and inspire their trust. Charismatic leaders stimulate their followers to think independently and to ask questions. They maintain open communication with subordinates and freely share recognition with them. They tend to generate high job performance and positive work attitudes among their followers.

Charismatic leaders also communicate a vision to their followers. They act to implement that vision, and they display a powerful communications style, such as a captivating tone of voice, animated facial expressions, and a dynamic way of interacting with other people. Research involving 115 employees and 32 managers in a government agency in the Netherlands demonstrated a high positive correlation between charismatic leadership, as perceived by subordinates, and employees' feelings of belongingness (Den Hartog, De Hoogh, & Keegan, 2007).

In a study of 25 middle-level managers at a cell phone company in Germany, investigators found that the managers could be trained to become more inspirational leaders. The training program, which lasted a day and a half, involved instruction in charismatic leadership behaviors and in preparing and delivering inspirational speeches. Feedback, both positive and negative, was offered on the content and delivery of speeches (Frese, Beimel, & Schoenborn, 2003).

Charismatic leaders are the ones who launch new enterprises, direct organizational change, and stimulate impressive gains in employee productivity. But charismatic leaders can also misuse their power over others. They can be insensitive to the needs of their followers and act only for personal gain.

THE ROLE OF POWER

Power in leadership behavior may be manifested in two ways: (1) the power that leaders have over their subordinates and (2) the power that motivates leaders. Leaders may exert different kinds of power, depending on the situation, the nature of their followers, and their personal characteristics.

Types of Power

Psychologists have proposed five types of leadership power (Yukl & Taber, 1983). These are the first three:

1. *Reward power.* Organizational leaders have the ability to reward subordinates with pay raises and promotions. This power gives leaders a means of control over employees and can affect employee behavior.

2. *Coercive power.* Organizational leaders have an equally strong source of power in their ability to punish subordinates by firing them, by withholding promotions and raises, and by keeping them in undesirable jobs.

3. *Legitimate power.* Legitimate power derives from the organization's formal power structure. The hierarchy of control legitimizes the right of the leader to direct and supervise the activities of followers and the duty of followers to accept that supervision.

These three sources of power are derived from and defined by the formal organization to which leaders and subordinates belong. They are types of power dictated or prescribed by the organization. The next two types of power derive from the leaders themselves and are earned or merited by the leaders' personal characteristics as these are perceived by followers. We might call these attributes *respect* as well as power.

4. *Referent power.* Referent power refers to the degree to which employees identify with their leaders and the leaders' goals, accept those

goals as their own, and work with their leaders to achieve the goals.

5. *Expert power.* Expert power refers to the extent to which leaders are believed to have the skills necessary to attain the group's goals. If employees acknowledge their leader's expertise, then they are more likely to become willing and supportive subordinates.

Uses of Power

As you may know from your own experience, coercive power can be counterproductive. Leaders who rely primarily on coercive power in dealing with subordinates are less likely to be effective than are leaders who exercise the other types of power. People who work for coercive leaders tend to rank low in job satisfaction, productivity, and commitment to the organization. In order, the types of leadership power that research has shown to be most effective are expert power, legitimate power, and referent power.

How does power motivate organizational leaders? High-level executives and middle-level managers often show a great personal need for power. Effective managers tend to demonstrate a higher need for power than do less effective managers. However, the most effective managers do not seek power for personal gain. Their power need is directed toward the organization and is used to achieve organizational goals. As a result, they are usually successful in establishing and maintaining a good work climate, high morale, and high team spirit among their subordinates.

Managers motivated by the need for personal power serve themselves rather than their organization. They are capable of creating loyalty among subordinates, but it is a loyalty toward them, not toward the organization. These managers are more effective than those who show no need for power, but they are not as effective as those whose power is oriented toward the organization.

THE ROLE OF EXPECTATIONS

Leaders' expectations about their employees' job performance can influence that performance. For example, managers who expect high performance tend to get high performance, and those who expect poor performance tend to get poor performance.

Pygmalion effect A self-fulfilling prophecy in which managers' expectations about the level of their employees' job performance can influence that performance.

Consideration leadership functions Leadership behaviors that involve awareness of and sensitivity to the feelings of subordinates.

Initiating structure leadership functions Leadership behaviors concerned with organizing, defining, and directing the work activities of subordinates.

This type of self-fulfilling prophecy was first observed in the classroom. In a classic demonstration, teachers were told that some of their students had a high level of potential and others had a low level of potential. In reality, there were no such differences between the two groups; the students were equal in their abilities. The differences existed only in the teachers' expectations, as created by the experimental situation. Yet, the group of students with the allegedly high potential later scored significantly higher on IQ tests than did the other group. The teachers had subtly communicated their expectations to their students, thereby affecting the students' academic performance (Rosenthal & Jacobson, 1968).

This expectancy effect was labeled the **Pygmalion effect**, named after Pygmalion, a king of Cyprus who fell in love with an ivory statue of a beautiful woman named Galatea. In answer to Pygmalion's prayers, the statue came alive, turning his fantasy into reality.

The self-fulfilling prophecy has been widely demonstrated in the workplace. A meta-analysis of 17 studies involving nearly 3,000 employees in a variety of jobs showed that the phenomenon was particularly strong in the military. The self-fulfilling prophecy was more prevalent among men than women. It was also found extensively among disadvantaged employees—those employees considered by management, and by themselves, to have low expectations (McNatt, 2000); their job performance usually matched their expectations. Other research involving 30 squads of soldiers in the Israel Defense Force (the Israeli army) confirmed these findings. Women recruits who were held in low esteem by their female superior officers tended to perform poorly (Davidson & Eden, 2000).

Expectations of co-workers can also influence employees. A study of 166 engineers, software development specialists, research scientists, physicians, and pharmacists in Taiwan showed that when they believed their co-workers expected them to be creative, their own self-reported identity as a creative person was higher than when co-workers had no such expectations (Farmer, Tierney, & Kung-McIntyre, 2003).

Researchers who conducted a survey of 584 blue-collar workers and 158 white-collar workers found that employees came to believe they had creative abilities on the job when their supervisor served as a model and used verbal persuasion to enhance employee self-confidence and expectations. In other words, the supervisor can create a self-fulfilling prophecy among the workers that they can be more creative, which has the effect of leading to an actual increase in creativity on the job (Tierney & Farmer, 2002).

LEADERSHIP FUNCTIONS

A comprehensive research program to identify the functions of leaders on the job identified a variety of leadership tasks and behaviors and grouped them in two categories: **consideration** and **initiating structure** (Fleishman & Harris, 1962).

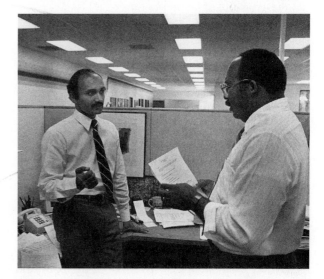

Effective managers balance consideration behaviors (sensitivity to subordinates' needs) with initiating structure behaviors (providing a framework within which to meet the company's goals).

The Consideration Dimension

The functions in the consideration dimension involve awareness of and sensitivity to the feelings of subordinates. These functions are allied with the human relations approach to management. Leaders high in consideration understand and accept subordinates as individuals with unique motivations and needs. Successful leaders must relate to each employee by being considerate of that person's feelings. This necessarily places an additional burden on managers. They must be sympathetic, warm, and understanding of their employees while maintaining production levels and other organizational goals.

The effects of such consideration behaviors on employees can have highly beneficial results for leaders and their organizations. In a study of 115 employees of a credit union, investigators found that when disagreements occurred between managers and employees, those managers who communicated openly and showed concern for their workers were perceived as more trustworthy and were less likely to be blamed for the disagreement. Employees who worked for managers who were perceived as trustworthy were far more likely to make contributions to their organizations beyond job requirements, as compared to employees who did not find their managers to be trustworthy (Korsgaard, Brodt, & Whitener, 2002).

Note the similarity between the consideration leadership function and the leadership styles proposed by some of the theories described earlier in this chapter. High consideration relates to the person-oriented leader in contingency theory, to participative leadership in path–goal theory, and to the leadership condition in the leader–member exchange model.

Newsbreak

The Company Canoe Race

A Japanese company and an American company decided to have a canoe race on the Missouri River. Each company's team practiced long and hard to reach peak performance before the race. On the day of the race, the Japanese company's team won by a mile.

The American company's team was crushed; they felt discouraged and depressed. The company's management prepared a mission statement and made it their goal to uncover the reason for the defeat. A measurement team of senior management personnel was formed. They would investigate and recommend appropriate action.

They found that the Japanese company's team had eight people rowing and one person steering, whereas their team (the American company) had one person rowing and eight people steering. So the American company hired a consulting firm for an enormous amount of money to advise them. The consulting company concluded that too many people were steering the boat and not enough people were rowing.

To prevent another humiliating loss to the Japanese company's team the following year, the American company's rowing team was reorganized. The new management structure included four steering managers, three area-steering superintendents, and one assistant area-steering superintendent liaison. The group then implemented a new performance system intended to give the one person rowing the boat greater incentives to work harder. The system was called the Rowing Team Quality-First Program, designed to give the rower empowerment and job enrichment. The program was kicked off with meetings, dinners, and free pens and T-shirts for the rower.

The next year, the Japanese company's team won the boat race by two miles. The American company's management fired the rower for poor performance, halted funds for the development of a new canoe, sold the paddles, and canceled capital investment for new equipment. They gave awards for high performance to the steering managers and distributed the money saved as bonuses to the senior executives.

Source: An Internet legend of unknown source, provided by Marty Salo.

The Initiating Structure Dimension

The functions in the initiating structure dimension include tasks traditionally associated with a leadership role—organizing, defining, and directing the work activities of subordinates. Sometimes this aspect of a manager's job conflicts with the demands of the consideration dimension. To accomplish a job (to initiate structure), managers must assign specific tasks to employees, direct the way in which the tasks should be performed, and monitor the work to ensure that it is being done properly.

Such work activities may call for some authoritarian behavior and decision making, and there may not be time or opportunity for leaders to consider their subordinates' needs or feelings. A certain amount of work must be accomplished at a specified level of quality in a fixed time. The organization's success and the manager's job depend on meeting these standards consistently. Thus, it is not always easy for managers to balance the behaviors of consideration and initiating structure.

The leadership functions in the initiating structure dimension are similar to those of the task-oriented leader in contingency theory, directive leadership in path–goal theory, autocracy in normative decision theory, and supervision in the leader–member exchange model.

Although the consideration and initiation dimensions were developed more than 50 years ago, recent research reveals that they remain valid descriptors of leadership behavior. In a meta-analysis of 322 studies, researchers found that consideration showed a significant positive correlation with the quality of the leader's performance and the performance of his or her group or organization. Initiating structure was related to leader satisfaction and to group performance. Taken together, both dimensions were linked to leader effectiveness and to the subordinates' level of motivation (Judge, Piccolo, & Ilies, 2004).

CHARACTERISTICS OF SUCCESSFUL LEADERS

The characteristics required for successful leadership vary with a manager's level in the organizational hierarchy. The CEO of an automobile manufacturing company performs different functions and thus needs different abilities from those of a supervisor on the auto-painting assembly line. In general, the

A first-line supervisor at an automobile plant meets with subordinates to discuss problems and hear grievances.

higher the position on the corporate ladder, the fewer consideration activities and the more initiating structure activities are required. A high-level executive needs fewer human relations skills than a supervisor, because the executive typically controls and interacts directly with fewer subordinates. The corporate vice president may deal with only a half-dozen department heads, whereas the first-line supervisor may have 100 or more workers to manage. Therefore, leaders at different levels have different functions, characteristics, and problems on the job.

First-Line Supervisors

I-O psychology research on first-line supervisors suggests that supervisors with the most productive work groups have the following qualities:

- Effective supervisors are person-centered. They rate higher in the consideration function than do unsuccessful supervisors.
- Effective supervisors are supportive. They are more helpful to employees and more willing to defend them against criticism from higher management than are less effective supervisors.
- Effective supervisors are democratic. They hold frequent meetings with employees to solicit their views and encourage participation. Less effective supervisors are more autocratic.

- Effective supervisors are flexible. They allow employees to accomplish their goals in their own way whenever possible, consistent with the goals of the organization. Less effective supervisors dictate how a job is to be performed and permit no deviation.
- Effective supervisors describe themselves as coaches rather than directors. They emphasize quality, provide clear directions, and give timely feedback to their workers.

Managers and Executives

At higher levels of an organization, managers and executives engage in fewer consideration behaviors and more initiating structure behaviors. In other words, they are less people-oriented and more work-oriented. Successful executives share other characteristics. We discuss the impact of college attendance, personality, the role of power, and the importance of mentoring. We also note the characteristics of unsuccessful executives.

College Experience and Intelligence. College attendance correlates positively with later job success at the executive level. Employees with a college background rise faster and higher through the management ranks than do those who did not attend college. College grades correlate positively with assessment-center ratings of management potential and later advancement on the job. People who earn higher grades in college show greater potential for promotion, obtain their first promotion early in their career, and rise higher in management than those who earn lower grades. The quality of the college attended is a less useful predictor of later job performance.

A more valid predictor of potential and actual promotion is college major. Those who major in humanities and social sciences receive superior ratings in assessment-center exercises and job performance and move faster and farther up the corporate ladder. Those who major in business administration rank second. Mathematics, science, and engineering majors are third. Humanities and social science majors excel in decision making, creativity in solving business problems, intellectual ability, written communications skills, and motivation for advancement. They, and the business majors, rank higher in interpersonal skills, leadership ability, oral communications skills, and flexibility than the math, science, and engineering majors.

For many years it was thought, or assumed, that intelligence was highly related to leadership, that leaders were characteristically more intelligent than their subordinates. Recent research does not support this assumption. Studies have shown a low correlation between intelligence and leadership. In other words, intellectual abilities have not been found to be significantly related to the prediction of performance in leadership positions (see, for example, Fiedler, 2002; Judge, Colbert, & Ilies, 2004).

Personality. Various aspects of personality, especially the Big Five factors, have been related to job performance. Psychologists studied 17 chief executive officers of major corporations. They found personality to be an important component of job success at the highest level of management. The factor of conscientiousness was related to a sense of control among the CEOs' top management teams. The factor of emotional stability influenced team cohesion and intellectual flexibility. Agreeableness on the part of the CEO was related to the top management team's feeling of cohesion. Extraversion was related to leader dominance. Openness to experience was related to team risk taking (Peterson, Smith, Martorana, & Owens, 2003).

A study of managers in China found that, in contrast to most of the results of research conducted in the United States, the Big Five personality factors were not useful predictors of effective leadership on the job. Among the Chinese managers, for example, extraversion was negatively related to leadership, contrary to the findings of studies with U.S. managers. This finding supports the suggestion of cultural differences in the characteristics of successful leaders (Shao & Webber, 2006).

In a study of 571 bank tellers employed by the same firm in the Hong Kong office and the U.S. office, investigators found that managers were far more likely to form relationships of high trust and commitment with subordinates when the subordinates' personalities were similar to their own. Thus, similarity in personality was shown to lead to a high leader–member exchange (Schaubroeck & Lam, 2002).

The Role of Power. Power is an important motivating force for successful executives. In a classic study, psychologist David McClelland proposed a leadership motive pattern (LMP), informally described as empire building. Executives with a high LMP are believed to be effective managers. They have a high need for power, a lower need for affiliation with other people, and considerable self-control. They have a greater need to influence people than to be liked (McClelland, 1975).

Research on the LMP found it to be highly predictive of success for managers in nontechnical jobs. The managers' need for achievement (the need to perform well) also predicted success in nontechnical positions. In addition, managers high in the LMP prefer jobs that are high in prestige and status.

Mentoring. People who acquire the support or sponsorship of mentors within the company are often the ones more likely to advance in the corporate hierarchy. A mentor is a coach or counselor who provides support and advice to a younger protégé. Managers fortunate enough to have had good mentors are far more likely to receive pay increases and promotions, compared to those who do not have mentors. A meta-analysis of 43 studies supported the career-enhancing value of career mentoring, which focuses on aspects of the work, and of psychosocial mentoring, which involves role modeling, counseling, and friendship. Employees who received mentoring had more positive attitudes toward their job and organization and were more successful in terms of promotions and pay raises than were employees who did not receive mentoring (Allen, Eby, Poteet, Lentz, & Lima, 2004).

Studies in U.S. organizations have indicated that the quality and effectiveness of the mentoring provided to employees by their managers can be improved with appropriate training. Also, allowing both managers and subordinates to participate in the process of matching mentor to employee can be helpful (Allen, Eby, & Lentz, 2006; Heslin, Vanderwalle, & Latham, 2006).

Unsuccessful Executives. It is just as important for organizations to know what characteristics lead some managers to fail as it is to understand what makes others succeed. Such failure is usually referred to as "derailment," such as when a train unexpectedly leaves the track.

Executives who once showed management potential but who are later dismissed or retired early typically fail because of personality factors rather than job performance. Derailed executives are judged by their superiors to lack consideration behaviors. Insensitive, arrogant, and aloof, they display an abrasive and domineering leadership style and are overly ambitious to attain personal rather than organizational goals.

One I-O psychologist described unsuccessful executives in terms of flaws or fallacies in their thinking (Sternberg, 2003):

- *Unrealistic optimism fallacy:* Believing they are so smart that they can do whatever they want
- *Egocentrism fallacy:* Believing they are the only ones who matter, that the people who work for them don't count
- *Omniscience fallacy:* Believing they know everything and seeing no limits to their knowledge
- *Omnipotence fallacy:* Believing they are all-powerful and therefore entitled to do what they want
- *Invulnerability fallacy:* Believing they can get away with doing what they want because they are too clever to get caught; even if they are caught, believing they will go unpunished because of their importance

PRESSURES AND PROBLEMS OF LEADERS

First-Line Supervisors

Just as leadership characteristics vary with a manager's level in the organizational hierarchy, so do the pressures and problems. In some ways, first-line supervisors have more difficult jobs than executives, yet they receive less formal training in how to manage other people. In fact, supervisors may receive no training at all, and they are not selected as carefully as people who begin their careers at higher level management positions. Often, the most competent workers are chosen to be supervisors, without any assessment of their leadership potential.

Supervisors promoted from the ranks face conflicting demands and loyalties. Before promotion, they were accepted by those who worked with them and shared their attitudes and values. They may have socialized with co-workers off the job. Their work group gave them a sense of identity and belonging that provided a measure of emotional security.

After they become supervisors, they can no longer enjoy the same relationship with co-workers

Self-managing work teams   Employee groups that allow the members of a work team to manage, control, and monitor all facets of their work, from recruiting, hiring, and training new employees to deciding when to take rest breaks.

and friends. Even if they try to remain part of the group, their former co-workers do not respond to them in the same way because of the changed relationship. This costs newly promoted supervisors the emotional security that comes from group affiliation and identification.

Supervisors are the point of contact between management and workers; they try to weigh the conflicting needs of both sides. If supervisors expect to establish and retain the loyalty and cooperation of their workers, they must present management's needs and decisions to the workers and must present the workers' needs to management, thereby serving as a buffer and an open channel of communication. In practice, often supervisors must be more responsive to the demands of their superiors if they hope to keep their jobs.

The trend toward increased worker participation complicates the job of first-line supervisors. They stand to lose what little autonomy they have by being forced to share leadership and decision-making power with subordinates. **Self-managing work teams** are another threat to supervisory power and autonomy. In these programs, instead of sharing power, supervisors must abandon their traditional responsibilities and act as resource persons rather than leaders. If the work groups are less effective than expected, the supervisor will be blamed. If the work groups are effective, top management usually attributes the favorable results to the workers, not to the supervisor.

A study was conducted of 102 management teams, each consisting of a manager and at least two employees, in a large U.S. hotel chain. Leader behaviors believed to be empowering (such as leading by example, coaching, expressing concern for the team, and allowing participative decision making) correlated positively with overall team performance. The more the managers displayed empowering behaviors toward their subordinates, the more effectively the team performed its job (Srivastava, Bartol, & Locke, 2006).

Computer technology in the workplace has also made supervision more difficult. First-line supervisors are responsible for hardware they often are not trained to understand. In addition, computers can control and monitor quantity and quality of production and provide top management with data on employee performance, output, and other aspects of office or manufacturing processes, thus bypassing any input from the first-line supervisor.

Managers and Executives

A department or section head faces stresses that are different from those of the CEO. Middle-level managers, despite comfortable salaries and fringe benefits, typically express considerable discontent. A frequent complaint is the lack of influence in formulating company policy, policy they are expected to implement without question. Middle managers also complain about having insufficient authority and resources to carry out company policy. They must fight for recognition from superiors and compete for support for their ideas and projects. As a result, middle managers often experience considerable frustration as they vie for the few top management slots in the hierarchy.

Another source of dissatisfaction is the feeling of obsolescence that comes to middle-level managers in their late thirties and early forties. Most of them have reached a plateau and will receive no additional promotions. That realization often becomes part of a general midlife crisis, a period of self-examination for middle managers who feel threatened by younger subordinates, by changing cultural values, and by redefined organizational goals. Their productivity, creativity, and motivation may decline, and they may in effect retire on the job, making little further contribution to the organization.

Employee participation in decision making is another source of stress for middle managers. Although middle managers have no influence in decisions affecting their own jobs, they see that assembly-line, production, and office workers have gained the right to participate in decision making and job design. Participatory democracy leads to drastic changes in the ways managers can exert

> **Achievement motivation theory** The theory of motivation that emphasizes the need to accomplish something, to do a good job, and to be the best.

If you ask people why they work, you will probably get some strange looks—and no wonder! Most people don't have a choice; they work in order to survive. Some people are fortunate enough to love what they do, and many other people get a lot more from their work than just a paycheck. But what *motivates* people to work well, to do the best job they are capable of doing? How do organizations get people to work more productively, enhance their feelings of satisfaction and involvement, and increase their commitment to the organization? Motivation is one of the major problems facing organizations today.

Employers have made tremendous strides in applying the findings of I-O psychology to recruit, select, and train their workers and to provide effective leadership. But none of these functions can improve the quality of the work being performed if employees are not motivated to do the best job possible.

The study of motivation is important to you for two reasons. First, as a consumer you are often the victim of dissatisfied workers who produce faulty products or who process your requests improperly. Second, you will likely spend one third to one half of your waking hours at work for 40 to 45 years. That is a long time to feel frustrated, dissatisfied, and unhappy, especially as these feelings will carry over to your family and social life and affect your physical and emotional well-being.

Psychologists have studied motivation, job satisfaction, job involvement, and organizational commitment. They have proposed various theories to explain employee motivation—why people behave as they do on the job. Some of these theories emphasize the impact of factors in the workplace. Other theories focus on personal characteristics. The theories have stimulated a great deal of research and have spawned a number of techniques to modify work behavior. Thus, they may provide options for making your work life more satisfying and fulfilling.

CONTENT THEORIES OF MOTIVATION

Content theories of motivation focus on the importance of the work itself and the challenges, growth opportunities, and responsibilities work provides for employees. These theories deal with the content of motivation, that is, with the specific needs that motivate and direct human behavior. In the next section, we will describe process theories, which do not focus directly on work but rather deal with the cognitive processes we use in making decisions and choices about work.

We describe here four content models: achievement motivation theory, needs hierarchy theory, motivator–hygiene (two-factor) theory, and job-characteristics theory.

Achievement Motivation Theory

The need for achievement, or **achievement motivation**, is a characteristic of successful executives. This desire to accomplish something, to do a good job, and to be the best typifies many people, not only business leaders. People who have a high degree of the need for achievement derive great satisfaction from working to accomplish some goal, and they are motivated to excel in whatever task they undertake.

Since the early 1950s, achievement motivation has been studied intensively by David McClelland and his colleagues (Atkinson & Feather, 1966; McClelland, Atkinson, Clark, & Lowell, 1953). Their research, conducted in a number of countries, shows that successful business managers consistently display a high need to achieve, regardless of the culture. For example, in Poland, which was then a Communist country, the level of concern for achievement was almost as high as in the United States. McClelland concluded that the economic growth of organizations and societies can be related to the level of the achievement need among employees and citizens (McClelland, 1961).

McClelland's research identified three major characteristics of people who have a high need to achieve:

1. They favor a work environment in which they are able to assume responsibility for solving problems.
2. They tend to take calculated risks and to set moderate, attainable goals.

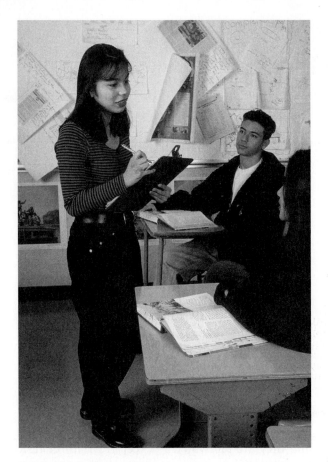

People high in the need for achievement are motivated to excel. They derive satisfaction from working hard to accomplish their goals.

3. They need continuing recognition and feedback about their progress so that they know how well they are doing.

Studies have shown a high positive correlation between the achievement motivation scores of executives and the financial success of their companies. Research also shows that managers high in the need to achieve display more respect for their subordinates. These managers are more receptive to new ideas and are more accepting of participative management programs than are managers low in the need to achieve. The need for achievement is positively related to subsequent promotions among middle- and upper-level managers. Also, entrepreneurs—both men and women—have been found to score significantly higher in the need to achieve than male and female employees who are not entrepreneurs.

In a study involving 846 employees in high-tech industries in Israel and in England, the investigator found a significant positive relationship between the need for achievement and job performance. The higher the measured achievement motivation, the higher was the employee's job performance (Baruch, 2004).

Additional research has suggested two types of goals, mastery and performance, that can satisfy the need for achievement (Barron & Harackiewicz, 2001). Mastery refers to developing competence and self-satisfaction through acquiring knowledge and skills. Performance goals involve developing competence by performing better than other people, such as co-workers, who are in the same situation. Both types of goals can be satisfied by doing one's job to the best of one's abilities. A study of more than 600 college students in the Netherlands found that two thirds of them preferred mastery of knowledge and skills over the attainment of performance goals. In other words, the college students were more highly motivated to achieve for self-satisfaction than to show that they could perform better than other students (Van Yperen, 2006).

In a study of 170 employees of an energy company in the Netherlands, researchers showed that employees with a strong mastery orientation were more effective on the job than were those with a strong performance orientation. Also, those with a high mastery orientation established higher quality leader–member exchanges (LMXs) with their supervisor, which, in turn, were linked to higher job satisfaction and intrinsic motivation. In contrast, employees with a strong performance orientation established lower quality LMXs and correspondingly were lower in job satisfaction and intrinsic motivation (Janssen & Van Yperen, 2004).

A research program involving 200 information systems employees in Taiwan delineated three dimensions of achievement motivation that were important in these high-tech jobs: perseverance, competition, and level of difficulty of controlling the task. All three were instrumental in satisfying the need to achieve (Chen, 2008).

In general, achievement motivation theory provides a plausible explanation for the motivation of some employees and is considered to have widespread application in the workplace.

Needs hierarchy theory   The theory of motivation that encompasses physiological, safety, belonging, esteem, and self-actualization needs.

Motivator–hygiene (two-factor) theory   The theory of motivation that explains work motivation and job satisfaction in terms of job tasks and workplace features.

Needs Hierarchy Theory

Abraham Maslow developed the **needs hierarchy theory** of motivation in which human needs are arranged in a hierarchy of importance (Maslow, 1970). Needs hierarchy theory suggests that people always want what they do not yet have. Consequently, the needs that are already satisfied no longer provide any motivation for behavior and new needs must rise to prominence. Once people have satisfied their lower level needs, they can pay attention to higher level needs. The needs, from lowest to highest, are as follows:

- *Physiological needs:* The basic human needs, including food, air, water, and sleep, and the drives for sex and activity
- *Safety needs:* The needs for physical shelter and for psychological security and stability
- *Belonging and love needs:* The social needs for love, affection, friendship, and affiliation that involve interaction with and acceptance by other people
- *Esteem needs:* The needs for self-esteem and for esteem, admiration, and respect from other people
- *Self-actualization need:* The need for self-fulfillment, for achieving our full potential and realizing our capabilities

These needs should be satisfied in the order presented. People who are hungry or who fear for their physical safety are too busy attempting to satisfy these needs to be concerned about self-esteem or self-fulfillment. In times of economic hardship, when jobs are scarce, most people are so intent on survival that they cannot attend to higher needs such as self-actualization. However, once people reach a sufficient level of physical and economic security, they can move on; that is, they will be motivated to satisfy the next level of needs.

The belonging needs can be important motivating forces on the job. Workers can develop a social support network and a sense of belonging through interactions with co-workers. Esteem needs can be satisfied by buying a bigger house or car, which contributes to the feeling of success, and through on-the-job rewards such as praise from the boss, a promotion, an office with a window, or a reserved parking space. To satisfy the self-actualization need, employees should be provided with opportunities for growth and responsibility so that they can exercise their abilities to the utmost. A routine and boring job will not satisfy the self-actualization need, no matter how high the salary.

Maslow's theory has received little research support and is judged to have low scientific validity and applicability. Its complexity makes it difficult to test empirically. Nevertheless, the self-actualization concept became popular with managers and executives who accepted this high-level need as a potent motivating force.

Motivator–Hygiene (Two-Factor) Theory

The **motivator–hygiene (two-factor) theory**, which deals with both motivation and job satisfaction, was proposed by Frederick Herzberg. The theory has inspired a great deal of research and has led many organizations to redefine the way many jobs are performed in order to increase employee motivation (Herzberg, 1966, 1974).

According to Herzberg, there are two sets of needs: the motivator needs, which produce job satisfaction, and the hygiene needs, which produce job dissatisfaction. The motivator needs (the higher needs) motivate employees to high job performance. Motivator needs are internal to the work itself. They include the nature of the individual job tasks and the worker's level of responsibility, achievement, recognition, advancement, and career development and growth. Motivator needs are similar to Maslow's self-actualization need. They can be satisfied by stimulating, challenging, and absorbing work. When these conditions are met, job satisfaction will result. However, when these conditions are not met—when work is not challenging—the result is not necessarily job dissatisfaction.

Job dissatisfaction is produced by the hygiene needs (the lower needs). The word *hygiene* relates to the promotion and maintenance of health. Hygiene

Job enrichment An effort to expand the scope of a job to give employees a greater role in planning, performing, and evaluating their work.

Job-characteristics theory The theory of motivation that states that specific job characteristics lead to psychological conditions that can increase motivation,

performance, and satisfaction in employees who have a high growth need.

needs are external to the tasks of a particular job and involve features of the work environment, such as company policy, supervision, interpersonal relations, working conditions, and salary and benefits. When the hygiene needs are not satisfied, the result is job dissatisfaction. However, when the hygiene needs are satisfied, the result is not necessarily job satisfaction, but merely an absence of dissatisfaction. Hygiene needs are similar to Maslow's physiological, safety, and belonging needs. Both Maslow and Herzberg insisted that these lower needs must be satisfied before a person can be motivated by higher needs.

A survey of more than 3,200 workers in Britain showed that factors such as money and recognition (hygiene needs) were not the primary sources of motivation. In line with Herzberg's theory, the motivator needs played a more important role in the job performance of these employees (Bassett-Jones & Lloyd, 2005).

Herzberg's theory focused attention on the importance of internal job factors as motivating forces for employees. If the motivator needs stimulate employees to perform at their best and to develop a positive attitude toward the job, then why not redesign the job to maximize opportunities to satisfy motivator needs? This effort, called **job enrichment**, expands jobs to give employees a greater role in planning, performing, and evaluating their work, thus providing the chance to satisfy their motivator needs. Herzberg suggested the following ways of enriching a job:

1. Remove some management controls over employees and increase their accountability and responsibility for their work, thus increasing employee autonomy, authority, and freedom.

2. Create complete or natural work units where possible; for example, allow employees to produce a whole unit instead of one component of that unit. This policy increases the likelihood that employees will regard their work as meaningful within the total organizational process.

3. Provide regular and continuous feedback on productivity and job performance directly to employees instead of through their supervisors.

4. Encourage employees to take on new, challenging tasks and to become experts in a particular task or operation.

All these proposals have the same goals of increasing personal growth, fulfilling the needs for achievement and responsibility, and providing recognition. Proper job enrichment, therefore, involves more than simply giving the workers extra tasks to perform. It means expanding the level of knowledge and skills needed to perform the job.

Job-Characteristics Theory

The job enrichment movement led two psychologists to ask which specific job characteristics could be enriched. J. Richard Hackman and G. R. Oldham developed the **job-characteristics theory** of motivation based on their research on objective measures of job factors that correlated with employee satisfaction and attendance (Hackman & Oldham, 1976, 1980). Evidence suggested that certain characteristics influence behavior and attitudes at work, but these characteristics do not influence all employees in the same way. For example, the research documented individual differences in the need for growth. People with a high growth need were found to be more affected by changes in job characteristics than were people with a low growth need. Also, changes in these job characteristics did not seem to influence employee attitudes and behavior directly but were filtered by the employees' cognitive processes, that is, their perceptions of the changes.

The presence of certain job characteristics causes employees to experience a positive emotional state when they perform their job well. This condition motivates them to continue to perform well, on the expectation that good performance will lead to good feelings. The strength of an employee's motivation to perform well depends on the strength of the need to grow and develop. The stronger the need, the more the person will value the positive emotional feelings that result from good job performance. Thus, the job-characteristics theory states that specific job characteristics lead to psychological

Valence-instrumentality-expectancy (VIE) theory The theory of motivation that states that people make choices that are based on their perceived expectations that certain rewards will follow if they behave in a particular way.

conditions that lead, in turn, to higher motivation, performance, and satisfaction—if employees have a high growth need to begin with.

The core job characteristics identified by Hackman and Oldham are as follows:

1. *Skill variety:* the extent to which workers use various skills and abilities on the job. The more challenging a job, the more meaningful it will be.

2. *Task identity:* the unity of a job—that is, whether it involves doing a whole unit of work or completing a product instead of making only part of a product on an assembly line.

3. *Task significance:* the importance of a job to the lives and well-being of co-workers or consumers. For example, the job of aircraft mechanic affects the lives of more people in a more significant way than does the job of postal clerk.

4. *Autonomy:* the amount of independence employees have in scheduling and organizing their work.

5. *Feedback:* the amount of information employees receive about the effectiveness and quality of their job performance.

Jobs can be redesigned to maximize these characteristics in a manner similar to that proposed earlier by Herzberg:

• Combine small, specialized tasks to form larger work units; this enhances skill variety and task identity.

• Arrange tasks in natural, meaningful work units to make the worker responsible for an identifiable unit; this enhances task identity and task significance.

• Give workers responsibility for direct contact with clients or end users; this enhances skill variety, autonomy, and feedback.

• Give workers authority, responsibility, and control over the job tasks; this increases skill variety, task identity, task significance, and autonomy.

• Arrange for workers to learn regularly how well they are performing the job; this increases feedback.

Hackman and Oldham developed the Job Diagnostic Survey (JDS) to measure three aspects of the theory: (1) employees' perceptions of the job characteristics, (2) employees' level of the growth need, and (3) employees' job satisfaction. The JDS is a self-report inventory consisting of short descriptive phrases about the various job characteristics. Respondents rate how accurately each statement describes their job. A revised version, using positively worded items only, has been found to be more valid than the original version.

The job-characteristics theory continues to stimulate research. Studies on job enrichment programs based on this theory have been more supportive and have shown that adding challenge, complexity, and responsibility to some jobs results in greater employee satisfaction, self-efficacy, and motivation.

As you can see, the content theories of motivation share a common core or central concept. They focus on enlarging, enriching, or redefining jobs to provide greater employee responsibility. They note the importance of opportunities for growth, self-actualization, personal achievement, and increased motivation through increasing the amount of accountability, challenge, control, and autonomy at work. Enlarging the scope of a job can provide personal satisfaction and greater motivation to perform well. Boring and routine jobs can be stultifying and decrease satisfaction and motivation. You might keep these conclusions in mind when you apply for your next job.

PROCESS THEORIES OF MOTIVATION

Process theories focus on the cognitive processes that are part of decision making. We describe three process models: valence-instrumentality-expectancy (VIE) theory, equity theory, and goal-setting theory.

Valence-Instrumentality-Expectancy (VIE) Theory

The **valence-instrumentality-expectancy (VIE) theory**, originated by Victor Vroom, asserts that people make choices based on their perceived

> **Equity theory** The theory of motivation that states that people's motivation on the job is influenced by their perception of how fairly they are treated.

expectancy that certain rewards will follow if they behave in a certain way (Vroom, 1964). In the workplace, employees will choose to perform at the level that results in the greatest payoff or benefit. They will be motivated to work hard if they expect this effort to lead to positive outcomes such as a promotion or pay raise and if those outcomes will be instrumental in leading to other desired results.

The psychological value, or valence, of the reward varies with the individual. In other words, one's personal perception of the importance of the outcome determines its strength as a motivator. A high salary and increased responsibility have a positive valence for many people. Dangerous working conditions have a negative valence for most people. An outcome may not be as satisfying as expected, but it is the level of expectancy that determines whether a person will work hard to obtain that outcome.

The three facets of the VIE theory are related as follows:

1. Employees must decide whether they expect certain job behaviors—such as coming to work on time, following safe procedures, or improving productivity—to have a high probability of leading to a particular outcome (*expectancy*).
2. Employees must determine whether that outcome will lead to other outcomes—for example, whether a good attendance record leads to a bonus (*instrumentality*).
3. Employees must decide whether those outcomes have sufficient value to motivate them to behave a certain way (*valence*).

Think of your experience in school. If you have decided that getting high grades in the courses you take in your major is important, then that outcome has a high valence for you. If you're not so concerned about your grades in your other courses, then earning high grades in them has a low valence for you. If you want high grades in your major, you have probably developed the expectancy that attending classes, studying hard, and doing more than the minimum requirements will be instrumental in

achieving your goal. Such calculations are not difficult for most of us to make. Indeed, we may not even be aware of them, but they motivate us and guide our behavior nonetheless.

The VIE theory has received a great deal of research support. It appears to agree with personal experience and common sense. The greater our expectation of receiving a reward, assuming it is of sufficient value, the harder we will work for it.

Equity Theory

J. Stacy Adams advanced the **equity theory**, the notion that motivation is influenced by our perception of how equitably or fairly we are treated at work (Adams, 1965). He proposed that in any work environment—whether office, shop, factory, or classroom—we assess our inputs (how much effort we put into the work) and our outcomes (how much reward we receive for the work). We calculate, perhaps unconsciously, the ratio of outcome to input and mentally compare it with what we believe are the ratios for our co-workers. If we think we are getting less than other people, the feeling of tension or inequity that results will motivate us to take action, to do something to bring about a state of equity. If we perceive that we are receiving the same ratio of reward-to-effort that others are receiving, then a state of equity exists.

Other psychologists have extended the equity theory, suggesting three behavioral response patterns to situations of perceived equity or inequity (Huseman, Hatfield, & Miles, 1987; O'Neil & Mone, 1998). These three types are the benevolent, equity-sensitive, and entitled patterns. The level of reward received by each type affects motivation, job satisfaction, and job performance.

Benevolent people, described as altruistic, are satisfied when they are underrewarded compared with co-workers, and they feel guilty when they are equitably rewarded or overrewarded. Equity-sensitive persons (the type described by the equity theory) believe that everyone should be rewarded fairly. They feel distressed when underrewarded and guilty when overrewarded. Entitled persons

Newsbreak

The Work Ethic: Let's Hear It for Cal Ripken!

On September 8, 1995, a baseball player made history. He did it by showing up for work. Cal Ripken, Jr., showed up for work 2,131 times—every time his team, the Baltimore Orioles, played a major league baseball game. And no one has beaten his record since.

The 42,000 fans in Oriole Park at Camden Yards stadium went wild the night Ripken broke the previous record, held by Lou Gehrig, for the longest streak of consecutive games played. The President of the United States witnessed the historic moment and praised Ripken's discipline, determination, and constancy. A television reporter summed up the excitement when he described Ripken as "a paragon of the work ethic."

The *work ethic* is a familiar term, and it has been a guiding rule and way of life for generations of American workers. It drives, pushes, goads, and motivates people to work hard like Cal Ripken, to do the best job they can, to be on time, and to show up for work every day. If you are curious about the great driving force of the nineteenth and twentieth centuries that led to unimagined heights of industrial, agricultural, and commercial productivity and economic success, then the work ethic is where you should begin.

The work ethic wasn't always so popular. There was a time when people were not motivated to perform a job well, or even to do it at all. To the ancient Greeks and Romans, there was nothing noble about work. It was a curse of the gods that brutalized the mind and ruined an otherwise good day. The early Hebrews agreed. Work was a punishment from God, although it was also a necessary evil, a way of improving society and atoning for sin.

The early Christians put a more positive spin on work, viewing it as a way to serve God by sharing the proceeds of one's work with people who were less fortunate. Wealth was a means to charity. Work became holy, and idleness sinful.

But it was John Calvin, the sixteenth-century French Protestant leader, who gave us the ultimate work ethic. Work alone pleases God, he declared, but to achieve that end, work must be methodical and disciplined. "Not leisure and enjoyment but only activity serves to increase the glory of God."

To Calvin, and others who refined what came to be called the Protestant work ethic, work was an emblem of faith. And so was wealth. It was OK to make a lot of money and not feel guilty about it, as long as you did not enjoy it. Old-fashioned, puritanical, nose-to-the-grindstone toil for its own sake became the motivation that drove millions of people to work hard all their lives and to feel virtuous for doing so. And it still drives many people each and every day to do the best job they can. And to show up for every game.

Sources: Todd, R. (1996, January). All work, no ethic. *Worth Magazine*, pp. 78–84; Bair, J., & Sherer, S. J. (1995, Fall). What happened to the work ethic? *College Park Magazine*, pp. 18–22; Robinson, 2007.

believe that everything they receive is their due. They are satisfied only when they are overrewarded and are distressed when underrewarded or equitably rewarded.

It seems intuitively correct that if we believe we are being treated fairly in comparison to others, in accordance with our expectations, then we will be motivated to maintain our level of job performance. In contrast, if we think we are being treated unfairly, then we will try to reduce that inequity by reducing our level of performance. Consider the example of major league baseball players (infielders and outfielders). If they have their salaries cut or lose at arbitration during their first year as free agents, they are likely to perform at lower levels during the following season. They may reduce their inputs (batting averages and runs batted in) if they believe that their outcomes (salaries) are too low.

Not all research supports the equity theory, but some studies have shown that employee perceptions of inequity are linked to increased levels of resentment, absenteeism and turnover, and burnout.

> **Goal-setting theory** The theory of motivation based on the idea that a person's primary motivation on the job is defined in terms of the desire to achieve a particular goal.

Goal-Setting Theory

Developed by Edwin Locke, **goal-setting theory** has a commonsense appeal and is clearly relevant to the workplace. Locke argued that our primary motivation in a work situation is defined in terms of our desire to achieve a particular goal (Locke, 1968; Locke & Latham, 1990). The goal represents what we intend to do at a given time in the future. For example, we may set the goal of graduating from college with honors, or achieving the highest sales record in the company, or getting a pay raise within a year so we can buy a new house.

Setting specific and challenging performance goals can motivate and guide behavior, spurring people to perform in more effective ways. Research has shown that having goals leads to better performance than not having goals. Specific goals are more powerful motivating forces than general goals. Goals that are difficult to attain are greater motivators than goals that are easy to attain. However, difficult goals may spur greater motivation toward attaining the goals at the expense of other behaviors, such as helping co-workers, and this type of behavior has the potential for reducing overall organizational effectiveness. In addition, goals that are too difficult, perhaps beyond a person's capabilities, are worse than having no goals in terms of their impact on motivation and job performance.

An important aspect of the goal-setting theory is individual goal commitment, which is defined in terms of the strength of a person's determination to reach a goal. Three types of factors influence goal commitment: external, interactive, and internal. The external factors that affect goal commitment are authority, peer influence, and external rewards. Complying with the dictates of an authority figure such as a boss has been shown to be an inducement to high goal commitment. Goal commitment increases when the authority figure is physically present, supportive, and trusted. Peer group pressure and external rewards such as pay increases also strengthen goal commitment.

The interactive factors that influence commitment to reaching goals are competition and the opportunity to participate in setting goals. These factors have been shown to be an inducement to setting higher goals and to working harder to reach them. Internal cognitive factors that facilitate goal commitment are self-administered rewards and expectation of success. Commitment to the goal is reduced when the expectation of achieving it declines.

Other personal and situational factors have been related to high goal commitment. These include the need for achievement, endurance, aggressiveness, and competitiveness (so-called Type A behavior), success in achieving difficult goals, high self-esteem, and an internal locus of control. In addition, a meta-analysis of 65 studies found that two of the Big Five personality factors are related to performance motivation, as described by the goal-setting theory. People who score high in conscientiousness and low in neuroticism display high levels of motivation induced by goal setting (Judge & Ilies, 2002).

The goal-setting theory has generated considerable supportive research. Setting goals has been found to produce substantial increases in employee output. In general, the motivating effects of setting goals are strongest for easy tasks and weakest for more complex tasks. These effects generalize across a variety of organizations, jobs, and tasks. Goal-setting theory has been shown to be one of the most practical theories of employee motivation (Latham & Locke, 2007; Latham, 2004; Locke & Latham, 2002).

The process theories are concerned with factors and processes internal to the employee. Instead of focusing on characteristics of the work itself, as with content theories, process theories deal with our thoughts and perceptions about our jobs, our calculations about what we stand to gain in return for our efforts, and the decisions we make based on those calculations. We can be motivated to perform at high levels by our expectations of getting the greatest benefit (VIE theory), or by how fairly we perceive we are rewarded relative to our co-workers (equity theory), or by setting challenging goals (goal-setting theory)—or perhaps by some combination of all

Job satisfaction   Our positive and negative feelings and attitudes about our jobs.

three, at different times and in different situations. Process theories share the common theme that how we perceive the work situation will determine how motivated we are to perform at a high level in that situation.

Since the 1990s, interest in work motivation theories has shifted away from developing new theories and more toward extending, empirically testing, and applying proposed ideas in the workplace. The number of purely theoretical articles published in the leading behavioral science journals declined considerably, whereas the number of empirical studies increased (Steers, Mowday, & Shapiro, 2004). Does it follow that theories of work motivation are no longer a focus of I-O psychology? No. Although the theories described here have some limitations, most are useful in describing some aspect of employee motivation. The diversity of ideas derived from these theories, which are now being tested in and applied to the workplace, shows the progress being made in understanding the multiple facets of employee motivation (see Locke & Latham, 2004).

JOB SATISFACTION: THE QUALITY OF LIFE AT WORK

Job satisfaction refers to the positive and negative feelings and attitudes employees hold about a job, and it is the most frequently studied independent variable in I-O psychology. It depends on many work-related factors, ranging from an assigned parking space to work overload to the sense of fulfillment employees get from daily tasks (see, for example, Pearson, 2008). A study of 1,114 police officers in Alabama related several factors to job satisfaction: the opportunity to make a contribution to society, good pay, adventure and excitement, autonomy on the job, respect from peers, and job security (Carlan, 2007). Personal factors can also influence job satisfaction: age, health, length of job experience, emotional stability, social status, leisure activities, and family and other social relationships. Motivations and aspirations, and how well these are satisfied by our work, also affect our attitudes toward our jobs.

Assembly-line workers tend to have low job satisfaction. Routine, repetitive work offers little opportunity for personal growth and development.

Also, how much or how little employees contribute to their work roles, beyond the basic requirements of the job, has been shown to affect employee attitudes (Harrison, Newman & Roth, 2006).

Job satisfaction influences psychological well-being even after workers retire from their jobs. Surveys of more than 2,000 people in the United States, conducted over an 8-year period, found that those who reported low job satisfaction reported improved psychological health after retirement. Those who reported high satisfaction from their jobs reported positive well-being both before and after retirement (Wang, 2007).

Changing one's job can affect attitudes toward and satisfaction with a job. A survey of 2,522 high-level managers showed that job satisfaction increased immediately after taking a new job (the so-called honeymoon effect) but declined with the first year or two (the so-called hangover effect) (Boswell, Boudreau, & Tichy, 2005).

For some employees, job satisfaction is a stable, enduring characteristic, independent of the features of the job. Changes in job status, pay, working conditions, and goals have little effect on the job satisfaction of these people. Their personal tendency toward happiness (satisfaction) or unhappiness (dissatisfaction) varies little over time and circumstances. Researchers who studied more than 5,000 workers in a customer service organization found that job performance, as measured by supervisor ratings, was highest among employees who also scored high in job satisfaction and psychological well-being (Wright, Cropanzano, & Bonett, 2007).

I-O psychologists have suggested, based on research conducted with twins, that attitudes toward work and the satisfactions expected from it may have a hereditary component. In other words, these feelings may be influenced more by genetic endowment than by features of the work environment. Nevertheless, it is clear that some people are generally more satisfied with life and, thus, with their work. People who have positive attitudes toward their work are likely to have positive feelings about their personal and family life.

So it is generally accepted that job satisfaction and life satisfaction are positively related, but which one causes the other? Or are both influenced by some third factor? Research shows a positive and reciprocal relationship between job satisfaction and life satisfaction in the short term; that is, each one influenced the other. Over time, however, the impact of life satisfaction on job satisfaction was significantly stronger, which indicates that life satisfaction may be the more influential of the two factors. However, it does not follow that attempts to improve job satisfaction are useless. Remember that the two are interrelated. Job satisfaction still has an effect on life satisfaction.

Measurement of Job Satisfaction

The approach used most often to measure employee attitudes is the anonymous questionnaire, typically distributed to employees through the company's e-mail network. Because participation is voluntary, not all workers will complete a questionnaire. There is no way of knowing which employees responded and which did not, or how those who failed to respond differ from those who did respond. It might make a difference if more good workers than poor workers completed the questionnaires.

Two popular attitude surveys are the Job Descriptive Index (JDI) and the Minnesota Satisfaction Questionnaire (MSQ). The JDI contains scales to measure five job factors: pay, promotion, supervision, the nature of the work, and the characteristics of one's co-workers. It can be completed in 15 minutes and has been published in several languages. The MSQ is a rating scale for various levels of satisfaction and dissatisfaction, ranging from "very satisfied" to "very dissatisfied." It covers 20 job facets including advancement, independence, recognition, social status, and working conditions. The MSQ takes 30 minutes to complete; a 10-minute form is also available. These questionnaires have high construct validity.

Job Satisfaction Polling Data

Every year the Gallup Poll organization asks a representative sample of U.S. workers the following question: On the whole, would you say you are satisfied or dissatisfied with the work you do?

The results show consistently that only 10% to 13% of the workers questioned each year say that they are dissatisfied with their jobs. Thus, the majority of people are assumed to be satisfied with their jobs. However, when more specific questions are asked about job satisfaction, the results are different. For example, when factory workers are asked if they would like to change jobs, many say yes, even though they claim to be satisfied with their present jobs. When people say they are satisfied, they often mean that they are not dissatisfied. Therefore, when I-O psychologists consider data on job satisfaction, they must examine the kinds of questions that are asked.

Some job satisfaction studies survey a representative national sample of workers. Others deal with targeted populations, such as the workers in a particular industry, or with specific facets of job satisfaction. Job satisfaction varies with type of occupation. For example, assembly-line workers are significantly less satisfied with their jobs than are office workers. Managers in government agencies are significantly less satisfied than are managers in private industry and business.

Employees of companies on *Fortune* magazine's list of 100 best companies to work for in the United States report high levels of job satisfaction that tend to remain stable over time. Research also shows a high correlation between these employees' positive attitudes toward their companies and the companies' financial performance. The more satisfied workers seem to be, the better is the organization's economic health (Fulmer, Gerhart, & Scott, 2003). To find out more about the top 100 companies and

TABLE 8-1	
Ten Most Satisfying and Ten Least Satisfying Jobs	
Most Satisfying Jobs	**Least Satisfying Jobs**
Clergy	Laborer (excluding construction)
Firefighter	Clothing salesperson
Physical therapist	Hand packer or packager
Author	Food preparer
Special education teacher	Roofer
Teacher	Cashier
Educational administrator	Furniture/home furnishings salesperson
Painter or sculptor	Bartender
Psychologist	Freight or materials handler
Power plant engineer	Food server

to learn how the ratings were determined, go to the Web site http://www.greatplacetowork.com

Table 8-1 shows the 10 most satisfying and 10 least satisfying jobs in rank order, based on a nationwide U.S. survey of more than 27,000 employed adults (Bryner, 2007).

Personal Characteristics and Job Satisfaction

Many characteristics of the job and the workplace affect job satisfaction. By redesigning job and work environments, management can increase job satisfaction and productivity. Jobs can be redesigned to maximize opportunities to satisfy the needs for achievement, self-actualization, and personal growth. Jobs can be enriched to enhance the motivator needs and the core job characteristics, and to provide higher levels of responsibility. Personal characteristics linked with job satisfaction include, among others, age, gender, race, cognitive ability, job experience, use of skills, job congruence, organizational justice, personality, job control, and occupational level.

Age. In general, job satisfaction increases with age; the lowest job satisfaction is reported by the youngest workers. This relationship holds for blue-collar and white-collar employees and for men and women. In a study of 234 accountants, researchers found that so-called Baby Boomers (born between 1946 and 1964) scored higher in job satisfaction than those born later (Generation X or Generation Y)

(Westerman & Yamamora, 2007). Many young people are disappointed with their first jobs because they fail to find sufficient challenge and responsibility. Why does job satisfaction tend to increase with age when the typical reaction to a first job is often disappointment? Three possible explanations have been suggested:

1. The most strongly dissatisfied young workers may drop out of the workforce or change jobs so frequently in their search for satisfaction that they are no longer counted in surveys. This means that the older the sample of employees studied, the fewer dissatisfied people are likely to be included.

2. A sense of resignation develops in some workers as they grow older. They may give up looking for fulfillment and challenge in their work and seek these satisfactions elsewhere. Therefore, they tend to report less dissatisfaction with their jobs.

3. Many older workers have greater opportunities to find fulfillment and self-actualization on the job. Age and experience usually bring increased confidence, competence, esteem, and responsibility. In turn, these feelings lead to a greater sense of accomplishment. In other words, older workers are more likely to have better jobs than are younger workers.

Gender. The research evidence about possible differences in job satisfaction between men and women

Job congruence   The match between a person's abilities and the requirements of a job.

is inconsistent and contradictory. Psychologists have found no clear pattern of differences in job satisfaction. It may not be gender, as such, that relates to job satisfaction as much as the group of factors that vary with gender. For example, women are typically paid less than men for the same work, and their opportunities for promotion are fewer. Most women believe that they have to work harder and be more outstanding on the job than men before they receive comparable rewards. Obviously, such factors can influence a person's satisfaction.

Race.   In general, more White than non-White employees report satisfaction with their jobs. However, before a person can be concerned with job satisfaction, he or she must have a job. Although there is a large, thriving middle class among Black and ethnic minority employees, large numbers of people who want to work are unemployed, are employed irregularly, or are too discouraged to seek employment. Many who have full-time work are confined to low-level jobs that offer marginal pay and little opportunity for advancement or fulfillment. Thus, the primary concern for many workers is not satisfaction but finding a job that pays a decent wage.

Cognitive Ability.   Cognitive ability does not appear to be a significant determinant of job satisfaction, but it may be important when related to the type of work a person chooses. For many jobs, there is a range of intelligence associated with high performance and satisfaction. People who are too intelligent for their work may find insufficient challenge, which leads to boredom and dissatisfaction. People whose jobs are not sufficiently challenging for their level of intelligence report greater dissatisfaction with their work.

A factor sometimes related to intelligence is level of education. Some studies have shown that education has a slight negative relationship to job satisfaction. The higher the level of formal education, the more likely a person is to be dissatisfied with the job. One explanation is that better-educated persons have higher expectations and believe that their work should provide greater responsibil-

ity and fulfillment. Many jobs do not satisfy these expectations. Employees with college degrees are somewhat more satisfied with their jobs than employees who attended college but did not graduate. This finding may be related to the fact that many higher level positions are open only to college graduates.

Job Experience.   During the initial stage of employment, new workers tend to be satisfied with their jobs. This period involves the stimulation and challenge of developing skills and abilities, and the work may seem attractive just because it is new. Early satisfaction wanes unless employees receive feedback on their progress and tangible evidence of their achievements. After a few years on the job, discouragement is common, often being brought on by the feeling that advancement in the company is too slow.

Job satisfaction appears to increase after a number of years of experience and to improve steadily thereafter. The relationship between job satisfaction and length of work experience parallels the relationship with age. They may be the same phenomenon under different labels.

Use of Skills.   A common complaint, particularly among college graduates in engineering and science, is that their jobs do not allow them to exercise their skills or apply the knowledge acquired during their college training. Surveys of engineers show high dissatisfaction with job factors such as pay, working conditions, supervisors, and opportunities for promotion. Other studies show that people are happier at work if they have the chance to use their abilities. When working conditions or the actions of co-workers interfere with work quality, job satisfaction declines.

Job Congruence.   **Job congruence** refers to the match between the demands of a job and the abilities of the employee. The higher the congruence—the closer the fit between a person's skills and attributes and the job's requirements—the greater the job satisfaction. Conversely, a poor fit between job demands and personal skills reduces the potential for job satisfaction.

Organizational Justice. Organizational justice refers to how fairly employees perceive themselves to be treated by their company. When workers believe they are being treated unfairly (a perceived lack of organizational justice), their job performance, job satisfaction, and organizational commitment are likely to decline. Under these circumstances, employees also report higher levels of stress, and they are more likely to file grievances or seek other jobs. Employees who work for large organizations or for companies with an authoritarian culture are likely to have a low opinion of the level of organizational justice in their workplace. Consequently, they may retaliate against the organization by reducing their productivity and job performance (Cohen-Charash & Mueller, 2007; Cropanzano, Bowen, & Gilliland, 2007).

Considerable research has shown that participation in decision making can contribute to an increase in feelings of organizational justice, which, in turn, can lead to increased job satisfaction and commitment to the organization (Mayer, Nishii, Schneider, & Goldstein, 2007; Wiesenfeld, Swann, Brockner, & Bartel, 2007).

Personality. Research suggests that employees who are more satisfied in their work are better adjusted and more emotionally stable. Although the relationship seems clear, the cause-and-effect sequence is not. Which comes first, emotional stability or job satisfaction? Emotional instability or job dissatisfaction? Emotional instability can cause discontent in every sphere of life, and prolonged job dissatisfaction can lead to poor emotional adjustment. A meta-analysis of studies involving thousands of employees concluded that overall happiness, or emotional satisfaction, takes precedence. Happier people rate themselves higher in job satisfaction than do those who are less happy. Happier people also show higher levels of job performance and earn higher incomes (Boehm, & Lyubomirsky, 2008).

Two personality factors related to job satisfaction are alienation and locus of control. Employees who feel less alienated and who have an internal locus of control are more likely to be high in job satisfaction, job involvement, and organizational commitment. A meta-analysis of 135 studies of job

satisfaction confirmed the positive relationship between internal locus of control and job satisfaction. The study also found that high self-esteem and self-efficacy, and low neuroticism, are significantly related to high job satisfaction (Judge & Bono, 2001).

Two dimensions of the Type A personality are related to job satisfaction. *Achievement striving* (the extent to which people work hard and take work seriously) is positively related to job satisfaction and job performance. *Impatience/irritability* (intolerance, anger, hostility, and a sense of time urgency) is negatively related to job satisfaction. The higher the impatience score, the lower the job satisfaction.

Job satisfaction appears to be highest among employees with a high degree of social and institutional trust, defined as a belief that people and organizations are basically fair and helpful and can be trusted. Job satisfaction was also found to be high among employees who scored high on the factors of conscientiousness and positive affectivity (which corresponds to extraversion in the Big Five personality factor model) and low on negative affectivity (neuroticism in the Big Five model) (Brief & Weiss, 2002; Ilies & Judge, 2003; Judge, Heller, & Mount, 2002).

In an unusual research program, investigators studied the self-evaluations of 384 employed adults; the evaluations included psychological measures of self-esteem, self-efficacy, locus of control, and neuroticism. Earlier in this long-term study, investigators had assessed these factors in childhood. People who scored high in esteem and efficacy and low in neuroticism, and showed an internal locus of control, showed significantly higher job satisfaction in their middle adult years than did people who scored in the opposite direction. Thus, personality factors measured in childhood showed a direct relationship to job satisfaction measured some 30 years later (Judge, Bono, & Locke, 2000).

Job Control. Based on the description of motivational theories in this chapter, you might predict that people who can exercise greater control over their job duties will be more highly motivated to perform well and will experience greater satisfaction. In fact, this prediction was supported in a study of 412 workers in customer service centers in England. Those who scored high on a questionnaire called the Job Control Scale were found, 1 year later,

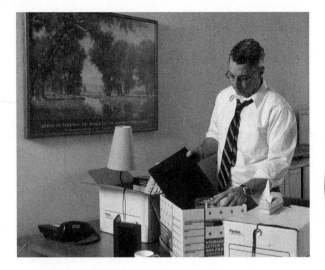

Unemployment can lead to anxiety that may persist even after a new job has been found.

to have better mental health and higher levels of job performance and job satisfaction than did those who reported a low level of job control (Bond & Bunce, 2003).

In a 9-year study of 3,125 workers in Japan, researchers found a fourfold increase in the risk of suicide among those who reported low control on the job. A study of 2,221 workers in Canada linked high job control to lower levels of stress and greater physical health (Smith, Frank, Bondy, & Mustard, 2008; Tsutsumi et al., 2007).

Occupational Level.   The higher the occupational or status level of a job, the higher the job satisfaction. Executives express more positive job attitudes and feelings than do first-line supervisors, who, in turn, are usually more satisfied than their subordinates are. The higher the job level, the greater is the opportunity for satisfying motivator needs. Also, high-level jobs offer greater autonomy, challenge, and responsibility. Satisfaction of Maslow's esteem and self-actualization needs also increases with each level in the organizational hierarchy.

Job satisfaction varies with job category. High job satisfaction is more likely to be reported by entrepreneurs (self-employed persons) and by people in technical, professional, and managerial jobs. The least satisfied employees work in manufacturing and service industries and in wholesale and retail businesses.

The Impact of Unemployment

No job satisfaction exists without a job. I-O psychology research confirms the obvious. Losing one's job or being laid off is stressful for employees and their families. In Japan, layoffs are considered so traumatic that they are called *kubi kiri*, which means "beheading." Specific consequences of layoffs can include feelings of guilt, resentment, depression, and anxiety about the future, as well as physical complaints, alcohol abuse, drug abuse, divorce, spouse and child abuse, and thoughts of suicide.

Employees with higher level jobs appear to suffer more greatly from unemployment. Employees with lower level jobs seem to be more adaptable. Executives, managers, and professionals tend to become defensive and self-critical. Losing a job typically leads to significant changes in lifestyle, expectations, goals, and values. The psychological contract these employees believed they had with their employer has been breached. They can no longer rely on this unwritten agreement: If I work hard and show loyalty to the company, then the company will respond with job security, pay raises, and promotions. Many people who have lost their jobs feel a sense of betrayal. In a study of 756 employees who lost their jobs, investigators found that over a 2-year period the feeling of loss of personal control was especially harmful. In many cases it led to chronic physical health problems and impaired emotional functioning (Price, Choi, & Vinokur, 2002). Other researchers found that people who lost their jobs after the age of 50 had twice the risk of strokes or heart attacks than those of the same age who were still employed (Gallo et al., 2006).

Negative reactions to layoffs can be minimized if management is honest with employees about the reasons for the dismissals. Well-informed employees are more likely to view the layoffs as fair, to continue to speak positively about the company, and to express no intention of suing for wrongful termination. Finding a new position typically reverses the negative effects of losing one's job. However, the nature of the new job relative to the old one can make a difference. A study of 100 workers found that those who were dissatisfied with their new job continued to experience most of the negative effects associated with being dismissed from their previous job (Kinicki, Prussia, & McKee-Ryan, 2000).

Prosocial behavior Behaviors directed toward supervisors, co-workers, and clients that are helpful to an organization.

When large-scale layoffs occur in an organization, the employees who keep their jobs are also affected. Often they worry that they will be among the next to be dismissed. A report from the U.S. Department of Labor noted that half of the layoff survivors questioned reported increased job stress, lower morale, and reduced job commitment. Also, 60% reported greatly increased workloads because workers remaining on the job still had to meet production goals even though there were fewer workers. The layoff survivors reported a decrease in feelings of commitment to the organization since their friends and co-workers had been dismissed (Shah, 2000).

A survey of 283 employees in a company undergoing a major reorganization showed that their sense of job insecurity, from worry about being laid off, was related to a decrease in their organizational commitment and an increase in their stress levels and health problems. Employees who reported a high sense of job involvement experienced health problems and greater stress than did employees who were less involved with their jobs (Probst, 2000). Another survey, involving 1,000 employed men and women in the United States under age 60, indicated that those who felt insecure about their jobs were twice as likely to report health problems as those who felt secure. Black workers who felt insecure about their jobs showed four times the level of reported depression as White workers (Swanbrow, 2006).

In a study of 1,297 workers in Finland, investigators reported that those who were concerned about being downsized experienced decreased levels of work motivation and well-being and a high level of stress. Even rumors about the possibility of company downsizing were sufficient to cause measurable increases in stress (Kalimo, Taris, & Schaufeli, 2003). A meta-analysis of more than 28,000 employees in 50 samples reported that feelings of job insecurity correlated highly with health problems, negative attitudes toward employers, and expressed intention to seek employment elsewhere (Sverke, Hellgren, & Naswall, 2002).

Job Satisfaction and On-the-Job Behavior

Several factors influence job satisfaction. Now let us consider those aspects of our behavior at work that can be affected by the level of job satisfaction.

Productivity. Ample research has demonstrated a strong and significant relationship between job satisfaction and job performance: The higher the reported satisfaction, the higher the level of performance (see, for example, Judge, Thoresen, Bono, & Patton, 2001). When 4,467 employees, 143 managers, and 9,903 customers of a restaurant chain were surveyed, the results showed that employee satisfaction affected not only customer satisfaction but also the restaurant's level of profitability. When employees reported high job satisfaction, so did customers, who were then likely to spend more money at the restaurant (Koys, 2001).

Most job satisfaction research has focused on individual employees, but I-O psychologists have also considered collective measures of job satisfaction, that is, the satisfaction level of a business unit such as a work team, section, or department. A meta-analysis of 7,939 business units in 36 companies demonstrated that employee satisfaction at the collective level was positively related to customer satisfaction and loyalty, and to employee productivity and safety on the job. High collective job satisfaction was also related to a reduction in turnover rates (Harter, Schmidt, & Hayes, 2002).

Prosocial and Counterproductive Behavior. High job satisfaction has been related to **prosocial behavior**, that is, to helpful behaviors directed at customers, co-workers, and supervisors to the benefit of employees and their organization. A number of studies have related prosocial behavior to high job performance and productivity (Grant, 2008).

Does it follow that low job satisfaction is related to antisocial actions or to counterproductive behavior that may thwart organizational goals? Negative employee behavior can interfere with production and lead to faulty products, poor service, destructive rumors, theft, and sabotaged equipment.

Newsbreak

Grades Slipping? Your Fault—Or Your Parents'?

How good are you at assessing your parents' moods? Can you sense when they seem worried or upset about something, like maybe losing a job? Psychologists have learned that children from ages 10 to 17 are keenly aware when their parents experience feelings of insecurity about their work. For example, when children believe that their fathers are uneasy about their work situation, the children's attitudes toward their schoolwork changes and their grades are likely to drop. However, this effect was found only with fathers' jobs. When mothers experience job insecurity, children do not seem to be affected.

At Queen's University in Canada, psychologists investigated this situation in college students, even though they were no longer living with their parents at home. Would college students pick up on their parents' job anxiety and insecurity even though they didn't see or talk to them every day? And if so, would their own work, their academic performance, be altered?

The subjects in this experiment were 120 undergraduates younger than 21. A questionnaire surveyed their perception of their parents' level of job security. Parents were asked to complete a questionnaire about their perceived level of job security. It included such items as this: "I am not really sure how long my present job will last."

The results showed that college students were sensitive to their parents' feelings about their work, even though they no longer had daily contact with them. Like the younger children studied, the college students' grades fell with a decline in their parents' job security. Again, the effect was greater with fathers than with mothers.

In another study of 250 college students in Singapore, psychologists found that parents' feelings of job insecurity influenced their college-age children. The parents' economic concerns about losing their jobs led their children to report financial anxiety and feelings of being driven to seek financial rewards as a way of overcoming this newly acquired sense of inadequacy, which was seen as a direct reflection of their parents' concerns.

So if you're a parent, remember that being laid off, or even fearing a layoff, can have consequences for your children. And if you're a college student, maybe you should think twice before calling home to ask a parent how he or she is doing at work, or to ask for money!

Sources: Barling, J., Zacharatos, A., & Hepburn, C. G. (1999). Parents' job insecurity affects children's academic performance through cognitive difficulties. *Journal of Applied Psychology, 84,* 437–444; Lim, V., & Sng, Q. (2006). Does parental job insecurity matter? Money anxiety, money motives, and work motivation. *Journal of Applied Psychology, 91,* 1078–1087.

Employees may view these behaviors as a way of striking back at an organization because of real or imagined grievances.

Studies have shown a positive relationship between job dissatisfaction and counterproductive behavior for workers over the age of 30. This does not mean that older workers engage in more negative behaviors than do younger workers; the frequency of negative behaviors is higher for employees younger than 30. What the research indicates is that only in older workers has counterproductive behavior been related to job dissatisfaction.

Absenteeism. Absenteeism is widespread and costly for organizations. On any given workday in the United States, up to 20% of employees do not show up for work. Absenteeism costs businesses more than $30 billion a year.

Absenteeism has plagued industry since the invention of machines. In textile mills in Wales in the 1840s, the absenteeism rate was approximately 20%. During the 2-week period following each monthly payday, absenteeism often reached 35%. Throughout the nineteenth century in England, workers typically took off Mondays—"Saint

Merit pay   A wage system in which pay is based on level of performance.

salaries are higher than those of their colleagues are likely to be more satisfied with their pay. You may recognize this as a real-world example of the equity theory of motivation, discussed earlier in this chapter.

A meta-analysis of 203 studies conducted over a 35-year period revealed a strong positive correlation between pay satisfaction and job performance. Employees who were more satisfied with their pay rated higher in job performance than did those who were less satisfied with their pay (Williams, McDaniel, & Nguyen, 2006).

Most people develop personal standards of comparison that are based on the minimum salary they consider acceptable, the pay they believe their job deserves, and on the amount they think co-workers are being paid. Thus, satisfaction with pay is determined by the discrepancy between standards and actual salary. A study of 362 employees in the United States and in Belgium found that the higher employees believed their co-workers were being paid, the less satisfied they were with their own pay (Harris, Anseel, & Lievens, 2008).

Of course, for some groups in American society there is little pay equity, either actual or perceived. In general, women are paid less than men for the same or similar work, and many ethnic minority employees are paid less than Whites. Also, you might think that a family-member CEO of a family-controlled company would have a higher salary than a CEO who is not a member of the family or a family-controlled company. A study of 253 family-owned companies over a 4-year period revealed, however, that CEOs who were family members actually received lower pay and bonuses than CEOs who were not related to the family (Gomez-Mejia, Larraza-Kintana, & Makri, 2003).

Merit Pay

Merit pay, or pay for performance, means that the better performing workers in an organization are paid more than the less productive workers. This wage system is fine in theory but it does not translate well to the realities of the workplace. I-O psychologists

have studied various influences on the size of the pay raises given under merit pay plans. They have found widespread disagreement among managers about the behaviors that they consider important in making decisions about a worker's pay increase. A worker in one department might receive a sizable raise for job behaviors that bring no recognition in another department. Supervisors who receive substantial pay raises tend to recommend larger raises for their subordinates than do supervisors who receive smaller pay raises.

Pay raises are also related to the degree to which managers rely on their subordinates' expertise and support and to whether managers consider such dependence a threat. For example, a manager who is low in self-esteem may want subordinates to provide praise or positive feedback and therefore may be reluctant to give them low pay increases. The manager may fear that if subordinates do not receive a sufficient salary, they will withhold their support or reduce their productivity to make the manager look bad.

There is also evidence that not everyone who receives a merit pay increase reacts to it positively. The effects of merit pay raises were studied over an 8-month period among more than 1,700 hospital employees at all levels from housekeepers to physicians. The effect of the pay increases on employee motivation and job performance was greater among employees who scored low in positive affectivity than among employees who scored high in positive affectivity. In other words, greater pay for better performance was considered to be of greater value by employees who were more introverted and pessimistic and less energetic. Perhaps they needed the recognition and appreciation of the merit pay raise more than did those whose higher positive affectivity (greater energy and optimism) were more independent of the circumstances of their employment (Shaw, Duffy, Mitra, Lockhart, & Bowler, 2003).

Cross-cultural differences have also been cited in the effectiveness of merit pay. In a large-scale study of more than 28,000 employees in 37 countries, researchers found that merit pay was much

Wage-incentive system   The primary pay system for production workers in which the more units produced, the higher is the wage.

Unequal Pay for Women—and for Men, Too

Patti Landers was delighted when she got a job as an engineer with the Boeing Company in her home town of Seattle, Washington. Working at Boeing was a family tradition; her father, brother, and husband all had jobs with the aircraft manufacturer. Years before, her grandparents had worked there. It seemed like a great opportunity, and it was, until Patti compared the amount of her paycheck with what the men in her family were earning—and found a big, big difference. She felt cheated; so in the year 2000 she and 37 other women filed a sex discrimination lawsuit against the company.

Boeing denied the allegation that women were paid less than men for doing the same work. But *Business Week* magazine obtained more than 12,000 pages of company documents showing that Boeing had conducted several internal studies that confirmed that men were paid more than women for the same job. Yet Boeing still fought the lawsuit, even though their own documents—which they had hidden in a secure room with an electronic cipher lock—proved that they had known about the pay inequities for 10 years.

Company policies such as these are nothing new. Most businesses have typically paid women less than men for performing the same or similar jobs. What is new is a study showing that *both women and men* who manage work groups composed mostly of women are paid less than those who manage work groups composed mostly of men.

A study of 2,178 managers in 512 companies demonstrated that in work groups that are 40% to 50% women, managers are paid substantially less than managers with work groups that have a majority of men. As the percentage of female employees in a work group increases, the pay of their manager decreases. The researchers concluded that pay is unequal for men, too, if the group they manage is composed mostly of women.

Eight years after Patti Landers filed her sex discrimination lawsuit, Boeing agreed to pay $72.5 million to settle the case, far more money than they saved by paying women less than men for the same work in the first place.

Sources: Holmes, S. (April 26, 2004). A new black eye for Boeing: Internal documents suggest years of serious compensation gaps for women. *Business Week*, pp. 90–92; Ostroff, C., & Atwater, L. (2003). Does whom you work with matter? Effects of referent group gender and age composition on managers' compensation. *Journal of Applied Psychology, 88*, 725–740; usatoday.com, February 26, 2008.

---

more effective as a motivator in so-called poorer countries than in so-called richer ones (Van De Vliert, Van Yperen, & Thierry, 2008).

Wage-Incentive Pay Systems

Wage-incentive systems are the primary pay scheme for production workers. Through a time-and-motion analysis of a production job, an average or standard number of units produced in a given time can be determined. The wage-incentive system is based on this rate. In theory, the system provides an incentive for high job performance—the more units produced, the higher the wage—but it seldom works in practice. Many work groups establish their own standard for a good shift's production. Regardless of the incentive offered they will not produce more; rather, they will spread out the work to comfortably fill the hours. Surveys show that most workers prefer a straight hourly payment system.

JOB INVOLVEMENT AND ORGANIZATIONAL COMMITMENT

Closely related to motivation and job satisfaction is job involvement, that is, the intensity of a person's psychological identification with a job. Usually, the higher one's identification or involvement with a job, the greater is one's job satisfaction. Job involvement is related to several personal and organizational variables.

Personal Factors

Personal characteristics related to job involvement include age, growth needs, and belief in the traditional work ethic. Older workers are usually more involved with their jobs, perhaps because they have more responsibility and challenge and more opportunity to satisfy their growth needs. Older workers are also more likely to believe in the value of hard work. Younger workers, typically in entry-level positions, hold less stimulating and challenging jobs.

Growth needs are important in job involvement. It follows, then, that the job characteristics most relevant to job involvement are stimulation, autonomy, variety, task identity, feedback, and participation—the characteristics that allow for the satisfaction of the growth needs.

Social factors on the job can influence job involvement. Employees who work in groups or teams report stronger job involvement than employees who work alone. Participation in decision making is related to job involvement, as is the extent to which employees support organizational goals. Feelings of success and achievement on the job enhance an employee's level of job involvement.

The relationship between job involvement and job performance is unclear. Employees with high job involvement are more satisfied with, and more successful at, their jobs. Their rates of turnover and absenteeism are lower than those of employees with low job involvement. However, psychologists cannot state with certainty that high job involvement correlates with high performance.

Another variable allied with motivation and job satisfaction is organizational commitment, that is, the degree of psychological identification with or attachment to the company for which a person works. Organizational commitment has the following components:

- Acceptance of the organization's values and goals
- Willingness to exert effort for the organization
- Having a strong desire to remain affiliated with the organization

Organizational commitment is related to both personal and organizational factors. Older employees who have been with a company more than 2 years and who have a high need to achieve are more likely to rate high in organizational commitment. A meta-analysis of 3,630 employees in 27 separate studies showed that the longer a person had been employed by a company, the stronger was the link between organizational commitment and job performance. The researchers suggested that taking measures to increase organizational commitment early in new employees could lead to better job performance (Wright & Bonett, 2002). Scientists and engineers appear to have less organizational commitment than do employees in other occupational groups. In addition, government employees have lower organizational commitment than employees in the private sector. Government employees are also likely to be lower in job satisfaction.

Job satisfaction is related to workplace conditions. For some employees, an exercise facility at the workplace fosters a positive attitude toward the job.

Organizational Factors

Organizational factors associated with high organizational commitment include job enrichment, autonomy, opportunity to use skills, and positive attitudes toward the work group. Organizational commitment is influenced by employees' perception of how committed the organization is to them. The greater the perceived commitment to employees, the higher the employees' expectations that if they work to meet organizational goals, they will be equitably rewarded.

A study of 746 employees of a university showed that those who scored high in organizational commitment were more dedicated to a company-sponsored program designed to improve work quality than were those who scored low in organizational commitment (Neubert & Cady, 2001). There is also a positive relationship between perceived organizational support and organizational commitment, diligence, innovative management, job performance, and attendance. Organizational commitment is positively related to the amount of support received from supervisors and co-workers and to the degree of satisfaction with supervisors (Bishop & Scott, 2000; Liden, Wayne, & Sparrowe, 2000).

Studies have confirmed a positive relationship between organizational justice and organizational commitment. People who believe their employer treats them fairly are more likely to feel a commitment to the company than are people who believe they are being treated unfairly (Simons & Roberson, 2003).

Gender seems to be related to organizational commitment. The more women in a work group, the lower the commitment of the men. With women, however, the reaction is the opposite. The more men there are in a work group, the higher the level of organizational commitment among the women.

Types of Commitment

I-O psychologists have identified three kinds of organizational commitment: affective, or attitudinal, commitment; behavioral, or continuance, commitment; and normative commitment (Esnape & Redman, 2003; Meyer & Allen, 1991). In *affective commitment*, the type we have been discussing, the employee identifies with the organization, internalizes its values and attitudes, and complies with its demands. Affective commitment correlates highly with perceived organizational support, as was shown in research with 333 retail employees studied over a 2-year period and 226 employees studied over a 3-year period (Rhoades, Eisenberger, & Armeli, 2001). The results demonstrated that perceived organizational support was a primary factor in the development of affective commitment.

In a review and meta-analysis of more than 70 studies, researchers also found a strong positive link between perceived organizational support and affective commitment (Rhoades & Eisenberger, 2002). A study of 211 employee–supervisor dyads showed that supervisor support and recognition was related to perceived organizational support, which, in turn, was related to organizational commitment (Wayne, Shore, Bommer, & Tetrick, 2002). The importance of supervisor support in increasing perceived organizational support was also demonstrated in a study of 493 retail sales employees. That study also found that high perceived organizational support was strongly related to reduced turnover (Eisenberger, Stingchamber, Vandenberghe, Socharski, & Rhoades, 2002).

Other research involving 413 postal workers found a reciprocal relationship between perceived organizational support and affective commitment, which suggests that each factor strengthens the other. The more employees believe their company cares for them and supports their needs, the more strongly they identify with the company and internalize its values and attitudes; and vice versa (Eisenberger, Armeli, Rexwinkel, Lynch, & Rhoades, 2001).

Studies conducted in the United States and in France have demonstrated a high positive correlation between affective organizational commitment and an employee's mood and job performance (Herrbach, 2006; Hunter & Thatcher, 2007; Luchak & Gellatly, 2007).

In *behavioral commitment*, the employee is bound to the organization only by peripheral factors such as pension plans and seniority, which would not continue if the employee quit. There is no personal identification with organizational goals and values. Research suggests that affective commitment is positively related to job performance, but behavioral commitment is negatively related to job performance.

Normative commitment involves a sense of obligation to remain with the employer, a feeling that develops when employees receive benefits such as tuition reimbursement or specific skills training.

Organizational Citizenship Behavior

Organizational citizenship behavior (OCB) means putting forth extra effort, doing more for an employer than the minimum requirements of the job. It includes such behaviors as "taking on additional assignments, voluntarily assisting other people at work, keeping up with the developments in one's field or profession, following company rules even when no one is looking, promoting and protecting the organization, and keeping a positive attitude and tolerating inconveniences at work" (Bolino & Turnley, 2003, p. 60).

Good organizational citizens are model employees whose behavior can help ensure the success of an organization. Studies in a variety of businesses—insurance agencies, paper mills, and fast-food restaurant chains—have demonstrated that employees who are high in organizational citizenship behaviors are more productive and offer better service, which is related to higher customer satisfaction and greater company profits (see, for example, Bergeron, 2007; Koys, 2001; Walz & Niehoff, 2000).

Research has related several factors to OCB. For example, studies of U.S. workers showed that high OCB correlated with the strength of friendships with co-workers, a strong sense of empathy, and high job satisfaction and affective commitment (Bowler & Brass, 2006; Joireman, Kamdar, Daniels, & Duell, 2006; Payne & Webber, 2006). A large-scale study of more than 116,000 managers and team members from 33 countries found that supportive leadership facilitated OCB in work teams (Euwema, Wendt, & Van Emmerik, 2007). Similar results were obtained from a survey of 1,000 U.S. bank employees, which showed the importance of support from supervisors in developing OCB (Dineen, Lewicki, & Tomlinson, 2006).

Other research has shown that people who display organizational citizenship behaviors score high on the factors of conscientiousness, extraversion, optimism, and altruism. They are also team-oriented. In a study of 149 nurses in Canada, investigators identified a strong cognitive component to organizational citizenship behavior. Good organizational citizens based their behaviors on deliberate, rational calculations as to how they would benefit from displaying such behaviors on the job (Lee & Allen, 2002). Essentially they seemed to be saying, "What's in it for me if I behave this way on the job?" But is this a question people routinely ask in almost any situation—on the job, in the classroom, or in evaluating relationships with other people? What do you think?

Summary

Content theories of motivation deal with internal needs that influence behavior. Process theories focus on cognitive processes involved in making decisions. **Achievement motivation theory** posits the need to accomplish something and to be the best in whatever one undertakes. **Needs hierarchy theory** suggests five needs (physiological, safety, belonging, esteem, and self-actualization), each of which must be satisfied before the next becomes prominent. **Motivator–hygiene theory** proposes motivator needs (the nature of the work and its level of achievement and responsibility) and hygiene needs (aspects of the work environment such as pay and supervision). An outgrowth of motivator–hygiene theory is **job enrichment**, the redesign of jobs to maximize motivator factors. **Job-characteristics theory**, a theory based on individual differences in growth needs, suggests that employee perceptions of job characteristics influence motivation.

The **valence-instrumentality-expectancy (VIE) theory** describes a person's perceived expectation of the rewards that will follow certain behaviors. **Equity theory** deals with the ratio of outcome to input and how equitably that ratio compares with those of co-workers. **Goal-setting theory** suggests that motivation is defined by a person's intention to achieve a particular goal.

Job satisfaction, which can be measured through questionnaires and interviews, may be partly an inherited characteristic reciprocally related to overall life satisfaction. Job satisfaction increases with age, length of job experience, and occupational level. Differences by gender in reported job satisfaction are inconsistent. Job satisfaction appears unaffected by cognitive ability, assuming a job is sufficiently challenging. Other factors affecting job satisfaction include **job congruence**, organizational justice, use of skills, personality, and control. Losing one's job can be damaging to self-esteem and health. Large-scale layoffs also affect the workers remaining on the job.

Research shows a significant relationship between job satisfaction and job performance. The higher the job satisfaction, the higher the performance—a relationship that holds for individuals and for business units such as work teams. Job satisfaction can result in **prosocial behavior**; job dissatisfaction can lead to counterproductive behavior that interferes with organizational goals. Absenteeism is higher among younger workers and in companies with liberal sick-leave policies. Absenteeism is high in low-status jobs and in high-paying jobs and can be caused by low positive affectivity and high levels of stress and depression. Turnover is allied with low job involvement, low organizational commitment, poor promotion opportunities, and dissatisfaction with pay and supervision. In functional turnover, low performers quit; in dysfunctional turnover, high performers quit.

Research has demonstrated a positive relationship between pay and job satisfaction. An important factor in pay satisfaction is its perceived equity and relationship to job performance. Both blue-collar workers on **wage-incentive systems** and managers on **merit pay** systems report pay dissatisfaction. Merit pay can lower motivation because of perceived unfairness; that is, some workers believe their true abilities are not sufficiently rewarded.

Job involvement (intensity of psychological identification with work) is related to job satisfaction. These factors affect job involvement: personal characteristics such as age, growth needs, and belief in the work ethic; and job characteristics such as level of challenge and opportunity for employee participation. Organizational commitment is also related to job satisfaction and is greater among older employees and those high in achievement motivation. In addition, other variables contribute to organizational commitment: job enrichment, autonomy, perceived organizational support, organizational justice, and a positive attitude toward the work group. Organizational commitment can be affective, behavioral, or normative.

Organizational citizenship behavior involves doing more for an employer than the job requires. Such behavior can lead to higher job performance and can be influenced by personality, supportive leadership, and self-serving decisions.

Key Terms

achievement motivation theory	job enrichment	needs hierarchy theory
equity theory	job satisfaction	prosocial behavior
goal-setting theory	merit pay	valence-instrumentality-
job-characteristics theory	motivator–hygiene (two-factor)	expectancy theory
job congruence	theory	wage-incentive systems

Review Questions

1. Explain the differences between content theories and process theories of motivation. What do these types of theories have in common?

2. What two types of goals can satisfy the need for achievement?

3. Describe the characteristics of people who are high in the need for achievement.

4. What are the needs in Maslow's needs hierarchy theory? Which needs can be satisfied on the job?

5. Distinguish between motivator needs and hygiene needs and describe how each type affects job satisfaction.

6. How would you enrich the job of an automobile assembly-line worker?

7. In what ways does the motivator–hygiene theory differ from the job-characteristics theory? In what ways are they similar?

8. Give an example of how the VIE theory can be applied to your job as a student.

9. According to equity theory, what are three ways of responding to perceived equity or inequity? Which way best describes you?

10. How can goal-setting theory be applied to the workplace? Give an example of how it would work.

11. How do I-O psychologists measure job satisfaction? What personal characteristics can influence level of job satisfaction?

12. Describe some effects of being laid off from a job. How does job loss affect the company employees who were not laid off?

13. What is prosocial behavior and how does it relate to job satisfaction?

14. Discuss the relationship between job satisfaction and job performance for individual employees and for work groups.

15. Why is it difficult to conduct research on absenteeism?

16. What organizational policies may contribute to a high absenteeism rate?

17. Distinguish between functional turnover and dysfunctional turnover.

18. How does a merit pay system differ from a wage-incentive pay system? What are the problems with each of these approaches?

19. Explain the difference between job involvement and organizational commitment.

20. What personal and organizational factors can influence organizational commitment?

21. Describe three types of organizational commitment.

22. What is organizational citizenship behavior and what factors can influence it?

23. Give two examples of organizational citizenship behavior and explain what you think motivates the behavior.

Additional Reading

Ellingson, J. E., Gruys, M. L., & Sackett, P. R. (1998). Factors related to the satisfaction and performance of temporary employees. *Journal of Applied Psychology, 83*, 913–921. Discusses job satisfaction among temp employees (a large but rarely studied subject group) and relates it to whether the decision to undertake temporary work is voluntary or involuntary.

Hart, P. M. (1999). Predicting employee life satisfaction. *Journal of Applied Psychology, 84*, 564–584. Reports on personality correlates (such as neuroticism, extraversion, and job satisfaction) that relate to overall life satisfaction in a group of police officers.

Latham, G. (2007). *Work motivation*. Thousand Oaks, CA: Sage. A comprehensive review of the history, theory, research, and practical issues involved in employee motivation and job satisfaction.

Organ, D., Podsakoff, P., & Mackenzie, S. (2006). *Organizational citizenship behavior*. Thousand Oaks, CA: Sage. Describes prosocial organizational behavior and relates it to variables such as conscientiousness, commitment, morale, and satisfaction with management.

Uchitelle, L. (2006). *The disposable American: Layoffs and their consequences*. New York: Knopf. Deals with the psychological effects of layoffs among white-collar and blue-collar employees, problems with retraining, and feelings of loyalty towards one's organization.

Wright, T. A., & Cropanzano, R. (2000). Psychological well-being and job satisfaction as predictors of job performance. *Journal of Occupational Health Psychology, 5*(1), 84–94. Analyzes the idea that the so-called happy worker is a more productive worker. Relates happiness (psychological well-being) and job satisfaction to job performance.

CHAPTER 9

The Organization of the Organization

Bureaucracy A formal, orderly, and rational approach to organizing business enterprises.

All of us live and work within the framework of some kind of organization, a context that provides written and unwritten, formal and informal rules about how its members conduct themselves. You grew up in an organization called a family. Your parents established a culture that defined the guidelines by which the family functioned—the acceptable attitudes, values, and behaviors that made your family a unique organization, different from the families of your friends and acquaintances.

Perhaps a family in the house across the street had a culture based on orthodox religious beliefs and unusually strict standards of behavior, whereas a family next door was more moderate in its beliefs or reared its children more permissively. These families operated within different organizational styles. They established a structure based on a specific set of expectations, needs, and values that were expected to hold for all family members.

Various organizational styles are also evident in your college classes. One professor may be stern, even dictatorial, allowing no student discussion. Another may operate in a more democratic fashion, asking students to participate in decision making about course content and requirements.

Differences in organizational style in the workplace range from the rigid, hierarchical bureaucracy of the military and the civil service to the open, participatory approach that fosters high employee involvement. Bureaucracies regulate and prescribe what workers do and how they do it; little deviation is tolerated. The modern organizational style, which attempts to humanize the workplace, has led to a modification of many traditional bureaucratic practices. Increasing numbers of organizations are treating their employees as integral members of the company and requesting their input in long-range planning and decision making. This shift in organizational style has brought about radical changes in the way work is organized and performed and has led to an improvement in the quality of work life for many employees.

Organizational psychologists study these changing trends in organizational life to determine their impact on employee satisfaction and behavior. In chapters 7 and 8 we described how the nature of leadership and the motivation of workers can affect job satisfaction, job performance, and organizational efficiency. In this chapter we describe the impact of organizational factors.

BUREAUCRATIC ORGANIZATIONS OF THE PAST

The bureaucratic approach and the participatory approach represent two extremes in organizational style. People tend to think of **bureaucracies** in negative terms, as bloated, inefficient structures, top-heavy with layers of management and wrapped in miles of red tape that frustrates creativity. As everyday experiences in trying to deal with organizations of this type show, there is much truth to this view. Yet the bureaucratic organizational style was once as revolutionary as the modern participative style, and it was considered just as humanistic in its intentions. Bureaucracies were devised to improve the quality of work life, and for a while they did.

As a movement of social protest, bureaucracy was designed to correct the inequities, favoritism, and cruelty that characterized organizations at the beginning of the Industrial Revolution. Companies were owned and managed by their founders, who had absolute control over the terms and conditions of employment. Employees were at the mercy of the owners' whims, prejudices, and decrees.

To correct these abuses, Max Weber (1864–1920), a German sociologist, proposed a new organizational style that would eliminate social and personal injustice (Weber, 1947). Bureaucracy was to be a rational, formal structure organized along impersonal and objective lines—an orderly, predictable system that would function like an efficient machine, unaffected by the prejudices of the factory owners. Workers would have the opportunity to rise from one organizational level to the next on the basis of their ability, not because of their social class or whether the boss liked them. Bureaucracy was a socially responsible improvement over the earlier system and served in its day to humanize the workplace.

The few executives at the top of the organization chart have little contact with lower level employees and may have little awareness of their working conditions and personal concerns.

The first practical application of the bureaucratic organizational style appeared in the United States even before Weber published his ideas on bureaucracy. The organization chart, which may be the most famous symbol of the bureaucratic approach, came into being in the 1850s. A general superintendent for the New York & Erie Railroad, Daniel McCallum, prepared a chart for his company and insisted that all workers abide by it (Chandler, 1988). McCallum's idea of formalizing the position and status of all employees in a hierarchical structure quickly became popular and was soon adopted by most U.S. companies. Thus, when Weber formally promoted the rules by which bureaucracies should operate, he was describing an organizational style already widely accepted in the United States.

Weber's ideas about bureaucracy, as depicted on the organization chart, involved breaking down or decentralizing the organization into component parts and operations. Each operation would be linked to others in a fixed rank order of control. The concept of division of labor, fostered by the scientific management approach, simplified jobs and made them more specialized. Responsibility or authority for each operation was delegated downward through the hierarchy, and communication flowed upward through the same channels. This arrangement effectively cut employees off from contact with other levels and sectors of the organization.

Organization charts look nice and give managers the feeling that employees are in their proper places and that the organization is running smoothly. However, these neat lines and boxes on paper do not always reflect daily operations on the job. There is an organization within the organization—an uncharted complex of informal social groupings of workers—that can interfere with the most rigid rules of the most dictatorial structure. Often it is through these informal groups and networks that the work of an organization is (or is not) accomplished.

And bureaucracies have problems. A bureaucratic management tends to ignore human needs and values. Managers in bureaucracies treat employees as inanimate, impersonal boxes on the chart, as interchangeable as the machines they operate. Bureaucracies do not recognize human motivations, such as the needs for personal growth and responsibility, self-actualization, and participation in decision making.

Employees in a bureaucracy have no individual identity and no control over their work or over the organizational policies that influence the quality of their working life. The ideal employees for a bureaucracy are docile, passive, dependent, and childlike. Decisions are made for them, for their own good, because they are considered incapable of deciding for themselves. By being forced to channel all communications through their immediate super-visor, workers are isolated from higher management and prevented from making suggestions about company practices that affect their jobs and their well-being. Employees in these situations score low on measures of job satisfaction, job performance, and organizational commitment.

Bureaucracies can be criticized not only for their smothering effects on workers but also for their harmful effects on themselves. Just as they prevent personal growth for employees, bureaucracies minimize opportunities for organizational growth, in part because of the barriers to upward communication. Bureaucracies foster rigidity and permanence and do not adapt quickly or well to the kinds of changing social conditions and technological innovations characteristic of today's workplace. The orderly bureaucratic structure operates to preserve existing conditions. New developments are viewed as threats. For all its initial revolutionary fervor and humanistic intentions, then, the bureaucracy has not been successful in meeting human needs and changing times.

HIGH-INVOLVEMENT MANAGEMENT AND EMPLOYEE PARTICIPATION

A major criticism of bureaucracy is its tendency to treat workers as docile, passive, and dependent. The participative organizational style takes a different view of human nature, summarized by the Theory Y position of McGregor's Theory X/Theory Y formulation as described in chapter 7. Theory X describes a view of human nature compatible with the rigid requirements of a bureaucracy, which stifles individual motivation and the potential for growth. Workers need strict supervision because they are incapable of acting on their own initiative. This traditional, low-involvement organizational approach has the employees doing the work, middle managers controlling them, and only top management involved in strategy, planning, and long-range leadership.

In contrast, Theory Y assumes that employees are motivated to seek and accept responsibility for their work. In this view, people have a high level of creativity, commitment, and need for personal growth. Theory Y and other motivational conceptions supporting a participative approach suggest that organizations must decrease workers' dependency and subordination in order to take better advantage of their potential. Jobs and organiza-

tions must become less rigid in design and structure; they must allow employees to help determine how best to perform their tasks. Jobs should be enriched to increase challenge and responsibility. Leaders should become less autocratic and more responsive to employee input. Decision making should involve participation at all levels. And organizations must become more flexible, capable of changing in response to employee needs and to social, technological, and economic conditions.

This high-involvement management style rests on three assumptions about people, participation, and performance:

1. *Human relations.* People should be treated fairly and with respect. People want to participate, and when they are allowed to do so, they will accept change and become more satisfied with and committed to the organization.

2. *Human resources.* People are a valuable resource because they have knowledge and ideas. When they participate in decision making, the result is better solutions to organizational problems. Organizations must promote the personal development of their employees because it makes them more valuable to the company.

3. *High involvement.* People can be trusted to develop the knowledge and skills to make important decisions about the management of their work. When people are allowed to make such decisions, the result is an improvement in organizational performance.

The kind of work behavior stimulated by high-involvement management has been labeled, simply, "taking charge." Taking charge in this context involves employees in making decisions about how their work should be performed and then implementing those decisions by actively restructuring the way they do their job. There is ample research to demonstrate that employee involvement and participation in decision making correlates with increases in job satisfaction and performance and with lower rates of turnover (Combs, Liu, Hall, & Ketchen, 2006; Pereira & Osburn, 2007; Zatzick & Iverson, 2006).

In a nationwide survey of thousands of workers in England, high-involvement management was positively related to higher pay (Forth & Millward, 2004). Research conducted in a large U.S. retail organization on 2,755 employees in 215 work groups reported that a sense of "psychological ownership" was fostered by a climate that

> **Total quality management (TQM)**
> Participative management programs characterized by increased employee involvement and responsibility.

emphasized self-determination, participative management, and recognition. This feeling of psychological ownership correlated with positive employee attitudes toward the organization and with the organization's improved profitability (Wagner, Parker, & Christiansen, 2003).

High-involvement management calls for active employee participation in decision making and policymaking at all levels, and it can lead to greater opportunities for personal growth and fulfillment and increased organizational effectiveness. These changes in organizational style have been expressed in various quality-of-work-life programs.

TOTAL QUALITY MANAGEMENT

Total quality management (TQM) refers, in general, to the kinds of participative management programs we have been describing. They are characterized by increased employee involvement,

Newsbreak

Look Out! The Employees Are Taking Over

It's happening everywhere. Employees are taking on more responsibility and making decisions only their bosses used to make. Jobs have been enlarged, expanded, and enriched; workers have been empowered, that is, given the freedom to take charge and do their work in their own way.

Take the case of a major department store. A salesperson overheard a customer tell a companion that the suit she had bought 3 weeks ago was now on sale. She wished she had waited for the sale so she could have bought it for less. The alert salesperson asked for the customer's name and credited her account with the difference between the sale price and the original price. The salesperson acted on his own initiative, without asking his supervisor for an OK. Without even telling his supervisor! He was empowered to make these decisions for himself.

Nordstrom, the department store that prides itself on both customer and employee satisfaction, posts the following rules for its new employees:

Rule #1: Use your good judgment in all situations.

There will be no additional rules.

The rule says to use your good judgment. This means that decisions and the responsibility for them are in the hands of the employees, not the supervisors. This is nothing short of a revolution in the workplace.

A commercial printing company in Wisconsin encourages its printing press operators to make their own decisions. A corporate spokesperson explained: "Just as each lawyer is a partner and runs his own part of the business, I said each pressman is going to run his own press. I'd rather have 50 people out there thinking independently than for me to sit up here from the top and say, 'This is the way we're going to do it.'"

At Compaq Computers, three-person teams assemble and test new computers. Each worker is capable of performing different tasks and coping with challenges. Previously, the computers were built on an assembly line, with each worker performing one small task repeatedly. Under the new system, the number of completed units per worker increased 50%. Profits improved, and employees reported greater satisfaction with their jobs. They feel important—and they are. The employees are taking over!

Quality-of-work-life (QWL) programs
Organizational programs based on active employee participation in decision making and policy making.

responsibility, and participation in jobs that have been expanded, enriched, and enlarged. They adhere to the Theory Y approach to leadership in which employee ideas and decisions play a vital role in the effective functioning of the organization. The overall goal of TQM is to improve the quality of the work being performed within the organization by improving the quality of the employees' working life. For that reason, TQM programs are sometimes called **quality-of-work-life (QWL) programs**. These programs have been implemented—in most cases with great success—to change the nature of leadership from Theory X to Theory Y and to improve employee motivation, job satisfaction, job involvement, and organizational commitment (see www.managementhelp.org/quality/tqm/tqm.htm).

An ambitious quality-of-work-life program was undertaken by General Motors (GM) with the support of top management and the United Auto Workers union. The program began when company and union officials agreed to form a labor–management committee to assess QWL projects. All projects had to consider extrinsic factors (physical working conditions) as well as intrinsic factors (employee involvement and satisfaction). Teams of I-O psychologists, managers, and employees were empowered to enlarge jobs, redesign production facilities, and revise the old low-involvement bureaucratic organizational structure.

The program began at a GM assembly plant in Fremont, California, which had been closed because of the poor quality of the cars assembled there. Absenteeism stood at 20%, on-the-job use of alcohol and illicit drugs was widespread, and more than 800 employees had filed grievances against the company. The plant reopened 3 years later as New United Motors Manufacturing Incorporated (NUMMI), a joint venture of GM and Toyota that was committed to participative management (see www.nummi.com).

NUMMI employees work in teams of four to six members and perform a variety of tasks throughout the workweek. Cars are built on the traditional assembly line, but employees rotate from one job to another, mastering new skills in the

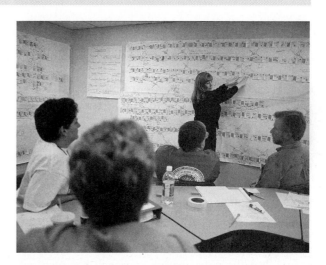

Under a quality-of-work-life program, small teams of workers meet periodically to discuss problems of productivity and employee involvement.

process. They solve production problems and devise ways to increase productivity on their own, without being told what to do by their supervisors. Artificial status barriers have been eliminated. Workers and managers eat in the same cafeteria, and all begin the workday with a group exercise period. Most of the employees who worked in the old GM plant like the high-involvement participative organizational style, and the quality of the cars produced has improved markedly.

Encouraged by NUMMI's success, General Motors adopted the participatory approach for its Saturn Motors plant in Spring Hill, Tennessee. Workers are organized into teams of about a dozen members, and they make all major decisions about their work, including the hiring of new employees. Management perks, such as reserved parking places, were eliminated. Communication is encouraged across all levels without employees having to obtain permission from supervisors or union shop stewards. Absenteeism is reported to be less than 1%, a rate similar to that of Japanese auto plants and less than a tenth of other U.S. auto plants. Productivity increased markedly in all GM plants that instituted QWL programs. Ford and Chrysler

Self-managing work teams Employee groups that allow the members of a work team to manage, control, and monitor all facets of their work, from recruiting, hiring, and training new employees to deciding when to take rest breaks.

started similar programs and reported increases in worker productivity.

The major factor driving these advances in the auto industry and other sectors of the economy is increased worker involvement and participation. Management has seen that taking an interest in what workers have to say really does pay off.

Success or Failure?

Although there are many reports of successful QWL programs, some have failed. Consider Volvo, which has been building cars by the team approach for decades. At Volvo's plants with QWL programs, productivity is lower than at standard assembly plants, but the participative approach has resulted in substantial improvements in quality and reductions in turnover and absenteeism.

More than 20 years ago, Volvo expanded the concept of worker participation at a new car assembly factory in Sweden. Instead of having employee teams build a portion of each car, which then moves on to the next team, the teams at the new plant were expected to build an entire car. The results were dismal. It took 50 hours to assemble a car at the new plant, compared to 37 hours at the plant where teams worked on portions of a car. At a Volvo plant in Belgium that used a traditional assembly line, it took 25 hours to assemble a car. Absenteeism at the plant in Sweden was high because many employees did not realize the demands the redesigned job would entail. In addition, the training period to provide workers with the skills required to assemble an entire car turned out to be longer than anticipated.

Other QWL programs have failed because some employees have no desire to participate in decision making or to assume responsibility for determining the best way to perform their jobs. Some workers prefer, or need, more rather than less direct supervision. Also, QWL efforts can be doomed when managers continue to try to control their subordinates instead of working with them to share power and authority. QWL programs have a high probability of failure when they do not have the forceful advocacy and commitment of senior executives and when supervisors and union shop stewards view such programs as a threat to their power. Managers and supervisors must give up some of the power and authority by which they once directed and controlled their subordinates. They must also learn to share power and to function willingly as coaches, guides, mentors, and resource persons. Many managers find this a difficult adjustment to make.

Two characteristics of today's workplace may tend to dampen the positive effects of QWL programs: diversity and the growing number of contingent workers. Although the workforce as a whole is becoming increasingly diverse, some organizations remain dominated by a majority of White males. Women and ethnic minority employees are often left out of the informal social network through which majority employees share job-related information and social support. Thus, minority employees have fewer opportunities to participate in decision making and in efforts to restructure and redesign their jobs. In addition, an organization's permanent, full-time staff may actively exclude contingent employees (like temporary or contract employees, or virtual workers) from participative programs.

Self-Managing Work Teams

Self-managing work teams allow employees to manage, control, and monitor all facets of their work, from recruiting, hiring, and training new employees to deciding when to take rest breaks. These autonomous work teams have become highly popular in business and industry today.

An early analysis of the first self-managing work teams yielded the following behavioral characteristics:

- Employees assume personal responsibility and accountability for the outcomes of their work.
- Employees monitor their own performance and seek feedback on how well they are accomplishing their tasks and meeting organizational goals.

Modern organizations invite employee participation in decision making.
(Courtesy of Ford Motor Company.)

- Employees manage their performance and take corrective action when necessary to improve their performance and the performance of other group members.

- Employees seek guidance, assistance, and resources from the organization when they do not have what they need to do the job.

- Employees help members of their team and employees in other teams to improve job performance and raise productivity for the organization as a whole.

Self-managing work teams require a level of employee maturity and responsibility not called for in supervisor-managed groups. Self-managing work groups also need clear direction from the organization about production goals, a support staff to provide technical expertise, and adequate material resources. In some cases, engineers and accountants are added to the self-management teams so that the teams can deal with a full range of problems. The teams operate, in effect, like miniature businesses within the larger organization.

Self-managing work teams also depend on the maturity and responsibility of managers, who must be willing to surrender authority to their subordinates. Indeed, management support is the most critical variable in determining the effectiveness of these groups. The extent of managerial support is also highly predictive of employee satisfaction.

The term *self-managing* is not quite accurate because all such teams require an external team leader (an employee of the organization who is outside the work group) to serve as a mediator, liaison, and buffer between the work group and the organization. In-depth critical-incident interviews with 19 external team leaders and 38 team members of a Fortune 500 company revealed that successful external team leaders displayed two kinds of behaviors: one focused on the organization and the other on the team (Druskat & Wheeler, 2003). Organization-focused behaviors involve a high degree of social and political awareness of the needs, values, and concerns of management. Leaders must make sure that team members are aware of those concerns and responsive to them. Team-focused behaviors involve building trust among the group members and showing respect, concern, and care for them. Thus, some type of leadership is necessary for self-managing work teams to function efficiently; a hands-off approach was not found to be effective.

Many studies of self-managing work teams showed their positive effects on productivity, quality of work, turnover, and job satisfaction (Morgeson, Johnson, Campion, Medsker, & Mumford, 2006; Zhang, Hempel, Han, & Tjosvold, 2007). Note, however, that self-managing work teams also have their problems. Converting from traditional bureaucratic management to self-management is difficult, expensive, and time-consuming, and many organizations underestimate the extent of the investment required. In particular,

they underestimate the amount of training and meeting time involved and have unrealistic expectations about how soon self-managing teams can become productive. The need to monitor and review the progress of self-managing work teams can also dampen the initial enthusiasm for this approach.

Virtual Self-Managing Work Teams

Employees who are members of a virtual self-managing work team may work in geographically separate offices, or home offices, for different units of the same company or even in different companies but linked by the same project. They meet by electronic means to perform a specific task; they may rarely assemble in person. Their efforts are wired through information systems such as the Desktop Videoconferencing System (DVCS).

Through e-mail and other means of telecommunication, the DVCS re-creates the face-to-face interactions and dynamics of actual group meetings. Cameras mounted on computer monitors bring team members into visual contact, allowing their verbal contributions to be supplemented and enlivened by facial expressions and gestures that can be viewed by all team members. An important element of context is thus added to the team members' words and opinions.

Virtual work teams have the potential to increase productivity, job satisfaction, job involvement, and organizational or team commitment. Group members must manage their own projects and evaluate their own performance. Managers must master the means of communication and keep team members "in the loop." Attendance must be mandatory, so that all team members have an opportunity to participate.

In a study of 54 successful virtual teams from 33 organizations, researchers found that team leaders consistently displayed certain behaviors and practices that were not shown by leaders of unsuccessful teams. The successful leaders developed and maintained the trust of their team members by making frequent use of communications technology, managing the virtual meetings, actively monitoring team progress, and ensuring that the contributions of individual team members were recognized by the rest of the organization (Malhotra, Majchrzak, & Rosen, 2007).

A Shorter Workday? What If Everyone Wants to Go Home Early?

Did you know that Harman Automotive is the most famous automobile rearview mirror factory in the history of I-O psychology? The plant, located in Bolivar, Tennessee, was the first real-life experiment in employee empowerment; Workers were given control over their own jobs. When this bold venture began, more than a quarter of a century ago, it was so phenomenally successful that the Big Three automakers used it as a model when they planned and implemented similar changes in their workplaces.

So many corporate presidents, foundation executives, and university scholars descended on the plant to see the miracle firsthand that the workers soon felt overwhelmed. They were so busy conducting tours that they had little time left for making rearview mirrors. They decided to limit the visitors to one group a week.

And then it all went wrong. Workers decided that they wanted to go home as soon as they met their daily production quota. Managers agreed. They called it "earned idle time." Well, this was fine for the assemblers and polishers, who, by working in teams, could finish their mirrors in half a day. But it caused friction with the workers who ran the huge metal-casting machines. They had to remain on the job for the full shift to tend to their equipment.

So before long, everybody was demanding a shortened workday. Some managers bent the rules to allow their workers to leave early. Other managers refused. Many employees began to cut corners on quality so they could finish work in the morning and take most of the day off. Some workers devised shipping cartons with raised false bottoms so they would appear to be completely filled with mirrors when they were not. The temptation of paid time off was too great.

One worker said, "It turned us into thieves." A Harvard professor who had helped design the system lamented, "We were too idealistic."

Morale plummeted. Quality and quantity of product dropped. Absenteeism and turnover soared. Applicants for the jobs were easily attracted, however. Everybody had heard about the plant where you could get a full day's pay for a half day's work. The first question new hires asked was, "When can I go home?"

And one day in 1996, everybody went home early. Harman Automotive was forced to close.

ORGANIZATIONAL CHANGE

The employee participation programs we have discussed call for radical changes in organizational style. However, bureaucratic organizations by definition are resistant to change. When a structural change is to be introduced into an organization, it often meets with hostility, production slowdowns, strikes, or increased absenteeism and turnover. Whether the change involves new equipment, work schedules, procedures, office layout, or reassignment of personnel, it will usually be resisted at first.

Some organizations are able to change with the cooperation and support of employees and managers. The factor most responsible for determining whether change will be received positively or negatively is the way in which change is proposed and implemented. If change is imposed on employees in an autocratic manner and they are given no explanation or opportunity to participate, then they are likely to react negatively. However, when managers make an effort to explain the nature of the forthcoming change, the reasons for implementing it, and the benefits workers and management can expect from it, then workers are likely to respond positively and accept the change. As you might expect, the higher the leader–member exchange (LMX), the more accepting employees were found to be of organizational change (Furst & Cable, 2008).

A study of 130 public housing employees showed that their openness to change was positively affected by the amount of information they received from management and by the degree of their participation

> **Organizational development (OD)** The study and implementation of planned organizational changes.

in the planning process. Employees who were the least receptive to change also showed lower job satisfaction, were more likely to quit, and displayed greater irritation with aspects of their jobs (Wanberg & Banas, 2000).

Similar findings resulted from a study of two utility companies that were introducing major changes designed to reduce costs and to offer faster customer service. The changes would alter the ways in which many jobs were performed. Employees participated in the change process through their representation on a steering committee that worked closely with management. Before and during the time the changes were formulated and introduced, more than 100 employees were surveyed. The most significant finding was that employee trust in management increased over the period of the surveys. The researchers suggested that this greater trust was related to employees' beliefs that they had been given ample opportunity to participate in planning for the change and that management had explained and justified the plan sufficiently (Korsgaard, Sapienza, & Schweiger, 2002).

In another example of organizational change, a merger of companies resulted in job losses due to layoffs. Survey data showed that social support from co-workers was the most important coping resource for employees who were not laid off. Another finding was that employees' perceived control over their own job tenure was lowest during the initial stage of the organizational change, a time when layoffs were being rumored but not yet implemented. Once the layoffs had occurred, employees' perceived control increased (Fugate, Kinicki, & Scheck, 2002)

A study of 265 nurses also illustrated the importance of organizational commitment in accepting change. This survey showed that affective commitment and normative commitment were more important in employee support for organizational change than was behavioral commitment (Herscovitch & Meyer, 2002). In a study of 553 employees in 25 companies, researchers found that self-efficacy was a major factor in accepting organizational change. The more strongly employees

believed that they could adapt to the change, the more committed they became to it (Herold, Fedor, & Caldwell, 2007).

Are the positive effects of worker participation in planning and implementing change permanent, or do they disappear once the researchers leave the office or factory? To study this question, two I-O psychologists visited a plant more than 4 years after it had undergone a radical change from a centralized bureaucracy to a flexible, innovative, participatory democracy. The change had been guided by the company president (a psychologist), with full worker participation, and was considered successful in terms of increased corporate profits, productive efficiency, and employee satisfaction.

The consulting psychologists in this classic study found that the benefits were evident 4 years later and that some of the effects were even greater than during the period immediately following the change. The increase in job satisfaction was accompanied by a higher concern with maintaining production levels (Seashore & Bowers, 1970). When properly introduced, then, a change in work procedures or in the entire organizational climate can have long-lasting positive effects.

Organizational Development (OD)

I-O psychologists have focused considerable attention on the problems of total organizational change and on systematic ways to bring about planned change. This effort, called **organizational development (OD)**, involves techniques such as sensitivity training, role playing, group discussion, and job enrichment as well as survey feedback and team building.

In the survey feedback technique, surveys are conducted periodically to assess employee feelings and attitudes. The results are communicated to employees, managers, and work teams throughout the organization. Their task is to provide feedback to higher management by suggesting explanations for the questionnaire findings and by recommending ways to correct the problems identified by employees in the surveys. The team building technique is based

Change agents   Organization development facilitators who work with business groups to implement change and develop group confidence and effectiveness.

Socialization   The adjustment process by which new employees learn their role in the organizational hierarchy, their company's values, and the behaviors considered acceptable by their work group.

on the fact that many organizational tasks are performed by small work groups or teams. To enhance a team's morale and problem-solving abilities, OD consultants (called **change agents**) work with the groups to develop self-confidence, group cohesiveness, and working effectiveness.

Outside consultants, or change agents, are usually able to view an organization's structure, functions, and culture with greater objectivity than in-house managers. Change agents' first task is diagnosis: They use questionnaires and interviews to determine the organization's problems and needs. Change agents evaluate strengths and weaknesses and develop strategies for solving problems and for coping with future changes. However, they must be cautious about introducing change without allowing employees to participate in the process.

Implementation of the recommended strategies, a process called intervention, begins with top management. Unless organizational change has management support, the chance of success is small. The specific intervention techniques depend on the nature of the problem and on the organizational climate. The OD process is flexible and can be adapted to the needs of the situation. In general, regardless of the specific techniques applied, the OD process helps to free the typical bureaucratic organization from its rigidity and formality, thereby allowing more responsiveness and open participation.

OD techniques have been applied by many public and private organizations. Although research results are mixed, some significant increases in productivity have been documented. Job satisfaction seems to be negatively related to OD, however, perhaps because the emphasis is on improvements in productivity rather than on employee considerations.

SOCIALIZATION OF NEW EMPLOYEES

Organizations are constantly undergoing change through the addition of new employees at all levels of the workforce. New workers come with different levels of ability, motivation, and desire to perform their job well. They bring various needs and values that affect the organizations for which they work. At the same time, the culture of the organization makes its impact on the new employees. They have much to learn beyond the necessary job skills. They must learn their role in the hierarchy, the company's values, and the behaviors considered acceptable by their work group.

This learning and adjustment process is called **socialization**, and it is not unlike a rite of passage in which members of a society enter a new stage of life. Those who cope successfully with this adjustment process are generally happier and more productive employees.

Poor socialization to an organization—that is, a negligent or haphazard introduction to company policies and practices—can undermine the accomplishments of the most sophisticated employee selection system. An organization can recruit and hire qualified people and then lose them in the early stages of employment because of an inadequate reception. Improper socialization can foster frustration, anxiety, and dissatisfaction for new employees, which can lead to low job involvement and organizational commitment, low motivation and productivity, and to dismissal or quitting.

Positive interactions between current and new employees should be part of a company's socialization program.

Role ambiguity   A situation that arises when job responsibilities are unstructured or poorly defined.

Role conflict   A situation that arises when there is a disparity between job demands and the employee's personal standards.

On the other hand, successful socialization of new employees has been shown by much research to correlate positively with job satisfaction and job performance, organizational identification and commitment, and low intention to quit (Ashforth, Sluss, & Saks, 2007; Klein & Weaver, 2000; Saks, Uggersle, & Fassina, 2007).

Socialization involves several organizational strategies. Ideally, the company should provide new employees with challenging jobs that offer opportunities for growth and development, the mastery of skills, self-confidence, success experiences, positive interactions with superiors, feedback, and co-workers who have high morale and a positive attitude toward the organization.

A study of 154 newly hired accountants found that early socialization links with supervisors (instead of forming links only with co-workers at the same level) fostered the learning of job and social roles and the establishment of organizational commitment (Morrison, 2002). A long-term study of 101 new employees involved surveying them when they were graduating college seniors and conducting follow-up surveys 6 months after graduation and 2 years after graduation. Results showed that the new employees tended to internalize the values of their employer when they received positive social support from more experienced co-workers who served as role models (Cable & Parsons, 2001).

Although institutionalized socialization strategies are effective in teaching new hires about the organization, most new employees are not passive learners in this rite-of-passage process. Many are highly proactive, taking an enthusiastic role in seeking the information they believe they need to adapt to their work environment. In a study of 118 newly hired workers during their first 3 months on the job, researchers found that those high in extraversion and openness to new experiences demonstrated significantly higher proactive socialization behaviors than did those lower in these personality attributes. The extraverted employees were more likely to take steps to build relationships and to obtain feedback from co-workers and managers (Wanberg & Kammeyer-Mueller, 2000).

Research involving 70 newly hired employees for high-tech project teams found that newcomers who rated high in self-efficacy held higher expectations about how well they would perform their new job. The study also showed that newcomers' performance expectations were enhanced when they were provided with early success experiences, challenging goals, and positive role models on which to base their own job behaviors (Chen & Klimoski, 2003). In a meta-analysis of 70 samples of new hires, investigators found that those high in self-efficacy were far more likely to have successful socialization experiences than were those low in self-efficacy (Bauer, Bodner, Erdogan, Truxillo, & Tucker, 2007).

Socialization occurs more quickly when there is greater interaction between new and established employees. Interactions can include asking questions, having informal conversations, and taking coffee breaks together as well as formal activities such as mentoring and performance appraisals. However, some evidence indicates that socialization programs should not rely on the employees who are being replaced by the newcomers. Departing employees may teach their successors established and perhaps inefficient job performance techniques and thus discourage innovation.

In a study of 261 new employees of a large consulting firm, researchers compared the effectiveness of a social-based, in-person orientation program with a self-guided, computer-based orientation program that provided the same information. The results showed clearly that the computer-based approach hindered rather than helped the employees adjust to their new organizations (Wesson & Gogus, 2005).

I-O psychologists have identified two factors that relate to socialization: **role ambiguity** (when the employee's work role is poorly structured or defined) and **role conflict** (when there is a disparity between job demands and the employee's personal standards). High levels of role ambiguity and role conflict are associated with low levels of job satisfaction, satisfaction

> **Organizational culture** The organization's pattern of beliefs, expectations, and values as manifested in company and industry practices.

with supervisor, and organizational commitment, and with a high rate of turnover. To resolve role ambiguity and role conflict, many new employees act on their own to obtain information about the job and organization from their co-workers and supervisors.

Resocialization Due to Job Changes

Most of the research cited here has dealt with new college graduates entering their first full-time job. But nowadays, most people can expect to change jobs several times during their working life. Throughout your career, you are likely to experience new rites of passage, new socialization experiences (or resocialization) every time you join a different organization. Common sense suggests that having had one or more prior jobs should make socialization to the next job easier. Also, performance, job satisfaction, and organizational commitment might be expected to be higher among workers who have had previous jobs because of their experience in adjusting to different organizations. Research, however, has not always supported these expectations. Sometimes common-sense notions and intuitive beliefs are not supported by scientific study. This shows the importance of careful I-O research.

What about employees who stay with the same company but are transferred from one location to another? Do they also need resocialization? Yes, because each unit of the organization has different values, expectations, and acceptable behaviors. Usually there is no formal socialization process for transferees, but there is an informal one in which employees seek feedback from peers and supervisors to test the adequacy of their job behaviors in their new situation.

ORGANIZATIONAL CULTURE

A major organizational factor to which new employees must be socialized is the culture of the group they are joining. Just as nations have cultural characteristics—beliefs, customs, and behaviors that distinguish them from other nations—so do organizations. **Organizational culture** may be defined as a general pattern of beliefs, expectations, and values, some conscious and some unconscious, that are expected to guide the behavior of all members of an organization.

An organization's culture is influenced by the type of industry of which it is part; different companies within the same industry can be expected to have a common organizational culture. For example, steel manufacturers share cultural characteristics that are distinct from those of publishers, insurance companies, hospitals, Internet companies, or movie studios because of different market conditions, competitive environments, and customer expectations. Also, society expects different services from, say, an electric power company and a furniture manufacturer. There is a greater societal need for continuous and uninterrupted service from the former than from the latter. Different departments within a company, such as research, engineering, and marketing, can develop their own subcultures that may differ from the dominant organizational culture. Studies have shown that typical bureaucracies—that is, more rigid, formal, and hierarchical organizations—have stronger and better defined cultures than do companies that are less bureaucratic (Dickson, Resick, & Hanges, 2006).

Some I-O psychologists use the terms *organizational culture* and *organizational climate* interchangeably, arguing that the concepts share a fundamental similarity. Others note that climate is the surface manifestation of culture. Organizational climate is what people perceive when they observe the way a company functions, whereas organizational culture relates to deeper issues, the causes of an organization's operating style.

Recall from our descriptions of participatory management programs that organizational culture can influence a company's effectiveness. For example, companies with a culture of high involvement and high participation consistently outperform companies that do not favor employee participation and involvement.

Person–organization fit   The congruence between an employee's values and the organization's values.

Person–Organization Fit

I-O psychologists define **person–organization fit** as the degree of congruence between an employee's values and the organization's values. That agreement can be maximized through recruitment, selection, and socialization procedures.

Person–organization fit may be enhanced when the values of newcomers agree with those of their supervisors. This was demonstrated in a study of 154 new employees and 101 supervisors from 68 European companies based in the Netherlands. High congruence correlated with low turnover intentions. A high level of incongruence or disparity between employee and supervisor values was associated with a low level of organizational commitment from that employee (Van Vianen, 2000).

A related variable is personality. A person–organization fit should encompass not only similar values but also similar personalities. Most organizations are relatively homogeneous in terms of instilling a typical personality among its managers. A self-selection factor is involved here: Job applicants tend to be attracted to companies with whose structure, mission, and attitudes they seem comfortable. Think about a high-tech company staffed by people in their 20s who dress casually, put in long hours hunched over their computers, and bring their dogs to work. Now imagine a major investment banking firm with people in dark suits who work in elegant offices and conduct their business in hushed voices. The differences in personality are obvious!

The degree of person–organization fit affects the amount of influence a person has in the organization, but influence also varies with the personality of the individual and the nature of the working group. For example, extraverts have more influence in a team-oriented organization. Leaders high in conscientiousness have more influence in organizations in which employees work by themselves on technical tasks (Anderson, Spataro, & Flynn, 2008).

Some organizational psychologists advocate revising the typical approach to employee selection. They suggest that in addition to evaluating whether the applicants' knowledge, skills, and abilities are suitable for a particular job, companies should evaluate whether those applicants' personalities are compatible with the organization's culture and personality.

LABOR UNIONS

One aspect of organizational life that helps define a company's culture is the presence or absence of labor unions, in which workers act collectively to protect and promote their interests. Union members form a subculture within the larger organizational culture. Membership in a union can contribute to job satisfaction and productivity and have a powerful influence on employees' attitudes toward their jobs and their employers.

Studies of more than 3,500 labor union members in the United States and in Australia showed that workers most likely to join and support unions were unhappy with their organization's decision-making processes. They also expressed dissatisfaction with the performance appraisal system and believed that their company was not evenhanded in applying company policies. They thought that unions would be instrumental in developing fair and safe working conditions and improving wages and benefits (Buttigieg, Deery, & Iverson, 2007; Tetrick, Shore, McClurg, & Vandenberg, 2007).

The socialization of new union members is similar to the process of becoming acclimated to any new organization. Unions offer formal institutionalized socialization as well as informal individual socialization. The formal procedures include orientation lectures and training programs. Informal procedures involve attending union meetings with co-workers, being introduced to the shop steward, or having a work problem solved by the union. In a study of 322 union members in Singapore, researchers found that loyalty to the union, developed through socialization procedures, was a powerful motivating force. This loyalty led union members to behave in ways that promoted the interests of the union and other union members (Tan & Aryee, 2002).

Newsbreak

Gimme an Order of Fries With That—Sir!

When Tom White was hired by Foodmaker, the parent company of the Jack-in-the-Box fast-food chain, he did no work at his level for 2 months. Although his job title was vice president, he spent this introductory period learning about the company's culture, starting from the bottom up. This meant cooking fries, flipping burgers, and mastering the socialization program called "on boarding."

In addition, he was assigned a mentor and coach who showed him the Foodmaker way of doing things and who closely monitored his progress to make sure he would fit in. Finally, after 8 weeks of experiencing in person more of the company's operations than most executives see in 8 years, Tom was permitted to start his new job.

"It was probably the first time," he said, "that I've taken a new position and from day one knew my duties and how to get things done in the organization. Without the on-boarding program, I would probably be 6 months to a year behind where I am now."

Corporate consultants report that few companies give their executives this type of opportunity to acquaint themselves with the organizational culture before undertaking their new job duties. The result is a high washout rate. Up to half of all new high-level executives quit or are dismissed within 3 years.

In a survey of 46 executives who had recently changed jobs, one third of the executives said they would need as long as a year to adjust to their new company. They agreed that the toughest part was adapting to the corporate culture. One human resources director described organizational culture as the "framework in which you get your job done—or not!"

Source: Sweeney, P. (1999, February 14), Teaching new hires to feel at home. *New York Times.*

A review of pay scales in the United States shows that unionized employees are paid wages up to 33% greater than nonunion employees. In addition to higher pay, membership in a labor union can result in better and safer working conditions, job security, and fringe benefits—all of which contribute to satisfaction of what Maslow called the lower order needs. Union membership can also satisfy higher order needs for status, belonging, and esteem and can provide a sense of power through the knowledge that unionized employees have an important bargaining tool: the threat of a strike. Some union members report a greater loyalty to their union than to their company.

Unions initially resisted quality-of-work-life programs because they feared such efforts would erode union loyalty. This resistance has been declining as more union members participate in and support QWL programs and other forms of worker participation.

Organized labor currently faces a crisis of declining membership. At the end of World War II,

in 1945, more than 35% of the U.S. workforce belonged to unions. By 2007, that figure had fallen to 12.1%, which nevertheless accounts for approximately 15.7 million union members in the United States. Men are more likely than women to join unions; Black workers are more likely than White, Asian, or Hispanic workers to join unions. Almost 40% of government employees belong to unions as compared to less than 10% of private sector employees. For information on current workplace issues from the standpoint of labor unions, see the Web site of the AFL-CIO at www.aflcio.org

The Grievance Process

One aspect of union activity that affects employee attitudes and behaviors is the grievance process. Specified in union contracts, the grievance process establishes a formal mechanism for airing and resolving worker complaints. The number and focus of worker grievances serve as indications of job dissatisfaction and can pinpoint the causes of problems in the workplace. Grievance procedures provide employees with a means of upward communication to management and an approved way of venting frustrations that might otherwise be expressed in work slowdowns, stoppages, or sabotage. Thus, the grievance process can be useful for both workers and managers.

The number of grievances varies with the nature of the job. Monotonous and repetitive assembly-line jobs performed under uncomfortable conditions by unskilled workers are associated with a high grievance rate. Social factors are also important. Highly cohesive work groups tend to file more grievances than do groups that lack a sense of unity. First-line supervisors who are low in consideration behaviors are the targets of more grievances than are supervisors who are high in consideration. In general, when a complaint is resolved in favor of the worker, job satisfaction rises along with the perception that the grievance system is fair and unbiased. When a grievance is settled in favor of management, labor–management relations often deteriorate.

INFORMAL GROUPS: ORGANIZATIONS WITHIN THE ORGANIZATION

Informal work groups develop within every organization. Such groups have tremendous power to shape employee attitudes, behavior, and productivity. Workers come together informally to establish and promote a set of norms and values, a subculture within the larger organizational culture. These informal groups do not appear on the organization chart and are beyond the control of management. Often, management is not aware of their existence.

Informal groups determine for new employees how they will come to perceive management and other aspects of organizational culture. These groups can work for or against the organization by encouraging cooperation with company policies and procedures or by thwarting productivity and management goals.

The Classic Hawthorne Studies

The Hawthorne studies provided empirical evidence of informal work groups. A team of 14 workers in the telephone-bank wiring room of the

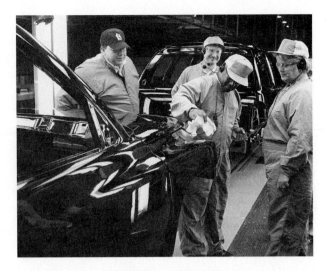

Members of informal work groups usually have similar backgrounds and interests and may determine for themselves an acceptable standard of productivity, which may differ from the one set by management.

Western Electric Company plant was observed for 6 months. The observer noticed that the group developed its own standards of behavior and productivity. The workers shared many interests, engaged in rough but friendly teasing, and stood ready to help one another on the job. They valued one another's friendship and acceptance and displayed many of the characteristics of a family. They avoided doing anything that might bring disapproval from the group.

In terms of productivity, the group determined what it considered to be a fair and safe output for the day. Management had set one standard, with an incentive to be paid for meeting or exceeding the daily level (an employee could make more money by working faster). But the group set its own standard, which was below the company's level. The workers believed that if they met or exceeded management's demands, the company would then raise the standard and force them to work harder. Therefore, the informal work group set a leisurely, easily attainable production goal; they were willing to forgo the opportunity to earn extra money. The workers admitted to the observer that they were capable of producing more but to do so would have defied the group's norms. The group had assumed such prominence in the workers' lives that they considered group acceptance more important than extra pay.

Social loafing　The idea that people do not work as hard in a group as they do when working alone.

Group cohesiveness　The focus, closeness, and commonality of interests of a small work group.

Social Loafing

Another effect of informal work groups is the phenomenon known as **social loafing**, the idea that people do not work as hard in a group as they do when working alone. One explanation for social loafing is that people believe they can get lost in the crowd and that their slower work pace will not be noticed. Also, people tend to expect, on the basis of past experience, that others in the group will goof off, so they might as well do so too.

Social loafing is less likely to occur when workers believe that their supervisors are aware of how hard they work as individuals. Social loafing is more likely to occur when workers believe their personal efforts are not recognized by their supervisors. Men are more likely to engage in social loafing than are women. Workers in Eastern cultures (which are more collectivist or group-oriented) are less likely to practice social loafing than are employees from Western, more individualistic, cultures.

Workers are likely to engage in social loafing under the following conditions:

- When their individual outputs cannot be evaluated
- When working on tasks that are not meaningful or personally involving
- When working with strangers
- When they expect their co-workers to perform well on the task
- When their work groups are less cohesive

Group Cohesiveness

Informal groups exist in every type of organization. They are characterized by personal interactions that occur over an extended period; frequent interactions are necessary to the development of a degree of closeness, called **group cohesiveness**, and a commonality of interests. Groups must also have a focus, such as workers in the same department who share a physical workspace. The groups cannot be too large or the sense of personal and direct contact will be lost.

Most of us have a need for affiliation and companionship, and this need can be satisfied by an informal work group. The group also serves as a source of information about work procedures and about what constitutes an acceptable day's output. Group closeness also influences employee perceptions of organizational issues. For example, employees who form personal relationships in a work group tend to interpret organizational events in a similar way. Employees in less cohesive groups tend to interpret the same events in a different way.

Group norms and standards are pervasive throughout organizational and personal life. The group can influence political and racial attitudes, style of dress, even where to eat or go on vacation. Because group membership satisfies so many needs, employees strive to be accepted by group members. Deviant behavior is rarely encountered, except from new workers who need time to absorb the group's ways.

Informal groups tend to attract and retain people with similar personality characteristics and to take on a consistent affective or emotional tone. As a result, group members tend to have similar moods and feelings about their work. A group's affective tone influences the group's work performance. A negative affective tone is related to a low level of helping behaviors, which is manifested in rude and uncooperative behavior. Positive affective tone is related to a low level of absenteeism.

Positive affective tone is also positively related to organizational spontaneity and organizational citizenship behavior, described as helping co-workers, protecting the organization, making constructive suggestions, developing personal skills, and spreading goodwill. Positive affect in a group is likely to be stronger when the group is small and the members work in physical proximity. In that situation, the mood of the individual employee is influenced by the collective mood of the group over time.

The greater the cohesiveness, the greater is the group's power over its members and the greater is the pressure on group members to conform. Several factors influence cohesiveness. As the group gets larger and there is less opportunity for frequent contact among group members, cohesiveness declines. Larger groups generally splinter into subgroups or competing groups. Diversity of background, interests, and lifestyles reduces group cohesiveness.

Working conditions are also important. Employees who work under a wage-incentive system that rewards on an individual rather than a team basis find that personal competition reduces feelings of closeness. Team rewards enhance group cohesiveness by encouraging cooperation; everyone works for a common goal.

Outside pressures and threats affect group cohesiveness. Just as citizens of a nation under attack usually cooperate to submerge personal or regional differences, so will a work group faced with an unfair supervisor or an unpopular policy. A meta-analysis of 64 studies identified three components of group cohesiveness: interpersonal attraction, task commitment, and group pride. Researchers found a strong positive relationship between high group cohesiveness and high job performance (Beal, Cohen, Burke, & McLendon, 2003). A study of 447 military employees in Canada also showed that high group cohesiveness was related to high job performance and satisfaction and low levels of stress (Ahronson & Cameron, 2007).

TECHNOLOGICAL CHANGE AND ORGANIZATIONAL STRUCTURE

The widespread use of computer-aided manufacturing and office equipment has changed the ways in which daily work is performed and has affected the formal and informal structure of organizations (O'Kane, Palmer, & Hargie, 2007). Computer technology creates the need for greater coordination and integration of an organization's basic units, which requires the development of new reporting hierarchies. For example, at one plant in which operations were computerized, the engineering staff was reorganized so that it reported to the marketing department, a unit with which it previously had had no direct contact. The change was necessary to coordinate customers' needs (marketing) and the development of new products (engineering).

Formalization of the Workplace

Computer technology requires greater formalization of work procedures. Rules for entering data into computer files must be precise; they permit no employee discretion or deviation. These formal procedures reduce opportunities for individuality in structuring and organizing work. Computers also change the source of decision-making authority, although the direction of the change is not always clear. In practice, automating an office or manufacturing plant sometimes results in greater centralization of decision making, restricting it to fewer levels on the organization chart. In other cases it results in decentralization, giving greater decision-making authority to the worker at the video display terminal. For some jobs, computer operators may be more knowledgeable than their supervisors about the equipment's capabilities. A shift in power from supervisors to employees can disrupt traditional working relationships and leave managers with a reduced understanding of the work they are supposed to be managing.

Virtual Meetings

Computers are also changing the procedures for the meetings that result in corporate decisions. Instead of asking a group of employees to sit around a table and discuss a problem, some organizations hold virtual meetings in which interaction takes place through computers. Participants express their ideas simultaneously and anonymously and comment on one another's work. Anecdotal evidence from organizations as diverse as hotels, banks, plastics companies, and aircraft manufacturers indicates that virtual meetings are shorter and less stressful. Leaders are able to stick to an agenda because employees do not digress or waste time at the computer to the extent they do in person.

This type of electronic brainstorming typically involves groups of up to 12 participants, who are instructed to submit as many ideas as they can, to avoid criticizing others' ideas, and to try to combine and improve the ideas generated by other group members. Thus, the process eliminates two problems inherent in face-to-face group brainstorming: (1) production blocking, which is the inability of more than one member to generate ideas at the same time and (2) evaluation apprehension, which is the reluctance of some members to offer their own ideas for fear of being publicly criticized or embarrassed. Software packages for electronic brainstorming allow the members of the virtual group to enter their ideas at any time without interruption and to do so anonymously. Such groups tend to generate more ideas than traditional face-to-face groups, and the ideas are often of higher quality, apparently as a result of being exposed to the ideas of the other group members (Dennis & Williams, 2005; DeRosa, Smith, & Hantula, 2007; Kerr & Tindale, 2004).

Loss of Group Cohesiveness

Computers can force changes in an organization's informal structure by disrupting traditional lines of communication and power. For example, in companies where employees have side-by-side workstations, workers communicate freely and easily about work-related and personal matters. Where such jobs are automated, workers are often separated by partitions that inhibit talking and socializing.

A reduction in the chances for personal interaction lessens a group's cohesiveness. Even though workers have found ways to use their computers for informal communication, this approach lacks the closeness and the privacy afforded by face-to-face contact. It also eliminates nonverbal cues, such as tone of voice, facial expressions, hand gestures, and other forms of body language that can be as informative as the words themselves. In addition, many companies routinely monitor the messages on their internal e-mail system, an action that discourages its use for promoting the personal and social interactions necessary to maintain group cohesiveness.

In addition to reducing group cohesiveness, computer use on the job has led to employees' growing sense of isolation, both on and off the job. Instead of walking into the neighboring office or down the hall to consult with a colleague in person, co-workers ask questions without leaving their cubicle, and thus without any meaningful personal contact. Instead of talking around the water cooler, employees are chatting online. Even lunch breaks are at risk as growing numbers of employees rush back to their computer terminals rather than visit with co-workers or run errands. A survey of 1,000 employees found that 14% ate by themselves at their desks so they could log on during their free time (Fickenscher, 2000).

Ideas once shared during informal gatherings of employees or generated and exchanged during spontaneous meetings are being lost, along with the opportunities to network and build social support. This situation is especially true for the millions of employees who work at home. Many of these telecommuters spend their entire workday connecting with other people only by electronic means.

Surveys of employees who do business with others online rather than in person reveal that they trust the people with whom they deal in person more than they trust the people they interact with only by electronic means. Those who engage with others face to face spend time getting to know one another through conversation about conventional topics such as family and other personal (nonwork) matters, which can lay a foundation for trust and friendship. Interacting with people only through e-mail, text-messaging, or videoconferencing is not the same as being there in person. Such electronic relationships are less personal and less humanized.

The depersonalized nature of communicating through electronic means can affect business negotiations. The greater distrust of a party who is known only online can impede and distort the negotiating process. In surveys of international bankers, researchers found that bankers thought communicating by telephone when engaged in important negotiations was a more real and beneficial way to establish a good personal and working relationship than communicating only online (Bargh & McKenna, 2004).

Excessive Internet Use

An additional problem brought on by electronic communication involves the amount of time spent online on nonwork-related activities. Surveys have shown that this so-called cyberslacking is widespread in the workplace, with the average office worker sending and receiving up to 100 e-mails per day. In addition, employees spend up to 20% of their working hours on Internet shopping, bill paying, surfing, and logging on to pornographic or social networking sites. Younger and better educated workers seem to spend considerably more time cyberslacking than older and less educated workers (Heller, 2007; Phillips & Reddie, 2007).

Psychologists have suggested that excessive Internet use can lead to a form of addiction. The Center for Internet Studies surveyed 18,000 users and found that nearly 6% met the criteria for compulsive Internet use—characteristics similar to those that define compulsive gambling (DeAngelis, 2000). These people were especially hooked on chat rooms, pornography sites, online shopping, and e-mail. One third of them said they logged on regularly as a form of escape or to alter their mood. For more information on Internet addiction log on to the Center for Online Addiction at www.netaddiction.com

Later surveys revealed that 14% of Americans said they found it difficult to stay away from Internet use for more than a few days at a time; 12% said they often remained online longer than they had planned. Almost 9% of those surveyed reported that they tried to conceal their nonwork-related Internet use from their employers, family, and friends, and 8% said they used the Internet to escape from problems and negative moods (Brandt, 2006; Payne, 2006). The governments of China, South Korea, Thailand, and Vietnam have laws to curb excessive Internet use among the young. China has established treatment centers of people considered Internet addicts (Cha, 2007).

Electronic Monitoring

Employer monitoring of computer use has a disruptive effect on the employee–employer relationship and, as a result, on the organization as a whole. Workers may come to view their bosses as watchdogs who always spy on their behavior. To examine the pervasiveness of electronic snooping in the workplace, the American Management Association surveyed more than 300 major U.S. companies. They found that electronic surveillance

---

Newsbreak

Compulsive Multitasker? What Your Laptop Says About You

Charles Lax is always "on," no matter where he is or what he's doing. When the 44-year-old venture capitalist from Boston flew to Los Angeles for a conference on telecommunications, he wasn't really all there. Only part of him was listening to the presentation he paid $2,000 to attend. He was also surfing the Internet on his laptop while checking his mobile device (part phone, part pager, part Internet tool) for his e-mail. Even as the presentation continued he could not disconnect himself from his electronic devices long enough to concentrate on it. If he did so, he risked facing the one situation he dreaded most: boredom.

"It's hard to concentrate on one thing," he said. "I think I have a condition."

He does. Experts who study such persistent multitasking—the need to be constantly "on," to be always wired or connected—have given it a label, to make it official. They call it online compulsive disorder, or OCD. You've seen OCD people in your classes or your workplace. They may be sitting in a meeting room or a lecture hall and exchanging messages with someone across the room on a handheld device, or at their desk talking on two phones simultaneously, or watching their child's soccer game and reading the news on some information Web site.

Psychologists who have studied OCD find that people with the condition have a short attention span, become frustrated when given long-term projects or assignments, thrive on the constant fixes of information, and have a physical craving for the stimulation they receive from checking voicemail or e-mail or answering the phone. Or even better, doing all three at once. Does this mean they are more productive than people who prefer to do one thing at a time? Not according to David Meyer, a psychology professor at the University of Michigan. His research shows that multitaskers hinder their own productivity when they try to do more than two things at the same time. He found that people who switch back and forth between two tasks spend 50% longer to complete them than if they worked on one task at a time. But that behavior would not supply the rush or fulfill the need for excitement and exhilaration that people with OCD constantly crave.

"It's instant gratification," Lax told a telephone interviewer. "I use it when I'm in a waiting situation—if I'm standing in line. Being able to send an e-mail in real time is just so . . ." He stopped. "Can you hold for a second? My other line is ringing."

Source: Richtel, M. (2003, July 6). The lure of data. *New York Times*.

of employees had grown rapidly and that more than half of U.S. companies had fired employees for misusing the Internet on the job. Approximately 84% of those employees were dismissed for accessing pornography and other inappropriate sites. Among those fired for e-mail abuse, 64% were let go because they violated company policies, 62% for using offensive or inappropriate language in the e-mails, and 22% for violating confidentiality rules.

Two thirds of the companies surveyed reported routinely monitoring Internet connections and using software to block inappropriate Web sites. Nearly half tracked the content, number of keystrokes, and amount of time employees spent at their keyboards, 43% stored and reviewed employee computer data, and 10% monitored social networking sites.

In another survey 1,000 Internet users were questioned. The results showed that 10% believed that their work had suffered as a result of the excessive amount of time they spent surfing Web sites. Another 13% blamed easy access to the Internet as being responsible for their inability to stay focused on their jobs (Fickenscher, 2000).

Despite such findings, other survey research has indicated that employees who know their computer use is being monitored are not less likely to continue to use their computers for nonwork activities than those who do not know their computer activities are being monitored (Everton, Mastrangelo, & Jolton, 2003). Perhaps the first group of employees are compulsive Internet users who will continue their addictive behavior despite

Newsbreak

Cyberslacking: Big Brother Is Watching You

It pays to be careful when you log on at work these days. What you say could get you fired. That was the painful lesson learned by Michael Smyth, who used to be a sales manager until he messaged his boss one day and referred to the boss's superior as a "back-stabbing bastard." Smyth thought his e-mail was private and personal, just like sending a letter through the regular mail. But it wasn't. A co-worker found a printout of the message and brought it to the attention of the "back-stabbing bastard." Smyth was fired right away. He sued for wrongful discharge, arguing that his communication was private, but a judge turned down his claim.

The judge ruled that Smyth forfeited any and all reasonable expectations of privacy when he used the company network, even though his message was clearly intended for only one person. A lawyer for the company pointed out that a warning appears on the screen every time employees log on, reminding them that their mail might be intercepted and read by anyone else on the network.

So be careful what you say online at work. You don't know who might be monitoring your mail. And be careful where you surf. That can get you in trouble, too.

Andrew Quinn, systems manager in charge of monitoring for a Canadian company, checks every e-mail employees send and receive as well as every Web site with which they connect. "Look at this guy," he told a visiting reporter. "He's sending out jokes on e-mail. That's all he's been doing for the last hour!" What does that tell you about his job productivity?

The *New York Times* fired 23 workers at its Virginia office for sending and receiving obscene messages. Xerox fired 40 workers when records showed that they had spent up to 8 hours a day on pornography sites. Other workers misuse their work time conducting personal business, day-trading, planning trips, shopping, and playing computer games. This so-called cyberslacking has caused meltdowns of company networks, costing many hours of downtime and hundreds or thousands of dollars for repair. Sometimes the situation gets so bad that business has to be conducted over that low-tech device known as the telephone.

Sources: Guernsey, L. (1999, December 16). The Web: New ticket to a pink slip. *New York Times*; You've got inappropriate mail (2000, April 5). *New York Times*; Seglin, J. L. (1999, July 18). You've got mail; you're being watched. *New York Times*.

the consequences, not unlike gamblers or alcoholics. Employees who are monitored for Internet use also report higher levels of depression, tension, and anxiety, and lower levels of productivity than do employees who are not monitored by their employers (Rosen, 2000).

Some employees, particularly those in food service and health care industries, cannot find privacy anywhere—even in the bathroom. Sensing devices on soap dispensers and faucets determine whether employees are adhering to basic sanitary requirements and practices by washing their hands. One employer said, "If an employee fails to wash up, his badge may start flashing as a black mark goes directly into his file on the main computer." In addition, up to 35% of large companies have installed video cameras as a security measure

to prevent employee or customer theft or to monitor job performance.

In a study of 370 high school and college students holding summer jobs, researchers asked how they felt about video cameras watching them as they worked. Those who had been told about the electronic monitoring in advance thought it was fair and said they felt more valued by their employers. Those who were not told in advance thought procedure was unfair and they felt devalued by their employers (Hovorka-Mead, Ross, Whipple, & Renchin, 2002).

Employees who are being watched and monitored in any fashion by any means often complain that their privacy and dignity are being violated. Employers argue that they need to ensure that their workers are, in fact, working.

Summary

Organizational psychologists study organizational climates and styles and the ways they affect employees. The classic organizational style is **bureaucracy**, which was intended to be a rational structure in which rules of conduct and lines of authority were fixed and in which subjectivity and personal bias had no place. Bureaucracies ignored human needs and could not adapt easily to social and technological change. The more modern organizational style, a high-involvement participatory approach, is concerned with employees' intellectual, emotional, and motivational characteristics. Workers participate in decision making at all levels. **Total quality management (TQM)** programs restructure job and management requirements to enhance worker participation, involvement, and responsibility. In **self-managing work teams**, a work group controls all aspects of the job through an external team leader who serves as a buffer between the group and the organization. Virtual self-managing work teams are linked electronically; its members may never have a face-to-face meeting.

Employees and managers may resist changes in work methods, equipment, or policies. If workers are allowed to participate in decisions about the change, they are more likely to support it. **Organizational development (OD)** involves techniques for introducing large-scale changes. The

process is carried out by **change agents** who diagnose problems, devise appropriate strategies, and implement the interventions.

New employees undergo an adjustment period called **socialization**. A socialization program should include a challenging job, appropriate training and feedback, a considerate supervisor, co-workers with high morale and organizational commitment, and a suitable orientation program. Resocialization occurs any time an employee joins a different organization.

Organizational culture is the pattern of beliefs, values, and expectations that guide the behavior of the organization's members. **Person–organization fit** refers to the congruence between an employee's personality and values and the organization's culture and values.

Membership in a labor union can affect job satisfaction and productivity and can satisfy lower level needs through pay, job security, and fringe benefits. Membership can also satisfy belonging, esteem, status, and power needs.

Informal work groups, which influence employee attitudes and behavior, exist beyond management control. They operate by their own standards with regard to productivity and worker–management relations. **Social loafing** means that people do not work as hard in a group as they do when working alone. **Group cohesiveness** refers to the degree of closeness of a group. The higher the group cohesiveness, the higher the job performance and job satisfaction.

Computer use has produced changes in organizational structure by causing a power shift from supervisors to employees. Meetings can now be held online (virtual meetings), which reduces group cohesiveness and increases social isolation. Cyberslacking involves excessive use for personal reasons of e-mail and the Internet on the job. Electronic surveillance can reduce employees' trust in their organization.

Key Terms

bureaucracy
change agents
group cohesiveness
organizational culture
organizational development (OD)

person–organization fit
quality-of-work-life (QWL)
    programs
role ambiguity
role conflict

self-managing work teams
social loafing
socialization
total quality management (TQM)

Review Questions

1. List the formal and informal organizations to which you belong, for example, family, study groups, part-time jobs, social organizations, and chat rooms. How does each of these influence your thinking and behavior?

2. Why was the development of the bureaucratic organizational style considered to be a revolutionary and humanistic change to the workplace?

3. Describe the problems and weaknesses of bureaucracies for the individual employee and for the organization.

4. According to McGregor's Theory Y, what are workers like? How does this differ from the Theory X view of workers?

5. If your company employed 2 managers and 50 workers to produce mountain bikes, how would you convert the operation to a high-involvement management system?

6. What are the requirements and advantages of TQM programs? Why do some fail?

7. If self-managing work teams are designed to function autonomously, why are external team leaders necessary, and what do they do?

8. How can self-managing work teams function when group members work in different locations instead of together in one facility?

9. What factors influence the ways in which employees accept major organizational change?

10. Describe the procedures involved in OD. What is the role of change agents?

11. In what ways can an organization facilitate the socialization of its new employees?

12. What are the results of the poor socialization of a new employee?

13. Define role ambiguity and role conflict. How do they relate to socialization?

14. Define organizational culture and give an example of how it can affect job satisfaction and performance.

15. What advantages does membership in a labor union provide to employees?

16. In what ways can the labor union grievance process benefit workers and employers?

17. What organizational conditions are likely to lead to social loafing? Does social loafing occur when people work alone rather than in groups?

18. Describe three components of group cohesiveness.

19. Is there likely to be greater group cohesiveness in larger groups or in smaller groups? Offer an explanation for your answer.

20. How has computer technology affected work procedures, the conduct of meetings, and the brainstorming process?

21. Keep track of the number of hours you spend each day on e-mail or Internet use for purposes other than school or work. Would you describe yourself as an excessive user of online activities?

Does this use contribute to or detract from your quality of life?

22. How extensive is electronic monitoring in the workplace? Give some examples of how it is carried out.

23. What would be your reaction if you learned that your employer was monitoring your computer use? Would it change your behavior? If so, how? Do you think your employer has the right to monitor your Internet activities at work?

Additional Reading

Ashkansay, N. M., Wilderom, C. P. M., & Peterson, M. F. (Eds). (2000). *Handbook of organizational culture and climate*. Thousand Oaks, CA: Sage. Reviews international research, theory, and practice. Includes basic concepts, measurement, assessment, and applications of organizational culture/climate theory to everyday management and human resources problems such as organizational commitment and socialization.

Bowers, C., Salas, E., & Jentsch, F. (Ed.). (2006). *Creating high-tech teams*. Washington, DC: APA Books. Explores state-of-the-art technology and its effect on the functioning of work groups; explores communication patterns, group decision making, and virtual teamwork.

Boyett, J. H., & Boyett, J. T. (2000). *The guru's guide to entrepreneurship*. New York: Wiley. Profiles 70 highly successful entrepreneurs including the founders of Microsoft, Amazon.com, McDonald's, and Wal-Mart. Describes their organizational styles, including sharing information and perks with employees, and offers self-tests to assess your potential to start and run a business.

Hodgkinson, G., & Healey, M. (2008). Cognition in organizations. *Annual Review of Psychology*, 59 387–417. Surveys the literature on the analysis of cognition in industrial-organizational psychology, especially applications to the information-processing challenges facing the twenty-first century workforce.

Ilgen, D., Hollenbeck, J., Johnson, M., & Jundt, D. (2005). Teams in organizations. *Annual Review of Psychology, 56*, 517–543. Reviews the literature on the structure and functions of work teams and embedded informal groups, including the bonding process among members and the groups' effects on the organization.

Schein, E. H. (1999). *The corporate culture survival guide*. San Francisco: Jossey-Bass. A readable, practical guide to the creation and evolution of organizational cultures, showing how to guide the inevitable changes. Emphasizes the importance of appropriate leadership in understanding values and shared assumptions in new, midlife, and mature companies.

Williams, K. (2007). Ostracism. *Annual Review of Psychology*, *58*, 425–452. Reviews the social-psychological research on ostracism, social exclusion, and rejection; these ideas are relevant to the functioning of informal groups within organizations as well as to communication between superiors and subordinates.

PART FOUR

Characteristics of the Workplace

We have described some of the effects of the social and psychological climate in which work takes place. The structure of the organization, its style of leadership, and the motivations of employees all influence productivity and job satisfaction. But the more tangible aspects of the workplace—physical features, working hours, safety issues, and concerns about physical and emotional health—also are influential.

Chapter 10 deals with physical conditions of work, including lighting, noise, temperature, color, and music. Work hours and work schedules are discussed, along with factors such as fatigue, monotony, and sexual harassment. Accidents, violence, alcoholism, and drug abuse are covered in chapter 11. Psychologists help to determine the causes of workplace accidents and violence and ways to prevent them. Dependence on alcohol or illicit drugs is both a personal tragedy and a personnel problem. Psychologists design employee assistance programs for troubled workers at all occupational levels. Chapter 12 considers the stresses that result from various physical and psychological conditions of work, including conflicts between the demands of the job and those of home and family. Psychologists have developed ways of preventing such stress and of treating it on and off the job.

CHAPTER 10

Working Conditions

CHAPTER OUTLINE

PHYSICAL WORKING CONDITIONS

Look around. Are you in the dorm? An Internet café? The library? An office? What is it like? Comfortable and quiet? Noisy and distracting? Bright and attractive? Cold and drab? These are just some of the physical characteristics of a work environment that can determine how well employees are able to do their jobs. Whatever the task—studying, repairing an engine, designing software—our surroundings can affect our skill, motivation, and satisfaction.

An organization can recruit and select the best employees, train them thoroughly, provide outstanding leaders and an optimal organizational climate to maximize job performance, but if the physical working conditions are uncomfortable, productivity will suffer. Uncongenial work settings can lead to decreased productivity, lower job satisfaction, more mistakes and accidents, and increased absenteeism and turnover.

When a workplace is made more comfortable or working hours are made more flexible, productivity usually increases, at least temporarily. But be careful in interpreting such changes in performance. What, precisely, caused the greater produc-

tivity? Was it physical changes such as a new climate-control system, brighter lighting, or better soundproofing? Or was it a more subtle psychological factor such as employees' more positive attitude toward management for instituting the changes?

Although the results may be beneficial for the company, whatever the cause, management needs to be able to explain the reasons for any improvements in productivity or satisfaction. Suppose the improvements occurred because employees are pleased that their company is treating them as human beings rather than cogs in a machine. If so, the company will want to know whether there are other ways to improve satisfaction and productivity that do not involve expensive alterations to the physical workplace.

In many industries people work at peak efficiency under what appear to be intolerable conditions. And there are many instances of poor performance and low morale in well-equipped, lavishly decorated surroundings. The effects of changes in physical working conditions may be influenced or modified by how employees perceive, accept, and adapt to these changes. Therefore, the physical features of the workplace must be considered in light of complex psychological factors.

Newsbreak

Complaints About Your Job? Maybe You're Experiencing Bad Workplace Design

What do you think is the number one complaint of people who work in offices? What is it about their workplace that bothers them more than anything else? Take a guess. According to the International Facility Management Association, the number one office complaint relates to temperature—the workplace is too cold. And the number two complaint? The office is too hot!

Here are the rest of the top 10 complaints reported by office workers:

- Poor janitorial service
- Not enough conference space

- Not enough storage or filing space at the workstation
- Poor quality of indoor air
- Lack of privacy at the workstation
- Inadequate parking
- Computer problems
- Too much noise in the workplace

Do any of these apply to your work or study area?

Work Sites

The physical work environment includes many factors, from the size of the parking lot and location of the building to the amount of natural light and noise in the work area. Inadequate parking spaces or a parking lot located too far from the building can so irritate employees that their attitude toward the organization is negative before they reach their workstation.

The location of the work site, whether in the downtown of a large city or in a more remote suburban area, can also affect employees' satisfaction with their jobs. For example, suburban office parks are often isolated from the shops, restaurants, and other services found in cities. Surveys show that young, single employees typically prefer living and working in cities, whereas married people tend to prefer the quieter suburbs as better places to work and rear children.

Organizations offer various amenities to attract and retain dedicated employees. Some companies have turned themselves into vacation resorts with on-site spas, gyms, nurseries, shops, banks, medical clinics, and upscale dining rooms. For example, Google provides gourmet meals for employees—without charge. The Nielsen Company's facility in Florida features a five-star cafeteria with a glass wall overlooking a nature preserve where a resident alligator delights visitors from northern states. On "family friendly" days each month, pizza and hot dogs are served to employees' children (Rexrode, 2007).

Why would organizations spend money on what used to be considered frills? At the luxury-laden Citicorp office complex in Tampa, Florida, an employee said, "You spend so much of your life at work; it's nice that you can have things like a fitness center or child-care facility. For me, it builds loyalty." And loyal employees are less likely to quit, take time off, or be sloppy about their work.

Office and Workplace Design

Once inside their place of employment, workers may find physical features that create dissatisfaction or frustration. One source of complaints is the ventilating, heating, and air conditioning systems in glass-wall, fixed-window buildings. Temperatures are often uncomfortably hot on the sunny side of the building and too cool on the shady side. Other irritants are slow elevators in high-rise buildings,

Landscaped offices have no floor-to-ceiling dividers. These cubicles may enhance communication and work flow, but they can be noisy and distracting.

the quality of the food in the company cafeteria, and inconvenient or poorly maintained restrooms.

Office size and design can be related to employee satisfaction and productivity. The layout of a set of offices will affect the behavior of managers who rely on spontaneous encounters as a way of obtaining and exchanging information. The closer their offices, the more likely they are to meet throughout the workday. Physical separation, such as placing suites of management offices on different floors of a building, decreases the amount of contact.

In studies of office workers in South Korea, researchers found that the more personal control workers had over their desk and office space, and the easier the access to meeting rooms, the higher was workers' job satisfaction and group cohesiveness (Lee & Brand, 2005). Research on office workers in the United States showed that greater satisfaction with the layout of their workstations was related to higher job performance and increased collaboration with co-workers (Robertson & Huang, 2006).

The size of an office building can influence working relationships. The smaller the building, the closer the relationships among employees tend to be. In very large buildings, where employees have fewer interactions, relationships tend to be more formal and impersonal. All these factors, none of which involves actual job tasks, can impair

Environmental psychology The study of the effect of workplace design on behavior and attitudes.

productive efficiency. An unpopular location, poor design, or inconvenient layout can reduce morale and foster negative attitudes.

Workplace design and location are especially critical for disabled employees who may be barred from certain jobs not because of lack of ability, but because they do not have access to the work area. Steep flights of stairs, narrow doorways, and inadequate restrooms may prevent them from being employed. The 1973 Rehabilitation Act and the 1990 Americans with Disabilities Act require the removal of architectural barriers. All parts of a building must be accessible to persons in wheelchairs.

Compliance with the laws has meant modifications to elements of the physical plant, such as automatic doors, ramps and elevators, handholds, wider doorways and corridors, and lower wall telephones and speakerphones. Surveys show that 60% of these required changes cost less than $100 and 90% cost less than $1,000. Many disabled employees do not need any physical modifications of an office workspace. IBM, which has hired disabled workers for more than 40 years, took the lead in redesigning workstations to provide job opportunities for these employees.

Environmental Psychology: Landscaped Offices and Cubicles

The field of **environmental psychology** studies the relationships between people and their physical environment. Combining architecture and psychology, environmental psychologists are concerned with natural and built environments and their impact on behavior. For example, research on office design and layout has focused on communications between and within departments, flow of job tasks among groups, relationships between managers and subordinates, and work group cohesiveness.

One early result of environmental psychology research was the landscaped office. In contrast to private, separated offices, the landscaped office consists of a huge open space with no floor-to-ceiling walls to divide the area into separate rooms. All employees, from clerks to corporate officers, are grouped into cubicles, functional work units that are set off from others only by planters, screens or partitions, or cabinets and bookcases.

Inexpensive to construct and maintain, landscaped offices are believed to facilitate communication and work flow. The openness is supposed to enhance group cohesiveness and cooperation and reduce psychological barriers between employees and managers. Research on employee reactions has revealed both advantages and disadvantages. Employees report that landscaped offices are pleasant and conducive to socializing. Managers report improved communication. Complaints relate to lack of privacy, noise, and difficulty in concentrating. Because cubicles are typically separated only by low dividers, work areas tend to lack the personal touches—such as photos, plants, posters, or souvenirs—that contribute to feelings of individuality and comfort.

In studies of 779 cubicle workers in the United States and in Canada, investigators found that those who were more satisfied with their work environment were also more likely to be satisfied with their jobs as a whole. This finding reinforces the importance of the physical environment to employees' well-being and effectiveness (Veitch, Charles, Farley, & Newsham, 2007). A study of employees in Turkey who worked in cubicles found that those who had access to a window that provided natural light and an outdoor view were significantly more satisfied with their workspace than those who had no window. In addition, workers in cubicles with partitions 1.4 meters (4 feet, 7 inches) in height expressed greater satisfaction with their space than those with lower walls. Men in the Turkish study were more satisfied working in cubicles than were women (Yildirim, Akalin-Baskaya, & Celebi, 2007).

Despite the problems with landscaped offices, many organizations have invested considerable money in them and are reluctant to bear the additional expense of reconverting to more private offices. For companies with large numbers of employees at computerized workstations, the landscaped office has become standard.

Newsbreak

Does Anyone Get Work Done in Those *Dilbert*-Style Cubicles?

Can you get any work done at work? Maybe not if you work in a cubicle, as the comic strip *Dilbert* reminds us daily. Cubicle designers and managers may insist that the open office plan, with its low walls surrounding individual workstations, allows the free flow of ideas, but tell that to the employees who spend many hours each workday in that setting. They'll likely tell you that they find it hard to concentrate on their job because of all the nonwork activities and conversations going on around them. Cubicle dwellers will complain to anyone who will listen about being forced to hear of other workers' family problems, medical problems, financial problems, or the cute thing their dog did yesterday. Some say it's easier to work at home—the office is more suitable for socializing.

Sue Weidermann, a management consultant in Buffalo, New York, found that in one large law firm the employees who worked in cubicles were interrupted by noise, visual distractions, or co-workers who just wanted to have a conversation, an average of 16 times a day. And none of these interruptions was related to work. Interruptions that did relate to the job occurred an average of 5 times a day. Ms. Weidermann observed that after an interruption, it took an employee 2.9 minutes to settle down and return to work, which means that approximately an hour of every workday was spent trying to refocus on the job tasks.

Kathi Heering used to work for a bank but found that she couldn't concentrate in her cubicle. She pleaded with her boss to construct the cubicle walls a few inches higher, so that co-workers couldn't lean over them so easily to chat, but the boss refused. He claimed that the low walls "fortified communication." Unfortunately, the communication was not about work. Now Kathi does her job from home where she enjoys a luxury that she did not have at the office. It's called a door. Whenever her family or her dogs intrude on her work, she simply closes the door.

Source: Laboring to work at work (2004, May 8). *Wall Street Journal.*

As real estate costs escalate, organizations are trying to squeeze more employees into smaller facilities. The size of the typical office cubicle or individual workstation is steadily shrinking. Some employees who travel frequently no longer have a permanently assigned work area but only a temporary space. For example, consultants who spend much of their time on-site at a client's workplace will phone ahead to reserve a cubicle for their next visit to the home office. Because the practice is not unlike booking a hotel room, it has come to be known as "hoteling" or "free addressing."

Capital One, a banking company headquartered in Richmond, Virginia, began a hoteling program for its employees in 2005; it became so popular that within 2 years some 1,600 employees nationwide chose not to have desks of their own. When they did need office time, they simply plugged in their laptops to empty docking stations. Otherwise they worked at home or while traveling. Companies with similar programs include, among others, IBM, American Express, Microsoft, and Sun Microsystems.

Lighting

In addition to studying general issues of workspace design, I-O psychologists have conducted extensive research on specific environmental factors such as lighting, noise, and temperature. These aspects of the work environment are analogous to the hygiene needs proposed by Herzberg. All of these environmental factors have been found to affect job satisfaction.

Continued exposure to inadequate illumination while reading or performing detailed operations can be harmful to a person's eyesight. Research confirms that inadequate lighting is a source of distress. High glare, dim bulbs, and a lack of natural light have negative effects on job performance.

Intensity.   Intensity, or level of brightness, is the most common factor associated with illumination. The optimal level of intensity varies with the nature of the task and the age of the worker. Older workers generally need brighter light than do younger workers for satisfactory performance of the same task. A job involving the precise manipulation of small parts, as in electronics assembly, requires brighter light than an assembly line in a bottling plant. Lighting engineers have recommended minimum intensity levels for a variety of work areas, including office buildings (see Table 10-1).

Distribution of light.   Another important factor in illumination is the distribution of light over the work area. Ideally, lighting should be distributed uniformly throughout the visual field. Illuminating a workstation at a much higher intensity than its surroundings leads to eyestrain because of the natural tendency of the eyes to move. When a person looks from a brightly lit area to a dimly lit area, the pupils of the eyes dilate. Returning the gaze to the brighter area causes the pupils to contract. This constant reaction of the pupils leads to eyestrain. When you are sitting at your desk, you should have overhead lighting as well as a desk

lamp focused on your work. This arrangement will give a uniform distribution of light throughout the room. Similarly, it is less fatiguing to the eyes to have additional lighting in the room where you are watching television or staring at your computer screen.

Uniform illumination throughout a work area can be provided by indirect lighting in which all light is reflected. Thus, no light will strike the eyes directly. In contrast, direct lighting, with bulbs located at various points in the ceiling, tends to focus or concentrate the light on specific areas, causing bright spots and glare.

Glare.   Glare reduces visual efficiency and contributes to eyestrain. Glare is caused by light of a brighter intensity than that to which the eye is accustomed. This brightness may come from the light source or from reflective surfaces. Glare can lead to an increase in errors in detailed work in as short a time as 20 minutes. It can obscure vision, something you may have experienced when driving at night and confronting an oncoming car that has its high-beam headlights on. Glare is also a problem with the video display terminals for computers.

There are several ways to reduce or eliminate glare. Extremely bright light sources can be shielded or kept out of the visual field. Workers can be supplied with visors or eyeshades. Reflective or glossy surfaces can be painted with a dull, matte finish.

TABLE 10-1	
Recommended Lighting Levels for Office Workplaces	
Description	**Range of Footcandles***
General Offices and Private Offices	56–70
Accounting, Bookkeeping, Drafting	120–150
Conference Rooms	10–70
Corridors, Elevators, Escalators, Stairways	16–20
Lobbies, Reception Areas	10–30
Bathrooms	24–30

* A footcandle of light (a standard candle at a distance of 1 foot) is approximately the brightness produced by a 100-watt bulb 10 feet above your head on a dark night.

Source: Commonwealth of Pennsylvania Lighting Recommendations. www.pacode.com/secure/data/034/chapter27/chap27toc.html

Natural light.   There is a definite psychological component with regard to the preference for natural (full-spectrum) light instead of artificial light. People who work in windowless offices and receive no natural light express a strong desire for windows, regardless of the adequacy of the artificial illumination in their work area. Most workers want to see outside, and they believe that natural light is better for the eyes than is artificial light. People also may have a physiological need for a certain amount of full-spectrum or natural light. Several European countries have laws requiring employers to ensure that all employees can see natural light from their work areas.

Noise

Noise is a common complaint in modern life. Noise makes us irritable and nervous, interferes with sleep, and produces physiological effects such as hearing loss. Noise has been documented as an occupational hazard for industrial employees such as riveters, boilermakers, aircraft mechanics, and foundry and textile workers. Businesses have been faced with employee claims of hearing damage that total millions of dollars each year.

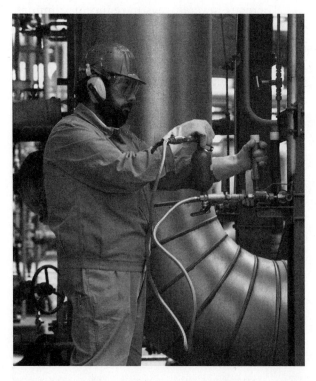

The excessive noise levels in some industrial plants can cause hearing loss.

The National Institute for Occupational Safety and Health (NIOSH) reports that 30 million Americans are routinely exposed to noise levels that eventually will affect their hearing. NIOSH also estimates that at least 20% of U.S. employees work in environments that can endanger their hearing. For example, more than 90% of coal miners experience hearing loss by age 50. At least 75% of farmers suffer hearing impairment from continued exposure to noisy farm machinery. A past president of the National Hearing Conservation Association asserted that hearing loss was one of the most common workplace conditions.

The basic unit for measuring noise is the *decibel* (db), which is a measure of the subjective or perceived intensity of a sound. Zero decibels is the threshold of hearing, the faintest sound most of us can hear. Table 10-2 shows decibel levels in familiar situations. Some loudness levels are threats to hearing. A worker exposed regularly over a long period to decibel levels above 85 can expect to experience some hearing loss. Exposure to levels over 120 db can cause temporary deafness. Brief exposure to levels in excess of 130 can cause permanent deafness. The U.S. government has established maximum permissible sound levels for industrial workers: exposure

TABLE 10-2	
Decibel Levels for Familiar Sounds	
Source of Noise	**Decibel Level**
Breathing	10
Whisper from 5 feet away	30
Quiet office	40
Conversation 3 feet away	70
City traffic	80
Kitchen appliances	95
Average factory	100
Power lawnmowers	110
Crying babies	110
Noisy restaurant	110
Pneumatic hammers 3 feet away	120
Electronically amplified rock band	140
Jet aircraft at takeoff	150

to 90 db for an 8-hour day, 100 db for a 2-hour period, and 110 db for a 30-minute period.

When people are exposed to sounds in the 95 to 110 db range, blood vessels constrict, heart rate changes, and the pupils of the eyes dilate. The constriction of the blood vessels continues for some time after the noise ceases, a condition that alters the blood supply throughout the body. Continuous exposure to loud noise is associated with stress, high blood pressure, and impaired emotional well-being.

In a study of 40 female clerical workers, 3 hours' exposure to the noise of a typical open-office arrangement produced measurable physiological signs of stress. The noise also reduced the employees' motivation to work (Evans & Johnson, 2000). Researchers studying the physiological effects of high noise levels tracked blood pressure changes in workers in Israel over a 4-year period. They found that workers who had more complex jobs showed greater increases in blood pressure than those with less complex jobs (Melamed, Fried, & Froom, 2001).

Noise interferes with communication. If the background noise in an office is low (between 50 and 60 db), then two people can conduct a conversation without raising their voices at a distance of up to 5 feet. As the background noise level rises, workers must talk louder or must leave their workstations and come closer together to be heard. The decibel level of the average factory forces workers and supervisors to shout; it is likely that important information is lost in transmission.

Color

Exaggerated claims have been made about the benefits of color for homes, offices, and factories. Some people have suggested that certain colors increase productivity, reduce accidents, and raise employee morale. These claims are not supported by empirical evidence, and there is no validity to any purported relationship between a specific color and productivity, fatigue, or job satisfaction.

Nevertheless, there is a role for color in the workplace. Color can provide a more pleasant working environment and can be an aid in safety practices. Many manufacturing plants use color as a coding device. Fire equipment is red, danger areas yellow, and first-aid stations green. Color-coding allows these areas to be identified quickly. Color can prevent eyestrain because colors differ in their reflective properties. A white wall reflects more light than a dark

one. Thus, the appropriate use of color can make a workroom or office seem brighter or darker. Colors also create different illusions of size. A room painted a darker color seems smaller than it actually is. Light-colored walls give the feeling of space and openness.

On U.S. Navy submarines, the 24 Trident missile tubes, which run through all four decks, are painted reddish-orange. The color is darker for tubes at one end of the ship than the other to create the illusion of depth. This makes the cramped quarters appear more spacious than they are. The captain of the USS *Tennessee* told an interviewer, "That's the psychologists looking out for us."

Interior decorators claim that blues and greens are cool colors and that reds and oranges are warm colors. Anecdotal evidence suggests that these colors influence our perception of temperature. In one example, an office was repainted from a drab brown to a bright blue. When winter approached, the employees complained that they were cold even though the indoor office temperature was the same as it had been during previous winters. The temperature was raised 5 degrees, but the complaints persisted. The office was repainted in warm colors, and the employees said they were too hot. The temperature was lowered 5 degrees to where it had been before, and complaints ceased.

If a work area is dingy, then repainting it may improve employee morale. A fresh coat of paint in any color can make workers feel better about their environment. But there is little I-O psychologists can conclude with assurance about the effects of color on employee behavior.

Music

The use of music at work is as old as work itself. Workers traditionally sang on the job, even in noisy factories at the time of the Industrial Revolution. During the late 1800s and early 1900s, quieter industries, such as cigar making, encouraged singing on the job. Some companies hired musicians to play for the workers, and by the 1930s many organizations supported their own bands and singing groups.

Many claims have been made about the effects of music on productivity and morale. Employees are supposed to be happier and more efficient when they listen to music at work. Studies conducted by firms that supply recorded music support these claims, but such research often lacks scientific rigor and control. Early research on music

Put a Little Red in Your Life

If you start to feel a little drowsy or a little queasy after dinner, maybe it's not what you ate or drank. Maybe it's the color of your dining room. That's the suggestion of one painting contractor, who wrote in the magazine *Paint Dealer* that beige walls create gas and stagnation in the human digestive tract. Should you paint your dining room walls blue? No, that's not a good idea either. Decorators consider blue to be an appetite suppressant. You'll lose weight if you have your meals in a blue room. What about red? Yes! According to the same decorators, red increases your appetite, heart rate, passion, and energy.

And so it goes—various and sometimes competing claims that the right color will improve your life, or ruin it. Here's an ad from one manufacturer.

Cool colors, like blue and green, cool and soothe your mind, body, and spirit. It's no wonder we flock to the ocean and mountains to rejuvenate our senses. These blue-based tones are best used in rooms where you want peace and serenity to prevail. Warm colors, like red, orange, and yellow, convey an energy and passion unmatched by their cooler counterparts. Use these high-power hues in rooms where you anticipate activity and motivation, such as a kitchen, child's playroom, or exercise space. You may find your life becomes more than just living. It becomes a sensory experience full of color and feeling!

Do you believe that? Or do you think they're in the business of selling paint?

---

showed that most employees liked the idea of having music during working hours and believed it would make them more productive. Research results depend partly on the kind of work involved. Music has been found to increase production slightly for assembly-line jobs that are reasonably simple and repetitive. Workers regard this type of job as monotonous and not sufficiently demanding to fully engage their attention. Thus, music can provide a focus for these workers, something to occupy the mind and to help the workday pass more quickly and enjoyably. For more demanding work, there is no evidence that music increases productivity because the complexity of the work requires more concentrated attention.

Most of the music piped into factories, offices, corridors, elevators, and waiting rooms is supplied by Muzak, which has been in business since 1934. The company estimates that its background music is played to 100 million people in more than 250,000 companies in a dozen countries. It has more than a million tunes in its database and provides customized pop-rock programs to companies such as Gap, Old Navy, and Harry Winston. Another music provider, PlayNetwork, supplies the music you hear in Starbucks and TGI Fridays.

Muzak-style sound is intended to humanize the work environment by giving people an emotional lift. A different program is created for each type of business and each workday. The tempo corresponds to changes in mood and energy levels and is designed to be more stimulating at midmorning and midafternoon. Critics consider such music to be bland, even a form of noise pollution.

Temperature and Humidity

Most people have experienced the effects of temperature and humidity on morale, efficiency, and physical well-being. Some are happier and have more vitality in cold weather, whereas others prefer hot weather. Some people are depressed by rainy days, and others barely notice them. Most employees work in facilities where temperature and humidity are controlled. But workers in construction, shipbuilding, and other industries are frequently exposed to temperature extremes.

Recall that the number one complaint of office workers was that the workplace was too cold, and the number two complaint was that it was too hot. But if employees tried to raise or lower the temperature of their office area, they would probably find that the

Nominal working hours The prescribed number of hours employees are supposed to spend on the job; not all of these hours are actually spent performing job tasks.

thermostats are fakes—they are there only to provide the illusion of control. Employees may believe that by changing the thermostat they have initiated some action to correct the sensation of being too hot or too cold, and often that action satisfies them, even though the actual temperature remains the same.

Research shows that for people who work outdoors or in facilities that are not air-conditioned (such as warehouses or automobile repair shops), unusually high temperatures seem to have no significant effect on mental work but do lead to lower performance on strenuous physical tasks. Even if productivity holds steady, workers must expend more energy under difficult climate conditions to maintain the same output. Usually, they will need more frequent rest breaks. Motivation is also a factor. Highly motivated workers are better able to maintain production under temperature extremes than are poorly motivated workers.

Automated office equipment has been found to interfere with climate-control systems. A single computer terminal does not generate much heat, but when dozens of terminals, printers, and fax machines are operated in the same area, heat and static electricity levels increase. The drier air also leads to complaints about eye irritation from employees who wear contact lenses.

WORK SCHEDULES

A vital part of the overall work environment is the amount of time workers spend on the job. There is no standard, universal work schedule. The 40-hour workweek common in the United States is not the norm in every country. Americans spend more hours on the job than do workers in other industrialized nations. Employees in the United States work almost 2 weeks longer each year than employees in Japan, and 14 weeks longer each year than workers in Norway. Not only do Americans work more hours, they also take fewer annual vacation days. A survey of 1,000 employees conducted by Expedia found that 12% of them did not plan to take any vacation days. On average, U.S. workers receive 16 vacation days per year but take only 14 of them.

Contrast that with the vacation policies of other nations: Italy, 42 days; France, 37 days; Germany, 35 days; England, 28 days; and Japan, 25 days.

Vacations can be good for you. A study conducted with 221 workers in Germany showed that their complaints about health and exhaustion decreased significantly during their vacation time. However, these beneficial effects dissipated within 2 weeks after returning to work (Fritz & Sonnentag, 2006).

In general, managers work longer hours than employees at other levels, but they seem to be well rewarded for their efforts. In a survey of 47 male managers, researchers found that they averaged a 56.4-hour workweek, and 28.6% of them worked more than 61 hours per week. Those who put in the greatest number of hours were paid significantly more than those who worked less, receiving, on average, a $204,993 annual salary compared with $162,285. Those who worked longer hours also reported significantly higher job satisfaction and job involvement. The negative side was a feeling of alienation from one's family and a high level of conflict between work and family (Brett & Stroh, 2003).

Although Americans continue to work long hours, they do so in ways that are different from previous generations of workers. The traditional 5-day, 40-hour week in which all employees of an organization arrived and left at the same time is being replaced by alternative work schedules such as permanent part-time employment, the 4-day workweek, flexible hours, and shift work.

Working Hours

At one time in the United States, people routinely worked 10 hours a day, 6 days a week. The 5-day, 40-hour week became the norm in 1938 with the passage of the Fair Labor Standards Act. The United States became the first country to formally establish a 5-day, 40-hour workweek, but this is not necessarily the most efficient work schedule. Workers have accepted it as normal, but in the past they accepted 60 hours and then 48 hours as normal.

There is a difference between **nominal working hours** (the prescribed number of hours employees are supposed to spend on the job) and actual working hours (the amount of time employees devote to job duties). The two rarely coincide. Some research shows that employees spend no more than half the workweek actually performing required job tasks. Some of the lost time is scheduled by the company as rest pauses, but most of the lost time is unauthorized and beyond the control of the organization. When employees arrive at the workplace, it may take them a long time to begin work. They may check their e-mails, send text messages, surf the Web, or sharpen pencils (whether needed or not). Throughout the workday they visit with co-workers, take coffee breaks, and exceed the length of the lunch period. Managers lose time waiting for meetings to begin or calls to be completed, or spend time sending personal e-mails.

An interesting relationship has been documented between nominal and actual working hours. When nominal (prescribed) working hours are increased, actual working hours decrease. In other words, the longer the workday or workweek, the lower is worker productivity. This finding holds even for highly motivated workers. In the early days of World War II in England, patriotic fervor reached a peak. Dangerously low in supplies and equipment, the nation was fighting for survival. The government extended the workweek in defense plants from 56 to 69 1/2 hours. At first, productivity increased 10%, but it soon fell 12% below the previous level. Other consequences of increasing nominal working hours included greater absenteeism and more frequent accidents. In the 69 1/2-hour workweek, actual working hours were only 51. With the shorter 56-hour workweek, actual working hours had been 53. A study conducted by the U.S. Bureau of Labor Statistics during World War II showed that the 7-day workweek that was adopted by many U.S. companies during the war resulted in no greater production than the 6-day week. One day of the 7 days was lost time.

This relationship between nominal and actual working hours also applies to overtime when employees are asked to work beyond the normal workday for a markedly higher rate of pay. Much of the extra time is unproductive, because people tend to adjust to the longer workday by performing at a slower pace. If productivity drops when the number of required working hours is increased, will productivity rise if the workday is shortened? Some research indicates that it will, but other studies show that a decrease in nominal working hours has no effect on actual working hours. In a case of historical interest, during the Great Depression of the 1930s a U.S. manufacturing plant reduced nominal working hours by more than 9 hours a week, yet actual working hours fell only 5 hours a week. Another plant reduced the workweek by 10 1/2 hours, and hourly production rose 21%.

In research conducted in Sweden with white-collar workers, investigators found that overtime resulted in fewer hours of sleep for these employees and greater self-reported feelings of exhaustion (Dahlgren, Kecklund, & Akerstedt, 2006).

Permanent Part-Time Employment

Part-time or half-time employment is the most widespread form of alternative work schedule. More than 25% of the U.S. workforce holds part-time jobs. Part-time employment has grown faster than full-time employment, particularly in service and retail trades. By shifting to part-time employment, organizations reduce the costs of keeping full-time staffs (which require higher salary and benefit packages) and increase their scheduling flexibility.

Some jobs require workers to punch a time clock at the beginning and end of each work shift.

Flextime A system of flexible working hours that combines core mandatory work periods with elective work periods at the beginning and end of the workday.

Management recognizes that full-time employment does not mean that the organization is actually getting a full day's work from each employee. Furthermore, much work, such as writing and independent research, can be performed satisfactorily part time. A lower-level assembly-line job or a clerical job can be performed by two persons, each working half time.

The U.S. Department of Health and Human Services found that supervisors of part-time employees were strongly in favor of part-time employment. Welfare caseworkers in Massachusetts who worked 20 hours a week had a lower turnover rate and higher caseload contact than did full-time employees. State government agencies in Wisconsin found that actual working hours among permanent, part-time social workers, attorneys, and research analysts equaled or exceeded the actual working hours of full-time employees.

Part-time employment is attractive to people with family responsibilities and to disabled persons who have mobility problems. Most part-time employees are women, and they tend to be concentrated in lower level jobs and receive lower rates of pay than do full-time employees. In a large-scale study including 794 employees of a grocery store chain, 200 hospital workers, and 243 retail employees, researchers found that those who had chosen part-time employment were far more satisfied with their jobs, performed their work better, and were more committed to their organization than were those who were assigned to part-time work against their will (Holton, Lee, & Tidd, 2002).

The Four-Day Workweek

Another way to alter the workweek significantly is to reduce it to 4 days. This usually involves 4 days at 10 hours a day (a 40-hour week) or 4 days at 9 hours a day (a 36-hour week with no reduction in pay). Union leaders, management consultants, and many companies that have tried the 4-day workweek are enthusiastic about it. Typically, initiatives to shorten the workweek came not from employees but from management, for reasons such as these: the possibility of increasing worker productivity and efficiency, the use of the shorter workweek as an incentive to recruit workers, and the hope of reducing absenteeism, which in many organizations is unusually high on Mondays and Fridays.

Comments from managers and employees on the 4-day workweek have been positive. They cite improved job satisfaction and productivity, reduced absenteeism, and easier work scheduling. A nationwide Gallup Poll supported the appeal of the 4-day week. Some 45% of the men surveyed indicated that they would like a 4-day schedule. Women who did not work outside the home opposed the 4-day workweek by a ratio of two to one. Women who did work outside the home were far more favorable to the idea of a 4-day workweek.

Flexible Work Schedules

Another type of alternative work schedule permits employees to decide for themselves when to begin and end the workday. In the 1960s, several companies in Germany tried a flexible working hours (**flextime**) schedule to deal with traffic congestion at rush hours. Under this plan, the workday is divided into four segments, two of which are mandatory and two optional (see Figure 10–1).

In this example, employees can report to work any time between 7:30 and 9:00 a.m. and leave any time between 4:00 and 5:30 p.m. The mandatory work periods are the morning hours from 9:00 a.m. until the lunch break and the afternoon hours from lunch to 4:00 p.m. Thus, employees work a minimum 6 1/2-hour workday. The optional daily maximum is 9 1/2 hours. How long each employee works is established individually as a function of the company's needs.

Flextime offers several advantages. Rush-hour traffic congestion around plants and offices is reduced. Because employees spend less time and energy commuting, they are often more relaxed at

FIGURE 10-1   A typical flexible work schedule.

work, more satisfied with their jobs, and more likely to begin work promptly. Many workers make only minor changes in their work habits under a flextime schedule. The inflexible demands of car pools, commuter timetables, and family life hold them to schedules much like those they had before flextime. However, employees believe that having the choice of when to arrive and leave work enhances their personal freedom. Studies have found that flextime schedules decreased absenteeism and improved workers' productivity and their satisfaction with the job and the work schedule.

Flexible working hours appear to be most appropriate for jobs such as research and development, clerical and data entry, and light and heavy manufacturing. For some assembly-line and shift-work operations, flextime is difficult to implement because of the interdependence of the work teams. Overall, flextime is a fair, sensible, and low-cost alternative work schedule that is popular with employers and employees.

Surveys conducted by the Families and Work Institute have consistently shown that employees with flexible work plans were significantly less likely to leave their companies and were more productive than employees who had no flexible options. The surveys also reported that 72% of low-wage workers without flexible working hours call in sick when they need time off to deal with child-care problems or family crises. Under a plan of flexible working hours, they might not have to use illness as an excuse to tend to personal needs (see www.familiesandwork.org).

Rest Breaks

Ever since the Hawthorne studies, management has recognized the importance of authorized rest breaks. Their beneficial effects have been amply demonstrated, but there is a more insistent reason for granting them. Why? Because employees will take breaks whether or not the company sanctions them. If the time is going to be taken anyway, the organization might as well appear benevolent and offer the rest pauses as a fringe benefit.

When authorized rest pauses are introduced, unauthorized breaks decline, though they do not disappear. Other benefits of rest periods include increased morale and productivity and reduced fatigue and boredom. This is another instance of how a decrease in nominal working hours can result in an increase in efficiency.

Workers who engage in heavy physical labor need rest pauses because muscles in continuous use will tire and become less effective. Rest pauses also reduce repetitive motion injuries to hands and wrists. For sedentary and intellectual work, a rest break provides a change of stimulation. It allows boredom to dissipate and provides the opportunity to think about something else or to socialize with co-workers. Rest pauses may also result in more

Many jobs are repetitive and physically demanding; workers should be given formal rest periods to reduce boredom and fatigue.

Newsbreak

The Modern Flextime Virtual Mom

Amey Stone is a financial writer for *Business Week Online* and the mother of two small children. Her schedule is hectic but she gets to choose when she works. "I manage my own time," she wrote, "and as long as I get my work done and my editors know how to reach me, I don't think they really care where I am from 9 a.m. to 5 p.m. Most of the time I assume they would rather not know why, for example, I'm rushing out the door at 2 p.m. on a Wednesday or e-mailing after midnight on a Thursday." Most of the time she works from home, balancing the demands of her job and those of her family, and her hours may seem odd to those who are tied to their workplace from 9 to 5, Monday through Friday.

"I get the flexibility to plan my workweek so that I can attend my daughters' doctors' appointments, dance recitals, and the occasional after-noon play date. But I also get to keep a full-time salary and the status and potential for advancement that goes along with it."

Nevertheless, sometimes her life presents hard choices. "The downside is that I have to be a lot of things to a lot of people at the same time. Of course, I can't be both Involved Mom and Devoted Employee all day every day. The roles are in too great a conflict for me to manage them simultaneously for more than a few minutes at a time. Worst of all, some other roles I've signed on for—Loving Wife, Loyal Best Friend, and Devoted Daughter—sometimes get short shrift. But the truth is, if I didn't work, I couldn't do it all anyway. So for me, working full time flextime gives me the freedom, financial security, and sense of accomplishment I need to keep a lot of balls in the air."

It works for her. Would it work for you?

Source: Stone, A. (2005, May 4). One mom's solution: Flextime. Retrieved from *Business Week Online*.

---

positive attitudes toward management. When a rest program is implemented, workers tend to believe that it is an expression of management's concern for them as individuals.

Research on data entry clerks and computer operators showed that those who reported higher levels of fatigue and boredom on the job tended to take longer rest breaks than did those who felt less fatigued and bored. Also, psychologists have found that computer workers who do stretching exercises during rest breaks, particularly for arms and shoulders, perform better after the breaks than do workers who engage in no physical movement during their breaks (Jett & George, 2003).

In a study of data entry workers in Canada, researchers found that microbreaks lasting only 30 seconds, when taken regularly every 20 minutes, reduced physical discomfort in back, shoulder, and forearm muscles to a greater extent than taking microbreaks whenever the workers felt like it or having no breaks at all. With regularly scheduled rest breaks, there was no decline in productivity levels (McLean, Tingley, Scott, & Rickards, 2001).

In research conducted with 800 workers in the Netherlands and in Germany, investigators found that the need for recovery from the demands of a job was highest for workers with low control over hazardous jobs and little organizational support. This higher need for recovery time was linked to greater fatigue and lower psychological well-being (Sonnentag & Zijlstra, 2006).

A much longer rest break—the off hours between workdays—was the subject of another research study. A survey of 147 workers in Germany showed that workers who believed they had sufficiently recovered from the previous day's work were more involved in their work the next day. Workers who felt greater stress on the job needed more time to recover from the workday than did those who experienced less stress (Sonnentag, 2003).

Shift Work

Many industries operate around the clock. Workers in electric and natural gas utilities, transportation, steel, automotive assembly, hospital services, and telecommunications typically work one of three shifts: usually 7:00 a.m. to 3:00 p.m., 3:00 p.m. to 11:00 p.m., or 11:00 p.m. to 7:00 a.m. Some companies assign workers to one shift permanently, whereas others rotate assignments, switching workers each week or month to a different shift. Employees working evening or all-night shifts usually receive extra pay to compensate for the inconvenience of the working hours. About 25% of the blue-collar and white-collar workforces perform shift work.

How does shift work affect job performance? Research shows that workers are less productive on the all-night shift than on the day shift. Night-shift workers are also more prone to make errors and to have more serious accidents. Accidents in nuclear power plants in the United States and in Russia occurred during the night shift. A nuclear power plant in Pennsylvania was closed by the Nuclear Regulatory Commission when night-shift control room personnel were found to be asleep on the job.

In a study of 1,867 oil industry employees in Britain, shift workers reported greater levels of stress, increased exposure to adverse and risky working conditions, lower feelings of job control, less social support from supervisors, and higher levels of conflict at work than those who worked regular hours during the standard workday (Parkes, 2003).

Disruption of the normal sleep–wake cycle has physiological and psychological consequences. Humans develop a diurnal rhythm, a regular daily cycle of bodily activities that is consistent from one 24-hour period to the next. When this rhythm is disrupted, the body undergoes dramatic changes and sleep becomes difficult. The effect on sleep is the major complaint of employees who do night-shift work, that is, they are unable to sleep during the day because of daylight and household routines. Family life suffers, and everyday activities such as shopping become difficult to schedule. Night-shift workers and those on a rotating-shift schedule report a high incidence of stomach disorders, sleep disorders, cardiovascular complaints, marital problems, and irritability. In a study of nurses in Australia, researchers showed that a 30-minute nap break during the night shift reduced sleepiness on the job and increased response speed and reaction times, both of which are critical functions in the nursing profession (Smith, Kilby, Jorgensen, & Douglas, 2007).

Fewer problems are encountered with the fixed-shift system than with the rotating-shift system, even when the fixed shift occurs at night. Workers permanently assigned to one shift are more likely to adjust to a new diurnal rhythm. With the rotating-shift system, workers must readjust every week or so, whenever the shift schedule is changed; this system does not give the body time to adjust to one schedule before being forced to begin another.

There are other ways to alleviate some of the problems associated with shift work. When the rotating-shift system must be used, changes from one shift to another should be made as seldom as possible—for example, every month instead of every week. Another way to ease the change from one shift to another is to lengthen the time off between shift changes. A longer interim period makes the change less abrupt and allows employees to rest before starting a new schedule. Because the night shift is the most difficult for employees and the least productive for employers, it could be shortened to make it less stressful.

A potentially harmful form of shift work that affects many people is the erratic work schedule of commercial airline pilots. Commercial pilots often change from night flights to day flights and back, sleeping at irregular intervals and disrupting their bodily rhythms. Studies of civilian and military pilots and flight crews working unusually long and erratic hours (such as 10 to 24 hours continuously) confirm the harmful effects of severe disturbances of diurnal rhythms. Airline personnel reported considerable fatigue, slept poorly following their work periods, and took unauthorized naps in the cockpit for up to 2 hours. Examinations of aircraft flight recorders (so-called black boxes) revealed that deviations in pilot performance correlated positively with subjective feelings of fatigue.

Psychologists conducting research for NASA's Fatigue Countermeasures Program found that allowing pilots 40-minute rest periods during low workload portions of long flights resulted in significantly increased alertness. Flight crews that were not supposed to nap during the study period did so anyway, although most of the personnel who took unauthorized naps were not aware of having done so.

Newsbreak

Asleep on the Job? Good for You!

There was a time when you could be fired for falling asleep on the job. But now a growing number of companies are urging their employees to do just that. A national survey in 2008 found that 34% of U.S. companies allowed their employees to nap during their authorized breaks and 16% provided lounges and encouraged workers to "power nap" when they felt sleepy. Why are companies encouraging employees to go to sleep during working hours? The answer is that employees will be more alert and efficient when they wake up.

Sleep researchers have demonstrated that no matter how soundly we sleep at night, most of us become drowsy in early afternoon, whether we've eaten heavily at lunchtime or not. A sleepy worker is not efficient or productive and is likely to make mistakes or cause accidents.

Worse, many of us don't get enough sleep at night, so we begin the workday feeling sluggish. A study by the National Sleep Foundation reported that 64% of U.S. workers fail to sleep the recommended 8 hours a night. And 32% of the people report sleeping fewer than 6 hours per night. This widespread lack of sleep affects how well people perform their jobs.

The same study found that 61% of the population said that a bad night's sleep impairs their decision-making ability, and 37% felt that it prevented them from doing their best work. The obvious antidote is to make up the sleep at work, to take brief power naps during the day to restore alertness and efficiency.

The work of the National Sleep Foundation is changing many corporate cultures. It has a slogan: *Be productive. Take a nap!*

Sources: Korkki, P. (2007, August 19). The yawn after lunch is perfectly normal. *New York Times*; Flora, C. (2008, February 4). Nap your way to the top. Retrieved from *Psychology Today Online*.

For information, in English and Spanish, on sleep and alertness problems (including jet lag, insomnia, shift work, and the effects of caffeine) see the Web site for the National Sleep Foundation at www.sleepfoundation.org You can also participate in a Sleep in America public opinion poll.

PSYCHOLOGICAL AND SOCIAL ISSUES

Other important factors in the work environment relate to the nature of the job and its impact on employees. Does your job provide you with a sense of satisfaction and achievement, or does it make you tired, bored, and ill? The design of a job can affect motivation and satisfaction. Some quality-of-work-life programs have been successful in improving morale and motivation, but jobs designed to be so simple that they make no demands on intelligence, need for achievement, or attention will lead to boredom, fatigue, and inefficiency.

Job Simplification

Simplified, fragmented, and repetitive work affects mental and physical health. For example, assembly-line workers complain more about their physical health and visit company medical facilities more often than workers who do less repetitive work. Psychologists suggest that people who hold such jobs on a rigid work schedule are more anxious, depressed, and irritable than workers doing the same kinds of jobs on a more flexible schedule. Simplified and repetitive work can lead to the deterioration in cognitive functioning usually associated with old age. People who do this type of work are prone to absentmindedness and disorientation.

A meta-analysis of 259 research studies involving 219,625 employees demonstrated that simplifying jobs led to lower supervisor ratings of performance and lower job satisfaction. Providing more autonomy in jobs led to better performance, higher job satisfaction, and lower levels of exhaustion (Humphrey, Nahrgang, & Morgeson, 2007).

The history of **job simplification** dates from the beginnings of mass production systems in the early twentieth century. If relatively expensive consumer goods such as automobiles were to be produced cost-effectively in sufficient quantities to meet consumer demand, then old-style production methods, such as building each unit by hand, would have to change. Mass production called for product consistency and standardization so that parts would be interchangeable. It also required fractionation of job tasks. It was no longer economically or technically feasible for one person to make an entire product. The work had to be meticulously divided so that each worker produced only a small part of the finished product. The ideal was to reduce every manufacturing process to the simplest elements that could be mastered by an unskilled or semiskilled employee.

Job simplification offered tremendous economic advantages to industry and to consumers by permitting the lowest possible cost per unit produced. When Henry Ford established his automobile assembly line, he was able to sell cars at a price within reach of people who previously could not afford them. The same was true for other consumer goods. The factory-produced chair in which you are sitting costs considerably less than a chair handmade by a skilled furniture craftsperson. This was an additional advantage of job simplification: Industry no longer had to rely on the skilled trades, the workers who required years of apprenticeship, expected high wages, and were apt to be independent of mind. The typical assembly line could be staffed by workers who had little skill and could be quickly trained to perform the job. The process made workers more docile and easier to manage. Because they had few marketable skills, they knew they could easily be replaced. Workers were as interchangeable as the parts they produced.

There is no denying that job simplification had a stimulating impact on the U.S. economy. More jobs became available, and people had more money to buy the plentiful consumer goods. The more people bought, the more factories had to be built, which, in turn, meant even more jobs. New prod-

ucts required additional businesses to advertise, sell, and service them. Such economic growth could not have occurred if production methods had remained limited to the handcrafted approach.

Assembly-line workers have paid a price for their role in this industrial development. The farther removed workers are from the finished product, the less meaning and value they attach to their jobs. The carpenter who shaped a table from a piece of lumber knew the pride and fulfillment of achievement and the challenge of using skill and imagination. There is little challenge and satisfaction in operating a machine that attaches bumpers to automobiles day after day, year after year. The worker is an adjunct to the machine, pressing a button or pushing a lever or watching in case something goes wrong. The work has little meaning and quickly becomes frustrating and monotonous. Workers soon grow apathetic, morale declines, and the quantity and quality of production deteriorate.

Job simplification also affects white-collar and managerial jobs because computers have turned many offices into electronic assembly lines. In white-collar jobs, work is increasingly fragmented and simplified. As a result, office workers are becoming cheaper to train and easier to replace.

Recall from chapter 9 how jobs can be enlarged, enriched, and expanded to provide employees with greater responsibility and challenge. The quality-of-work-life programs discussed are real-world examples of making jobs more complex rather than simpler. Expanding the job has clear benefits for both employees and employers.

Boredom and Monotony

Two inevitable consequences of job fractionation and simplification—boredom and monotony—are important components of the psychological work environment. Boredom results from the continuous performance of a repetitive and uninteresting activity and can lead to restlessness, discontent, and a draining of interest and energy. However, what is boring for one person may be exciting for another. Although most people find assembly-line work to be monotonous, for example, others do not. And some workers in jobs that appear to be challenging also report feelings of boredom. The relevant factor is motivation. The data entry clerk who is highly motivated to process entries without making errors will be less bored than the worker who lacks this motivation.

One obvious way to alleviate boredom is to enlarge the scope of a job, to make it more complex, stimulating, and challenging. Management can also alter work schedules and the physical and social conditions of the workplace to reduce boredom. Attention to noise reduction, lighting, and pleasant surroundings can help combat the negative effects of repetitive and monotonous work. A congenial informal work group helps, as do rest pauses to provide a change of activity. The greater the change in activity during rest pauses or lunch breaks, the less disruptive will be the effects of boredom (Mann, 2007).

Physical Fatigue

Psychologists describe two types of fatigue: psychological fatigue, which is similar to boredom, and physiological fatigue, which is caused by excessive use of the muscles. Both types of fatigue can cause poor job performance and lead to errors, accidents, and absenteeism. Prolonged or heavy physical labor produces measurable physiological changes. People whose jobs require heavy lifting and hauling consistently show cardiovascular, metabolic, and muscle fatigue as well as a decline in the ability to maintain their initial productivity level.

Psychological or subjective fatigue is more difficult to assess but is no less disturbing to employees. You are no doubt aware of experiencing strain, irritability, and weakness when you are excessively tired, or of finding it difficult to concentrate, think coherently, and work effectively.

On-the-job research has shown that productivity parallels reported feelings of fatigue. High reported fatigue is a reliable indicator that production will shortly decline. With most physically demanding work, employees say that they are most tired at the beginning of the work period, just before the lunch break, and again at the end of the workday. Thus, fatigue does not build up over the course of the work period but appears and disappears throughout the working hours. This suggests that factors other than physical labor (motivation, for example) can influence feelings of fatigue.

An employee experiencing psychological fatigue finds it difficult to concentrate, think coherently, and work effectively.

Often a person leaves the job at the end of the shift feeling exhausted but finds that the fatigue disappears on arriving home and anticipating some pleasurable activity.

A major survey of nearly 29,000 employees confirmed the strong relationship between physical fatigue and productivity. Fully 38% of those surveyed said they had experienced fatigue, decreased energy, and poor sleep during the 2 weeks prior to the survey. The results also revealed that fatigue was higher among women than men, higher in workers younger than 50, and higher in Whites than in African Americans (Ricci, Chee, Lorandeau, & Berger, 2007).

In research conducted in the Netherlands with 322 university employees and 555 nurses, researchers found that as the demands of a job increased, greater feelings of job control reduced fatigue. Also, as the demands of a job increased, reported feelings of fatigue led to a decrease in job satisfaction (Van Yperen & Hagedoorn, 2003; Van Yperen & Janssen, 2002).

Studies in Japan and in Australia showed that fatigue can be reduced if working hours are kept to fewer than 260 per month and if workers perceive that they have a high level of organizational support (Nagashima et al., 2007; Samaha, Lai, Samaha, & Wyndham, 2007).

Research on physiological fatigue indicates that workers can undertake greater amounts of physical labor when the work pace is more gradual. Too rapid a rate of heavy work dissipates the body's energy too quickly so that the worker must then function at a slower pace for the remainder of the work period. An analogy can be made with long-distance runners who pace themselves so that they do not use all their energy before covering the desired distance.

Rest periods are necessary for jobs that involve heavy physical labor, and they should be taken before fatigue is complete. The greater the amount of fatigue at the time of the rest break, the longer the recovery period must be. For some jobs, more frequent rest breaks are needed. Rest periods must provide total relaxation, not merely a stoppage of work. The manual laborer, more than the office worker, will benefit from pleasant cafeterias and comfortable lounges in which to relax.

Ethnic and Gender Harassment

Another social-psychological condition of the workplace that affects productivity, job satisfaction, and emotional and physical health is on-the-job harassment, whether based on race, ethnicity, gender, or other personal characteristics. Harassment may come from co-workers or supervisors, or it may be part of the corporate culture.

Ethnic Harassment. The population of a typical workplace, like the population of many countries, has become increasingly diverse. As organizations employ more people of various racial and ethnic groups, harassment is on the rise. Ethnic harassment is an obvious source of stress. It may be manifested at work as slurs or derogatory comments about a person's racial or ethnic group and may result in the exclusion of the person from work groups or social activities.

A study of 575 Hispanic men and women provided evidence of harassment on the job. Verbal slurs, derogatory comments, and offensive ethnic jokes were found to be more common than behaviors intended to exclude a person on ethnic grounds. People who were targets of verbal harassment reported a lowering of their sense of psychological well-being (Schneider, Hitlan, & Radhakrishnan, 2000). Hispanic workers who speak Spanish on the job report more exclusion, harassment, and discrim-

ination than those who speak English on the job (Bergman, Watrous-Rodriguez, & Chalkley, 2008).

Sexual and Gender Harassment. Women at all levels in an organization face harassment on the job ranging from suggestive remarks and obscene jokes to threats of job loss and physical assaults. A distinction can be made between sexual harassment and gender harassment. Sexual harassment involves unwanted sexual attention and coercion. Gender harassment refers to behavior that reflects an insulting, hostile, and degrading attitude toward women. Thus, gender harassment does not necessarily involve sexual harassment. Gender harassment is directed toward all women, whereas sexual harassment is targeted toward a specific woman. To report incidents of sexual harassment and to receive advice on dealing with it, call the toll-free Job Survival Hotline of 9 to 5, a working women's advocacy group (1-800-522-0925). Their Web site, www.9to5.org, focuses on issues of economic fairness, harassment, and work–family policies.

Gender and sexual harassment have occurred in many workplaces and have resulted in costly and embarrassing lawsuits for prominent organizations. Chevron paid $2.2 million to four female employees who were further harassed following their initial filing of sexual harassment charges. Mitsubishi was ordered to pay $34 million to several hundred women who charged that the company's Illinois plant failed to respond to their sexual harassment complaints.

A review of harassment claims filed with the Equal Employment Opportunity Commission (EEOC) showed that several types of companies were likely to be the target of lawsuits because they ignored reports of harassment. These include family-owned businesses, firms too small to maintain human resources or personnel departments, factories located in rural areas, and so-called male-dominated industries such as construction. Younger women in low-level jobs, single or divorced women, and women in predominantly male environments report more harassment than do middle-age or older married women whose jobs are not in male-dominated organizations.

Studies have shown that minority women are far more likely than majority women to experience harassment on the job. Women of all races who are seen as violating female stereotypes (such as being assertive, aggressive, or behaving in other so-called masculine ways) are more likely to be sexually harassed than are those who behave in ways that are traditionally considered feminine (Berdahl, 2007; Berdahl & Moore, 2006). Sexual harassment on the job also occurs more frequently in workplaces where the male employees have a habit of drinking heavily, even off the job (Bacharach, Bamberger, & McKinney, 2007).

The reported incidence of sexual harassment can be affected by the wording of the survey questions. A meta-analysis of 55 samples (consisting of 86,578 respondents) found two distinct approaches to measuring the incidence of sexual harassment. The *direct query survey* allows respondents to define what behaviors constitute sexual harassment and to describe freely what happened to them. The *behavioral experiences survey* provides respondents with a list of incidents defined by the researcher as constituting sexual harassment; respondents then select the experiences or behaviors that correspond to their personal situation. These approaches reveal striking differences in the reported incidence of harassment. Women who responded to surveys that used the direct query approach reported the incidence of harassment at approximately 35%, whereas women who responded to surveys that used the behavioral experiences approach reported the incidence of harassment at approximately 62% (Ilies, Hauserman, Schwochau, & Stibal, 2003). These findings provide another example of the importance of knowing how a survey was conducted and how the questions were phrased before evaluating and applying the results.

The same meta-analysis compared the incidence of sexual harassment in four work environments: academic, the private sector, government, and the military. The reported incidence of sexual harassment was highest in the military setting; the results were the same for both types of survey questions. More women in the military reported being harassed than women in any other work environment. The lowest reported incidence was in academia.

Survey data from 22,372 women in all branches of the military services in the United States revealed that 4% of them reported actual or attempted rape by other military personnel. Those most likely to report such physical assaults were lower in rank, hence in status and power (Harned, Ormerod, Palmieri, Collinsworth, & Reed, 2002).

A meta-analysis of gender differences in defining harassment involved 62 research studies. Women perceived a wider range of behaviors as potentially harassing than did men. For example, 89% of women perceived sexual touching as harassment; only 59 percent of men shared that view. Men were significantly more likely to believe that physical sexual contact initiated by a woman was a compliment; women were more likely to believe that physical sexual contact initiated by a man was a threat and an instance of harassment (Rotundo, Nguyen, & Sackett, 2001). Thus, there is disagreement about the behaviors that are considered harassing. Another point to keep in mind is that not all incidents of harassment on the job are reported.

In a study of 315 male and 262 female police officers in New Zealand, researchers found that gender harassment was a significantly greater source of psychological distress for women than for men. The researchers suggested that harassment is more harmful for women who work in traditionally male occupations such as police departments, because in those situations such behaviors can make women feel that "they need to over-perform to be accepted and recognized within the organization. High performance demands are in turn associated with psychological distress" (Parker & Griffin, 2002, p. 13).

Like ethnic harassment, gender harassment can lead to physical ailments (gastrointestinal disorders, headaches, and weight loss) as well as psychological problems (fear, depression, anxiety, and loss of self-esteem). It also has a negative effect on job satisfaction and productivity. Many studies link harassment to low job satisfaction and high stress (Willness, Steel, & Lee, 2007). A study of 11,521 women in the U.S. military showed that sexual harassment led to a significant increase in turnover. Those who had experienced harassment were far more likely to leave the service than those who had not been harassed (Sims, Drasgow, & Fitzgerald, 2005).

Sexual harassment affects even those employees who are not being personally harassed. In a study of 1,702 male and female university employees, investigators found that simply observing incidents of sexual harassment on the job led to lower reported psychological well-being, lower organizational commitment and job satisfaction, and increased intentions to look for work elsewhere among both men and women (Miner-Rubino & Cortina, 2007).

Research shows that most incidents of sexual harassment on the job are not reported out of fear of retaliation, a fear that may be justified. A study of 6,417 men and women in the U.S. armed forces showed that those who reported sexual harassment to their superiors faced retaliatory measures that led to greater psychological distress and lower job satisfaction. The higher the rank of the perpetrator of the offense, the less likely that the organization took punitive measures or corrective action against the harasser (Bergman, Langhout, Palmieri, Cortina, & Fitzgerald, 2002). A study of 622 female nurses in Turkey revealed that 80% of those who had been sexually harassed on the job (almost always by male physicians) did not report the incidents to the hospital administration for fear of retaliation (Celik & Celik, 2007).

Another source of sexual harassment in the workplace comes not from co-workers or superiors but from the organization's customers and clients. A survey of 3,839 female employees found that such harassment led to decreases in job satisfaction and organizational commitment, increases in stress, and a tendency to avoid the predatory client, which had negative repercussions for both the employee and the organization (Gettman & Gelfand, 2007).

Gender and sexual harassment remain serious problems in the workplace, despite the ongoing publicity given to the issues. Training programs designed to make employees more aware of and sensitive to the feelings of others have had limited effects. A strong organizational culture in which the consequences of sexual harassment on the job are swift and severe can reduce but not eliminate the problem. A committed organizational leadership is also important. A study of 2,749 men and women in the military showed that women who viewed their leaders as making honest and sincere efforts to stop harassment were significantly more willing to report harassment than those whose leaders were more tolerant of harassment. In addition, women who viewed their leaders as sincere about the issue were more satisfied with the procedure for filing complaints about harassment and felt more committed to the organization (Offermann & Malamut, 2002).

For current news about sexual harassment and links to related sites see the Web site for the National Organization for Women (NOW) at www.now.org/issues/harass It describes current cases as well as actions being taken to combat on-the-job harassment. For the federal government's policy on sexual harassment, and links to the proper way to file a charge of employment discrimination, see www.eeoc.gov/facts/fs-sex.html

Telecommuting: The Virtual Workplace at Home

Many employees now work at home, thanks to advances in personal computers, telecommunications, and fax machines. This move toward telecommuting—the decentralizing of work—has affected hundreds of U.S. companies in life insurance, data processing, financial services, airline and hotel reservations, and mail-order merchandising. The U.S. Office of Personnel Management estimates that 45 million workers in the United States telecommute at least part time. Men in their early 40s make up 65% of this workforce. Telecommuting is particularly attractive to employees with day-care or dependent-care problems and to disabled workers.

Companies that provide for telecommuting cite gains in productivity, reduced costs for office overhead, and, obviously, a decline in absenteeism. People working at home may have fewer interruptions than people working in offices and may be

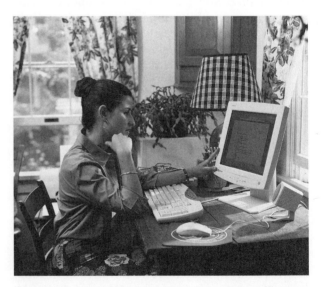

A growing number of employees work from a home office, an option that is particularly attractive to people with day-care concerns.

able to concentrate better. They can perform their job in bad weather or when feeling poorly, whereas office-based employees in those situations might hesitate to come to work. Research at IBM comparing virtual-office telecommuters with in-house office employees found that telecommuting was associated with high productivity and job satisfaction as well as increased psychological well-being. IBM's flexible telework program has been so successful that 40% of its 330,000 employees have chosen to work away from the office, either at home or on the road (Cooney, 2007).

In general, women in virtual offices are more productive than men in virtual offices, but both groups seem pleased that they don't have to spend time commuting. They enjoy being able to schedule their work outside traditional office hours, and they report fewer distractions and a more comfortable working environment. In a study of 26 highly educated white-collar workers in Sweden, researchers found that the blood pressure levels of both men and women were significantly higher when they worked at the office than when they worked at home. This finding suggested to the researchers that working at home was less stressful for these workers (Lundberg & Lindfors, 2002).

Los Angeles County administrators estimated that their telecommuting program involving 2,600 workers saved $11 million a year in increased productivity, reduced absenteeism, decreased overtime pay, and reduced office space. They also claimed that the program cut commuting time by 1.4 million hours, thereby eliminating 7,500 tons of carbon monoxide from car exhausts. An AT&T poll of 1,005 home-based workers found that 80% believed they were more productive than when working in company offices. In addition, 61% said they got sick less often, and 79% appreciated the chance to wear casual clothes while working. Surveys at other companies found increases of up to 30% in productivity as well as a significant reduction in the nonproductive work time spent socializing. Telecommuting does not appear to be related to any decrease in an employee's opportunity for promotion.

A survey of 10,000 U.S. workers found that 73% of the telecommuters were satisfied with their employer, as compared to only 64% of those who worked in the company offices (Coombes,

2008). In a meta-analysis of 46 studies of nearly 13,000 workers, researchers found that telecommuting was related to increased feelings of autonomy, positive relationships with supervisors, higher performance ratings, greater job satisfaction, and reduced stress and turnover intentions. Nevertheless, telecommuting also appeared to lead to poor relationships with co-workers; this is not surprising as the teleworkers spent so little time socializing in the office (Gajendran & Harrison, 2007). A survey of information technology workers in Egypt found that, in principle, far more of them favored telecommuting than opposed it (Abdel-Wahab, 2007).

Not everyone likes the idea of working at home. Not only do some people miss the social interaction, but they may not be sufficiently disciplined to work steadily without supervision. Some spouses object to having a partner work at home. Children may provide an additional distraction. Some managers believe they will lose their authority over subordinates if the subordinates are not physically present. And labor unions are concerned about the declining loyalty of members who do not work together on the job.

To deal with potential feelings of isolation, some companies have established programs to enable teleworkers to develop and maintain relationships with other telecommuters and with office employees. IBM has set up so-called mobility centers where telecommuters can have office time with other employees. IBM clubs also encourage telecommuting employees to meet co-workers through company-organized social outings in settings far removed from the traditional workplace.

Some telecommuters feel pressured to work harder than they did in their traditional offices. Others say that by working at home, they are never free of the job. When the phone or fax or e-mail summons them after working hours, they feel compelled to respond. For these reasons, nearly 20% of telecommuting programs fail. Another reason for unsuccessful programs is that some telecommuters do not get the technical support they need from employers. Despite these difficulties, many employees prefer working at home. Human resources managers view telecommuting as one of the most important workplace trends of the twenty-first century.

Summary

Physical working conditions include factors such as the location of the factory or office building, parking facilities, heating and air-conditioning systems, elevators, child-care facilities, cafeterias, and rest rooms. **Environmental psychology** is concerned with the impact of these workplace features on employee behaviors and attitudes. In the landscaped office, employees are grouped in functional units with no floor-to-ceiling barriers.

Light distribution and glare must be considered in designing illumination for work spaces. Noise in the work area can lead to deafness and to physiological effects such as increased muscle tension and high blood pressure. Color is a useful coding device that can create differing illusions of size and temperature and improve the aesthetic appearance of the workplace. Some employees like music on the job, but research shows that it does not influence productivity. Optimal temperature and humidity ranges have been established for different kinds of workplaces. The comfort level of a workspace also depends on humidity level and air circulation.

Temporal working conditions include the number of hours worked and how those hours are arranged. Much scheduled work time is lost to unauthorized breaks. When **nominal working hours** are reduced, production tends to increase. Part-time employment offers opportunities to combine career, family, educational, leisure, and other pursuits, and may result in greater productivity. The 4-day workweek seems to result in lower absenteeism and higher morale, but it has little effect on productivity. **Flextime** is popular with employees and increases productivity and job satisfaction. Rest pauses are taken whether or not they are officially sanctioned. In manual labor they are necessary to rest the muscles. For sedentary workers, rest pauses provide a change of pace and help alleviate boredom. Shift work disrupts the body's diurnal rhythm and can lead to social and psychological difficulties. In general, productivity is lower on the night shift; serious accidents and errors are higher.

Social-psychological working conditions relate to the design of the job and its effects on employees. **Job simplification** has made many jobs so unchallenging that they are boring and lead to psychological and physiological fatigue that reduces productivity and job satisfaction. Repetitive, boring work is also tiring. Boredom can be relieved by enlarging the job scope, improving working conditions, and scheduling rest pauses. Ethnic and gender harassment occur frequently in the workplace. Harassment causes harmful physical and emotional effects on employees as well as reducing their job satisfaction and productivity.

Advances in computer and telecommunications technology have made working at home possible for many types of employees. Telecommuting is associated with higher productivity, lower absenteeism, and corporate savings on office space.

Key Terms

environmental psychology	job simplification
flextime	nominal working hours

Review Questions

1. Why is it difficult to interpret the effects of a change in the physical work environment that has led to an increase in productivity?

2. What are the major complaints made by office workers about their work environment?

3. In what ways can the size and design of offices and the size of an office building affect productivity and the nature of the working relationships among co-workers?

4. Describe advantages and disadvantages of landscaped offices.

5. What is a foot-candle of light? Why is it a bad idea to illuminate a workstation at a much higher level of intensity than its surroundings?

6. How many decibels does it take to cause permanent deafness? What other physiological changes occur as a result of exposure to high noise levels?

7. In what ways can the use of different colors be helpful in the workplace?

8. Describe the history of music provided for workers on the job. For what kinds of jobs does music lead to an increase in productivity?

9. What are the effects of exposure to very high temperatures on the job? Why do some organizations put fake thermostats in their offices?

10. What is the difference between nominal working hours and actual working hours?

11. What was the effect on actual working hours when nominal working hours were increased in some companies during the years of World War II?

12. What are the advantages to employees and employers of permanent part-time employment, of a 4-day workweek, and of flexible working hours?

13. If you had a job that required shift work, which shift schedule would you choose? Explain the reason for your choice.

14. When did job simplification begin? What did it involve? How did it benefit the U.S. economy?

15. Is there a relationship between job simplification and boredom or monotony on the job? If so, explain it.

16. How would you reduce boredom and fatigue in an automobile assembly plant? In an office where employees work at computer terminals?

17. Distinguish between ethnic harassment, sexual harassment, and gender harassment.

18. What are the effects of sexual harassment on female employees? On co-workers who observe the harassment?

19. In what type of work environment has sexual harassment been found to occur most frequently?

20. Why are most incidents of sexual harassment not reported? What factors can reduce sexual harassment at work?

21. Why do some employees dislike telecommuting?

22. Would you rather telecommute for your job or work in the office or factory? Why?

Additional Reading

Bell, P., Green, T., Fisher, J., & Baum, A. (2001). *Environmental psychology* (5th ed.). Ft. Worth, TX: Harcourt College Publishers. A standard textbook on environmental psychology; covers the influence of physical workplace features on employee behaviors and attitudes.

Hochschild, A. R. (1997). *The time bind: When work becomes home and home becomes work.* New York: Metropolitan/Holt. Describes an organization in which employees routinely put in 10-hour workdays and identify more with colleagues and subordinates than with family members, deriving greater social support from office relationships than from relationships outside the workplace.

Peirce, E., Smolinski, C. A., & Rosen, B. (1998). Why sexual harassment complaints fall on deaf ears. *Academy of Management Executive, 12*(3), 41–54. Discusses reasons why many organizations are slow to respond to employees' complaints of sexual harassment, forcing victims to seek help through the court system.

Rothausen, T. J., Gonzalez, J. A., Clarke, N. E., & O'Dell, L. L. (1998). Family-friendly backlash. *Personnel Psychology, 51*, 685–706. Discusses the positive and negative effects on employees of employer-provided on-site child care facilities.

CHAPTER 11

Employee Safety and Health Issues

Some jobs can kill you or make you sick, and some jobs lead to a high rate of accidents. Shops, offices, and factories can be dangerous places. Every year more than 5,000 accidental deaths occur on the job. The number of disabling injuries, although not fully documented, is thought to be in excess of 4 million each year. Research by the U.S. Bureau of Labor Statistics indicates that for every disabling work injury reported, at least 10 are not reported by companies attempting to hide a poor safety record. The monetary cost of these injuries is staggering, not only to employees and their organizations, but also to the nation as a whole. Billions of dollars are forfeited through lost time and wages and paid out in medical benefits and workers' compensation claims.

In some types of jobs the health of workers can be undermined by their exposure to toxic chemicals in the workplace. Disabling illnesses caused or aggravated by these on-the-job conditions generally do not kill or maim as suddenly or dramatically as accidents, but they impose emotional and economic costs and shorten the lives of thousands of workers.

Although accidents are the primary cause of death on the job, murder is the second; for women it is the leading factor, accounting for 42% of women's on-the-job fatalities. Injuries from deliberate acts of violence are becoming more widespread.

In this chapter we focus on these and other aspects of workplace health and safety, discussing what I-O psychologists have learned about accidents and violence on the job and what organizations can do about the problem. We also deal with alcohol and drug abuse, both of which have adverse effects on employee health, safety, and job performance. In addition, we examine health issues related to the use of computers. For more information, check out the Work, Stress and Health Office of the American Psychological Association at www.apa.org/pi/work and the Society for Occupational Health Psychology at sohp.psy.uconn.edu/Index.html

THE SCOPE OF WORK-RELATED HEALTH PROBLEMS

The toll from work-related diseases is as shocking as the accident rate. These illnesses are more insidious than a sudden, traumatic accident because they develop slowly over years before the worker experiences physical symptoms. For example, coal miners develop a unique respiratory condition

called black lung disease, a progressively crippling disorder caused by prolonged inhalation of coal dust. Chemical industries pose health perils to their workers, dangers that are not fully known. Up to 10 million workers are exposed daily to chemicals for which safe thresholds have not been established. The U.S. Environmental Protection Agency (EPA) has designated as toxic more than 16,000 chemical substances regularly used in the workplace. Some 150 of these are neurotoxins; they are capable of causing damage to the human brain and nervous system.

Miners, mill workers, and shipyard workers who are exposed to asbestos on the job face the danger of lung cancer at seven times the national rate. Textile workers are at risk for brown lung disease, caused by inhaling cotton dust. Medical technicians face dangers from radiation exposure. Office workers face the potentially harmful effects of indoor pollutants.

Astronauts working in the International Space Station report a variety of symptoms, including nausea and headaches, which have been traced to chemical fumes and an accumulation of deadly carbon dioxide. Chemists employed by the BP Amoco research center near Chicago, Illinois, were developing a rare form of brain cancer at eight times the national average. It was traced to two chemical agents used routinely in their work. The American Academy of Asthma estimates that approximately 15% of the people with asthma in the United States acquired their disease from chemicals on the job such as latex, nickel, chrome, and mercury. Occupational asthma has now become the single most common work-related respiratory disorder.

An alarming increase in the incidence of job-related cancers among women has been documented among textile workers and workers at dry-cleaning plants. Breast cancer is on the increase among nurses and medical technicians who deal with X-rays and chemotherapy agents. A higher than normal rate of spontaneous abortion (miscarriage) has been found among oncology nurses and among women working in the chemical industry.

Table 11-1 lists a few of the frequently used hazardous substances, their health effects, and the types of workers who are regularly endangered.

The accident figures cited do not include workers killed or injured commuting to and from the workplace. More than 90% of employees killed on the job are men, though they constitute little more than half of the workforce. There is an obvious reason for this

TABLE 11-1

Hazardous Substances and On-the-Job Diseases

Potential Dangers	Potential Diseases	Workers Exposed
Arsenic	Lung cancer, lymphoma	Smelter, chemical, oil refinery workers; insecticide makers and sprayers
Asbestos	White-lung disease (asbestosis); cancer of lungs and lining of lungs; cancer of other organs	Miners; millers; textile, insulation, and shipyard workers
Benzene	Leukemia; aplastic anemia	Petrochemical and oil refinery workers; dye users; distillers; painters; shoemakers
Bischloromethylether (BCME)	Lung cancer	Industrial chemical workers
Coal dust	Black lung disease	Coal miners
Cotton dust	Brown lung disease (byssinosis); chronic bronchitis; emphysema	Textile workers
Lead	Kidney disease; anemia; central nervous system damage; sterility; birth defects	Metal grinders; lead smelter workers; lead storage-battery workers
Radiation	Cancer of thyroid, lungs, and bone; leukemia; reproductive effects (spontaneous abortion, genetic damage)	Medical technicians; uranium miners; nuclear power and atomic workers
Vinyl chloride	Cancer of liver, brain	Plastic industry workers

occurrence: more men than women work in construction and heavy industry, where an accident can have the most severe consequences. More men than women work as long-distance truck drivers, an occupation that contributes to 20% of all on-the-job fatalities every year. Obviously, some jobs are more dangerous than others, which means that some workers are subject to greater risk of injury or death at work.

In 1970, the U.S. Congress passed the Occupational Safety and Health Act establishing the Occupational Safety and Health Administration (OSHA) in the Department of Labor. OSHA's purpose is to ensure safe working conditions by developing and enforcing federal safety standards and by sponsoring research on the causes and prevention of accidents and diseases in the workplace. Although progress has been made, OSHA has been so poorly funded that it has not been able to carry out its mandate to make workplaces safer. More than 40 years after OSHA was established, it still has so few safety

inspectors that on average a company can expect to be visited only once every 84 years.

Many jobs are not dangerous but they can cause considerable pain and discomfort. In a questionnaire study of more than 800 employees in the Netherlands, researchers found that sitting down while working led to low back pain. Forced standing on the job produced pain in the legs, chest, and lower back, and repetitive movements were associated with arm, chest and back pains (Roelen, Schreuder, Koopmans, & Groothoff, 2008).

UNDERSTANDING ACCIDENT STATISTICS

Statistics do not lie, but sometimes the people who use statistics distort ideas in their own interests, backing up the distortions with data. This is the situation with accident statistics. The major problem

Working in a Sick Building May Make You Sick

Many people spend their working days sealed off from fresh air, trapped in closed environments. They can't open the windows—in many buildings they're not designed to open—and they breathe only filtered cooled or heated air. Cooling and heating systems in modern office buildings may be cost-efficient to operate, but the results can be dangerous. What we inhale can make us sick.

According to the World Health Organization, the physical complaints brought on by these artificial environments include eye, ear, and throat irritations, dry nasal membranes, skin inflammations, fatigue, headaches, nausea, and dizziness. Consider a few examples. In a sealed office building in San Francisco, California, most of the 250 employees complained of headaches, sinus problems, allergic skin reactions, and general discomfort shortly after the building opened. The symptoms disappeared when the air filtration system was modified to allow more fresh air to circulate. In another new building, workers became sleepy and dazed most afternoons, especially on hot days. The problem was traced to the roof, where melting tar released fumes that were drawn into the air conditioning system and dispersed throughout the building. Bacterial infections have also been transmitted through ventilation and air conditioning systems.

When hundreds of employees in a new $37-million, 10-story county office complex in Florida developed symptoms of asthma, the building had to be abandoned. Experts concluded that construction flaws, a faulty air conditioning system, a leaky roof, and vinyl wallpaper had combined to make the building a breeding ground for mildew and other contaminants.

Sealed buildings contain an alarming number of chemicals that are not dissipated or diluted by fresh air. Solvents, adhesives, cleaning fluids, fire-retardant materials, paint additives, formaldehyde in insulation, and chemicals in carpeting, wall coverings, and draperies can all be toxic. Copy machines produce ozone, which has been linked to headaches and upper respiratory tract infections. Solvents in carbonless paper are dangerous. Long-term exposure to electronic equipment has been related to headaches, eye problems, and neurological disorders. Harmful levels of microwaves and other sources of radiation have been linked to eye damage, memory loss, thyroid dysfunction, and leukemia. Perhaps some buildings should carry this warning: *Caution*: Working here may be hazardous to your health. For more information on the sick building syndrome, visit the Web site www.epa.gov/iaq/pubs/sbs.html

is defining when an accident is really an accident, which is not as ridiculous as it sounds.

How severe must an accident be for it to be included in an organization's accident statistics? Suppose a bakery worker drops a 100-pound sack of sugar. Is this an accident? Technically, yes. However, whether the company lists it as an accident depends on the consequences, not on the act itself. If the sack does not split and spill sugar all over the equipment and if no one is hurt, the episode will not be recorded as an accident. But what if the sack falls on the worker's foot and breaks a few bones? Is this considered an accident? Not necessarily. Many companies would not list this as an accident, even though the worker is

injured and requires medical treatment. The worker may not be able to walk for a while, but if the company provides a desk job until the injury heals, then the employee will not have lost time from work. So an accident resulted in an injury, yet it will not be included in the accident statistics, and the company's safety record will remain intact. The definition of an accident in this case depends on whether the injured worker must miss time from work.

A few years ago, a large U.S. meat-packing firm was fined nearly $3 million for failing to report more than 1,000 job-related injuries among its workers. Statistics on railroad accidents investigated by a Washington-based journalist contradicted official government reports. Where Amtrak cited 494 injuries in 25 train wrecks, the independent journalist found 1,338 injuries. This failure to record all job-related injuries, not just those that keep workers off the job, led the U.S. Bureau of Labor Statistics to conclude that accidents are significantly underreported.

Incomplete reporting makes research on the causes and prevention of accidents more difficult. The statistics provided by business and industry show the results of only a small proportion of accidents and provide little information on their causes. By concentrating only on lost-time accidents, the data provide an inaccurate picture of overall safety patterns.

An organization likes to boast about having a good safety record. It shows that the company is a caring employer, doing all it can to promote a safe working environment for its employees. To preserve a good safety record and a favorable public image, a company may resort to extreme measures such as closed-door investigations, incomplete reporting, and outright distortion of facts. Sometimes, however, it is the employees who distort the facts. Some fail to report minor accidents for fear of acquiring a reputation as careless or accident-prone. Others fear disciplinary action if the accident was their fault because they failed to follow prescribed operating procedures or to activate safety devices.

The underreporting and cover-up of accidents has been documented in many countries. In Japan, workers tend to conceal evidence of job-related injuries because of personal shame. To avoid losing face, Japanese workers attempt to hide even major injuries such as broken bones or to insist that they occurred at home. Managers conspire to conceal workplace injuries because they may represent negligence on their part as well.

Another problem with accident statistics has to do with how researchers collect their data. For example, in a study in Denmark, factory workers kept a daily log of their on-the-job accidents. Then, 28 days later, they were asked to write down the number of accidents that had occurred during that month. The two sets of figures did not agree, even though the same employees were providing data about themselves. In the later reports (retrospective data), the workers recorded only about one third of the accidents that they had listed in their daily logs. The researchers concluded that they simply forgot to report the rest (Anderson & Mikkelsen, 2008).

CAUSES OF ACCIDENTS

Human error is the factor responsible for most accidents, whether they occur in the workplace, on the highway, or in the home. However, conditions of the work environment and the nature of the job tasks can also contribute to accidents.

Workplace Factors

Workplace conditions that affect employee safety include type of industry, hours of work, lighting, temperature, equipment design, safety devices, and work pressure.

Type of Industry.   The frequency and severity of accidents vary as a function of type of industry. A steel mill provides more opportunities for accidents than does a bank. The greater the physical demands made on the worker, the higher the accident rate. Also, stressful and tiring work seems to result in more accidents.

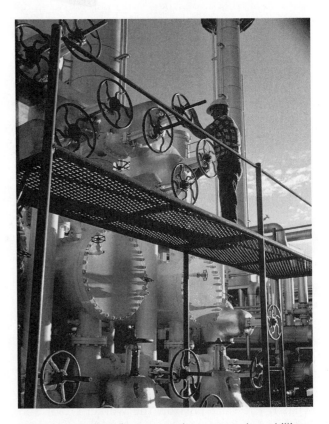

A hazardous work environment such as a natural gas drilling plant must be designed so that emergency controls are within easy reach.

Industries such as construction, highway transportation, farming, and mining are high in frequency and severity of accidents. Industries such as warehousing, aircraft and automobile manufacturing, and communications have a low frequency and severity of accidents. Cement and steel companies report a low frequency of accidents, but when accidents do occur, they are usually severe. Electric utilities also record few accidents, but these tend to be severe because of the high voltages involved. Wholesale and retail businesses have high accident rates, but lost-time injuries are rare.

Even parking lots can be dangerous. Data collected over a 9-year period by the U.S. Bureau of Labor Statistics showed that more than 200 employees were killed each year in parking lots. Some 36% were homicides, 11% were suicides, and the rest were due to various kinds of accidents (Fayard, 2008).

Accident data for some high-risk industries are listed in Table 11-2.

Hours of Work. A reasonable assumption might be that the higher the number of hours worked, the higher the accident rate, but research does not provide clear support for this idea. However, shift work seems to be related to accident rates. In general, fewer accidents occur during the night shift than during the day shift, although when accidents do occur during the night shift, they are usually more serious. The occurrence of fewer accidents during the night shift may be related to level of illumination. The artificial lighting provided at night can be better for work than the natural lighting conditions during the day.

Researchers found that U.S. workers on night shifts believe that their chances of being hurt in an accident are significantly lower than the chances of day-shift workers, when they perceive that their company supports a climate of high awareness of safety (Huang, Chen, Dearmond, Cigularov, & Chen, 2007). Other researchers found that workers who have been injured on the job face a greater risk of being fired or of being unable to work full time if (once they return to work after the injury) they work the night shift (Dembe, Delbos, Erickson, & Banks, 2007).

Lighting.   Good lighting can lead to a reduction in accidents. The insurance industry estimates that poor lighting is a causal factor in one fourth of all industrial accidents. Accidents are higher in plants that continue production through dusk before the nighttime lighting is turned on. Dusk is also a time of frequent automobile accidents. The relationship between level of illumination and accident rates in industry has been firmly established. An alert management can easily correct the problem of a poorly lit work area.

Temperature.   Studies of factory workers show that accident rates are lowest when the workplace

---

TABLE 11-2

Jobs That Can Kill: Risk Levels for Business and Industry

Industry	Fatal injuries per 100,000 workers
Agriculture	29.6
Mining	27.8
Transportation	16.3
Construction	10.8
Utilities	6.2
Wholesale trade	4.8
Professional and business service	3.1
Manufacturing	2.7
Government	2.3
Finance	1.2

Source: U.S. Bureau of Labor Statistics, 2007. Retrieved from www.stats.bls.gov/IIF/home.htm

temperature is maintained at 68 to 70 degrees F. Accidents increase when the temperature varies significantly, either warmer or cooler. Studies of coal miners show that minor accidents are three times more frequent under high temperatures (approaching 85 degrees F) than under low temperatures (approaching 62 degrees F). Workers seem to become more careless under the discomfort of higher temperatures. Older workers are more affected than younger workers by climatic extremes and are more likely to have accidents at higher temperatures.

Equipment Design. Another physical factor related to accidents is the design of the tools, equipment, and machines used on the job. For example, if an engineer locates a machine's stop button where it is difficult to reach, the consequences can be deadly for the worker who needs to shut down the machine immediately. Poor placement of switches and controls, inadequate warning lights for system malfunctions, and dials that are difficult to read have all been blamed for accidents.

Engineering psychologists strive to match equipment requirements with the capabilities of the human operators (see chapter 13). Their work on safe workplaces and equipment has been highly effective, particularly with regard to cumulative trauma disorders and repetitive motion injuries such as carpal tunnel syndrome. These injuries are caused by continuous and repeated motions of hands and wrists and can affect shoulders and back as well. Repetitive motion injuries are prevalent among office workers who use computer terminals and among certain types of factory workers. Redesigning keyboards, providing chairs and armrests that support good posture, and allowing rest pauses are all effective in reducing repetitive motion injuries.

Cumulative trauma disorders also occur in grocery store checkout clerks who are required to make frequent, repetitive wrist movements using electronic scanners. Every product must be moved over or in front of the scanner so that the price of the item will be registered. The optimum workstation design for checkout clerks is one in which the cashier stands and is able to use both hands interchangeably to distribute the workload between both wrists. This reduces the type of injury likely to occur if only one hand is used. The next time you are in a checkout line, notice whether the cashier uses one hand or two when passing items by the scanner.

Safety Devices. Also important in the design of safe machinery is the development of built-in safety devices and other aids to prevent accidents. Safety devices function to keep a worker's hand away from sharp moving parts or to automatically disconnect the power supply in an emergency, but they must not interfere with the operation of the machine.

Personal protective equipment—such as respirators, safety glasses with shatterproof lenses, steel-tipped shoes, ear protectors, and padded gloves—can be provided to protect workers in dangerous jobs, but too often they are not used. Sometimes the reasons are practical; for example, workers object to using a safety device that interferes with job performance. A respirator can hinder communication among workers. Thick gloves make it hard to press buttons on a control panel.

Another reason safety equipment is often not used is that it can be uncomfortable. Workers who use respirators for jobs performed under high-temperature conditions may find that the device causes skin irritation when clamped to their face. A survey of employees in an automobile glass factory showed that only 30% considered respirators comfortable enough to wear. Comfort obviously influences workers' decisions about whether to use equipment that may protect them from harm but that causes considerable discomfort.

Work Pressure. Accidents can be caused by the pressure to maintain a production schedule or adhere to a timetable. Workers often perceive the threat of disciplinary action or dismissal if they fail to keep to a schedule. Shutting down a production line or power plant because workers think conditions are unsafe costs the company huge sums of money. The employee or manager who assumes the responsibility for such an action may be punished.

Airline pilots who refuse to fly in bad weather or because ice is forming on the aircraft's wings cause passengers to miss connecting flights. Also, they are held responsible for reducing the company's on-time performance record. When pilots see their colleagues reprimanded for similar behavior, they feel considerable pressure to take off on time despite the weather.

Personal Factors

Proper attention to equipment design and to the physical and social conditions of the work environment can

On-the-Job Stress/Off-the-Job Drinking

Everyone knows that driving after having a few drinks is not a smart thing to do, but surely there can be no harm in having a few drinks *after* driving. Right? Wrong! At least it would be wrong if you drive a bus, a semitrailor, or a cable car for the San Francisco, California, Municipal Railway System (Muni).

A 5-year study of 1,836 drivers for the Muni system found that the more drivers drank in their off-the-job hours, the more likely they were to have an accident or serious injury at work. Drivers who reported having more than 10 drinks a week after work were far more likely to file claims against the company for work-related injuries. Also, the amount of drinking after work was directly related to job stress. The more on-the-job stress the workers reported, they more they drank off the job as a way of relieving the stress.

This situation was expensive for Muni. Workers' compensation claims linked to after-hours drinking was costing the company more than $250,000 a year. That's a high price to pay for drinking off the job, and a good reason for companies to identify and monitor employees who show serious job stress. These employees can be offered counseling and shown ways of coping with stress other than drinking.

Source: Drinking after work could affect job (2002, September 22). *St. Petersburg (FL) Times.*

help reduce the frequency and severity of accidents. Overall, however, the human element is the more important cause to consider. Personal factors such as these contribute to accidents: alcohol and drug use, cognitive ability, health, fatigue, work experience, job insecurity, age, and personality characteristics.

Alcohol and Drug Use.   Large numbers of employees use alcohol or illegal drugs on the job. An employee with a drinking or drug problem is much more likely to be involved in an accident than is an employee without such a problem. Even drinking off the job can lead to accidents at work. A study of more than 380,000 general aviation pilots showed that pilots with DWI (driving while intoxicated) convictions were 3.5 times more likely to have alcohol-related problems while flying than those who had no DWI convictions (McFadden, 2002).

Cognitive Ability.   It seems reasonable to assume that workers with a lower measured level of intelligence would have more accidents than workers with a higher measured level of intelligence. However, research does not fully support this idea. Some studies have found that cognitive ability is related to accident-free behavior only in certain jobs, such as those requiring judgment and decision making as opposed to those involving repetitive manual labor.

Health.   I-O psychologists have documented a relationship between health and accidents. Employees who are in poor health or who are frequently ill tend to be highly susceptible to accidents. Workers with physical disabilities—with overall good health and with jobs commensurate with their abilities—do not have a disproportionate share of accidents. Those disabled employees are usually highly motivated to work well and safely. One physical characteristic related to accidents is vision. In general, people who have good eyesight have fewer accidents than do people who have poor eyesight.

Fatigue.   Fatigue causes a decrease in productivity and an increase in accidents. During a typical 8-hour workday, periods of increased productivity are accompanied by decreased accidents. In the 10-hour workday in many heavy industries, a sharp rise in the accident rate has been reported during the last 2 hours of the shift, presumably because of fatigue.

Fatigue is a factor in highway accidents, a subject of study by I-O psychologists because highways are the workplace for bus and truck drivers. Fatigued bus and truck drivers who fall asleep at the wheel are involved in at least 10% of the collisions involving other vehicles. Fatigue contributes to one fourth of all single-car accidents.

Work Experience.   A shorter time on the job tends to mean a higher accident rate. After some months on the job, the accident rate usually drops and continues to decline as work experience increases. This was shown in a 12-year study of 171 firefighters. Firefighters with more experience on the job had fewer less severe injuries from accidents than did those with less experience on the job (Liao, Arvey, Butler, & Nutting, 2001). However, the relationship between accidents and time on the job is not always clear. Although most studies have reported fewer accidents among employees with greater experience, such findings may be biased by self-selection. Workers who have had many job-related accidents are likely to have been fired or transferred or to have quit to look for safer employment. Therefore, we cannot conclude with certainty that longer work experience, by itself, leads to a reduction in the accident rate. In some cases, the decrease in accidents among experienced workers can be explained by the fact that those who had more accidents dropped out.

Job Involvement, Empowerment, and Autonomy.   In a study of 14,466 workers from more than 2,000 companies, researchers found that employees who scored higher in job involvement, which means they had greater autonomy and responsibility for their work, also scored higher in job satisfaction (an issue discussed in chapter 8). These researchers also reported a positive relationship between high job satisfaction and safety awareness. Thus, they concluded that high job involvement leads to a lower accident rate (Barling, Kelloway, & Iverson, 2003).

Research with 531 workers in 24 work groups within a chemical company showed that groups whose workers felt more empowered (who had greater power and authority over their work) had significantly better safety records than groups whose workers did not feel so empowered. The empowered groups performed safety checks and other safety-related behaviors more frequently than did the nonempowered groups (Hechanova-Alampay & Beehr, 2001).

Similarly, a study of 161 factory workers in Australia demonstrated that workers who were high in feelings of job autonomy had significantly higher safety records over an 18-month period than did those who had a low degree of job autonomy (Parker, Axtell, & Turner, 2001).

Job Insecurity.   Research was conducted on 237 food-processing plant employees in an organization that had already laid off some of its workers. The results showed that the workers who reported feeling insecure about their jobs and their future with the company had less motivation to adhere to safe working practices and to comply with safety policies. This lack of diligence, in turn, contributed to an increase in workplace accidents and injuries among these insecure employees (Probst & Brubaker, 2001).

Age.   The link between age and accidents is similar to the relationship between experience and accidents, because there is an obvious relationship between age and length of work experience. Other factors that interact with age are physical health and attitudes toward the job. Overall health, as well as specific abilities such as vision and hearing, deteriorates with age. However, older workers have greater job knowledge and more highly developed skills. Even though reaction time and eye–hand coordination may no longer be as good, older workers usually have a more complete grasp of the job's demands. Their attitudes toward safety tend to be more serious. When older workers do have accidents, however, they are likely to be more costly in terms of physical consequences and time lost from work.

Personality Characteristics.   A popular belief is that people who have a great many accidents have some unique set of personality traits that distinguish them from people who rarely have accidents. Research does not support this contention, although some studies have found that people who have a high number of accidents manifest characteristics such as neuroticism, hostility, anxiety, social maladjustment, and a sense of fatalism. One study of 219 civilian production workers and 263 U.S. Army mechanics found that those who scored low in conscientiousness were more likely to make a cognitively based mistake or error that led to an accident while performing a routine task than were those who scored high in conscientiousness (Wallace & Vodanovich, 2003). A meta-analysis of accident studies showed that people who scored low in agreeableness had more accidents on the job than people who scored high (Clarke & Robertson, 2008). However, any relationship between personality variables and accident frequency is not strong. There is no basis for concluding that people who have frequent accidents have a personality pattern that is clearly different from that of accident-free individuals.

Accident proneness   The idea that some people have personality traits that predispose them to have accidents, and that most accidents are caused by or involve these same few people. This theory is not supported by research.

Temporary emotional states can contribute to accidents. The person who is angry with a spouse or boss or is preoccupied with money problems is likely to be less attentive on the job and hence more susceptible to accidents. This was demonstrated in research involving 127 U. S. Army soldiers who had been involved in automobile accidents during the previous 5 years and 273 other soldiers who had not been involved in accidents. The difference between the two groups was clear. Those who had experienced accidents reported heightened emotions just before the accident. These emotionally stressful states covered a wide range, from divorce and illness to being disturbed by a passenger in the car (Legree, Heffner, Psotka, Medsker, & Martin, 2003).

A study of 243 health care workers showed that those whose family problems and responsibilities caused conflicts with their work roles were far less likely to comply with safety regulations than those who reported little or no conflicts (Cullen & Hammer, 2007).

Accident Proneness

The theory of **accident proneness** holds that certain people are more likely than others to have accidents. In addition, the theory posits that most accidents are caused by or involve the same few people. The theory also assumes that accident-prone persons are likely to have accidents regardless

Newsbreak

It's Only a Game—But You Can Still Get Hurt

Baseball players have accidents all the time. Some are are serious and some are trivial. Some result from doing dumb things. Other "accidents" are deliberate and malicious: Players act to hurt players on the other team so their own team can win, or just because it feels good.

An analysis of 27,667 HPB events in major league games (when batters are hit by pitches) revealed some interesting findings. The number of HBPs has increased over the past 25 years. They occur most often in these situations:

- The batter is a better player than the pitcher.
- The pitcher's team is losing.
- The previous batter had hit a home run.
- The pitcher's teammate had been hit by a pitch in the previous inning.
- The batter is Latino.
- The pitcher is from the South.

Do these so-called on-the-job accidents sound like coincidences to you? Or just plain bad luck or chance events?

But baseball players also do dumb things, just like the rest of us. One player was put on the disabled list because he developed athlete's foot from tying his shoes too tight. Another had to sit out a game because he had rubbed chili sauce in his eyes. One guy stuck his hand inside an air conditioner to see why it wasn't working. It turned out that it was working and he cut his hand badly. Then there was the player who strained his back putting on his socks, another who dislocated a finger when he punched out a watercooler, and the one who burned his chest while ironing the shirt he was wearing!

Well, stuff happens in life, and sometimes people get hurt and there's not always a reason for it. But then again—sometimes there is.

Sources: Timmerman, T. (2007) "It was a tough pitch": Personal, situational, and target influences on hit-by-pitch events across time. *Journal of Applied Psychology, 92,* 876–884; True baseball injuries. Retrieved from www.funny2.com/baseball.htm

of the type of situation. An effective way to test this theory is to compare accident records for the same people for two different periods to determine if the people who had accidents in one period also had accidents in the other. Correlations from studies of this type are low, which indicates that a person's past accident record is not a valid predictor of future accidents.

In a classic study, a psychologist reexamined accident statistics that had originally been interpreted as supporting the accident-proneness theory (DeReamer, 1980). The driving records of 30,000 people showed it was found that fewer than 4% of them accounted for 36% of the accidents over a 6-year period. These data suggested that a small group of drivers were involved in a large number of accidents. If they could be prevented from driving, then the accident rate could be cut by more than one third. The data were reanalyzed by comparing accident records for the first 3 years of the period with accident records for the second 3 years of the period. It was found that the accidents during the two different periods did not involve the same drivers. Those identified as safe drivers during the first period accounted for more than 96% of the accidents in the second period, a finding that is highly damaging to the accident-proneness theory. More recent attempts to measure and validate the concept of accident proneness also have been unsuccessful (see As, 2001; Haight, 2001).

The theory no longer enjoys the credibility it once had, although evidence suggests that some workers may be predisposed to have more accidents in a particular type of work. Accident proneness may be specific to the work situation and not a general tendency over all situations, which limits the theory's predictive value.

Newsbreak

Don't Look Back—The Driver Behind You May Be Asleep

That's a chilling thought to remember the next time you travel on an interstate highway. Take a look at those 40-ton 18-wheelers barreling along all around you and think of this statistic: 78% of all truck drivers have a sleep disorder. It's called obstructive sleep apnea, and it causes a sleeping person to stop breathing momentarily and to awaken briefly. Someone with this disorder can wake up literally hundreds of times each night and not know it. The next day, however, the person will be sleepy.

"If someone wakes up every 2 or 3 minutes throughout the night," said psychologist William Dement, director of the Sleep Research Center at Stanford University, "it's as though they had very little sleep or no sleep at all." And then that person climbs into the cab of a truck and drives at speeds up to 80 miles an hour, trying to keep awake for the duration of a 10- or 12-hour workday. No wonder fatigue is a major factor in truck accidents, when three of four drivers have such disturbed sleep.

Drivers who fall asleep at the wheel of their rig account for up to 1,500 highway deaths a year. This figure means that even though trucks represent only 3% of the traffic on the nation's highways, they are involved in 13% of all fatalities.

In case you're wondering whether you might be suffering from obstructive sleep apnea, don't worry. The disorder is three times higher among truck drivers than in the general population. One cause may be irregular work and sleep patterns. Long-distance drivers may work half the night, sleep for 2 hours, then continue driving. Other factors are lack of regular exercise and a tendency to be overweight.

There are cures for sleep apnea, but first you have to know you have it. Most truckers don't know. They may wonder why they feel so tired during the day, but there is a natural tendency to shrug it off, gulp another cup of coffee, and keep on trucking. That's their job.

Sources: Gavzer, B. (1999, May 16). Is the long haul too long? *Parade Magazine*; Park, A., et al. (2006). Impaired performance in commercial drivers, *American Journal of Respiratory and Critical Care Medicine, 174,* 446–454.

ACCIDENT PREVENTION

An organization can take several steps to safeguard its employees and reduce accidents in the workplace. These include reporting accidents properly, paying attention to workplace design, conducting safety training, ensuring management support, and promoting safety publicity campaigns.

Accident Reports

An accident prevention program is no better than the quality of its accident reports. All accidents, regardless of the consequences, should be investigated and described in detail. A comprehensive accident report should include the following items:

- Precise time and location of the accident
- Type of job and number of employees performing it
- Personal characteristics of the accident victim
- Nature of the accident and known or suspected causes
- Results of the accident—such as personal injuries and damage to plant, equipment, and supplies

Workplace Conditions

Although most accidents are caused by human error, conditions in the physical work environment are potential sources of accidents. Lighting in the workplace must be adequate for the job tasks, and temperature must be maintained at a comfortable level. Work areas should be clean and orderly. Many accidents have been traced to poor housekeeping. Oil or grease spots on the floor, electrical cables underfoot, and equipment stored in hallways or stairwells can cause serious accidents that can easily be prevented. First-aid kits, fire extinguishers, and other safety equipment should be located conveniently throughout a work area and painted in vivid and easily identified colors.

Controls that are hard to reach or that require excessive force to operate, and displays that are excessively complicated and so easily misread, are design mistakes that are ready sources of accidents. Emergency controls must be made accessible and easy to operate.

Engineering psychologists suggest two general principles for the design of safety devices. First, the machine should not function unless the safety device is engaged, for example, a power saw that

---

Newsbreak

Do Teens Have More Accidents at Work? Do Guys?

Do you hold a job while you are attending school? The chances are good that you do, and you probably had an outside job during your high school years too. Some 75% of high school seniors in the United States are employed, and nearly half of them work more than 20 hours a week. Research shows that 16- to 19-year-olds are the group at the highest risk for on-the-job accidents.

Michael Frone, a psychologist at the Research Institute on Addiction, in Buffalo, New York, wanted to know why. What characteristics of the high-school and college-age populations could be related to these accidents and injuries? He started his

research by investigating substance abuse (no surprise, given his place of employment). He surveyed 319 adolescents and found that the use of marijuana and alcoholic beverages on the job showed a positive correlation with accidents and injuries.

But he also found other causes. One was simply being a guy. That's right. Male teenagers had more work-related injuries than female teenagers did. A high accident rate was also associated with heavy workloads, boring jobs, poor physical health, and a negative emotional outlook. It's hard enough being 18 or 19, but it appears to be extra hazardous on the job.

Source: Frone, M. (1998). Predictors of work injuries among employed adolescents. *Journal of Applied Psychology, 83*, 565–576.

will not operate unless the hand guard is in place. Second, the safety device must not interfere with production or cause the employee to work harder to maintain the same output.

A large-scale analysis of accidents in the aircraft and nuclear industries concluded that at least half of all accidents were attributable to poor design of features of the work environment (Kinnersley & Roelen, 2007).

Safety Training

Most organizational training programs devote time to accident prevention. Workplace dangers and hazards are pointed out and information is presented on the causes and results of past accidents. Rules for safe operating procedures are taught, along with the location of emergency and first-aid equipment. Periodic drills may be held to maintain awareness of safe working habits. When a company has an increase in accidents, it may mean that retraining of the workforce is necessary. Experienced workers can become careless and need refresher courses to update their work habits. In general, companies that systematically continue safety training efforts are rewarded with substantial reductions in accidents and in hours lost from work. The money saved easily pays the cost of the training programs.

In a study on the effectiveness of a computer-based safety training program for workers in an electronics manufacturing firm, researchers found that workers under the age of 44 performed better on a test of the safety information than workers over the age of 44. They also found that both age groups performed equally well when the computer-based training included pictures and audio narrations along with the printed texts instead of the printed text material alone. The researchers noted that most safety training programs today are presented online (Wallen & Mulloy, 2006).

For more information on work-related health and safety issues, see the Web sites for the Occupational Safety and Health Administration (www.osha.gov) and the National Institute for Occupational Safety and Health (www.cdc.gov/niosh/).

Management Support

Supervisors play a key role in any successful program for safety training and awareness. Because of their close association with workers, they must be alert to unsafe working conditions and practices. Supervisors are in the best position to remind employees of safe working habits, to arrange proper maintenance of equipment and the work environment, and to foster a climate of safety within the organization. They are also able to recommend when retraining is advisable. If supervisors do not insist on adherence to safe working procedures, then any safety training program will be less than maximally effective. By example as well as instruction, supervisors can maintain employee motivation to work safely and to prevent accidents.

Research involving 703 workers on the offshore oil-drilling platform of a company in Britain illustrated the significant impact supervisors can have on safe job performance. The greater the care and concern supervisors expressed for the safety of their subordinates, the more attention these workers paid to safety-related issues (Mearns & Reader, 2008).

A study of 381 workers and 36 supervisors in a maintenance and repair center in Israel showed that leaders could be trained to improve safety practices on the job. Supervisors were provided with feedback about safety-related episodes over a period of 8 weeks. This training led to a significant increase in the supervisors' safety awareness, which, in turn, led to a significant decrease in the accident rate among their workers. It also led to an increase in the workers' use of safety-related equipment (Zohar, 2002).

Other research confirms the vital role of the supervisor in establishing an appropriate climate for safety on the job. A study of 127 transportation teams in the U.S. Army showed that high quality leader-member exchange relationships (LMXs) led to a positive safety climate characterized by a greater emphasis on safe job behaviors. Low LMXs did not lead to greater safety awareness (Hofmann, Morgeson, & Gerras, 2003).

Studies conducted in Canada on a variety of jobs also demonstrated the importance of a supervisory emphasis on safe practices on the job. The results showed that transformational leadership led to an enhanced safety climate at work and a consequent reduction in injuries on the job (Barling, Loughlin, & Kelloway, 2002; Kelloway, Mullen, & Francis, 2006).

Supervisors cannot be expected to practice safety awareness, however, unless their superiors reinforce that concern. If higher management tolerates sloppy accident reporting or expresses even a neutral attitude toward safety, this does not encourage attention

Safety devices such as face shields should be easy to use and should not interfere with production.

to safe practices. Active high-level management support of safety is a key dimension of an appropriate organizational climate. All levels of supervision must demonstrate to subordinates that safety is everyone's responsibility.

In a study of 1,590 employees in 10 manufacturing and mining companies in Australia, the attitude toward safety promoted by management was shown to be significantly related to safe job performance (Griffin & Neal, 2000). And research on 534 production workers in 53 work groups in Israel found that the group safety climate created by the immediate supervisor significantly affected the rate of on-the-job injuries. The higher the group perceived its safety climate, the lower its accident rate (Zohar, 2002).

A study of 136 production workers showed that a strong company-wide safety climate can significantly reduce the anticipated adverse effects of job insecurity on compliance with safe job practices. The author suggested that organizations that focus on production, perhaps at the expense of safety, send a message to their employees that high productivity is the best way to keep their jobs. On the other hand, organizations that support a safe working environment send a message to their employees that compliance with safety practices is necessary to retain their jobs (Probst, 2004).

Research on more than 10,000 workers in various jobs in Australia and in the United States confirmed the importance of a positive organizational safety climate in increasing safe working practices and reducing accident rates (Huang,

Chen, Dearmond, Cigularov, & Chen, 2007; Neal & Griffin, 2006; Wallace, Popp, & Mondore, 2006).

In a study of 1,127 nurses working in U.S. hospitals, researchers found that a positive safety climate helped reduce errors such as administering an incorrect dose or the wrong medication. This, in turn, reduced the incidence of unintended health consequences for the patients. Good safety practices also reduced the number of back injuries among nurses and led to an increase in job satisfaction (Hofmann & Mark, 2006). A study of workers in Australia whose jobs required considerable driving found that they were more motivated to drive safely when the believed their supervisor placed a high value on safety (Newnam, Griffin, & Mason, 2008).

Thus, pertinent I-O research today demonstrates that all levels of management must establish and reinforce a climate of safety to keep accidents and injuries at a minimum.

Safety Publicity Campaigns and Contests

To motivate employees to follow the safe work habits they have been taught, many organizations conduct publicity and promotional campaigns with posters and booklets, charts showing the number of accident-free days, and contests with appealing prizes.

Posters and Booklets. Posters are a frequently used device, but their effectiveness depends on the kind of message depicted. Negative themes coupled with gruesome pictures of mangled bodies ("Don't do this or this is what will happen!") are particularly ineffective. Fear-oriented appeals create resentment and anger toward the company and the message. The most effective safety posters stress positive themes (for example, "Wear hard hat in this area" or "Hold on to railing").

Warning signs and posters should be as conspicuous as possible, placed where they will be seen by the appropriate employees. For greatest effectiveness, signs should be in large, bold print with the lettering in high contrast against the background. The use of color, prominent borders, easily recognized pictorial symbols, and flashing lights are also desirable. I-O psychologists recommend the following criteria for posters and warning signs:

- *Signal word.* Warnings should have signal or key words that are appropriate to the level of danger, for example, DANGER, WARNING, or CAUTION.

```
WARNING                          (Signal word)
UNDERGROUND GAS LINE             (Hazard statement)
EXPLOSION AND FIRE POSSIBLE      (Consequences)
NO DIGGING                       (Instructions)
```

FIGURE 11-1   Effective warning poster.

- *Hazard statement.* Warnings should tell clearly what the dangers are.
- *Consequences.* Warnings should tell clearly the results of failing to comply.
- *Instructions.* Warnings should tell workers what to do or what not to do to avoid the danger.

The example in Figure 11-1 meets these criteria.

Booklets of safety instructions and rules are relatively ineffective in encouraging safe working practices, no matter how widely they are distributed. It is easy to ensure that all workers receive a booklet, but it is far more difficult to make them read it.

Safety Contests.   Safety contests can be effective in maintaining interest in accident prevention. Some contests reward workers on an individual basis for accident-free work over a given period. Other contests operate on a group basis, rewarding a work crew or department. In a competitive contest, one work unit can be pitted against another to see which has fewer accidents. Such contests may make workers more conscious of safe operating procedures and thus reduce accident rates, but the effects may not last much longer than the life of the contest. One solution is to hold continuous contests, changing the awards frequently enough to maintain employee interest. An obvious disadvantage of safety contests is that they encourage workers, supervisors, and managers to suppress the accurate reporting of accidents.

Safety in Home Offices.   With an increasing number of employees now telecommuting, the problem of safety in home offices has become a national concern. Home-based workers report computer-related discomfort and injury to necks, backs, shoulders, and arms from poorly designed chairs and awkwardly positioned keyboards and monitors. Other dangers include overloaded power outlets, poor lighting, and hazards from children's toys underfoot or outstretched power cords.

Safety experts suggest that many accidents in these offices go unreported because employees do not want to risk losing the opportunity to work at home. OSHA has raised the issue of safety for home work environments. Should employers be held liable when employees are injured while working at home, or is safety at a home office the responsibility of the employee who chooses to work at home?

THE SCOPE OF WORKPLACE VIOLENCE

Murder is the second leading cause of death on the job and the primary cause of death for women in the workplace. In addition, every year more than 2 million employees are physically assaulted at work or threatened with assault. The office, shop, and factory have become dangerous places. This phenomenon is occurring worldwide, from peaceful Finland to war-torn Iraq. For example, in a study of 116 nurses in Iraq, researchers found that 49 of them (more than 40%) had been physically attacked in the hospitals in which they worked (Abuairub, Khalifa, & Habbib, 2007). Research conducted in Finland showed that workplace violence had increased significantly over the past decade, whereas rates of violence in other areas of daily life had remained unchanged. Most of the acts of violence against women on the job are committed by male co-workers (Heiskanen, 2007).

You are no doubt aware of the stories of disgruntled ex-employees who have been fired but return to the office or store or factory with guns and kill or wound former co-workers and the supervisor who fired them. Because of the publicity given such incidents that have occurred in post offices, the phrase "going postal" has become a generic, shorthand description of the phenomenon. In fact, postal workers are less likely to be harmed on the job than many other types of workers.

It is important to put such events in perspective. You need not fear that the person at the next desk is looking at you suspiciously. Although disturbed workers have, indeed, gone on murderous rampages, three fourths of workplace fatalities involve deliberate robberies rather than random, vengeful acts. Victims of violence are typically taxicab drivers, convenience store clerks, pizza delivery drivers, and owners of small inner-city grocery and liquor stores. Ex-employees or co-workers commit approximately one third of workplace homicides. Women are especially vulnerable to workplace violence. Many are murdered by boyfriends or husbands who choose the women's workplaces as the sites of their actions.

Some companies provide security for female employees who are being stalked by abusive partners. For a detailed examination of the risk factors and prevention strategies associated with workplace violence see www.osha.gov/SLTC/workplaceviolence/

Levels of Workplace Violence.   I-O psychologists have described different levels of violence in the workplace. They begin with incivility, which involves the display of disrespect and condescension toward, or the degradation of, one person or group by another person or group. Incivility does not involve physical violence but it can make the workplace an unpleasant and stressful environment. In a study involving nearly 2,000 public sector workers, researchers found that 71% of them reported at least one instance of incivility over a 5-year period. As many as one third of these acts were instigated by people in positions of power within the organization. Women were more often the targets of incivility than were men, but the effects for all employees were lower job satisfaction, greater psychological distress, and psychological withdrawal from the job (Cortina, Magley, Williams, & Langhout, 2001; Lim, Cortina, & Magley, 2008).

Another level of violence in the workplace is unruliness, which includes the following aggressive and violent behaviors:

- Threatening or bullying other employees
- Punching, kicking, throwing, or damaging something in anger
- Using profanity in a loud and harsh manner
- Exhibiting emotional and irrational behavior when thwarted
- Defacing or destroying company property

None of these behaviors involves homicide or physical assault, yet the tendency toward unruliness may contribute to an atmosphere of violence and in some instances may become a significant precursor to violence.

Bullying in the workplace has been documented in many nations and cultures, and it can have unpleasant consequences for its victims. In a survey of more than 7,000 male and female workers in France, investigators reported that being the victim of bullying at work, or simply seeing others being bullied, was related to symptoms of depression (Niedhammer, David, & Degioanni, 2006). A study of 877 white-collar employees in Turkey demonstrated that more than half (55%) had been victims of bullying episodes at work; some 47% reported witnessing acts of bullying. In most instances, the perpetrator was the victim's superior. The majority of those who reported bullying and tried to take action to stop it were dissatisfied by the lack of organizational support they received. This, in turn, led to feelings of anxiety, depression, and stress (Bilgel, Aytac, & Bayram, 2006).

Research conducted in Norway on workplace bullying showed that victims were more likely to score high on measures of emotional instability than were those who had not been bullied (Giaso, Matthiesen, Nielsen, & Einarsen, 2007). This finding leads to an interesting question: Were the victims bullied because they were less emotionally stable than other workers, or did the emotional problems arise later, as a result of being bullied?

Research on Workplace Violence.   Some research on workplace violence attempts to define the characteristics of people believed most likely to commit destructive acts; these are shown in Table 11-3. A

TABLE 11-3
Characteristics of Violent Employees
• Male between the ages of 30 and 50 • Alcohol or drug abuser • Past history of violent behavior, serious psychiatric disorder, and impulsive behavior • History of trauma, abuse, and neglect • A loner with few social outlets • Identifies strongly with the job • Expresses feelings of shame or humiliation

telephone survey of 300 employed adults found that alcohol abuse correlated positively with committing acts of violence. Heavy drinking also correlated positively with becoming a victim of violence (McFarlin, Fals-Stewart, Major, & Justice, 2000).

Other factors have been related to violence at work, including the location of the workplace. A survey of 250 plants in a variety of locations found that the highest level of aggressive behavior occurred in plants located in communities with high crime rates. The lower was the community's crime rate, the lower the level of aggression within the workplace located in that community (Dietz, Robinson, Folger, Baron, & Schulz, 2003). It has also been shown that the incidence of workplace violence is greater in highly stressful working environments (Bowling & Beehr, 2006).

Another factor involves imitation. In a study of 149 employees of group health care facilities, researchers found that those who saw co-workers engage in aggressive behavior, or who themselves were targets of aggressive behavior, were more likely to engage in aggressive behavior on the job (Glomb & Liao, 2003).

Research on 489 men in their 30s who worked for a variety of organizations revealed that employees who perceived themselves as victims were highly likely to demonstrate aggression on the job. This effect of perceived victimization was stronger among whose who had a history of alcohol abuse or antisocial behavior in other settings (Jockin, Arvey, & McGue, 2001). In a related study involving 141 government employees, those who felt victimized were less likely to seek revenge if the offender held a higher status position within the organization. Those who felt victimized by people in lower status positions were more likely to seek revenge against the perpetrator of the aggressive act (Aquino, Tripp, & Bies, 2001).

Other research on predictors of workplace aggression has explored the impact of individual differences. One study of 115 workers in two companies found that the measured trait of anger, defined as a stable personality trait that predisposes a person to experience anger in almost any situation, was directly linked to aggression on the job. The higher the level of the trait of anger, the higher the incidence of workplace aggression (Douglas & Martinko, 2001). A meta-analysis of 57 studies confirmed the importance of anger as a predisposition to instigating acts of workplace violence (Hershcovis, et al., 2007).

Researchers have identified other factors related to initiating workplace violence: low scores on tests of cognitive ability, agreeableness, and the need for achievement, as well as higher scores on self-report measures of job dissatisfaction and negative emotions (Diefendorff & Mehta, 2007; Dilchert, Ones, Davis, & Rostow, 2007; Mount, Ilies, & Johnson, 2006). A 23-year research program involved 930 employed adults in New Zealand. Those who had shown behavioral problems in childhood and adolescence were far more likely to commit violent acts on the job as adults than were those who had not exhibited behavior problems as children. In addition, subjects who had scored low on agreeableness and conscientiousness at age 18 were more likely to commit workplace violence than those who scored high on these factors (Roberts, Harms, Caspi, & Moffitt, 2007).

Ways to Deal with Workplace Violence.   Ideally, companies would not hire anyone who is prone to violence, but employee selection techniques are not yet sufficiently accurate to accomplish that goal. Even if human resources directors or personnel managers had the selection techniques to identify applicants with violence-prone personality profiles, not all such people would commit acts of violence on the job. Indeed, unless they were faced with sudden adverse situations (for example, receiving a poor performance evaluation or a harsh reprimand or being fired), they might never exhibit even minor unpleasant behaviors.

I-O psychologists recommend several positive steps to deal with workplace violence: Managers can be trained to recognize potentially violent workers. Difficult employees can be offered counseling. Supervisors can be taught tactful ways of communicating bad news such as disciplinary actions or terminations. OSHA has developed more tangible suggestions for reducing workplace violence, including installing metal detectors, alarm systems, extra lighting, video surveillance cameras, and bulletproof barriers. The agency also recommends hiring more security guards.

As usual, support from the organization is beneficial. In a study of 225 health care workers in Canada, researchers investigated two types of organizational support: *instrumental support*, which involved directly helping employees in need, and *informational support*, which involved providing employees with information they could use to help themselves deal with problems of aggression. The results showed that both types of organizational support led to a reduction in negative psychological health consequences of experiencing aggression in the workplace. Instrumental support was found to be more powerful than informational support because it also led to a reduction in physical health problems and negative affect that resulted from aggression on the job (Schat & Kelloway, 2003).

ALCOHOLISM IN THE WORKPLACE

More than 14 million people in the United States are known to be afflicted with alcoholism, although the actual figure may be higher. The U.S. Public Health Service considers alcoholism to be a major health threat, along with heart disease and cancer. Alcoholism is defined as an illness characterized by an inability to control the consumption of alcohol to the extent that intoxication is inevitable once drinking has begun. Medically, alcoholism is an addiction, that is, a pathological drug dependence that is harmful to health and that interferes with normal functioning.

Up to 10% of the U.S. workforce is estimated to be alcoholic at a cost to employers in excess of $100 billion a year. This cost is attributable to absenteeism, tardiness, errors and accidents, low productivity, inefficiency, and, often, the dismissal of valuable employees in whom money and training time was invested. Although there is no dispute that alcoholism is a serious problem for American business, not everyone agrees on the extent of alcoholism in the workforce. It is possible that the problem is overstated by therapists, consultants, and directors of rehabilitation programs, the people whose livelihood depends on the idea that alcoholism is rampant and that their programs can cure it.

Alcoholic employees work at all levels of organizational life. According to the National Institute on Alcohol Abuse and Alcoholism (NIAAA), more than 70% of known alcoholics are professional, semiprofessional, or managerial employees. More than half of all alcoholics have attended college. The greatest incidence of alcoholism is in the age group of 35 to 55 years.

Researchers in England studied 422 workers from a variety of occupations and found that negative affect was positively related to alcohol consumption. The higher the negative emotions, the greater the amount of alcohol consumed (Jones, O'Connor,

Connor, McMillan, & Ferguson, 2007). Research involving 1,481 New York City firefighters found that the higher their level of stress, as related to critical incidents on the job, the greater the level of drinking (Bacharach, Bamberger, & Doveh, 2008).

The Drug Free Workplace Act of 1988 makes employers who hold $25,000 or more in federal government contracts responsible for the prevention of substance abuse on the job. The law requires these employers to notify employees that the possession, sale, or use of alcohol or illegal drugs on the job is prohibited. If employees are convicted of alcohol or drug offenses, employers are required to impose disciplinary action such as mandatory treatment programs, suspension without pay, or discharge.

Effects on Job Performance

Alcoholics tend to believe that drinking will not affect their behavior at work and that no one will detect a difference in the way they perform their jobs. This is not true. The debilitating effects of excessive drinking are evident almost immediately. In the beginning stages, however, only a trained observer will notice them.

Although behavioral changes occur gradually, after a few years of steady drinking an employee's job performance and efficiency will have deteriorated so greatly that the changes will be obvious to supervisors and co-workers. The downward path of an alcoholic's behavior is depicted in Figure 11-2. The signs of altered job performance include excessive absenteeism, long lunch breaks, lies, errors, and low productivity. In the middle phase, gross changes occur that can no longer be overlooked. By this time, the alcoholic has usually received a warning from supervisors and is no longer being considered for promotion.

As the performance curve shows, everything goes downhill—career, family life, reputation, and financial stability. Ironically, each crisis precipitated by excessive drinking provides yet another reason to continue drinking. Unless the person recognizes the problem and accepts help, this cycle can lead to career failure, imprisonment, hospitalization, or an early death. When a worker's superiors continue to ignore excessive drinking, mistakenly believing that they are being kind or helpful, they are only prolonging the problem. Intervention at an early stage is vital to an alcoholic's recovery.

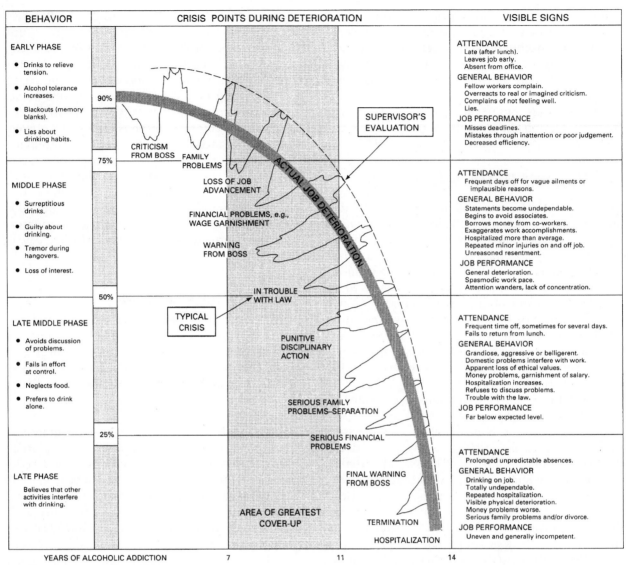

FIGURE 11-2 Deterioration in behavior and job performance of an alcoholic as a function of time. (From A. Carding, "Booze and business," *Administrative Management*, 1967, *30*, 21. Copyright Doyle Lindley, Bechtel Corporation. Reproduced by permission.)

The Alcoholic Executive

The plight of any employee with a drinking problem is tragic, but when the alcoholic is an executive, the cost to the company is greater. When an organization loses an executive because of a drinking problem, it is deprived of someone in whom it has invested considerable training, a high salary and fringe benefits, and significant responsibilities, a person whose judgment and decision-making abilities have been considered important to the organization's success.

Alcoholic executives, more than lower level employees, are adept at concealing their problem for a longer period. They may be aided by their subordinates, who are often willing to cover up for their bosses' indispositions. Thus, alcoholic executives can escape detection longer than people in the accounting office, the warehouse, or on the assembly line. There is another comfort for alcoholic executives: They are not as apt to be fired as are lower level employees. Although management recognizes the problem of alcoholism on the factory

Employee assistance programs (EAPs) Counseling and rehabilitative services for various employee problems, notably alcohol and drug abuse.

Newsbreak

Is Your Manager an Alcoholic in Denial?

Brian's a hard charger. That's what Brian Early's friends and colleagues used to say about the mid-twenties accounts manager. They also used to say that sometimes he drank more than he could handle. They didn't realize that Brian was drinking most of the time. "I was getting up the next morning and smoking dope just to get rid of the headache" from a hangover, he admitted.

But Brian was able to hide his problem from his co-workers and bosses because he had layers of protection, like most managers. He arranged his own workday and travel schedule, was often out of the office on legitimate business—where he could drink without been seen by colleagues—and he had a support staff who did much of the work that he was supposed to be doing. Also, even if his subordinates suspected that he was drinking heavily, they feared retaliation if they went over his head to complain about his behavior.

Like many alcoholics, Brian denied he had a problem. A psychologist who counsels alcoholic executives wrote, "Their work becomes the foundation of their denial." The person says, in effect, "I can't be an alcoholic because I'm handling all these things at work." In the end, it was not Brian's boss who told him he had to get help. It was his wife, before she left him. That got his attention. He checked into a treatment center, endured the symptoms of withdrawal, and has not had a drink for 22 years. He carved out a successful new career, and, yes, his wife returned to him. But Brian never forgot the way he had once behaved. He regularly attends support group meetings and is always on guard against the kinds of stresses that led him so easily to drink. And he likes to say he holds one comforting thought: "My worst day today is still better than my last day drunk."

Source: Olsen, P. (2003, May 25). Detoured but not stopped by alcohol. *New York Times.*

floor, it is more reluctant to admit that it exists in the office next door.

Laboratory studies of the process of negotiation, a skill widely practiced by high-level managers and executives, showed that people who negotiate deals while under the influence of alcohol make costly mistakes for their organization. Subjects who conducted negotiations while intoxicated (having a blood alcohol level of 0.05) were significantly more aggressive in their dealings with others than were negotiators who were sober. Those who had been drinking were far more likely to insult, mislead, and threaten the people with whom they were bargaining. In addition, they were found to be cognitively impaired, which led them to make errors of judgment, focus on irrelevant

information, and misinterpret or ignore key points of the problem under consideration (Schweitzer & Kerr, 2000).

Rehabilitation Programs

Many federal government agencies and more than half of the largest U.S. corporations sponsor formal alcoholic rehabilitation programs. These efforts, called **employee assistance programs (EAPs)**, return as much as 20 dollars for every dollar invested in them in terms of reduced absenteeism, reduced health care costs, and higher productivity. Most EAPs offer counseling services for various employee problems, but their major concerns are alcohol and drug abuse.

Employers can offer a strong motivation for alcoholic employees to seek treatment because they hold out the hope of retaining a job. Psychologists and physicians who work with alcoholics agree that fear of losing one's job can carry more weight than threats from spouses or the possibility of an early death. To alcoholics, keeping their jobs may be their last defense against admitting that they have a drinking problem. When that defense is jeopardized, the desire to seek and accept help is usually great.

Most programs to combat alcohol abuse follow a three-step process suggested by the National Council on Alcoholism:

1. *Education of managers and supervisors.* Management learns that alcoholism is not a moral or ethical issue but a medical problem, a treatable illness.

2. *Early detection of alcoholic employees.* Managers are trained to detect the symptoms of alcoholism and the resulting behavioral and performance changes. Early detection improves the alcoholic worker's chances for recovery.

3. *Referral of alcoholic employees for help.* Some companies rely on in-house physicians and psychologists to supervise rehabilitation programs for alcoholic employees. Other companies refer employees to outside clinics. Most organizations provide for treatment on company time and continue the workers' salaries while they are in treatment programs.

An especially effective treatment approach involves co-workers who are members of Alcoholics Anonymous. That organization has a high success rate in dealing with alcoholism because its members know the effects firsthand. There is some evidence, albeit weak, to suggest that recovering alcoholics become better workers. Their performance no longer suffers from their drinking, and they may expend extra effort, realizing that this is their last chance. However, even if the job performance of recovering alcoholics does not improve, at least the company has reclaimed experienced workers who would otherwise have been lost.

Information on databases, research programs, and other resources is available from the National Institute on Alcohol Abuse and Alcoholism of the National Institutes of Health at www.niaaa.nih.gov

DRUG ABUSE

The use of illegal drugs on the job is a serious problem. Marijuana is the principal substance used, but the use of amphetamines, opiates, cocaine, PCP, and Ecstasy has also been reported in the workplace. In addition, prescription drugs such as tranquilizers, painkillers, and stimulants are sometimes overused. Data show that 1 of every 10 current and prospective employees has used or will use drugs. The National Institute of Drug Abuse reports that the use of illegal drugs is more widespread among younger employees, ages 18 to 25. Research shows that more than 14% of all employees use illicit drugs on the job. Drug use is higher among men than women, and the highest rates of drug use on the job are among restaurant workers (17.4%) and construction workers (15.1%).

Consider some recent findings on the extent of drug use by workers (Frone, 2006; Office of Applied Studies, Substance Abuse and Mental Health Services Administration, U.S. Department of Health and Human Services, 2007).

- 11.3% use marijuana
- 4.9% use psychotherapeutic drugs
- 1.0% use cocaine
- 0.7% use methamphetamines
- 0.3% use heroin
- 0.3% use OxyContin

Although drug abuse has been detected at all corporate levels, it is highest among skilled and semi-skilled workers and lowest among managerial and professional personnel. The overuse of prescription drugs is highest among middle-age and older workers. Drug users are found in all types of jobs. One nuclear power plant caught security guards using drugs. The U.S. Navy discovered that the majority of one aircraft carrier's crew regularly smoked marijuana. And an oil company learned that crews of its offshore drilling rigs in the Gulf of Mexico were often under the influence of illegal drugs.

A survey of 2,790 U.S. workers showed a relationship between work overload and substance abuse in the workplace. Drugs, rather than alcohol, were more likely to be used in response to job stress. One reason suggested reason for this finding is that drugs are more difficult to detect, being less obvious than the smell of alcohol on an employee's breath (Frone, 2008).

The drug-dependent worker may present a more serious problem than the alcoholic worker in terms of the disruptive effects on production and efficiency. Drug users are potentially more dangerous because they may attempt to sell drugs to other workers to finance their own habit.

Effects on Job Performance

Behavioral effects of drug use on the job vary with the type of drug taken. In general, however, the new user shows marked changes in behavior. Negligence develops about appearance, personal hygiene, and dress. Some users take to wearing dark glasses. Emotional outbursts are common, along with a tendency to borrow money. Users are also likely to show impairment in judgment and of reflexes, sluggishness of movement, dilation or contraction of the pupils of the eyes, bloodshot eyes, and, in extreme cases, needle marks on the arms or elsewhere on the body. These behavioral changes affect job performance.

In addition, drug abusers have been found to have up to four times the number of accidents, three times the number of absences, three times the number of health benefit claims, and five times the number of workers' compensation claims. They are far more likely to be late for work and they rate low in job satisfaction.

Researchers administered questionnaire surveys to 470 adults when they were in their mid-twenties and again when they were in their early thirties. The researchers found that early use of drugs was highly predictive of later drug abuse. In other words, the adults who reported drug problems in their twenties continued to abuse drugs into their early thirties. Their continuing drug abuse led to job instability, lowered job satisfaction, and a reduced tendency to conform to generally accepted societal norms. However, those who received early social support for confronting their drug problem were less likely to be using drugs by the time of the second survey. Also, they were more likely to rate themselves higher in job satisfaction than were those who did not receive early social support (Galaif, Newcomb, & Carmona, 2001).

Depending on what there is to steal from an organization, drug use can lead to an increase in employee theft. Thus, drug users are likely to become marginal employees who are a burden to management and a threat to the morale and safety of co-workers. In hazardous occupations, such as construction and transportation, drug users, like alcoholics, can be a menace to the public. Proponents of on-the-job drug screening argue that public safety is the best reason for mandatory drug testing. The public has a right to expect that operators of buses, trains, and airplanes will not have their judgment or reaction time impaired by drugs.

The U. S. Department of Labor reports that small businesses (with 24 or fewer workers) are more strongly affected by employee drug abuse than are large companies (500 or more workers). Only 13% of known drug users work for large organizations; 44% work for smaller companies. The practical explanation for this finding is that smaller companies are less likely to have programs designed to detect or combat drug use on the job. Therefore, drug users at a smaller company are less likely to get caught. In addition, a mistake made by a drug-impaired employee at a small company (say, 1 worker out of 25) can be more economically devastating and potentially dangerous than an error made by one employee out of 1,000.

Drug Screening Programs and Policies

The chances are high that you will be tested for drug use when you next apply for a job. Most companies that test for drug use refuse to hire applicants who test positive. Drug testing is a standard part of the employee selection process, and the results of a drug test can override your performance on all other selection measures.

Testing for Drug Use. Psychologists have suggested the following guidelines to make drug testing programs as equitable as possible:

1. The organization should issue a statement to employees describing its policy on drug abuse and testing.

2. If employees belong to a union, the company's drug policies and testing procedures should be submitted to collective bargaining before being put into effect. Employers who refuse to bargain with the union are subject to charges of unfair labor practices.

3. Drug testing procedures should apply to all employees. No specific group should be singled out for testing.

4. Current employees should be tested only in documented cases of job impairment or because of other valid indications of probable cause.

5. Employees should be informed in advance of drug testing procedures, including the drugs being screened for, the types of tests, and the consequences of refusing to be tested.

6. Positive test results should be confirmed by a second test.

7. Results of drug tests should be kept confidential.

In a telephone survey of 1,484 people employed full-time or part-time, researchers found that those who had used marijuana during the previous month were significantly more likely to believe that employer drug testing was unfair than were workers who had not used marijuana during the previous month. These researchers also reported that workers who held safety-sensitive jobs—where impaired performance could cause injury to the public, to co-workers, or to the employee—were significantly more likely to believe that drug testing by their company was fair, as compared to those who did not have safety-sensitive jobs (Paronto, Truxillo, Bauer, & Leo, 2002).

Drug testing is controversial. Some people argue that testing infringes on employees' rights to privacy, confidentiality, and security from unreasonable search and seizure. Primarily for these reasons, some organizations have been reluctant to institute widespread drug testing programs and instead prefer to reassign workers in dangerous jobs to alternative tasks if they are known to be drug users.

The validity of drug testing is also an issue. The Centers for Disease Control & Prevention (CDC) report that mass drug screening, particularly with inexpensive and unsophisticated tests, can incorrectly indicate the presence of drugs in up to two thirds of the cases. This high rate of false positives means that a disturbingly large number of job applicants and employees are mistakenly labeled as drug users. Lack of accuracy of the tests can be attributed to false readings, laboratory errors, and cheating by employees. Other substances in urine or blood samples can mimic the presence of drugs. Poppy seeds can falsely indicate the use of opiates. Marijuana can be inaccurately indicated by over-the-counter cough and cold products such as Contac or by painkillers such as Advil and Nuprin.

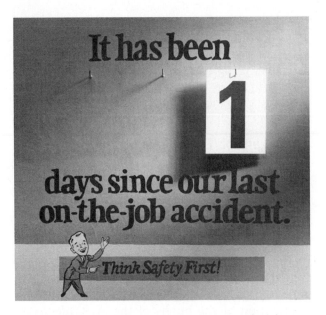

Drug users are highly likely to have accidents on the job. (Reproduced by permission of Partnership for a Drug-Free America.)

An herbal tea that is a normal part of the diet in certain South American countries can lead to a positive test for cocaine. Laboratory technicians can inadvertently mix up samples; the U.S. Army once found that half the urine samples of a group of 60,000 soldiers had been so carelessly handled by the lab that none of the test results could be considered reliable.

People being tested for drug use may try to cheat the system by substituting someone else's drug-free urine or by adding an adulterant such as laundry bleach to mask traces of drugs. For this reason, most employers insist that employees urinate in the presence of an observer, a practice most people find offensive.

Dealing with Drug Use. The first step taken by many organizations to deal with drug use on the job is a clear and direct statement to employees and job applicants about the policy concerning drug use and drug testing and the consequences of violating that policy. The second step is to screen all applicants, not only with drug testing but also by paying attention to gaps in employment history, criminal conviction records, dishonorable military discharges, and physical signs of addiction.

The third and most difficult step is to detect employees using or selling drugs on the job. One

Carpal tunnel syndrome A repetitive motion disorder that may involve numbness, tingling, or pain in fingers, hands, and forearms.

company hired an ex-addict to work at various jobs throughout the organization and identify drug users. Another hired private detectives to pose as employees. Some employers have used drug-sniffing dogs to detect the presence of drugs in the workplace and in employees' cars in the company parking lot.

Most organizations differentiate between occasional users of soft drugs and addicts or pushers of hard drugs. If occasional users have a good performance record and agree to accept help, companies usually arrange for a treatment program. If users refuse help, they will likely be fired. Drug pushers are typically subject to arrest.

Workers who are treated successfully for drug problems and return to their jobs show reduced absenteeism, accidents, sick leave, and claims for health benefits. In general, EAPs report success rates of up to 80%, with success defined as remaining drug-free and maintaining satisfactory job performance for 1 year after treatment. Once drug users have lost their jobs, the recovery rate drops to about 5%, a clear indication of the importance of detecting and treating a worker's substance abuse problem while he or she is still employed.

Research involving 260 city government employees showed the usefulness of group training for building acceptance of and trust in EAPs. Group training specifically oriented toward drug abuse problems significantly increased the tendency for employees to seek help for up to 6 months after the end of the training program (Bennett & Lehman, 2001). For more information about drug abuse issues in the workplace see the Web site of the National Institute on Drug Abuse at www.nida.nih.gov

COMPUTER USE AND PHYSICAL HEALTH ISSUES

Some employees who work with computers report a high incidence of back pain, physical fatigue, and visual disturbances. These problems can often be eased by altering the design of the work area and correcting poor lighting conditions. The city government of San Francisco, California, passed legislation to regulate the use of video display terminals in the workplace in order to reduce eyestrain, muscle fatigue, and repetitive motion injuries. The law follows guidelines recommended by engineering psychologists and requires that (1) workers be provided with adjustable chairs and adequate lighting and (2) computer terminals be equipped with detachable keyboards and adjustable screens. In addition, employees whose jobs do not include regular rest breaks must be given 15 minutes of alternative work every 2 hours.

Carpal tunnel syndrome, a repetitive motion disorder of the wrist, has plagued workers in many occupations for decades. Any job that requires repeated identical or similar motions can lead to this painful, crippling nerve injury. Once reported mainly by blue-collar workers such as meat cutters, carpenters, jackhammer operators, and assembly-line workers, it received little recognition or publicity. With the advent of computers, white-collar workers, such as newspaper reporters and editors, started feeling those characteristic shooting pains in hands and forearms accompanied by tingling and numbness in the fingers. That was when carpal tunnel syndrome became famous. And when media people started hurting, they wrote articles about this newfound condition. Psychologists and medical researchers began to study it, and OSHA became alarmed. For more information about carpal tunnel syndrome see the Web site for the National Institute of Neurological Disorders and Strokes at www.ninds.nih.gov/disorders/carpal_tunnel/carpal_tunnel.htm

Repetitive strain injuries affect millions of people throughout the world who work at a variety of jobs. In a study of 936 employees at call centers throughout England, researchers found that employees who reported a heavier workload involving more frequent repetitions of hand and arm movements experienced more pain in the upper body, lower back, and arms than did those with less physically strenuous jobs. The researchers also showed that a 10-minute rest break every hour could significantly reduce these symptoms (Sprigg, Stride, Wall, Holman, & Smith, 2007).

Of 8,594 workers in Norway who participated in a survey, up to 60% reported health problems

Protective exclusion The practice of barring certain groups of employees, such as women of childbearing age, from potentially hazardous jobs because of fear of lawsuits.

including pains in neck, shoulders, lower back, and arms as well as general fatigue. All of those polled attributed their discomfort to various aspects of the physical demands of their jobs (Mehlum, Kjuus, Veiersted, & Wergeland, 2006).

People who manufacture computer chips face other health concerns. Their work is potentially dangerous because it exposes them to arsenic, cyanide, acids, and noxious solvents. Some workers claim that the job causes headaches and loss of concentration, and they are concerned about long-term health effects. Research to date neither confirms nor refutes these charges. Nevertheless, companies such as AT&T have taken the precaution of transferring pregnant women from areas that manufacture computer chips to other workstations. Other companies inform employees of the hazards and offer the opportunity for a transfer.

Some studies have shown a higher rate of miscarriages among pregnant women who work with computers more than 20 hours a week, compared to pregnant women who do other kinds of office work. Research on animals has related the low-frequency, pulsed, electromagnetic radiation emitted by video display terminals to miscarriages and birth defects. However, the evidence with human subjects is less certain.

Psychologists suggest that a source of the problem may be the stressful assembly-line atmosphere in which many computer operators function rather than the radiation emitted by the display screens. In research conducted with pregnant women in several occupations, clerical employees had a higher miscarriage rate than did managerial and professional employees who spent a comparable amount of time at a computer terminal. The jobs of the managerial and professional women may have

been less stressful and more satisfying. Research on pregnant workers in several countries found no significant evidence linking increased risk of miscarriages or birth defects to working with computers.

This health concern raises a problem of discrimination. Some companies practice what is called **protective exclusion**, barring women of childbearing age from certain jobs (such as computer chip production) because they fear eventual lawsuits should it be shown that computer work is related to miscarriages, birth defects, or other health problems. In some companies, female job applicants have been asked to supply urine samples that were tested, without the applicants' knowledge or consent, for evidence of pregnancy. In instances where women were not hired because of such a policy they can claim sex discrimination.

In 1991, the U.S. Supreme Court struck down the practice of protective exclusion as a form of sex discrimination and ruled that employers could not exclude women from jobs in which exposure to toxic substances might harm a developing fetus. The case before the court involved the Johnson Controls battery plant, which had excluded women of childbearing age (except those who could prove they were sterile) from high-paying assembly-line jobs that exposed them to potentially harmful lead fumes. Some women had undergone surgery to be rendered sterile rather than transfer to lower paying jobs. It is interesting that the company's fetal-protection policy had never been applied to men, even though the men's sperm was at risk of becoming malformed, a condition that could lead to birth defects.

Computers emit other forms of radiation, including X-rays and infrared, magnetic, and electrostatic fields. The long-term effects of these emissions have not been determined.

Summary

Many workplaces can be hazardous to physical health. Toxic chemicals in factories, mines, refineries, plants, and modern office buildings can cause debilitating health problems, even death, for thousands of workers. The goal of the Occupational Safety and Health Administration is to enforce federal industrial safety standards to protect workers from accidents and health problems on the job. One problem with research on accidents is that organizations distort accident data through incomplete reporting in an effort to maintain good safety records.

Workplace factors that can affect employee safety include type of industry, work schedules, lighting, temperature, and equipment design. Personal factors such as these also contribute to accidents: alcohol and drug use, health, fatigue, work experience, job insecurity, age, job involvement, and personality variables such as conscientiousness. The theory of **accident proneness** has little research support.

To prevent accidents, organizations should practice complete reporting and analysis of accidents, consider the design of the job and work environments, provide managerial support for safe work practices, provide safety training and a strong safety climate, and sponsor safety publicity campaigns.

Workplace violence is increasing. Behaviors expressing incivility, anger, bullying, and hostility threaten workers at all levels. Factors related to workplace violence include the level of violence in the community, being a target or victim of workplace aggression, and the psychological trait of anger. Those most likely to commit acts of violence are men between the ages of 30 and 50 with a history of substance abuse, psychiatric disorders, or behavioral problems in childhood and adolescence.

Alcoholism on the job has been linked to tardiness, absenteeism, low productivity, and emotional problems. Organizations try to assist alcoholic employees through **employee assistance programs (EAPs)** and by training managers to detect signs of alcoholism in their workers. Drug use on the job has been found at all occupational levels. In general, organizations treat employees who use drugs more severely than they do alcoholic employees. The use of drug testing in employee selection is widespread, although the tests may not be accurate and may violate privacy rights. Effects of prolonged computer use, such as **carpal tunnel syndrome** and other repetitive strain injuries, can be reduced by scheduling rest breaks.

Key Terms

accident proneness
carpal tunnel syndrome

employee assistance programs
  (EAPs)

protective exclusion

Review Questions

1. In what ways can your workplace affect your health? Give specific examples.
2. Describe some of the symptoms and causes of sick building syndrome.
3. Why is it difficult to define an on-the-job accident as an *accident*?
4. What physical conditions of the workplace can contribute to accidents?
5. In what ways can the design of equipment and safety devices reduce workplace accidents?
6. Explain how each of the following contributes to accidents in the workplace: alcohol and drug use; health; age and work experience; organizational safety climate; and job insecurity.
7. What roles do personality characteristics and job involvement play in workplace accidents?
8. What three industries are the most dangerous for employees? What are the three safest industries?
9. Discuss the effects of safety training and management support in reducing accidents on the job.
10. Describe how you would design a warning poster to caution employees about the dangers of getting too close to a high-voltage cable.
11. Describe different levels of violence in the workplace. Indicate the relative incidence of each type and some of the overall effects of workplace violence.

12. Describe the background, social, and personality characteristics of a person likely to commit an act of violence in the workplace.

13. What kind of person is most likely to be a victim of bullying on the job?

14. Define the personality trait of anger and describe how it relates to workplace violence.

15. Describe personal, background, and job-related factors that are likely to be linked with alcoholism.

16. Why is it easier for an alcoholic executive to escape detection than for a lower level employee with alcoholism?

17. Describe the three-step process of the National Council on Alcoholism to combat alcohol abuse on the job.

18. What factors influence drug abuse in the workplace? What are the effects of drug use among employees?

19. Discuss arguments for and against drug testing in the workplace. Do you think it is fair for an employer to require you to take a drug test as a condition for employment?

20. How, and why, do employers treat alcoholics differently from drug users?

21. How is prolonged computer use related to physical health problems? How can such potential problems be reduced on the job?

Additional Reading

Fox, S., & Spector, P. (Eds.). (2005). *Counterproductive work behavior*. Washington, DC: APA Books. Reviews actions that are harmful to employees and organizations such as bullying, emotional abuse, incivility, retaliation, and aggression; assesses environmental issues in the workplace as well as personal characteristics of employees as contributing factors.

Kelloway, E., Barling, J., & Hurrell, J. (Eds.). (2006). *Handbook of workplace violence*. Thousand Oaks, CA: Sage. A sourcebook on violence and aggression in the workplace including bullying, harassment, physical violence, and cyberaggression; covers causes and prevention in a great variety of work situations.

Lewis, G. W., & Zare, N. C. (1999). *Workplace hostility: Myth and reality*. Philadelphia: Taylor & Francis. Offers a profile of the at-risk employee, including behavioral warning signs for the potential for violence (such as attendance records, job performance problems, and verbal and nonverbal cues). Suggests courses of action for the organization including referral for psychological evaluation, legal action, and the development and implementation of corporate antiviolence policies.

Schwenk, C. R., & Rhodes, S. L. (Eds.). (1999). *Marijuana and the workplace*. Westport, CO: Quorum. Reviews research on the effects of marijuana use on job performance and behavior in the workplace. Covers issues such as motivation, attention, learning and memory, and psychomotor skills as well as violent behavior, socially deviant behavior, and criminal conduct.

CHAPTER 12

Stress in the Workplace

> **Stress**   Physiological and psychological
> responses to excessive and usually
> unpleasant stimulation and to threatening
> events in the environment.

OCCUPATIONAL HEALTH PSYCHOLOGY

In chapter 11 we described how work can be harmful to employees' health. Accidents and violence on the job and exposure to noxious chemicals in factories and sealed office buildings account for substantial numbers of injuries and deaths every year. Another danger—**stress**—affects millions of employees, but it operates in more silent and subtle ways. Whereas poorly designed chairs and toxic fumes are physical agents that affect health, productivity, and morale, stress is a psychological agent that influences physical and emotional well-being and our ability to perform our jobs.

Stress-related diseases are widespread among employees throughout the world. An online survey of 1,848 people in the United States, conducted by the American Psychological Association, found that 74% cited work as their primary source of stress, an increase from 59% just one year earlier. More than half of those polled said they had considered quitting their job because of the stress and that stress made them less productive at work. The survey also found that highly stressed workers miss more days on the job than those who report less stress (Anderson, 2008; Holland, 2008).

As many as half of all visits to physicians are precipitated by stress. A major share of physical complaints may be psychosomatic—that is, actual physical disorders caused by or related to emotional factors such as stress on the job. Physical problems associated with stress include high blood pressure (hypertension), ulcers, colitis, arthritis, skin diseases, allergies, headaches, neck and lower back pain, and cancer. Stress has been linked to an increase in infectious diseases and may be implicated in disorders that involve suppression of the immune system.

Stress in the workplace is also costly to employers, as reflected in lower productivity, reduced motivation, and increased errors and accidents. High stress is related to increases in turnover intentions and counterproductive behavior, such as theft and drug and alcohol abuse. Job stress contributes to spiraling health care costs. The estimated expenditure for only two stress-related conditions—heart disease

With portable electronic equipment, employees are always connected to their office. Constant job-induced stress may reduce efficiency and lead to physical complaints.

and ulcers—is approximately $45 billion a year, which makes stress more costly for organizations than accidents. For every worker killed in a job-related accident, at least 50 experience some form of heart disease. In a study of more than 10,000 government employees in Britain, conducted over a 12-year period, researchers found that the risk of coronary heart disease was 68% greater among people who reported chronic job stress than among those who reported no stress. This relationship between stress on the job and heart disease was significantly greater among people under age 50 than for those closer to retirement age (Chandola et al., 2008).

In survey of more than 1 million workers in Britain, more than half of the people reported physical health problems that resulted from the stress of unusually long working hours. British psychologists conclude that job stress accounts for 60% of all workplace accidents in that country (Cartwright, 2000).

Other research shows that employees who report the greatest amount of job stress cost their employers significantly more in health care benefits than employees who report little stress on the job. A survey of 14 university employees who completed daily Internet diary accounts of stressful events over the course of one semester showed that the job stress increased over the period of the study.

Occupational health psychology The field of study dealing with the health effects of job stress and other aspects of employee well-being.

Individual sources of job stress remained relatively minor over time, but as these stressful events accumulated, the overall effect became more severe. And as stress levels increased, job satisfaction and morale decreased (Fuller et al., 2003).

In research on more than 24,000 workers in Canada, investigators found a significant positive correlation between job stress and depression. The higher the work stress, the greater the feelings associated with depression (Blackmore, et al., 2007). A survey of 630 workers in Malaysia and Pakistan found that high stress in the workplace led to low job performance, high absenteeism, and greater intention to quit (Jamal, 2007). Even psychothera-

pists experience job stress. A study of therapists in the United States and in South Korea indicated that both groups reported higher levels of stress than did a sample of nontherapists (Kim, 2007).

Stress affects employees at all levels and in all types of jobs. It is unlikely that you can avoid the consequences of stress during your career, any more than you can avoid them in college. Some level of stress will probably affect the quality of your working life and, in turn, other aspects of daily living.

Continuing problems of workplace stress led to a field of study called **occupational health psychology**. Concern for occupational health and

Newsbreak

The Job of a War Correspondent—Glamorous or Traumatic?

Military forces in combat experience high levels of stress, both during wartime and for a long time after. But what about the war reporters we see on television and the Internet, the men and women in flak jackets and helmets who brave combat conditions to bring the war home to the rest of us? According to Anthony Feinstein, a psychiatrist at the University of Toronto, war correspondents also experience high levels of stress. Feinstein studied 140 reporters from six major news organizations who had covered combat in several wars. When he compared them with 107 other journalists from the same organizations who had never covered war situations, he found striking differences between the two groups.

War reporters had been severely traumatized by the events they had witnessed, often to a degree that impaired their normal functioning. They showed substantially higher rates of serious

depression and posttraumatic stress disorder (PTSD) than those who had not reported from war zones. The PTSD often persisted for years. The war reporters also exhibited a wide range of social and emotional problems with symptoms such as flashbacks, recurring nightmares, irritability, and difficulty concentrating. Also, they were frequently unable to adjust to civilian society back home. They were reluctant to spend time with old friends, unless they had shared similar experiences, and had difficulty maintaining personal relationships. Some sought solace in alcohol.

Nevertheless, the war reporters in this study claimed to know little about PTSD and did not recognize their symptoms as typical of stress. They were aware that something was wrong, and that they were deeply troubled, but they remained, as the researcher described it, "surprisingly unaware of what afflicted them."

Sources: Feinstein, A. (2002). A hazardous profession: War, journalists, and psychopathology. *American Journal of Psychiatry, 159(9)*, 1570–1579; Goode, A. (2002, September 17). War horrors take a toll on reporters at the front. *New York Times.*

employee well-being can be traced to the early years of industrial psychology practice. The German psychologist, Hugo Münsterberg, who taught at Harvard University, helped found the field of industrial psychology. Among the issues he considered were accidents and worker safety. During World War I (1914–1918), the British government established the Industrial Fatigue Research Board to study problems of inefficiency and fatigue in manual laborers. Since then, a great deal of research has been conducted on all aspects of employee health.

In 1990, psychologist Jonathan Raymond proposed the term *occupational health psychology* for this field. The Academy of Management formed the Health and Well-being Focus Group in its organizational behavior division. Similarly, the American Psychological Association and the National Institute for Occupational Safety and Health (NIOSH) launched programs to support the formal development of the field of occupational health psychology. International conferences were convened, graduate school programs established at major universities, and publication of the *Journal of Occupational Health Psychology* was begun.

The goal of occupational health psychology is to understand and combat the harmful effects of stress on employee health and safety. Much of the research discussed in this chapter is an outgrowth of this effort. For more information on occupational health psychology visit the NIOSH Web site at www.cdc.gov/niosh For general information on stress, see www.stress.org (the American Institute of Stress) and www.workhealth.org (the Job Stress Network, home page of the Center for Social Epidemiology).

PHYSIOLOGICAL EFFECTS OF STRESS

Some students feel stress every time they take an exam. People undergo stress when a car runs a stop sign and almost hits them or when a shadowy figure follows them down a dark street. When incidents like these happen, people become anxious, tense, and fearful. Stress involves physiological and psychological responses to excessive and usually unpleasant stimulation and to threatening events in the environment.

Dramatic physiological changes occur during stress. Adrenaline, released from the adrenal glands, speeds up all bodily functions. Blood pressure rises, heart rate increases, and extra sugar is released into the bloodstream. The increased blood circulation brings additional energy to the brain and muscles, making the person stronger and more alert to cope with the threat. A stressful situation mobilizes and directs one's energy, boosting it beyond its normal level. With the excess energy of this so-called fight-or-flight response, an organism (human or other animal) will either fight the source of the stress (perhaps an attacker or a predator) or flee from it.

Most of the research conducted on the fight-or-flight phenomenon has been conducted on male subjects. Only more recently have enough data been compiled on female subjects to support the idea that they respond differently to stress. Researchers characterize women's response to stress as tend-and-befriend. *Tending* involves nurturing activities designed to protect themselves and their offspring from the stress; *befriending* refers to the development of social groups or networks that help defend against stress (Taylor, et al., 2000). Although behavioral responses to stress may vary by gender, the physiological changes induced by stress (noted in the previous paragraph) are experienced by both men and women.

Psychosomatic Disorders

Most people will not encounter extreme emergency situations on the job. Few jobs expose workers to threatening events such as those faced by police officers, firefighters, or soldiers in combat. For most of us, the stresses we face on the job are psychological or emotional in nature, such as an argument with the boss, the belief that we have been treated unfairly, or concern about a promotion. These constitute what are commonly referred to as hassles or insults of everyday life. Individually, they are low-level sources of stress, but they are hard on the body because they accumulate. Each stress adds to the previous one and can tax the body's energy reserves because of the physiological changes it produces. If stressors occur frequently in the workplace, the body remains in a state of high physiological arousal and alertness for long periods, a condition that can lead to physiological damage as well as psychosomatic illnesses.

Psychosomatic disorders are not imaginary; they involve specific tissue and organ damage. Although their origin lies in psychological and emotional factors, they have a definite physical impact on the body. Furthermore, the illnesses brought about by stress can serve as new sources of stress. When physical health declines, resistance is lowered and bodily energy is reduced. As a result, motivation and job performance are bound to suffer. In a large-scale meta-analysis of more than 300 research articles dealing with stress, investigators found that chronic stressors such as worry over losing one's job, or the fear of unemployment, can suppress the body's immune system. This leaves the individual more vulnerable to disease with fewer physiological resources with which to combat it (Segerstrom & Miller, 2004).

Not all employees are affected by stress in the same way. Consider air-traffic controllers, who have highly stressful jobs. Hour after hour they exercise constant vigilance, tracking aircraft at various speeds and altitudes converging on or departing from the same point. Their work is hectic, difficult, and demanding, and has the additional burden of making them responsible for thousands of lives throughout each workday. Research on air-traffic controllers confirms the physiological effects of the pressures of their job. As the number of aircraft in their sector increases, coronary arteries become more constricted and blood pressure rises. The incidence of hypertension among air-traffic controllers is three times higher than normal for their age group. So this seems to be a classic example of the deadly effects of stress. Most of us would guess that the rate of heart attacks, strokes, and other stress-related disabilities is many times higher among air-traffic controllers than among the rest of the population. But research indicates that this is not so. On some measures, air-traffic controllers are healthier than the general population. Although some air-traffic controllers show a pattern of disease and early death, others are apparently unaffected.

Job Satisfaction and Feelings of Control

What makes the difference? Why don't job pressures affect all air-traffic controllers in the same way? The difference seems to lie in the level of job satisfaction controllers get from their work. Those who report being very satisfied with their jobs show fewer harmful effects of stress. Those who are very dissatisfied with their jobs show many more stress-related effects.

A study of 1,886 business managers in the United States identified two kinds of daily work stress (Cavanaugh, Boswell, Roehling, & Boudreau, 2000):

1. *Challenge-related stress*, which includes time pressure and a high level of responsibility that lead to feelings of fulfillment and achievement
2. *Hindrance-related stress*, which includes excessive job demands and constraints (such as red tape, poor support from higher management, and job insecurity) that interfere with achieving goals

Thus, not all stress is considered harmful. Challenge-related stress is motivating and positively related to job satisfaction. Hindrance-related stress is associated with frustration and low job satisfaction. High job satisfaction contributes to health and longevity. Although both types of stress cause similar physiological changes, only hindrance-related stress was shown to lead to detrimental health effects. Identification of these two types of stress explains why some people in high-stress jobs, such as air-traffic controllers, maintain generally good health.

Consider another high-stress occupation—that of corporate executive. Many people assume that executives experience enormous job stress and consequently have a higher rate of heart attacks than does the general population. Research does not support this position. High-level executives have 40% fewer heart attacks than do middle-level managers, who are popularly assumed to work under less stressful conditions. The primary reason top executives are relatively less affected by job stress is that they have more autonomy and control over their work than do middle-level managers. Being able to control workplace events can significantly reduce perceived job stress. People with low levels of job control are far more likely to develop heart disease than are those with greater control over the demands and responsibilities of their job. A study of 3,504 employees in the United States showed that those who reported a great degree of control and autonomy on the job scored higher in job satisfaction and in overall life satisfaction than those whose jobs provided little or no autonomy and control (Thompson & Prottas, 2005).

In research on 97 government employees in Britain, investigators found that reorganizing employees' jobs to give them more choice and control over their work tasks resulted in significant

Hardiness   A personality variable that may explain individual differences in vulnerability to stress. So-called hardy persons believe they can control the events in their lives and thus may be more resistant to stress.

improvements in their self-reported mental health, job performance, and absence rates for illness over a 1-year period (Bond & Bunce, 2001). A comparison of workers in the United States and in China found that lack of autonomy and control was a major source of stress for American but not for Chinese workers. This finding suggests the importance of cultural differences in response to workplace stress (Liu, Spector, & Shi, 2007).

INDIVIDUAL DIFFERENCES IN RESPONDING TO STRESS

A thorough examination of the causes of stress on the job must take into account personal factors that can render employees vulnerable to stress. Not all stressors at work affect people the same way. A source of stress that can ruin the health of one worker may have no noticeable effect on that of a colleague.

We have mentioned two factors that may reduce a person's susceptibility to stress: high job satisfaction and control over the conditions of one's work. Several other variables have been related to employees' vulnerability to the effects of stress. One factor involved in coping with stress is social support, a person's network of family and social ties. The person who lives alone or is emotionally alienated from others is more likely to be sensitive to stress than is someone who has strong ties to family, friends, and colleagues. Family support can help compensate for negative feelings about one's job and can enhance self-esteem, acceptance, and worth. Social support on the job, such as a cohesive work group or a good relationship with one's boss, can also reduce the effects of stress. This was demonstrated in a study of 61 nurses and 32 accountants in Britain. Low social support from colleagues and supervisors at work was linked to elevated heart rate not only during the workday but also during the evening hours after the work period had ended (Evans & Steptoe, 2001).

In general, the lower the level of available social support, the greater the health risks. Variations in social support over the course of the workday have been found to affect blood pressure. Studies of men and women in various occupations showed that blood pressure rose when social support was low and dropped when social support was high. In a study of more than 500 city employees in Germany, the researcher found that employees who scored high in organizational commitment (their degree of involvement in and emotional attachment to their employing organization) were less affected by symptoms related to job stress than were employees who were less committed (Schmidt, 2007).

General physical health is related to susceptibility to stress. People in better physical condition experience fewer harmful effects from a stressful work environment than do people in poorer physical condition. Physical exercise is a good way to improve general well-being. Many companies provide exercise facilities to help employees alleviate stress.

Our level of ability to perform a job can make us more or less resistant to stress. Employees with high skill levels usually find their work less stressful than do employees with lower skill levels. You may have noticed this effect in your college classmates. Students who are barely able to keep up with the course work are usually more anxious about exams than are students who have less difficulty mastering the required material.

Personality Factors

Personality factors have been related to tolerance of stress. Among the variables that may account for individual differences in vulnerability to stress are hardiness, the Big Five factors, self-efficacy, locus of control, organization-based self-esteem, self-control, and negative affectivity.

People characterized as being high in **hardiness** have attitudes that may make them more resistant to stress. Hardy people believe they can control or influence the events in their lives. They are deeply committed to their work and to other activities of

Newsbreak

Business Travel: Perils of the Road Warrior

Have you been in an airport lately? Then you know how stressful air travel has become. Long lines at security checkpoints, flight delays, canceled departures, cramped aisles and seats. And if you think it's stressful taking a flight every now and then for vacation or to go home for the holidays, what must it be like for employees whose jobs require that they travel frequently? Some employees make more than 100 business trips a year, often covering several cities in a week's time: a meeting in New York on Monday, a Denver conference on Tuesday, a presentation in Germany on Wednesday. Sound glamorous? Maybe if you travel on a corporate jet. For most business travelers who don't have that perk, travel is a major source of stress.

A survey of frequent business travelers conducted by Hyatt Hotels found that one of every three employees said they would like to stop traveling, but they were sure it would hurt their careers. More than half said that in the future they would turn down a job that required so much travel. Those with families were particularly inconvenienced. They carried the additional burden of guilt for being away from home and missing so many of their children's activities.

Other surveys show that flight delays are a source of stress for up to 50% of all business travelers. Long waits for baggage are an annoyance for 30%. Questionnaires completed by customers of the Hilton Hotel chain indicated that more than half did not sleep well, despite the luxurious and well-equipped accommodations.

An additional problem for business travelers is becoming ill while away from home. A study of international business travelers conducted by Coca-Cola reported that diarrhea is the most common health complaint, followed by colds and other respiratory ailments linked to poor air quality on airplanes. Half of all business travelers admitted to overeating while on the road, and one fourth said they drank more than usual. The World Bank noted that their employees who travel frequently account for 80% more of the organization's medical claims than their employees who do not travel. Frequent travelers are also three times more likely to seek psychological help for anxiety and acute stress reactions than are employees who rarely travel. Even spouses of frequent business travelers develop problems. Their rate of insurance claims for psychological disorders is twice as high as for spouses of nontravelers. Clearly, it's not easy being a road warrior.

Sources: DeFrank, R. S., Knonpaske, R., & Ivancevich, J. M. (2000). Executive travel stress: Perils of the road warrior. *Academy of Management Executive, 14*(2), 58–71; Sharkey, J. (2000, January 12). Business travel. *New York Times*; Tugend, A. (2004, May 25). All stressed out and everywhere to go. *New York Times.*

interest, and they view change as exciting and challenging rather than threatening.

Hardiness can be assessed by a 20-item scale designed to measure three components: control, commitment, and challenge (Kobasa, 1979, 1982). Hardy persons develop fewer physical complaints under highly stressful conditions than do persons who are not hardy. For example, among a group of 88 adults who lost their jobs, which is considered to be a highly stressful life event, those who scored higher in hardiness used a variety of coping techniques, such as problem solving and positive reap-

praisals of their employment options, to a greater extent than did those who scored low in hardiness (Crowley, Hayslip, & Hobdy, 2003). In a study of 1,571 recruits for the U.S. Marine corps, researchers found that recruits who scored high on hardiness at the beginning of their 13-week basic training period reported significantly fewer stress reactions at the end of the training, when compared with those who scored low in hardiness (Vogt, Rizvi, Shipherd, & Resick, 2008). Thus, hardiness may moderate the effects of stress through the way people evaluate and interpret the experiences and events in their lives.

Locus of control   One's belief about the source of one's rewards. People with an internal locus of control believe that job performance, pay, and promotion are under their control and dependent on their own behavior. People with an external locus of control believe such events depend on outside forces such as luck.

Organization-based self-esteem   A personality dimension relating to our assessment of our adequacy and worth with regard to our place in the employing organization.

Research carried out in Australia on 211 male and female managers in a major department store showed that of the so-called Big Five personality factors, extraversion and neuroticism influenced reactions to stress. Managers scoring high in extraversion and low in neuroticism were the least affected by job stress (Grant & Langan-Fox, 2007).

Self-efficacy refers to the belief in one's ability to accomplish a task. It is the sense of how adequate, efficient, and competent a person feels about coping with life's demands. People who are high in self-efficacy are less bothered by stress than are people who are low in self-efficacy. For example, 2,293 U.S. Army soldiers were subjected to both psychological and physical stress associated with overly long workdays and unusual physical demands. Soldiers who scored high in self-efficacy in this study reacted more positively to work stressors than did soldiers who scored low (Jex, Bliese, Buzzell, & Primeau, 2001).

In a study of 226 U.S. bank tellers, researchers reported that employees high in self-efficacy who believed that they had a high level of control over their jobs were more resistant to psychological stress than were employees with low self-efficacy (Schaubroeck, Lam, & Xie, 2000). Even when tellers who scored low in self-efficacy had high perceived control over their jobs, they still experienced the effects of stress. Thus, the researchers concluded that the determining factor in stress tolerance was self-efficacy, a finding confirmed in a follow-up study of 217 employees of a survey research company (Schaubroeck, Jones, & Xie, 2001).

The personality variable of internal or external **locus of control** influences a person's reaction to stress. People who rate high on internal control believe that they can influence the forces and events that shape their lives. People who rate high on external control believe that life is determined by other people and by outside events and forces such as luck or chance. In a study of 361 nurses in Germany, nurses who scored high in external locus of control reported experiencing higher levels of stress and burnout on the job than those who scored high in internal locus of control (Schmitz, Neumann, & Oppermann, 2000).

Self-esteem, which is similar to self-efficacy, refers to how people feel about themselves. In the workplace this concept is referred to as **organization-based self-esteem (OBSE)**. People high in OBSE have a high sense of personal adequacy and see themselves as important, effective, and worthwhile members of their organizations. Research shows that people low in OBSE are more affected by job stress than people high in OBSE. Workers low in OBSE are likely to be more susceptible to the effects of role conflict (a major workplace stressor) and to poor support from their supervisors. Workers low in OBSE also tend to be more passive in coping with stress. An online survey of 171 people from several countries found that those who rated low in OBSE experienced greater stress induced from the perceived need to respond quickly to e-mails than did those who scored higher in self-esteem (Hair, Renaud, & Ramsay, 2007).

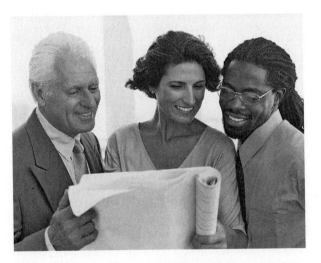

People high on the personality variable of hardiness may be more resistant to stress. They are committed to their work, believe they can control events in their lives, and view changes as exciting and challenging.

Negative affectivity   A personality dimension characterized by a generalized life and job dissatisfaction and by a focus on negative aspects of life events.

Self-control is a personality characteristic we all have to some degree. People who exercise a high level of self-control tend to restrain behaviors, desires, and emotions that might interfere with what they believe is expected of them. For example, if you are high in self-control, you will work diligently on a project your boss or professor has assigned, instead of procrastinating and wasting time by playing video games or reading magazines. Research on 551 government employees in Germany found that those high in self-control on the job reported greater stress and anxiety than those low in self-control. The researchers identified two components of self-control—impulse control and resisting distractions—that were strongly involved in workplace stress (Schmidt & Neubach, 2007). Nevertheless, some degree of self-control is necessary if you want to succeed at your job. Low self-control may result in less stress, but you may well not pass the course or get the promotion if you fail to do what is expected of you.

Another personality characteristic that influences vulnerability to stress is **negative affectivity**, which is related to neuroticism, one of the Big Five personality dimensions. People who measure high in negative affectivity are likely to experience distress and dissatisfaction in all areas of life, not just on the job. They focus on the negative aspects of their experiences and dwell on their failures, weaknesses, and shortcomings. Although some research has found that people high in negative affectivity are likely to show high levels of stress, as measured by self-report inventories, other studies have failed to confirm such an effect (Spector, Chen, & O'Connell, 2000).

Construction work can be stressful not only because of physical hazards, but also because of external factors such as completion deadlines.

farm worker, and miner. Other occupations ranked as stressful were police officer, firefighter, computer programmer, dental technician, electrician, plumber, social worker, telephone operator, and city bus driver. NIOSH ranked college professor as one of the least stressful jobs. In general, clerical and blue-collar workers experience more stress than do managerial and professional employees, largely because they have less opportunity to make decisions about their work and less control over working conditions.

Type of Occupation

Stress levels differ as a function of occupation. The NIOSH ranked 130 jobs in terms of the level of stress they engender. These jobs were ranked with the highest stress levels: laborer, secretary, clinical laboratory technician, nurse, first-line supervisor, restaurant server, machine operator,

Gender Differences

Women consistently report higher levels of job stress than men. Female employees cite headaches, anxiety, depression, sleep disturbances, and eating disorders more frequently than male employees. Women also report more smoking and use of alcohol and drugs in response to workplace stress. Women in

Newsbreak

Flipping Burgers? Making Every Second Count

Try saying this fast: "Hi! May I take your order, please?" Try again, only faster: "HimayItakeyourorderplease." Talk about stress! Say it fast, as fast as you can, over and over, several hundred times a day. Your boss is holding a stopwatch to make sure you're not speaking too slowly. That's what happened at Wendy's, the fast-food chain striving to become the fastest in the world.

"Every second is business lost," explained a Wendy's manager, eyeing the clock. He was pleased. His store had knocked 8 seconds off the average takeout delivery time. A survey of 25 fast-food restaurants found that customers' cars idled an average of 203.6 seconds from the instant they arrived at the menu board until they left the pickup window with their food. At Wendy's, they cut that average down to 150.3 seconds, which put them 16.7 seconds ahead of McDonald's and 21 seconds ahead of Burger King. But that's still not fast enough. For every 6 seconds saved at the drive-through, sales rise by 1%. A store that can increase its drive-through efficiency by 10% stands to grow its sales more than $50,000 a year.

If the timer beeps before you've finished your task, you know you're falling behind. If you can't take an order, make change, and deliver the food in less than a minute, you're too slow. If you can't cook 300 burgers in less than 7 seconds each, you should get out of the kitchen. Every second counts, and the boss is counting.

Source: Faster food (2000, May 19). *St. Petersburg (FL) Times.*

highly stressful jobs are more likely to experience spontaneous abortion and shorter menstrual cycles than women in less stressful jobs. On the positive side, research in the United States and in Spain, has demonstrated that women are far more likely than men are to take advantage of social support networks to help them cope with stress (Gonzalez-Morales, Peiro, Rodriguez, & Greenglass, 2006; Nelson & Burke, 2000).

Women homemakers also experience high levels of stress. The demands of family and the roles of wife and mother can lead to overwork, to dissatisfaction and a sense of loss of control, and to conflict with the need to seek employment outside the home. Many women homemakers report feeling depressed because they believe that more demands are placed on them than on women with paying jobs.

WORK–FAMILY BALANCE

Both men and women report conflicts in trying to achieve a balance between the demands of family and the demands of the job, but the difficulties are usually greater for women. Work–family conflict has been documented among workers in many countries (see, for example, Lu, Kao, Chang, Wu, & Cooper, 2008; Song, Foo, & Uy, 2008; Yang, Chen, Choi, & Zou, 2000). The intensity of that conflict may vary from one culture to another. This was demonstrated in two large-scale studies of nearly 8,000 managers from some 20 nations. Western, or Anglo, cultures included the United States, Canada, Australia, England, and New Zealand. Eastern cultures included Hong Kong, Taiwan, China. Latin cultures included Argentina, Brazil, Colombia, Ecuador, Mexico, Peru, and Uruguay.

The results showed that for managers in the Western, more individualistic, cultures, there was a greater relationship between the number of hours worked and the strength of the work–family conflict than for managers in more collectivist Eastern and Latin cultures. The researchers suggested that "Anglos view working extra hours as taking away from their families, which may provoke feelings of guilt and greater levels of work–family pressure." Employees in the other collectivist Eastern or Latin cultures were more accepting of the necessity of working longer hours because, in general, earning a living was more difficult (Spector, et al., 2004, p. 135).

Similar findings were obtained in a study of 276 Latino immigrants from collectivist cultures who worked at a U.S. poultry processing plant. They reported high levels of stress associated with the physical working conditions (noise, high-speed production line, constant pressure to work faster) but little work–family conflict (Grzywacz et al., 2007).

The stressors associated with trying to achieve a suitable work–family balance are apparently independent of type of job and working conditions, and they affect managerial as well as nonmanagerial employees. A study of 75 university employees who completed daily Internet surveys for a 2-week period showed that the predominant emotional reactions to their work–family conflict were guilt and hostility, which they experienced both at home and on the job (Judge, Ilies, & Scott, 2006). In research on 18,366 workers in Finland, investigators found that work–family conflict resulted in a greater number of absences for blue-collar workers but not for higher level white-collar workers (Vaananen et al, 2008).

Today, more than 60% of all women who have children under age 6 hold jobs outside the home. These working women are essentially holding two full-time jobs: one in the office, shop, or factory and the other at home. Spouses may help out, but the primary responsibility for family life remains with women. It is typically the woman who is called when a child becomes ill or who must adjust her work schedule when an elderly parent needs care.

A survey of 513 workers at a Fortune 500 company in the United States found that the greater the numbers of hours worked, the higher the reported feeling that work was interfering with family life, and the higher the levels of reported stress. Employees who worked longer hours identified strongly with their careers. They believed that they had insufficient time each day to accomplish all of their work and that their bosses expected them to put in extra hours (Major, Klein, & Ehrart, 2002).

Later research, based on daily e-mail questionnaires to 106 college employees over a 2-week period, confirmed that work–family conflict increased with the number of hours worked. Employees' subjective perceptions of their workload (how hard they believed they were working) also affected the reported strength of their work–family difficulties. A heavy workload and similar negative job experiences carried over into the employees' home lives. The greater the stress at work, the more the employees withdrew from their families at home (Ilies, et al., 2007).

As you might expect, women are reported to be more affected than men by work–family conflicts,

Both men and women report conflicts between the demands of family life and the demands of the job, but the difficulties are usually greater for women.

primarily because so many women come home from work to their second job—caring for their children and spouse and managing their household. In a study of 623 men and women employed outside the home, researchers found that women devoted an average of 7 hours more each week to their families than men did. In addition, the men averaged 2 hours a week more personal free time than the women did (Rothbard & Edwards, 2003).

Despite this gender gap in work–family relationships, in general, women with paying jobs outside the home enjoy better health than full-time homemakers. Employed women score higher on measures of psychological well-being and have a lower risk of cardiovascular illness. The psychological and physical health advantages for employed women are greatest for women in high-status careers (Nelson & Burke, 2000). Also, work–family conflict diminishes significantly for women over age 50; children are grown and may no longer be living at home. Work–family conflict increases with the number of children at home and when women are also responsible for the care of aging parents (Gordon, Whelan-Berry, & Hamilton, 2007; Premeaux, Adkins, & Mossholder, 2007).

Organizational Assistance for Work–Family Conflicts

As research continues on work–family conflicts, and as the data showing potentially harmful effects accumulate, organizations have instituted measures to deal with these effects. For example, providing

Newsbreak

Balancing Work and Family: The Stress Never Ends

Susan R., manager at AT&T in Basking Ridge, New Jersey, experiences stress daily caused by work overload, both on and off the job. When she leaves her office at 5 p.m., the workday is far from over. For many women like Susan, the most difficult part of the day is just beginning. She must leave precisely at 5 p.m., not a minute later, even if she's in the middle of a meeting. "It's a frantic rush to get out of the office," she said. "It's so stressful." What's her hurry? She has to pick up her 4-year-old son from his day-care center, then drive across town at the height of rush hour traffic to collect her 7-year-old daughter from her after-school program. If she's not on time, she'll be met by a fretting child and a harried teacher (who's probably late picking up her own children), and then docked for a late fee.

Next, a quick stop at the grocery store to buy food for dinner and a dash home to let the dog out. Then, prepare the meal, referee fights between the children, pay attention to her husband (who doesn't do much to help), supervise the children's homework, do the laundry, and so it goes.

By the time she's gotten the kids to bed, Susan has put in more than a 12-hour workday. No wonder she's exhausted and stressed out. And she's not alone. Even for wives whose husbands share more of the child-care and household duties, the primary responsibility rests with the woman. And if she's a single working mom, the situation can be worse.

How do they do it all? Where do they find the time and energy? "They steal it from themselves," said a sociologist who studied the lives of 300 mothers who had jobs outside the home. In order to spend time with their children, these women cut down on sleep and on their own free time. Today, working mothers sleep nearly 6 hours less per week and have 12 fewer hours for their own activities than do mothers who do not have outside jobs. "There's no time for hobbies or socializing," one woman said. "I can't tell you the last time I went out." Having it all—a family and a job—can lead to a lot of stress along the way.

Sources: Kelly, A. L., (1999, June 13). For employed moms, the pinnacle of stress comes after work ends. *New York Times*; Working moms don't shirk times with kids (2000, March 28). *St. Petersburg (FL) Times.*

day-care facilities at the workplace can relieve some of the concerns of employees with young children. Other approaches include reducing work hours and providing flexible work scheduling and opportunities for telecommuting (see, for example, Ford, Heinen, & Langkamer, 2007; Golden, 2006; Golden, Veiga, & Simsek, 2006; Valcour, 2007).

Flexible work scheduling and supportive supervision are highly effective ways in which organizations can help reduce work–family conflicts among employees. Both supportive bosses and flexible working hours lead to increases in employee perceptions of having some personal control over their work and family demands. These feelings of greater control lead, in turn, to lower levels of conflict and stress and higher job satisfaction.

Another source of organizational support involves maternity or paternity leave. The 1993 U. S. Family and Medical Leave Act provides up to 12 weeks of parental leave. There is some evidence, however, that women in high-paying, high-status professional and managerial jobs are penalized for taking too much parental leave. Extended time off has been associated with fewer subsequent promotions, smaller pay increases, and lower performance evaluations.

Organizations that try to assist their employees in reducing work–family conflicts may benefit financially from these initiatives. A study of 231 Fortune 500 companies found that companies that offered programs to reduce work–family conflict had higher stock prices and thus a higher shareholder return compared to companies that did not offer such benefits (Arthur, 2003). However, the higher share price may have resulted from the publicity given the organizations that offered such benefits, or it may have been related to other factors. As noted in chapter 2, correlation does not necessarily imply causation.

Work overload   Too much work to perform in the time available or work that is too difficult for the employee to perform.

Life Is Unfair: When Co-workers Work Less but Get the Same Pay

If your boss allows your co-workers to leave work early to take their children to the dentist or to watch siblings perform in a school play, is that fair to the employees who don't have children? Is it fair to give a flexible work schedule to a woman who has children but to deny it to a woman or man who has no kids? Should only employees without children at home be asked to work late or on weekends to finish a project?

A growing number of childless adults in the workplace are concerned about fairness. They are part of an increasingly vocal backlash against so-called family friendly organizational policies and benefits established to help reduce work–family conflicts by providing special assistance to employees with children. Today there are more childless adults in the workforce than ever before and many of them believe they are being taken advantage of—exploited—because they receive fewer benefits than workers with children.

Do you think some employees merit special consideration just because they have children? Or do they deserve extra help precisely because the responsibility of children at home can affect their on-the-job performance?

Source: Brown, P. (2007, October 13). The revolt of the childless. *New York Times*.

STRESSORS IN THE WORK ENVIRONMENT

Many aspects of the work environment can induce stress. These include, among others, work overload and work underload, organizational change, role conflict and role ambiguity, and burnout.

Work Overload and Underload

Psychologists use the term **work overload** to describe the common condition of overwork. They have identified two types: quantitative overload and qualitative overload.

Quantitative overload is the condition of having too much work to do in the time available. It is an obvious source of stress and has been linked to stress-related ailments such as coronary heart disease. The key factor seems to be the degree of control workers have over the rate at which they work rather than the amount of work itself. In general,

the less control employees have over their work pace, the greater the stress. *Qualitative* overload involves work that is too difficult. Having insufficient ability to perform a job is stressful. Even employees with considerable ability can find themselves in situations in which they cannot cope with the job's demands.

A study of 94 employees of an accounting firm in Britain showed that work overload was directly linked to self-reported psychological stress, burnout, and the belief that work was interfering with family life (Harvey, Kelloway, & Duncan-Leiper, 2003). Questionnaire surveys of 241 workers in Canada showed that employees who felt they had job demands that were significantly higher than those of other workers performed less physical exercise than those who felt they had lower job demands (Payne, Jones, & Harris, 2002). The combination of high job demands and little exercise is consistent with the relationship between work–related stress and coronary heart disease.

Work underload   Work that is too simple or insufficiently challenging for a worker's abilities.

Role ambiguity   A situation that arises when job responsibilities are unstructured or poorly defined.

Role conflict   A situation that arises when there is a disparity in job requirements or between a job's demands and the employee's personal standards.

The opposite condition, **work underload**—having work that is too simple or is insufficient to fill a worker's time or challenge a worker's abilities—is also stressful. In a study of 63 musicians in a symphony orchestra, researchers found that the musicians faced both overload and underload—overload when the job tasks were too difficult and underload when the tasks did not make full use of the their skills (Parasuraman & Purohit, 2000). Other research relates work underload to increased boredom and monotony (also a factor in stress) and to reduced job satisfaction.

Thus, an absence of challenge in the workplace is not necessarily beneficial. A certain level of job stress can be stimulating, invigorating, and desirable. Your goal as an employee should be to find the optimum level under which you can function and remain in good health and to avoid the extremes of work overload and work underload.

Organizational Change

Another stressor is change. Employees who consider change exciting and challenging are less vulnerable to stress than are those who view change as a threat. The way people perceive or respond to change, rather than the change itself, is the source of the stress. Many people resist change, preferring the familiar so that they know what to expect. A study of 375 employees in Australia confirmed that organizational change was a direct cause of feelings of uncertainty, which in turn were related to job dissatisfaction and intention to quit (Rafferty & Griffin, 2006).

As an example of a frequent change in the workplace, consider the relationship between employees and supervisors. Once a relationship has been established, assuming it is positive, all parties feel comfortable with it because each knows what to expect from the other. The situation is predictable, safe, and secure. When the supervisor leaves and employees face a new boss, they no longer know what behaviors will be tolerated, how much work will be expected, or how their job performance will be evaluated. Such changes in the work environment can be stressful, as can be changes such as revised work

procedures, required training courses, and new workplace facilities. Company mergers may lead to concerns about job security, new managers, and different organizational policies.

A stressful change for many older employees is the presence of younger workers and workers of diverse ethnic backgrounds who bring to the workplace unfamiliar attitudes, habits, and cultural values. Higher level managers may experience stress when changes are made in the organizational culture, for example, encouraging employee participation in decision making.

Role Ambiguity and Role Conflict

An employee's role in the organization can be a source of stress. **Role ambiguity** arises when the scope and responsibilities of a job are unstructured or poorly defined. The employee is not sure what is expected or even what to do. This stress is particularly relevant to new employees, whose job guidelines may be unclear. Adequate orientation and socialization programs for new employees can reduce role ambiguity. A meta-analysis of 169 studies involving more than 35,000 employees showed that role ambiguity was one of the strongest workplace stressors linked to low job performance (Gilboa, Shirom, Fried, & Cooper, 2008).

I-O psychologists have proposed three components of role ambiguity:

1. Performance criteria ambiguity—uncertainty about the standards used to evaluate a worker's job performance
2. Work method ambiguity—uncertainty about the methods or procedures appropriate to the successful performance of the job
3. Scheduling ambiguity—uncertainty about the timing or sequencing of work

For most jobs it would not be difficult for supervisors to alleviate role ambiguity by establishing and promoting consistent standards and procedures.

Role conflict arises when a disparity exists in job requirements or between a job's demands and the employee's values and expectations. For example, when a supervisor is told to allow subordinates to participate in decision making and at the same time is pressured to increase production, the supervisor faces an obvious conflict. To meet production goals immediately may require authoritarian behavior, yet meeting participation goals requires democratic behavior.

When a job requires behaviors that contradict an employee's moral code, such as when a salesperson is asked to sell a product known to be inferior or dangerous, role conflict can develop. The salesperson can quit, but the threat of unemployment may be a greater stressor than the role conflict.

Bad Bosses, Technology, and Other Stressors

Supervisors and managers can be major sources of stress to their subordinates. Poor leadership behaviors can lead to stress; for example, supervisors fail to support their employees or refuse to allow participation in decision making.

Problems of career development—such as failing to receive an anticipated promotion—may also lead to stress. If an employee's career aspirations are not satisfied, frustration can be intense. Overpromotion can be stressful when employees are advanced beyond their level of competence to positions with which they cannot cope; this can lead to qualitative overload. The fear of failure on the job can induce considerable stress. To many workers, performance appraisal is a source of stress. Few people like being evaluated relative to others. Also, a poor evaluation can have a significant impact on a career.

Taking responsibility for subordinates can be a stressor for supervisors and managers. Evaluating employees for salary, promotion, or termination decisions; providing incentives and rewards; and managing work output on a daily basis can lead to stress. Managers are much more likely to report stress-related physical complaints than are employees such as accountants whose daily responsibilities do not include supervising others.

Despite their importance to the workplace, computers can be a source of stress. A study in Sweden of 25 employees between the ages of 18 and 24 showed that they had misgivings about using computers even though they recognized the advantages. The employees said that computer access generally improved the quality of life but that computers also caused stress, information overload, and a lack of personal connection to other people. They also believed that computers demanded that they always be available to respond quickly to e-mail and to information on the Internet (Gustafsson, Delive, Edlund, & Hagberg, 2003). A study of computer use in Austria involved 26 people using the Internet. Researchers found that interruptions and delays in system response time during online searches produced signs of physiological stress, including increased heart rate and increased emotional activity as measured by skin conductance (Trimmel, Meixner-Pendleton, & Haring, 2003).

A person otherwise free of stress on the job can be adversely affected by a boss or co-worker who is experiencing stress (a so-called stress carrier). The anxiety exhibited by one stressed employee can easily affect other people. In a study of 109 women working in a variety of jobs, researchers found that interpersonal conflicts at work were a source of stress and were related to affective well-being. Interpersonal conflicts outside the workplace were perceived as not nearly so stressful (Potter, Smith, Strobel, & Zautra, 2002).

Physical working conditions are common sources of job stress. Temperature extremes, poor lighting, shift work, and indoor pollution contribute to stress. Assembly-line work is associated with stress because it is repetitious, monotonous, noisy, and lacks challenge and control. Similarly, computer-controlled performance monitoring can be stressful. Machine pacing of mail sorting and repetitive keyboard tasks increase stress and are related to absenteeism, poor performance, and muscle fatigue. Automated monitoring of keystrokes and keyboard time is stressful—like having an ever-vigilant supervisor looking over one's shoulder.

Burnout

Earlier in this chapter, we described some of the long-term physical health consequences of stress, those psychosomatic disorders that arise from prolonged exposure to stressful conditions. In addition, there are long-term psychological consequences such as tension, depression, irritability, anxiety, low self-esteem, resentment, psychological fatigue, and neuroticism. High job stress has also been linked to spouse abuse, child abuse, and aggressive behaviors on the job such as overt hostility and sabotage. Other effects of work stress are burnout and some types of workaholism.

Burnout A condition of job stress that results from overwork.

The effects of job stress that result from overwork can be seen in the condition called **burnout**. Employees affected by burnout become less energetic and less interested in their jobs. In general, they are emotionally exhausted, as demonstrated in a survey of 64 firefighters. The researchers found that emotional exhaustion was linked to the deterioration of job performance that is so characteristic of burnout (Halbesleben & Bowler, 2007). Employees experiencing burnout are apathetic, depressed, irritable, and bored. They tend to find fault with all aspects of their work environment, including co-workers, and they react negatively to the suggestions of others. The quality of their work deteriorates but not necessarily the quantity.

These employees tend to become rigid about their work; they follow rules and procedures compulsively because they are too exhausted to be flexible or to consider alternative approaches. In time, the burned-out employee has an impact on the emotional health and efficiency of co-workers and subordinates. Advanced burnout is characterized by even lower energy, self-esteem, self-efficacy, and job involvement, as well as by an increase in physical stress symptoms, turnover, and social withdrawal at the very time social support is most needed. Deterioration in job performance becomes noticeable, and poor performance appraisals are usually the result (Cropanzano, Rupp, & Byrne, 2003; deCroon, Sluiter, Blonk, Broersen, & Frings-Dresen, 2004; Van der Ploeg, Dorresteijn, & Kleber, 2003).

In a survey of more than 3,000 workers in Finland, researchers found that physical illnesses, including heart disease in men and musculoskeletal disease in women, were strongly related to burnout (Honkonen et al., 2006).

Three components of the burnout syndrome have been proposed (Maslach, Schaufeli, & Leiter, 2001):

1. Emotional exhaustion—the feeling of being drained and empty that is caused by excessive psychological and emotional demands, often brought about by work overload or unrealistically high expectations
2. Depersonalization—a feeling of callousness and cynicism and a reduced sensitivity toward others
3. Reduced sense of personal accomplishment (inefficacy)—the feeling that one's actions and efforts are wasted and worthless

The Maslach Burnout Inventory was developed to measure this condition (Maslach & Jackson, 1986). It consists of four subscales to assess the components of emotional exhaustion, depersonalization, a reduced sense of personal accomplishment, and a related factor called personal involvement. Studies show the inventory to have high reliability and validity. High scores on the burnout subscales have been related to exhaustion and to work overload in various occupations. Here are sample items from the Maslach Burnout Inventory. Do they apply to anyone you know?

- I feel emotionally drained by my work.
- I feel used up at the end of the workday.
- I feel like I'm at the end of my rope.
- I worry that this job is hardening me emotionally.

Age is a significant predictor of burnout. The condition of burnout is an early-career phenomenon, more likely to occur among younger workers than among those over age 40. Women are no more likely than men to experience burnout, but marital status is related to the condition. Single and divorced persons have been found to be more likely than married persons to experience emotional exhaustion. Emotional exhaustion also has been related to lack of opportunity for promotion. Burnout typically strikes employees who are highly dedicated and committed to their work—those who put in overtime, take work home, or come to the office on weekends.

Other factors have been related to burnout: feelings of time pressure, high levels of role conflict and role ambiguity, and lack of social support from supervisors. Research conducted in Australia showed that symptoms of burnout were related to high work–family conflict and low job satisfaction (Thompson, Brough, & Schmidt, 2006). In a study of 374 workers in Germany who were employed in industrial jobs, human service jobs (teachers and nurses), and in transportation (air-traffic controllers), researchers found that excessive job

Workaholism So-called addiction to work because of anxiety and insecurity or because of a genuine liking for the job.

demands and lack of job resources were significantly related to exhaustion and disengagement from work (Demerouti, Bakker, Nachreiner, & Schaufeli, 2001).

Research involving 1,010 police officers in Israel whose jobs included dealing with terrorist attacks (a highly stressful situation that could be considered a component of burnout) found that the stressors they reported were low pay, unfair treatment by supervisors, work overload, and insufficient resources with which to do their job. The ever-present possibility of being killed or seriously injured on the job were rated much lower as factors contributing to burnout (Malach-Pines & Keinan, 2007).

Another study conducted in Germany involved 591 flight attendants, travel agents, and shoe sales clerks. The results showed that dealing with customers contributed to job stress and burnout. Four customer-related social stressors were described: disproportionate customer expectations; verbally aggressive customers; hostile, humorless, or unpleasant customers; and unclear customer demands, which lead to employee role ambiguity (Dormann & Zapf, 2004).

An additional cause of burnout in the workplace is the feeling that one is being treated unfairly relative to other employees. This was demonstrated significantly in a study of 466 university employees (see Maslach & Leiter, 2008).

In a study of 40 managers of large companies and 125 other employees in a variety of clerical, managerial, and professional jobs, investigators found that burnout was negatively associated with decision-making opportunities in one's work. Burnout (particularly the depersonalization component) was more likely to occur when employees were given little choice about participating in making decisions relating to their jobs. Thus, the less influence they believed they had over their jobs, the greater the effects of burnout (Posig & Kickul, 2003). A study of health care workers in Sweden also indicated that high job demands and little control over work-related decisions contributed to burnout, as did a lack of support from superiors (Peterson, Demerouti, Bergstrom, Asberg, & Nygren, 2008).

Several personality characteristics have been related to burnout. A study of 296 nurses in acute care hospitals demonstrated that nurses who scored high on the Big Five personality factor of neuroticism were far more likely to experience burnout than were those who scored low on this factor. Nurses high in extraversion and agreeableness were less likely to develop burnout, primarily because these qualities allowed them to engage in more interpersonal and social activities, such as talking with co-workers about their job stresses. That type of interpersonal relationship provided social support, which was not experienced by those who scored low in extraversion and agreeableness (Zellars & Perrewe, 2001). The likelihood of experiencing burnout on the job is higher among people who score low in hardiness, high in external locus of control, or low in self-esteem.

Burnout affects people in different ways. Some employees affected by burnout may feel insecure and have unfulfilling personal lives. Because they lack self-esteem and recognition off the job, they try to find it on the job. By working hard and making significant contributions to the company, they earn esteem and tangible rewards and also prove to themselves that they are worthwhile. The price for prolonged overwork is an accumulation of stress and the depletion of the body's energy. This condition, in turn, leads to physical and psychological problems.

Workaholism

Employees also experience burnout are sometimes described as **workaholics**, people who are addicted to their work. However, not all people labeled as workaholics strive to perform well because they are driven by anxiety and insecurity. Some genuinely like their work and derive satisfaction from it. To them, work is not an unhealthful compulsion that gradually wears them down. Rather, work provides a healthful, enriching, and stimulating focus for their lives. These workaholics are happy, well-adjusted people who enjoy their jobs. They seldom take vacations because they feel no need to escape from their work. Because of their intense sense of commitment, however, they can be a source of stress to others.

Psychologists estimate that 5% of all employees are workaholics and that the majority of these are

Job engagement The true enjoyment of work that characterizes people who score high in energy, involvement, and efficacy.

content. These healthy workaholics are likely to have supportive families, autonomy and variety on the job, and tasks that match their levels of knowledge, skills, and abilities. Workaholics who lack these qualities tend to be discontent and dissatisfied. They are more susceptible to burnout and to the negative effects of stress. There is a distinction, then, between healthy and unhealthy workaholics. Healthy workaholics, or work enthusiasts, are highly committed to and involved with their work; they derive such intense enjoyment from their work that it seems inappropriate to characterize them as having a type of addictive behavior. I-O psychologists have proposed a new label for employees who truly love their work; they are described as being high in **job engagement** (Maslach, Schaufeli, & Leiter, 2001).

Job engagement is defined in terms of the three components of burnout—emotional exhaustion, depersonalization, and inefficacy—but people who score high in job engagement are described as high in energy, involvement, and efficacy. They are vigorous, resilient, willing to commit fully to their work, seldom fatigued, and persistent in the face of difficulties. They are enthusiastic about their work and take pride in it. Work is the center and focus of their lives and they are both unwilling and unable to detach themselves from it. Work is the source of their satisfaction, challenge, and fulfillment.

Research conducted in the Netherlands found that job engagement and experiencing joy in one's work were major factors contributing to employee well-being (Schaufeli, Taris, & Van Rhenen, 2008). Consistent with these findings, a study of workers in Norway showed that high self-efficacy and high extraversion were both related to joy in work and job engagement (Burke, Matthiesen, & Pallesen, 2006).

To take an online test to determine whether you are a healthy or unhealthy workaholic, go to Workaholics Anonymous at www.workaholics-anonymous.org/

STRESS-MANAGEMENT PROGRAMS

Both organizations and individuals can be active in managing workplace stress. Organizational stress-management interventions include altering the organizational climate and providing treatment under employee assistance programs (EAPs). Individual techniques for dealing with stress include relaxation training, biofeedback, and behavior modification.

Organizational Efforts

Controlling the Organizational Climate. Because one of the stressors of modem organizational life is planned change, the organization should provide sufficient support to enable employees to adapt to change. Stress can be prevented or reduced by allowing employees to participate in decisions about changes in work practices and in organizational structure. Participation helps employees accept change and allows them to express their opinions and air their complaints.

Providing Control. Employees' belief that they can exercise some control over their work greatly reduces the effects of stress. This was demonstrated in a nationwide survey of 2,048 U.S. workers. The results showed that workers who perceived fewer constraints on their job and greater decision-making ability, reported lower levels of job stress (Ettner & Grzywacz, 2001). Organizations can improve employees' sense of control by enriching, enlarging, and expanding jobs to provide greater responsibility and decision-making authority.

Defining Employee Roles. To reduce the stress caused by role ambiguity, managers should tell subordinates clearly what is expected of them and what their job responsibilities are.

Eliminating Work Overload and Work Underload. Appropriate employee selection and training programs, equitable promotion decisions, fair distribution of work, and proper matching of job requirements with employee abilities can help eliminate the stress of work overload and work underload.

Providing Social Support. Social support networks can reduce personal vulnerability to stress effects. A study of 211 traffic police officers found that burnout

Relaxation training A stress-reduction technique that concentrates on relaxing one part of the body after another.

was lowest among those who reported receiving the greatest support from their supervisors and their families (Baruch-Feldman, Brondolo, Ben-Dayan, & Schwartz, 2002). Organizations can enhance social support by promoting cohesive work groups and by training supervisors to show empathy and concern for subordinates.

Allowing Pets at Work. A growing number of companies allow their employees to bring their pets (usually dogs) to work with them. A study of 193 people who worked for employers with pet-tolerant policies found that those who brought pets to work reported lower levels of stress than those who did not bring their pets or who had no pets (Wells & Perrine, 2001).

Providing Stress-Management Programs. Employee assistance programs can include in-house counseling on managing stress. Evaluative research has been conducted on EAPs that teach individual stress control techniques such as relaxation, biofeedback, and cognitive restructuring. Studies show that these programs can reduce the level of physiological arousal associated with high stress. Participants who master behavioral and cognitive stress-relief techniques report less tension and fewer sleep disturbances, and an improved ability to cope with workplace stressors.

In a study of 130 employees in the Netherlands who participated in a corporate stress-management training program, researchers found significant reductions in anxiety and psychological distress, and improvements in assertiveness. These effects lasted up to 6 months. Social workers and other employees who received 2 days of training in managing stress were found to be just as effective in helping other employees reduce stress as were highly trained clinical psychologists (de Jong & Emmelkamp, 2000). In a meta-analysis of 36 studies of organizational stress-management programs, relaxation techniques were reported as the most frequently used method to reduce stress (Richardson & Rothstein, 2008).

A study was conducted to compare a live instructor with a computer-based stress-management program. Both approaches resulted in significant reductions in stress when stress was measured immediately after the instruction. However, many more people dropped out of the computer-based program, citing time constraints and technical problems with the software. The instructor-led program kept more people in attendance, which reduced their stress levels over a longer period of time (Eisen, Allen, Bollash, & Pescatello, 2008).

Providing Fitness Programs. The number of organizations offering wellness or physical fitness programs to promote occupational health is now well over 80%. By enhancing their physical and emotional well-being, employees may become less vulnerable to the effects of stress. The focus is on counseling employees to change or modify unhealthful behaviors and to maintain a healthful lifestyle. Although such programs are sponsored by the organization, the responsibility for healthful behaviors—such as exercising, eating properly, and stopping smoking—rests with the employee. A meta-analysis of 17 studies involving more than 7,700 employees found that organizational fitness and wellness programs reduced stress and had the additional benefits of increasing job satisfaction and lowering absenteeism rates (Parks & Steelman, 2008).

Individual Efforts

Some individual techniques for dealing with stress can be taught in company-sponsored EAPs or stress reduction programs. Others can be adopted personally, such as a program of physical exercise. Exercise can increase stamina and endurance, reduce risk factors for coronary heart disease, and dissipate excess energy and tension. Many companies sponsor physical fitness programs and provide exercise facilities and running tracks at the workplace. Other individual techniques for reducing stress are relaxation training and biofeedback.

Relaxation Training. As early as the 1930s, **relaxation training** was promoted as a way to reduce stress. Clients are taught to concentrate on one part of the body after another, systematically tensing and relaxing the muscles. By focusing on

Biofeedback   A stress-reduction technique that involves electronic monitoring of physiological processes so that people can learn to control muscle tension, blood pressure, and brain waves.

the sensations produced by the relaxed state, they are able to achieve progressively deeper relaxation. Psychologists have proposed several refinements of this basic technique. In autogenic training, participants learn to relax by imagining that their limbs are growing warm and heavy. In meditation, participants concentrate on deep, regular breathing and the repetition of a phrase or sound. The relaxation-response approach combines these two techniques. The quieting reflex technique teaches subjects to achieve the relaxed state more quickly. Feedback on muscle tension can be combined with these approaches, along with self-measurement of blood pressure before and after relaxation exercises.

Biofeedback.   **Biofeedback** is a popular technique for dealing with the effects of stress. It involves electronic measurement of physiological processes

Newsbreak

Take a Vacation—and Don't Call the Office!

Workers in the United States don't take enough time off as a way of slowing down and recharging to help avoid stress, work overload, and burnout. Europeans take much more annual vacation time than Americans do. Workers in the United States get fewer paid vacation days than French or German workers, and many U.S. workers do not even use the days to which they are entitled. A survey conducted by Expedia, the online travel service, of 2,019 adults found that at least 30% gave up earned vacation time every year. On average, every full-time U.S. worker misses out on 3 vacation days a year, and each year workers tend to take less time off than they did the year before.

The Expedia survey also showed that 32% of the people who took vacations managed to take their work with them, checking e-mail or office voicemail regularly. They carried the stress of their job with them. Consequently, companies such as RadioShack, concerned about employee burnout, are trying to induce employees to change their behavior by introducing what they call a guilt-free vacation program. The program has one simple rule: Don't call the office while you're on vaca-tion. Other companies *insist* that employees at all levels actually take their vacations instead of accumulating the time for extra pay.

But is a forced vacation the best way to relieve stress and prevent burnout? Dov Eden, a management professor at Tel Aviv University in Israel, studied several thousand employees before and after their vacations. The results were not encouraging. The benefits from the break dissipated after only 3 weeks. Employees quickly returned to their prevacation levels of stress. It was as if they had never been away. And many people don't ever get away from their work. Eden says, "Using cell phones and checking company e-mail at poolside is not a vacation. People who do this are shackled to electronic tethers."

James Quick, a professor of organizational behavior at the University of Texas at Arlington, discovered that the incidence of heart attacks rises on Monday mornings, when people return to work from their weekend break. He suggested that a longer vacation may bring an even greater risk. So what's the choice? Your work may be stressful, but now it appears that your vacation can also be harmful to your health!

Sources: Galant, D. (2000, July 12). Now for the hard part: It's over. *New York Times*; Yahoo Financial News, June 6, 2004. Retrieved from www.biz.yahoo.com; Rosenbloom, S. (2006, August 10). Please don't make me go on vacation. *New York Times*; Burning out? Try logging off (2007, November 30). *Science Daily.* Retrieved from www.sciencedaily.com/news/health_medicine/workplace_health/

such as heart rate, blood pressure, and muscle tension. These measurements are converted into signals, such as flashing lights or beeps, which provide feedback on how a bodily process is operating.

Using the feedback, people then learn to control their internal states. For example, suppose that a light is activated on a monitor whenever your heart is beating at a relaxed rate. With practice, you can learn to keep the light on by maintaining that relaxed heart rate. Precisely how you learn to do this has not been established, but with enough practice, you can control your heart rate and soon will no longer need feedback from the light to do so.

Biofeedback can be used to control muscle tension, blood pressure, body temperature, brain waves, and stomach acid. By reducing the physiological changes that accompany stress, people can reduce the incidence of stress-related disorders.

Summary

Occupational health psychology is concerned with the effects of stress in the workplace. Stress lowers employees' productivity, increases absenteeism and turnover, and causes physiological changes. Prolonged stress can be a factor in the psychosomatic origins of illnesses, including heart disease, gastrointestinal distress, arthritis, skin diseases, allergies, headaches, and cancer. Factors that can reduce stress include high job satisfaction, control, high autonomy and power, social support, good health, job skills, and certain personality characteristics.

People high in **hardiness** believe they can control life events, make a commitment to work, and view change as stimulating; they are less vulnerable to the effects of stress. Similarly, people high in self-efficacy, internal **locus of control** and self-esteem, and low in negative affectivity, are less vulnerable to stress.

Causes of stress may include work–family conflicts, **work overload** and **work underload**, organizational change, **role ambiguity** and **role conflict**, computer use, contact with stress carriers, and physical conditions of the workplace. Consequences of stress may be long-term effects such as psychosomatic disorders and short-term effects on health, behavior, and job performance.

Burnout is related to prolonged overwork, feelings of time pressure, high role conflict and role ambiguity, and lack of social support. It results in lower productivity, exhaustion, irritability, rigidity, and social withdrawal. Employees who are high on the Big Five factor of neuroticism are more likely to experience burnout. Employees affected with burnout are sometimes considered to be **workaholics** who are compulsively driven to work hard out of insecurity and lack of fulfillment in their personal lives. Healthy workaholics, who score high in **job engagement**, derive satisfaction from work and are free of the stress effects of burnout.

Organizational techniques for coping with stress include control of the organizational climate, clear definition of employee roles, elimination of work overload and underload, social support, stress-management programs, and wellness and physical fitness programs. Individual techniques such as physical exercise, **relaxation training**, and **biofeedback**, help employees reduce stress.

Key Terms

biofeedback
burnout
hardiness
job engagement
locus of control
negative affectivity

occupational health psychology
organization-based self-esteem
    (OBSE)
relaxation training
role ambiguity
role conflict

stress
work overload
work underload
workaholism

Review Questions

1. How can you tell when you are experiencing stress? Describe some of the mental and physical problems that can be caused by stress.

2. Describe the history and purpose of occupational health psychology.

3. What physiological changes occur in the body in reaction to stress?

4. Explain how the cumulative effect of minor hassles and insults of everyday life can affect health.

5. What are the major job-related factors that can prevent the harmful effects of job stress?

6. Explain why air-traffic controllers and senior executives may be less affected by stress than middle-level managers?

7. Describe the roles of social support, general physical condition, and the ability to perform a job well as these relate to a person's vulnerability to the effects of stress.

8. How do the following personality characteristics account for individual differences in reactions to stress: hardiness, locus of control, and negative affectivity?

9. What is self-efficacy? How can it affect our reactions to stress and our ability to cope with stressful situations at work?

10. Define the concept of organization-based self-esteem. How can it influence a person's reaction to job stress?

11. What types of occupations are high in stress? Which ones rank low in stress?

12. Why are work–family conflicts generally greater for women than for men?

13. In what ways do work–family conflicts differ among Western, Eastern, and Latin cultures? In your opinion, what accounts for these differences?

14. How can organizations reduce problems associated with work–family conflicts?

15. Explain the differences between qualitative work overload and quantitative work overload.

16. How can work underload be as stressful as work overload?

17. Describe how the following can be a source of stress: organizational change, role ambiguity, role conflict.

18. Do you think the widespread use of computers in the workplace adds to job stress? If so, how?

19. Do you think computers, cell phones, and other personal electronic devices at work and in everyday life make our lives more stressful or less stressful? Why?

20. What are the major causes and components of burnout? What personality characteristics are related to burnout?

21. Define job engagement. How does it differ from workaholism? Describe the characteristics of a person who scores high in job engagement.

22. What approaches do organizations take to treat job stress?

23. How do you deal with stress in your life?

Additional Reading

Allen, D. (2001). *Getting things done: The art of stress-free productivity.* New York: Viking. Offers advice on decision making to minimize stress and maximize productivity. Suggests dividing tasks into categories: do it yourself, delegate it, defer action on it, or drop it.

Maslach, C., Schaufeli, W. B., & Leiter, M. P. (2001). Job burnout. *Annual Review of Psychology, 52,* 397–422. Burnout, the prolonged response to chronic emotional and interpersonal job stressors, is described in terms of exhaustion, cynicism, and inefficacy. Describes recent research on "engagement," the antithesis of burnout, which suggests possible interventions to alleviate the burnout syndrome.

Nelson, D. B., & Burke, R. J. (2000). Women executives: health, stress, and success. *Academy of Management Executive, 14*(2), 107–121. Explores the unique health issues of women with high-level jobs outside the home. Describes stressors, ways of coping, and effects on organizational effectiveness.

Pitt-Catsouphes, M., Kossek, E., & Sweet, S. (Eds.). (2006). *The work and family handbook*. Mahway, NJ: Erlbaum. Focuses on work–family balance from an historical perspective to the twenty-first century; reviews legal issues and government polices, the changing nature of the workforce, the role of the community, problems of single parents, and increasing demands for leisure time.

Wright, T. A., & Cropanzano, R. (2000). The role of organizational behavior in occupational health psychology. *Journal of Occupational Health Psychology, 5,* 5–10. Introduces a special section of nine articles highlighting the effects on organizations of employee health and psychological well-being.

PART FIVE

Engineering Psychology

Engineering psychologists are involved in designing the comfortable, safe, and efficient environments in which we live and work. From the adjustability of office chairs and the brightness level of the data displayed on computer monitors to the controls of cars or cell phones, psychologists work to make jobs less stressful and employees more productive. Chapter 13 describes the contributions of engineering psychologists to the design of tools, equipment, work areas, and other aspects of daily life so that they are compatible with employees' abilities and needs.

CHAPTER 13

Engineering Psychology

CHAPTER OUTLINE

THE DEVELOPMENT OF ENGINEERING PSYCHOLOGY

We have discussed various ways in which I-O psychologists contribute to the organizational goals of increasing employee efficiency, productivity, and job satisfaction. We have considered how employees with the best abilities can be recruited and selected, trained for their jobs, and supervised and motivated effectively. We have described techniques that can be applied to optimize the quality of work life and the conditions of the work environment. But we have mentioned only briefly a factor as influential as any of these—the design of the machines and equipment people use to do their jobs and the workspaces in which those tasks are performed.

Machines, tools, equipment, and workstations must be compatible with the workers who use them. Think of a team operation, a person and a machine functioning together to perform a task that could not be accomplished by either working alone. If the person and the machine are to work

Newsbreak

It's Your Choice, Part 1: Believe the Person or the Machine?

At 11:40 on the night of July 1, 2002, two aircraft were on a collision course over southern Germany. Unless one or both of them took evasive action immediately, they would collide in less time than it will take you to read this paragraph. One plane was a cargo jet with a crew of two. The other was a chartered airliner from Russia with 71 people on board, including 43 children. Both planes were equipped with computerized collision avoidance systems that instantly recognized the impending disaster and triggered audible and visible warnings in each cockpit with urgent instructions for the pilots.

The automated systems told the pilot of the cargo jet to dive to a lower altitude, an action he took immediately. A similar system told the Russian pilot to climb to a higher altitude, but he hesitated, first contacting an air-traffic controller to ask for additional instructions.

Two controllers were scheduled to be on duty that night, but one was taking a break while the other tried to keep track of the five aircraft in his sector. The controller also had a computerized alarm system, which at that instant could have provided him with the information that the two planes were on a collision course. But the system had been shut down for routine maintenance. There was no backup.

When the Russian pilot reported the alarm in his cockpit, the controller told him to dive, which was the opposite of what his warning system was telling him to do. So now, with 70 lives in his hands, he had conflicting instructions: go up or go down. Was he to believe the human—the air-traffic controller—or was he to believe the insistent alarm from the machine? He chose to believe the human. It was the wrong choice. A minute later, the two planes smashed into each other. Everyone aboard was killed.

There is a postscript to this tragedy. Many months later, on February 26, 2004, the unfortunate air-traffic controller answered a knock on the door of his house near Zurich, Switzerland. The visitor, whose wife and two children had died in the crash, stabbed the man to death. Three years later, four employees of the Swiss air-traffic control system were found guilty of creating a "culture of negligence" that contributed to the collision. Three were given suspended prison sentences and the fourth was fined. In this tragedy, the machines worked as they were designed to do; it was the people who failed.

Sources: Johnson, G. (2002, July 14). To err is human. *New York Times;* Revenge suspected as motive for killing of air controller (2004, February 26). *Chechen Times.* Retrieved from www.chechentimes.net/; Silence for slain air controller (2004, March 5). BBC News, World Edition. Retrieved from www.news.bbc.co.uk; Four guilty over Swiss air crash (2007, April 9). BBC News, World Edition. Retrieved from www.news.bbc.uk

Engineering psychology   The design of machines and equipment for human use and the determination of the appropriate human behaviors for the efficient operation of the machines. The field is also called human factors, human engineering, and ergonomics.

smoothly in this person–machine system, they must be compatible, so that each makes use of the strengths of the other and, where necessary, compensates for the weaknesses of the other.

This pairing of operator and machine is the province of **engineering psychology**, also called human factors or human engineering. British psychologists use the term *ergonomics*, which is derived from the Greek word *ergon*, meaning work, and *nomos*, meaning natural laws. In conjunction with engineers, engineering psychologists apply their knowledge of psychology to the formulation of natural laws of work. Thus, engineering psychology is the science of designing or engineering machines and equipment for human use and of engineering human behavior for the efficient operation of the machines.

Until the 1940s, the design of machinery, equipment, and industrial plants was solely the responsibility of engineers. They made design decisions on the basis of mechanical, electrical, space, and size considerations. They paid little attention to the workers who would have to operate the machines. The machine was considered to be a constant factor, incapable of being changed to meet human needs; the employee would have to adapt. No matter how uncomfortable, tiring, or unsafe the equipment was, the human operators—the only flexible part of the person–machine system—had to adjust, to make the best of the situation and fit themselves to the machine's requirements.

Adapting the worker to the machine was accomplished through time-and-motion study, a forerunner of engineering psychology, in which jobs were analyzed to determine how they could be simplified. But this approach to designing machines while ignoring the needs of the people who operated them could not be maintained. Machines were becoming too complex, requiring levels of speed, skill, and attention that threatened to exceed human capacities to monitor and control them.

Impetus of Military Needs.   The weapons developed for use in World War II placed greater demands on human abilities, not only muscle strength but also sensing, perceiving, judging, and making split-

second decisions. For example, pilots of sophisticated fighter aircraft were allowed little time to react to a dangerous situation, to determine a course of action, and to initiate the appropriate response. Radar and sonar operators also required high levels of skill. In general, the wartime equipment worked well, but mistakes were frequent. The most precise bombsight ever developed was not leading to accurate bombing. Friendly ships and aircraft were being misidentified and fired upon. Whales were mistaken for submarines. Although the machinery seemed to be functioning properly, the system—the interaction of the person and the machine—clearly was not.

It was this wartime need that spurred the development of engineering psychology, similar to the way the screening and selection needs of the army in World War I gave rise to mass psychological testing. Authorities recognized that human abilities and limitations would have to be taken into account while designing machines if the overall system was to operate efficiently. Psychologists, physiologists, and physicians soon joined engineers to design aircraft cockpits, submarine and tank crew stations, and components of military uniforms.

An example of this early work helped American pilots stay alive. At the time, there was no consistent or standard arrangement of displays and controls within the cockpits of different models of aircraft. A pilot accustomed to one type of plane who was suddenly assigned to another would be confronted by a different set of displays and controls. The lever to raise the wheels in the new plane might be in the same place as the lever to operate the flaps in the old plane. Imagine trying to drive a car in which gas pedal and brake pedal are reversed. In an emergency you would probably step on what you thought was the brake pedal but would be stepping on the gas instead.

There was also no consistency in the operating characteristics of aircraft controls. Within the same cockpit, one control might be pushed upward to turn something on and another switched downward to turn something on. Separate controls with identical knobs were often placed close together so that a pilot whose attention was diverted would not be able to distinguish among the controls by touch alone. As these problems were recognized, they were corrected. Nevertheless, many pilots were killed because their machines had been designed poorly from the reference point of the pilot, whose job was to direct and control the aircraft's power.

Inadequate attention to the human factor also led to other kinds of accidents as the machines and equipment designed for work, and for pleasure, became more complicated. In 1979, a disastrous situation occurred at the nuclear power plant at Three Mile Island, Pennsylvania. The accident occurred during the night shift when the operators were less alert, but part of the problem involved a lack of attention to human needs. In the power plant's control room, instrument dials and controls had been placed too far apart. When operators detected a dangerous reading on one of the displays, valuable time was lost because the employees had to run to another part of the room to activate controls to correct the malfunction. To prevent a recurrence, the Nuclear Regulatory Commission ordered modification of the control rooms of nuclear power plants to consider the abilities and the limitations of the human operators.

To deal with human factors in aircraft accidents, 66% of which can be traced to pilot error, the National Transportation Safety Board added engineering psychologists to its staff. Their job is to investigate pilot and crew fatigue, shift work schedules, health issues, stress, and equipment design—all of which can contribute to accidents.

Much human factors research has been conducted on passenger cars to make them safer. Variables studied include the brightness of automobile and motorcycle headlights; the position, color, and brightness of brake lights; and the layout of dashboard controls and displays. Since 1985, passenger cars driven in the United States must have a brake light mounted in the rear window. This requirement is a result of human factors research on 8,000 vehicles that showed that a high-mounted brake light reduced the incidence of rear-end collisions by 50%.

The work of human factors specialists influences many other aspects of our lives. They are studying ways to make license plates and traffic signs more legible and noticeable at night. They investigate the effects of alcohol on driver behavior and conduct research on driver reaction time—how drivers perceive and comprehend risky situations and make decisions about responding.

Another problem engineering psychologists are tackling is the effect on visibility of tinting or solar film on car windows. Research results show that the detection of objects, such as pedestrians or other cars, through the rear window while backing up is significantly reduced when that window is tinted. In some cases, a tinted window admits only half of the available light, a finding that has led many states to regulate the use of solar film for safe visibility. Older drivers are more affected by dark window tints than are younger drivers. One study found that drivers between the ages of 60 and 69 experienced a greater reduction in contrast sensitivity to light than did drivers between the ages of 20 and 29 (LaMotte, Ridder, Yeung, & DeLand, 2000).

Research has demonstrated that text messaging or talking on cell phones while driving reduces reaction time and can lead to a higher accident risk among drivers of all ages. These and similar research findings are instigating state regulation of cell phone use.

Design for Ergonomic Needs. Engineering psychologists contribute to the design of a variety of other products, including dental and surgical implements, cameras, toothbrushes, and bucket seats for cars. They have been involved in the redesign of the mailbags used by letter carriers. Why? Because more than 20% of letter carriers report musculoskeletal problems such as low back pain from carrying mailbags slung over their shoulders. A mailbag with a waist-support strap, and a double bag that requires the use of both shoulders, have been shown to reduce muscle fatigue.

The most well-developed human factors programs in the United States and in European and Asian nations are in the automobile, electronics, and food industries, as well as in the design of workstations for a variety of businesses. The following companies have been active in applying human factors findings to their workplaces and products: General Motors, Daimler Benz, SAAB, Volvo, IBM, and other computer makers.

An analysis of the economic benefits to corporations of applying ergonomic research showed net gains between 1% and 12% over the cost of the human factors intervention. These financial gains almost always accrued in less than a year after incorporating human factors changes. One example is the introduction of the high-mounted brake light on automobiles, which cost the industry about

Time-and-motion study An early attempt to redesign work tools and to reshape the way workers performed routine, repetitive jobs.

Newsbreak

Engineering Psychology Is a Hot Career Choice—Seriously

Recent years have seen a growing demand for engineering psychologists and a growing number of students interested in the field, not only for the job opportunities but because, as one graduate student wrote, "The purpose of engineering psychology is to deliberately make someone's life better." After developing a new global positioning system (GPS) system for an automobile company, one psychologist was proud that drivers would be safer because of her work. She said, "That's satisfying in a way that publishing a paper is not."

The primary reason why the demand for engineering psychologists is so strong is the realization on the part of industry leaders that psychologists help them develop better products that are easier, more pleasant, and safer for customers and clients to use. In turn, this means that the company can sell more items. "People are really starring to understand that there is a need for psychologists, for specialists, who can evaluate data on a prod-

uct's or a system's use and provide recommendations. Engineers [alone] can't account for every interaction within a system because they aren't so familiar with the *human* system."

The salaries of engineering psychologists reflect the demand. The average pay for a graduate with a master's degree in private industry is more than $90,000 a year. Those with a PhD earn an average of $111,000 annually. Consultants with a doctorate typically earn approximately $180,000 a year. And the added benefit is actually making a difference in people's everyday lives. Not many jobs offer that kind of satisfaction.

To learn more about the field of human factors, check out the Web sites of the Human Factors and Ergonomics Society at www.hfes.org/web and Division 21 (Applied Experimental and Engineering Psychology) of the American Psychological Association at www.apa.org/divisions/div21

Source: Packard, E. (2007). Postgrad growth area: Engineering psychology. *Gradpsych, 5*(2), 34–36.

$10 per car. The annual return on that modest initial investment has been approximately $434 million in lower car repair costs resulting from the 50% drop in rear-end collisions (Stanton & Baber, 2003).

Because the field of engineering psychology is a hybrid, it is not surprising that its practitioners have diverse backgrounds. The membership of the Human Factors and Ergonomics Society consists primarily of psychologists and engineers, but it also includes professionals from medicine, sociology, anthropology, computer sciences, and other behavioral and physical sciences. During the past decade there has been a substantial increase in the number of master's-level

psychologists undertaking careers in engineering psychology. The growth of the field remains dynamic, and its work extends to many types of organizations.

TIME-AND-MOTION STUDY

Time-and-motion study was an early attempt to redesign work tools and equipment and to reshape the way workers performed their jobs. It stemmed from the efforts of three pioneers who focused on ways to make physical labor more efficient.

The first systematic attempt to study the performance of specific job tasks began in 1898 when

Frederick W. Taylor, the promoter of scientific management, undertook an investigation of the nature of shoveling at the request of a large U.S. steel manufacturer. Taylor observed the workers and found that they were using shovels of many sizes and shapes. As a result, the loads being lifted by each man ranged from $3\frac{1}{2}$ pounds to 38 pounds. By experimenting with different loads, Taylor determined that the optimum shovel—the one with which workers were most efficient—held $21\frac{1}{2}$ pounds. Lighter or heavier loads resulted in a decrease in total daily output. Taylor introduced shovels of different sizes for handling different materials, for example, a small one for heavy iron ore and a larger one for ashes. These changes may sound trivial, but Taylor's work saved the company more than $78,000 a year, an enormous sum at that time. With the new shovels, 140 men could accomplish the same amount of work that previously required 500 men. By offering an incentive of higher pay for greater productivity, the company allowed workers to increase their wages by 60% (Taylor, 1911).

Taylor's work was the first empirical demonstration of the relationship between work tools and worker efficiency. The next pioneers in the field were Frank Gilbreth, an engineer, and Lillian Gilbreth, a psychologist, who did more than anyone else to promote time-and-motion study. Whereas Taylor had been concerned primarily with tool design and incentive wage systems, the Gilbreths were interested in the mechanics of job performance. Their goal was to eliminate all unnecessary motion (Gilbreth, 1911).

It began when Frank Gilbreth at age 17 was working as an apprentice bricklayer. During his first day on the job, he noticed that the bricklayers made many unnecessary motions in doing their work. He thought he could redesign the job to make it faster and easier, and within a year he was the fastest bricklayer on the job. Once he persuaded his co-workers to try his methods, the entire crew was accomplishing far more work without becoming exhausted.

Gilbreth designed a scaffold that could be raised or lowered so that the worker would always be at a height convenient to the task. By analyzing the hand and arm movements involved in laying bricks and changing to the most efficient ones, he found that workers could lay 350 bricks an hour instead of 120. This increase in productivity was not brought about by forcing men to work faster but by reducing the number of motions needed for laying each brick from 18 to $4\frac{1}{2}$.

Frank and Lillian Gilbreth organized their household and their personal lives around the principles of time-and-motion economy. Every activity was scrutinized for wasted motion. For example, Frank Gilbreth always buttoned his vest from the bottom up because it took 4 seconds less than buttoning it from the top down. He used two brushes, one in each hand, to lather his face for shaving, a savings of 17 seconds. He tried shaving with two razors simultaneously but lost more time bandaging cuts than he had saved in shaving. The efforts to schedule the activities of the 12 Gilbreth children were recounted in a popular book and movie, *Cheaper by the Dozen.* To learn more about the life and work of Taylor, go to www.netmba.com/mgmt/scientific/ For more about Frank and Lillian Gilbreth, see gilbrethnetwork.tripod.com/bio.html and www.webster.edu/~woolflm/gilbreth2.html

Time-and-motion engineers (sometimes called *efficiency experts*) have applied the Gilbreths' techniques to many types of jobs, with the goal of reducing the number of motions required. The familiar operating room procedure of having nurses place each tool in the surgeon's hand is an outgrowth of time-and-motion analysis. Previously, surgeons sought out tools themselves, a practice that greatly increased operating time.

The next time you see a United Parcel Service track stop to make a delivery, watch how the driver behaves. Every move has been dictated by time-and-motion analysis to ensure a fast delivery. Drivers carry packages only under their left arm, step out of the truck with their right foot, cover 3 feet per second when they walk, and hold their truck's keys with the teeth face up. Unnecessary and wasteful motions have been eliminated. These procedures allow the drivers to work faster and more efficiently without creating extra work and stress.

The most significant results of time-and-motion analysis have been with routine and repetitive work. In a typical motion study a worker's movements are recorded on video and analyzed with a view to modifying or eliminating inefficient and wasteful motions. (The same technique is applied by sports psychologists and coaches to analyze the performance of athletes.)

Newsbreak

You May Be Efficient, But Lillian Gilbreth Did It Better

Lillian Moller thought she was so plain that no one would marry her so she decided to have a career. This was an unpopular notion for a 22-year-old woman in the year 1900. She graduated from the University of California at Berkeley that year and was the first woman to be chosen as the school's commencement speaker. She stayed on at Berkeley to study for her PhD in English literature with a minor in psychology. In 1904, her plans were upset when she met a handsome, charismatic, wealthy owner of a construction company.

Frank Gilbreth was 10 years older than Lillian. He lived in Boston, where Lillian and some friends had stopped on their way to Europe. When they returned, Frank was waiting at the dock with flowers. He traveled to California to meet her parents and set the date for the wedding. Frank wanted a wife, children, and all the pleasures of domesticity, but he also desired a partner for his work. At his urging, Lillian changed her major to psychology and enrolled in graduate school at Brown University. She worked alongside him at construction sites, climbing ladders and striding across steel girders. A fearless and fast learner, Lillian was soon helping Frank with decisions that would make construction work more efficient. She encouraged Frank to give up the construction business and become a management consultant, so they could apply their ideas about work performance and efficiency to a broad range of jobs.

But the times decreed that women couldn't do such things. That was made clear to Lillian in 1911, when she and Frank wrote a book, *Motion Study.* The publisher refused to list her as co-author, claiming that a woman's name would detract from the book's credibility. The same thing happened a year later with their next book. In 1914, Lillian completed her PhD in psychology, but when she tried to publish her dissertation in book form, the publisher would not let her use her first name, insisting that hardheaded business-

men would never buy a book on the psychology of management written by a woman. Consequently, the title page listed the author as L. M. Gilbreth.

Twenty years later, with a thriving consulting business and 12 children to rear, Lillian Moller Gilbreth was widowed. She tried to carry on the work, but most of the business executives for whom she and Frank consulted now cut her off. They had been willing to tolerate her as a wife helping her husband but wanted nothing to do with her on her own.

If she could no longer apply time-and-motion study in the workplace, the business she and Frank had built, she decided to teach others how to do it. She organized workshops on industrial management, attracting participants from many countries. These workshops, and the quality of her trainees, enhanced her reputation so that eventually business and industrial organizations began to seek her advice.

Over the years, Lillian Gilbreth became immensely successful and influential. She was awarded several honorary degrees, received appointments to presidential commissions, and won accolades from the male-dominated engineering community. One business leader called her "the world's greatest woman engineer." She and Frank earned an additional measure of fame with the 1950 movie *Cheaper by the Dozen* about how they brought up 12 children according to the principles of time-and-motion study. (A remake, starring Steve Martin, was released in 2003.)

Lillian Gilbreth died in 1972, in her nineties, still at work in the field of scientific management. She applied her ideas to all types of problems. The next time you open your refrigerator, notice the shelves on the inside of the door. That was her idea. Does your trash can have a foot pedal to operate the lid? That was her idea, too. Lillian Gilbreth's contributions in applying the principles of time-and-motion economy were so extensive that they touched

Person–machine system   A system in which human and mechanical components operate together to accomplish a task.

everyday tasks not only at home, but in factories, shops, and offices, making work for everyone a little easier. Her influence and popularity remain secure, even in the twenty-first century, through the publication of another biography (Lancaster, 2004).

Sources: Kelly, R. M., & Kelly, V. P. (1990). Lillian Moller Gilbreth (1878–1972). In A. N. O'Connell & N. F. Russo (Eds.), *Women in psychology: A bio-bibliographic sourcebook* (pp. 117–124). New York: Greenwood Press; Lancaster, J. (2004). *Making time: Lillian Moller Gilbreth: A life beyond "Cheaper by the dozen."* Boston: Northeastern University Press.

Guidelines for Efficient Work

Based on years of research, psychologists have developed guidelines for efficient work. Rules for increasing the ease, speed, and accuracy of manual jobs include the following:

1. Minimize the distance workers must reach to get tools and supplies or to operate machines.
2. Both hands should begin and end their movement at the same time. Movements should be as symmetrical as possible. The right hand should reach to the right for one item as the left hand reaches to the left for another item.
3. Hands should never be idle except during authorized rest breaks.
4. Hands should never do tasks that can be performed by other parts of the body, particularly legs and feet. A foot control can often be used, thus relieving the hands of one more operation.
5. Whenever possible, work materials should be held by a mechanical device, such as a vise, instead of being held by hand.
6. The workbench or worktable should be of sufficient height that the job can be performed when standing or when sitting on a high stool. Alternating positions relieves fatigue.

You might think that these guidelines for simplifying jobs would be received with enthusiasm. After all, the company reaps a greater output and employees' jobs are made easier. Although management has generally been pleased with the results of time-and-motion study, workers and labor unions have been suspicious, even hostile. They have argued that the only reason for time-and-motion study is to force employees to work faster. This would lead to lower pay and to dismissals, because fewer workers would be needed to maintain production levels. These concerns do have some validity. Other worker complaints are that job simplification leads to boredom, to a lack of challenge and responsibility, and to low motivation, which is manifested in lower productivity.

Time-and-motion analysis is most applicable today for routine tasks such as assembly-line jobs. When operations, equipment, and functions are more complex and the total relationship between person and machine must be considered, a more sophisticated approach to the person–machine interaction is needed.

PERSON-MACHINE SYSTEMS

A **person–machine system** is one in which both components work together to accomplish a task. Neither part is of value without the other. A person pushing a lawnmower is a person–machine system. A person driving a car or playing a video game is a more complex person–machine system. At a more sophisticated level, an airliner and its crew of specialists, each responsible for a different operation, is a person–machine system. An air-traffic control network includes a number of separate person–machine systems, each an integral part of the whole. If one part—mechanical or human—fails, all other parts of the system will be affected.

In all person–machine systems, the human operator receives input on the status of the machine from

An airplane cockpit is a complex person–machine system. Displays present information on the machine's status. The flight engineer processes the information and initiates action by operating the appropriate controls.

the displays. On the basis of this information, the operator regulates the equipment by using the controls to initiate some action (see Figure 13-1). Suppose you are driving a car on a highway at a constant speed. You receive input from the speedometer (a display), process this information mentally, and decide that you are driving much faster than the speed limit. Through the control action of easing your foot off the accelerator, you cause the computer-aided fuel injection system to reduce the flow of gasoline to the engine, which slows the speed of the car. This decrease in speed is displayed on the speedometer for your information, and so the process continues.

A driver also receives information from the external environment, such as a sign noting a change in the speed limit or a slow car blocking the lane. The driver processes this information and dictates a change in speed to the machine. Verification

of the altered status of the machine—the new speed—is displayed on the speedometer. The principle is the same for even the most sophisticated person–machine systems. It is the total system that is the starting point for the engineering psychologist's job.

Person–machine systems vary in the extent to which the human operator is actively and continuously involved. In flying an airplane or controlling traffic at a busy airport, operators are necessary most of the time. Even when an airplane is on automatic pilot, the flight crew must be prepared to assume control in an emergency. In other person–machine systems, humans interact less extensively. Many large-scale production processes, such as those in oil refineries, are highly automated. Some products and components can be assembled entirely by industrial robots. Although this automated equipment can operate itself, it cannot design, build, or maintain itself, or replace its own lightbulb. Humans remain important components of such automated manufacturing systems even when they are not directly or continuously operating the equipment.

Automation has complicated the task of engineering psychologists. Employees who are required to monitor automated equipment find that task to be more fatiguing and boring than the job of actually running a machine. Engineering psychologists must design monitoring equipment to keep observers alert and vigilant so that they can detect errors and malfunctions and respond immediately and appropriately.

In general, the definition and requirements of person–machine systems are the same regardless of the degree of involvement of the worker with the machine. No one has yet developed a machine that can design, build, and maintain other machines. Humans are still vital to the system.

FIGURE 13-1 A person–machine system. (Adapted from "Human Factors in the Workplace" by W. C. Howell, 1991. In M. D. Dunnette and L. M. Hough (Eds.), *Handbook of Industrial and Organizational Psychology*, 2nd ed., vol. 2, p. 214. Palo Alto, CA: Consulting Psychologists Press.)

Allocating Functions

The initial step in the design of a person–machine system involves making decisions about the division of labor between the human operator and the machine. To do that, each step or process in the functioning of the total system must be analyzed to determine its characteristics: the speed, accuracy, and frequency with which it is performed; and the stress under which it occurs. After evaluating this information, the engineering psychologist can proceed to match the requirements of the system with the abilities of the person and of the machine. Each component—person and machine—has its advantages and its limitations.

Research by psychologists, physiologists, and physicians has provided considerable information about human strengths and weaknesses, revealing those functions for which humans are superior or inferior to machines. In general, machines are better than humans in performing the following functions:

- Machines can detect stimuli such as radar wavelengths and ultraviolet light that are beyond human sensory capacities.
- Machines can monitor reliably for lengthy periods as long as the stimulus in question is programmed or specified in advance for the machine.
- Machines can make large numbers of rapid, accurate calculations.
- Machines can store and retrieve huge amounts of information with a high level of accuracy.
- Machines can apply greater physical force continuously and rapidly.
- Machines can engage in repetitive activities with no performance deterioration as long as proper maintenance is applied.

Of course, machines are not perfect. They have several weaknesses and limitations:

- Machines are not very flexible. Even the most sophisticated computer can do only what it is programmed to do. When the system requires the ability to adapt to changing circumstances, machines are at a disadvantage.
- Machines cannot learn from errors or modify their behavior on the basis of past experience. Any change in operation must be built into the system or initiated by the human operator.
- Machines cannot improvise; they are unable to reason or to examine unprogrammed alternatives.

As early as the 1930s, many industrialists, such as Thomas Watson, the founder of IBM, began to change drastically the nature of work by taking workers away from jobs that machines could perform better and more efficiently. As Watson put it, "Machines should work. People should think" (quoted in Boff, 2006, p. 391). As more and more systems have become automated, the tendency has been to eliminate the worker from the system as much as possible and to let the machine do both the working and the thinking.

Automation: Reducing the Human Role

Some engineers believe that they should automate every possible function in a person–machine system, relegating the operator to a peripheral role. However, fully automated systems can fail, sometimes with disastrous results. Consider modern mass transit systems. In some subway lines, drivers do not control the train's speed or bring the train to a stop at station platforms. Those functions are controlled by computer.

In a study of the Metrorail system in Miami, Florida, trains failed to stop at stations 10% of the time, forcing drivers to press an emergency button to stop the train quickly, usually overshooting the station platform. If the driver doesn't intercede, the train proceeds automatically to the next station, delivering its passengers to the wrong place. Drivers in this system have been reduced to little more than monitors who act only when the machine malfunctions. They say they find it hard to remain alert when they have so little to do. The job is boring, lacking challenge and responsibility, and it rarely requires drivers to use their skills. As the operators become more dependent on the computer-controlled equipment, they become less capable of making crucial decisions in emergencies. No matter how thoroughly they have been trained, if their job skills are rarely used, those skills will deteriorate.

A similar problem has been found in the airline industry. Consider the different philosophies behind the design of the European-built Airbus and the U.S.-built Boeing 777. The Airbus is largely computer controlled and limits the actions pilots are allowed to take in flying the

Newsbreak

It's Your Choice, Part 2: Believe Your GPS or Yourself?

Would you drive your car into a lake if your friend sitting in the passenger seat told you that was the right way to get to your destination? Probably not. But suppose a machine you trusted, a system that had always given you good advice in the past—your global positioning system (GPS)—told you to turn off the road and go down a dirt lane directly into a lake you could clearly see? Would you do it? Would you ignore the clear evidence of your own senses and drive your car into the water? People have done so, and their only explanation (after they were saved from drowning) was that their GPS told them to turn there, and so they did.

Then there was the case of the 32-year-old employee of a high-tech company in California's Silicon Valley, who, on a business trip to New York state, drove his rental car onto railroad tracks, following instructions from his GPS. He did not just cross the tracks, he drove straight down them, bouncing along until he saw—you guessed it—an oncoming train. He jumped out of the car just before it was demolished in a fiery crash. His excuse, when the police asked why he was driving down the tracks, was that the GPS had told him to turn in that direction.

A similar thing happened to a 20-year-old student in England who told police, "I put my complete trust in the sat nav [satellite navigation system] and it led me right into the path of a speeding train." Another driver in England made a sudden U-turn, or tried to, at a speed of nearly 80 miles per hour on a freeway. His GPS had ordered an immediate turn to get to his hotel.

A bus driver in Seattle ignored several large warning signs announcing that the underpass ahead had only a 9-foot clearance. His bus, which he had been driving for some time, was almost 12 feet high. His automated navigation system sent him straight ahead; as a result, he sheared off the top of the bus from front to back, injuring five members of a high school softball team.

A growing number of drivers are ignoring highway and warning signs, failing to believe what they see with their own eyes. Or maybe they've stopped looking because they have become so convinced that a machine can guide them better than they can do on their own. Maybe machines are taking over the "thinking" function that people used to exercise in evaluating information and making decisions. Think about these examples the next time a machine tells you to do something.

Source: For other examples, enter "GPS caused accidents" on Google, but not while you're driving.

plane. In general, Airbus pilots are unable to override the computer. In the Boeing airplane, pilots can take the controls themselves at any time to negate or override the onboard computer. Even so, all large passenger aircraft today have such efficient flight computers, navigational equipment, and automatic pilots that much of the human pilot's time is spent monitoring the informational displays rather than actively controlling and flying the plane. As a result, pilots can easily become bored and inattentive. The Federal Aviation Administration (FAA) has officially expressed concern that pilots' basic flying skills are deteriorating because they rely so much on automation. In other words, too many functions in modern aircraft are being allocated to the machine component of the system and not enough to the human.

A team of engineering psychologists in Britain argued that while many pilots "agree that modern aircraft are easier to fly, closer inspection suggests that their workload has shifted rather than reduced, so pilots now have to carry out more supervisory tasks. This means that there is increased likelihood of pilots spending more time . . . interacting with the automation, rather than focusing their efforts on the primary task of flying the aircraft" (Baxter, Besnard, & Riley, 2007, p. 418).

In a study of 30 pilots from a major U.S. airline, investigators found that automated systems increasingly communicate only with other machine parts of the system, making decisions and initiating actions without interacting with the pilot. In experimental tests in flight simulators, pilots under time pressure were unable to detect situations in which flight systems were initiating inappropriate or incompatible control decisions that could have harmful consequences for the aircraft. The human part of the person–machine system was being bypassed in critical decision-making situations (Olson & Sarter, 2001).

For information on a variety of issues in engineering psychology see www.ergonomics.ucla.edu and www.ergonomics.org.uk/ (the home page of The Ergonomics Society).

THE DESIGN OF WORKSPACES AND TOOLS

As an example of the harmful effects of poor workspace design, consider the U.S. Army's M-l Abrams tank. The interior of a tank, which is the crew's workspace, can influence job performance—in this case, the tank crew's fighting efficiency. The M-1 tank was designed without benefit of engineering psychology research and thus without regard for the needs and abilities of the crew. When the tank was tested, 27 of the 29 test drivers developed such severe neck and back pains that they required medical attention. Also, the drivers were unable to see the ground in front of the tank for a distance of 9 yards, making it difficult to avoid obstacles or to cross trenches.

When the engine and turret blowers were operating, more than half the tank's gunners, loaders, and drivers reported that they could not hear one another well enough to communicate because the noise of the machinery was too loud. All crew members reported visibility problems at their workstations. When drivers and tank commanders rode with an open hatch, they found that the front fenders had been so poorly designed that they did not protect the crew from rocks, dirt, and mud churned up by the tank's treads. It was obvious that the designers of the M-l tank had given no consideration to the human factor, to the people who would have to operate the machine.

Effective design of the human operator's workspace, whether it is a bench for an electronic parts assembler, a display screen for a newspaper copywriter, or a locomotive cab for a driver, involves the following principles from time-and-motion study and engineering psychology research:

1. All materials, tools, and supplies needed by the workers should be placed in the order in which they will be used so that the paths of the workers' movements will be continuous. Knowing that each part or tool is always in the same place saves the time and annoyance of searching for it.

2. Tools should be positioned so that they can be picked up ready for use. For example, for a job requiring the repeated use of a screwdriver, that tool can be suspended just above the work area on a coil spring. When the tool is needed, the worker can reach up without looking and pull it down ready for use.

3. All parts and tools should be within a comfortable reaching distance (approximately 28 inches). It is fatiguing for workers to change positions frequently to reach beyond the normal working area.

As an example of good workspace design, see Figure 13-2, which illustrates the workstation of a radar operator or power plant monitor. Typically, the worker is seated before a panel or console of lights, dials, and switches. The job involves monitoring and controlling the operation of complex equipment. The monitoring console is designed so that operators can see and reach everything necessary for successful job performance without leaving their chair or reaching excessively beyond normal seated posture.

Another important consideration in workspace design is the size and shape of individual hand tools that must be used repeatedly. If tool designers apply principles of engineering psychology, they can improve even basic tools such as hammers to make them easier, safer, and less tiring to use. Hand tools should he designed so that workers can use them without bending their wrists; hands are less vulnerable to injury when the wrists can be kept straight. One general principle of good tool design from a human factors standpoint is to bend the tool, not the wrist, as shown in the design of pliers

We don't buy just any seats. We design them.

GM begins with detailed studies of the human body. Biomedical research. The kind of comprehensive investigation of anatomy da Vinci undertook in the 1500s.

As a leader in the field of Human Factors Engineering, we design interiors scientifically to minimize the possible distractions from your driving.

It may take us two years and countless clay models to arrive at a more comfortable, durable seat for new GM cars and trucks. But we think it's worth it.

And we believe old Leonardo would have thought so, too.

We believe in taking the extra time, giving the extra effort and paying attention to every detail. That's what it takes to provide the quality that leads more people to buy GM cars and trucks than any other kind. And why GM owners are the most loyal on the road.

That's the GM commitment to excellence.

Chevrolet • Pontiac • Oldsmobile • Buick • Cadillac • GMC Truck

Leonardo da Vinci gave us a great idea for bucket seats.

Let's get it together. Buckle up.

Nobody sweats the details like GM.

Engineering psychologists help design components for various workspaces. (Reproduced by permission of General Motors Corporation.)

in Figure 13-3. Workers can perform most tasks faster with bent-handled pliers than with straight-handled pliers (Duke, Mirka, & Sommerich, 2004).

Hand tools that have been designed properly can enhance productivity, satisfaction, and physical health. In contrast, the continuous use of tools that require bending the wrist while working can lead to nerve injuries, such as carpal tunnel syndrome, caused by the repetitive motion. Carpal tunnel syndrome, which can be painful and debilitating, is also prevalent among people who spend a great deal of time playing the piano, knitting, or playing video games, a finding that may influence your choice of hobbies.

In a study of 87 clerical employees in a municipal office building, researchers investigated the effects of

FIGURE 13-2 Monitoring console work arrangement. (From K. Kroemer, H. Kroemer, & K. Kroemer-Elbert, *Ergonomics: How to design for ease and efficiency*, 2nd ed., Upper Saddle River, NJ: Prentice Hall, 2000, p. 384.)

redesigning workstations to apply ergonomic principles. Human factors alterations were made in four areas: seating, keyboards, computer relocations, and computer screen modifications. Changes included new chairs and chair cushions, back supports, wrist support pads, and glare guards for computer monitors. Most of the changes were simple and inexpensive, yet they resulted in significant benefits to the workers, who reported decreased upper back pain and greater satisfaction with the design and efficiency of the workstations (May, Reed, & Schwoerer, 2004).

Sometimes changes in workplaces are rejected or ignored by workers, even when the change has been shown to make their job easier or less stressful. For example, four companies in Sweden introduced new worktables that could be raised or lowered by employees so that they could change from a sitting position to a standing posture position, thereby reducing the strain on neck, back, and shoulder muscles. Of the 165 employees who were surveyed or interviewed about the new tables, a majority considered the tables an improvement in their work environment and appreciated having the

Avoid short tool handles that press into the palm of the hand. The palm is very soft and easily damaged.

Avoid narrow tool handles that concentrate large forces onto small areas of the hand.

Tools and jobs should be designed so that they can be performed with straight wrists. Hands are stronger and less vulnerable to injury when the wrists are kept straight.

FIGURE 13-3 Application of human factors principles to the design of pliers. (From "Ergonomics," 1986, *Personnel Journal*, *65*(6), p. 99.)

Human anthropometry   A branch of engineering psychology concerned with the measurement of the physical structure of the body.

opportunity to vary their posture throughout the workday. However, although they liked the change, more than 60% changed the table height only once a month or less. Only 20% changed the height daily. Thus, not all changes in workspace design fulfill their intended purpose of making jobs easier or less taxing to perform (Wilks, Mortimer, & Nylen, 2006).

Human Anthropometry

A branch of engineering psychology called **human anthropometry** focuses on measurement of the physical structure of the human body. Complete sets of body measurements have been compiled from a large, representative sample of the population in the performance of various activities. Specific data include height (standing and sitting), shoulder breadth, back height, chest depth, foot and hand length, knee angle, and so on (see Figure 13-4). These measurements are applied in the design of work areas to determine, for example, normal and maximum reaching distances, tool and desk height and arrangement, size and shape of seats, and viewing angles for video display terminals.

As the workforce becomes more globalized, the design of efficient workstations must consider that so-called average body measurements and dimensions may vary with workers from different cultures. This was demonstrated in a study comparing anthropometric measurements of Chinese workers (to represent Asians) and German workers (to represent Caucasians). Chinese workers were typically found to have longer torsos and shorter legs than German workers, as well as larger heads and longer arms. Thus, the same workstations, ergonomic chairs, tools, and uniforms would not be suitable for both groups (Shan & Bohn, 2003). A similar conclusion was reached in a study of body measurements of 400 female workers in an agricultural region of India. These data were compared with body measurements of women from the United States, Britain, China, Egypt, Japan, Korea, Mexico, and Taiwan.

All 76 body dimensions were found to be smaller for the Indian women than for women from other nations. These differences meant that agricultural tools, such as a simple hand scythe, that had been designed for the typical worker were too large and unwieldy for the workers in India to use safely and efficiently (Dewangen, Owary, & Datta, 2008).

Millions of people work at a desk or workbench. The seats they use, if improperly designed, can cause back and neck pain and lead to fatigue, which, in turn, reduces productive efficiency. Research has been conducted on every conceivable aspect of the design of workplace seating, and guidelines are available for various kinds of jobs. For example, in a study of 80 bus drivers in Scotland, psychologists found that the drivers spent 60% of their time actually driving the bus, sitting upright with their back unsupported. Well over half of the drivers reported lower back pain. The psychologists concluded that the backrest portion of the driver's seat was poorly designed and needed to be reshaped to provide better back support (Okunribido, Shimbles, Magnusson, & Pope, 2007). Research involving 30 employees in Canada whose job involved sitting at computer workstations also found that the back support of the chair was inadequate. Adding a backrest in the form of a lumbar pad against the small of the back greatly reduced pressure on the spine; consequently, the employees reported enhanced feelings of comfort (Carcone & Keir, 2007).

Another problem affecting seating has more to do with people than with the seats. You may have noticed that seats are getting larger and wider, because we are! With the notable exception of seats in airplanes, seats have become roomier; think of the seats in stadiums, movie theaters, and subway cars. The ferries crossing Puget Sound in Washington state used to hold 250 people in seats 18 inches wide. Because the operators had to install wider seats, each boat now carries only 230 people. Even car seats for children have become too small for the children

FIGURE 13-4 Typical postures used in gathering body measurements (anthropometric data). (From R. S. Bridger, *Introduction to ergonomics*, 2nd ed., London & New York: Taylor & Francis, 2003, p. 64.)

they were designed to protect. Research carried out at Baltimore's Johns Hopkins Hospital found that more than 250,000 children under the age of 6 were too overweight to fit safely into their car seats. Most of these children had reached obesity by the age of 3 (Nordquist, 2006).

For another look at poor human factors design of consumer items from maps to toothbrushes, log on to www.baddesigns.com/index.shtml

DISPLAYS: PRESENTING INFORMATION

In person–machine systems, operators receive inputs from the machine through the physical senses. For example, in driving a car you receive information on the operating status of the machine from visual displays (speedometer, temperature indicator, gas gauge) and from auditory displays

Quantitative visual displays Displays that present a precise numerical value, such as speed, altitude, or temperature.

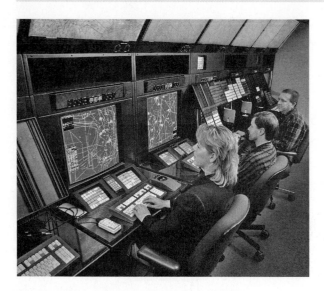

Visual displays in an air-traffic control tower present information in words, symbols, and graphics.

(the chime alerting you to fasten your seat belt or remove the ignition key). More informally, you receive inputs tactilely, such as when a balky engine causes the car to vibrate.

One of the earliest decisions to be made about the presentation of information in the design of a person–machine system relates to selecting the most effective means of communication. Visual presentation of information, the mode most frequently used, is more appropriate in the following instances:

- The message is long, difficult, and abstract.
- The environment is too noisy for auditory messages.
- The auditory channels of communication are overloaded.
- The message consists of many different kinds of information that must be presented simultaneously.

The auditory presentation of information is more effective in these instances:

- The information is short, simple, and straight-forward.

- The message is urgent; auditory signals typically attract attention more readily than visual ones do.
- The environment is too dark or otherwise does not allow for visual communication.
- The operator's job requires moving to different locations. The ears can receive messages from all directions, whereas the eyes must be focused on the display to receive messages.

Visual Displays

A common error made in the visual presentation of information is to provide more input than the operator needs to run the system. For example, most drivers do not need a tachometer to indicate engine revolutions per minute (rpm). Although this unneeded information may not be a major concern in a passenger car, in an airplane, where large amounts of vital information must be displayed, any unnecessary input adds to the display problem and is potentially confusing for the pilot. The engineering psychologist must ask: Is this information needed to operate the system? If the system can function without it, then that is one less item for the busy human operator to confront. If the information is vital to the operation of the equipment, what is the most effective way to display it? Three types of visual displays commonly used in person–machine systems are quantitative, qualitative, and check reading.

Quantitative Displays. **Quantitative visual displays** present a precise numerical value. In situations dealing with speed, altitude, or temperature, for example, the operator must know the precise numerical value of a condition of the system. A pilot must know if the altitude is, for example, 10,500 feet, as dictated by the flight plan. An approximate indication of altitude instead of an exact one could lead the plane into the path of another aircraft or into a mountain in fog.

There are basically two ways to present quantitative information visually: through analog displays or digital displays. An analog display, such as you see on many clocks and speedometers, contains a

Qualitative visual displays Displays that present a range rather than a precise numerical value. They are frequently used to show whether components, such as engine temperature, are operating in the safe or unsafe range.

Check reading visual displays Displays that tell the operator whether the system is on or off, safe or unsafe, or operating normally or abnormally.

range of numbers and an arrow or pointer indicating the time of day or the speed at which a vehicle is traveling. The numbers on a clock face range from 1 to 12; the numbers on a speedometer may range from 0 to 130 miles per hour. Digital displays, such as you see on your cell phone, digital video recorder, microwave, and many other electronic devices, display only the number pertinent at the moment. The clock may display only 3:45 or the speedometer may display only 60.

Digital displays can be read faster and with fewer errors than any other type of display. Nevertheless, they cannot be used in all situations. If the information being presented changes rapidly or continuously, a number may not remain in place long enough to be read and processed by the human operator. Digital displays are also unsuitable when it is important to know the direction or the rate of change—for example, whether engine temperature is rising or falling, or whether it is rising rapidly or slowly.

Qualitative Displays. **Qualitative visual displays** are appropriate when a precise numerical reading is not necessary. For example, most drivers do not need to know the precise temperature of their car's engine. All drivers need to know is whether the temperature is in the safe operating range. With many components of person–machine systems, the operator needs to know only whether the system is functioning within the proper range and whether the values are increasing or decreasing over time. A typical qualitative display is shown in Figure 13-5. Operating ranges are often color coded with the dangerous, or hot, portion in red and the safe portion in green. Such a display permits quick, accurate verification of the system's status and reduces the amount of technical information the operator must absorb.

When several qualitative displays must be checked frequently, consistent patterning makes them easier to read accurately (see Figure 13-6). Placing the dials so that they always face the same way in the normal operating range makes it easier to scan the display and detect an abnormal reading. Unpatterned displays force the operator to read

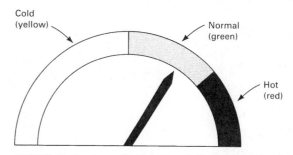

FIGURE 13-5 A qualitative visual display. (Adapted from *Human Factors in Engineering and Design* (p. 76) by E. J. McCormick, 1976, New York: McGraw-Hill.)

each dial separately. Patterned displays are used in aircraft cockpits, power plant control rooms, and automated manufacturing plants.

Check Reading Displays. **Check reading visual displays** are the simplest kind of visual display. They tell the operator whether the system is on or off, safe or unsafe, or operating normally or abnormally. Think of the engine temperature gauge in your car; a warning light is sufficient to indicate whether you can continue to drive safely or should stop because the engine is in danger of overheating. This kind of display is sometimes referred to as *go/no go*. Either the system is in condition to operate (to go) or it is not.

The most common check reading display is the warning light. When the light is not illuminated, the system is functioning satisfactorily. When the light comes on, it indicates a system malfunction serious enough to require the operator to take immediate corrective action. Among the considerations in the design of warning lights is level of brightness. On a display panel that contains several sources of light, it is vital that a warning light be at least twice as bright as the background to get the operator's attention. Location of warning lights is also important. They should be centrally located within the operator's field of vision. Warning lights too far to one side of a console may not be noticed when the worker is paying attention to more centrally located displays and controls. Also, flashing lights attract attention more quickly than continuous warning lights.

Auditory displays Alarms or warning signals in person–machine systems. Auditory displays can be more compelling than visual displays.

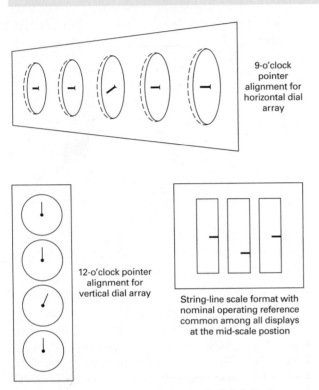

9-o'clock pointer alignment for horizontal dial array

12-o'clock pointer alignment for vertical dial array

String-line scale format with nominal operating reference common among all displays at the mid-scale postion

FIGURE 13-6 Patterned and unpatterned dial displays with pointers aligned for rapid reading. (From K. Kroemer, H. Kroemer, & K. Kroemer-Elbert, *Ergonomics: How to design for ease and efficiency*, 2nd ed., Upper Saddle River, NJ: Prentice Hall, 2000, p. 491.)

Visual displays today include more than the familiar lights, dials, and gauges. Much information is displayed on video screens and in words, symbols, and graphics. The electronic flight information system used in aircraft and in air-traffic control radar screens combines lines, numbers, and pictorial symbols to present precise information about location. Adding color to cockpit displays reduces errors and response times for aircraft crew members who are reading and processing information.

An experiment conducted in Wales asked 98 university students to search for and identify various signs, symbols, and icons on their computer screens. The researchers found that it took them longer to respond to the more visually complex displays than to the simpler displays. Also, performance was slower between 2 and 3 p.m., which is also the time when traffic accidents increase. Thus, although changes in the design of visual displays can improve recognition and response time overall, there are certain times of day when worker efficiency declines, regardless of workplace conditions (McDougall, Tyrer, & Folkard, 2006).

Not all visual displays are high-tech. For example, every day millions of people use the common push/pull door signs as they enter and exit stores, factories, and office buildings. Some doors need to be pushed, others pulled. To determine how best to display this basic information visually, so that users will follow directions accurately, a study was conducted with 60 participants under laboratory conditions and 1,100 participants in the real world. Eleven different kinds of signs were tested. The most effective signs (those quickly identified or eliciting the greatest compliance) combined a drawing of a hand with an arrow and the word *push* or *pull* displayed horizontally (see Figure 13-7). Even a simple visual display can be improved through engineering psychology research.

Engineering psychologists have studied how people of different body sizes approach doors, open them, and push or pull on door handles. A study of 2,400 human–door interactions showed that people who are shorter and of lesser body weight use greater force to push or pull on doors than do taller and heavier people. The researchers also learned that most people push on doors at some point between the center of the door and the side that opens, but generally closer to the center than at the point where the handles are located. Such findings can influence decisions about where to place the handles as well as the location of push/pull signs (Chang & Drury, 2007).

Auditory Displays

An **auditory display** can be more compelling than a visual display for several reasons:

- Our ears are always open, but our eyes are not.

Most effective (word plus symbol)

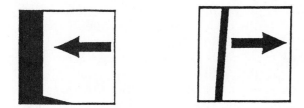

Least effective (symbol only)

FIGURE 13-7   Most effective and least effective door pull signs. (Adapted from T. J. B. Kline & G. A. Beitel, "Assessment of push/pull door signs: A laboratory and a field study." *Human Factors*, 1994, 36, 688.)

- We can receive auditory information from all directions.
- Our visual sense is often taxed to capacity.

In general, horns, whistles, and sirens have greater attention-getting ability than bells, buzzers, and the human voice. But no matter how loud or effective an auditory alarm seems, it is only as good as the human operator's response to it. Recall the case of the Russian airline pilot, described at the beginning of this chapter, who chose not to believe what the auditory collision warning system told him to do.

Ignoring alarm systems is not unusual; people often fail to respond properly. For example, in a long-term study of employees monitoring the daily operation of nuclear power plants in Canada, researchers found that more than 50% of the alarms did not provide useful or meaningful information for the human operator, so that he or she could initiate some corrective action. These so-called nuisance alarms added clutter or confusion to a critical and demanding job (Mumaw, Roth, Vicente, & Burns, 2000). A study of highly trained registered

nurse-anesthetists in 24 surgical cases found that almost half of the auditory alarms from the medical equipment were ignored. No corrective action was taken because none was needed. The surgical team had learned that the warnings were probably nuisance alarms (Seagull & Sanderson, 2001).

Research has been conducted on smoke alarms, devices most of us have in our homes and workplaces. Researchers found that the commonly used high frequency beeping signal is significantly less effective when people are asleep than is a voice alarm or an alarm using a lower frequency signal. Changing the type of auditory signal for smoke alarms would save many lives. Data show that three times as many people die by fire when they are asleep and thus do not hear the alarm, than are killed by fire when awake (Bruck & Ball, 2007).

Sometimes even the most carefully designed person–machine system does not work as intended because the human operator violates the conditions under which the system was designed to function. On the night of May 17, 1987, aboard the navy frigate USS *Stark* on duty in the Persian Gulf, a radar operator was monitoring a complex system that was tracking all nearby radar signals. The system had visual and auditory warning devices to alert the operator if hostile radar was detected. The system designers believed that with both visual and auditory displays, there was no way the operator could miss a warning. If the operator was looking away from the visual display screen, the auditory signal—a rapid beeping—would surely be noticed.

Yet, when hostile radar was detected that night and the visual warning signal flashed on the screen, the operator was looking away and the auditory signal failed to sound. That operator, or an operator from an earlier shift, had disconnected the auditory alarm because it was annoying. Because the ship was in enemy territory, the alarm was beeping frequently, and the sailor decided that it was a nuisance.

With the auditory alarm disabled and the visual warning signal unseen, a jet fighter plane from Iraq fired a missile at the USS *Stark*, killing 37 U.S. sailors. In this case, the equipment portion of the person–machine system functioned satisfactorily, but the human operator did not.

Auditory signals can transmit complex information. One example is the shipboard use of sonar for detecting underwater objects. A high frequency sound is transmitted from beneath the ship through

Jack, the Virtual Equipment Tester

"In his 15 years on the job," wrote a reporter for the *New York Times*, "Jack has been trapped in coal mines and forced to lift and carry objects that could break his back, and once while pregnant—yes, pregnant—was stuffed into a car to see if he could fit behind the wheel and reach the pedals. Jack never complains, however, because Jack is a piece of software, a virtual reality representation of a person who can take on various forms. Jack can walk, avoid obstacles, reach, and lift. But if he cannot perform a certain task, an image of the character will signal a problem, sometimes by turning a body part a different color on a computer screen. Jack rolls with the punches so that we don't have to."

By wearing virtual reality helmets, real people—like designers of cars or aircraft cockpits or workstations—can see through Jack's eyes as he becomes a driver or pilot, a factory worker or office manager. Thus, engineering psychologists or human factors engineers can see how something works, or fails to work, before they actually build it. For example, they might find answers to questions such as these: By reaching to change a radio station in a sports car, could the driver accidentally nudge the gearshift lever into neutral? Does the farmer driving the redesigned tractor have a clear view of the blades that are tilling the soil behind it? When the John Deere company learned that Jack couldn't see those blades from the new tractor cab, it was no big deal to change the design at that stage. But had the tractors already started rolling off the assembly line, it would have been tremendously expensive to redesign them.

Good ol' Jack never fails. And Jack never gets tired or cranky or comes in late or stays home with the flu. And he costs only $25,000. In today's market, Jack's a bargain.

Source: Jack is put through the wringer so you won't be (2000, May 11). *New York Times.*

---

the water. When the sound strikes a large enough object, the signal is reflected back to the ship and reproduced as the familiar pinging sound heard in old war movies. The job of interpreting the message or information that the sound conveys can be difficult. Extensive training is required to learn to discriminate among the sound's various qualities. With sonar, if the detected object is moving away from the ship, the reflected sound is of a lower frequency than is the transmitted sound. An object moving toward the ship provides a higher frequency of returning sound.

Humans can receive and interpret a variety of information through the auditory sense. We are capable of responding to formal signaling procedures (warning horns, whistles, and buzzers) and to informal cues (the misfire of a car engine or the beep of the computer that lost your term paper).

Tactile Displays

Tactile communication, through the skin senses, is used daily by people throughout the world. Visually impaired persons read through the Braille system of tactile displays by passing their fingers over raised dots or points on a flat surface. This has been shown to be a rapid and efficient way to receive information; persons skilled in Braille can read up to 200 words per minute.

Engineering psychologists have conducted considerable research on the use of dynamic, or changing, tactile displays as a way of presenting information. One effective technique involved vibrations on the surface of the skin. Subjects learned learn to perceive many distinct sensations when a vibrating stimulus was applied to different areas of the chest for different durations and levels of intensity. Although this early research, now more than 50 years old, showed promise for developing effective displays, interest in the topic lagged.

In the early years of this century, however, psychologists report a renewed focus on tactile displays of information for use in the workplace, on the battlefield, and in everyday life (see Jones & Sarter, 2008; Simonite, 2007). Several promising devices have been developed to present various types of information to the skin, especially to the hands, for drivers and other workers whose visual capacity may be overloaded (Spence & Gallace, 2007).

One such device is the vibrating vest that "writes" messages on the skin of a person's back. It was designed for use by police, firefighters, and soldiers for situations in which radio or other means of audio or visual communication is not possible—a firefighter in a burning building whose radio has malfunctioned and where smoke has obscured vision. Strapped directly to the person's back, under clothing, the vest contains 16 small vibrating motors connected to a wireless transceiver. In experimental tests of the device, subjects have learned to respond to up to 15 distinct commands, each associated with vibration on a particular area of the back. Similar devices have been developed for hands and have been shown to be effective even when the subject's hands are busy operating controls. As visual and auditory displays become more numerous and complex in certain work environments, tactile displays can be used as an additional source of communication.

CONTROLS: TAKING ACTION

In person–machine systems, once human operators receive input through the displays and mentally process that information, they must communicate some control action to the machine. They transmit their control decisions through devices such as switches, pushbuttons, levers, cranks, steering wheels, mouses, joysticks, trackballs, and foot pedals. Engineering psychologists analyze the nature of each task to determine whether it involves, for example, turning on a light or activating some other system component. Does the task involve a fine adjustment, such as selecting one radio frequency from the spectrum of frequencies? Does the task require frequent and rapid readjustment of a control, or is a single setting sufficient? How much force must the operator exert to accomplish the job? If the control must be activated in cold temperatures, will wearing gloves interfere with proper operation? If the control must be activated under low lighting conditions, can it be easily identified by shape alone?

Guidelines for Controls. For a task that requires two discrete settings of a control, such as "on" and "off," a hand or foot pushbutton is suitable. For four or more discrete settings, a group of finger pushbuttons or a rotary selector switch is preferable. For continuous settings, knobs or cranks are the best choice. For selecting elements on a computer display, devices such as a mouse, light pen, or touch pad can be used. A selection of controls and the actions for which they are appropriate are shown in Figure 13-8. In addition, controls should satisfy the following two criteria:

1. *Control–body matching.* Although some controls can be activated with the head or the elbow, most of them are activated by hands and feet. Engineering psychologists recommend that no one limb be given too many tasks to perform. The hands are capable of greater precision in operating controls, and the feet are capable of exerting greater force.

2. *Control–task compatibility.* A control action should imitate the movements it produces. For example, pulling an airplane's control column to the right pulls the plane to the right; the control movement and the machine's response are parallel. To lower aircraft flaps or landing gear, the control moves downward. Typically, we turn a control knob to the right (clockwise) to turn a machine on. Most people would have difficulty adjusting to a knob that turned to the left to activate a machine.

Combining Related Controls. Wherever possible, engineering psychologists combine controls that perform similar or related operations. For example, simple radios have three control functions— on/off, volume, and station selection—yet there are only two controls. The on/off and volume controls, which perform related functions, are combined to reduce the number of separate actions required of the human operator and to save space on the control panel.

Identification of Controls. Controls must be clearly marked or coded to ensure their correct and rapid identification. Automobile manufacturers code instrument panels by using pictorial symbols to represent control functions (for example, a miniature wiper blade identifies the windshield wiper switch). On a crowded instrument panel, easily identifiable controls can minimize errors caused by activating the wrong control.

Shape coding Designing knobs for control panels in recognizably different shapes so that they can be identified by touch alone.

For transmitting discrete information

| Hand push button | Foot push button | Toggle switch 2-position | Toggle switch 3-position | Rotary selector switch |

For transmitting traditional continuous information

| Knob | Crank | Wheel | Lever | Pedal |

For transmitting cursor positioning information

| Mouse | Trackball | Digitizing tablet | Light pen |

FIGURE 13-8 Control devices and the type of information they best transmit. (From M. S. Sanders & E. J. McCormick, *Human factors in engineering and design*, 6th ed., p. 261. New York: McGraw-Hill, 1987. Copyright 1987, McGraw-Hill Book Co. Used with permission.)

Shape coding means designing each knob on a console or control panel in a recognizably different shape (see Figure 13-9). This allows for rapid visual identification of the correct control and permits identification by touch in low-lighting conditions or when the eyes must focus elsewhere. Sometimes the control's shape symbolizes its function. In U.S. Air Force planes the landing flap control looks like a landing flap, and the landing gear control looks like a tire. Each control is unique in touch and appear-

ance, and the control functions can be learned quickly. Standardizing the controls on all aircraft reduces the opportunity for pilot error.

Placement of Controls. Once the kind and shape of the controls have been selected, engineering psychologists determine their placement on the control panel. In doing so, they consider the control's relationship to an informational display. A primary requisite for control location is consistency or uniformity

FIGURE 13-9 Recommended handle shapes for coding. (From W. Woodson, B. Tillman, & P. Tillman, *Human factors design handbook*, 2nd ed., New York: McGraw-Hill, 1992, p. 439.)

of placement. For example, we expect the gas pedal to be located to the right of the brake pedal on automobiles and the Enter key to be on the right side of the keyboard. The greater the standardization of control arrangement, the easier and safer it is for people to work with different models of the same system. This sounds like common sense, but it took many years before engineering psychology research was accepted and for aircraft instrument panels to be standardized. This basic design principle is still being ignored in many consumer products.

Consider the kitchen range. Typically, there are four burners on top and four knobs on a panel to control the burners. However, there is little consistency in the relationship between control knobs and burners. A survey of 49 electric and gas ranges revealed six different knob–burner operating linkages. Although lack of standardization in ranges does not create as serious a problem as lack of standardization in airplanes, it can lead to burns and other accidents. With a gas range, you receive immediate feedback when you turn a knob to activate a burner; however, with an electric range, you could touch a burner—thinking it was cold—but find out it had been turned on.

In the global marketplace, where a product manufactured in one country may be sold in many others, human engineers must be aware of cultural differences that may influence the product's use, such as the linkage between displays and controls. For example, research subjects in Taiwan preferred a different link between burner and control when operating a four-burner stove than subjects in the United States. The Taiwanese automatically reached for different knobs than the Americans to operate the same burners. This probably reflected the Taiwanese practice of reading characters vertically and from right to left, whereas English-speaking people read horizontally and from left to right. Thus, the so-called natural approach to the use of these controls differed for people in the two cultures.

Controls that are associated with emergency functions must be placed in the normal line of sight where they can be distinguished from other controls. Operators should be able to reach emergency controls quickly. Such controls should be protected with a cover or shield so that they cannot be activated accidentally.

When displays are associated functionally with controls—such as a dial that must be set by turning a knob—they should be placed as close together as possible. It is desirable to group related displays and controls according to function. In an aircraft cockpit, for example, displays and controls involving engine performance are grouped. When the order of operation is consistent, displays and controls can be grouped sequentially.

HUMAN FACTORS IN HEALTH CARE

We noted earlier how time-and-motion study, the precursor of human factors engineering, radically changed procedures in hospital operating rooms by having nurses place each surgical tool directly in the surgeon's hand, instead of the surgeon visually searching for and reaching out to grasp every tool. This change made surgery more efficient, faster, and safer for patients because it eliminated the possibility of the surgeon choosing and using the wrong instrument. The technology of modem medical care has since become much more complicated. A growing number of medical procedures are being automated. The health care professional, whether physician, nurse, or technician, is called upon to monitor a machine as it performs its functions.

For example, there are so-called smart intravenous pumps designed to shut themselves off, that is, to stop administering the chemical, drug, or nutrient to the patient if it reaches an unsafe level. Such equipment has to be programmed correctly for each patient and checked periodically. The attending health care employee must, like the pilot in the cockpit, detect a warning signal if a harmful level is reached. Bar-coding of medications has been developed and implemented to prevent incorrect prescriptions or dosages from being given to a patient. Again, a person must monitor the performance of the system for it to function correctly.

The U.S. Food and Drug Administration (FDA) requires developers of medical technology to demonstrate that the guidelines of engineering psychology have been applied in the design of new medical technology and drug delivery systems. This requirement ensures an ever greater involvement of human engineering specialists (see, for example, Alvarado & Cao, 2004; Martin, Norris, Murphy, & Crowe, 2008; Salas, Baker, King, & Battles, 2006). Engineering psychologists are currently involved with innovations in robotic surgery, virtual patients, and even the design of nurses' shoes.

In robotic surgery, surgeons operate from a computer console and monitor displays that present such information as the patient's vital health data, live X-ray and ultrasound images, and the organ or body part the surgical tools are working on. Surgeons see inside the patient and manipulate surgical tools indirectly. Their actions at the control panel are translated by the computer into delicate, tremor-free movements of scalpels and other surgical implements. Robotic surgery is used routinely for operations such as knee replacements, prostate gland removal, and open-heart surgery. Studies show that robotic surgery allows for smaller incisions, less invasive procedures, and more precise movements. In addition, robotic surgery helps surgeons avoid the fatigue of standing for lengthy operations and the weight of the heavy lead vests required because of continuous exposure to X-rays (Feder, 2008).

Another medical innovation in which engineering psychologists are involved is the virtual patient—a lifelike, computer-controlled, robotic dummy used in training medical students. "Help me," the dummy says to the students, "I don't feel well." Students can apply diagnostic and treatment procedures learned in the classroom without doing harm to a real patient. Virtual patients can be programmed for a variety of symptoms and conditions, some of which may require emergency procedures. After a training session, a computer display presents an immediate evaluation of the medical student's performance. Virtual patients have also been developed for dental students; they are programmed to shout, "Ow, that hurts!" if a student drills too close to sensitive nerves.

In Taiwan engineering psychologists studying foot and leg discomfort of nurses found that pain was reduced significantly when nurses wore compression hosiery during duty shifts, shoes with arch supports, and soles and heels of specified heights. In addition to reducing pain in feet and legs, these changes in apparel also reduced pain in the lower back, which led to notable changes in worker efficiency, alertness, and physical comfort at a relatively low cost (Chiu & Wang, 2007).

HUMAN FACTORS IN EVERYDAY LIFE

The findings of ergonomics research are evident in many areas of everyday life. The field of telematics, for example, refers to the wireless information technology you may already have in your car, such as a GPS navigation system, a satellite radio, or a built-in wireless phone. An automatic collision notification system, such as OnStar, knows where your car is at all times and alerts authorities when your airbag deploys. Soon to be available are e-mail and Internet access for your car, Bluetooth support, and built-in PDAs. The obvious problem with these devices, however, is that they can distract you and lead to accidents. Engineering psychologists are working to determine the nature and extent of these distractions and how best to equip the human operator to deal with them.

The use of cell phones while driving is a major contributor to accidents, but most governmental jurisdictions do not require information on cell phone use in traffic accident reports. A driver's chance of being involved in a car crash is four times greater when the driver is using a cell phone than when he or she is not using a cell phone (Strayer, 2006). Research on drivers in Japan showed that the primary cause of accidents was answering a phone call while driving. The second most frequent cause was placing a call while driving. Third was talking on the phone while driving. No significant differences were found between the use of handheld phones and hands-free phones; the nature of the distraction was similar in both cases (Green, 2003).

Research on use of GPS navigation systems while driving in urban traffic showed that drivers were able to make destination entries using a touch screen in an average time of 3.4 seconds. The average glance time at the screen to check on location was 1.32 seconds. The researchers of this study suggested that the ability to enter destinations by voice activation rather than manual activation would simplify the driver's task and reduce the time the driver's attention would be focused on the screen (Chiang, Brooks, & Weir, 2004).

Studies were conducted of auditory warning systems in automobiles on the road, as well as in a realistic driving simulator in a laboratory. Researchers found that an auditory warning system that sounded when drivers were too close to the car ahead led these drivers to maintain a greater distance behind other cars and thus reduced the number of rear-end collisions by 50% (Ben-Yaacov, Maltz, & Shinar, 2002; Lee, McGehee, Brown, & Reyes, 2002).

Some human factors research has focused on the voice menu systems of telephones. In a study of 114 people, ranging in age from 18 to over 60, investigators found that older people had greater difficulty than younger people identifying the menu choices they wanted. When a graphic aid was provided with the recorded spoken instructions, the performance of older people in selecting the appropriate menu options improved significantly (Sharit, Czaja, Nair, & Lee, 2003).

Desks and chairs for school classrooms have also been the subject of human factors research. Anthropometric measurements of 414 students in Greece, ages 6 to 18, indicated that school furniture was poorly designed for the use and comfort of the students. Chairs were too high and the seats too deep, and desks were also too deep for the reach of most students. This situation led to uncomfortable and unnatural sitting postures, and then to slumping and pressure on the spine and back (Gouvali & Boudolos, 2006; Panagiotopoulou, Christoulas, Papanckolaou, & Mandroukas, 2004). These findings supported a similar study in Michigan in which 80% of the students (ages 11 to 14) had seats that were too high and deep and desks that were too high. Attention to anthropometric measurements for students in these age ranges could have prevented discomfort and harm.

Have you noticed that passengers who fly first class often get leather seats while the rest have fabric-covered seats? If you are flying coach, do you envy the people in first class? You shouldn't. A study conducted in Germany reported that fabric upholstery was rated more comfortable because fabric breathes and leather does not. People are more likely to perspire in leather-covered seats (Bartels, 2003).

The Federal Aviation Administration (FAA) reports that the number of incidents in which aircraft in the process of landing have come close to colliding with other planes on the runway has increased to an average of one a day. To prevent these so-called incursions, the FAA sponsored a runway design competition. A group of engineering psychology graduate students had the winning design: They proposed lining runways with inexpensive wireless sensors that would provide an instant alert directly to the pilot if another aircraft or object was in the flight path. Under the current system, an air-traffic controller must be alert to possible obstructions and then inform the pilot. The new design, if implemented, would save time by bypassing the controller and providing information (an auditory alarm) directly to the pilot (Packard, 2007).

And what about the food-service industry? Ergonomics researchers have been working in that area, too. For example, research has shown that the physical stress of repeated scooping by employees in ice cream shops can be reduced if the ice cream is kept no colder than minus 14 degrees Celsius. Scooping is also less physically difficult if the edge of the scoop is sharpened at least once a month. In addition, the job is easier when an antifreeze liquid is encapsulated within the scoop, but as yet designers have not found a way to keep the antifreeze from leaking onto the ice cream, which definitely would not be good for business (Dempsey, McGorry, Cotnam, & Braun, 2000).

Newsbreak

Designing Cars for Aging Drivers: Let's Pretend

It's not easy to put on the Third-Age Suit, and it's not easy to move around and do normal things once it's on. There are goggles with scratched and yellowed lenses; a neck brace restraining the head and making it hard to turn; heavy padding on the back, shoulders, and around the waist; braces restricting the movements of the hands, wrists, and elbows; plastic gloves reducing the sense of touch; and restraints around ankles, knees, and feet to restrict mobility.

Once he puts on the suit, Eero Laansoo, a 35-year-old designer for the Ford Motor Company, gets in a car and tries to drive. But how can he with all those restrictions and restraints? That's precisely the point: to demonstrate to car designers, who are likely to be in their 20s and 30s, what it's like for an older person to get behind the wheel.

As we get older, we tend to become heavier, less flexible, and more bothered by stiff joints and failing vision. Twisting a knob can be painful, as can squeezing and lifting a door handle, or trying to twist around far enough to spot other cars behind or to the side. That's why Ford, guided by engineering psychologists, replaced some flush-mounted exterior door handles and made seats on some models more comfortable and higher so that older drivers could easily slide in and out. Ford engineers are also developing a blind-spot sensor that will let visually impaired drivers know if another vehicle is in the blind spot without having to squirm around to try to see it.

Boeing Aircraft Company was so impressed with Ford's Third-Age Suits, that it built one to help its engineers configure the interior of its 787 jets with older passengers in mind. As one young Boeing engineer put it, "We're designing airplanes for ourselves when we get older. We're not going to be decrepit, but we're going to be slower and less strong. And there will be more of us. We have to face up to that." Proper attention to the engineering psychology aspects of products we use in our daily lives will make it easier for all of us.

Source: Heller, J. (2006, February 26). New designs cater to needs of older drivers. *St. Petersburg Times.*

Ergonomics researchers in China found that spatulas used by restaurant cooks to turn over food while it is cooking can lead to carpal tunnel syndrome and other trauma disorders in the upper limbs. They tested spatulas with different handle lengths and various angles between the handle and the turning surface. Both factors significantly affected the twisting, or flexion, angle of the cook's wrist. The straighter the wrist could be held, the less physical strain occurred. The best spatula was found to be one that minimized the flexing of the wrist: 25 centimeters in length with a lift angle of 25 degrees. With a tool of those dimensions, the restaurant cooks were able to manage more food with less physical damage and pain (Wu & Hsieh, 2002).

Similar research findings of engineering psychologists are applied routinely to transportation, furniture design, kitchen items, home workspaces, and other consumer products to make them more comfortable and efficient and to minimize discomfort from long-term use.

HUMAN FACTORS AND COMPUTERS

Millions of people use computers on the job and in everyday life. When the human engineering aspects of the design of computer terminals and computer furniture are ignored, the result can be physical strain, discomfort, eyestrain, and blurred vision. Engineering psychologists have found that most employee complaints about visual disturbances result not from the terminals but from equipment components and from the design of the workstation. Equipment factors identified as potential hazards include the size of the screen, the degree of flicker of the characters on the screen, and the rate at which characters are generated.

In addition, level of illumination and glare in the workplace can be sources of eyestrain. The application of antiglare coatings and shields helps reduce the problem. The overall lighting of the work area can be decreased and walls can be painted in darker colors. Fluorescent overhead lights can be replaced by indirect lighting. All these changes enhance visual comfort for computer users.

Some evidence suggests that people read more slowly from computer screens than from paper. Research is focusing on specific factors of the display and the user—such as length of time spent at the terminal—to explain this phenomenon. I-O psychologists suggest that slower reading speed may be related to the quality of the image on the screen (size, type style, clarity, and contrast with background).

Many people have a better understanding of what they read on paper than what they read on the screen. This was shown in a study of 113 college students who read and answered questions about two magazine articles. One group was presented with the material on paper; the other group read the articles on a computer. More readers of the paper version reported that the articles were interesting and persuasive than did the readers of the computer version. The readers of the paper version also showed a higher degree of comprehension of the content of the articles (Greenman, 2000).

Complaints from computer users such as fatigue and pain in wrists, hands, shoulders, neck, and back can be related to a lack of attention to human engineering concerns. For example, desks and chairs used with computer equipment are often poorly designed for jobs that involve sitting for long periods. The best chair is adjustable, enabling computer operators to adapt it to their height, weight, and posture. Changing position periodically can reduce fatigue, and this is easier to do with an adjustable chair. Desks with split and adjustable tops that hold keyboard and display screen components at different heights can also contribute to user comfort. Comparisons of the standard flat keyboard and the split adjustable keyboard, using experienced typists as subjects, found no differences between the two designs in regard to causing musculoskeletal pain. However, people who used a padded wrist rest reported less pain in elbows and forearms than people who did not use a wrist rest.

Many people tend to move their middle fingers inadvertently when using a computer mouse. In a study of 100 graduate students, researchers found that 48% lifted their middle finger in the air during mouse-dragging movements and 23% extended the middle finger while moving the mouse. Such involuntary movements of the middle finger contributed nothing to the performance of the task but did contribute to reported pain in the forearm, wrist, and hand (Lee, McLoone, & Dennerlein, 2008).

A great deal of human factors research has been conducted on the design of computers and workstations. Some well-established guidelines are illustrated in Figure 13-10. For example, research findings indicate that a downward-sloping computer keyboard at an angle of 15 degrees decreases discomfort in the neck and shoulders. Locating the monitor too high or too low, or to the right or left instead of directly in front of the user, creates pain in the neck and lower back. Viewing angle has a significant effect on posture; an angle of approximately 17 degrees permits the best postural alignment of back, neck, and shoulders (see Psihogjos, Sommerich, Mirka, & Moon, 2001; Srmoneau & Marklin, 2001; Sommerich, Joines, & Psihogios, 2001; Szeto & Sham, 2008).

Studies have also been conducted on the standard mouse, comparing it with other types of control devices. The mouse requires extensive movement of wrist and forearm. Research conducted in Sweden suggests that a mouse is less comfortable to work with, and is related to lower productivity, than a virtual mouse shaped like the joystick used to play video games (Gustafsson & Hagberg, 2003). With the virtual mouse, the hand is maintained in a vertical position wrapped around the stick, with the thumb operating the click button. Thus, there is no strain on the muscles of the wrist and forearm.

The Ergonomics Group at the Eastman Kodak Company developed a questionnaire to determine the kinds of problems employees faced in their daily interaction with computers. The goal was to gather information from employees so that workstations could be redesigned to reduce fatigue, stress, and neuromuscular disorders. So sit down in front of your computer, answer yes or no to the questions in Table 13-1, and see how you score. If your answers to all the questions were yes, congratulations! You are working comfortably and are not experiencing computer-related physical problems. If you answered no to any of the questions, then something about your work area probably needs to be readjusted.

FIGURE 13-10 Guidelines for the design of computer workstations. (Adapted from M. S. Sanders & E. J. McCormick, *Human factors in engineering and design*, 6th ed., p. 358. New York: McGraw-Hill, 1987. Copyright 1987, McGraw-Hill Book Co. Used with permission.)

TABLE 13-1

Ergonomics Questionnaire on the Design of Workstations

Employees answer YES or NO

1. Are you able to view your computer screen without tipping your head forward or backward?
2. Are you looking straight ahead at your screen?
3. Is your copyholder next to your screen and at the same height and distance from your eyes?
4. Can you easily view your work without leaning forward and hunching your shoulders and back?
5. Are the screen contrast and brightness levels set correctly for your visual comfort?
6. Is the screen free of glare, reflections, or white spots that might be caused by the surrounding work environment?
7. Can you avoid bending your neck or hunching your shoulders when you hold your telephone?
8. When you work at your desk or keyboard, is your elbow at about a 90-degree angle?
9. Are your wrists almost straight (in a neutral posture) as you work?
10. Is your work area free of sharp edges that might rub against your wrists or forearms?
11. Can you reach frequently used items (such as your mouse, files, coffee mug, or pen) without stretching?
12. Can you sit all the way back in your chair without feeling pressure against the back of your knees?
13. Does your chair provide good support for the lumbar region of your back?
14. Are your feet fully supported by the floor or by a foot rest?
15. Do you take mini-breaks during the workday to stand up, stretch, and focus your eyes on something far away?

Source: Adapted from Eastman Kodak Company (2004). *Kodak's Ergonomic Design for People at Work* (2nd ed.). New York: Wiley, p. 131.

Newsbreak

Are Those Chocolate Chip Cookies Good for Your Laptop?

It happens every day. You're leaning over your computer, intent on surfing the Web or sending an e-mail, and you drop food on the keyboard. Chocolate chip cookie crumbs, pizza, cheese curls. Or worse—coffee or soda. The high-tech wonders of the workplace—these marvels of design and engineering—can be totally ruined by a diet cola. No joke! This is a serious problem as more and more people stay at their desks to eat lunch or take their laptops to the cafeteria.

All that food and drink is messing up sensitive electronics. At the Execuspace Company in Chicago, a woman trashed a $1,000 digital telephone when she spilled iced tea on it. Sticky liquids with sugar are the worst. They jam keys and pushbuttons, clog openings, and attract bugs. An exterminator in Chicago, whose business is obviously increasing, was quoted as saying "We're seeing more and more cockroach, mice, and ant problems in [office] cubi-

cles." To solve this growing problem, the Amherst-Merritt International Company of Dallas, Texas, is marketing a simple plastic sheath, called the Safeskin, that keeps stuff out of your keyboard.

In a survey of computer users in Britain, 46% of users claimed to clean their keyboards once a month, 10% said they never cleaned their keyboards, and 20% said they never cleaned their mouse. A microbiologist who examined 33 keyboards in a London office found that 4 of them contained more germs than the typical toilet seat.

But suppose you've already done the damage. Is it too late to save the mechanism and get rid of all those nasty germs? An official from Gateway advises, 'Take the keyboard into the shower [unplugged, of course]. Give it a good going over with warm water. Let it sit upside down for two weeks. There's a slight possibility it will work again."

Source: Desk dining may be hazardous to office's health (2000, April 18). *St. Petersburg (FL) Times;* Goldsmith, B. (2008, May 2). Computer keyboards can be dirtier than a toilet. Retrieved from www.news.yahoo.com

HUMAN FACTORS AND ROBOTS

The use of robots has created significant alterations in many work environments. Whereas computers affect jobs at all organizational levels, robots have largely changed the nature of manufacturing jobs. Workers most affected include mechanics, assemblers, welders, painters, assembly-line workers, and other semiskilled and unskilled industrial employees. Many of the robots used by U.S. companies are in the automotive industry where they do welding and painting jobs. Another use of industrial robots is in the manufacture of consumer appliances such as refrigerators and dishwashers. Robots are valuable in jobs that involve exposure to hazardous chemicals, such as spray painting epoxies on booster rockets. Robots also perform detailed and skilled jobs such as assembling computer components and undertaking maintenance operations in nuclear power plants. Tiny robots crawl around gaps in bundles of piping in power plants to inspect for cracks and defects and make the necessary repairs.

Robots consistently perform better than humans on routine, repetitive tasks. When programmed properly, robots are capable of producing more products of higher quality in a shorter time. One locomotive assembly plant reported that a team of 8 unskilled workers and their robots produced a locomotive frame in a day. Previously, it took 68 skilled machinists 16 days to produce a locomotive frame.

Industrial robots are also superior to humans in finding defects in components or products while these items are moving rapidly along a conveyor belt or assembly line. Some robots have been designed to inspect fruit; they accurately detect colors, shapes, and bruises. Other machines inspect sheets of aluminum or steel, faultlessly checking for defects in appearance and thickness. Robots work under difficult conditions such as extremes of noise and temperature without any deterioration in performance. The cost of a robot is typically one third that of the average industrial employee, and robots operate 24 hours a day, 7 days a week, without fatigue or errors.

Aside from freeing employees from dangerous and uncomfortable work environments, most of the advantages of industrial robots are on the side of management. Many workers fear losing their jobs to the machines or having to match their work habits to the pace of a robot. Consider the experience at a General Motors automobile assembly plant in New Jersey. In modernizing the production facility, management installed more than 200 robots for welding, painting, and sealing car windows. The workforce was reduced by 26% and the number of first-line supervisors by 42%. However, an increase of 80% in the number of skilled electricians, machinists, and carpenters was required to maintain the robots! Interviews with these skilled workers showed that they experienced greater challenge and responsibility, and the opportunity to upgrade their skills. The production workers who remained on the job reported a downgrading of responsibility and a reduction in the skills needed for their job. They felt they had become subordinate to the machines.

Thus, when robots are introduced into the workplace, employees' jobs necessarily change. In a robotized plant it is also likely that employees will be separated by greater physical distance, which reduces social contact and group cohesiveness. Some workers have felt so threatened that they have engaged in acts of sabotage. In a plant in Russia, management erected metal barricades around the machines to protect them from angry workers.

Robots are not solely machines; rather, they are a type of person–machine system. Once designed, built, programmed, and maintained, they work with little human contact or intervention. But obviously it requires people to design, produce, and monitor the machines.

Engineering psychologists are involved in designing hardware and software for industrial robots. Hardware includes control panels, workspace features, operator seating, illumination, and other physical aspects of the system. Software includes computer programs, languages, and informational displays. A critical issue for engineering psychologists is the division of labor, the allocation of functions, between the robot and the human operator. The following factors affect this decision: development costs, task complexity, safety issues, space limitations, and degree of accuracy required.

Robots are fast appearing in service industries. As security guards, robots patrol buildings at night and summon human guards when they sense intruders. Robot janitors clean offices, programmed (we hope) to avoid bumping into the robot security guards. Robots in hospitals deliver medications and charts and guide patients through hospital corridors, leading them to the correct department for X-rays and laboratory tests. In fast-food restaurants robots assist physically disabled workers in making pizza; the robots are programmed to respond to voice commands such as "cheese" and "pepperoni." Robots in Japan work as office receptionists—welcoming visitors, serving tea, and giving guided tours. Japan has been highly innovative in developing robots. Management estimates that each robot can replace up to 10 human workers, a major consideration in a nation with a diminishing workforce; 20% of the population is over age 65 and the birthrate is low (Tabuchi, 2008).

You are probably familiar with the most popular U.S. robot, the Roomba, a self-propelled, computer-controlled vacuum cleaner that scoots around the house on its own to clean floors. More than 2 million have been sold; some owners have become so attached to the machines that they've given them pet names.

The most surprising and upbeat use of a robot may be ASIMO (Advanced Step In Innovative Mobility), a 4-foot 3-inch robot manufactured by Honda. On May 15, 2008, this robot conducted the Detroit Symphony Orchestra in a sold-out performance of "The Impossible Dream," from the musical *Man of La Mancha*, the story of Don Quixote. The robot greeted the audience—"Hello, everyone"—before raising its baton. At the conclusion of the music the audience erupted in enthusiastic applause. ASIMO bowed and said that it was thrilling to perform with the orchestra in such a magnificent hall, but it did not play an encore.

For more information about robots, log on to www.robots.net and www.sciencedaily.com/news/computers_math/robotics/

Summary

Engineering psychology is concerned with the design of tools, equipment, and workspaces to make them compatible with the abilities of employees. Psychologists consider the limitations and capacities of workers as well as the characteristics of the equipment to produce an efficient **person–machine system**. A precursor to engineering psychology was **time-and-motion study**, pioneered by Frederick

Taylor and Frank and Lillian Gilbreth, which attempted to redesign tools and wage-incentive systems and to eliminate wasted motions on the job. Time-and-motion study is applied to routine jobs, whereas engineering psychology focuses on higher level jobs that involve more complex systems.

The initial step in designing a person–machine system is allocating functions between human operators and machines. Humans are superior in detecting a range of stimuli, detecting rare or low-level stimuli from a confusing background, sensing and recognizing unusual or unexpected stimuli, recalling relevant information, using past experiences in making decisions, responding quickly to diverse situations, using inductive reasoning, and showing flexibility in problem solving. Machines are superior to humans in detecting stimuli beyond human sensory powers, monitoring for long periods, calculating rapidly and accurately, storing and retrieving large amounts of data, applying physical force, and engaging in repetitive tasks with no performance deterioration. As systems become more automated, there is a danger of eliminating the human from the system and letting the machine do both the working and the thinking.

Workspace design involves principles of motion economy as well as data from **human anthropometry** (measurements of the body's physical structure). Three types of visual informational display are quantitative, qualitative, and check reading. **Quantitative displays** provide a precise numerical value, which may be presented in analog or digital displays. Analog displays contain a range of numbers with an arrow or pointer indicating the correct reading; digital displays present only the number pertinent at that moment. **Qualitative displays** provide an indication of relative operating conditions. **Check reading displays** tell whether a system is operating normally or abnormally or whether it is on or off. **Auditory displays** can attract attention more readily than can visual displays because the ears receive sound from all directions. Tactile displays present information through the skin senses at the same time the operator is receiving input from visual and auditory displays.

Controls to initiate action must be compatible with the task and the worker's abilities. Controls should be combined for similar or related operations, and they must be easily identifiable. Identification can be aided by pictorial symbols or by **shape coding**. Sometimes controls have to be modified for users from different cultures.

Engineering psychology research is being applied to health care through the development of life-saving technologies such as robotic surgery and virtual patients. Many aspects of our daily lives have been enhanced through engineering psychology.

Computers are person–machine systems that may cause problems for the human operator. Computer use can lead to a downgrading of human skills, job dissatisfaction, boredom, muscle strain, and pain, much of which can be eliminated by paying attention to human factors considerations in designing computer workstations. Robots have been developed to replace human workers in boring and dangerous factory jobs as well as in offices and other work environments.

Key Term

auditory displays	human anthropometry	quantitative visual displays
check reading visual displays	person–machine systems	shape coding
engineering psychology	qualitative visual displays	time-and-motion study

Review Questions

1. Describe the purpose of engineering psychology and its relationship to the person and the machine.

2. When did the field of human factors begin? How did its early efforts help save the lives of military pilots?

3. Give an example of how human factors research has reduced the chances of being involved in a car crash.

4. Why is human engineering considered to be an exciting career choice?

5. Who was Frederick Taylor and what did he do to improve the job of shoveling?

6. How did Frank and Lillian Gilbreth change the way jobs are performed?

7. How did the Gilbreths apply time-and-motion study to everyday life?

8. Describe several rules for increasing the ease, speed, and accuracy of manual jobs that developed from the findings of time-and-motion studies.

9. What is the relationship of displays, controls, and the human operator in a person–machine system? Give an example of a person–machine system.

10. What advantages do humans have over machines? In what ways are machines superior to humans?

11. How would you design a workspace for a person who is assembling and testing cell phones, so that the job can be performed rapidly and safely?

12. What is human anthropometry? How is it applied to workspace design? How is it used in the field of transportation?

13. What are the two primary ways of presenting quantitative information visually? Give examples of each from your own experience.

14. Under what conditions is the visual presentation of information superior to the auditory presentation of information?

15. Describe three types of visual displays and note what kind of information is best displayed on each.

16. What are some problems with auditory alarm systems? How would you correct these problems?

17. Describe how a tactile system of displaying information could work with firefighters in a smoke-filled building.

18. What is the field of telematics? Why is it important in engineering psychology?

19. What has human factors research learned about (a) the use of cell phones while driving, (b) leather versus fabric seating, and (c) furniture for the classroom?

20. How would you design a study to determine the most efficient ice cream scoop to minimize muscle strain?

21. What factors should be considered in designing a computer workstation?

22. What are the most frequent complaints expressed by computer users?

23. Would you rather read a magazine article on your computer screen or printed on paper? Which format provides for faster reading and better understanding?

24. Give examples of how the use of robots is changing how people work and live.

25. In your opinion, is new technology reducing the role and importance of the person in a person–machine system? Do you think the continuing development of automated systems works to our ultimate advantage or disadvantage?

Additional Reading

Carroll, J. M. (1997). Human-computer interaction. *Annual Review of Psycholog, 48,* 61–83. Reviews research and applications in the field of human–computer interaction focusing on the development of user-centered systems.

Nelson, N. A., & Silverstein, B. A. (1998). Workplace changes associated with a reduction in musculoskeletal symptoms in office workers. *Human Factors, 40,* 337–350. Identifies workplace factors associated with hand/arm and neck/shoulder/back complaints among office workers.

O'Brien, T. G., & Charlton, S. G. (Eds.) (1996). *Handbook of human factors testing and evaluation.* Hillsdale, NJ: Erlbaum. A sourcebook on assessing the components of a person–machine system.

Shih, H. M., & Goonetilleke, R. S. (1998). Effectiveness of menu orientation in Chinese. *Human Factors, 40,* 569–576. An example of cultural differences in human factors applications. Studies reading and writing flow (for example, vertical versus horizontal) in the effectiveness of computer menus.

Wickens, C., Lee, J., Liu, Y., & Becker, S. (2004). *An introduction to human factors engineering* (2nd ed.). Upper Saddle River NJ: Prentice Hall. A comprehensive textbook explaining and illustrating human factors principles.

PART SIX

Consumer Psychology

Not everyone works for an organization, but all of us are consumers of the products and services of many organizations. We buy cars, cosmetics, clothes, and cell phones. We vote for political candidates and express our opinions on issues in public opinion polls. We respond to appeals from charities and special interest groups.

We are bombarded by communications from all these organizations—messages from business, government, and other groups urging us to behave in one way or another. These thousands of advertising appeals appear on television, computer screens, and billboards and in the pages of magazines and newspapers.

Consumer psychologists are concerned with the interactions between consumers and organizations. Advertisers spend billions of dollars to influence our choices, and many of their persuasive techniques were devised by psychologists. Consumer psychology is also important to you as an employee. If people do not buy what your company produces, the company will not be in business for long.

Chapter 14 deals with the interactions between the producer and the consumer: the ways of studying consumer behavior and preferences; the nature of advertising; the importance of packaging, trademarks, and product images; the assessment of reactions to television programs; and types of advertising appeals for different segments of society.

C H A P T E R   1 4

Consumer Psychology

CHAPTER OUTLINE

THE SCOPE OF CONSUMER PSYCHOLOGY

There is no escaping the influence of consumer psychology. Pick up a magazine, turn on the radio or TV, go online, or drive down a billboard-lined road and you will be bombarded by thousands of advertising messages every day. Your phone company sends advertising flyers with your monthly bill. The supermarket prints ads on the back of your cash register receipt. Theaters showing popular films also run commercials. Public buildings post ads on the inside of the stall doors in restrooms.

Banks run ads on their ATMs and spew out money-saving coupons with your cash. Office buildings install high-resolution color monitors in elevators to beam ads to the captive audience. Cable TV presents a running band across the bottom of the screen to show news headlines, sports scores, weather and traffic reports, and—you guessed it—ads! You'll find high-tech ads running wherever people have to wait: supermarket checkout lines, gas pumps, the post office, doctors' offices. The next time you board an airplane you may find ads on the tray table, napkins, and airsickness bag. Airlines in Europe and Asia have put ads on the overhead bin doors and even on the plane's exterior. Plans are underway for huge advertising panels on the ground beside runways so that passengers can see the messages while their plane is coming in for a landing.

Scented paper forces you to smell a product, even if you do not look at the ad for it. Aromas of perfumes, chocolates, detergents, and leather automobile upholstery fill the glossy pages of magazines. More than a billion scent strips a year are distributed, creating severe problems for people who have allergies. Thanks to microchips the size of a grain of salt, it is possible to hear print ads. Several years ago, a popular brand of vodka spent $1 million on a Christmastime magazine ad that played "Jingle Bells" when readers turned the page and saw the ad. The company claimed that the ad produced the largest holiday season sales in its history. "With blinking lights, pop-up ads, kiss-on lipstick samples, scratch-off scents, melt-in-your-mouth taste strips . . . advertisers are stuffing magazines full of just about anything to make their advertisements stand out" (*New York Times*, April 22, 2008, p. C4).

None of us can pay attention to or respond to all the messages directed toward us as consumers, nor should we, if we want to maintain our sanity. We do not consciously perceive most of the messages around us, but even if we remain unaware of the details, we are certainly aware of the process of advertising—and many of us don't like it. A large-scale, nationwide survey conducted for the American Association of Advertising Agencies yielded results that did not make the ad agencies happy. Here are a few of the findings (Elliott, 2004):

- 54% of those surveyed said they deliberately avoided products that overwhelmed them with advertising
- 60% said their opinions about advertising were much more negative than they were a few years ago
- 61% reported that the amount of advertising they were exposed to was "out of control"
- 69% expressed interest in products and services that would help them eliminate or block ads
- 45% said that the amount of advertising and marketing detracted from the quality of everyday life

Although it is true that advertising can annoy us, it can also inform and even entertain us. Ads tell us about new products, new models of current products, product specifications and pricing, places to purchase the product, and sales. Some ads are attractive, clever, and funny. Advertising is part of daily life and a major topic of research. Indeed, consumer behavior has been of interest to psychologists since the beginning of the field. It was the study of consumer behavior that launched I-O psychology.

Industrial psychology dates from the early-twentieth-century work of Walter Dill Scott on advertising and selling. In 1921, John B. Watson, founder of the behaviorist school of psychology, began to apply his ideas about human behavior to problems in the business world. He proposed that consumer behavior could be conditioned—and, therefore, predicted and controlled—just like any other kind of behavior. Watson brought experimental and survey methods to marketing, and he insisted that advertisements should focus on style and image rather than substance and fact. He also pioneered the use of celebrity endorsements.

Since those early days, the field has continued to expand in scope and influence. In the late 1960s, the

Association for Consumer Research was founded and the first textbooks on consumer behavior were published. The Society for Consumer Psychology was founded in 1960 as Division 23 of the American Psychological Association. Besides psychology, researchers in the field of consumer behavior come from the disciplines of sociology, anthropology, economics, and business administration.

Paper

RESEARCH METHODS IN CONSUMER PSYCHOLOGY

People can lie or change mind

Most consumer psychology research relies on the techniques described in chapter 2, such as laboratory experiments and surveys. Research is conducted in settings such as university laboratories, downtown intersections, homes, shopping centers, the offices of manufacturers and advertising agencies, and online.

Surveys and Public Opinion Polls

The premise underlying the use of surveys is simple: Most people can and will express their feelings, reactions, opinions, and desires when somebody asks them. This assumption holds whether trying to determine reactions to a new brand of peanut butter or to a presidential candidate. The survey method often works well. Think of how accurately many pre-election polls have predicted election results or how successfully new products have been introduced on the basis of market testing. However, there have also been spectacular failures

in predicting election results and in forecasting a product's success. Table 14-1 shows advantages and disadvantages of different survey techniques.

Part of the difficulty is the complex and changeable nature of human behavior. Some people will tell a pollster on Friday that they intend to vote Republican and then will vote Democratic on Tuesday. Respondents may tell an interviewer that they drink expensive imported beer, but a glance inside their refrigerator would reveal cans of some generic brand. They may have claimed to drink the imported beer because they thought it would make them appear sophisticated.

Searches of trash cans have revealed that on average, people drink twice the amount of beer and liquor than they report in consumer surveys. Survey respondents consistently underreport the amount of junk food they eat and overreport the amount of fresh fruit and diet soft drinks they consume. People tend to respond to surveys and polls with statements they believe will enhance their status. On such vagaries, elections are lost and manufacturers go bankrupt.

A survey of 2,448 people who had received a mail-order catalog reported that 10% of those who had purchased products from the company said they had *never* purchased anything from that company. In addition, 40% of those who had made no purchases reported that they had, indeed, bought something. Whatever the cause of such false responses—memory lapses or deliberate distortions—the results highlight the problem of inaccurate responses to survey questions (Woodside & Wilson, 2002).

TABLE 14-1

Advantages and Disadvantages of Various Survey Techniques

	Mail	Telephone	Personal Interview	Online
Cost	Low	Moderate	High	Low
Speed	Slow	Immediate	Slow	Fast
Response rate	Low	Moderate	High	Self-selected
Geographic flexibility	Excellent	Good	Difficult	Excellent
Interviewer bias	N/A	Moderate	Problematic	N/A
Interviewer supervision	N/A	Easy	Difficult	N/A
Quality of response	Limited	Limited	Excellent	Excellent

Source: L. Schiffman & L. Kanuk (2004), *Consumer Behavior* (8th ed.). Upper Saddle River, NJ: Prentice Hall, p. 351.

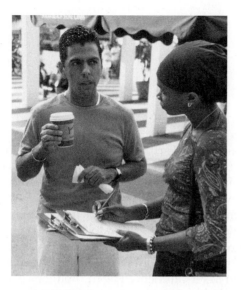

Much consumer psychology research relies on surveys. Shoppers may be asked about the products they are using, how often they purchase them, and why they have chosen a particular brand.

In a study on mail surveys, researchers found that sending postcards to potential respondents that contained a contact telephone number to establish the survey's validity significantly increased the response rate over simply mailing the survey without advance notice or contact information (McPheters & Kossoff, 2003). In another study, sending a photo of a woman who was identified as the researcher conducting the survey resulted in a significantly greater response rates than sending a photo of a man identified as the researcher (Dommeyer, 2008).

Response rates to telephone surveys have declined significantly since the development of caller ID systems and the federal "Do Not Call" registry. Research has shown that half of the people who own answering machines or subscribe to caller ID services screen their calls and tend not to answer those whose names they do not recognize. The tendency to screen calls is higher among 18- to 29-year-olds, single persons, African Americans, and people with young children at home. Call screening is also higher in large cities and their surrounding suburbs than in smaller cities and towns (Tuckel & O'Neill, 2002).

Many market researchers are now turning to online surveys, which have become a fast and less expensive way to obtain data on consumer behavior and attitudes. Web sites have been developed that offer incentives (such as the chance to win a vacation or a TV) to respond to surveys online. The Consumer Reports organization conducted its first annual online product survey in 2003, reaching 4 million online subscribers. The return rate was 25%, compared to 14% in previous years when questionnaires were sent by mail. The cost of the online survey was half that of the mailed surveys.

Newsbreak

Spring Break in Florida: Bring on the Ads!

Have you ever gone to Panama City, Florida, for spring break? About 300,000 college students descend on this town every April, and with them come hundreds of advertisers eager to market their products. It's a huge, lively bazaar where thousands of samples are given away in the hope that the students will become hooked on a particular brand or product and use it for the rest of their lives.

Wherever you look there's some advertising or promotional gimmick—all for free. Mouthwash, chewing tobacco, sunblock, bikinis, T-shirts, high-energy drinks, beef jerky, and much more. And everywhere you see ads, from restaurant menus to lampposts, hotel lobbies, and the beach itself. Shower curtains in motel rooms painted with the name of a body spray, tanning lotion samples placed on bed pillows, key cards to access hotel rooms decorated with ads. Contests on the beach offer ways to score bags of free loot. Even the beach balls display ads. There's no break from advertising!

Source: Copeland, L. (2007, May 28). An ocean of promotion for spring breakers: The selling never stops. *Washington Post.*

> **Focus groups** A method of surveying public opinion through the paid participation of 8 to 12 group members who meet to describe their reactions to a product, advertisement, or specific issues.

↘ Focus Groups

A widely used type of survey involves **focus groups**, which consist of small samples of consumers who meet in groups of 8 to 12 to describe their reactions to a product, package, or ad, or to the ideas and issues being promoted by a political candidate. Members of focus groups are usually paid for their participation and are selected to match the profile of the average voter or consumer of a particular type of product. For example, only pet owners would be selected for a focus group to test an ad for dog food. Only mothers of infants would be chosen to evaluate a new disposable diaper. Focus groups can be structured on the basis of age, income, educational level, or any other variable relevant to the product.

Focus groups are structured differently for different segments of the population. For example, an approach suitable for groups of adolescents must be modified for the lesser attention span of children or the perceptual and cognitive differences of the elderly. Focus group sessions are observed through one-way mirrors and videorecorded for later analysis. The data produced by focus groups—the comments and responses of the participants—are more qualitative than are those obtained from questionnaires in large-scale empirical surveys. Sometimes focus group members are not asked direct questions but are observed as they try to use a new product. In a session to evaluate a disposable razor, observers reported that many men cut themselves while shaving because the package directions were not clear.

As in surveys, participants in focus groups may distort their answers, saying what they think others want to hear or what they want others to hear. Consider the focus group that was discussing ads for a company that performed surgical hair replacements. The men in the group all insisted that they were not bothered, personally, by losing their hair. Yet they were all wearing hats—on a hot day in Atlanta, Georgia! Their behavior may have been more truly reflective of their attitude about hair loss than what they said to others in the group, but how could the observers know for sure?

Virtual focus groups conducted online function in a similar way as face-to-face groups and offer the advantages of lower cost and greater efficiency. They can sample a more diverse group of people who might lack the time and transportation to come to a central meeting place for the focus group session. Responses of members of actual and virtual focus groups may differ. Usually, in a face-to-face meeting, one person at a time expresses an opinion. Sometimes one individual will dominate the group. In an online meeting, all participants have the chance to speak simultaneously and thus tend to be less influenced by the opinions of others. When dealing with sensitive topics such as health issues, the privacy and anonymity of an online session enables people to speak more candidly.

✦ Motivation Research

Psychologists cannot uncover all human motivations by asking questions that permit people to mask or distort their true intentions and feelings. To probe these deeper, hidden motivations, some psychologists use in-depth interviews and projective techniques. The pioneer in this field of motivation research was Ernest Dichter (1907–1992), a psychologist born and trained in Vienna. Dichter immigrated to the United States in 1938. Building on Freudian psychoanalysis to discover unconscious motivations for neurotic behavior, he applied the approach to consumer behavior—why some people purchase particular products or decline to purchase other products.

Dichter's first success was with packaged cake mix, a product introduced around 1940. Everything needed to bake a cake was included in the box: sugar, flour, shortening, and dried egg. Just add water, stir, pour in a pan, and bake. The product promised a revolution in cake baking—an easy, quick, no fuss, and homemade cake with that just-baked aroma that never failed. The only problem was that consumers rejected it. Why? Dichter solved the problem for the General Mills organization by applying psychoanalytic techniques to uncover the real reason for customer resistance. Questioning a sample of female consumers, so-called typical homemakers of the day, he found that the women felt guilty about doing little or no work to bake a cake for their family. The solution? Give the consumer something to do, to help

Newsbreak

You Can Make a Living From Focus Groups

You can make a living from focus groups—if you tell them what they want to hear. Read this article from a popular magazine and draw your own conclusion.

"I have been many men in my career as a focus-group member. For a travel study, I was a hardy adventurer who'd backpacked through Mongolia. For a deodorant group, I claimed a glandular problem that caused me to sweat profusely, no matter the conditions. . . . It all began when I woke up to my status as a card-carrying member of the advertiser-horny 18-to-34-year-old, single-white-male segment of society. As such, my opinions are valuable. Focus groups pay serious money: anywhere from $75 to $300 an hour for sitting with a bunch of other guys and commenting on everything from alcohol packaging to the elastic waistband of your tighty-whities. These 'screenings' are constructed as theoretically perfect control groups, with men off the street full of fresh, unspoiled insights. To that end, most focus companies have a rule that no one can participate in a group more than once every six months. This is complete bunk. If you know how to game the system, you can do one of these a week, sometimes even more. . . . If [recruiters] ask you whether you've done [a focus group] in the past six months, just say no. They never check. If they ask you something off-the-wall, like 'Have you purchased a treadmill in the past year?' say yes; they wouldn't ask if that weren't the answer they wanted. If they ask you what brands you purchase most often, always name big ones: Sprint, Budweiser, Marlboro.

They're representing either one of those companies or a smaller one trying to figure out how to steal you away. And, most important, let the recruiters lead you. Before you answer a question you're not sure about, pause for a couple of seconds. They'll tip their hand every time."

"Once you're actually in the group, it's vital to be as invisible as possible. If you're tagged as an 'outlier' who has opinions that don't jibe with an advertiser's research, it's less likely you'll be invited back. You are not a human; you are a demographic stereotype. So act manly: Refer to any pink product packaging as 'feminine' or 'wussy,' or mention that you're always 'tossing down a few after work with my buddies.' In one group for Johnnie Walker Black, it was obvious the marketers wanted us to consider their beverage upscale, for special occasions. Recognizing this, I made up a story about learning my best friend was engaged and telling him, 'It's Johnnie Walker time!' The interviewer looked like he wanted to hug me."

"It's also important to be vague. During the focus group on travel, the interviewer asked me if there were any countries I might have moral qualms visiting. The correct answer was 'Oh, none at all.' But I blurted out, 'South Africa,' sharing some underdeveloped thoughts I had about apartheid. The interviewer's face sharpened, and he began to pepper me with questions. I had forgotten the cardinal rule: They don't want your opinion; they want you to confirm what they already think. You're whatever they want you to be, baby."

Source: Leitch, W. (2004, June 21) Group thinker. *New York.*

fulfill the urge to be creative. In this case, Dichter recommended that the company omit the dried egg and let the consumer add fresh eggs to the packaged mix. As a result, sales soared, Dichter became rich and famous, and his motivation research techniques became essential tools in the understanding of consumer behavior (see Smith, 2004; Stern, 2002).

We described some projective techniques in chapter 4, namely, the Rorschach Inkblot Test, the Thematic Apperception Test, and the sentence completion test. The theory behind the use of projective techniques is the same whether they are applied to employee selection or to consumer behavior. When people are presented with an ambiguous stimulus, such as an inkblot, it is assumed that they will project their needs, fears, and values onto the stimulus in the act of interpreting it. A classic example of the use of projective techniques to study consumer behavior involved the reaction of women to a new brand of roach killer packaged in small plastic trays. Surveys showed that consumers said they believed the plastic trays were far more effective than the old-style sprays, yet they continued to buy the sprays. To determine the reasons for this inconsistency, groups of women were asked to draw pictures of roaches and to write stories about them. The researchers reported the following about the possible motivation of the female consumers:

> The results were very informative—all the roaches in the pictures were male, 'symbolizing men who the women said had abandoned them and left them feeling poor and powerless.' The women were said to be expressing their built-up hostility by spraying the roaches and watching them squirm and die! (Foxall & Goldsmith, 1994, p. 162)

Direct questioning would not have revealed this motivation.

In theory, the projective approach to studying consumer behavior offers the same advantages as projective tests for employee selection, namely, the ability to reach deeper levels of motivation and to uncover feelings and desires that cannot be assessed by objective tests and questionnaires. However, projective tests are low in reliability and validity. There have been successful uses of projective techniques to study consumer behavior, but because the advertising industry does not publicize its failures, it is difficult to determine the extent of that success.

Observations of Shopping Behavior

Consumer surveys and the kinds of techniques used in motivation research share a basic weakness: They reveal only what people say they believe or will do. These expressed intentions do not always coincide with actual behavior. Because of this discrepancy, some consumer psychologists prefer to observe what people do when purchasing a product or when expressing their preference by selecting one brand over another. Common sense suggests that acceptance of a new product or advertising campaign will be reflected in subsequent sales figures.

For example, if sales of a toothpaste brand double in the 6 months after an ad campaign, then the campaign must have been successful. However, unless all other variables capable of influencing sales were controlled, the advertisers cannot conclude with certainty that the new advertising program was solely or even partially responsible for the boost in sales. Suppose the company's aggressive sales staff arranged for more prominent shelf display of the toothpaste during the 6-month period. That increased visibility could have contributed to higher

sales, independent of the ad campaign. Or suppose the company's leading competitor was faulted in a government report for adding an allegedly harmful ingredient to its toothpaste formula. That criticism could contribute to higher sales for all other toothpaste manufacturers. Thus, sales data can reflect factors other than the one being evaluated, and without adequate control over all possible influencing variables, the cause of any increase or decrease in sales cannot be determined precisely.

The most direct way to investigate purchasing behavior is to place video cameras or human observers in stores. Researchers have watched mothers with young children as they shopped for cereals and snack foods. More than 65% of the time, children ask for a particular product. And more than half the time, the mothers buy the products their children demand. Such data are especially valuable because they indicate that children, not adults, should be the target of ads for cereals and snack foods. Had the mothers been questioned directly in a survey, however, they might have said that *they* were the ones to choose these products, not wanting to appear to be dominated by their children or perhaps not realizing the extent of their children's influence.

Another observation of purchasing behavior resulted in a change in how a product was stocked. Supermarket observers noted that dog food was purchased by adults, but dog treats were more often selected by children or older persons. However, dog treats were usually stocked on the upper shelves. Hidden cameras caught children climbing on shelves to reach the dog cookies. Older women were observed using boxes of foil or other long objects to knock down a favorite brand of dog biscuit. By moving the dog treats to lower, more accessible shelves, sales improved almost overnight.

Although observations of actual purchasing behavior can be useful, they are costly and time-consuming. There are other problems as well. One relates to adequate sampling of shopping behavior. Stores in different locations attract customers with different needs and income levels. As you might expect, city and suburban shoppers preferred different kinds of stores, chose different types of products, and had differing amounts of disposable income for shopping. Another problem is the variety in types of shoppers in the same store at different times of the day or week. People who shop in the evenings and on weekends may have different buying habits from those of people who shop during the day. The research design must compensate for such problems by providing for observations at an adequate sample of locations and shopping hours, but this increases the cost of the research.

An additional problem with observations of purchasing behavior is the lack of experimental control over other influencing variables; this is a weakness of all types of observational research studies. In observing supermarket shopping patterns in urban and suburban locations, for example, it is difficult to determine whether any differences noted are a function of socioeconomic level, ethnic composition, shelf arrangement, or inventory. All these factors could affect the outcome of the research. Despite such limitations, however, direct observation of shopping behavior has often revealed valuable marketing information that would have been difficult to obtain any other way.

A useful variation on the observation of people when they shop is to observe them actually using a product. When the Kimberly-Clarke company found that sales of its Huggies baby wipes and baby lotions had declined, the company tried to find out why. Focus groups failed to provide useful answers, so the marketers tried a new approach. Consumers agreed to have a tiny camera placed on their eyeglasses. That way, the researchers could see exactly what these caregivers saw when using the baby products. In focus groups, women had talked about changing diapers at diaper tables, but in practice, "they changed them on beds, floors, and on top of washing machines in awkward positions. The researchers could see they were struggling with wipe containers and lotions requiring two hands. The company redesigned the wipe with a push-button

---

Newsbreak

Are You a Minivan or an SUV?

Consumer researchers indicate that different products attract different kinds of people. This seems particularly true for the kinds of automobiles people drive. A survey of 5,400 owners of minivans and sport utility vehicles (SUVs) revealed that what you drive tells the world a lot about your personality. And maybe that's why you chose it.

The research showed that SUV owners tend to be more restless, more devoted to pleasurable pursuits, less social, and more fearful of crime than are people who purchased minivans. Minivan owners tend to be more self-confident and sociable and more comfortable with the idea of being married and having children than are SUV drivers.

Both groups said they wanted to be "in control" of their vehicle, but they don't mean the same thing by that phrase. Minivan people want to be in control in terms of safety, the ability to maneuver well in traffic, and to park easily. SUV people want to be in control in the sense of dominating everyone around them.

It is not surprising, then, that SUV drivers have been found to be more aggressive and less con-cerned with behaving courteously to drivers of other vehicles. A French anthropologist who is a consultant to Ford, General Motors, and Daimler Chrysler said, "Sport utilities are designed to be masculine and assertive, often with hoods that resemble those on 18-wheel trucks and vertical metal slats across the grilles to give the appearance of a jungle cat's teeth. Sport utilities are designed to appeal to Americans' deepest fears of violence and crime."

SUVs are like weapons, he concluded, "armored cars for the battlefield." Their message is, "Don't mess with me."

What do you drive? And what do you call your car? Have you given it a name? Male or female? A study of college students in Colorado found that 25% named their cars and 50% thought of them as either masculine or feminine. These students scored high on personality tests that measured characteristics of road rage such as verbal and physical aggression and anger while driving.

So the kind of car you choose and the way you think of it may well reflect the kind of person you are.

Sources: Benfield, J., Szlemko, W., & Bell, P. (2007). Driver personality and anthropometric attribution of vehicle personality related to reported aggressive driving tendencies, *Personality and Individual Differences, 42,* 247–248; Morin, R. (2006, October 19). Personality of a car an indicator of road rage. *Washington Post*; Bradsher, K. (2000, July 17). Was Freud a minivan or an SUV kind of guy? *New York Times.*

one-handed dispenser and designed lotion and shampoo bottles that can be grabbed and dispensed with one hand" (Kiley, 2005, p.2). With these changes, sales increased. The marketers attributed this increase to learning how customers were actually using their products rather than listening to what they said in focus groups.

Neuromarketing

A newer research method in consumer psychology is neuromarketing, which involves measuring brain activity and functions in response to marketing and advertising programs. People serving as subjects are connected to devices that scan activity in various parts of the brain by means of electroencephalography (EEG), magnetic resonance imaging (MRI), and positron emission tomography (PET).

Neuromarketing is being used to test the effectiveness of advertising and the appeal of new products and promotional programs not by listening to what people say or by watching what they do, but by examining brain waves (Fugate, 2007). As one neuromarketer said, "We measure attention second by second; how emotionally engaged you are with what you're watching, whether it's a commercial, a movie, or a TV show" (Elliott, 2008).

In one study, brain waves were monitored as adult subjects watched presentations for different products on their computer screens. By reading how brain wave activity changed in response to the products, the researchers found that they could accurately predict what other products the subjects would say they would purchase, even before they saw them on the screen (Knutson, Ricks, Wimmer, Prelec, & Loewenstein, 2007).

In other research, men were shown 66 pictures of sports cars, sedans, and small cars; they rated sports cars as the most desirable. When sports cars were shown, brain images revealed increased activity in an area of the brain that contains the self-reward center, which is normally activated only by such stimuli as sex, chocolate, or cocaine. The sight of the sports car released opiates in the brain related to lust and pleasure, which shows just how deeply pleasurable the pictures of sports cars were perceived. Researchers learned how such stimuli could be used to get viewers' attention (Britt, 2004).

A study of 200 television viewers in England found that TV ads shown during the morning hours were far more stimulating to areas of the brain associated with attention, concentration, short-term and long-term memory, and positive emotional engagement than were the same commercials shown at night, during the so-called prime-time viewing hours. Perhaps prime time is not prime for advertisers after all (Haq, 2007).

Testing Reactions to Ads

A major research activity of consumer psychologists is testing the effectiveness of advertising and promotional campaigns. The most direct approach is to ask people for their reactions to an ad. Does the ad make them want to buy the product? Do they believe the ad? Which of two ads for a product do they find more interesting? In such research, the respondents must be a representative sample of the population for whom the product is intended. Asking single men or older women to pretest an ad for baby food is not likely to yield useful results. Consumer psychologists also use three other techniques for testing the effectiveness of advertisements: physiological measures, sales tests, and coupon returns.

Physiological Measures. TV commercials are designed to elicit emotional responses in viewers. Physiological measures of changes in the electrical activity of the muscles as influenced by those emotions are an effective way to determine a commercial's usefulness. For example, consumers can be exposed to a variety of TV commercials while their physiological responses are measured by electromyography (EMG), which detects changes in the electrical activity of the muscles. When applied to certain facial muscles, EMG measures a person's reaction to emotional stimuli. Some time later, these consumers can be asked to rate each commercial or ad on the basis of how much they liked it or how much pleasure (or other emotion) it aroused in them. If the results show that facial EMG data correlate strongly and positively with the ratings of the commercials, then the ads can be considered effective.

Sales Tests. Some marketers and consumer psychologists argue that the only meaningful test of advertising effectiveness is whether it results in higher sales. Recall, though, the limitations of using sales data as a measure of advertising success. The

Sales test technique A way of testing the effectiveness of an advertising campaign by introducing the new advertising in selected test markets.

sales test technique is designed to reduce those problems because it permits experimental control of extraneous variables. Sales tests have been found to be a highly accurate way of assessing the impact of advertising on sales.

In a sales test, an advertising campaign is introduced in selected test markets, such as a specific neighborhood, city, or other geographical area. Other locations, chosen to be as similar as possible to the test markets, serve as controls; the new advertising is not presented in these control areas. If the test and control areas are comparable, then any change in sales within the test areas can be attributed to the advertising campaign. Control over possible influencing variables is the major advantage of sales tests. The researcher is not measuring interest in an ad or what subjects say they remember, but whether people actually buy the product on the basis of the ad.

The use of sales tests for studying advertising effectiveness also has limitations. An adequate sales test is costly. It takes time to arrange, and it requires precise accounting of the purchasing behavior of a large number of people. Another problem involves the areas selected for the control group. By not exposing people in the control markets to its new ad campaign, the company risks losing sales to its competitors.

Coupon Returns. In some cases the effectiveness of magazine and newspaper advertising is tested by evaluating coupon returns. When coupons are returned to a manufacturer to obtain a product sample or to enter a contest, they provide a measure of reader interest. When coupons are used to purchase a product or receive a discount (cents-off coupons), they measure actual buying behavior. However, if the inducement to return the coupon is attractive (for example, when a mail-order retailer offered a free pair of sweat socks to introduce a house brand), there is a danger that people will respond even though they have no interest in the product. Many people just want to get something free. There are also people who send in coupons because they like to get mail in return. It is difficult to determine how many coupon returns come from

habitual coupon clippers and how many come from people genuinely interested in the product.

Coupon returns may indicate the attention-getting value of an ad, but they do not provide a direct measure of the ad's impact on sales. When coupons offer a reduced price for a product, they are effective in inducing people to change brands, at least temporarily. A price reduction obtained by redeeming a coupon at the supermarket promotes greater sales than an equivalent price markdown at the store.

In one study, more than 900 shoppers were given questionnaires as they left various stores and were asked to mail them to the researchers. The results showed that those who used coupons differed from those who did not. The high coupon users considered themselves to be smart shoppers, believed in the economic benefits of using coupons, were more price sensitive and value conscious, and were willing to invest the time required to obtain coupons in order to save money. High coupon users also reported that they enjoyed the shopping experience more than did low coupon users (Garretson & Burton, 2003).

THE NATURE AND SCOPE OF ADVERTISING

Sellers of goods and services select various approaches to encourage, persuade, stimulate, or manipulate consumers to buy their products. The most frequently used kind of advertising is the direct sell type, designed to elicit an immediate response from the consumer. Other advertising, however, serves different purposes.

Consumer Awareness. One type of advertising is designed to create consumer awareness of a new product, an improved product or package, or a price change. This type of advertising also tries to reinforce the brand name. Because so much purchasing behavior is linked to brand names, companies spend considerable sums creating and maintaining public awareness of company and product names.

Newsbreak

Coupons: Why Clip If You Can Download!

It started in 1895 when Asa Chandler of Atlanta, Georgia, distributed coupons for a free glass of Coca-Cola at his soda fountain. Today, an estimated 335 billion cents-off, free-product, and rebate coupons are distributed annually—an average of more than 3,000 for every U.S. household. Surveys show that three of every four Americans use coupons when making purchases. People cut them out of newspapers and magazines or download them from the Internet and take them to stores to redeem on purchases of toothpaste, headache remedies, cookies, and breakfast cereal. Pharmacies give them out for discounts on prescription drugs, department stores offer them for special sales, and bookstores send them via e-mail.

Coupons can save real money. The average family that uses coupons can count on saving approximately $700 a year, a substantial hourly payback rate for the time required to clip or print, assemble, and organize the coupons. Hard-core coupon users, who have been known to purchase several copies of the Sunday newspaper to get additional coupons,

save even more money. Coupon inserts are now the second most widely read part of the typical Sunday newspaper; only the front page is more popular.

The use of online coupons is growing by more than 50% a year, though they still represent only a small portion of all the coupons redeemed. Online coupons provide a major benefit to marketers and researchers: instant personal information about the person who is downloading the coupon. One source of online coupons is www.smartsource. com Users who log on to this Web site must register, providing details about themselves, family members, pets, income, and preferred stores. In return, they get free access to up to 35 coupons a day worth approximately $14. When they use a coupon, its code number tells the company who redeemed it, where it was redeemed, and for what product. Such data cannot be obtained from a coupon cut out from a newspaper supplement.

So log on and get your coupons, but you'll give away a bit of your privacy. Do you think it's a fair trade?

Sources: It all started with a coupon for a free Coke (1996, January 11), *St. Petersburg (FL) Times*; Paper coupons still popular as Internet tries to clip them (2006, August 29). *International Herald Tribune*.

Product Image.   Some advertising tries to establish an image for a product or service. Many products cannot be distinguished from one another on the basis of ingredients or quality, so advertisers try to create differences in terms of images, symbols, or feelings. For example, an automobile must do more than provide transportation; a lipstick must provide more than color. These items must, through their image, make the owners feel younger, sportier, or more attractive, or they enhance prestige and economic status. As the president of a firm that makes men's and women's fragrances said, "In the factory we make cosmetics. In the store we sell hope."

Institutional Advertising.   The goal of institutional advertising is to persuade the public that the company is a good neighbor and community benefactor. An oil company may conduct a campaign to promote highway safety rather than simply

to sell its brand of gasoline. Companies advertise that their products are good for the environment, that they contribute a share of their profits to charities, or that they support sports teams for children and adolescents. Institutional advertising can build public goodwill, boost sales, recruit employees, improve employee morale, and drive up the price of the company's stock.

Informational Advertising.   Advertising can be called informational when it enables consumers to make more intelligent purchasing decisions. Various types of information appear in such ads: price, quality, performance data, components or contents, availability, nutritional data, warranties, safety record. The use of informative advertising has increased from an average of 20% of all ads a decade ago to more than 65% today. Magazine ads tend to be more informative than television ads.

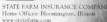

VISITORS TO MS. GAWEL'S CLASSROOM FIND OUT JUST HOW WILD IT REALLY IS.

To help awaken them to the plight of the world's rainforests, Julie Gawel's students created one of their own.

Julie, an art teacher at Killough Middle School in Houston, Texas, designed the multi-disciplinary program for her students utilizing reading, writing, science, and art. After researching the rainforest environment, the students practiced drawing its inhabitants; learning about paint, color mixing, and texture in the process. Then they transformed their classroom with wall-size murals and papier-mâché trees filled with a menagerie of plants and wildlife.

Finally, the students invited parents and local business leaders to their rainforest, where the children made presentations and passed along the lessons they learned about conservation.

For teaching her students how to be wild about art – and the world's rainforests – Julie Gawel is our newest Good Neighbor Award winner.

State Farm is pleased to contribute $5,000 in her name to Alief Independent School District.

GOOD NEIGHBOR AWARD
STATE FARM INSURANCE COMPANIES
Home Offices: Bloomington, Illinois
www.statefarm.com

The Good Neighbor Award was developed in cooperation with the National Art Education Association.

Institutional advertising promotes the idea that the company is a good neighbor and community benefactor. (Reproduced by permission of State Farm Insurance Companies.)

Advertising Placement. Outlets for advertising have changed over the past several years. For example, McDonald's devotes one third of its marketing budget to television ads, but only a few years ago that figure was two thirds. Companies are cutting back on the money earmarked for TV advertising and spending it instead on other media outlets in an effort to reach more targeted audiences. For McDonald's, the money the company used to spend on 30-second network spots now goes to closed-circuit sports programs piped into bars with a large Hispanic customer base, to ads in *Upscale* magazine (distributed to barbershops with a Black clientele), to in-store videos at Foot Locker, to print ads in women's magazines, and to pop-up ads on Web sites. What happened to TV advertising? Many consumers prefer to spend time in front of their computer

TABLE 14-2

Interest in Various Types of Television Advertising

Product	Percent of Viewers Ignoring These TV Ads	Percent of Ads Skipped by Using Personal Video Recorders
Beer	5	32
Soft drinks	22	83
Fast food	45	96
Automobiles	53	69
Credit cards	63	94
Upcoming TV programs	75	94

Source: Business Week, July 12, 2004.

instead of their TV. And when people do watch television, they find ways to ignore commercials. Table 14-2 shows the waning interest in TV ads for various consumer products.

[handwritten margin note: Paper: I've been a victim of this]

Types of Advertising Appeals

The major way in which an ad campaign can persuade you to buy a product is through its appeal, that is, what it promises to do for you. Look at some magazine ads. Which human needs or motivations does the product promise to satisfy? Psychologists have identified many human needs: the innate or primary needs, such as food, water, shelter, security, and sex; and the learned or secondary needs, such as power, status, achievement, esteem, and affiliation. These secondary motivations depend on personal experiences and thus vary from one person to another and from one culture to another.

To sell their products and services, advertisers must identify the relevant needs and direct their messages toward the appropriate segment of the population. Most ads attempt to satisfy more than one need. For example, an ad for imported beer can promise to quench thirst (a primary need) and to satisfy desires for status and belonging (secondary needs). Ads for mouthwash and deodorant promise users they will avoid embarrassing situations and thus be more likable. If you use the right cologne, you will find love and thus fulfill the needs for social support and self-esteem. Driving the right car can provide power, prestige, and achievement, along with the hope of attracting a mate. Advertisers use several techniques to appeal to these diverse human needs.

Celebrity Endorsements. A product endorsed by a celebrity entertainer or sports figure invites the audience to identify with that person's success. Advertisers often choose celebrities to sell products, although there is little published evidence of the impact of celebrity endorsements on actual purchasing, unless the celebrity is believed to be qualified to promote that product. A study of college students investigated the influence of celebrity status, attractiveness, trustworthiness, and perceived expertise on their expressed intentions to purchase particular items. Only the perceived expertise of the celebrities was positively related to buying intentions. For example, a tennis pro was considered to be a believable endorser of tennis rackets, a good-looking male movie star was an effective promoter of men's cologne, and a fashion model was an appropriate spokesperson for designer jeans.

Other research showed that the use of sports or entertainment celebrities in magazine ads did not lead to correct identification of the brand being advertised. Most of the people exposed to the ads could not recall the brand when they were shown the celebrity's picture (Costanzo & Goodnight, 2006).

Endorsement of a product by people presumed to be experts in that product category, but who are not celebrities, seems to be effective in selling the product. An online survey of 2,000 consumers found that 87% believed that a tooth whitener sold in stores was not as effective as a tooth whitener advertised as having been developed by dentists and available only in dentists' offices (Strauss, 2008).

Some celebrities endorse more than one product, which can cause problems for sponsors or manufacturers. Research shows that as the number of products endorsed by a celebrity increases, ratings of the celebrity's credibility decrease significantly. In addition, consumer attitudes toward the ads became significantly less favorable.

Positive and Negative Emotional Appeals.   Advertising appeals can be positive or negative. The message can suggest that something good will happen to you if you use the product or that something unpleasant will happen if you don't use the product. For example, an ad for deodorant soap might show a room full of happy people who are obviously desirable because they use the featured soap, or it might show a person sitting at home alone, dateless and dejected because he or she failed to bathe with the soap. A related approach is to make a person feel guilty for not buying the product, a tactic that is particularly effective with mothers of young children.

Negative appeals are effective for certain types of products, but they do not work when the consequences are overly unpleasant. Pictures of gruesome automobile accidents to promote safe driving or depictions of diseased lungs in antismoking campaigns have been shown to be ineffective. Such fear-laden appeals distract people from the message. The same holds true for guilt appeals. Strong appeals are significantly less effective than moderate appeals in inducing feelings of guilt. A strong guilt appeal can easily generate anger toward the ad and the company that sponsored it. A frequently used approach combines positive and negative appeals. First the negative consequences of not using the product are shown, then the positive consequences of using the product are presented.

Whereas negative appeals may not be effective in advertising, shock appeals (ads that deliberately startle or offend the audience) may work. A series of three ads—one to inform, one to instill fear, and one to shock—were shown to 105 college students. The messages related to the use of condoms as a way to prevent HIV/AIDS. The shock ad showed a nude couple embracing; the message read, "Don't be a f---ing idiot." The fear ad showed a driver license with the expiration date circled; the message read, "If you get the AIDS virus now, you and your license could expire at the same time." The information ad showed the acronym AIDS and the words "Acquired Immunodeficiency." The shock appeal produced significantly greater scores on recall, recognition, and attention paid to the message than the other types

of appeals. Also, more students in the shock-ad group and the fear-ad group took AIDS-related informational materials from items displayed on a table in the viewing room than did students in the information-ad group (Dahl, Frankenberger, & Manchanda, 2003).

Implied Superiority.   A widely used appeal is implied superiority; the superiority of one product over its competitors is not stated directly but is inferred by the consumer. For example, if all headache remedies take the same amount of time to bring relief, one company may claim that no competitor provides faster relief than its product. The claim is true—no one product is faster than another—but the phrasing may lead people to conclude that this brand is superior because it sounds as if it works faster. The ad also suggests, indirectly, that its claim is based on scientific research.

Trademarks

A familiar trademark can facilitate advertising effectiveness because it serves as a shorthand symbol of the feelings and images associated with the product. Key aspects of the product come to be identified with and exemplified by the trademark. Most trademarks are brand names—for example, Coca-Cola, Kleenex, and Xerox. When a trademark is well established in the marketplace, it alone, without any other advertising message, can stimulate consumers to recall the product.

In a survey of brand names and trademarks, executives were asked to rate them on the reputation,

Trademarks. (Reproduced by permission of Wal-Mart Stores, Inc. and AT&T Corporation.)

management strength, and investment potential of their companies. A second survey asked a random sample of more than 10,000 people to rate the brand names on product quality, corporate vision, and leadership. The rankings are shown in Table 14-3, in descending order of popularity. Only three names—Coca-Cola, Walt Disney, and Johnson & Johnson—appear on both lists. Otherwise, the companies selected by the executives are different from those selected by the random sample of consumers. Thus, it is clear that the "best" brand names depend on who is being asked to pick them.

Companies spend a great deal of time and money on the development of product trademarks and brand names. Identity consultants specialize in naming and renaming products and companies. For example, California Airlines changed its name to AirCal when focus-group interviews revealed that the new name had greater consumer impact. Allegheny Airlines changed its name to USAir (now US Airways) to make it sound more like a national than a regional carrier.

Research can tell manufacturers how recognizable their product name is to the consuming public and what it means to the target audience. This information is especially crucial for U.S. companies marketing products in other countries. Sometimes a trademark can have an unintended or unfavorable meaning in another language. The Chevrolet Nova, named for a star that suddenly increases in brightness and energy, became in Spanish "*no va*," which means "doesn't go"—not a very good name for a car.

Coca-Cola changed its product name in China when the company discovered that in Chinese, Coca-Cola meant "bite the wax tadpole." Pepsi had a similar problem. "Come alive with the Pepsi generation" translated into Chinese as "Pepsi will bring your ancestors back from the dead." Remember Kentucky Fried Chicken's "finger-lickin' good"? In Chinese it became "eat your fingers off." Oops. One U.S. airline boasted in Spanish-language magazines about the leather upholstery on its seats; in translation the message meant "sit naked." The Scandinavian vacuum cleaner company, Electrolux, pulled an ad that promised, "Nothing sucks like an Electrolux," when informed by its American distributors that this was not quite the image to associate with the brand.

A trademark can be so effective that it comes to stand for all brands of a product. For example, many people now use the word *kleenex* to mean any kind of facial tissue, *xerox* for any type of photocopier, and *fedex* for any express-mail carrier. When this type of usage occurs, the company can lose its identifiability and its exclusive share of the market.

Trademarks that have worked successfully for years may have to be altered to reflect changes in the culture of the marketplace. The image of Betty Crocker, the fictional woman trademark for many food products of General Mills, was updated in 1996 to reflect the greater racial and ethnic diversity of the American population. The new Betty Crocker, computer-generated hybrid of 75 real American faces, was designed to look multicultural in an attempt to depict more accurately American society.

TABLE 14-3

Rank Order of U.S. Companies by Reputation and Brand Name Recognition

By Executives	By Random Sample
Coca-Cola	**Johnson & Johnson**
Microsoft	**Coca-Cola**
Walt Disney	Hewlett-Packard
Campbell Soup	Intel
Johnson & Johnson	Ben & Jerry's
General Electric	Wal-Mart
FedEx	Xerox
Procter & Gamble	Home Depot
Hershey Foods	Gateway
Harley-Davidson	**Walt Disney**

Product Image

Often allied with a product's trademark is its image—the ideas, thoughts, and feelings associated with the product's personality. The development of a successful product image, one with which consumers will want to identify, can bring a company from obscurity to prosperity. Indeed, the image can be more important than the qualities of the product itself.

Sometimes product image is transmitted by a symbol, such as the tiny alligator on some popular knit shirts. The symbol is supposed to convey the image of the person wearing the product. In a classic study, the researcher compared consumer perceptions of a person wearing a plain knit shirt and the same person wearing shirts with alligator, fox, and polo-player logos. The person wearing the plain shirt was judged to be self-confident, tolerant, satisfied, and friendly. The same person in the shirt with the fox emblem was described as self-confident, enthusiastic, and a leader. In the polo-player shirt, the person was perceived as less self-confident, tolerant, enthusiastic, satisfied, and friendly than in any of the other shirts. In the shirt with the alligator, the same person was described as preppy but neither a leader nor a follower. The shirt was identical in all cases; the only difference was the logo (Swartz, 1983).

The most difficult problem in developing a product image is determining the qualities that will attract potential buyers. One technique for studying product image involves group interviews with selected samples of consumers in which they are questioned about their perceptions of various products. This in-depth approach attempts to elicit positive and negative feelings about the products. A more objective approach involves the adjective checklist, which is what was used in the study of the shirts with the logos. Consumers are given a list of descriptive adjectives and phrases and are asked to select those that characterize their feelings about the product or their concept of the person who would buy the product.

Product Packaging

Another important aspect of an advertising campaign is the product's package, the part of the product that

Newsbreak

You Bought All That Stuff? What Were You Thinking?

Do you find yourself shopping a lot, buying things you don't really want, and then wondering why you bought them? If so, you're certainly not alone. To the delight of store owners, it seems that many people buy stuff they don't need, and they have been called by many names—compulsive shoppers, shopaholics, or shopping addicts.

For some people, shopping serves as a kind of therapy; it makes them feel better when they're unhappy or depressed. Consider a study in which college students were shown one of two videos: people grieving after learning of a tragic death or a film from a nature show. When the students were later given the chance to buy a sporty water bottle, the subjects who had seen the sad video were willing to pay 300% more money to purchase it than those who had seen the more neutrally emotional video. The researchers reasoned that students who saw the sad video needed cheering up and believed that if they bought something, regardless of price, their action would make them feel better.

One psychologist wrote: "Shopping can temporarily take people's minds off their troubles [and] make us feel better about ourselves." Surveys show that about 6% of men and women in the United States are compulsive shoppers. A survey of college students found that those who shopped a great deal were motivated by such factors as low self-esteem. Apparently they thought that they could compensate for this feeling by purchasing high-status items such as the latest cell phone, hot clothing, or a fast car. The good feeling won't last long, however, perhaps not even long enough to use the item even once.

Sources: Childs, D. (2008, February 8). Retail Therapy: Does Sadness Mean Spending? Retrieved from abcnews.go.com; Bryner, J. (2008, March 3). Why We Buy: The Truth About Shopaholics. Retrieved from msnbc.com; Koran, L., Faber, R., Aboujaoude, E., Large, M., & Serpe, R. (2006). Estimated prevalence of compulsive buying behavior in the United States. *American Journal of Psychiatry, 163,* 1806–1812.

consumers see at the critical point of sale—the moment of deciding whether to purchase. Shoppers looking for a box of crackers on a supermarket shelf who are confronted by an array of competing brands may not remember the TV commercial they saw last night or the magazine ad they read last week. At the instant of purchase, the packaging may be the deciding factor.

There is an old saying about not judging a book by its cover, but many people make decisions on just that basis. People may evaluate others by their clothing or their car, and they may judge similarly the products they purchase. Often consumer attitudes are shaped not by the quality of an item but by the wrapping in which it is offered.

The most famous example is an early consumer study on the taste of coffee. Two groups of people were questioned. For one group, the coffee was poured from an ordinary electric coffeemaker. For the other group, the coffee was served from an ornately engraved antique silver urn. You guessed it. Consumers rated the taste of coffee poured from the silver urn much higher than the taste of coffee from the electric coffeemaker, though the coffee was the same in both cases. It was the container— the package—that accounted for the difference in the way people perceived the taste.

In other research on this concept, pills of two sizes were shown to groups of patients and physicians, who were asked to rate the potency of each drug. Both groups reported that they thought that the larger pill was the more potent. In fact, the larger pill was less than half as strong as the smaller pill.

Overall, the package must reinforce the product's image or personality as established by its advertising campaign. For example, a men's hair gel should not be packaged in a pink bottle with letters in script but in a sturdy box with bold stripes and colors. The design and matching of product and package can be determined through consumer research. Consumers may be asked to free-associate to the designs of current or proposed packaging, telling researchers the positive or negative images elicited by the designs. Researchers also use surveys and projective techniques to determine packaging impact and preference.

Packaging is an expensive part of the manufacturing and marketing process. In fact, packaging accounts for more than one third of the cost of most items in supermarkets. For every dollar you spend on food, drugs, cosmetics, clothing, and electronics, approximately 35 cents goes for the container, not for what is in it. And prices may rise as product packaging incorporates new electronic technologies. For example, bottles of Coors Light beer have labels that turn blue when the bottles are chilled to the proper drinking temperature. Huggies' Henry the Hippo bottles of hand soap flash a light for 20 seconds so that children will know how long to wash their hands. Tiny speakers are being developed that would become active when the product is moved. In the near future you might pick up a package of cheese at the grocery store and hear, "I go well with Triscuit crackers." Just imagine this scene: As you wheel your cart down the supermarket aisles, all the packages are shouting to get your attention.

Sex in Ads

Attractive and scantily clad models of both sexes are popular in advertising, so you might assume that their effectiveness is beyond question. However, the value of sexy images in ads has been accepted on faith, there is little empirical research support. Sex appeal does have a high attention-getting value. Studies using the eye camera show that most consumers reading magazines, when confronted with several ads on a page, will immediately look at the ad that contains an element of sex. But what then? In general, the information in the ad that features provocative pictures of women is read more often by women than by men. Men look at the pictures, but women read the message, which usually means that the ad is communicating with the wrong audience. Similar results have been found with ads featuring pictures of attractive men; the messages are read more often by men than by women, again attracting the wrong audience.

Research evidence suggests a very low rate of recall for information that accompanies sexy illustrations. One company published two versions of a magazine ad, each containing a mail-in coupon for additional information. One ad showed a bikini-clad young woman; the other ad did not. Coupon returns were significantly higher for the ad without the sexy model.

Laboratory research supports these field observations. In one study, male subjects viewed several ads; some of the ads had sexy illustrations and some did not. The men were then shown the same ads with the brand names deleted and were asked to identify the product or advertiser. They were questioned again 24 hours later. There was no difference in the rate of product recall for the ads with sexy images and for those without sexy images, and After 7 days, the men had forgotten significantly more of the information in the sexy ads than in the non-sexy ads.

In a study in which 324 male and female adults were shown a sexually explicit or a neutral television program, researchers found that those who saw the sexy program had significantly lower recall and recognition scores for nine ads that were shown during the program than did those who saw the neutral program. In another experimental condition, people who watched a violent television program reacted similarly to the group who saw the sexy program. Neither group could recall or recognize the products advertised during the program as well as could those who watched the neutral program (Bushman & Bonacci, 2002).

It appears, then, that although many people may enjoy looking at sexy ads, they are not likely to remember the product. Nevertheless, advertisers continue to rely on the shock value and their promotions—especially for fragrances, underwear, and jeans—grow more daring every year.

How do women feel about being depicted in advertising as sex objects? A survey of female college students in 2008 reported that this generation was not offended, nor were they inclined to boycott products that used such ads. This finding is a significant change from surveys in the 1990s when college-age women said they were offended and would not buy products whose ads portrayed women as sex objects (Zimmerman & Dahlberg, 2008).

Effectiveness of Advertising Campaigns

The most important question for the seller is whether its advertising campaign is effective in increasing the sales of its product or service. In many cases, neither the advertising agency nor the company knows the answer, because effectiveness is difficult to determine. Furthermore, companies are reluctant to go public with their failures and are apt to exaggerate their successes.

Research on television ad campaigns consistently shows that most people dislike commercials. Television viewers watch fewer than half the commercials broadcast. They leave the room during commercial breaks, turn off the sound or switch channels with the remote control device, and erase or fast-forward through commercials on video-recorded programs. A study of 360 television viewers in Hong Kong found that 81% avoided watching commercials (Tse & Lee, 2001).

Advertising agencies recognize that most people are not sitting through or paying attention to TV ads. They describe viewers as nomads because they wander or surf from one channel to another. In laboratory test situations where people watching commercials were unable to tune them out, channel surf, or leave the room, subjects typically misunderstood or forgot approximately one third of what they had seen when questioned immediately afterwards. A day later, they had forgotten or misunderstood three fourths of what they had seen. The figures were higher for magazine ads. Of course not everyone can avoid all commercials all the time. A study of advertising during a typical Super Bowl broadcast, where a 30-second advertising spot can cost millions of dollars, showed that movies promoted in ads during the game grossed nearly 40% more than movies released at the same time but not advertised during the Super Bowl telecast. In this instance, the ads were watched by enough people to more than pay for their cost (Yelkur, Tomkovick, & Traczyk, 2004).

Two organizations, the Nielsen Company and Arbitron, have long been in the business of tracking television viewing behavior and determining how many people watch commercials and can recall them. Their job was easier when most people watched TV at home, but nowadays people receive broadcasts on computers, ipods, BlackBerry smart phones, and large screens in public places.

A survey of more than 2,500 Americans over age 12 found that 35% spent some portion of their weekly television viewing time away from home. Among younger viewers (ages 12 to 17), 64% watched broadcasts away from home at least once a week, as did 23% of those over age 55. These people were far less likely to divert their attention from commercials than they were when watching at home. People who watch TV away from home are more likely to be a captive audience for advertising, because they cannot channel surf or use TiVo in a sports bar, doctor's office, or airport lounge (*New York Times*, April 13, 2007). To learn more about Internet ratings, see www.nielsen-netratings.com

Researchers conducted a study with 14,400 people in South Africa who viewed commercials in movie theaters and on television and 1,291,800 additional people who saw the same ads but only in the theater. The researchers found that the recall rate for ads in the movie theaters was higher than the recall rate for ads shown on television. This result was the same for young adults (the primary movie audience) and for older adults. The researchers suggested that perhaps people pay more attention to ads in the theaters because there is little opportunity to avoid them (Ewing, DuPlessis, & Foster, 2001).

How people feel about commercials in general can affect how well they remember them. In one study, the attitudes of 1,914 adults toward ads were measured. Although 45% of these subjects thought that advertising was informative, 77% believed that ads were annoying and manipulative and that many products failed to live up to advertising claims. These results tell advertisers that even people who think ads can be useful may also hold negative attitudes toward them. The same subjects were shown a series of magazine ads and were asked on the following day to recall them. People with highly favorable attitudes toward advertising recalled significantly more of the ads they had seen than did people with highly unfavorable attitudes toward advertising (Mehta, 2000).

Racial identification can be a factor in attitudes toward advertisements. A group of 160 Black adults participated in an experiment in which some of them viewed an ad featuring a White woman holding a garment bag and some viewed an ad featuring a Black woman holding the same bag. Their reactions were shown to depend on their level of identification with Black culture. Those with a high identification regarded the ad with the Black model more favorably. Those with a low identification with Black culture showed no preference for either model (Whittler & Spira, 2002).

Commercials today compared to a few years ago

Some advertisers recognize the buying power of women for products that are beyond the scope of the traditional homemaker role. (Reproduced by permission of Samsonite Corporation.)

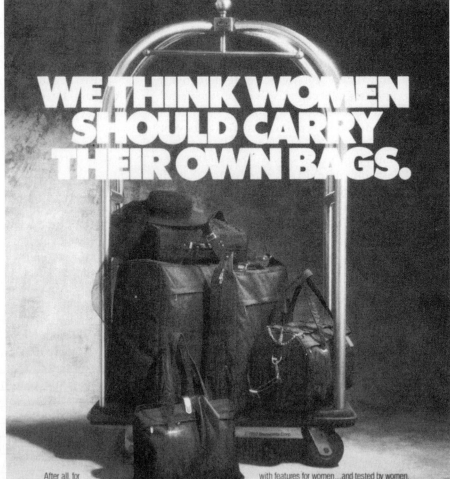

Much research has been conducted on the effectiveness of the controversial but widespread practice of placing advertisements in magazines for prescription drugs. A Gallup survey of 1,475 women over age 18, who described themselves as frequent magazine readers, showed that prescription ads were effective, especially among women who believed they had one of the symptoms described in the ad, which the drug claimed to cure. Half of those with such a symptom claimed to read the ads; 43% reported that they asked their physicians about the medication. Older respondents had a higher rate of recall for the ad content, and 62% of those surveyed, regardless of age, believed that prescription drug advertising provided vital information (Mehta & Purvis, 2003).

More recent research produced somewhat less positive attitudes toward prescription drug advertising. In two studies of more than 450 adult consumers, researchers found that nearly 70% thought that such ads did not provide adequate information on the risks or benefits of the medications. However, most respondents also believed that such ads motivated them to find out more about the drugs being promoted and the medical conditions associated with them (Friedman & Gould, 2007; Spake & Joseph, 2007).

Mass-market advertising is a relatively recent, but rapidly growing, phenomenon in China. Research on the effectiveness of advertising there, conducted in a telephone survey of 825 adults ages 18 to 64, found that people held more positive attitudes toward ads than adults surveyed in the United States. A majority of the Chinese respondents (69%) reported that they found advertising to be informative, and 56% said they often used ads when making purchasing decisions. Younger people exhibited the most positive attitudes; they found advertisements to be entertaining and informative. Those with greater formal education held more positive attitudes toward advertising than did those with less education (Zhou, Zhang, & Vertinsky, 2002).

Web-Based Advertising

The Internet provides another outlet for advertisers to spread their messages, although the effectiveness of their banner ads is still undetermined. One survey reported that 40% of the people who use the Internet do so primarily for shopping. Even consumers who do not actually make purchases from Internet sites find it a good source of consumer information. Popular purchases include computers, books, flowers, music, travel services, and investment products. Yet for all the success stories, particularly around the Christmas shopping season, many companies have been disappointed by the response to their Web sites.

Newsbreak

That Billboard *Is* Watching You

An electronic billboard on a New York City street has a tiny camera that watches you when you are looking at the ad. It takes your picture when you stop to check it out or even when you are just walking past. It's a relatively new way of finding out how many people pay attention to the ad. And here's the scary part: It can find out who you are. The camera records all kinds of information such as gender, approximate age, how long you stare at the ad—and then passes that information on to a central database.

The ultimate goal, say the developers of this means of testing advertising effectiveness, is to be able to show different ads to different people. A teenage boy, for example, would be the target of one advertising approach. After he passed by, different ads would be shown to the next pedestrians—say, a middle-age White woman or an older Asian man. This ability to gear ads electronically to different audiences is being used in Ikea stores in Europe, in McDonald's restaurants in Singapore, and in commuter train stations in Philadelphia. So the next time you spot a sidewalk billboard, don't be surprised if it's already spotted you!

Source: Billboards that look back (2008, May 31). *New York Times*.

Surveys of people with Internet access show that 66% have purchased products such as books, toys, music, or clothing from online sources and that 78% appreciate the convenience of online shopping. However, 75% of Internet users report that they do not like the idea of providing credit card or other personal information online. And 75% report frustrating or confusing experiences because of the lack of information in navigating some shopping sites (Horrigan, 2008).

On a global level, the number of Internet shoppers increased by 40% between 2006 and 2008 and more than 85% of those made purchases. The most frequently ordered items were books, clothing, shoes and accessories, DVDs and video games, airline tickets, and electronic equipment. The biggest buyers of books online were from developing nations such as China, Brazil, Vietnam, and Egypt. The highest percentages of online shopping were reported by South Korea, England, Germany, and Japan; the United States ranks eighth on the list (Nielsen news release, 2008).

Research with groups of employed adults and college students on the design of Web pages has shown that complexity has a negative influence on advertising effectiveness. The simpler the Web page design, the higher was the stated intent to purchase the product displayed. Also, simpler Web pages engendered more favorable attitudes toward the company and the ad (Bruner & Kumar, 2000; Stevenson, Bruner, & Kumar, 2000).

In a study of 311 adults who reviewed four hotel Web sites, researchers found that a high level of perceived interactivity with the site, as well as features such as a virtual tour of the facilities and an online reservation system, resulted in highly positive attitudes toward the companies and the sites. Web sites lacking these features did not receive positive ratings (McMillan, Hwang, & Lee, 2003).

An international study of 299 Internet users in 12 countries in Europe and South America, as well as the United States, revealed that consumer trust in a Web site was a major determinant in making the decision to purchase a product online. Trustworthiness was perceived to be higher when the site featured customer-service guarantees, reviews and testimonials from prior customers, and certification from an independent source such as a respected consumer organization (Lynch, Kent, & Srinivasan, 2001).

Men shop online more frequently than women. This finding was confirmed in a questionnaire study of 227 adults over age 18 who had made at least one purchase online. The women in the sample shopped online less often and reported that they found online shopping to be less emotionally satisfying and less convenient than men did. Women were less trusting and more skeptical of Web site advertising claims than men were (Rodgers & Harris, 2003). An international market research firm, Harris Interactive (www.harrisinteractive.com) suggested, on the basis of survey results, six types of online shoppers (see Table 14-4).

Increasing amounts of research data are being published on the effectiveness of Web site advertising. In one study, pop-up questionnaires on 13 sites that were advertising and selling a variety of products were completed by more than 13,000 people who had logged on. The effectiveness of banner ads was measured by length of visit to a site and number of clicks made to obtain additional information. The results showed that sites for so-called high-involvement products such as luxury cars provided more effective advertising (people spent more time on the site and clicked through more levels of information) than sites for low-involvement products such as baby diapers or diary products (Dahlen, Rasch, & Rosengren, 2003). Apparently, people spend more time tracking down information on products that are more important, attractive, and desirable to them than on products that are merely functional.

Do people who spend more time looking at ads on a Web site, or in any other medium, remember more of the ad content than do those who spend less time with the ad? A study conducted in New Zealand suggested yes. Some 149 university students were exposed to different ads on Web sites for various lengths of time (20 to 60 seconds per page). Then the students were given aided recall and recognition tests on the ads they had just seen. The longer a student was exposed to a Web page containing an ad, the more likely he or she was to recall and recognize the ad after the exposure (Danaher & Mullarkey, 2003).

Personal interviews with 105 residents of Seoul, South Korea, who used the Internet at least 1 hour per week, showed that their online time was greater for high-involvement products than low-involvement products. Overall, however, the researchers did not find Internet ads to be as effective as television ads for enticing new consumers to consider luxury products. TV ads were more effective for

TABLE 14-4
Six Types of Internet Shoppers

E-bivalent newbies
Approximately 5% of the online shopping population, this group is the newest to the Internet, is somewhat older, likes online shopping the least, and spends the least money online.

Time-sensitive materialists
Approximately 17% of online shoppers, this group is most interested in convenience and time-saving and is less likely to read product reviews, compare prices, or use coupons.

Clicks and mortar
Approximately 23% of online shoppers, this group tends to shop online but prefers to make purchases in stores, is more likely to include women homemakers, expresses concerns about privacy and security when buying online, and visits shopping malls more often than other groups.

Hooked, online, and single
Approximately 16% of online shoppers, this group is more likely to be young, single men with high incomes, has used the Internet the longest, likes to play games, download software, bank, invest, and shop online the most often.

Hunter-gatherers
Approximately 20% of online shoppers, this group is typically age 30 to 49 with two children and most often visits Web sites that provide analysis and comparison of products and prices.

Brand loyalists
Approximately 19% of online shoppers, this group is the most likely to connect directly to the site address of a company they know, expresses the greatest satisfaction with online shopping, and spends the most money online.

Source: Adapted from L. Schiffman & L. Kanuk (2004), *Consumer Behavior* (8th ed.). Upper Saddle River, NJ: Prentice Hall, p. 70, after www.harrisinteractive.com

all four products studied: luxury cars, expensive watches, fast food, and shampoo. Newspapers, magazines, and radio were also effective in enticing people to buy new products (Yoon & Kim, 2001).

Advertisers have been increasingly turning to social networking sites such as Facebook, MySpace, and YouTube, but results to date have been disappointing. A survey of 800 users of such sites found that 58% said that few ads matched their interests; 29% found none of the ads to be of interest. Only 7% reported that they responded to any of the ads on these sites (Loechner, 2008).

The click-through rates for ads on major sites such as Yahoo, Microsoft, and AOL are less than 1%. However, when ads were customized or targeted to specific viewers, based on the Web pages they visited and the kinds of information they sought through search engines, the click-through rates for ads increased by as much as 300%. If advertisers show people ads for items they're interested in, they will pay attention.

CONSUMER BEHAVIOR AND MOTIVATION

Consumers can be influenced by marketplace factors other than advertising when they make their purchasing decisions. A store's atmosphere and cleanliness, the ease of parking, the length of the aisles—all these things can affect buyer behavior. For example, research on supermarket shopping behavior found that people look down short aisles rather than walk down them. They are much more likely to walk down long aisles and to make more impulse buys as a result. Research also showed that products more likely to be purchased on impulse are those displayed at the ends of the aisles and near the checkout lanes. You can readily see where manufacturers would want to shelve their products for maximum visibility.

A meta-analysis of 32 studies showed that background music played in stores had a positive effect on the mood and behavior of customers. Music increased the amount of time people spent

Target + small Heros questioned it

Newsbreak

"Please Press 1—Your Call Is Very Important to Us"

How many times have you heard that while you've been waiting to reach an actual human on the phone? It happens when you're trying to reach tech support to find out why your new DVD player doesn't work or why your Internet service went out. Whatever the reason for your complaint, there's probably an automated system ready to frustrate you. "Press 1 if you're calling from your home phone." "Press 9 if you want to speak to a trained service provider."

There are more than 100,000 call centers in the United States and approximately another 10,000 outsourced to other countries. Most of them have one thing in common: They don't work very well and they confuse, anger, and alienate the consumer.

Two psychologists in Israel investigated how companies could soothe the tempers of the customers waiting for the next operator to become available. They had people place calls to be put on hold to see what would happen under various conditions. Some callers heard recorded music while they waited. Others heard periodic apologies interrupting the music, with a recorded voice saying,

"We are sorry to keep you waiting. Please hold and your call will be answered in the order it was received." People in the third group heard the same music but were given periodic updates about their place in line or the approximate number of minutes of waiting time.

You can guess the results. More people expressed satisfaction with their experience when they were given updates about their place in line. The most negative reaction was to the recorded apologies; people didn't believe the recorded voice was really sorry about their long wait.

Increasing numbers of dissatisfied callers are expressing their anger online and warning others to avoid companies that fail to offer good customer service. And there are ways to bypass an automated system to reach a live person faster. For example, www.gethuman.com tells you how to reach a representative at several hundred companies and organizations and offers the chance to rank companies that provide good telephone service. If more companies truly believed your call was important to them, they might have a person answer the phone within a reasonable period of time.

Sources: Munichor, N., & Rafaeli, A. (2007). Numbers or apologies? Customer reactions to telephone waiting time fillers. *Journal of Applied Psychology, 92,* 511–518; Tugend, A. (2008, May 24). Far from always being right, the customer is on hold. *New York Times.*

in the stores. The longer browsing time increased the likelihood of impulse buying. Customers lingered longer in stores when the music was slower, quieter, and more familiar than when it was fast, loud, and unfamiliar (Garlin & Owen, 2006). Observations of 220 encounters between customers and employees in coffee shops indicated that consumers' level of satisfaction was influenced by the way the employees smiled. Bigger smiles produced greater satisfaction than weaker smiles or no smiles (Barger & Grandey, 2006).

Personal factors that affect consumer behavior include the standard biographical variables—age, gender, educational level, socioeconomic status, and ethnic origin—along with cognitive variables such as perceived time available for shopping, attitudes toward shopping, purpose of the shopping

trip, and the shopper's mood and personality. For example, people who are self-conscious in public (overly concerned about the impression they make on others and what others think of them) tend to be concerned about the labels on the products they buy. Perhaps they believe that people will think more highly of them if they purchase national brands rather than store brands or generic brands.

Other factors that influence consumer behavior of interest to psychologists are brand placement, buying habits and brand loyalty, and the effect of product pricing.

Brand Placement

When you watch television or go to movies, it is impossible to avoid brand placement. When a film

Newsbreak

How Much Should I Tip?

Consumer psychologists try to amass as much information as possible about human behavior and motivation: where we shop, what we purchase, why we buy it, what ads we like, what ads turn us off. There's not much that escapes the scrutiny of consumer psychologists, even leaving a tip in a restaurant. To the people who serve meals and clear tables, tips make up the bulk of their income. Therefore, the amount a customer decides to leave for their service is vital to them.

How do you decide on the size of the tip you leave at a restaurant? Do you tend to tip excessively? Do you tip only a token amount and hurry to leave before the server notices? Here are several other factors that may influence the size of your tips:

- *How big was your bill?* The size of the tab you run up is the single best predictor of tip size. The larger the bill, the larger the tip.

- *How friendly was your server?* The first thing new servers should learn is the friendlier they are, the larger tip they receive. Waiters who smile and introduce themselves by name tend to make more money than those who do not. Also, waiters who crouch or bend down to your level while taking your order get better tips than those who remain standing. Female servers who draw smiley faces on the bill get higher tips than those who do not, but male servers who draw smiley faces get lower tips.

- *How professional was the service?* Studies show a weak relationship between customer evaluations of the quality of service and the size of the tip. Thus, friendliness may compensate for making a mistake with the order.

- *How attractive was the server?* As with many social activities, more attractive people fare better than less attractive people. In this case, they tend to receive somewhat larger tips, although the difference is not significant.

- *How many in your party?* Do you expect to leave a bigger tip when you are eating alone than when you're with a group? Tip size seems to decrease with the size of the party. Single diners leave an average of 20% of the bill. Two diners tip an average of 17% apiece. But when the group includes four or more, tip size drops to around 13%.

- *How often do you eat there?* Regulars at a restaurant tend to tip more than first-time customers or people who eat there only occasionally. Apparently, people feel differently about tipping when they expect to patronize the restaurant again.

- *Cash or charge?* People who charge meals leave larger tips than those who pay cash. Perhaps it doesn't seem like real money when you're using plastic.

A nationwide survey found that 30% of Americans do not know that it is customary to leave a 15% to 20% tip for a restaurant server. The professor of consumer behavior at Cornell University who conducted the survey was surprised by the results. He wrote that "a fair number of that 30% said 'I leave a buck or two.' I was shocked. I figured about 90% of the population would know that you leave 15% or 20%, and maybe there was that 10% of people living under a rock who didn't know."

Sources: Grimes, W. (1999, February 3). Tips: Check your insecurity at the door. *New York Times*; Sharkey, J. (2004, April 25). He parked your car. She retrieved it. Who gets a tip? *New York Times*; Surowiecki, J. (2005, September 5). Check, please. *New Yorker*.

character drives a particular sports car or drinks a certain brand of beer, you are seeing an example of brand placement within the context of the story, rather than as a separate commercial or ad. A review of 112 hours of prime-time television programs showed an average of 30 brand placement appearances every hour (Avery & Ferraro, 2000). Advertisers like brand placement in movies, TV shows, and video games because they know the audience is not going to mute it, zap through it, leave the room, or channel surf, the way they are likely to do when commercials come on. In addition, brand placement usually involves the use of the product by a popular star, and thus can have the impact of a celebrity endorsement.

Studies have shown that when the lead character in a movie is shown using, driving, or drinking the product, viewer recall of that brand is increased. Viewers tend to evaluate the product more positively when a well-known actor appears to use the product. People also report that brand placement enhances their viewing experience because it makes the movie or television program seem more realistic (Yang, Roskos-Ewoldson, Roskos-Ewoldson, 2004).

In a study of 105 children ages 6 to 12, researchers showed half the children a brief film clip in which the Pepsi-Cola soft drink was mentioned and spilled on a table. The other group of children saw the same film clip but instead of Pepsi, unbranded food and milk were used in the clip. Then the children were offered a choice between Coca-Cola and Pepsi, after which they were asked to describe the film clip. Significantly more of the children exposed to the brand placement selected Pepsi over Coke. This was true even for children who said they did not recall seeing Pepsi in the movie segment. Fewer younger children than older children were able to recall the brand they had seen, but there was no age difference in their choice of Pepsi over Coke. In this case, the brand placement was effective (Auty & Lewis, 2004).

Buying Habits and Brand Loyalty

Many of the stores in which people shop and the products they select are chosen on the basis of habit. Once people find a product they like, it is simpler to continue to buy it than to find a new one. To demonstrate the strength of shopping habits, one supermarket rearranged its display of canned soups. The soups had been grouped by brand name but were changed to alphabetical order by type of soup, thus intermixing all the different brands. Although signs were posted to explain the new arrangement, more than 60% of the customers were fooled. Habit led them to the space on the shelf where they had previously selected the desired soups. When questioned, customers said that the soups had been stocked in their usual order. They were amazed to find the wrong cans in their shopping cart. When consumers shop in new stores, where habit does not automatically lead them to the shelf locations of their preferred prod-

ucts, they tend to buy many more different brands than in the past.

The design of an ad campaign to change persistent buying habits presents a challenge. Studies show that consumer loyalty to major brands can remain unchanged up to 8 years. Sixteen brands that were top sellers in their product category in 1923 retained their primacy 60 years later: these included Campbell soups, Lipton teas, Kodak cameras, and Wrigley chewing gum. These findings reinforce the importance to advertisers of establishing brand preferences in childhood. Once committed, consumers tend to remain loyal to a particular brand for many years and to pass that loyalty on to their children.

Researchers conducted online interviews with 938 consumers of Ford and Volvo automobiles, IBM and Compaq computers, Grolsch and Heineken beers, and two brands of shampoo. Consumers felt more emotionally involved with their choice of car or beer brands than they did with computers or shampoo. Results also showed that those who bonded more with their car or beer had more years of education and a higher social class standing, and they expressed a stronger emotional connection to the product than those who bonded more with computer or shampoo brands (Smit, Bronner, & Tolboom, 2007).

Sometimes it is difficult for researchers to distinguish between buying habits and brand loyalty. Both can be defined in terms of repeat purchase behavior, which means the consumer is relatively impervious to ads for competing brands. Some companies—notably airlines, hotels, and car rental agencies—have developed effective brand loyalty programs by offering a rising scale of rewards for repeat business. For example, airline frequent-flyer plans offer rewards such as free flights, first-class upgrades, VIP check-in lines, early boarding, and sky-lounge memberships. These programs have been shown to be highly successful in inducing customer loyalty. Many people make longer or more circuitous flight arrangements on their chosen airline just to accumulate additional miles.

A survey of 643 adults showed that the promise of a low to moderate reward for buying a product, in an effort to establish brand loyalty, was more cost-effective than the offer of a higher reward in return for an intention to purchase. This finding contradicted the results of a survey of 300 brand managers who believed that offering high rewards would be more cost-effective for their company in establishing brand loyalty (Wansink, 2003).

Product Pricing

Price alone can be an important influence on buying behavior, independent of advertising and product quality. Consumers frequently use price as an index of quality based on the assumption that the more an object costs, the better it must be. Some manufacturers capitalize on this belief and charge a higher price than their competitors do for a product of equal quality. Identical products, differing only in price, are often judged solely by their cost; the more expensive product is typically rated higher in quality.

In a study using neuromarketing techniques, the brain activity of the subjects was measured by MRI while they sampled various wines. They were told that some of the wines were far more expensive than others; that information, though false, affected brain activity levels. The results showed that the part of the brain that responds to pleasurable experiences reacted more strongly to what the participants believed were the more expensive wines. Thus, the differences in the alleged prices of the wines were found to alter the level of cortical pleasure experienced by the drinkers (Plassmann, O'Doherty, Shiv, & Rangel, 2008).

Some consumers, however, do not consider price when shopping for certain items. Observations of supermarket shoppers revealed that most do not pay attention to price information when shopping for staples such as breakfast cereal, coffee, and soft drinks, and they cannot accurately report current prices. Because of different package weights and sizes, shoppers are often unable to make the calculations necessary to determine which of several

brands is the best buy. When supermarkets provide unit pricing information, such as cost per serving or cost per item, some shoppers consider this information in making purchasing decisions.

A popular technique to gain sales for a new product or package is to charge a low price as an introductory offer. The idea is that once shoppers purchase the product, they will continue to do so out of habit, even when the price is raised to the level of competing products. Research does not support this notion. Sales are usually high during the introductory price period but drop when the price is raised. In stores that do not lower the price during the introductory period, sales typically remain stable. Rebates are a more effective way of offering a price reduction as an inducement to purchase. A price decrease in the form of a rebate usually produces higher sales than an equal point-of-sale price reduction.

Targeted Advertising to Hispanics, Blacks, and Asians

Consumer psychologists recognize important differences in consumer values, attitudes, and shopping behavior among people of different ethnic groups. Studies of Whites, Blacks, Hispanic Americans, and Asian Americans have documented preferences for various products. In many large cities, Blacks and Hispanics account for the majority of the residents, so they form sizable markets with considerable purchasing power.

In 2002, Hispanics became the largest minority group in the United States, representing 15% of the population. The U.S. Census Bureau estimates that Hispanics will account for nearly one third of the U.S. population by 2050. Hispanics now outnumber Blacks and have become the fastest growing minority. Marketers are responding to this group in a variety of ways. More than 100 Hispanic-oriented advertising agencies create materials almost exclusively in the Spanish language. The Association of Hispanic Advertising Agencies estimates that this population spent more than $900 billion on consumer goods in 2007, an increase of $200 billion in only 2 years. The number of Spanish-language television and radio stations and Web sites is growing throughout the country, not just in traditionally Hispanic areas in Florida, California, and Texas, but in Boston, Minneapolis, Anchorage, Syracuse, and Portland, Oregon.

Supermarket shoppers may judge certain products to be superior solely on the basis of price.

Corporations such as Kraft, General Foods, and PepsiCo have created special organizational units to develop advertising targeted to appeal to Hispanics. Studies show that as a group, Hispanics have positive attitudes toward advertising and rely on it, more than do other minority groups, to provide information about consumer products and services (Torres & Gelb, 2002). Recognizing this characteristic, Procter & Gamble spends millions of dollars a year on advertising designed for Hispanic media outlets for products ranging from toothpaste to laundry detergent. The company established a 65-member bilingual team to identify the needs and desires of Hispanic consumers. One result of this market research was the finding that Hispanic consumers like to be able to smell certain household products, such as toiletries and detergents. This finding led Procter & Gamble to add new scents for Hispanic market.

In surveys of Hispanic and non-Hispanic teenage girls, researchers found that Hispanic teens expressed a significantly higher desire for uniqueness in clothing. The results also showed that Hispanic teens were more independent of family influences in their choice of fashions (Chattalas & Harper, 2007). Market researchers have identified other characteristics of Hispanic shoppers (see Table 14-5).

Blacks constitute nearly 13% of the U.S. population, which makes them a desirable market with rapidly increasing purchasing power. Black consumers, more than any other group, demonstrate a high level of brand loyalty. Once they select a brand they are highly unlikely to switch to a competing brand. Black households tend to spend a larger share of their income on food, clothing, entertainment, and health care than other groups. They also prefer to make more separate trips to grocery stores in the course of a week than do other groups. In general, Black consumers are more willing to pay more for what they consider to be products of higher quality. This includes a preference for high-fashion items and name-brand products that serve as a visible indicator of success. Blacks, in general, look to the media, movies, TV programs, and advertisements for cues as to which items of clothing, jewelry, and other products define success in the mainstream culture.

Surveys of Black and Hispanic consumers show that both groups are attracted to upscale images and attributes of products and the stores in which they shop. For Blacks, unlike Hispanics, family and friends are an important reference point and source of information in making purchasing decisions. These findings indicate the value of word-of-mouth advertising and of showing images of friends and family using a particular product in the ads.

Surveys indicate a general level of distrust of advertising in the Black community. Because many people appear to believe that ads are designed for a White audience, Black adult consumers have greater trust in Black-centered media outlets as sources of information about consumer products. Consequently, major companies are spending millions of dollars designing ads to appeal to the Black community for Black-oriented print media and radio and television programs. As with the Hispanic market, advertisers have learned that, contrary to

---

TABLE 14-5

Characteristics of Hispanic-American Shoppers

- Prefer well-known or familiar brands
- Buy brands perceived to be prestigious
- Are fashion conscious
- Prefer to shop at smaller, more personal stores
- Buy brands advertised by their own ethnic group stores
- Tend not to be impulsive buyers
- Tend to clip and use cents-off coupons
- Prefer to purchase the products and brands their parents bought
- Prefer fresh or freshly prepared food items rather than frozen foods

Source: Adapted from L. Schiffman & L. Kanuk (2004), *Consumer behavior* (8th ed.). Upper Saddle River, NJ: Prentice Hall, p. 441.

the popular saying, one size does *not* fit all. An ad that may be highly successful with White consumers may fail to reach other groups.

The Asian-American community in the United States is approximately 4% of the population, but it is another fast-growing segment. Asians have a reputation for being industrious, disciplined, and hard-working, eager to achieve a middle-class lifestyle. Thus, they constitute another desirable market for advertisers. Asians tend to be better educated than the general population and to be more computer literate. About 60% of this group earn more than $60,000 a year; approximately half have professional positions in the workforce.

Asians tend to value high quality, to buy established and well-known brands, and to remain loyal customers. They are a particularly diverse community of some 15 different groups with different buying and spending habits; thus, they can be expected to respond differently to advertising appeals. For example, almost 80% of the Vietnamese people living in the United States were not born in this country; in contrast, less than a third of the Japanese people in the United States were not born here. Most Vietnamese prefer to use their native language and are highly committed to maintaining their cultural traditions. They do not like to make purchases on credit, because owing money in their culture brings disapproval. In contrast, Korean and Chinese people who have spent more years in the United States are highly agreeable to the use of credit as being the "American way" of being a good consumer in the marketplace.

Advertising to Children and Teens

Children in the age group of 4 to 12 years, number 35 million; they control over approximately $15 billion in disposable income. Fast-growing spending categories for these young consumers are shoes, clothing, breakfast cereals, candy, soft drinks, and other snack foods. One explanation psychologists have advanced for the children's high degree of purchasing power is parental guilt. Consumer psychologists suggest that in single-parent families, in families with both parents employed outside the home, and in families in which parents have postponed childbearing until their thirties, children have been indulged with more money to spend and more influence over family purchasing decisions.

Many teenage shoppers are responsible for household grocery purchases.

Marketing to children involves techniques such as these: placing products on lower supermarket shelves, airing cartoon commercials on children's TV programs, and distributing in schools pencils, magazines, and book covers featuring a product's name or logo. But the primary way of reaching children in the marketplace is through electronic media. On average, children ages 2 to 11 view 25,000 TV ads per year.

Researchers who surveyed television-viewing habits of children reported these findings:

- Children ages 2 to 7 years are exposed to an average of 13,900 TV ads annually.
- Children ages 8 to 12 years are exposed to an average of 30,000 TV ads annually.
- Teens ages 13 to 17 years are exposed to an average of 29,000 TV ads annually.

At least half of all television commercials aired on children's shows are for food (34% for candy and snacks, 38% for cereal, 10% for fast foods), which many experts believe may be at least partly responsible for the marked increase in childhood obesity (Ganz, Schwartz, Angelini, & Rideout, 2007).

A study of children ages 3 to 5 years found that the foods they preferred were the items presented to them in a McDonald's wrapper. The researchers offered French fries, chicken nuggets, milk, hamburgers, and baby carrots, but more than three fourths of the children said that the items in the McDonald's wrappers (even the carrots!) tasted better than items in plain wrappers.

One third of the children in these studies ate at McDonald's more than once a week and three fourths had McDonald's toys at home. Those who ate at the fast-food restaurant more often and had more TVs at home showed the strongest preference for food in McDonald's wrappers. McDonald's spends more than $1 billion a year on targeted advertising to children; it works and it builds brand loyalty from an early age (Reinberg, 2007; Robinson, Borzekowski, Matheson, & Kraemer, 2007).

Teenagers spend an estimated $30 billion a year on clothing, cosmetics, and other personal items such as video games and DVDs. They have also assumed responsibility for much household spending. Many adolescents compile the household grocery list, make decisions about specific brands, and do the family shopping. More than 60% of teenage girls and 40% of teenage boys are believed to do routine grocery shopping.

In a study of nearly 200 teenagers, researchers found that half reported spending up to 3 hours a day watching television and one third reported spending the same amount of time listening to the radio (LaFerle, Edwards, & Lee, 2000). Teenagers also spend hours surfing the Web. So much advertising has been directed at adolescents about the importance of having the most popular brand of shoes, jeans, cell phones, and cars that they have changed the way they view themselves and their interactions with peers and adults. One child psychologist noted that "by the time children reach their teens, a developmental stage when they're naturally insecure and searching for a personal identity, they've been taught that material possessions are what matter" (Kersting, 2004, p. 61). They define themselves, all too often, by the images they see in movies and on TV. In a study of 150 children and teens ages 8 to 18, researchers found that they developed a keener appreciation of and need for material possessions when they entered the adolescent years, around ages 12 to 13. The typical decline in self-esteem at this period can be overcome, so advertisers believe, by encouraging teens to buy the right brands of clothing, accessories, personal electronics, and so on. Having these prestigious items allows teens to cope with their insecurities. The researchers found that by late adolescence, ages 16 to 18, as feelings of self-esteem began to rebound, the teenagers were placing less importance on material goods (Chaplin & John, 2007).

Advertising to the Over-50 Market

Changing demographic trends have produced another important market for advertisers: working people over the age of 50. This consumer segment, growing in numbers and affluence, will, by the year 2020, constitute more than one third of the population. The over-50 group now includes some Baby Boomers (people born between 1946 and 1964), a market of 76 million consumers with large disposable incomes that they are used to spending freely. People older than 50 have half the discretionary income in the United States, and people over 65 have twice the discretionary income of people between 25 and 34.

The over-50 group represents a multibillion dollar market for goods and services. Advertisers have responded by revising their image of older people in ads and by eliminating stereotypes about the older consumer. Ads featuring attractive older models now promote cosmetics, hair care products, luxury travel, automobiles, clothing, jewelry, health clubs, and investments.

Retired people over age 65 constitute a large market for clothing, home furnishings, travel, entertainment, and health care products and services. They tend to read more newspapers and magazines, and their television preferences include news and sports programs. Thus, they rely on mass media advertising. They also use the Internet for shopping. There are more Internet users over age 50 than under age 20. People in the over-50 group tend to shop online for books, stocks, and computer equipment more frequently than those under age 50.

Research conducted in Finland and the United States shows a modest gap in Internet use and online shopping activity between Baby Boomers and people older than 65. Baby Boomers are fully plugged in to the Internet and show no signs of the technology anxiety that some people over 65 exhibit. Still, many of those older than 65 are learning to use the Internet to stay in touch with friends, to keep current with news from around the world, and to make online comparisons of products. That means that advertisers are increasingly directing online ads to the older segment of the population, with positive results (Niemela-Nyrhinen, 2007; Reisenwitz, Iyer, Kuhlmeier, & Eastman, 2007).

Advertising to People With Disabilities

Approximately one in five Americans, representing 50 million people, has some form of physical or

Newsbreak

Marketing to Children: When Your Kids Nag You to Buy the Product

Does advertising exploit children? The answer is yes. In 2004, the American Psychological Association reported that ads directed at children under age 8 should be restricted, because young children tend to assume that what they see and hear is truthful and unbiased. Even advertisers admit that their marketing exploits children. The head of one ad agency said, "Advertising at its best is making people feel that without their product, you're a loser. Kids are very sensitive to that. If you tell them to buy something, they are resistant. But if you tell them they'll be a dork if they don't, you've got their attention. You open up emotional vulnerabilities, and it's easy to do that with kids."

Advertisers refer to a product's "nag factor"— how much they can get kids to nag their parents before they give in and purchase the product. One clinical psychologist reported that parents experience considerable emotional turmoil over how they should respond to such nagging. Parents feel guilty about surrendering and buying their children the junk food or violent video games they want, because the parents know these things are bad for their children. And the parents feel guilty if they don't agree to buy, thinking their decision might lead to a child's depression, anxiety, or lowered self-esteem if he or she doesn't get the right shoes or backpack.

Advertisers like to develop materialistic attitudes as early as possible, which, critics say, can lead children to grow up defining their self-worth in terms of their possessions instead of their personal qualities.

Critics charge that manipulation and deception in advertising occur on a massive scale. Psychologists agree, even though some of them help advertisers develop effective techniques to persuade children to buy products. As one psychologist put it, "The fake promises of popularity, success, and attractiveness that marketers routinely make for their products are such common lies that we have become inured to their dishonesty. Yet we know that when adults chronically deceive and manipulate a child it erodes the youngster's ability to trust others and to feel secure in the world."

Do children learn from a young age that advertising is not like real life and that they shouldn't take it seriously? Is part of growing up learning who and what to trust? And even if no psychologists were involved, wouldn't advertisers be doing the same thing? Here's the bottom line according to the advertising industry: If companies did not use advertising ploys to sell products, they would go out of business and would have to fire hundreds of thousands of employees, most of whom have children. Do you agree?

Sources: Clay, R. A. (2000, August). Advertising to children: Is it ethical? *Monitor on Psychology*, pp. 52–53; Kanner, A. D., & Kasser, T. (2000). Stuffing our kids: Should psychologists help advertisers manipulate children? *The Industrial-Organizational Psychologist, 38(1)*, 185–187; Ads that target kids are unfair, studies say (2004, February 24). *St. Petersburg (FL) Times.*

mental disability. That figure is expected to rise to one of four by the year 2020. The rate of disability increases with age. More than 40% of the population over 65 has some type of handicap compared to 19% of those between the ages of 16 and 64.

A growing number of advertisers, including Ford, Netflix, McDonald's, Verizon Wireless, Sears, and Honda feature people with disabilities in their advertising and target ads directly to this population because, disabled or not, they spend money. Surveys show that more than 75% of those with some form of disability eat out at least once a week;

69% travel for business or pleasure; and a large number buy products such as wheelchairs and hearing aids, as well as the same products bought by those who have no such disabilities. Thus, this segment of the consumer market is no longer being ignored. To learn more about this type of advertising, go to www.disaboom.com (Newman, 2007).

Advertising to the Gay Community

A visible and vocal consumer group, gay persons are better educated and more affluent than the general population. A survey of 20,000 gay men and women conducted by an opinion polling firm found that approximately 60% of gay men and women were college graduates, compared to about 20% of the U.S. population as a whole. As a large potential market of people with high discretionary incomes, they are increasingly coming to the attention of advertisers.

A survey conducted in San Francisco showed that the median household income of gay men and women was $87,500; 40% of those surveyed earned more than $100,000 a year. Almost all reported taking at least one overnight leisure trip within the past 2 years. Resort owners are capitalizing on this trend by advertising directly to gay consumers. Also, this market segment tends to spend more while on vacations than other consumers (*St. Petersburg (FL) Times*, June 27, 2006).

Interviews with 44 gay men in Canada found that they preferred making consumer purchases only from companies perceived as "gay positive." These were companies that advertised in gay media, supported gay and lesbian employee groups, and offered same-sex domestic partnership benefits. These companies also supported the gay community at large, for example, by making corporate contributions to AIDS charities. In addition, the survey showed that these gay consumers actively boycotted companies perceived as being homophobic or practicing discrimination in hiring (Kates, 2000).

Another survey of 372 gay men and women in the United States confirmed their status as a better-educated and more affluent segment of the population, but these upscale characteristics applied more often to men than to women. Questionnaire responses indicated that these gay consumers preferred to read the *Wall Street Journal*, *Business Week*, *Fortune*, *Money*, *The New Yorker*, *Sports Illustrated*, and *National Geographic*; they were less likely to read *TV Guide* or *Readers' Digest*. Television preferences included network news programs, CNN, *Late Night with David Letterman*, and *60 Minutes*. They rarely watched game shows, soap operas, or talk shows. Such information tells companies where to target their ads.

By 2005, the gay and lesbian market had grown so large that Viacom started Logo, a cable TV station, and a Web site, www.logoonline.com, both aimed at gay people. Some of the sponsors advertising on Logo include Anheuser-Busch, Continental Airlines, Dell, Eastman Kodak, eBay, and General Motors.

The Logo cable channel is seen by more than 23 million households, making it a major marketing outlet (*New York Times*, June 26, 2006).

Advertising to Muslim Americans

Until recently, advertisers tended to ignore the Muslin-American community because they did not see much potential for sales. Also, they feared a political backlash if they ran ads that appeared to offend the group. Now the Muslim-American market is recognized as being much larger than was previously thought, rapidly growing, and increasingly affluent. The approximately 6 million Muslim-Americans tend, on average, to be wealthier and better educated than the general population; more than half make more than $50,000 a year and a quarter earn more than $100,000 annually. Muslim-American families also have more children and spend some $170 billion dollars a year on consumer products. That is too big a market for advertisers to ignore.

More companies are finding ways to adapt their products to Muslim law, to make them acceptable under *halal*, an Arabic term meaning what is permissible; the term covers everything, from the ingredients in food products to the length of women's skirts. Pioneering attempts to reach the Muslim-American market begin in Detroit, Michigan. A McDonald's in Detroit has been serving *halal* Chicken McNuggets, a Walgreen's drugstore has signs in Arabic in the aisles, and an Ikea store offers meat prepared in accordance with Islamic law, publishes catalogs in Arabic, and provides female Muslim employees head coverings to wear.

One enterprising company has created an Islamic version of the Barbie Doll, with dark hair, brown eyes, and a white headscarf. Islamic Barbie, named Fulla, does not have a job or a boyfriend. Fulla spends her days cooking, reading, and praying. Bridges TV, a satellite and cable outlet begun in 2004 as a Muslim television network, gained a wider viewing audience when it changed its stated purpose to that of bridging the cultural gap between East and West. Mainstream U.S. firms target advertising to the Muslim audience in magazines such as *Azizah* and *Muslim Girl Magazine*, but the publishers first had to assure marketers that the outlets were not radical or political in nature. Wherever consumers are, whatever their special needs might be, advertisers have proven themselves adept at designing specific ad campaigns and venues.

Manufacturers and advertisers respond to changing markets with new products and new marketing techniques. Consumers need to remember the varied nature of advertising; sometimes advertising is valuable and informative and sometimes it is manipulative and deceptive. As a consumer, remember one of history's oldest lessons: *caveat emptor*. Let the buyer—whether of ideas, political philosophies, values, theories, research findings, and even psychology textbooks—beware.

Summary

Consumer psychology studies consumer behavior through research methods such as surveys, **focus groups**, and observations of behavior. Neuromarketing, a newer research method, involves measuring brain activity in response to various advertising and marketing programs. Testing of advertising effectiveness is done through direct questioning, physiological measures, sales tests, and coupon returns.

Seller of products and services use various kinds of advertising to influence consumers: direct sell, consumer awareness, product image, informational, and institutional. Advertising appeals can be positive, negative, or mixed; some appeals highlight celebrity endorsements. Many ads involve claims of implied superiority, which consumers tend to believe.

Trademarks can be effective advertising aids, as can the product image. Packaging can be influential at the point of purchase. Although sexy images are commonly used in ads because they attract people, they do not seem to influence how much of the advertising message is recalled. Most people dislike TV commercials, avoid watching them, and fail to remember three fourths of what they see.

Advertising on the Internet has increased; a simple Web page design is effective in getting people to purchase advertised products. Nevertheless, some consumer resistance to online shopping exists, typically related principally to credit card safety. Men shop more frequently online than women do. Trust in a Web site is also a factor in online shopping. People who spend more time looking at an online ad are more likely to recall the message and recognize the product. Ads placed on social networking sites have not been successful.

Brand placement (for example, having a product used by a character in a movie or TV program) is effective in influencing consumer opinion about a product. Brand loyalty can render buyers immune to advertising for competing products. Consumers often consider product price as an indication of quality. Many people believe that higher priced products are always better than lower priced products.

Hispanic, Black, Asian, and Muslim ethnic groups in the United States have become targeted audiences for advertising campaigns designed to appeal to their specific cultural needs and values. Such advertising occurs most often in magazine ads and television commercials. Other groups likely to receive targeted ads include children, teens, older persons, disabled persons, and gay men and women.

Key Terms

focus groups
sales test technique

Review Questions

1. What did John B. Watson contribute to the study of consumer behavior?

2. Describe some of the results of the nationwide survey by the American Association of Advertising Agencies on popular opinions toward advertising.

3. What are the advantages of online consumer surveys over surveys conducted by telephone or in person?

4. Describe how focus groups are conducted. Discuss advantages and disadvantages of focus groups compared to surveys.

5. How do virtual focus groups differ from those that meet in person? Which approach (live or virtual) do you think provides more useful information for a company developing a new product?

6. How did the study by Ernest Dichter on packaged cake mixes influence consumer research?

7. If you had the job of observing the behavior of consumers shopping for cookies at supermarkets in your city, how would you design the project? What problems would you have to resolve in conducting this research?

8. Describe techniques used by consumer psychologists to test reactions to advertising.

9. What is neuromarketing? What advantages does it offer over more traditional approaches to studying consumer behavior?

10. How effective is the use of coupons in determining the effectiveness of newspaper and magazine ads?

11. What are the advantages of obtaining coupons online compared to cutting coupons out of the newspaper?

12. Which appeals are more effective in advertising: positive or negative? Shock or fear appeals? Give an example of each type.

13. Describe advantages and disadvantages of using celebrity endorsements to sell products.

14. Describe the impact on consumer behavior of product packaging, product pricing, and the use of sex in advertisements.

15. What factors help people remember an ad they have seen? How effective are ads for prescription medications?

16. Why is TV advertising becoming less effective than it used to be?

17. How do people who watch television away from home differ from home viewers in terms of the effectiveness of commercials?

18. What are the advantages and disadvantages of advertising on the Web?

19. How do people who like online shopping differ from those who do not like online shopping?

20. What kinds of products are people more likely to purchase online? What are they least likely to buy online?

21. What is brand placement? How effective is brand placement when targeted at adults? At children?

22. How would you devise an ad campaign for upscale furniture if your target was a Hispanic consumer? A Black consumer? What media outlets would you use for your ads?

23. Describe the major differences between the consumer behavior of Hispanic and of Black persons.

24. What characteristics influence the consumer behavior of Asian Americans?

25. Do you think it is ethical to advertise to children under the age of 8? Why or why not?

26. How do the consumer behaviors of gay people differ from those of people who are not gay?

27. Why are consumers over age 50 considered desirable targets for advertisers? Which is the more effective way to reach older people about products: television or the Internet?

28. What are some of the problems and opportunities involved in advertising to Muslim Americans?

Additional Reading

Lewis, D., & Bridger, D. (2000). *The soul of the new consumer: Authenticity—What we buy and why in the new economy.* London: Nicholas Breakley. Market researchers present findings from consumer surveys on shopping experiences and television commercials. They describe the modern consumer as individualistic and well-informed.

Loken, B. (2006). Consumer psychology. *Annual Review of Psychology, 57,* 453–485. Reviews research on consumer psychology; cover brand categories and preferences, the effects of motivation and mood on judgments, and responses to advertising appeals.

Longinotti-Buitoni, G. L. (1999). *Selling dreams: How to make any product irresistible.* New York: Simon & Schuster. The CEO of Ferrari North America describes his research on the emotional link between a product's image and its function. He applies his ideas to cars, hotels, magazines, beauty products, wines, clothing, and electronics.

Simonson, I., Carmon, Z., Dhar, R., Drolet, A., & Nowlis, S. M. (2001). Consumer research. *Annual Review of Psychology, 52,* 249–275. Reviews theories of consumer behavior, social and cognitive influences, and research methods (including online behaviors, field experiments, and laboratory research).

Twitchell, J. B. (2001). *20 ads that shook the world: The century's most groundbreaking advertising and how it changed us all.* New York: Crown. A look back at classic ad campaigns for Coca-Cola, Volkswagen, Listerine, Nike, and Lydia E. Pinkham's Vegetable Compound, showing how a market can be created for a products we never knew we needed.

Underhill, P. (1999). *Why we buy: The science of shopping.* New York: Simon & Schuster. An urban geographer presents his findings based on 20 years of observations of shoppers in supermarkets, bookshops, and department stores.

References

Abdel-Wahab, A. (2007). Employees' attitudes toward telecommuting. *Behaviour & Information Technology, 26*, 367–375.

Abraham, J., Morrison, J., & Burnett, D. (2006). Feedback seeking among developmental assessment center participants. *Journal of Business Psychology, 20*, 383–394.

Abuairub, R., Khalifa, M., & Habbib, M. (2007). Workplace violence among Iraq hospital nurses. *Journal of Nursing Scholarship, 39*, 281–288.

Adams, J. (1965). Inequity in social exchange. In L. Berkowitz (Ed.), *Advances in experimental social psychology* (Vol. 2). New York: Academic Press.

Aguinis, H. (Ed.). (2004). *Test-score banding in human resource selection: Legal, technical, and societal issues.* Westport, CT: Praeger.

Ahronson, A., & Cameron, J. (2007). The nature and consequences of group cohesion in a military sample. *Military Psychology, 19*, 9–25.

Allen, D., Mahto, R., & Otondo, R. (2007). Web-based recruitment. *Journal of Applied Psychology, 92*, 1696–1708.

Allen, T., Eby, L., & Lentz, E. (2006). Mentorship behaviors and mentorship quality associated with formal mentoring programs. *Journal of Applied Psychology, 91*, 567–578.

Allen, T., Eby, L., Poteet, M., Lentz, E., & Lima, L. (2004). Career benefits associated with mentoring for protégés: A meta-analysis. *Journal of Applied Psychology, 89*, 127–136.

Alvarado, C., & Cao, C. (2004). The role of human factors in healthcare: 2020. *Proceedings of the Human Factors & Ergonomics Society 48th Annual Meeting.*

Andersen, L., & Mikkelsen, K. (2008). Recall of occupational injuries. *Safety Science, 46*, 255–260.

Anderson, C., Spataro, S., & Flynn, F. (2008). Personality and organizational culture as determinants of influence. *Journal of Applied Psychology, 93*, 702–710.

Anderson, N. (2008). Toward reducing work stress. *Monitor on Psychology, 39*(2), 9.

Anderson, N., Lievens, F., Van Dam, K., & Born, M. (2006). A construct-driven investigation of gender differences in a leadership-role assessment center. *Journal of Applied Psychology, 91*, 555–566.

Anger, W., Stupfel, J., Ammerman, T., Tamulinas, A., Bodner, T., & Rohlman, D. (2006). The suitability of computer-based training for workers with limited formal education. *International Journal of Training & Development, 10*, 269–284.

Antonioni, D. (1994). The effects of feedback accountability on upward appraisal ratings. *Personnel Psychology, 47*, 349–356.

Antonioni, D., & Park, H. (2001). The effects of personality similarity on peer ratings of contextual work behavior. *Personnel Psychology, 54*, 331–360.

Aquino, K., Tripp, T., & Bies, R. (2001). How employees respond to personal offense: The effects of blame attribution, victim status, and offender status on revenge and reconciliation in the workplace. *Journal of Applied Psychology, 86*, 52–59.

Arnold, K., Turner, N., Barling, J., Kelloway, E., & McKee, M. (2007). Transformational leadership and psychological well-being. *Journal of Occupational Health Psychology, 12*, 193–203.

Arthur, M. (2003). Share price reactions to work-family initiatives: An institutional perspective. *Academy of Management Journal, 46*, 497–505.

Arthur, W., Bennett, W., Edens, P., & Bell, S. (2003). Effectiveness of training in organizations: A meta-analysis of design and evaluation features. *Journal of Applied Psychology, 88*, 234–245.

Arthur, W., Day, E., McNelly, T., & Edens, P. (2003). A meta-analysis of the criterion-related validity of assessment center dimensions. *Personnel Psychology, 56*, 125–154.

Aryee, S., Chen, Z., Sun, L.-Y., & Debrah, Y. (2007). Antecedents and outcomes of abusive supervision. *Journal of Applied Psychology, 92*, 191–201.

As, S. (2001). *The measurement of accident proneness.* Groningen, Netherlands: Groningen University.

Ashforth, B., Sluss, D., & Saks, A. (2007). Socialization tactics, proactive behavior, and newcomer learning. *Journal of Vocational Behavior, 70*, 447–462.

Athavaley, A. (2007, June 20). A job interview you don't have to show up for. *Wall Street Journal.*

Atkins, P., & Wood, R. (2002). Self-versus others' ratings as predictors of assessment center ratings: Validation evidence for 360-degree feedback programs. *Personnel Psychology, 55*, 871–904.

377

Atkinson, J. W., & Feather, N. T. (1996). *A theory of achievement motivation.* New York: Wiley.

Atwater, L., & Brett, J. (2006). 360-degree feedback to leaders. *Group & Organization Management, 31,* 578–600.

Atwater, L., Brett, J., & Charles, C. (2007). Multi-source feedback. *Human Resource Management, 46,* 285–307.

Atwater, L., Waldman, D. A., Atwater, D., & Cartier, P. (2000). An upward feedback field experiment. *Personnel Psychology, 53,* 275–295.

Auty, S., & Lewis, C. (2004). The "delicious paradox": Preconscious processing of product placements by children. In L. Schrum (Ed.), *The psychology of entertainment media: Blurring the lines between entertainment and persuasion.* Mahwah, NJ: Erlbaum.

Avery, D. (2003). Reactions to diversity in recruitment advertising: Are differences Black and White? *Journal of Applied Psychology, 88,* 672–679.

Avery, D., & Hysong, S. (2007). A look in the mirror: Examining the ethnic/racial composition of our society. *The Industrial-Organizational Psychologist, 45*(1), 65–70.

Avery, D., & McKay, P. (2006). Target practice: An organizational impression management approach to attracting minority and female job applicants. *Personnel Psychology, 59,* 157–187.

Avery, D., McKay, P., & Wilson, D. (2008). What are the odds? How demographic similarity affects the prevalence of perceived employment discrimination. *Journal of Applied Psychology, 93,* 235–249.

Avery, D., McKay, P., Wilson, D., & Tonidandel, S. (2007). Unequal attendance: The relationships between race, organizational diversity cues, and absenteeism. *Personnel Psychology, 60,* 875–902.

Avery, R., & Ferraro, R. (2000). Verisimilitude or advertising? Brand appearance on prime-time television. *Journal of Consumer Affairs, 34,* 217–244.

Bacharach, S., Bamberger, P., & Doveh, E., (2008). Firefighters, critical incidents, and drinking to cope. *Journal of Applied Psychology, 93,* 155–169.

Bacharach, S., Bamberger, P., & McKinney, V. (2007). Harassing under the influence. *Journal of Occupational Health Psychology, 12,* 232–250.

Bailey, D. (2004). Number of psychology PhDs declining. *Monitor on Psychology, 35*(2), 18–19.

Balderrama, A. (2007). Generation Y: Too demanding at work? www.cnn.com

Bandura, A., & Locke, E. (2003). Negative self-efficacy and goal effects revisited. *Journal of Applied Psychology, 88,* 87–99.

Barger, P., & Grandey, A. (2006). Service with a smile and encounter satisfaction: Emotional contagion and appraisal mechanisms. *Academy of Management Journal, 49,* 1229–1238.

Bargh, J., & McKenna, K. (2004). The Internet and social life. *Annual Review of Psychology, 55,* 573–590.

Barling, J., Kelloway, E., & Iverson, R. (2003). High-quality work, job satisfaction, and occupational injuries. *Journal of Applied Psychology, 88,* 276–283.

Barling, J., Loughlin, C., & Kelloway, E. (2002). Development and test of a model linking safety-specific transformational leadership and occupational safety. *Journal of Applied Psychology, 87,* 488–496.

Barling, J., Zacharatos, A., & Hepburn, C. G. (1999). Parents' job insecurity affects children's academic performance through cognitive difficulties. *Journal of Applied Psychology, 84,* 437–444.

Barreto, A. (2007). Are you ready for Generation Y? Nine ways to recruit, train and retain Generation Y. www.ezinearticles.com

Barrett, J., & Kirk, S. (2000). Running focus groups with elderly and disabled elderly participants. *Applied Ergonomics, 31,* 621–629.

Barrick, M., Stewart, G., & Piotrowski, M. (2002). Personality and job performance: Test of the mediating effects of motivation among sales representatives. *Journal of Applied Psychology, 87,* 43–51.

Barron, K., & Harackiewicz, J. (2001). Achievement goals and optimal motivation: Testing multiple goal models. *Journal of Personality and Social Psychology, 80,* 706–722.

Baruch, Y. (2004). Prosocial behavior and job performance. *Social Behavior and Personality, 32,* 399–412.

Baruch-Feldman, C., Brondolo, E., Ben-Dayan, D., & Schwartz, J. (2002). Sources of social support and burnout, job satisfaction, and productivity. *Journal of Occupational Health Psychology, 7,* 84–93.

Bass, B., Avolio, B., Jung, D., & Berson, Y. (2003). Predicting unit performance by assessing transformational and transactional leadership. *Journal of Applied Psychology, 88,* 207–218.

Bassett-Jones, N., & Lloyd, G. (2005). Does Herzberg's motivation theory have staying power? *Journal of Management Development, 24,* 929–943.

Bauer, B., Bodner, G., Erdogan, B., Truxillo, D., & Tucker, J. (2007). Newcomer adjustment during organizational socialization. *Journal of Applied Psychology, 92,* 707–721.

Bauer, T., Erdogen, B., Liden, R., & Wayne, S. (2006). A longitudinal study of the moderating role of extraversion. *Journal of Applied Psychology, 91,* 298–310.

Baxter, G., Besnard, D., & Riley, D. (2007). Cognitive mismatches in the cockpit. *Applied Ergonomics, 38,* 417–423.

Beal, D., Cohen, R., Burke, M., & McLendon, C. (2003). Cohesion and performance in groups: A meta-analytic clarification of construct relations. *Journal of Applied Psychology, 88*, 989–1004.

Belkin, L. (2007, July 26). When whippersnappers and geezers collide. *New York Times.*

Belkin, L. (2007, November 1). Life's work: The feminine critique. *New York Times.*

Bell, M., & Berry, D. (2007). Viewing diversity through different lenses. *Academy of Management Perspectives, 21*(4), 21–25.

Bell, S. (2007). Deep-level composition variables as predictors of team performance. *Journal of Applied Psychology, 92*, 595–615.

Bellizzi, J. A. (2000). Drawing prospects to E-commerce Websites. *Journal of Advertising Research, 40*, 43–53.

Bennett, J., & Lehman, W. (2001), Workplace substance abuse prevention and help seeking: Comparing team-oriented and informational training. *Journal of Occupational Health Psychology, 6*, 243–254.

Bennett, R. J., & Robinson, S. L. (2000). Development of a measure of workplace deviance. *Journal of Applied Psychology, 85*, 349–360.

Ben-Yaacov, A., Maltz, M., & Shinar, D. (2002). Effects of an in-vehicle collision avoidance warning system on short- and long-term driving performance. *Human Factors, 44*, 335–342.

Berdahl, J. (2007). The sexual harassment of uppity women. *Journal of Applied Psychology, 92*, 425–437.

Berdahl, J., & Moore, C. (2006). Workplace harassment. *Journal of Applied Psychology, 91*, 426–436.

Bergeron, D. (2007). The potential paradox of organizational citizenship behavior. *Academy of Management Review, 32*, 1078–1095.

Bergman, A., Watrous-Rodriguez, K., & Chalkley, K. (2008). Identity and language. *Hispanic Journal of Behavioral Sciences, 30*, 40–68.

Bergman, M., Langhout, R., Palmieri, P., Cortina, L., & Fitzgerald, L. (2002). The (un)reasonableness of reporting: Antecedents and consequences of reporting sexual harassment. *Journal of Applied Psychology, 87*, 230–242.

Berry, C., Gruys, M., & Sackett. P. (2006). Educational attainment as a proxy for cognitive ability in selection. *Journal of Applied Psychology, 91*, 696–705.

Berry, C., Sackett, P., & Wieman, S. (2007). A review of recent developments in integrity test research. *Personnel Psychology, 60*, 271–301.

Bertoa, C., Anderson, N., & Salgado, J. (2005). The predictive validity of cognitive ability tests. *Journal of Occupational and Organizational Psychology, 78*, 387–409.

Bilgel, N., Aytac, S., & Bayram, N. (2006). Bullying in Turkish white-collar workers. *Occupational Medicine, 56*, 226–231.

Birkeland, S., Manson, T., Kisamore, J., Brannick, M., & Smith, M. (2006). A meta-analytic investigation of job applicant faking on personality measures. *International Journal of Selection and Assessment, 14*(4), 317–328.

Birnbaum, M. (2004). Human research on data collection via the Internet. *Annual Review of Psychology, 55*, 803–832.

Bishop, G. D., Enkelmann, H., Tong, E., Why, Y., Diong, S., Ang, J., & Kaader, M. (2003). Job demands, decisional control, and cardiovascular responses. *Journal of Occupational Health Psychology, 8*, 146–156.

Bishop, J. W., & Scott, K. D. (2000). An examination of organizational and team commitment in a self-directed team environment. *Journal of Applied Psychology, 85*, 439–450.

Blackmore, E., Stansfeld, S., Weller, I., Munce, S., Zagorski, B., & Stewart, D. (2007). Major depressive episodes and work stress. *American Journal of Public Health, 97*, 2088–2093.

Blau, F., & Kahn, L. (2007). The gender pay gap. *Academy of Management Perspectives, 21*(1), 7–23.

Bobko, P., Roth, P. L., & Potosky, D. (1999). Derivation and implications of a meta-analytic matrix incorporating cognitive ability, alternative predictors, and job performance. *Personnel Psychology, 52*, 561–589.

Boehm, J., & Lyubomirsky, S. (2008). Does happiness promote career success? *Journal of Career Assessment, 16*, 101–116.

Boff, K. (2006). Revolutions and shifting paradigms in human factors and ergonomics. *Applied Ergonomics, 37*, 391–399.

Bolino, M., & Turnley, W. (2003). Going the extra mile: Cultivating and managing employee citizenship behavior. *Academy of Management Executive, 17*(3), 60–71.

Bond, F., & Bunce, D. (2001). Job control mediates change in work reorganization intervention for stress reduction. *Journal of Occupational Health Psychology, 6*, 290–302.

Bond, F., & Bunce, D. (2003). The role of acceptance and job control in mental health, job satisfaction, and work performance. *Journal of Applied Psychology, 88*, 1057–1067.

Bono, J., & Anderson, M. (2005). The advice and influence networks of transformational leaders. *Journal of Applied Psychology, 90*, 1306–1314.

Bono, J., Foldes, H., Vinson, G., & Muros, J. (2007). Workplace emotions. *Journal of Applied Psychology, 92*, 1357–1367.

Bono, J., & Judge, T. (2003). Self-concordance at work: Toward understanding the motivational effects of transformational leaders. *Academy of Management Review, 46,* 554–571.

Booth-Kewley, S., & Friedman, H. S. (1987). Psychological predictors of heart disease. *Psychological Bulletin, 101,* 343–362.

Boswell, W., Boudreau, J., & Tichy, J. (2005). The relationship between employee job change and job satisfaction. *Journal of Applied Psychology, 90,* 882–892.

Boudreau, J., Boswell, W., Judge, T., & Bretz, R., Jr. (2001). Personality and cognitive ability as predictors of job search among employed managers. *Personnel Psychology, 54,* 25–50.

Bowler, W., & Brass, D. (2006). Relational correlates of interpersonal citizenship behavior. *Journal of Applied Psychology, 91,* 70–82.

Bowling, N., & Beehr, T. (2006). Workplace harassment from the victim's perspective. *Journal of Applied Psychology, 91,* 998–1012.

Braaksma, A. (2005, September 12). Some lessons from the assembly line. *Newsweek,* p. 17.

Braddy, P., Meade, A., & Kroustalis, C. (2006). Organizational recruitment website effects on viewers' perceptions of organizational culture. *Journal of Business and Psychology, 20,* 525–543.

Brandt, M. (2006, October 18). Internet addiction: Too much of a good thing? *Stanford Report.* www.news-service.stanford.edu/news/

Braunsberger, K., Wybenga, H., & Gates, R. (2007). A comparison of reliability between telephone and web-based surveys. *Journal of Business Research, 60,* 758–764.

Brett, J., & Stroh, L. (2003). Working 61 plus hours a week: Why do managers do it? *Journal of Applied Psychology, 88,* 67–78.

Bridger, R. S. (2003). *Introduction to ergonomics* (2nd ed.). London: Taylor & Francis.

Brief, A., & Weiss, H. (2002). Organizational behavior: Affect in the workplace. *Annual Review of Psychology, 53,* 279–307.

Britt, B. (2004). Automakers tap consumer brains. *Automotive News Europe, 9*(1), 1–22.

Broad, W., & Wade, N. (1982). *Betrayers of the truth.* New York: Simon & Schuster.

Brooks, M., Grauer, E., Thornbury, E., & Highhouse, S. (2003). Value differences between scientists and practitioners: A survey of SIOP members. *The Industrial-Organizational Psychologist, 40*(4), 17–23.

Brown, D., Cober, R., Kane, K., Levy, P., & Shalhoop, J. (2006). Proactive personality and the successful job search. *Journal of Applied Psychology, 91,* 717–726.

Brown, K. (2001). Using computers to deliver training: Which employees learn and why? *Personnel Psychology, 54,* 271–296.

Brown, M., Sturman, M., & Simmering, M. (2003). Compensation policy and organizational performance: The efficiency, operational, and financial implications of pay levels and pay structure. *Academy of Management Journal, 46,* 752–762.

Bruck, D., & Ball, M. (2007). Optimizing emergency awakening to audible smoke alarms. *Human Factors, 49,* 585–601.

Bruner, G. C., II, & Kumar, A. (2000). Web commercials and advertising hierarchy-of-effects. *Journal of Advertising Research, 40,* 35–42.

Brustein, D. (2008). The role of work in psychological health and well-being. *American Psychologist, 63,* 228–240.

Bryner, J. (2007). Survey reveals most satisfying jobs. www.livescience.com/health/070417_job_satisfaction.html

Buckley, M., Jackson, K., Bolino, M., Veres, J., & Feild, H. (2007). The influence of racial demography on panel interview ratings. *Personnel Psychology, 60,* 627–646.

Burke, R., Matthiesen, T., & Pallesen, S. (2006). Personality correlates of workaholism. *Personality & Individual Differences, 40,* 1223–1233.

Burnett, J. J. (2000). Gays: Feelings about advertising and media used. *Journal of Advertising Research, 40,* 75–84.

Bushman, B., & Bonacci, A. (2002). Violence and sex impair memory for television ads. *Journal of Applied Psychology, 87,* 557–564.

Butcher, J., Cabiya, J., Lucio, E., & Garrido, M. (2007). *Assessing Hispanic clients using the MMPI-2 and MMPI-A.* Washington, DC: American Psychological Association.

Buttigieg, D., Deery, S., & Iverson, R. (2007). An event history analysis of union joining and leaving. *Journal of Applied Psychology, 92,* 829–839.

Buttigieg, S. (2006). Gender and race differences in scores on the Wonderlic Personnel Test. *Applied HRM Research, 11*(1), 73–74.

Button, S. (2001). Organizational efforts to affirm sexual diversity: A cross-level examination. *Journal of Applied Psychology, 86,* 17–28.

Bycio, P., Hackett, R. D., & Allen, J. S. (1995). Further assessments of Bass's (1985) conceptualization of transactional and transformational leadership. *Journal of Applied Psychology, 80,* 468–478.

Cable, D., & Parsons, C. (2001). Socialization tactics and person-organization fit. *Personnel Psychology, 54,* 1–23.

Caligiuri, P. M. (2000). The Big Five personality characteristics as predictors of expatriates' desire to terminate the assignment and supervisor-rated performance. *Personnel Psychology, 53,* 67–88.

Callister, R. R., Kramer, M. W., & Turban, D. B. (1999). Feedback seeking following career transitions. *Academy of Management Journal, 42,* 429–438.

Campion, M., & Berger, C. (1990). Conceptual integration and empirical test of job design and compensation relationships. *Personnel Psychology, 43,* 525–554.

Campion, M., Outtz, J., Zedeck, S., Schmidt, F., Kehoe, J., Murphy, K., & Guion, R. (2001). The controversy over score banding in personnel selection: Answers to ten key questions. *Personnel Psychology, 54,* 149–185.

Cappo, J. (2003). *The future of advertising: New media, new clients, new consumers in the post-television age.* New York: McGraw-Hill.

Carcone, S., & Keir, P. (2007). Effects of backrest design on biomechanics and comfort during seated work. *Applied Ergonomics, 38,* 755–764.

Carlan, P. (2007). The search for job satisfaction: A survey of Alabama policing. *American Journal of Criminal Justice, 21,* 74–86.

Cartwright, S. (2000). Taking the pulse of executive health in the U.K. *Academy of Management Executive, 14*(2), 16–23.

Cascio, W. F. (1998). The virtual workplace. *The Industrial-Organizational Psychologist, 35*(4), 32–36.

Catano, V., Darr, W., & Campbell, C. (2007). Performance appraisal of behavior based competencies. *Personnel Psychology, 60,* 201–230.

Cavanaugh, M. A., Boswell, W. R., Roehling, M. V., & Boudreau, J. W. (2000). An empirical examination of self-reported work stress among U.S. managers. *Journal of Applied Psychology, 85,* 65–74.

Cawley, J., Rizzo, J., & Haas, K. (2007). Occupation-specific absenteeism costs associated with obesity and morbid obesity. *Journal of Occupational and Environmental Medicine, 49,* 1317–1324.

Celik, Y., & Celik, S. (2007). Sexual harassment against nurses in Turkey. *Journal of Nursing Scholarship, 39,* 200–206.

Cha, A. (2007, September 2). In China, stern treatment for young Internet addicts. www.washingtonpost.com

Chandler, A. D., Jr. (1988). Origins of the organization chart. *Harvard Business Review, 66*(2), 156–157.

Chandola, T., Britton, A., Brunner, E., Hemingway, H., Malik, M., Kumari, M., Badrick, E., Kivimaki, M., & Marmot, M. (2008). Work stress and coronary heart disease. *European Heart Journal, 29,* 640–648.

Chang, S.-K., & Drury, C. (2007). Task demands and human capabilities in door use. *Applied Ergonomics, 38,* 325–335.

Chaplin, L., & John, D. (2007). Growing up in a material world: Age differences in materialism in children and adolescents. *Journal of Consumer Research, 34,* 480–493.

Chapman, D., Uggerslev, K., Carroll, S., Piasentin, K., & Jones, D. (2005). Applicant attraction to organizations. *Journal of Applied Psychology, 90,* 928–944.

Chattalas, M., & Harper, H. (2007). Navigating a hybrid cultural identity: Hispanic teenagers' fashion consumption influences. *Journal of Consumer Marketing, 24,* 351–357.

Chattopadhyay, P., & George, E. (2001). Examining the effects of work externalization through the lens of social identity theory. *Journal of Applied Psychology, 86,* 781–788.

Chen, L.-H. (2008). Job satisfaction among information systems (IS) personnel. *Computers in Human Behavior, 24,* 105–118.

Chen, G., Kirkman, B., Kanfer, R., Allen, D., & Rosen, B. (2007). A multilevel study of leadership, empowerment, and performance in teams. *Journal of Applied Psychology, 92,* 331–346.

Chen, G., & Klimoski, R. (2003). The impact of expectations on newcomer performance in teams as mediated by work characteristics, social exchanges, and empowerment. *Academy of Management Journal, 46,* 591–607.

Chen, Z., Lam, W., & Zhong, J. (2007). Leader-member exchange and member performance. *Journal of Applied Psychology, 92,* 202–212.

Chiang, D., Brooks, A., & Weir, D. (2004). On the highway measures of driver glance behavior with an example automobile navigation system. *Applied Ergonomics, 35*(3), 215–223.

Chiang, K., & Dholakia, R. (2003). Factors driving consumer intention to shop online: An empirical investigation. *Journal of Consumer Psychology, 13,* 177–183.

Chiu, M.-C., & Wang, M.-J. (2007). Professional footwear evaluation for clinical nurses. *Applied Ergonomics, 38,* 133–141.

Church, A. (2001). Is there a method to our madness? The impact of data collection methodology on organizational survey results. *Personnel Psychology, 54,* 937–969.

Clarke, S., & Robertson, I. (2008). An examination of the role of personality in work accidents using meta-analysis. *Applied Psychology: An International Review, 57,* 94–108.

Clay, R. A. (2000). Advertising to children. *Monitor on Psychology, 31*(8), 52–53.

Clevenger, J., Pereira, G., Weichmann, D., Schmitt, N., & Harvey, V. (2001). Incremental validity of situational judgment tests. *Journal of Applied Psychology, 86,* 410–417.

Cohen-Charash, Y., & Mueller, J. (2007). Does perceived unfairness exacerbate or mitigate interpersonal counterproductive work behavior related to envy? *Journal of Applied Psychology, 92,* 666–680.

Colbert, A., Kristof-Brown, A., Bradley, B., & Barrick, M. (2008). CEO transformational leadership. *Academy of Management Journal, 51,* 81–86.

Collela, A., Paetzold, R., & Belliveau, M. (2004). Factors affecting co-workers' procedural justice inferences of the workplace accommodations of employees with disabilities. *Personnel Psychology, 57,* 1–23.

Collins, C., & Stevens, C. (2002). The relationship between early recruitment-related activities and the application decisions of new labor-market entrants: A brand equity approach to recruitment. *Journal of Applied Psychology, 87,* 1121–1133.

Combs, J., Liu, Y., Hall, A., & Ketchen, D. (2006). How much do high-performance work practices matter? *Personnel Psychology, 59,* 501–528.

Coombs, A. (2008, February 3). Seeking loyal devoted workers? Let them stay home. *Wall Street Journal.*

Cooney, M. (2007). Telecommute: Kill a career? www.networkworld.com/news/2007/011707-telecommute-career.html

Cortina, L., Magley, V., Williams, J., & Langhout, R. (2001). Incivility in the workplace: Incidence and impact. *Journal of Occupational Health Psychology, 6,* 64–80.

Costanzo, P., & Goodnight, J. (2006). Celebrity endorsements. *Journal of Promotion Management, 11*(4), 49–62.

Coy, P. (2004, March 22). The future of work: Flexible, creative, and good with people? You should do fine in tomorrow's job market. *Business Week,* pp. 50–52.

Craig, S., & Hannum, K. (2006). Research update: 360-degree performance assessment. *Counseling Psychology Journal: Practice & Research, 58,* 117–124.

Cropanzano, R., Bowen, D., & Gilliland, S. (2007). The management of organizational justice. *Academy of Management Perspectives, 21,* 34–48.

Cropanzano, R., & Greenberg, J. (1997). Progress in organizational justice: Tunneling through the maze. In C. Cooper & I. Robertson (Eds.), *International review of industrial and organizational psychology.* New York: Wiley.

Cropanzano, R., Rupp, D., & Byrne, Z. (2003). The relationship of emotional exhaustion to work attitudes, job performance, and organizational citizenship behaviors. *Journal of Applied Psychology, 88,* 160–169.

Crosby, F., Iver, A., Clayton, S., & Downing, R. (2003). Affirmative action: Psychological data and the policy debates. *American Psychologist, 58,* 93–115.

Crowley, B., Hayslip, B., Jr., & Hobdy, J. (2003). Psychological hardiness and adjustment to life events in adulthood. *Journal of Adult Development, 10,* 237–248.

Cullen, J., & Hammer, L. (2007). Developing and testing a theoretical model linking work-family conflict to employee safety. *Journal of Occupational Health Psychology, 12,* 266–278.

Cynkar, A. (2007). The changing gender composition of psychology. *Monitor on Psychology, 38*(6), 46–47.

Dahl, D., Frankenberger, K., & Manchanda, R. (2003). Does it pay to shock? Reactions to shocking and nonshocking advertising content among university students. *Journal of Advertising Research, 43,* 268–280.

Dahlen, M., Rasch, A., & Rosengren, S. (2003). Love at first site? A study of Website advertising effectiveness. *Journal of Advertising Research, 43,* 25–34.

Dahlgren, A., Kecklund, G., & Akerstedt, T. (2006). Overtime work and its effects on sleep, sleepiness, cortisol and blood pressure in an experimental field study. *Scandinavian Journal of Work, Environment, & Health, 32,* 318–327.

Danaher, P., & Mullarkey, G. (2003). Factors affecting online advertising recall: A study of students. *Journal of Advertising Research, 43,* 252–264.

Davidson, O. B., & Eden, D. (2000). Remedial self-fulfilling prophecy. *Journal of Applied Psychology, 85,* 386–398.

Davis, B. L., & Mount, M. K. (1984). Design and use of a performance appraisal feedback system. *Personnel Administrator, 29*(3), 91–97.

Davis-Blake, A., Broschak, J., & George, E. (2003). Happy together? How using nonstandard workers affects exit, voice, and loyalty among standard employees. *Academy of Management Journal, 46,* 475–485.

Day, D., Schleicher, D., Unckless, A., & Hiller, N. (2002). Self-monitoring personality at work: A meta-analytic investigation of construct validity. *Journal of Applied Psychology, 87,* 390–401.

Dayan, K., Kasten, R., & Fox, S. (2002). Entry-level police candidate assessment center: An efficient tool or a hammer to kill a fly? *Personnel Psychology, 55,* 827–849.

Dean, M., Roth, P., & Bobko, P. (2008). Ethnic and gender subgroup differences in assessment center ratings. *Journal of Applied Psychology, 93,* 685–691.

DeAngelis, T. (2000). Is Internet addiction real? *Monitor on Psychology, 31*(4), 24–26.

deCroon, E., Sluiter, J., Blonk, R., Broersen, J., & Frings-Dresen, M. (2004). Stressful work, psychological job strain, and turnover: A two-year prospective cohort study of truck drivers. *Journal of Applied Psychology, 89,* 442–454.

Deatherage, B. H. (1972). *Human engineering guide to equipment design.* Washington, DC: U.S. Government Printing Office.

De Cuyper, N., & De Witte, H. (2006). Autonomy and workload among temporary workers. *International Journal of Stress Management, 13,* 441–459.

Deery, S., Iverson, R., & Walsh, J. (2006). Toward a better understanding of psychological contract breach. *Journal of Applied Psychology, 91,* 166–175.

DeFrank, R. S., Konopaske, R., & Ivancevich, J. M. (2000). Executive travel stress. *Academy of Management Executive, 14*(2), 58–71.

de Jong, G. M., & Emmelkamp, P. M. G. (2000). Implementing stress management training. *Journal of Occupational Health Psychology, 5,* 309–320.

Dembe, A., Delbos, R., Erickson, J., & Banks, S. (2007). Associations between employees' work schedules and the vocational consequences of workplace injuries. *Journal of Occupational Rehabilitation, 17,* 641–651.

Dembowski, J. M., & Callans, M. C. (2000, April). Comparing computer and paper forms of the Wonderlic Personnel Test. Paper presented at the meeting of the Society for Industrial and Organizational Psychology, New Orleans, LA.

Demerouti, E., Bakker, A., Nachreiner, F., & Schaufeli, W. (2001). The job demands—resources model of burnout. *Journal of Applied Psychology, 86,* 499–512.

Den Hartog, D., De Hoogh, A., & Keegan, A. (2007). The interactive effects of belongingness and charisma on helping and compliance. *Journal of Applied Psychology, 92,* 1131–1139.

DeNisi, A. S., & Kluger, A. N. (2000). Feedback effectiveness. *Academy of Management Executive, 14*(1), 129–139.

Dennis, A., & Williams, M. (2005). A meta-analysis of group size effects in electronic brainstorming. *International Journal of e-Collaboration, 1,* 24–42.

DeRosa, D., Smith, C., & Hantula, D. (2007). The medium matters: Mining the long-promised merit of group interaction in creative idea generation tasks in a meta-analysis of the electronic group brainstorming literature. *Computers in Human Behavior, 23,* 1549–1581.

Detert, J., Trevino, L., Burris, E., & Andiappan, M. (2007). Managerial modes of influence and counterproductivity in organizations. *Journal of Applied Psychology, 92,* 993–1105.

Dewangen, K., Owary, C., & Datta, R. (2008). Anthropometric data of female farm workers from northeastern India and design of hand tools of the hilly region. *International Journal of Industrial Ergonomics, 38,* 90–100.

Dickson, M., Resick, C., & Hanges, P. (2006). When organizational climate is unambiguous, it is also strong. *Journal of Applied Psychology, 91,* 351–364.

Diefendorff, J., & Mehta, K. (2007). The relations of motivational traits with workplace deviance. *Journal of Applied Psychology, 92,* 967–977.

Dietz, J., Robinson, S., Folger, R., Baron, R., & Schulz, M. (2003). The impact of community violence and an organization's procedural justice climate on workplace aggression. *Academy of Management Journal, 46,* 317–326.

Dilchert, S., Ones, D., Davis, R., & Rostow, C. (2007). Cognitive ability predicts objectively measured counterproductive work behaviors. *Journal of Applied Psychology, 92,* 616–627.

Dineen, B., Ash, S., & Noe, R. (2002). A Web of applicant attraction: Person-organization fit in the context of Web-based recruitment. *Journal of Applied Psychology, 87,* 723–734.

Dineen, B., Lewicki, R., & Tomlinson, E. (2006). Supervisory guidance and behavioral integrity. *Journal of Applied Psychology, 91,* 622–635.

Dirks, K., & Ferrin, D. (2002). Trust in leadership: Meta-analytic findings and implications for research and practice. *Journal of Applied Psychology, 87,* 611–628.

Dommeyer, C. (2008). The effects of the researcher's physical attractiveness and gender on mail survey response. *Psychology & Marketing, 25,* 47–70.

Donovan, M. A., Drasgow, F., & Probst, T. M. (2000). Does computerizing paper-and-pencil job attitude scales make a difference? *Journal of Applied Psychology, 85,* 305–313.

Donovan, J. J., & Radosevich, D. J. (1999). A meta-analytic review of the distribution of practice effect. *Journal of Applied Psychology, 84,* 795–805.

Dormann, C., & Zapf, D. (2004). Customer-related social stressors and burnout. *Journal of Occupational Health Psychology, 9,* 61–82.

Douglas, S., & Martinko, M. (2001). Exploring the role of individual differences in the prediction of workplace aggression. *Journal of Applied Psychology, 86,* 547–559.

Drory, A., & Zaidman, N. (2007). Impression management behavior. *Journal of Managerial Psychology, 22,* 290–308.

Druskat, V., & Wheeler, J. (2003). Managing from the boundary: The effective leadership of self-managing work teams. *Academy of Management Journal, 46,* 435–457.

Duehr, E., & Bono, J. (2006). Men, women, and managers. *Personnel Psychology, 59,* 815–846.

Duke, K., Mirka, G., & Sommerich, C. (2004). Productivity and ergonomic investigation of bent-handle pliers. *Human Factors, 46,* 234–243.

Eagly, A., Johannesen-Schmidt, M., & Van Engen, M. (2003). Transformational, transactional, and laissez-faire leadership styles: A meta-analysis comparing men and women. *Psychological Bulletin, 129,* 569–591.

Eddleston, K., Veiga, J., & Powell, G. (2006). Explaining sex differences in managerial career satisfies preferences. *Journal of Applied Psychology, 91,* 437–445.

Eisen, K., Allen, G., Bollash, M., & Pescatello, L. (2008). Stress management in the workplace. *Computers in Human Behavior, 24,* 486–496.

Eisenberger, R., Armeli, S., Rexwinkel, B., Lynch, P., & Rhoades, L. (2001). Reciprocation of perceived organizational support. *Journal of Applied Psychology, 86,* 42–51.

Eisenberger, R., Stingchamber, F., Vandenberghe, C., Socharski, I., & Rhoades, L. (2002). Perceived supervisor support: Contributions to perceived organizational support and employee retention. *Journal of Applied Psychology, 87,* 565–573.

Eklund, J. A. E. (1995). Relationships between ergonomics and quality in assembly work. *Applied Ergonomics, 26*(1), 15–20.

Ellin, A. (2004, February 29). When it comes to salary, many women don't push. *New York Times.*

Elliott, S. (2004, April 14). Advertising: A survey of consumer attitudes reveals the depth of the challenge that the agencies face. *New York Times.*

Elliott, S. (2008, March 31). Is the ad a success? The brain wave tells all. *New York Times.*

Ellis, A., West, B., Ryan, A., & DeShon, R. (2002). The use of impression management tactics in structured interviews: A function of question type? *Journal of Applied Psychology, 87,* 1200–1208.

Ely, R. J. (1995). The power in demography. *Academy of Management Journal, 38,* 589–634.

Epitropaki, O., & Martin, R. (2004). Implicit leadership theories in applied settings: Factor structure, generalizability, and stability over time. *Journal of Applied Psychology, 89,* 293–310.

Erdogan, B., & Enders, J. (2007). Support from the top. Supervisors' perceived organizational support as a moderator of leader-member exchange to satisfaction and performance relationships. *Journal of Applied Psychology, 92,* 321–350.

Erickson, T. (2006). "What is it with you people and 8:30 a.m.?"—Generation Y's first impression of us. www.harvardbusinessonline

Ettner, S., & Grzywacz, J. (2001). Workers' perceptions of how jobs affect health: A social ecological perspective. *Journal of Occupational Health Psychology, 6*(2), 101–113.

Euwema, M., Wendt, H., & Van Emmerik, H. (2007). Leadership styles and group organizational citizenship behavior across cultures. *Journal of Organizational Behavior, 28,* 1035–1057.

Evans, D. (2003). A comparison of other-directed stigmatization produced by legal and illegal forms of affirmative action. *Journal of Applied Psychology, 88,* 121–130.

Evans, G. W., & Johnson, D. (2000). Stress and open-office noise. *Journal of Applied Psychology, 85,* 779–783.

Evans O., & Steptoe, A. (2001). Social support at work, heart rate and control: A self-monitoring study. *Journal of Occupational Health Psychology, 6*(4), 361–370.

Everton, W., Mastrangelo, P., & Jolton, J. (2003). Surfin' USA: Using your work computer for personal reasons. *The Industrial-Organizational Psychologist, 40*(4), 90–93.

Ewing, M., DuPlessis, E., & Foster, C. (2001). Cinema advertising reconsidered. *Journal of Advertising Research, 4*(1), 78.

Facteau, J., & Craig, C. (2001). Are performance appraisal ratings from different rating sources comparable? *Journal of Applied Psychology, 86,* 215–227.

Farmer, S., Tierney, P., & Kung-McIntyre, K. (2003). Employee creativity in Taiwan: An application of role identity theory. *Academy of Management Journal, 46,* 618–630.

Fassinger, R. (2008). Workplace diversity and public policy. *American Psychologist, 63,* 252–268.

Fayard, G. (2008). Work-related fatal injuries in parking lots, 1993–2002. *Journal of Safety Research, 39,* 9–18.

Feder, B. (2008, May 4). Prepping robots for the OR. *New York Times.*

Feinstein, A. (2002). A hazardous profession: War, journalists, and psychopathology. *American Journal of Psychiatry, 159,* 1570–1579.

Feldman, D., & Klass, B. (2002). Internet job hunting: A field study of applicant experiences with online recruiting. *Human Resource Management, 41,* 175–192.

Ferdman, B. (2003). Accounts of inclusion (and exclusion). *The Industrial-Organizational Psychologist, 40*(4), 81–86.

Fiedler, F. E. (1978). The contingency model and the dynamics of the leadership process. In L. Berkowitz (Ed.). *Advances in experimental social psychology.* New York: Academic Press.

Fiedler, F. E. (2002). The curious role of cognitive resources in leadership. In R. Riggio, S. Murphy, & F. Pirozzolo (Eds.), *Multiple intelligences and leadership* (pp. 91–104). Mahwah, NJ: Erlbaum.

Fitness, J. (2000). Anger in the workplace: An emotion script approach to anger episodes between workers and their superiors, co-workers, and subordinates. *Journal of Organizational Behavior, 21,* 147–162.

Fleishman, E., & Harris, E. (1962). Patterns of leadership behavior related to employee grievances and turnover. *Personnel Psychology, 15,* 43–56.

Florey, A. T., & Harrison, D. A. (2000). Responses to informal accommodation requests from employees with disabilities. *Academy of Management Journal, 43,* 224–233.

Ford, M., Heinen, B., & Langkamer, K. (2007). Work and family satisfaction and conflict. *Journal of Applied Psychology, 92,* 57–80.

Forth, J., & Millward, N. (2004). High-involvement management and pay in Britain. *Industrial Relations, 43,* 118–119.

Foxall, G. R., & Goldsmith, R. E. (1994). *Consumer psychology for marketing.* London: Routledge.

Frame, J. H., & Beaty, J. C., Jr. (2000, April). An investigation of high-technology survey methods at Hewlett-Packard. Paper presented at the meeting of the Society for Industrial and Organizational Psychology, New Orleans, LA.

French, H. (2003, July 25). Japan's neglected resource: Female workers. *New York Times.*

Frese, M., Beimel, S., & Schoenborn, S. (2003). Action training for charismatic leadership: Two evaluations of studies of a commercial training module on inspirational communication of a vision. *Personnel Psychology, 56,* 671–697.

Friedman, M., & Gould, J. (2007). Consumer attitudes and behaviors associated with direct-to-consumer prescription drug marketing. *Journal of Consumer Marketing, 24*(2), 100–109.

Friedman, M., & Rosenman, R. H. (1974). *Type A behavior and your heart.* New York: Knopf.

Fritz, C., & Sonnentag, S. (2006). Recovery, well-being, and performance-related outcomes. *Journal of Applied Psychology, 91,* 936–945.

Frone, M. (1998). Predictors of work injuries among employed adolescents. *Journal of Applied Psychology, 83,* 565–576.

Frone, M. (2003). Predictors of overall and on-the-job substance abuse among young workers. *Journal of Occupational Health Psychology, 8,* 39–54.

Frone, M. (2006). Prevalence and distribution of illicit drug use in the workforce and in the workplace. *Journal of Applied Psychology, 91,* 856–869.

Frone, M. (2008). Are work stressors related to employee substance use? *Journal of Applied Psychology, 93,* 199–206.

Fugate, D. (2007). Neuromarketing. *Journal of Consumer Marketing, 24,* 385–394.

Fugate, M., Kinicki, A., & Scheck, C. (2002). Coping with an organizational merger over four stages. *Personnel Psychology, 55,* 905–928.

Fuller, J., Stanton, J., Fisher, G., Spitzmueller, C., Russell, S., & Smith, C. (2003). A lengthy look at the daily grind: Time series analysis of events, mood, stress, and satisfaction. *Journal of Applied Psychology, 88,* 1019–1033.

Fulmer, I., Gerhart, B., & Scott, K. (2003). Are the 100 best better: An empirical investigation of the relationship between being "a great place to work" and firm performance. *Personnel Psychology, 56,* 965–993.

Furst, S., & Cable, E. (2008). Employee resistance to organizational change. *Journal of Applied Psychology, 93,* 453–462.

Gajendran, R., & Harrison, D. (2007). The good, the bad, and the unknown about telecommuting. *Journal of Applied Psychology, 92,* 1524–1541.

Galaif, E., Newcomb, M., & Carmona, J. (2001). Prospective relationships between drug problems and work adjustment in a community sample of adults. *Journal of Applied Psychology, 86,* 337–350.

Gallo, W., Teng, H., Falba, T., Kasl, S., Krumholz, H., & Bradley, E. (2006). The impact of late career job loss on myocardial infarction and stroke. *Occupational & Environmental Medicine, 63,* 683–687.

Ganz, W., Schwartz, N., Angelini, J., & Rideout, V. (2007). Food for thought: Television food advertising to children in the United States. Henry J. Kaiser Family Foundation Report.

Ganzach, Y. (1998). Intelligence and job satisfaction. *Academy of Management Journal, 41,* 526–539.

Ganzach, Y., Pazy, A., Ohayun, Y., & Brainin, E. (2002). Social exchange and organizational commitment: Decision-making training for job choice as an alternative to the realistic job preview. *Personnel Psychology, 55,* 613–637.

Garavan, T. (2007). Using assessment centre performance to predict subjective person-organization fit. *Journal of Managerial Psychology, 22*(2), 150–167.

Garlin, F., & Owen, K. (2006). Setting the tone with the tune: A meta-analytic review of the effects of background music in retail settings. *Journal of Business Research, 59,* 755–764.

Garretson, J., & Burton, S. (2003). Highly coupon and sale prone consumers: Benefits beyond price and savings. *Journal of Advertising Research, 43*(2), 162–173.

George, J., & Zhou, J. (2001). When openness to experience and conscientiousness are related to creative behavior: An interactional approach. *Journal of Applied Psychology, 86,* 513–524.

Gettman, H., & Gelfand, M. (2007). When the customer shouldn't be king: Antecedents and consequences of sexual harassment by clients and customers. *Journal of Applied Psychology, 92,* 757–770.

Giaso, L., Matthiesen, S., Nielsen, M., & Einarsen, S. (2007). Do targets of workplace bullying portray a general victim personality profile? *Scandinavian Journal of Psychology, 48,* 313–319.

Glomb, B., & Liao, H. (2003). Interpersonal aggression in work groups: Social influence, reciprocal, and individual effects. *Academy of Management Journal, 46,* 486–496.

Gilboa, S., Shirom, A., Fried, Y., & Cooper, C. (2008). A meta-analysis of work demand stressors and job performance. *Personnel Psychology, 61,* 227–271.

Gilbreth, F. B. (1911). *Motion study.* Princeton, NJ: Van Nostrand.

Gill, C., & Hodgkinson, G. (2007). Development and validation of the 5-factor model questionnaire (FFMQ). *Personnel Psychology, 60,* 731–766.

Golden, T. (2006). The role of relationships in understanding telecommuter satisfaction. *Journal of Organizational Behavior, 27,* 319–340.

Golden, T., & Veiga, J. (2008). The impact of superior-subordinate relationships on the commitment, job satisfaction, and performance of virtual workers. *Leadership Quarterly, 19*(1), 77–88.

Golden, T., Veiga, J., & Simsek, Z. (2006). Telecommuting's differential impact on work-family conflict. *Journal of Applied Psychology, 91,* 1340–1350.

Goldman, B. (2001). Toward an understanding of employment discrimination claiming: An integration of organizational justice and social information processing theories. *Personnel Psychology, 54,* 361–386.

Goldstein, H., Yusko, K., & Nicolopoulos, V. (2001). Exploring Black-White subgroup differences of managerial competencies. *Personnel Psychology, 54,* 783–807.

Gomez, C., & Rosen, B. (2001). The leader-member exchange as a link between managerial trust and employee empowerment. *Group and Organization Management, 26,* 53–69.

Gomez-Mejia, L., Larraza-Kintana, M., & Makri, M. (2003). The determinants of executive compensation in family controlled public corporations. *Academy of Management Journal, 46,* 226–237.

Gonzalez-Morales, M., Peiro, J., Rodriguez, I., & Greenglass, E. (2006). Coping and distress in organizations. *International Journal of Stress Management, 13,* 228–248.

Gordon, J., Whelan-Berry, K., & Hamilton, E. (2007). The relationship among work-family conflict and enhancement, organizational work-family culture, and work outcomes for older working women. *Journal of Occupational Health Psychology, 12,* 350–364.

Gosling, S., Vazire, S., Srivastava, S., & John, O. (2004). Should we trust Web-based studies? A comparative analysis of six preconceptions. *American Psychologist, 59,* 93–104.

Gouvali, M., & Boudolos, K. (2006). Match between furniture dimensions and children's anthropometry. *Applied Ergonomics, 37,* 765–773.

Gowan, M. A., Riordan, C. M., & Gatewood, R. D. (1999). Test of a model of coping with involuntary job loss following a company closing. *Journal of Applied Psychology, 81,* 75–86.

Graen, G., & Schliemann, W. (1978). Leader-member agreement. *Journal of Applied Psychology, 63,* 206–212.

Graff, G. (2007, March). Smile: You're on YouTube. *Washingtonian,* pp. 49–54.

Grant, A. (2008). Does intrinsic motivation fuel the prosocial fire? *Journal of Applied Psychology, 93,* 48–58.

Grant, S., & Langan-Fox, J. (2007). Personality and the occupational stressor-strain relationship. *Journal of Occupational Health Psychology, 12,* 20–33.

Green, P. (2003). Motor vehicle driver interfaces. In J. Jacko & A. Sears (Eds.), *The human-computer interaction handbook* (pp. 844–860). Mahwah, NJ: Erlbaum.

Greguras, G., Robie, C., Schleicher, D., & Goff, M. (2003). A field study of the effects of rating purpose on the quality of multi-source ratings. *Personnel Psychology, 56,* 1–21.

Griffin, M., & Neal, A. (2000). Perceptions of safety at work. *Journal of Occupational Health Psychology, 5,* 347–358.

Griffith, K., & Hebl, M. (2002). The disclosure dilemma for gay men and lesbians: "Coming out" at work. *Journal of Applied Psychology, 87,* 1191–1199.

Grow, B. (2004, March 15). Is America ready? *Business Week.*

Grzywacz, J., Arcury, T., Marin, A., Carrillo, L., Burke, B., Coates, M., & Quandt, S. (2007). Work-family conflict. *Journal of Applied Psychology, 92,* 1119–1130.

Gustafsson, E., Delive, L., Edlund, M., & Hagberg, M. (2003). The use of information technology among young adults: Experience, attitudes, and health beliefs. *Applied Ergonomics, 34,* 565–570.

Gustafsson, E., & Hagberg, M. (2003). Computer mouse use in two different hand positions: Exposure, comfort, exertion and productivity. *Applied Ergonomics, 34,* 107–113.

Haaland, S., & Christiansen, N. (2002). Implications of trait-activation theory for evaluating the construct validity of assessment-center ratings. *Personnel Psychology, 55,* 137–163.

Hackman, J. R., & Oldham, G. R. (1976). Motivation through the design of work. *Organizational Behavior and Human Performance, 16,* 250–279.

Hackman, J. R., & Oldham, G. R. (1980). *Work redesign.* Reading, MA: Addison-Wesley.

Hagg, G. (2003). Corporate initiatives in ergonomics: An introduction. *Applied Ergonomics, 34,* 3–15.

Haight, F. (2001). *Accident proneness: The history of an idea.* Irvine, CA: University of California Institute of Transportation Studies.

Hair, M., Renaud, K., & Ramsay, J. (2007). The influence of self-esteem and locus of control on perceived email-related stress. *Computers in Human Behavior, 23,* 2791–2803.

Halbesleben, J., & Bowler, W. (2007). Emotional exhaustion and job performance. *Journal of Applied Psychology, 92,* 93–106.

Hamburger University. www.mcdonalds.com/usa/work/burgers.html

Haq, A. (2007, October 8). This is your brain on advertising. *Business Week.*

Hardy, G., Woods, D., & Wall, T. (2003). The impact of psychological distress on absence from work. *Journal of Applied Psychology, 88,* 306–314.

Harned, M., Ormerod, A., Palmieri, P., Collinsworth, L., & Reed, M. (2002). Sexual assault and other types of sexual harassment by workplace personnel: A comparison of antecedents and consequences. *Journal of Occupational Health Psychology, 7,* 174–188.

Harris, K., Kacmar, K., Zivnuska, S., & Shaw, J. (2007). The impact of political skill on impression management effectiveness. *Journal of Applied Psychology, 92,* 278–285.

Harris, M. (2003). Speeding down the information highway: Internet recruitment and testing. *The Industrial-Organizational Psychologist, 41*(2), 103–106.

Harris, M., Anseel, F., & Lievens, F. (2008). Keeping up with the Joneses: A field study of the relationships among upward, lateral, and downward comparisons and pay level satisfaction. *Journal of Applied Psychology, 93,* 665–673.

Harrison, D., Newman, D., & Roth, P. (2006). How important are job attitudes? *Academy of Management Journal, 49,* 305–325.

Hart, P. M. (1999). Predicting employee life satisfaction. *Journal of Applied Psychology, 84,* 564–584.

Harter, J., Schmidt, F., & Hayes, T. (2002). Business-unit-level relationship between employee satisfaction, employee engagement, and business outcomes: A meta-analysis. *Journal of Applied Psychology, 87,* 268–279.

Harvey, S., Kelloway, E., & Duncan-Leiper, L. (2003). Trust in management as a buffer of the relationships between overload and strain. *Journal of Occupational Health Psychology, 8*(4), 306–315.

Hausknecht, J., Halpert, J., DiPaolo, N., & Gerrard, M. (2007). Retesting in selection. *Journal of Applied Psychology, 92,* 373–385.

Hausknecht, J., Trevor, C., & Farr, J. (2002). Retaking ability tests in a selection setting: Implications for practice effects, training performance, and turnover. *Journal of Applied Psychology, 87,* 243–254.

Heaphy, E., & Dutton, J. (2008). Positive social interactions and the human body at work. *Academy of Management Review, 33,* 137–162.

Hebl, M., King, E., Glick, P., Singletary, S., & Kazama, S. (2007). Hostile and benevolent reactions toward pregnant women. *Journal of Applied Psychology, 92,* 1499–1511.

Hechanova-Alampay R., & Beehr, T. (2001). Empowerment, span of control, and safety performance in work teams after workforce reduction. *Journal of Occupational Health Psychology, 6*(4), 275–282.

Heil, G., Bennis, W., & Stephens, D. (2000). *Douglas McGregor, revisited: Managing the human side of the enterprise.* New York: Wiley.

Heilman, M., & Okimoto, T. (2008). Motherhood: A potential source of bias in employment decisions. *Journal of Applied Psychology, 93,* 189–198.

Heiskanen, M. (2007). Violence at work in Finland. *Journal of Scandinavian Studies in Criminology and Crime Prevention, 8,* 22–40.

Heller, C. (2007, August 28). Cyberslacking 101. www.features.us.reuters.com/techlife/news

Hepworth, W., & Towler, A. (2004). The effects of individual differences and charismatic leadership on workplace aggression. *Journal of Occupational Health Psychology, 9*(2), 176–185.

Herbert, B. (2003, December 29). The white-collar blues. *New York Times.*

Heremelin, E., Lievens, F., & Robertson, I. (2007). The validity of assessment centers for the prediction of supervisory performance ratings. *International Journal of Selection and Assessment, 15*(4), 405–411.

Herold, D., Davis, W., Fedor, D., & Parsons, C. (2002). Dispositional influences on transfer of learning in multistage training programs. *Personnel Psychology, 55,* 851–869.

Herold, D., Fedor, D., & Caldwell, S. (2007). Beyond change management. *Journal of Applied Psychology, 92,* 942–951.

Herold, D., Fedor, D., Caldwell, S., & Liu, Y. (2008). The effects of transformational and change leadership on employees' commitment to change. *Journal of Applied Psychology, 93,* 346–357.

Herrbach, O. (2006). A matter of feeling? The affective tone of organizational commitment and identification. *Journal of Organizational Behavior, 27,* 629–643.

Herscovitch, L., & Meyer, J. (2002). Commitment to organizational change: Extension of a three-component model. *Journal of Applied Psychology, 87,* 474–487.

Hershcovis, M., Turner, N., Barling, J., Arnold, K., Dupre, K., Inness, M., LeBlanc, M., & Sivanathan, N. (2007). Predicting workplace aggression. *Journal of Applied Psychology, 92,* 228–238.

Herzberg, F. (1966). *Work and the nature of man.* Cleveland: World.

Herzberg, F. (1974). Motivator-hygiene profiles. *Organizational Dynamics, 3*(2), 18–29.

Heslin, P., Vanderwalle, D., & Latham, G. (2006). Keen to help? Managers' implicit person theories and their subsequent employee coaching. *Personnel Psychology, 59,* 871–902.

Hofmann, D., & Mark, B., (2006). An investigation of the relationship between safety climate and medication errors as well as other nurse and patient outcomes. *Personnel Psychology, 59,* 847–869.

Hofmann, D., Morgeson, F., & Gerras, S. (2003). Climate as a moderator of the relationship between leader-member exchange and content specific citizenship: Safety climate as an exemplar. *Journal of Applied Psychology, 88,* 170–178.

Hogan, J., Barrett, P., & Hogan, R. (2007). Personality measurement, faking, and employment selection. *Journal of Applied Psychology, 92,* 1270–1285.

Hogan, R., Curphy, G. J., & Hogan, J. (1994). What we know about leadership. *American Psychologist, 49,* 493–504.

Holland, K. (2008, March 30). High level of stress rampant in workplace. *New York Times.*

Hollingworth, H. L. (1929). *Vocational psychology and character analysis.* New York: Appleton.

Holton, B., Lee, T., & Tidd, S. (2002). The relationship between work status congruence and work-related attitudes and behaviors. *Journal of Applied Psychology, 87,* 903–915.

Hom, P., Roberson, L., & Ellis, A. (2008). Challenging conventional wisdom about who quits. *Journal of Applied Psychology, 93,* 1–34.

Honkonen, T., Ahola, K., Pertovaara, M., Isometa, E., Kalimo, R., Nykyri, E., Aromaa, A., & Lonnqvist, J. (2006). The association between burnout and physical illness in the general population. *Journal of Psychosomatic Research, 61,* 59–66.

Honor, J., Wright, C., & Sablynski, C. (2007). Puzzle interviews. *Applied HRM Research, 11*(2), 79–96.

Hoobler, J., & Brass, D. (2006). Abusive supervision and family undermining as displaced aggression. *Journal of Applied Psychology, 91,* 1125–1133.

Horrigan, J. (2007). A typology of information and communication technology users. Pew Internet & American Life Project. www.pewinternet.org

Horrigan, J. (2008, February 13). Online shopping. Pew Internet & American Life Project. www.pewinternet.org

Hosodo, M., Stone-Romero, E., & Coats, G. (2003). The effects of physical attractiveness on job-related outcomes: A meta-analysis of experimental studies. *Personnel Psychology, 56,* 431–462.

Hough, L. M., & Oswald, F. L. (2000). Personnel selection. *Annual Review of Psychology, 51,* 631–664.

House, R. J. (1971). A path-goal theory of leader effectiveness. *Administrative Science Quarterly, 16,* 321–338.

House, R. J., & Mitchell, T. (1974). Path-goal theory of leadership. *Journal of Contemporary Business, 3,* 81–97.

Hovorka-Mead, A., Ross, W., Jr., Whipple, T., & Renchin, M. (2002). Watching the detectives: Seasonal student employee reactions to electronic monitoring with and without advance notification. *Personnel Psychology, 55,* 329–362.

Howard, A., Erkers, S., & Bruce, N. (2007). The selection forecast 2006/2007: Slogging through the war for talent. intelligence.monster.com

Howell, J. M., & Hall-Merenda, K. E. (1999). The ties that bind. *Journal of Applied Psychology, 84,* 680–694.

Hsueh, Y. (2002). The Hawthorne experiments and the introduction of Jean Piaget in American industrial psychology, 1929–1932. *History of Psychology, 5,* 163–189.

Huang, X., & Iun, J. (2006). The impact of subordinate-supervisor similarity in growth-need strength on work outcomes. *Journal of Organizational Behavior, 27,* 1121–1148.

Huang, Y.-H., Chen, J.-C., Dearmond, S., Cigularov, K., & Chen, P. (2007). Roles of safety climate and shift work on perceived injury risk. *Accident Analysis & Prevention, 39,* 1088–1096.

Huffcutt, A., Conway, J., Roth, P., & Stone, N. (2001). Identification and meta-analytic assessment of psychological constructs measured in employment interviews. *Journal of Applied Psychology, 86,* 897–913.

Huffcutt, A., Weekley, J., Wiesner, W., DeGroot, T., & Jones, C. (2001). Comparison of situational and behavior description interview questions for higher-level positions. *Personnel Psychology, 54,* 619-644.

Humphrey, S., Nahrgang, J., & Morgeson, F. (2007). Integrating motivational, social, and contextual work design features. *Journal of Applied Psychology, 92,* 1332–1356.

Hunter, L., & Thatcher, S. (2007). Feeling the heat: Effects of stress, commitment, and job experience on job performance. *Academy of Management Journal, 50,* 953–968.

Huseman, R. C., Hatfield, J. D., & Miles, E. W. (1987). A new perspective on equity theory. *Academy of Management Review, 12,* 222–234.

Ilies, R., Hauserman, N., Schwochau, S., & Stibal, J. (2003). Reported incidence rates of work-related sexual harassment in the United States: Using meta-analysis to explain reported role disparities. *Personnel Psychology, 56,* 609–631.

Ilies, R., & Judge, T. (2003). On the heritability of job satisfaction: The mediating role of personality. *Journal of Applied Psychology, 88,* 750–759.

Ilies, R., Nahrgang, J., & Morgeson, F. (2007). Leader-member exchange and citizenship behaviors. *Journal of Applied Psychology, 92,* 269–277.

Ilies, R., Schwind, K., Wagner, D., Johnson, M., DeRue, D., & Ilgen, D. (2007). When can employees have a family life? *Journal of Applied Psychology, 92,* 1368–1379.

Iverson, R., & Deery, S. (2001). Understanding the "personological" basis of employee withdrawal: The influence of affective disposition on employee tardiness, early departure, and absenteeism. *Journal of Applied Psychology, 86,* 856–866.

Jackson, N. (2003, August 3). Opinions to spare? Click here. *New York Times.*

Jacobs, D. (2004). Douglas McGregor: The human side of enterprise in peril [book review]. *Academy of Management Review, 29,* 293–296.

Jamal, M. (2007). Job stress and job performance controversy revisited. *International Journal of Stress Management, 14,* 175–187.

Jamal, M., & Baba, V. (2003). Type A behavior, components and outcomes: A study of Canadian employees. *International Journal of Stress Management, 10,* 39–50.

James, E., Brief, A., Dietz, J., & Cohen, R. (2001). Prejudice matters: Understanding the reactions of Whites to affirmative-action programs targeted to benefit Blacks. *Journal of Applied Psychology, 86,* 1120–1128.

Jansen, P., & Stoop, B. (2001). The dynamics of assessment-center validity: Results of a nine-year study. *Journal of Applied Psychology, 86,* 741–753.

Janssen, O., & Van Yperen, N. (2004). Employees' goal orientations, the quality of leader-member exchange, and the outcomes of job performance and job satisfaction. *Academy of Management Journal, 47,* 368–384.

Jawahar, I. (2001). Attitudes, self-monitoring, and appraisal behaviors. *Journal of Applied Psychology, 86,* 875–883.

Jeanneret, P., & Strong, M. (2003). Linking O*NET job analysis information to job requirement predictors: An O*NET application. *Personnel Psychology, 56,* 465–492.

Jett, Q., & George, J. (2003). Work interrupted: A closer look at the role of interruptions in organizational life. *Academy of Management Review, 28,* 494–507.

Jex, S., Bliese, P., Buzzell, S., & Primeau, J. (2001). The impact of self-efficacy on stressor–strain relations: Coping style as an explanatory mechanism. *Journal of Applied Psychology, 86,* 401–409.

Jockin, V., Arvey, R., & McGue, M. (2001). Perceived victimization moderates self-reports of workplace aggression and conflict. *Journal of Applied Psychology, 86,* 1262–1269.

Johnson, J. W., & Ferstl, K. L. (1999). The effects of inter-rater and self-other agreement on performance improvement following upward feedback. *Personnel Psychology, 52,* 271–303.

Joireman, J., Kamdar, D., Daniels, D., & Duell, B. (2006). Good citizens to the end? It depends. Empathy and concern with future consequences moderate the impact of a short-term horizon on organizational citizenship behaviors. *Journal of Applied Psychology, 91,* 1307–1320.

Jones, F., O'Connor, D., Conner, M., McMillan, B., & Ferguson, E. (2007). Impact of daily moods, work hours, and iso-strain variables on self-reported health behaviors. *Journal of Applied Psychology, 92,* 1731–1740.

Jones, L., & Sarter, N. (2008). Tactile displays. *Human Factors, 50,* 90–111.

Judge, T., & Bono, J. (2000). Five-factor model of personality and transformational leadership. *Journal of Applied Psychology, 85,* 751–765.

Judge, T., & Bono, J. (2001). Relationship of core self-evaluations traits—self-esteem, generalized self-efficacy, locus of control, and emotional stability—with job satisfaction and job performance: A meta-analysis. *Journal of Applied Psychology, 86,* 80–92.

Judge, T., Bono, J., Ilies, R., & Gerhardt, M. (2002). Personality and leadership: A qualitative and quantitative review. *Journal of Applied Psychology, 87,* 765–780.

Judge, T., Bono, J., & Locke, E. (2000). Personality and job satisfaction. *Journal of Applied Psychology, 85,* 237–249.

Judge, T., & Cable, D., (2004). The effect of physical height on workplace success and income: Preliminary test of a theoretical model. *Journal of Applied Psychology, 89,* 428–441.

Judge, T., Colbert, A., & Ilies, R. (2004). Intelligence and leadership: A quantitative review and test of theoretical propositions. *Journal of Applied Psychology, 89,* 542–552.

Judge, T., & Erez, A. (2007). Interaction and intersection: The constellation of emotional stability and extraversion in predicting performance. *Personnel Psychology, 60,* 573–596.

Judge, T., Heller, D., & Mount, M. (2002). Five-factor model of personality and job satisfaction: A meta-analysis. *Journal of Applied Psychology, 87,* 530–541.

Judge, T., & Ilies, R. (2002). Relationship of personality to performance motivation: A meta-analytic review. *Journal of Applied Psychology, 87,* 797–807.

Judge, T., Ilies, R., & Scott, B. (2006). Work-family conflict and emotions. *Personnel Psychology, 59,* 779–814.

Judge, T., Piccolo, R., & Ilies, R. (2004). The forgotten ones? The validity of consideration and initiating structure in leadership research. *Journal of Applied Psychology, 89,* 36–51.

Judge, T., Thoresen, C., Bono, J., & Patton, G. (2001). The job satisfaction–job performance relationship: A qualitative and quantitative review. *Psychological Bulletin, 127,* 376–407.

Judge, T., Thoresen, C., Pucik, V., & Welbourne, T. M. (1999). Managerial coping with organizational change. *Journal of Applied Psychology, 84,* 107–122.

Kacmar, K., Andrews, M., Van Rooy, D., Steilberg, R., & Cerrone, S. (2006). Sure everyone can be replaced, but at what cost? Turnover as a predictor of unit-level performance. *Academy of Management Journal, 49,* 133–144.

Kacmar, K., Witt, L., Ziunuska, S., & Gully, S. (2003). The interactive effect of leader-member exchange and communications frequency on performance ratings. *Journal of Applied Psychology, 88,* 764–772.

Kaiser, R., Hogan, R., & Craig, S. (2008). Leadership and the fate of organizations. *American Psychologist, 63,* 96–110.

Kalev, A., Dobbin, F., & Kelly, E. (2006). Best practices of best guesses? Assessing the efficacy of corporate affirmative action and diversity policies. *American Sociological Review, 71,* 589–617.

Kalimo, R., Taris, T., & Schaufeli, W. (2003). The effects of past and anticipated future downsizing on survivor well-being: An equity perspective. *Journal of Occupational Health Psychology, 8*(2), 91–109.

Kammeyer-Mueller, J., & Wanberg, C. (2003). Unwrapping the organizational entry process: Disentangling multiple antecedents and their pathways to adjustment. *Journal of Applied Psychology, 88,* 779–794.

Kanner, A. D., & Kasser, T. (2000). Stuffing our kids. *The Industrial-Organizational Psychologist, 38*(1), 185–187.

Kark, R., Shamir, B., & Chen, G. (2003). The two faces of transformational leadership: Empowerment and dependency. *Journal of Applied Psychology, 88,* 246–255.

Kates, S. M. (2000). Out of the closet and out on the street! *Psychology and Marketing, 17,* 493–513.

Katkowski, D., & Medsker, G. (2001). SIOP income and employment: Income and employment of SIOP members in 2000. *The Industrial-Organizational Psychologist, 391,* 21–36.

Keller, R. (2006). Transformational leadership, initiating structure, and substitutes for leadership. *Journal of Applied Psychology, 91,* 202–210.

Kelloway, E., Mullen, J., & Francis, L. (2006). Divergent effects of transformational and passive leadership on employee safety. *Journal of Occupational Health Psychology, 11,* 76–86.

Kelly, R. M., & Kelly, V. P. (1990). Lillian Moller Gilbreth (1878–1972). In A. N. O'Connell & N. F. Russo (Eds.), *Women in psychology* (pp. 117–124). New York: Greenwood.

Kerr, N., & Tindale, R. (2004). Group performance and decision making. *Annual Review of Psychology, 55,* 623–655.

Kersting, K. (2004). Driving teen egos and buying through branding. *Monitor on Psychology, 35*(6), 60–61.

Khanna, C., & Medsker, G. (2007). 2006 income and employment survey results for the Society for Industrial and Organizational Psychology (SIOP). *The Industrial-Organizational Psychologist, 45*(1), 17–32.

Kiley, D. (2005, November 14). Shoot the focus group. *Business Week.*

Kim, E. (2007). Occupational stress. *International Journal of Stress Management, 14,* 111–120.

Kim, Y., & Kang, J. (2001). The effects of ethnicity and product on purchase decision making. *Journal of Advertising Research, 41*(2), 39.

King, E., Shapiro, J., Hebl, M., Singletary, S., & Turner, S. (2006). The stigma of obesity in customer service. *Journal of Applied Psychology, 91,* 579–593.

Kinicki, A., McKee-Ryan, F., Schriesheim, C., & Carson, K. (2002). Assessing the construct validity of the Job Descriptive Index: A review and meta-analysis. *Journal of Applied Psychology, 87,* 14–32.

Kinicki, A., Prussia, G., & McKe-Ryan, F. (2000). A panel study of coping with involuntary job loss. *Academy of Management Journal, 43,* 90–100.

Kinnersley, S., & Roelen, A. (2007). The contribution of design to accidents. *Safety Science, 45,* 31–60.

Klein, H., & Kim, J. S. (1998). A field study of the influence of situational constraints, leader-member exchange, and goal commitment on performance. *Academy of Management Journal, 41,* 88–95.

Klein, H., & Weaver, N. (2000). The effectiveness of an organizational-level orientation training program in the socialization of new hires. *Personnel Psychology, 53,* 47–66.

Klein, H., Wesson, M. J., Hollenbeck, J. R., & Alge, B. J. (1999). Goal commitment and the goal-setting process. *Journal of Applied Psychology, 84,* 885–896.

Klein, K., Conn, A., & Sorra, J. (2001). Implementing computerized technology: An organizational analysis. *Journal of Applied Psychology, 86,* 811–824.

Kluger, J. (2004, April 5). Just too loud. *Time.*

Knutson, B., Ricks, S., Wimmer, G., Prelec, D., & Loewenstein, G. (2007). *Neural predictors of purchases. Neuron, 53,* 147–156.

Kobasa, S. C. (1979). Stressful life events, personality, and health. *Journal of Personality and Social Psychology, 37,* 1–11.

Kobasa, S. C. (1982). The hardy personality. In G. Sanders & J. Suls (Eds.), *Social psychology of health and illness* (pp. 3–32). Hillsdale, NJ: Erlbaum.

Kodak's ergonomic design for people at work (2nd ed.). (2004). New York: Wiley.

Kolmstetter, E. (2003). I-O's making an impact: TSA transportation security screener skill standards, selection system, and hiring process. *The Industrial-Organizational Psychologist, 40*(4), 39–46.

Korkki, P. (2007, September 2). The care and feeding of references. *New York Times.*

Korsgaard, M., Brodt, S., & Whitener, E. (2002). Trust in the face of conflict: The role of managerial trustworthy behavior and organizational context. *Journal of Applied Psychology, 87,* 312–319.

Korsgaard, M., Sapienza, H., & Schweiger, D. (2002). Beaten before begun: The role of procedural justice in planning change. *Journal of Management, 28,* 497–516.

Koys, D. (2001). The effects of employee satisfaction, organizational citizenship behavior, and turnover on organizational effectiveness: A unit-level longitudinal study. *Personnel Psychology, 54,* 101–114.

Krajewski, H., Goffin, R., Rothstein, M., & Johnston, N. (2007). Is personality related to assessment center performance? *Journal of Business Psychology, 22,* 21–33.

Kraut, R., Olson, J., Banaji, M., Bruckman, A., Cohen, J., & Couper, M. (2004). Psychological research online: Report of the Board of Scientific Affairs' Advisory Group on the Conduct of Research on the Internet. *American Psychologist, 59,* 105–117.

Kravitz, D. (2003). More women in the workplace: Is there a payoff in firm performance? *Academy of Management Executive, 17*(3), 148–149.

Kravitz, D., & Klineberg, S. L. (2000). Reactions to two versions of affirmative action among Whites, Blacks, and Hispanics. *Journal of Applied Psychology, 85,* 597–611.

Kroemer, K., Kroemer, H., & Kroemer-Elbert, K. (2000). *Ergonomics: How to design for ease and efficiency* (2nd ed.). Upper Saddle River, NJ: Prentice Hall.

Kroustalis, C., Behrend, T., Meade, A., & Surface, E. (2007). Influence of post-survey action on current survey responses. Paper presented at the 22nd annual meeting of the Society for Industrial and Organizational Psychology, New York.

Kuegler, T. (2000). *Advertising and marketing* (3rd ed.). Rocklin, CA: Prima Publishing.

Kuncel, N., Hezlett, S., & Ones, D. (2004). Academic performance, career potential, creativity, and job performance: Can one construct predict them all? *Journal of Personality and Social Psychology, 86,* 148–161.

Kwak, H., Fox, R., & Zinkhan, G. (2002). What products can be successfully promoted and sold via the Internet? *Journal of Advertising Research, 42*(1), 23–39.

LaFerle, C., Edwards, S. M., & Lee, W.-N. (2000). Teens' use of traditional media and the Internet. *Journal of Advertising Research, 40*(3), 55–65.

Lam, S., Yik, M., & Schaubroeck, J. (2002). Responses to formal performance appraisal feedback: The role of negative affectivity. *Journal of Applied Psychology, 87,* 192–201.

LaMotte, J., Ridder, W., Yeung, K., & DeLand, P. (2000). Effect of aftermarket automobile window tinting films on driver vision. *Human Factors, 42,* 327–336.

Lancaster, J. (2004). *Making time: Lillian Moller Gilbreth: A life beyond "Cheaper by the dozen."* Boston: Northeastern University Press.

Landrum, R., & Harrold, R. (2003). What employers want from psychology graduates. *Teaching of Psychology, 30*(2), 131–133.

Latham, G. (2004). The motivational benefits of goal setting. *Academy of Management Executive, 18,* 126–129.

Latham, G., & Locke, E. (2007). New developments in and directions for goal-setting research. *European Psychologist, 12,* 290–300.

Lawler, E. (1986). *High-involvement management.* San Francisco: Jossey-Bass.

Lawler, E. (2007). Why HR practices are not evidence-based. *Academy of Management Journal, 50,* 1033–1036.

Le, H., Oh, I., Shaffer, J., & Schmidt, F. (2007). Implications of methodological advances for the practice of personnel selection: How practitioners benefit from meta-analysis. *Academy of Management Perspectives, 21*(3), 6–15.

LeBlanc, M., & Kelloway, E. (2002). Predictors and outcomes of workplace violence and aggression. *Journal of Applied Psychology, 87,* 444–453.

Lee, D., McLoone, H., & Dennerlein, J. (2008). Observed finger behaviors during computer mouse use. *Applied Ergonomics, 39,* 107–113.

Lee, J., McGehee, D., Brown, T., & Reyes, M. (2002). Collision warning timing, driver distraction, and driver response to imminent rear-end collisions in a high-fidelity driving simulator. *Human Factors, 44,* 314–334.

Lee, K., & Allen, N. (2002). Organizational citizenship behavior and workplace deviance: The role of affect and cognitions. *Journal of Applied Psychology, 87,* 131–142.

Lee, S., & Brand, J. (2005). Effects of control over office workspace on perceptions of the work environment and work outcomes. *Journal of Environmental Psychology, 25,* 323–333.

Lefkowitz, J. (1970). Effect of training on the productivity and tenure of sewing machine operators. *Journal of Applied Psychology, 54,* 81–86.

Legree, P., Heffner, T., Psotka, J., Medsker, G., & Martin, D. (2003). Traffic crash involvement: Experiential driving knowledge and stressful contextual antecedents. *Journal of Applied Psychology, 88,* 15–26.

Lemov, R. (2005). *World as laboratory: Experiments with mice, mazes and men.* New York: Hill & Wang.

Levashina, J., & Campion, M. (2007). Measuring faking in the employment interview. *Journal of Applied Psychology, 92,* 1638–1656.

Levin, D., & Linn, S. (2004). The commercialization of childhood: Understanding the problem and finding solutions. In T. Kasser & A. Kanner (Eds.), *Psychology and consumer culture: The struggle for a good life in a materialistic world* (pp. 213–232). Washington, DC: American Psychological Association.

Lewis, K. (2000). When leaders display emotion: How followers respond to negative emotional expression of male and female leaders. *Journal of Organizational Behavior, 21,* 221–234.

Liao, H., Arvey, R., Butler, R., & Nutting, S. (2001). Correlates of work injury frequency and duration among firefighters. *Journal of Occupational Health Psychology, 6*(3), 229–242.

Liden, R. C., Wayne, S. J., & Sparrowe, R. T. (2000). An examination of the mediating role of psychological empowerment on the relations between the job, interpersonal relationships, and work outcomes. *Journal of Applied Psychology, 85,* 407–416.

Lievens, F., Harris, M., Van Keer, E., & Bisqueret, C. (2003). Predicting cross-cultural training performance: The validity of personality, cognitive ability, and dimensions measured by an assessment center and a behavior description interview. *Journal of Applied Psychology, 88,* 476–489.

Lim, S., Cortina, L., & Magley, V. (2008). Personal and work group incivility. *Journal of Applied Psychology, 93,* 95–107.

Lim, V. (2003). Managing HIV at the workplace: An empirical study of HIV and HR managers in Singapore. *Journal of Occupational Health Psychology, 8*(4), 235–246.

Liu, C., Spector, P., & Shi, L. (2007). Cross-national job stress. *Journal of Organizational Behavior, 28,* 209–237.

Locke, E. A. (1968). Toward a theory of task motivation and incentives. *Organizational Behavior and Human Performance, 3,* 157–189.

Locke, E. A., & Latham, G. P. (1990). *A theory of goal setting and task performance.* Upper Saddle River, NJ: Prentice Hall.

Locke, E. A., & Latham, G. P. (2002). Building a practically useful theory of goal setting and task motivation: A 35-year odyssey. *American Psychologist, 57,* 705–717.

Locke, E. A., & Latham, G. P. (2004). What should we do about motivation theory? Six recommendations for the 21st century. *Academy of Management Review, 29,* 388–403.

Loechner, J. (2008, May 30). Target social network ads to capture clicks. Center for Media Research. www.mediapost.com/blogs/research_brief/?p=1718

Lord, R., Brown, D., & Freiburg, S. (1999). Understanding the dynamics of leadership: The role of follower self-concepts in the leader-follower relationship. *Organizational Behavior and Human Decision Processes, 78,* 167–203.

Lord, R., & Maher, K. (1993). *Leadership and information processing: Linking perceptions and performance.* London: Routledge.

Lu, L., Kao, S.-F., Chang, T.-T., Wu, H.-P., & Cooper, C. (2008). Work-family demands, work flexibility, work-family conflict and their consequences at work. *International Journal of Stress Management, 15,* 1–21.

Luchak, A., & Gellatly, I. (2007). A comparison of linear and nonlinear relations between organizational commitment and work outcomes. *Journal of Applied Psychology, 92,* 786–793.

Lundberg, U., & Lindfors, P. (2002). Psychophysiological reactions to telework in female and male white-collar workers. *Journal of Occupational Health Psychology, 7*(4), 354–364.

Lynch, P., Kent, R., & Srinivasan, S. (2001). The global Internet shopper: Evidence from shopping tasks in 12 countries. *Journal of Advertising Research, 41*(3), 15–31.

Lyness, K., & Heilman, M. (2006). When fit is fundamental: Performance evaluations and promotions of upper-level female and male managers. *Journal of Applied Psychology, 91,* 777–785.

Lyness, K., & Thompson, D. (2000). Climbing the corporate ladder. *Journal of Applied Psychology, 85,* 86–101.

Madigan, J., & Dickson, M. (2007). Good science—good practice. *The Industrial-Organizational Psychologist, 44*(3), 93–96.

Maier, G., & Brunstein, J. (2001). The role of personal work goals in newcomers' job satisfaction and organizational commitment: A longitudinal analysis. *Journal of Applied Psychology, 86,* 1034–1042.

Mainiero, L., & Gibson, D. (2003). Managing employee trauma: Dealing with the emotional fallout from September 11th. *Academy of Management Executive, 17*(3), 130–143.

Major, V., Klein, K., & Ehrart, M. (2002). Work time, work interference with family, and psychological distress. *Journal of Applied Psychology, 87,* 427–436.

Malach-Pines, A., & Keinan, G. (2007). Stress and burnout in Israeli police officers during a Palestinian uprising. *International Journal of Stress Management, 14,* 160–174.

Malhotra. A., Majchrzak, A., & Rosen, B. (2007). Leading virtual teams. *Academy of Management Perspective, 21,* 60–70.

Mann, S. (2007). The boredom boom. *The Psychologist, 20*(2), 90–93.

Marcus, B., Lee, K., & Ashton, M. (2007). Personality dimensions explaining relationships between integrity tests and counterproductive behavior. *Personnel Psychology, 60,* 1–34.

Margulies, A. (2004). 2004 SIOP tour: Hamburger University. *The Industrial-Organizational Psychologist, 41*(3), 168–169.

Markham, S., Scott, K., & McKee, G. (2002). Recognizing good attendance: A longitudinal, quasi-experimental field study. *Personnel Psychology, 55,* 639–660.

Martell, R., & Desmet, A. (2001). A diagnostic-ratio approach to measuring beliefs about the leadership abilities of male and female managers. *Journal of Applied Psychology, 86,* 1223–1231.

Martin, D., Brooks, R., Ortiz, D., & Veniegas, R. (2003). Perceived employment barriers and their relation to workforce-entry intent among people with HIV/AIDS. *Journal of Occupational Health Psychology, 8*(3), 181–194.

Martin, J., Norris, B., Murphy, B., & Crowe, J. (2008). Medical device development. *Applied Ergonomics, 39,* 271–283.

Maslach, C., & Jackson, S. E. (1986). *Maslach Burnout Inventory manual* (2nd ed.). Palo Alto, CA: Consulting Psychologists Press.

Maslach, C., & Leiter, M. (2008). Early predictors of job burnout and engagement. *Journal of Applied Psychology, 93,* 498–512.

Maslach, C., Schaufeli, W., & Leiter, M. (2001). Job burnout. *Annual Review of Psychology, 52,* 397–422.

Maslow, A. (1970). *Motivation and personality* (2nd ed.). New York: Harper & Row.

Maslyn, J., & Uhl-Bien, M. (2001). Leader-member exchange and its dimensions: Effects of self-effort and others' effort on relationship quality. *Journal of Applied Psychology, 86,* 697–708.

Maurer, T., Solamon, J., Andrews, K., & Troxtel, D. (2001). Interviewee coaching, preparation strategies, and response strategies in relation to performance in situational employment interviews. *Journal of Applied Psychology, 86,* 709–717.

Maurer, T., Weiss, E., & Barbeite, F. (2003). A model of involvement in work-related learning and development activity: The effects of individual, situational, motivational, and age variables. *Journal of Applied Psychology, 88,* 707–724.

May, D., Reed, K., & Schwoerer, C. (2004). Ergonomic office design and aging: A quasi-experimental field study of employee reactions to an ergonomics intervention program. *Journal of Occupational Health Psychology, 9*(2), 123–135.

Mayer, D., Nishii, L., Schneider, B., & Goldstein, H. (2007). The precursors and products of justice climates: Group leader antecedents and employee attitudinal consequences. *Personnel Psychology, 60,* 929–963.

Mayer, R. C., & Davis, J. H. (1999). The effect of the performance appraisal system on trust for management. *Journal of Applied Psychology, 84,* 123–136.

McClelland, D. C. (1961). *The achieving society.* New York: Free Press.

McClelland, D. C. (1975). *Power.* New York: Irvington.

McClelland, D. C., Atkinson, J. W., Clark, R. A., & Lowell, E. L. (1953). *The achievement motive.* New York: Appleton-Century-Crofts.

McCormack, K. (2007). Careers: The goods on Generation Y. www.businessweek.com

McDaniel, M., Hartman, N., Whetzel, D., & Grubb, W. (2007). Situational judgment tests, response instructions, and validity. *Personnel Psychology, 60,* 63–91.

McDaniel, M., Morgeson, F., Finnegan, E., Campion, M., & Braverman, E. (2001). Use of situational judgment tests to predict job performance: A clarification of the literature. *Journal of Applied Psychology, 86,* 730–740.

McDougall, S., Tyrer, V., & Folkard, S. (2006). Searching for signs, symbols, and icons. *Journal of Experimental Psychology: Applied, 12,* 118–128.

McElroy, J., Morrow, P., & Rude, S. (2001). Turnover and organizational performance: A comparative analysis of the effects of voluntary, involuntary, and reduction-in-force turnover. *Journal of Applied Psychology, 86,* 1294–1299.

McFadden, K. (2002). DWI convictions linked to a higher risk of alcohol-related aircraft accidents. *Human Factors, 44,* 522–529.

McFarlin, S. K., Fals-Stewart, W., Major, D. A., & Justice, E. M. (2000, April). Alcohol use and workplace aggression. Paper presented at the meeting of the Society for Industrial and Organizational Psychology, New Orleans, LA.

McGregor, D. (1960). *The human side of enterprise.* New York: McGraw-Hill.

McKay, P., Avery, D., & Morris, M. (2008). Mean racial-ethnic differences in employee sales performance. *Personnel Psychology, 61,* 349–374.

McKay, P., Avery, D., Tonidandel, S., Morris, M., Hernandez, M., & Hebl, M. (2007). Racial differences in employee retention. *Personnel Psychology, 60,* 35–62.

McKay, P., & McDaniel, M. (2006). A reexamination of Black-White mean differences in work performance. *Journal of Applied Psychology, 91,* 538–554.

McKinney, A., Mecham, K., D'Angelo, N., & Connerly, M. (2003). Recruiters' use of CPA in initial screening decisions. *Personnel Psychology, 56,* 823–845.

McLean, L., Tingley, M., Scott, R., & Rickards, J. (2001). Computer terminal work and the benefit of microbreaks. *Applied Ergonomics, 32,* 225–237.

McMillan, S., Hwang, J., & Lee, G. (2003). Effects of structural and perceptual factors on attitudes toward the Web site. *Journal of Advertising Research, 43*(14), 400–410.

McNatt, D. B. (2000). Ancient Pygmalion joins contemporary management. *Journal of Applied Psychology, 85,* 314–322.

McPheters, R., & Kossoff, J. (2003). Effects of differential enhancements on mail response rates. *Journal of Advertising Research, 43*(1), 14–16.

Mearns, K., & Reader, T. (2008). Organizational support and safety outcomes. *Safety Science, 46,* 388–397.

Mehlum, I., Kjuus, H., Veiersted, K., & Wergeland, E. (2006). Self-reported work-related health problems from the Oslo health study. *Occupational Medicine, 56,* 371–379.

Mehta, A. (2000). Advertising attitudes and advertising effectiveness. *Journal of Advertising Research, 40*(3), 67–72.

Mehta, A., & Purvis, S. (2003). Consumer response to print prescription drug advertising. *Journal of Advertising Research, 43*(2), 194–206.

Melamed, S., Fried, Y., & Froom, P. (2001). The interactive effect of chronic exposure to noise and job complexity on changes in blood pressure and job satisfaction: A longitudinal study of industrial employees. *Journal of Occupational Health Psychology, 6*(3), 182–195.

Meyer, J. P., & Allen, N. J. (1991). A three-component conceptualization of organizational commitment. *Human Resource Management Review, 1,* 61–98.

Miner-Rubino, K., & Cortina, L. (2007). Beyond targets: Consequences of vicarious exposure to misogyny at work. *Journal of Applied Psychology, 92,* 1254–1269.

Mitchell, M., & Ambrose, M. (2007). Abusive supervision and workplace deviance and the moderating effects of negative reciprocity beliefs. *Journal of Applied Psychology, 92,* 1159–1168.

Morgeson, F., Campion, M., Dipboye, R., Hollenback, J., Murphy, K., & Schmitt, N. (2007). Reconsidering the use of personality tests in personnel selection contexts. *Personnel Psychology, 60,* 683–729.

Morgeson, F., Johnson, M., Campion, M., Medsker, G., & Mumford, T. (2006). Understanding reactions to job redesign. *Personnel Psychology, 59,* 333–363.

Morrison, E. (2002). Newcomers' relationships: The role of social network ties during socialization. *Academy of Management Journal, 45,* 1149–1160.

Morrison, E. W., & Phelps, C. C. (1999). Taking charge at work. *Academy of Management Journal, 42,* 403–419.

Mount, M., Ilies, R., & Johnson, E. (2006). Relationship of personality traits and counterproductive work behaviors. *Personnel Psychology, 59,* 591–622.

Moutafi, J., Furnham, A., & Crump, J. (2007). Is managerial level related to personality? *British Journal of Management, 18*(3), 272–280.

Muchinsky, P. (2004). When the psychometrics of test development meet organizational realities: A conceptual framework for organizational change, examples, and recommendations. *Personnel Psychology, 57,* 175–209.

Mumaw, R., Roth, E., Vicente, K., & Burns, C. (2000). There is more to monitoring a nuclear power plant than meets the eye. *Human Factors, 42,* 36–55.

Munson, L. J., Hulin, C., & Drasgow, F. (2000). Longitudinal analysis of dispositional influences and sexual harassment. *Personnel Psychology, 53,* 21–46.

Münsterberg, H. (1913). *The psychology of industrial efficiency.* Boston: Houghton Mifflin.

Nagashima, S., Suwazono, Y., Okubo, Y., Uetani, M., Kobayashi, E., & Kido, T. (2007). Working hours and mental and physical fatigue in Japanese workers. *Occupational Medicine, 57,* 449–452.

Naglieri, J., Drasgow, F., Schmit, M., Handler, L., Prifitera, A., Margolis, A., & Velasquez, R. (2004).

Psychological testing on the Internet: New problems, old issues. *American Psychologist, 59,* 150–162.

Neal, A., & Griffin, M. (2006). A study of the lagged relationships among safety climate, safety motivation, safety behavior, and accidents at the individual and group levels. *Journal of Applied Psychology, 91,* 946–953.

Nelson, D. L., & Burke, R. J. (2000). Women executives. *Academy of Management Executive, 14*(2), 107–121.

Nemanich, L., & Keller, R. (2007). Transformational leadership in an acquisition. *Leadership Quarterly, 18,* 49–68.

Neubert, M., & Cady, S. (2001). Program commitment: A multi-study longitudinal field investigation of its impact and antecedents. *Personnel Psychology, 54,* 421–448.

Neuman, G. A., & Wright, J. (1999). Team effectiveness. *Journal of Applied Psychology, 84,* 376–389.

Newman, A. (2007, October 30). Web marketing to a segment too big to be a niche. *New York Times.*

Newnam, S., Griffin, M., & Mason, C. (2008). Safety in work vehicles. *Journal of Applied Psychology, 93,* 632–644.

Ng, T., & Feldman, D. (2008). The relationship of age to ten dimensions of job performance. *Journal of Applied Psychology, 93,* 392–423.

Ng, T., Sorensen, K., & Eby, L. (2006). Locus of control at work. *Journal of Organizational Behavior, 27,* 1057–1087.

Niedhammer, I., David, S., & Degioanni, S. (2006). Association between workplace bullying and depressive symptoms in the French working population. *Journal of Psychosomatic Research, 61,* 251–259.

Nielsen news release (January 28, 2008). Over 875 million consumers have shopped online—the number of Internet shoppers up 40% in two years. Retrieved from www.nielsen.com

Niemela-Nyrhinen, J. (2007). Baby boom consumers and technology. *Journal of Consumer Marketing, 24*(5), 305–312.

Noguchi, Y. (2004, June 6). Hola! Stay in touch? Telecom companies are eager to help Hispanic families do just that. *Washington Post.*

Nordquist, C. (2006, April 3). American children getting too fat for car safety seats. Medical News Today. www.medicalnewstoday.com

Offermann, L., & Malamut, A. (2002). When leaders harass: The impact of target perceptions of organizational leadership and climate on harassment reporting and outcomes. *Journal of Applied Psychology, 87,* 885–893.

O'Kane, P., Palmer, M., & Hargie, O. (2007). Workplace interactions and the polymorphic role of e-mail. *Leadership & Organization Development Journal, 28,* 308–324.

Okunribido, O., Shimbles, S., Magnusson, M., & Pope, M. (2007). City bus driving and low back pain. *Applied Ergonomics, 38,* 29–38.

Olson, G., & Olson, J. (2003). Human-computer interaction: Psychological aspects of the human use of computing. *Annual Review of Psychology, 54,* 491–516.

Olson, W., & Sarter, N. (2001). Management by consent in human-machine systems: When and why it breaks down. *Human Factors, 43,* 255–266.

O'Neil, B., & Mone, M. (1998). Investigating equity sensitivity as a moderator of relations between self-efficacy and workplace attitudes. *Journal of Applied Psychology, 83,* 805–816.

Ones, D., & Viswesvaran, C. (2007). A research note on the incremental validity of job knowledge and integrity tests for predicting maximal performance. *Human Performance, 20,* 293–303.

Ozer, D., & Benet-Martinez, V. (2006). Personality and the prediction of consequential outcomes. *Annual Review of Psychology, 57,* 401–421.

Packard, E. (2007). Psychology students design safer runways. *GradPsych, 5*(4), 6.

Panagiotopoulou, G., Christoulas, K., Papanckolaou, A., & Mandroukas, K. (2004). Classroom furniture dimensions and anthropometric measures in primary school. *Applied Ergonomics, 35*(2), 121–128.

Parasuraman, S., & Purohit, Y. S. (2000). Distress and boredom among orchestra musicians. *Journal of Occupational Health Psychology, 5,* 74–83.

Parker, S. (1998). Enhancing role-breadth self-efficacy. *Journal of Applied Psychology, 83,* 835–852.

Parker, S., Axtell, C., & Turner, M. (2001). Designing a safer workplace: Importance of job autonomy, communications quality, and supportive supervisors. *Journal of Occupational Health Psychology, 6*(3), 211–228.

Parker, S., & Griffin, M. (2002). What is so bad about a little name-calling? Negative consequences of gender harassment for over-performance demands and distress. *Journal of Occupational Health Psychology, 7*(3), 195–210.

Parker, S., Griffin, M., Sprigg, C., & Wall, T. (2002). Effect of temporary contracts on perceived work characteristics and job strain: A longitudinal study. *Personnel Psychology, 55,* 689–719.

Parker, S., Williams, H., & Turner, N. (2006). Modeling the antecedents of proactive behavior at work. *Journal of Applied Psychology, 91,* 636–652.

Parkes, K. (2003). Shiftwork and environment as interactive predictors of work perceptions. *Journal of Occupational Health Psychology, 8*(4), 266–281.

Parks, K., & Steelman, L. (2008). Organizational wellness programs. *Journal of Occupational Health Psychology, 13,* 58–68.

Paronto, M., Truxillo, D., Bauer, T., & Leo, M. (2002). Drug testing, drug treatment, and marijuana use: A fairness perspective. *Journal of Applied Psychology, 87,* 1159–1166.

Payne, J. (2006, November 14). Caught in the Web. www.washingtonpost.com

Payne, N., Jones, F., & Harris, P. (2002). The impact of working life on health behavior: The effect of job strain on the cognitive predictors of exercise. *Journal of Occupational Health Psychology, 79*(4), 342–353.

Payne, S., & Webber, S. (2006). Effects of service provider attitudes and employment status on citizenship behaviors and customers' attitudes and loyalty behavior. *Journal of Applied Psychology, 91,* 365–378.

Pearson, Q. (2008). Role overload, job satisfaction, and psychological health among employed women. *Journal of Counseling & Development, 86,* 57–63.

Pereira, G., & Osburn, H. (2007). Effects of participation in decision making on performance and employee attitudes. *Journal of Business Psychology, 22,* 145–153.

Peterson, N., Mumford, M., Borman, W., Jeanneret, P., Fleishman, E., Levin, K., Campion, M., Mayfield, M., Morgeson, F., Pearlman, K., Gowing, M., Lancaster, A., Silver, M., & Due, D. (2001). Understanding work using the occupational information network O*NET: Implications for practice and research. *Personnel Psychology, 54,* 451–492.

Peterson, R., Smith, D., Martorana, P., & Owens, P. (2003). The impact of chief executive officer personality on top management team dynamics: One mechanism by which leadership affects organizational performance. *Journal of Applied Psychology, 88,* 795–807.

Peterson, U., Demerouti, E., Bergstrom, G., Asberg, M., & Nygren, A. (2008). Work characteristics and sickness absence in burnout and nonburnout groups. *International Journal of Stress Management, 15,* 153–172.

Phillips, J., & Reddie, L. (2007). Decisional style and self-reported e-mail use in the workplace. *Computers in Human Behavior, 23,* 2414–2428.

Piccolo, R., & Colquitt, J. (2006). Transformational leadership and job behaviors. *Academy of Management Journal, 49,* 327–340.

Plassmann, H., O'Doherty, J., Shiv, B., & Rangel, A. (2008). Marketing actions can modulate neural representations of experienced pleasantness. *Proceedings of the National Academy of Sciences, 105,* 1050–1054.

Ployhart, R., Weekley, J., Holtz, B., & Kemp, C. (2003). Web-based and paper-and-pencil testing of applicants in a proctored setting: Are personality, biodata, and situational judgment tests comparable? *Personnel Psychology, 56,* 733–752.

Posig, M., & Kickul, J. (2003). Extending our understanding of burnout: Test of an integrated model in nonservice occupations. *Journal of Occupational Health Psychology, 8*(1), 3–19.

Posthuma, R., Morgeson, F., & Campion, M. (2002). Beyond employment interview validity: A comprehensive narrative review of recent research and trends over time. *Personnel Psychology, 55,* 1–81.

Potter, P., Smith, B., Strobel, K., & Zautra, A. (2002). Interpersonal workplace stressors and well-being: A multi-wave study of employees with and without arthritis. *Journal of Applied Psychology, 87,* 789–796.

Powell, G., & Butterfield, D. (2002). Exploring the influence of decision-makers' race and gender on actual promotion to top management. *Personnel Psychology, 55,* 397–428.

Premeaux, S., Adkins, C., & Mossholder, K. (2007). Balancing work and family. *Journal of Organizational Behavior, 28,* 705–727.

Price, R., Choi, J., & Vinokur, A. (2002). Links in the chain of adversity following job loss: How financial strain and loss of personal control lead to depression, impaired functioning, and poor health. *Journal of Occupational Health Psychology, 9*(4), 302–312.

Probst, T. (2000). Wedded to the job. *Journal of Occupational Health Psychology, 5,* 63–73.

Probst, T. (2004). Safety and insecurity: Exploring the moderating effect of organizational safety climate. *Journal of Occupational Health Psychology, 9*(1), 3–10.

Probst, T., & Brubaker, T. (2001). The effects of job insecurity on employee safety outcomes: Cross-sectional and longitudinal explorations. *Journal of Occupational Health Psychology, 6*(2), 139–159.

Psihogios, J., Sommerich, C., Mirka, G., & Moon, S. (2001). A field evaluation of monitor placement effects in VDT users. *Applied Ergonomics, 32,* 313–325.

Rafferty, A., & Griffin, M. (2006). Perception of organizational change. *Journal of Applied Psychology, 91,* 1154–1162.

Ragins, B., & Cotton, J. (1999). Mentor functions and outcomes. *Journal of Applied Psychology, 84,* 529–550.

Ragins, B., & Cornwell, J. (2001). Pink triangles: Antecedents and consequences of perceived workplace discrimination against gay and lesbian employees. *Journal of Applied Psychology, 86,* 1244–1261.

Ragins, B., Singh, J., & Cornwell, J. (2007). Making the invisible visible: Fear and disclosure of sexual orientation at work. *Journal of Applied Psychology, 92,* 1103–1118.

Ray, B. (2006). Who's afraid of the big bad boss? www.fsu.edu/news/2006/12/04/bad.boss/

Reilly, R. R., Smither, J. W., & Vasilopoulos, N. L. (1996). A longitudinal study of upward feedback. *Personnel Psychology, 49,* 599–612.

Reinberg, S. (2007, August 6). Foods taste better with McDonald's logo, kids say. *Washington Post.*

Reisenwitz, T., Iyer, R., Kuhlmeier, D., & Eastman, J. (2007). The elderly's Internet usage. *Journal of Consumer Marketing, 24,* 406–418.

Rexrode, C. (2007, August 6). Mind the (generation) gap. *St. Petersburg (FL) Times,* p. D1.

Rexrode, C. (2007, December 23). Come and get it: Way to worker's heart may be via onsite cafeteria. *St. Petersburg (FL) Times*, p. F1.

Rhoades, L,. & Eisenberger, R. (2002). Perceived organizational support: A review of the literature. *Journal of Applied Psychology, 87,* 698–714.

Rhoades, L., Eisenberger, R., & Armeli, S. (2001). Affective commitment to the organization: The contributions of perceived organizational support. *Journal of Applied Psychology, 86,* 825–836.

Ricci, J., Chee, E., Lorandeau, A., & Berger, J. (2007). Fatigue in the U.S. workforce. *Journal of Occupational & Environmental Medicine, 49,* 1–10.

Richardson, K., & Rothstein, H. (2008). Effects of occupational stress management intervention programs. *Journal of Occupational Health Psychology, 13,* 69–93.

Richtel, M. (2000, July 6). The lure of data: Is it addictive? *New York Times.*

Roberts, B., Caspi, A., & Moffitt, T. (2003). Work experiences and personality development in young adulthood. *Journal of Personality and Social Psychology, 84,* 582–593.

Roberts, B., Harms, P., Caspi, A., & Moffitt, T. (2007). Predicting the counterproductive employee in a child-to-adult prospective study. *Journal of Applied Psychology, 92,* 1427–1436.

Robertson, M., & Huang, Y.-H. (2006). Effect of a workspace design and training intervention on individual performance, group effectiveness, and collaboration. *Work: Journal of Prevention, Assessment, & Rehabilitation, 27,* 3–12.

Robie, C., & Brown, D. (2007). Measurement equivalence of a personality inventory administered on the internet versus a kiosk. *Applied HRM Research, 11*(2), 97–106.

Robie, C., Brown, D., & Bly, P. (2005). The big five in the USA and Japan. *Journal of Management Development, 24,* 720–736.

Robinson, R. (2007, June 29). The Iron Horse and Ripken. *New York Times.*

Robinson, T., Borzekowski, D., Matheson, D., & Kraemer, H. (2007). Effects of fast food branding on children's taste preferences. *Archives of Pediatrics & Adolescent Medicine, 16,* 792–797.

Rodgers, S., & Harris, M. (2003). Gender and e-commerce: An exploratory study. *Journal of Advertising Research, 43*(3), 322–330.

Roelen, C., Schreuder, K., Koopmans, P., & Groothoff, J. (2008). Perceived job demands relate to self-reported health complaints. *Occupational Medicine. 58,* 58–63.

Roethlisberger, F. J., & Dickson, W. J. (1939). *Management and the worker.* Cambridge, MA: Harvard University Press.

Rogelberg, S. G., Luong, A., Sederburg, M. E., & Cristol, D. S. (2000). Employee attitude surveys. *Journal of Applied Psychology, 85,* 284–293.

Rose, D., Sidle, S., & Griffith, K. (2007). A penny for your thoughts: Monetary incentives improve response rates for company-sponsored employee surveys. *Organizational Research Methods, 10,* 225–240.

Rosenthal, R., & Jacobson, L. (1968). *Pygmalion in the classroom.* New York: Holt.

Rospenda, K. (2002). Workplace harassment, services utilization, and drinking outcomes. *Journal of Occupational Health Psychology, 7*(2), 141–155.

Roth, P., Bevier, C., Bobko, P., Switzer, F., & Tyler, P. (2001). Ethnic group differences in cognitive ability in employment and educational settings: A meta-analysis. *Personnel Psychology, 54,* 297–330.

Rothbard, N., & Edwards, J. (2003). Investment in work and family roles: A test of identity and utilitarian motives. *Personnel Psychology, 56,* 699–736.

Rotundo, M., Nguyen, D., & Sackett, P. (2001). A meta-analytic review of gender differences in perception of sexual harassment. *Journal of Applied Psychology, 86,* 914–922.

Rotundo, M., & Sackett, P. (1999). Effect of rater race on conclusions regarding differential prediction in cognitive ability tests. *Journal of Applied Psychology, 84,* 815–822.

Rowold, J. (2007). Individual influences on knowledge acquisition in a call center training context in Germany. *International Journal of Training & Development, 11,* 21–34.

Ryan, A., West, B., & Carr, J. (2003). Effects of the terrorist attacks of September 11, 2001, on employee attitudes. *Journal of Applied Psychology, 89,* 647–659.

Rynes, S., Brown, K., & Colbert, A. (2002). Seven common misconceptions about human resource practices: Research findings versus practitioner beliefs. *Academy of Management Executive, 16*(3), 92–102.

Rynes, S., Giluk, T., & Brown, K. (2007). The very separate worlds of academic and practitioner periodicals in human resource management. *Academy of Management Journal, 50,* 987–1008.

Sacco, J., Scheu, C., Ryan, A., & Schmitt, N. (2003). An investigation of race and sex similarity effects in interviews: A multilevel approach to relational demography. *Journal of Applied Psychology, 88,* 852–865.

Sackett, P., Borneman, M., & Connelly, B. (2008). High-stakes testing in higher education and employment. *American Psychologist, 63,* 215–227.

Saks, A. (2002). So what is a good transfer of training estimate? *The Industrial-Organizational Psychologist, 39*(3), 29–30.

Saks, A., & Ashforth, B. (2002). Is job search related to employment quality? *Journal of Applied Psychology, 87,* 646–654.

Saks, A., & Belcourt, M. (2006). An investigation of training activities and transfer of training in organizations. *Human Resource Management, 45,* 629–648.

Saks, A., Uggerslev, K., & Fassina, N. (2007). Socialization tactics and newcomer adjustment. *Journal of Vocational Behavior, 70,* 413–446.

Salas, E., Baker, D., King, H., & Battles, J. (2006). Opportunities and challenges for human factors and ergonomics in enhancing patient safety. *Human Factors, 48,* 1–5.

Salas, E., & Cannon-Bowers, J. (2001). The science of training: A decade of progress. *Annual Review of Psychology, 52,* 471–499.

Salgado, J., Anderson, N., Moscoso, S., Bertua, C., & Fruyt, F. (2003). International validity generalization of general mental ability and cognitive abilities: A European community meta-analysis. *Personnel Psychology, 56,* 573–605.

Salgado, J., Anderson, N., Moscoso, S., Bertua, C., Fruyt, F., & Rolland, J. (2003). A meta-analytic study of general mental ability validity for different occupations in the European community. *Journal of Applied Psychology, 88,* 1068–1081.

Salzberg, B. (2007, October 25). Shaping the workforce of the future. *Business Week.*

Samaha, E., Lai, S., Samaha, N., & Wyndham, J. (2007). Psychological lifestyle and coping contributors to chronic fatigue in shiftworker nurses. *Journal of Advanced Nursing, 59,* 221–232.

Sanders, M. S., & McCormick, E. J. (1987). *Human factors in engineering and design* (6th ed.). New York: McGraw-Hill.

Sarchione, C. D., Cuttler, M. J., Muchinsky, P. M., & Nelson-Gray, R. O. (1998). Prediction of dysfunctional job behavior among law enforcement officers. *Journal of Applied Psychology, 83,* 904–912.

Sarter, N., & Schroeder, B. (2001). Supporting decision making and action selection under time pressure and uncertainty: The case of in-flight icing. *Human Factors, 43,* 573–583.

Savicki, V. (2002). *Burnout across 13 cultures: Stress and coping in child and youth care workers.* Westport, CT: Praeger/Greenwood.

Schat, A., & Kelloway, E. (2003). Reducing the adverse consequences of workplace aggression and violence: The buffering effects of organizational support. *Journal of Occupational Health Psychology, 8*(2), 110–122.

Schaubroeck, J., Jones, J., & Xie, J. (2001). Individual differences in utilizing control to cope with job demands: Effects on susceptibility to infectious disease. *Journal of Applied Psychology, 86,* 265–278.

Schaubroeck, J., & Lam, S. (2002). How similarity to peers and supervisor influences organizational advancement in different cultures. *Academy of Management Journal, 45,* 1120–1136.

Schaubroeck, J., Lam, S., & Cha, S. (2007). Embracing transformational leadership. *Journal of Applied Psychology, 92,* 1020–1030.

Schaubroeck, J., Lam, S., & Xie, J. (2000). Collective efficacy versus self-efficacy in coping responses to stressors and control. *Journal of Applied Psychology, 85,* 512–525.

Schaufeli, W., Taris, T., & Van Rhenen, W. (2008). Workaholism, burnout, and work engagement. *Applied Psychology: An International Review, 57,* 173–203.

Schiffman, L., & Kanuk, L. (2004). *Consumer behavior* (8th ed.). Upper Saddle River, NJ: Prentice Hall.

Schleicher, D., Venkataramani, V., Morgeson, F., & Campion, M. (2006). So you didn't get the job; now what do you think? Examining opportunity-to-perform fairness perceptions. *Personnel Psychology, 59,* 559–590.

Schmidt, F. L., & Hunter, J. E. (1998). The validity and utility of selection methods in personnel psychology. *Psychological Bulletin, 124,* 262–274.

Schmidt, F. L., & Hunter, J. E. (2004). General mental ability in the world of work: Occupational attainment and job performance. *Journal of Personality and Social Psychology, 86,* 162–173.

Schmidt, K. (2007). Organizational commitment. *International Journal of Stress Management, 14,* 26–40.

Schmidt, K., & Neubach, B. (2007). Self-control demands: A source of stress at work. *International Journal of Stress Management, 14,* 398–416.

Schminke, M., Ambrose, M. L., & Cropanzano, R. S. (2000). The effect of organizational structure on perceptions of procedural fairness. *Journal of Applied Psychology, 85,* 294–304.

Schmitt, N., & Kunce, C. (2002). The effects of required elaboration of answers to biodata questions. *Personnel Psychology, 55,* 569–587.

Schmitz, N., Neumann, W., & Oppermann, R. (2000). Stress, burnout, and locus of control in German nurses. *International Journal of Nursing Studies, 37*(2), 95–99.

Schneider, K. T., Hitlan, R. T., & Radhakrishnan, P. (2000). An examination of the nature and correlates of ethnic harassment experiences in multiple contexts. *Journal of Applied Psychology, 81,* 3–12.

Scholz, U., Dona, B., Sud, S., & Schwarzer, R. (2002). Is general self-efficacy a universal construct? Psychometric findings from 25 countries. *European Journal of Psychological Assessment, 18*(3), 242–251.

Schriesheim, C. A., Neider, L. L., & Scandura, T. A. (1998). Delegation and leader-member exchange. *Academy of Management Journal, 41,* 298–318.

Schweitzer, M. E., & Kerr, J. L. (2000). Bargaining under the influence. *Academy of Management Executive, 14*(2), 47–57.

Scott, W. D. (1903). *The theory and practice of advertising.* Boston: Small.

Scotter, J., Moustafa, K., Burnett, J., & Michael, P. (2007). Influence of prior acquaintance with the rate on rater accuracy and halo. *Journal of Management Development, 26,* 790–803.

Seagull, J., & Sanderson, P. (2001). Anaesthesia alarms in context: An observational study. *Human Factors, 43,* 66–78.

Seashore, S. E., & Bowers, D. G. (1970). Durability of organizational change. *American Psychologist, 25,* 227–233.

Segerstrom, S., & Miller, G. (2004). Psychological stress and the human immune system: A meta-analytic study of 30 years of inquiry. *Psychological Bulletin, 130,* 601–630.

Seibert, S., Crant, J., & Kraimer, M. (1999). Proactive personality and career success. *Journal of Applied Psychology, 84,* 416–427.

Seibert, S., Kraimer, M., & Crant, J. (2001). What do proactive people do? A longitudinal model linking proactive personality and career success. *Personnel Psychology, 54,* 845–874.

Seifert, C., Yukl, G., & McDonald, R. (2003). Effects of multi-source feedback and a feedback facilitator on the influence behavior of managers toward subordinates. *Journal of Applied Psychology, 88,* 561–569.

Shah, P. P. (2000). Network destruction. *Academy of Management Journal, 43,* 101–112.

Shalley, C. E., Gilson, L. L., & Blum, T. C. (2000). Matching creativity requirements and the work environment. *Academy of Management Journal, 43,* 215–223.

Shan, G., & Bohn, C. (2003). Anthropometrical data and coefficients of regression related to gender and race. *Applied Ergonomics, 34,* 327–337.

Shanock, L., & Eisenberger, R. (2006). When supervisors feel supported. *Journal of Applied Psychology, 91,* 689–695.

Shao, L., & Webber, S. (2006). A cross-cultural test of the five-factor model of personality and transformational leadership. *Journal of Business Research, 59,* 936–944.

Shapiro, D., Kirkman, B., & Courtney, H. (2007). Perceived causes and solutions of the translation problem in management research. *Academy of Management Journal, 50,* 249–266.

Sharit, J., Czaja, S., Nair, S., & Lee, C. (2003). Effects of age, speech rate, and environmental support in using telephone voice menu systems. *Human Factors, 45,* 234–251.

Shaw, J., Duffy, M., Mitra, A., Lockhart, D., & Bowler, M. (2003). Reactions to merit pay increases: A longitudinal test of a signal sensitivity perspective. *Journal of Applied Psychology, 88,* 538–544.

Sherony, K., & Green, S. (2002). Co-worker exchange: Relationships between co-workers, leader-member exchange, and work attitudes. *Journal of Applied Psychology, 87,* 542–548.

Shin, S., & Zhou, J. (2003). Transformational leadership, conservation, and creativity: Evidence from Korea. *Academy of Management Journal, 46,* 703–714.

Shipper, F., Hoffman, R., & Rotondo, D. (2007). Does the 360 feedback process create actionable knowledge equally across cultures? *Academy of Management Learning & Education, 6*(1), 33–50.

Shore, L., Cleveland, J., & Goldberg, C. (2003). Work attitudes and decisions as a function of manager age and employee age. *Journal of Applied Psychology, 88,* 529–537.

Simon, E. (2007, November 5). Employer study of applicants' personalities. news.yahoo.com

Simoneau, G., & Marklin, R. (2001). Effect of computer keyboard shape and height on wrist extension angle. *Human Factors, 43,* 287–298.

Simonite, T. (2007, January 3). Vibrating vest could send alerts to soldiers. www.newscientist.com/article/dn1084b

Simons, T., Friedman, R., Liu, L., & Parks, J. (2007). Racial differences in sensitivity to behavioral integrity. *Journal of Applied Psychology, 92,* 650–665.

Simons, T., & Roberson, Q. (2003). Why managers should care about fairness: The effects of aggregate justice perceptions on organizational outcomes. *Journal of Applied Psychology, 88,* 432–443.

Simonson, I., Carmon, Z., Dhar, R., Drolet, A., & Nowlis, S. (2001). Consumer research. *Annual Review of Psychology, 52,* 249–275.

Sims, C., Drasgow, F., & Fitzgerald, L. (2005). The effects of sexual harassment on turnover in the military. *Journal of Applied Psychology, 90,* 1141–1152.

Sitzmann, T., Brown, K., Casper, W., Ely, K., & Zimmerman, R. (2008). A review and meta-analysis of the nomological network of trainee reactions. *Journal of Applied Psychology, 93,* 280–295.

Sitzmann, T., Kraiger, K., Stewart, D., & Wisher, R. (2006). The comparative effectiveness of Web-based and class-room instruction. *Personnel Psychology, 59,* 623–664.

Skitka, L., & Sargis, E., (2006). The Internet as psychological laboratory. *Annual Review of Psychology, 57,* 529–555.

Smit, E., Bronner, F., & Tolboom, M. (2007). Brand relationship quality and its value for personal contact. *Journal of Business Research, 60,* 627–633.

Smith, D. (2004, April 14). When flour power invaded the kitchen. *New York Times.*

Smith, D., & Ellingson, J. (2002). Substance versus style: A new look at social desirability in motivating contexts. *Journal of Applied Psychology, 87,* 211–219.

Smith, D., Hanges, P., & Dickson, M. (2001). Personnel selection and the 5-factor model: Reexamining the effects of applicant's form of reference. *Journal of Applied Psychology, 86,* 304–315.

Smith, P., Frank, J., Bondy, S., & Mustard, C. (2008). Do changes in job control predict differences in health status? *Psychosomatic Medicine, 70,* 85–91.

Smith, S., Kilby, S., Jorgensen, G., & Douglas, J. (2007). Napping and nightshift work. *Sleep & Biological Rhythms, 52,* 117–125.

Smither, J., London, M., Flautt, R., Vargas, Y., & Kucine, I. (2003). Can working with an executive coach improve multi-source feedback ratings over time? A quasi-experimental study. *Personnel Psychology, 56,* 23–44.

Smither, J., & Walker, A. (2004). Are the characteristics of narrative comments related to improvement in multi-rater feedback ratings over time? *Journal of Applied Psychology, 89,* 575–581.

Smithikrai, C. (2007). Personality traits and job success: An investigation in a Thai sample. *European Journal of Selection and Assessment, 15*(1), 134–138.

Smith-Jentsch, K. H., Jentsch, F. G., Payne, S. C., & Salas, E. (1996). Can pre-training experiences explain individual differences in learning? *Journal of Applied Psychology, 81,* 110–116.

Smith-Jentsch, K. H., Salas, E., & Brannick, M. (2001). To transfer or not to transfer? Investigating the combined effects of trainee characteristics, team leader support, and team climate. *Journal of Applied Psychology, 86,* 279–292.

Snape, E., & Redman, T. (2003). An evaluation of a 3-component model of occupational commitment: Dimensionality and consequences among United Kingdom human resource management specialists. *Journal of Applied Psychology, 88,* 152–159.

Sommerich, C., Joines, S., & Psihogios, J. (2001). Effects of computer monitor viewing angle and related factors on strain, performance, and preference outcomes. *Human Factors, 43,* 39–55.

Song, Z., Foo, M.-D., & Uy, M. (2008). Mood spillover and crossover among dual-earner couples. *Journal of Applied Psychology, 93,* 443–452.

Sonnentag, S. (2003). Recovery, work engagement, and proactive behavior: A new look at the interface between nonwork and work. *Journal of Applied Psychology, 88,* 518–528.

Sonnentag, S., & Zijlstra, F. (2006). Job characteristics and off-job activities as predictors of need for recovery, well-being, and fatigue. *Journal of Applied Psychology, 91,* 330–350.

Spake, D., & Joseph, M. (2007). Consumer opinion and effectiveness of direct-to-consumer advertising. *Journal of Consumer Marketing, 24,* 283–293.

Spector, P. E., Chen, P. Y., & O'Connell, B. J. (2000). A longitudinal study of relations between job stressors and job strains while controlling for prior negative affectivity and strains. *Journal of Applied Psychology, 85,* 211–218.

Spector, P. E., et al. (2004). A cross-national comparative survey of work-family stressors, working hours, and well-being: China and Latin America versus the Anglo world. *Personnel Psychology, 57,* 119–142.

Spence, C., & Gallace, A. (2007). Recent developments in the study of tactile attention. *Canadian Journal of Experimental Psychology, 61,* 196–207.

Sprig, C., Stride, C., Wall, T., Holman, D., & Smith, P. (2007). Work characteristics, musculoskeletal disorders and the mediating role of psychological strain. *Journal of Applied Psychology, 92,* 1456–1466.

Srivastava, A., Bartol, K., & Locke, E. (2006). Empowering leadership in management teams. *Academy of Management Journal, 49,* 1239–1251.

Stajkovic, A. D., & Luthans, F. (1998). Self-efficacy and work-related performance. *Psychological Bulletin, 124,* 240–261.

Stajkovic, A. D., & Luthans, F. (2003). Behavioral management and task performance in organizations: Conceptual background, meta-analysis, and test of alternative models. *Personnel Psychology, 56,* 155–194.

Stanton, E. (2002, December 29). If a résumé lies, truth can loom large. *New York Times.*

Stanton, N., & Baber, C. (2003). On the cost-effectiveness of ergonomics. *Applied Ergonomics, 34,* 407–411.

Stark, S., Chernyshenko, O., Chan, K., Lee, W., & Drasgow, F. (2001). Effects of the testing situation on item responding. *Journal of Applied Psychology, 86,* 943–953.

Steers, R., Mowday, R., & Shapiro, D. (2004). The future of work motivation theory. *Academy of Management Review, 29,* 379–387.

Stern, B. (2002). The importance of being Ernest: A tribute to [Ernest] Dichter. *Journal of Advertising Research, 42,* 19–23.

Sternberg, R. (2003). WICS: A model of leadership in organizations. *Academy of Management Learning and Education, 2,* 386–401.

Stevenson, J. S., Bruner, G. C., II, & Kumar, A. (2000). Web page background and viewer attitudes. *Journal of Advertising Research, 40,* 29–34.

Stewart, G., & Nandkeolyar, A. (2007). Exploring how constraints created by other people influence intraindividual variations in objective performance measures. *Journal of Applied Psychology, 92,* 1149–1158.

Stone, G., Besser, D., & Lewis, L. E. (2000). Recall, liking, and creativity in TV commercials. *Journal of Advertising Research, 40,* 7–18.

Strauss, A. (2008, January 10). The smile boutique in the dentist's office. *New York Times.*

Strayer, P. (2006). Cell phones and driver distraction. American Psychological Association convention presentation.

Subedi, B. (2006). Cultural factors and beliefs influencing transfer of training. *International Journal of Training & Development, 10,* 88–97.

Sutton, R. I., & Rafaeli, A. (1998). Untangling the relationship between displayed emotions and organizational sales. *Academy of Management Journal, 31,* 461–487.

Sverke, M., Hellgren, J., & Naswall, K. (2002). No security: A meta-analysis and review of job insecurity and its consequences. *Journal of Occupational Health Psychology, 7*(3), 242–264.

Swanbrow, D. (2006). Job insecurity takes toll on worker health. www.ur.umich.edu/0506/Apr03_06/00.shtml

Swartz, T. A. (1983). Brand symbols and message differentiation. *Journal of Advertising Research, 23,* 59–64.

Szeto, G., & Sham, K. (2008). The effects of angled position of computer display screen on muscle activities of the neck-shoulder stabilizers. *International Journal of Industrial Ergonomics, 38,* 9–17.

Tabuchi, H. (2008, March 2). Japan looks to a robot future. www.msnbc.com

Tan, H., & Aryee, S. (2002). Antecedents and outcomes of union loyalty: A constructive replication and an extension. *Journal of Applied Psychology, 87,* 715–722.

Tangirala, S., Green, S., & Ramanujam, R. (2007). In the shadow of the boss's boss: Effects of supervisors' upward exchange relationships on employees. *Journal of Applied Psychology, 92,* 309–320.

Taris, T., & Schreurs, P. (2007). How may nonresponse affect findings in organizational surveys? *International Journal of Stress Management, 14,* 249–259.

Taylor, F. W. (1911). *Scientific management.* New York: Harper.

Taylor, P., Kan Shi, W.-D., & Borman, W. (2008). The transportability of job information across countries. *Personnel Psychology, 61,* 69–111.

Taylor, S. E., Klein, L. C., Lewis, B. P., Gruenewald, T. L., Gurung, R. A. R., & Updegraff, J. A. (2000). Biobehavioral responses to stress in females. *Psychological Review, 107,* 411–429.

Tenopyr, M. L. (1992). Reflections of a pioneering woman in industrial psychology. *Professional Psychology, 23,* 172–175.

Tepper, B., Duffy, M., & Shaw, J. (2001). Personality moderators of the relationship between abusive supervision and subordinates' resistance. *Journal of Applied Psychology, 86,* 974–983.

Tepper, B., Moss, S., Lockhart, D., & Carr, J. (2007). Abusive supervision, upward maintenance communication, and subordinates' psychological distress. *Academy of Management Journal, 50,* 1169–1180.

Tetrick, L., Shore, L., McClurg, L., & Vandenberg, R. (2007). A model of union participation. *Journal of Applied Psychology, 92,* 820–828.

Tett, R., & Christiansen, N. (2007). Personality tests at the crossroads. *Personnel Psychology, 60,* 967–993.

Thee, M. (2007, December 7). Cell phones challenge poll sampling. *New York Times.*

Thompson, B., Brough, P., & Schmidt, H. (2006). Supervisor and subordinate work-family values. *International Journal of Stress Management, 13,* 45–62.

Thompson, C., & Prottas, D. (2005). Relationships among organizational family support, job autonomy, perceived control, and employee well-being. *Journal of Occupational Health Psychology, 10,* 110–118.

Thompson, J. (2005). Proactive personality and job performance. *Journal of Applied Psychology, 90,* 1011–1017.

Thompson, L., Surface, E., Martin, D., & Sanders, M. (2003). From paper to pixels: Moving personnel surveys to the Web. *Personnel Psychology, 56,* 197–227.

Tierney, P., & Farmer, S. (2002). Creative self-efficacy: Its potential antecedents and relationship to creative performance. *Academy of Management Journal, 45,* 1137–1148.

Tierney, P., Farmer, S., & Graen, G. B. (1999). An examination of leadership and employee creativity. *Personnel Psychology, 52,* 591–620.

Tippins, N., Beaty, J., Drasgow, F., Gibson, W., Pearlman, K., Segall, D., & Shepherd, W. (2006). Unproctored Internet testing in employment settings. *Personnel Psychology, 59,* 189–325.

Toegel, G., & Conger, J. (2003). 360-degree assessment: Time for reinvention. *Academy of Management Learning and Education, 2,* 297–311.

Torres, I., & Gelb, B. (2002). Hispanic-targeted advertising. *Journal of Advertising Research, 42*(6), 69–76.

Tourangeau, R. (2004). Survey research and societal change. *Annual Review of Psychology, 55,* 775–801.

Treadway, D., Ferris, G., Duke, A., Adams, G., & Thatcher, J. (2007). The moderating role of subordinate political skill on supervision. *Journal of Applied Psychology, 92,* 848–855.

Trimmel, M., Meixner-Pendleton, M., & Haring, S. (2003). Stress response caused by system response time when searching for information on the Internet. *Human Factors, 45,* 615–621.

Tse, A., & Lee, R. (2001). Zapping behavior during commercial breaks. *Journal of Advertising Research, 42*(3), 3–28.

Tsutsumi, A., Kayaba, K., Ojima, T., Ishikawa, S., Kawakami, N., and the Jichi Medical School Cohort Study Group (2007). Low control at work and the risk of suicide in Japanese men. *Psychotherapy and Psychosomatics, 76,* 177–185.

Tuckel, P., & O'Neill, H. (2002). The vanishing respondent in telephone surveys. *Journal of Advertising Research, 42*(5), 26–51.

Vaananen, A., Kevin, M., Kouvonen, A., Kumpulainen, R., Ala-Mursula, L., Kivimaki, M., Toivanen, M., Linna, A., & Vahtera, J. (2008). Work-family characteristics as determinants of sickness absence. *Journal of Occupational Health Psychology, 13,* 181–196.

Valcour, M. (2007). Work-based resources as moderators of the relationship between work hours and satisfaction with work-family balance. *Journal of Applied Psychology, 92,* 1512–1523.

Van der Ploeg, E., Dorresteijn, S., & Kleber, R. (2003). Critical incidents and chronic stressors at work: Their impact on forensic doctors. *Journal of Occupational Health Psychology, 8*(2), 157–166.

Van der Zee, K., Bakker, A., & Bakker, P. (2002). Why are structured interviews so rarely used in personnel selection? *Journal of Applied Psychology, 87,* 176–184.

Van De Vliert, E., Van Yperen, N., & Thierry, H. (2008). Are wages more important for employees in poorer countries with harsher climates? *Journal of Organizational Behavior, 29,* 79–94.

Van Dierendonck, D., Schaufeli, W., & Buunk, B. (2001). Burnout and inequity among human service professionals: A longitudinal study. *Journal of Occupational Health Psychology, 6*(1), 43–52.

Van Vianen, A. E. M. (2000). Person-organization fit. *Personnel Psychology, 53,* 113–149.

Van Yperen, N. (2006). A novel approach to assessing achievement goals in the context of the 2×2 framework. *Personality and Social Psychology Bulletin, 32,* 1432–1445.

Van Yperen, N., & Hagedoorn, M. (2003). Do high job demands increase intrinsic motivation or fatigue or both? The role of job control and job social support. *Academy of Management Journal, 46,* 339–348.

Van Yperen, N., & Janssen, O. (2002). Fatigued and dissatisfied or fatigued but satisfied? Goal orientations and responses to high job demands. *Academy of Management Journal, 45,* 1161–1171.

Vecchio, R., & Brazil, D. (2007). Leadership and sex-similarity. *Personnel Psychology, 60,* 303–335.

Vecchio, R., & Bullis, R. (2001). Moderators of the influence of supervisor-subordinate similarity on subordinate outcomes. *Journal of Applied Psychology, 86,* 884–896.

Vedantam, S. (2008, January 20). Most diversity training ineffective, study finds. *Washington Post.*

Veitch, J., Charles, K., Farley, K., & Newsham, G. (2007). A model of satisfaction with open-plan office conditions. *Journal of Environmental Psychology, 27,* 177–189.

Velada, R., Caetano, A., Michel, J., Lyons, B., & Kavanagh, M. (2007). The effects of training design, individual characteristics and work environment on transfer of training. *International Journal of Training & Development, 11,* 282–294.

Venkatesh, V., & Johnson, P. (2002). Telecommuting technology implementations: A within- and between-subjects longitudinal study. *Personnel Psychology, 55,* 661–685.

Vera, D., & Crossan, M. (2004). Strategic leadership and organizational leaving. *Academy of Management Review, 29,* 222–240.

Viswesvaran, C., Schmidt, F., & Ones, D. (2003). The moderating influence of job performance dimensions on convergence of supervisory and peer ratings of job performance: Unconfounding construct-level convergence and rating difficulty. *Journal of Applied Psychology, 87,* 345–354.

Vogt, D., Rizvi, S., Shipherd, J., & Resick, P. (2008). Longitudinal investigations of reciprocal relationship between stress reactions and hardiness. *Personality & Social Psychology Bulletin, 34,* 61–73.

Vroom, V. (1964). *Work and Motivation.* New York: Wiley.

Vroom, V., & Jago, A. (2007). The role of the situation in leadership. *American Psychologist, 62,* 17–24.

Waclawski, J., Church, A., & Berr, S. (2002). The 2002 SIOP member survey results. *The Industrial-Organizational Psychologist, 40*(1), 16–27.

Wagner, S., Parker, C., & Christiansen, N. (2003). Employees that think and act like owners: Effects of ownership beliefs and behaviors on organizational effectiveness. *Personnel Psychology, 56,* 847–871.

Waldman, D., & Korbar, T. (2004). Student assessment center performance in the prediction of early career success. *Academy of Management Learning and Education, 3*(2), 151–167.

Walker, A. G., & Smither, J. W. (1999). A five-year study of upward feedback. *Personnel Psychology, 52,* 393–423.

Wallace, J., Popp, E., & Mondore, S. (2006). Safety climate as a mediator between foundation climates and occupational accidents. *Journal of Applied Psychology, 91,* 681–688.

Wallace, J., & Vodanovich, S. (2003). Workplace safety performance: Conscientiousness, cognitive failure, and their interaction. *Journal of Occupational Health Psychology, 8*(4), 316–327.

Wallen, E., & Mulloy, K. (2006). Computer-based training for safety. *Journal of Safety Research, 37,* 461–467.

Walsh, M. (2002, November 19). Number of women in upper ranks rises a bit. *New York Times.*

Walz, S., & Niehoff, B. (2000). Organizational citizenship behaviors: Their relationship to organizational effectiveness. *Journal of Hospitality and Tourism Research, 24*(3), 301–319.

Wanberg, C. R., & Banas, J. T. (2000). Predictors and outcomes of openness to changes in a reorganizing workplace. *Journal of Applied Psychology, 85,* 132–142.

Wanberg, C. R., & Kammeyer-Mueller, J. D. (2000). Predictors and outcomes of proactivity in the socialization process. *Journal of Applied Psychology, 85,* 373–385.

Wang, M. (2007). Profiling retirees in the retirement transition and adjustment process. *Journal of Applied Psychology, 92,* 455–474.

Wansink, B. (2003). Developing a cost-effective brand loyalty program. *Journal of Advertising Research, 43*(3), 301–310.

Wardell, J. (2008, January 28). McDonald's given power to award British school qualifications. *Washington Post.*

Wated, G., & Sanchez, J. (2006). The role of accent as a work stressor on attitudinal and health-related work outcomes. *International Journal of Stress Management, 13,* 329–350.

Wayne, S., Shore, L., Bommer, W., & Tetrick, L. (2002). The role of fair treatment and rewards in perceptions of organizational support and leader-member exchange. *Journal of Applied Psychology, 87,* 590–598.

Weber, M. (1947). *The theory of social and economic organization.* New York: Oxford University Press.

Wells, M., & Perrine, R. (2001). Critters in the cube farm: Perceived psychological and organizational effects of pets in the workplace. *Journal of Occupational Health Psychology, 69*(1), 81–87.

Wells, W., Burnett, J., & Moriarty, S. (2003). *Advertising: Principles and practice* (6th ed.). Upper Saddle River, NJ: Prentice Hall.

Wesson, M., & Gogus, C. (2005). Shaking hands with a computer: An examination of two methods of organizational newcomer orientation. *Journal of Applied Psychology, 90,* 1018–1026.

Westerman, J., & Yamamora, J. (2007). Generational preferences for work environment fit. *Career Development International, 12,* 150–161.

Whittler, T., & Spira, J. (2002). Model's race: A peripheral cue in advertising messages? *Journal of Consumer Psychology, 12*(4), 291–301.

Wiesenfeld, B., Swann, W., Brockner, J., & Bartel, C. (2007). Is more fairness always preferred? Self-esteem moderates reactions to procedural justice. *Academy of Management Journal, 50,* 1235–1253.

Wilk, S., & Cappelli, P. (2003). Understanding the determinants of employer use of selection methods. *Personnel Psychology, 56,* 103–124.

Wilks, S., Mortimer, M., & Nylen, P. (2006). The introduction of sit-stand worktables. *Applied Ergonomics, 37,* 359–365.

Williams, M., McDaniel, M., & Nguyen, N. (2006). A meta-analysis of the antecedents and consequences of pay level satisfaction. *Journal of Applied Psychology, 91,* 392–413.

Willness, C., Steel, P., & Lee, K. (2007). A meta-analysis of the antecedents and consequences of workplace sexual harassment. *Personnel Psychology, 60,* 127–162.

Witt, L., Burke, L., Barrick, M., & Mount, M. (2002). The interactive effects of conscientiousness and agreeableness on job performance. *Journal of Applied Psychology, 87,* 164–169.

Witt, L., & Ferris, G. (2003). Social skill as moderator of the conscientiousness-performance relationship: Convergent results across four studies. *Journal of Applied Psychology, 88,* 809–820.

Wogalter, M., Conzola, V., & Smith-Jackson, T. (2002). Research-based guidelines for warning design and evaluation. *Applied Ergonomics, 33,* 219–230.

Wolburg, J., & Pokyrwczynski, J. (2001). A psychographic analysis of Generation Y college students. *Journal of Advertising Research, 41*(5), 33–53.

Woodside, A., & Wilson, E. (2002). Respondent inaccuracy. *Journal of Advertising Research, 42*(5), 7–20.

Woodson, W., Tillman, B., & Tillman, P. (1992). *Human factors design handbook* (2nd ed.). New York: McGraw-Hill.

Wright, T., & Bonett, D. (2002). The moderating effects of employee tenure on the relation between organizational commitment and job performance: A meta-analysis. *Journal of Applied Psychology, 87,* 1183–1190.

Wright, T., Cropanzano, R., & Bonett, D. (2007). The moderating role of employee positive well-being on the relation between job satisfaction and job performance. *Journal of Occupational Health Psychology, 12,* 93–104.

Yakubovich, V., & Lup, D. (2006). Stages of the recruitment process and the referrer's performance effect. *Organizational Science, 17,* 710–723.

Yang, M., Roskos-Ewoldson, B., & Roskos-Ewoldson, D. (2004). Mental models for brand placement. In L. Shrum (Ed.), *The psychology of entertainment media: Blurring the lines between entertainment and persuasion* (pp. 79–98). Mahwah, NJ: Erlbaum.

Yang, N., Chen, C. C., Choi, J., & Zou, Y. (2000). Sources of work-family conflict. *Academy of Management Journal, 43,* 113–123.

Yelkur, R., Tomkovick, C., & Traczyk, P. (2004). Super Bowl advertising effectiveness: Hollywood finds the games golden. *Journal of Advertising Research, 44*(3), 143–159.

Yildirim, K., Akalin-Baskaya, A., & Celebi, M. (2007). The effects of window proximity, partition height, and gender on perceptions of open-plan offices. *Journal of Environmental Psychology, 27,* 154–165.

Yoon, S., & Kim, J. (2001). Is the Internet more effective than traditional media? Factors affecting the choice of media. *Journal of Advertising Research, 41*(6), 53–61.

Yrle, A., Hartman, S., & Galle, W. (2002). An investigation of relationships between communication style and leader-member exchange. *Journal of Communications Management, 6*(3), 257–268.

Yukl, G., & Taber, T. (1983). The effective use of managerial power. *Personnel, 60*(2), 37–44.

Zaslow, J. (2007, April 20). The most-praised generation goes to work. *Wall Street Journal,* pp. W1, 7.

Zatzick, C., & Iverson, R. (2006). High-involvement management and workforce reduction. *Academy of Management Journal, 49,* 999–1015.

Zellars, K., & Perrewe, P. (2001). Affective personality and the content of emotional social support: Coping in organizations. *Journal of Applied Psychology, 86,* 459–467.

Zellars, K., Tepper, B., & Duffy, M. (2002). Abusive supervision and subordinates' organizational citizenship behavior. *Journal of Applied Psychology, 87,* 1068–1076.

Zhang, Z.-X., Hempel, P., Han, Y.-L., & Tiosvold, D. (2007). Transactive memory system links work team characteristics and performance. *Journal of Applied Psychology, 92,* 1722–1730.

Zhao, H., & Seibert, S. (2006). The Big Five personality dimensions and entrepreneurial status. *Journal of Applied Psychology, 91,* 259–271.

Zhao, H., Wayne, S., Glibkowski, B., & Bravo, J. (2007). The impact of psychological contract breach on work-related outcomes. *Personnel Psychology, 60,* 647–680.

Zhou, D., Zhang, W., & Vertinsky, I. (2002). Advertising trends in urban China. *Journal of Advertising Research, 42*(3), 73–82.

Zimmerman, A., & Dahlberg, J. (2008). The sexual objectification of women in advertising. *Journal of Advertising Research, 48,* 71–79.

Zimmerman, R. (2008). Understanding the impact of personality traits on individuals' turnover decisions. *Personnel Psychology, 61,* 309–348.

Zohar, D. (2002). Modifying supervisory practices to improve subunit safety: A leadership-based intervention model. *Journal of Applied Psychology, 87,* 156–163.

Glossary

Accident proneness The idea that some people have personality traits that predispose them to have accidents, and that most accidents are caused by or involve these same few people. This theory is not supported by research.

Achievement motivation theory The theory of motivation that emphasizes the need to accomplish something, to do a good job, and to be the best.

Adverse impact When a group of job applicants or employees is treated markedly worse than the majority group in staffing decisions.

Apprenticeship A training method for skilled crafts and trades involving classroom instruction and on-the-job experience.

Aptitude tests Psychological tests to measure specific abilities, such as mechanical or clerical skills.

Assessment center A method of selection and training that involves a simulated job situation in which candidates deal with actual job problems.

Attribution A source of error in performance appraisal in which raters attribute or assign positive or negative explanations to an employee's behavior.

Auditory displays Alarms or warning signals in person–machine systems. Auditory displays can be more compelling than visual displays.

Authoritarian leadership A leadership style in which a leader makes all decisions and tells followers what to do.

Average rating error A source of error in performance appraisal in which a rater is unwilling to assign very good or very poor ratings. Consequently, most ratings fall in the middle of the rating scale.

Banding A controversial practice of grouping test scores for minority job applicants to equalize hiring rates.

Behavior modeling A management training technique in which trainees attempt to imitate the job behaviors of successful supervisors.

Behavior modification A training program of positive reinforcement to reward employees for displaying desirable job behaviors.

Behavioral observation scales (BOS) A performance appraisal technique in which appraisers rate the frequency of critical employee behaviors.

Behaviorally anchored rating scales (BARS) A performance appraisal technique in which appraisers rate critical employee behaviors.

Biodata inventory An employee selection technique covering an applicant's past behavior, attitudes, preferences, and values.

Biofeedback A stress-reduction technique that involves electronic monitoring of physiological processes, so that people can learn to control muscle tension, blood pressure, and brain waves.

Bureaucracy A formal, orderly, and rational approach to organizing business enterprises.

Burnout A condition of job stress that results from overwork.

Business games A training method that simulates a complex organizational situation to encourage the development of problem-solving and decision-making skills.

Career self-management A lifelong approach to learning and skill enhancement initiated by the employee rather than by the organization.

Carpal tunnel syndrome A repetitive motion disorder that may involve numbness; tingling; or pain in fingers, hands, and forearms.

Case studies A method of executive training in which trainees analyze a business problem and offer solutions.

Change agents Organization development facilitators who work with business groups to implement change and develop group confidence and effectiveness.

Charismatic leadership A leadership style characterized by a self-promoting personality, a high energy level, and a willingness to take risks. Charismatic leaders stimulate their followers to think independently.

Check reading visual displays Displays that tell the operator whether the system is on or off, safe or unsafe, or operating normally or abnormally.

Computer-assisted instruction (CAI) A computer-based training method in which trainees learn material at their own pace and receive immediate feedback on their progress.

Computerized adaptive tests A means of administering psychological tests in which an applicant's response to an item determines the level of difficulty of succeeding items.

Concurrent validity   A way to establish criterion-related validity that involves administering a test to employees on the job and correlating their scores with job performance data.

Consideration leadership functions   Leadership behaviors that involve awareness of and sensitivity to the feelings of subordinates.

Constant bias   A source of error in performance appraisal based on the different standards used by raters.

Construct validity   A type of validity that attempts to determine the psychological characteristics measured by a test.

Content validity   A type of validity that assesses test items to ensure that they adequately sample the skills the test is designed to measure.

Contingency theory   A leadership theory in which a leader's effectiveness is determined by the interaction between the leader's personal characteristics and the characteristics of the leadership situation.

Control group   In an experiment, this is the group of research participants that is not exposed to the independent variable.

Correlation   The relationship between two variables. The strength and direction of the relationship is expressed by the correlation coefficient.

Criterion-related validity   A type of validity concerned with the relationship between test scores and subsequent job performance.

Critical-incidents technique   A means of identifying specific activities or behaviors that lead to desirable or undesirable consequences on the job.

Democratic leadership   A leadership style in which a leader and followers discuss problems and make decisions jointly.

Dependent variable   In an experiment, this is the resulting behavior of the subjects, which depends on the manipulation of the independent variable.

Descriptive statistics   Ways of describing or representing research data in a concise, meaningful manner.

Diversity training   Training programs to make employees aware of their personal prejudices and to teach them to be more sensitive to the concerns and views of others.

Employee assistance programs (EAPs)   Counseling and rehabilitative services for various employee problems, notably alcohol and drug abuse.

Engineering psychology   The design of machines and equipment for human use and the determination of the appropriate human behaviors for the efficient operation of the machines. The field is also called human factors, human engineering, and ergonomics.

Environmental psychology   The study of the effect of workplace design on behavior and attitudes.

Equity theory   The theory of motivation that states that our motivation on the job is influenced by our perception of how fairly we are treated.

Equivalent-forms method   A way to determine test reliability that involves administering similar forms of a new test to the same group of subjects and correlating the two sets of scores.

Executive coaching   A management training technique involving personal sessions with a coach to improve a particular aspect of job performance.

Experimental group   In an experiment, this is the group of research participants exposed to the independent variable.

Experimental method   The scientific way to determine the effect or influence of a variable on the subjects' performance or behavior.

Face validity   A subjective impression of how well test items seem to be related to the requirements of a job.

Fixed-alternative questions   Survey questions to which respondents limit their answers to the choices or alternatives presented. They are similar to multiple-choice questions on college exams.

Flextime   A system of flexible working hours that combines core mandatory work periods with elective work periods at the beginning and end of the workday.

Focus groups   A method of surveying public opinion through the paid participation of 8 to 12 group members who meet to describe their reactions to a product, advertisement, or specific issues.

Forced-choice technique   A performance appraisal technique in which raters are presented with groups of descriptive statements and are asked to select the phrase in each group that is most descriptive or least descriptive of the worker being evaluated.

Forced-distribution technique   A performance appraisal technique in which supervisors rate employees according to a prescribed distribution of ratings, similar to grading on a curve.

Frequency distribution   A graphic representation of raw data that shows the number of times each score occurs.

Goal-setting theory   The theory of motivation based on the idea that a person's primary motivation on the job is defined in terms of desire to achieve a particular goal.

Group cohesiveness   The focus, closeness, and commonality of interests of a small work group.

Group tests   Psychological tests designed to be administered to a large number of people at the same time.

Halo effect The tendency to judge all aspects of a person's behavior or character on the basis of a single attribute.

Hardiness A personality variable that may explain individual differences in vulnerability to stress. So-called hardy persons believe they can control the events in their lives and thus may be more resistant to stress.

Hawthorne studies A long-term research program at the Hawthorne, Illinois, Western Electric Company plant. It documented the influence of a variety of managerial and organizational factors on employee behavior.

Human anthropometry A branch of engineering psychology concerned with the measurement of the physical structure of the body.

Implicit leadership theory A leadership theory that describes a good leader in terms of one's past experiences with different types of leaders.

Impression management Acting deliberately to make a good impression, to present oneself in the most favorable way.

Inadequate information error A source of error in performance appraisal in which supervisors rate their subordinates even though they may not know enough about them to do so fairly and accurately.

In-basket technique An assessment center exercise that requires job applicants to process memos, letters, and directives found in a typical manager's in-basket.

Independent variable In an experiment, this is the stimulus variable that is manipulated to determine its effect on the subjects' behavior.

Individual tests Psychological tests designed to be administered to one person at a time.

Inferential statistics Methods for analyzing research data that express relationships in terms of probabilities.

Initiating structure leadership functions Leadership behaviors concerned with organizing, defining, and directing the work activities of subordinates.

Integrity tests Paper-and-pencil tests designed to detect employee theft, assess attitudes toward dishonesty, and measure relevant personality variables such as a tendency toward delinquency.

Interest tests Psychological tests to assess a person's interests and preferences. These tests are used primarily for career counseling.

Interpersonal affect Feelings or emotions toward another person. In performance appraisal, the emotional tone of the relationship between manager and employee, whether positive or negative, can influence the assigned ratings.

I-O psychology The application of the methods, facts, and principles of the science of psychology to people at work.

Job analysis The study of a job to describe in specific terms the nature of the component tasks performed by the workers.

Job congruence The match between a person's abilities and the requirements of a job.

Job engagement The true enjoyment of work that characterizes people who score high in energy, involvement, and efficacy.

Job enrichment An effort to expand the scope of a job to give employees a greater role in planning, performing, and evaluating their work.

Job rotation A management training technique that assigns trainees to various jobs and departments over a period of a few years.

Job satisfaction Our positive and negative feelings and attitudes about our jobs.

Job simplification The reduction of manufacturing jobs to the simplest components that can be mastered by unskilled or semiskilled workers.

Job-characteristics theory The theory of motivation that states that specific job characteristics lead to psychological conditions that can increase motivation, performance, and satisfaction in employees who have a high growth need.

Leaderless group discussion An assessment center exercise in which job applicants meet to discuss an actual business problem under the pressure of time. Usually, a leader emerges from the group to guide the discussion.

Leader–member exchange A leadership theory that focuses on how the leader–follower relationship affects the leadership process.

Locus of control One's belief about the source of one's rewards. People with an internal locus of control believe that job performance, pay, and promotion are under their control and dependent on their own behavior. People with an external locus of control believe such events depend on outside forces such as luck.

Management by objectives (MBO) A performance appraisal technique that involves a mutual agreement between employee and manager on goals to be achieved in a given period.

Mass psychogenic illness A stress-related disorder manifested in a variety of physical symptoms that spread rapidly among a group of workers; popularly called assembly-line hysteria.

Matched group design A method for ensuring similarity between experimental and control groups that matches subjects in both groups on characteristics, such as age, job experience, and intelligence, that could affect the dependent variable.

Mean The arithmetic average; a way of describing the central tendency of a distribution of data.

Median The score at the midpoint of a statistical distribution; half the scores fall below the median and half above.

Merit pay A wage system in which pay is based on level of performance.

Merit rating Objective rating methods designed to provide an objective evaluation of work performance.

Meta-analysis The large-scale reanalysis of the results of previous research studies.

Mode The most frequently obtained score in a distribution of data.

Most-recent-performance error A source of error in performance appraisal in which a rater tends to evaluate a worker's most recent job behavior rather than behavior throughout the period since the last appraisal.

Motivator–hygiene (two-factor) theory The theory of motivation that explains work motivation and job satisfaction in terms of job tasks and workplace features.

Naturalistic observation The scientific observation of behavior in its natural setting, without any experimental manipulation of the independent variable.

Needs assessment An analysis of corporate and individual goals undertaken before designing a training program.

Needs hierarchy theory The theory of motivation that encompasses physiological, safety, belonging, esteem, and self-actualization needs.

Negative affectivity A personality dimension characterized by a generalized life and job dissatisfaction and by a focus on negative aspects of life events.

Nominal working hours The prescribed number of hours employees are supposed to spend on the job; not all of these hours are actually spent performing job tasks.

Normal distribution A bell-shaped distribution of data in which most scores fall near the center and few fall at the extreme low and high ends.

Objective tests Tests for which the scoring process is free of personal judgment or bias.

Occupational health psychology The field of study dealing with the health effects of job stress and other aspects of employee well-being.

On-the-job training Training that takes place directly on the job for which the person has been hired.

Open-end questions Survey questions to which respondents state their views in their own words. They are similar to essay questions on college exams.

Organizational culture The organization's pattern of beliefs, expectations, and values as manifested in company and industry practices.

Organizational development (OD) The study and implementation of planned organizational changes.

Organization-based self-esteem A personality dimension relating to our assessment of our adequacy and worth with regard to our place in the employing organization.

Paired-comparison technique A performance appraisal technique that compares the performance of each worker with that of every other worker in the group.

Path–goal theory A leadership theory that focuses on the kinds of behaviors leaders should exercise to allow their subordinates to achieve personal and organizational goals.

Peer rating A performance appraisal technique in which managers or executives at the same level assess one another's abilities and job behaviors.

Performance appraisal The periodic, formal evaluation of employee performance for the purpose of making career decisions.

Personality tests Psychological tests that assess personal traits and feelings.

Person–machine system A system in which human and mechanical components operate together to accomplish a task.

Person–organization fit The congruence between an employee's values and the organization's values.

Power tests Tests that have no time limit. Applicants are allowed as much time as they need to complete the test.

Predictive validity An approach to establishing criterion-related validity in which a new test is administered to all job applicants, and all applicants are hired regardless of test scores. Later, when a measure of job performance can be obtained, test scores are correlated with job performance to see how well the test predicted job success.

Proactivity A tendency to take action to try to influence or change one's environment.

Probability The idea that the differences between the means of experimental and control groups could have occurred by chance.

Probability sampling A method for constructing a representative sample of a population for surveys or polls. Each person in the population has a known probability or chance of being included in the sample.

Protective techniques A personality assessment technique in which test-takers project their feelings onto an ambiguous stimulus such as an inkblot.

Prosocial behavior Behaviors directed toward supervisors, co-workers, and clients that are helpful to an organization.

Protective exclusion The practice of barring certain groups of employees, such as women of childbearing age, from potentially hazardous jobs because of fear of lawsuits.

Pygmalion effect A self-fulfilling prophecy in which managers' expectations about the level of their employees' job performance can influence that performance.

Qualitative visual displays Displays that present a range rather than a precise numerical value. They are frequently used to show whether components, such as engine temperature, are operating in the safe or unsafe range.

Quality-of-work-life (QWL) programs Organizational programs based on active employee participation in decision making and policymaking.

Quantitative visual displays Displays that present a precise numerical value, such as speed, altitude, or temperature.

Quota sampling A method for constructing a representative sample of a population for surveys or polls. Because the sample must reflect the proportions of the larger population, quotas are established for various categories such as age, gender, and ethnic origin.

Race norming A controversial practice, now outlawed, of boosting test scores for minority job applicants to equalize hiring rates.

Random group design A method for ensuring similarity between experimental and control groups that assigns subjects at random to each condition.

Ranking technique A performance appraisal technique in which supervisors list the workers in their group in order from highest to lowest or best to worst.

Rating scales A performance appraisal technique in which supervisors indicate how or to what degree a worker possesses each relevant job characteristic.

Rational validity The type of validity that relates to the nature, properties, and content of a test, independent of its relationship to job performance measures.

Realistic job previews A recruitment technique that acquaints prospective employees with positive and negative aspects of a job.

Recognition technique A technique for testing advertising effectiveness by asking people if they recognize a particular ad, where they saw it, and what they can recall about it.

Relaxation training A stress-reduction technique that concentrates on relaxing one part of the body after another.

Reliability The consistency or stability of a response on a psychological test.

Reverse discrimination The phenomenon that may occur when recruiting, hiring, promoting, and making other human resources decisions in favor of members of a minority group result in discrimination against members of the majority group.

Role ambiguity A situation that arises when job responsibilities are unstructured or poorly defined.

Role conflict A situation that arises when there is a disparity in job requirements or between a job's demands and the employee's personal standards.

Role-playing A management training technique in which trainees play the role of a supervisor, acting out various behaviors in situations with subordinates.

Sales test technique A way of testing the effectiveness of an advertising campaign by introducing the new advertising in selected test markets.

Scientific management A management philosophy concerned with increasing productivity that regarded workers as extensions of the machines they operated.

Scientific method A controlled, objective, and systematic approach to research.

Selection ratio The relationship between the number of people to be hired (the number of jobs) and the number available to be hired (the potential labor supply).

Self-managing work teams Employee groups that allow the members of a work team to manage, control, and monitor all facets of their work, from recruiting, hiring, and training new employees to deciding when to take rest breaks.

Self-ratings A performance appraisal technique in which managers assess their own abilities and job performance.

Self-report personality inventories Personality assessment tests that include questions dealing with situations, symptoms, and feelings. Test-takers are asked to indicate how well each item describes themselves or how much they agree with each item.

Shape coding Designing knobs for control panels in recognizably different shapes so that they can be identified by touch alone.

Situational interviews Interviews that focus not on personal characteristics or work experience but on the behaviors needed for successful job performance.

Situational judgment tests A means of assessing behavior and performance in job-related situations.

Situational testing An early term for the assessment-center technique for employee selection and performance appraisal. Employees are placed in a simulated job setting so that their behavior under stress can be observed and evaluated.

Skewed distribution An asymmetrical distribution of data with most scores at either the high or the low end.

Social loafing The idea that people do not work as hard in a group as they do when working alone.

Socialization The adjustment process by which new employees learn their role in the organizational hierarchy, their company's values, and the behaviors considered acceptable by their work group.

Speed tests   Tests that have a fixed time limit, at which point everyone taking the test must stop.

Split-halves method   A way to determine test reliability that involves administering a new test to a group of subjects, dividing in half the total number of items, and correlating the two sets of scores.

Standard deviation   A measure of the variability of a distribution, the standard deviation is a precise distance along the distribution's baseline.

Standardization   The consistency or uniformity of the conditions and procedures for administering a psychological test.

Standardization sample   The group of subjects used to establish test norms. The scores of the standardization sample serve as the point of comparison for determining the relative standing of the persons being tested.

Statistical significance   The level of confidence in the results of an experiment. Significance is based on the calculation of probability values.

Stress   Physiological and psychological responses to excessive and usually unpleasant stimulation and to threatening events in the environment.

Structured interviews   Interviews in which a predetermined list of questions are asked of every person applying for a particular job.

Subjective tests   Tests that contain items such as essay questions. The scoring process can be influenced by the personal characteristics and attitudes of the scorer.

Survey research method   Interviews, behavioral observations, and questionnaires designed to sample what people say about their feelings or opinions, or how they say they will behave in a given situation.

Test norms   The distribution of test scores of a large group of people similar in nature to the job applicants being tested.

Test-retest method   A way to determine test reliability that involves administering a new test twice to the same group of subjects and correlating the two sets of scores.

Theory X/Theory Y   The Theory X approach to management assumes that people are lazy and dislike work and therefore must be led and directed. Theory Y assumes that people find satisfaction in their work and function best under a leader who allows them to participate in working toward both personal and organizational goals.

360-degree feedback   A multisource approach to performance appraisal that combines ratings from several sources such as superiors, subordinates, peers, and self.

Time-and-motion study   An early attempt to redesign work tools and to reshape the way workers performed routine, repetitive jobs.

Total quality management (TQM)   Participative management programs characterized by increased employee involvement and responsibility.

Transactional leadership   A leadership style that focuses on the social interactions between leaders and followers, based on followers' perceptions of and expectations about the leader's abilities.

Transformational leadership   A leadership style in which leaders are not constrained by their followers' perceptions but are free to act to change or transform their followers' views.

Unstructured interviews   Interviews in which the format and questions asked are left to the discretion of the interviewer.

Valence-instrumentality-expectancy (VIE) theory   The theory of motivation that states that people make choices that are based on their perceived expectations that certain rewards will follow if they behave in a particular way.

Validity   The determination of whether a psychological test or other selection device measures what it is intended to measure.

Validity generalization   The idea that tests valid in one situation may also be valid in another situation.

Vestibule training   Training that takes place in a simulated workspace.

Wage-incentive system   The primary pay system for production workers in which the more units produced, the higher is the wage.

Work analysis   The study of certain tasks and skills that workers can transfer from one job to another.

Work overload   Too much work to perform in the time available or work that is too difficult for the employee to perform.

Work underload   Work that is too simple or insufficiently challenging for a worker's abilities.

Workaholism   So-called addiction to work because of anxiety and insecurity or because of a genuine liking for the job.

Credits

Name Index

Subject Index